Life Skills
Progression™  LSP™

· · · · · · · · · · · · · · · · · · ·

Life Skills Progression™ LSP

An Outcome and Intervention Planning Instrument
for Use with Families at Risk

• • • • • • • • • • • • • • • • • • •

by

LINDA WOLLESEN, M.A., RN, LMFT
Los Gatos, California

and

KAREN PEIFER, PH.D., M.P.H., RN
Denver, Colorado

·P·A·U·L·H·
BROOKES
PUBLISHING C₀ ®

Baltimore • London • Sydney

Paul H. Brookes Publishing Co.
Post Office Box 10624
Baltimore, Maryland 21285-0624

www.brookespublishing.com

Typeset by A.W. Bennett, Inc., Hartland, Vermont.
Manufactured in the United States of America by
Versa Press, Inc., East Peoria, Illinois.

Second printing, September 2011.

Library of Congress Cataloging-in-Publication Data

Wollesen, Linda.
    Life skills progression™ (LSP) : an outcome and intervention planning instrument for use with
    families at risk / by Linda Wollesen and Karen Peifer.
        p.   cm.
    Includes bibliographical references and index.
    ISBN-13: 978-1-55766-830-1 (paper cover)
    ISBN-10: 1-55766-830-2 (paper cover)
    1. Maternal and infant welfare—United States.   2. Child welfare—United States.   I. Title:
    Life skills progression™ (LSP).   II. Peifer, Karen.   III. Title.

    HV699.W64   2005
    362.7–dc22   2005020595

British Library Cataloguing in Publication data are available from the British Library.

Contents

Contents of CD-ROM

Life Skills Progression™ (LSP): An Outcome and Intervention Planning Instrument for Use with Families at Risk features a CD-ROM containing printable versions of the following PDF files:

About the Authors

Linda Wollesen, M.A., RN, LMFT, has focused her 35-year career on public health nursing and collaborative community-based services to low-income and ethnically diverse families. She worked as a nursing visitor in housing projects in East Los Angeles, nursing supervisor in Santa Clara, and program manager in Santa Cruz County, all in California. Her clinical expertise includes services and care coordination for children and infants who have special needs or who are in foster care. Most recently, she supervised a research replication site for the David Olds Nurse-Family Partnership in Monterey County.

In addition to earning a bachelor's degree in Nursing from California State University at Los Angeles, Ms. Wollesen received her master's degree in marriage, family, and child counseling from the University of Santa Clara and is a licensed therapist.

Ms. Wollesen is the author of the Life Skills Progression™ (LSP) instrument and pioneered the reliability and content work for the tool with the support of a fellowship from ZERO TO THREE: National Center for Infants, Toddlers and Families. She is currently the director for Life Skill Outcomes, LLC, which provides LSP training and best practice consultation and developed an LSP database for use by programs using the LSP. She conducts training nationally in the areas of maternal/child outcome data management and clinically for reflective function and other best practice interventions.

Karen Peifer, Ph.D., M.P.H., RN, became the program evaluation coordinator for the San Mateo County Prenatal To Three Initiative soon after finishing her doctorate in public health from the University of California at Berkeley. The Prenatal To Three Initiative is one of the premier multidisciplinary home visitation programs in the state of California that serves high- and moderate-risk low-income families. She directed and coordinated the evaluation efforts of this program. It is from this experience that she started working with Linda Wollesen on the Life Skills Progression™ (LSP) instrument and the writing of this book. She has taught nursing students at San José State University and has taught research methods to students in the Justice Studies Department. Currently, she is teaching graduate student nurses at the University of Colorado in Denver. Her research interests continue to be the social and emotional development of young children and the advancement of nursing in the field of infant mental health.

Foreword

Home visiting programs serve thousands of families annually across the United States for purposes ranging from the prevention of child maltreatment to the promotion of healthy child development and the educational development of parents. Some programs seek to accomplish multiple goals, whereas others seek to achieve just one or two. Some programs focus on first-time, teenage, or low-income parents, whereas other programs are offered to every family in a community. No matter their structure or goals, however, home visiting programs can only benefit children and families if program content is linked to program goals and if the program content is delivered with fidelity and with sufficient intensity by home visitors who know when to persevere with a day's lesson and when to put it aside to help a family handle a sudden crisis.

It is precisely this ability of home visiting programs to tailor services for families that constitutes their magic. The exemplary home visitor adjusts his or her plan to take into account the ongoing needs of the family and its needs on the day of the visit, as well as the constraints imposed by community context and home environment. Unlike many other service strategies, home visiting builds an intimacy that allows the home visitor to learn a great deal about families, and it is that wealth of knowledge and extra context that permit home visitors to tailor services most effectively for families.

Nevertheless, too much tailoring of services can sometimes mean that important issues are not addressed. For example, home visitors may shy away from broaching difficult or unpleasant issues such as mental illness, substance abuse, or domestic violence in families—especially if the visitors worry that doing so may result in some families leaving the program entirely. In other cases, home visitors and families may spend a disproportionate percentage of time on one or two issues, and other important issues may not receive the time and attention they deserve. Sometimes, for example, home visitors may find themselves spending more time attending to the problems of the parents than focusing on children's development.

What programs need are tools to ensure that important aspects of family and child functioning are discussed and progress is monitored routinely. That is one of the main purposes of the Life Skills Progression™ (LSP) developed by Linda Wollesen. The LSP should become a useful part of every home visitor's tool chest.

The LSP does not take the place of in-depth screening instruments that home visiting programs use to identify families eligible for services or to determine their levels of functioning and need. Instead, the LSP organizes that information. When used routinely by home visitors and supervisors, it should provide a quick way to see where a family stands on a wide range of family functioning. Undertaking that routine review of family functioning should help program staff align the services they provide with program goals and with family needs. In other words, the LSP should help home visitors and their supervisors become increasingly thoughtful, reflective, and planful in working with families.

In addition, of course, the LSP may make it easier for home visitors to raise difficult issues with families. If the LSP is used routinely, then perhaps discussions of difficult topics such as domestic violence, family planning, depression, or substance abuse can become just another part of ongoing program services. The LSP will remind home visitors to check if such issues are present, and the routine use of the tool may make it easier to raise the issues with families at a moment when the families are not in crisis. This volume includes a wide range of practical suggestions that indicate how staff and managers in home visiting programs can and should use the LSP regularly to improve program services.

Like most human services programs today, home visiting programs face increasing calls from public and private funders for evidence of effectiveness. Most home visiting programs cannot afford to take on the additional data collection and analysis costs inherent in sophisticated program evaluations. An ideal solution, therefore, is to use measures that are helpful in the delivery of program services as well as in program evaluation. This is precisely how the authors of this book propose the LSP can be used, and they include a wide range of practical recommendations for employing the LSP in evaluation. The LSP can show a family's progress over time on most of the dimensions of family functioning that are part of typical evaluations of home visiting programs. When results are aggregated across all of the families served by a program, those results can show the effects of the program. Seeing results in black and white can encourage families, cheer staff who may sometimes wonder if their efforts are making a difference, and reassure managers and funders that the program is indeed benefiting families.

Sometimes home visiting seems more like an art than a science. However, the LSP and this book suggest that collecting, organizing, and reviewing data and information on an ongoing basis can shift the balance from art toward science—a move that should lead to greater benefits for more parents and children.

Deanna Gomby, Ph.D.
Deanna Gomby Consulting
Sunnyvale, California

Preface

One fifth of American children live in poverty. And for the last several decades, those of us working with families who live in poverty have fought for funding—our own type of poverty. When did the first budget cuts and hiring freezes happen? The 1960s, I think. I can't remember a time when I didn't spend as much time finding ways to fund services as I spent on ensuring quality of service.

I am still puzzled by why this should be true. As a nation we are a caring people. However, we are more afraid of the sudden violence of terrorists than we are of the slow, ugly effects of poverty. The walls of social isolation between upper- and middle-income families and low-income families render invisible the dangers of poverty. *We* can't understand why *they* can't just do what they need to do to not be poor. . . . Education is free, jobs are available, just go to work and get off welfare. . . . Just say no and stop having children if you can't afford to feed them! Those of us who work in the barrios and ghettos, whose passion is to see low-income parents and their babies find a better way, who *know* how hard it is to climb out of poverty, have been too busy doing the work to successfully advocate for prevention and early intervention services. Our programs continue to lie at the bottom of the federal and state funding priorities as more money is spent on wars than on health and preventive services for our own citizens.

In the 1990s, home visitation services were thought to be a promising practice, but studies have continued to show only modest results, with the exception of one program that demonstrated a 79% decrease in child abuse in a longitudinal controlled study. The first time I heard David Olds present his study, I cried with relief that someone had finally proved that what *we* do in home visitation is important, improves outcomes, and saves money. My relief was short-lived, however, because I knew that what he had demonstrated for one nurse visitation program could not be generalized to any other visitation program. There was no *we* linked to the outcomes of his study, even for nursing visitation. When I read the Packard Foundation's *The Future of Children—Home Visiting: Recent Program Evaluations* (Gomby & Culross, 1999) and realized that most of us were not demonstrating significant outcomes—or at least the studies showed we didn't—I frankly didn't believe it. I believed instead that the problem is not our inability to produce outcomes, but our inability to demonstrate the outcomes we produce! My experience in the field didn't reflect "modest outcomes."

As the Olds Nurse-Family Partnership (NFP) model expanded past clinical trials to other sites, I worked for 5 years to find the 3 million dollars it would take to fund a site in my area. I wanted to see where the magic was in that model, to see what the rest of us weren't doing or didn't know and to see what data were collected. The new funding source that I wanted to tap was California First 5, funded by new tobacco taxes, which required child outcomes. I needed to find a way to demonstrate child outcomes, but child outcomes depended on parent skills and outcomes. There were no outcome tools that measured individual parent and infant/ toddler outcomes, and so my reflective process began and I wrote the Life Skills Progression™ (LSP) outcome tool. The LSP became the outcome instrument for the Monterey County NFP funding.

I began thinking outcomes. *What were the outcomes that we wanted to see for our mothers and infants? What did the family look like when we first met them? What life skills did the parents need to parent well, to move out of poverty, and to benefit from health and social services? What are the discrete steps of progress toward these life skills that we had not described but work with unconsciously all the time?* The thought process that went into the LSP was lengthy, but the time it took to actually write the first draft was amazingly short. One Saturday morning I felt compelled to try to define the main home visitation outcomes for parents and babies, and to capture the sequential steps from "as bad as it gets" to "as good as it can be." Four intense hours later, the rough format for the LSP was in place. The next day I showed it to a colleague who had been my best source of reflection, and I felt like a child showing my homework: "Look at what I did!"

Because I had the support of the director of nurses within the health agency, funding was found to test the LSP for reliability. It looked very good! That allowed us to pilot the tool within the agency, build the database (a painful experience), obtain the funding for the NFP replication, expand the pilots to other visitation programs, and gain the experience needed to refine the tool. At that point, magic happened: Joy Browne, Ph.D., from the University of Colorado Medical School–NICU, reviewed the LSP and encouraged me to apply for a ZERO TO THREE fellowship, and I was accepted. Kathryn Barnard, Ph.D., became a mentor for the project, and the fellowship provided me with the professional support needed to carry out the content validity review for final refinement. Vicky Youcha, Ed.D., facilitated the application to Paul H. Brookes Publishing Co. Meanwhile, simply by word of mouth, other agencies around the country began asking for training to use the LSP.

What evolved is a utilization-focused outcome evaluation tool for high-risk families with young children that is as useful clinically to the home visitor as it is for collecting cohort outcome data. The LSP is used by the visitor to sort and organize information gathered from visits, screening tools, and observations into a useable summary of a parent's and child's status. When completed sequentially in 6-month increments, the LSP makes progress visible. When done for a caseload, intermediate outcomes become available for statistical analysis. Data collected on a caseload can be analyzed to reveal progressive intermediate outcomes when compared with the baseline measure.

It is my dearest wish that the LSP, as it is used across the United States, will show the effective outcomes of home visitation so that policy and budget makers come to understand its value and fund our programs. I hope that the outcomes will prove so compelling that universal visitation, *at least* for families living in poverty, will be funded nationally. My second wish is that visitors and supervisors use the LSP to reflect together in ways that improve and empower interventions. As I train staff in different models (e.g., nursing, social work, parent educator and paraprofessional, national systems, stand-alone community-based organizations), I am aware of the need and potential benefit of learning what works best from the various service models. Finally, I wish that the LSP will become just the starting place for defining what parent–child outcomes are and what progress toward those outcomes looks like. The LSP's greatest potential service is its power to change how we think together for the benefit of disadvantaged families and the health of our country.

Linda Wollesen

REFERENCE

Gomby, D., & Culross, P. (1999). *The future of children—Home visiting: Recent program evaluations.* The David and Lucile Packard Foundation, retrieved from http://www.futureofchildren.org

Acknowledgments

Perhaps the greatest gift we can give to another person is to cause thoughtful reflection. Our profound respect and thanks go to the two people who had the greatest effect on the thought process behind the LSP. First, we thank Deanna Gomby, Ph.D., for her dedication to home visitation research, and particularly for her integrity and honesty in telling us about the "modest" outcomes being demonstrated and for the positive effect the challenge has produced. The field of home visitation is better because of it, and we are more thoughtful and more dedicated to demonstrating outcomes and to identifying successful interventions because of her work. Second, our deep appreciation goes to David Olds, Ph.D., for showing us how to demonstrate significant outcomes through his work with the nursing model. The quality of both the interventions and longitudinal outcomes developed and demonstrated in the Nurse-Family Partnership model has truly set the standard for home visitation services and has given us hope that significant outcomes are possible. We are also grateful for the challenge he has issued the field by raising the question of what type of visitor is likely to produce the best outcomes; the final answer for this is yet to be demonstrated.

For the more concrete supports provided for the development of the LSP, I thank the professionals in several agencies in Monterey County, California, who helped pilot the tool and thought with me all along the way. Special thanks to Lin McCray for all of those creative lunches we had and to Alene Guthmiller, my farsighted Director of Nursing who ran the gauntlet for me many times and was willing take the risk of funding the pilot work. My fondest appreciation to Carole Singley and Jan Paulsen, the colleagues who proved that we are truly "better together." We are grateful also to the home visitation staff of Monterey Public Health Nursing, Parents as Teachers, and Early Head Start for the use of "one more form," for their thoughtful comments and questions, and especially for their stories about parent successes. The usefulness of the pilot and national data would not have been possible without the preliminary reliability study and encouragement provided by Brad Richardson, Ph.D., whose wise friendship and dedication made all the difference in the final product.

The piloting of the LSP would not have been possible without the funding windfall created by the actor/filmmaker–turned–child advocate Rob Reiner, who dreamed of the tobacco tax initiative that became the California First 5. The world needs more champions like you! And an outcome tool is only part of the good funded by First 5.

Without the concrete support of ZERO TO THREE; Joy Browne, Ph.D.; the ZTT Fellowship experience; Kathryn Barnard, Ph.D., who was a mentor for the LSP project; Vicky Youcha, Ed.D.; and the wise comments and encouragement from the other 2000 Fellows, the validity study process and final LSP product would not have happened. But the greatest gift from the ZTT Fellowship is the professional friendship with my dearest ally and reflective function partner, Sandra Smith, M.P.H., author of the *Beginnings Guides*. The guidance that friendship has brought to the clinical usefulness of the LSP just keeps spiraling. Magic happens when nurse–home visitors and health educators think together collaboratively. Some of the most encouraging support and valuable critiques have come from Joanne Martin, Dr.P.H., assistant professor with the University of Indiana University School of Nursing and current ZTT Fellow. Joanne's work as past acting director of Healthy Families America and her deep knowledge of both public health and home visitation systems continue to add depth to the usefulness of the LSP to the visitation field on a national level.

Finally, my thanks to my co-author Karen Peifer, Ph.D., for her contributions to the evaluation information in the text. As a nurse-evaluator, Karen adds a perspective to the use of the LSP as an evaluation tool that will be helpful to visitation programs. Wally Anderson and Hope Maltz gave their technical expertise in the development of a user-friendly LSP database. Wally Anderson deserves extra applause for his enthusiastic contributions to the development and piloting of the LSP training and trainer materials. So few people speak both technical and program language; his ability to do both well is amazing. The editorial staff at Paul H. Brookes Publishing Co., particularly Jessica Allan and Jan Krejci, have patiently worked their magic to turn the tool into the book. Their support and dedication go beyond polishing a book or marketing a product; they reflect Brookes's value on the importance of the work with young families.

The collaborative contributions of so many colleagues makes this process an exciting and satisfying life experience. I have learned so much from all of you and I am so blessed by your friendships.

Linda Wollesen

I would like to concur with my co-author in thanking the many people who have contributed to our thinking about the many subjects addressed in the book and to the process of birthing this project. A project such as the LSP requires many hands to mold and shape it. My thinking as an evaluator of home visitation programs and my entry into the field came through my work with the Prenatal to Three Program in San Mateo County. Dr. Harriet Kitzman (University of Rochester) and Dr. Teh-wei Hu (University of California, Berkeley) have greatly influenced my professional development in research and program evaluation through working with this program. Sheryl Parker (deceased) and Dr. Maryjo Hansell guided me through the practicalities of conducting a thorough program evaluation with a real-life, ever-changing, and growing program. I hope that the many lessons I learned during those 4 years are reflected in sections of this book. In addition, Dr. Linda Perez and Mary Newman, M.S., helped me understand many of the intricacies of working with high-risk families and cultivated my interest in pursuing further research in this area.

Last and not least, I want to thank Cherleen (Cheri) Pearce, M.A., for her many hours reading and editing early drafts of the book. She gently helped Linda and me with our understanding, or lack thereof, with regard to commas, apostrophes, run-on sentences, as well as organizational issues. Not really understanding the content of the book, she made us laugh when she asked if a "disorganized baby" was one who got in trouble for not putting her toys away and said we were being unfair. Her insights, humor, and assistance were invaluable in the birthing of this project.

Karen Peifer

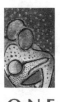

ONE

An Introduction to the
Life Skills Progression™ (LSP)

• • • • • • • • • • • • • • • •

Anyone can count the seeds of an apple, who can count the apples in a seed?

Early American proverb

• • • • • • • • • • • • • • • •

SUPPORTING AND MEASURING FAMILY PROGRESS

This book is about counting both the "seeds" and the "apples" of family change, and reaffirming the belief that change for the good does happen and that it can be facilitated. Societal change for the better does not just accidentally happen; it takes work. Determined parents, wanting a better life for themselves and their children, make positive change happen using the relationships, resources, and information provided by home visitors, friends, family, and other sources accessible to them.

The problems facing low-income families are multiple, complex, and interrelated and often span several generations of family members. Home visits to families during pregnancy and after the birth of the child by nurses, parent educators, and trained community workers have become the method used to build relationships, offer support, and provide information and referrals. Complex lives make it difficult for anyone, family or home visitor, to notice incremental progress in life skills as parents adjust to new parenthood. As a result, the structured measurement of family progress is an even more challenging task.

The conceptual complexity of outcome measurement, and our own confusion as to what the outcomes of home visitation services are, or should be, is the product of diverse interventions and program evaluations focused primarily on long-term outcomes. The "financial feet" of many of our programs are held to the fire of demonstrating whether they have produced fast and significant change in what have been termed *ultimate health*

1

outcomes (Halfon et al., 2000). These ultimate outcomes include important goals such as the Healthy People 2010 markers (U.S. DHHS, n.d.) and are highly desirable. They target such things as reduced infant mortality, child abuse, teen pregnancy, drug use, and maternal depression. The Rand Corporation and Wellness Foundation publication, the *California Health Report,* described a useful conceptual framework for the "determinants of health and well-being" (Halfon et al., 2000). The report used a modification of the work of Evans and Stoddart (1994) and expands on it. Halfon and associates (2000) described the interlinked chain of structures, processes and outcomes as a "critical pathway" that describes the influences of structural determinants, process determinants, intermediate outcomes, and ultimate health outcomes. How this theory of change and health outcomes fits with what home visitors and parents do is important and will be described in more detail in Chapter 2. However, the critical pathway model helps build a conceptual bridge for how home visitation programs can learn to connect the dots between parental outcomes and the ultimate health outcomes. This connection will not happen unless we focus with more clarity than we have in the past on what constitutes positive parental outcomes. This process includes defining the steps of personal growth for parents, recognizing them in parents, and linking them to the interventions that may have been the significant catalyst for growth.

Health theorists, evaluators, and epidemiologists look at population data, trends, and ultimate outcomes. The home visitor looks at individual parents, at her caseload, at program goals, and at the community in which she works. Then she asks how to get to the ultimate outcomes from individual parent and program outcomes. Outcomes have not generally focused on the skills or progress of individual parents. As a result, many individual parental intermediate outcomes have not been well defined, and have not been tracked over time or tallied to describe caseload characteristics and cohort progress over time. The Life Skills Progression (LSP) fills the gap in intermediate outcome measurement by defining and quantifying periodic pictures of parent and child outcomes. With this tool, a profile of parent and cohort progress begins to emerge and can be mapped over time.

The LSP measures a parent's life skills. The definition of a life skill is an ability, behavior, or attitude needed to achieve and maintain a healthy and satisfying life for families. The LSP describes individual parent and infant/toddler progress using 43 individual categories of life skills that reflect the array of basic skills needed to live and parent well. The LSP tracks important infant developmental and regulatory outcomes. Only when we capture the complex interrelationships of life skills and parental progress in achieving them will we truly understand what influences the long-term outcomes of families living in poverty.

The information summarized in the LSP provides clinically useful and succinct outcome information about individual parents and entire caseloads to home visitation and social service programs. Some families can independently identify their needs, utilize new information, and locate needed community resources. Many cannot. Home visitation programs generally target the most challenged families in our country in order to support the parents' need to master life skills.

Home visitors encounter parents struggling with the concurrent challenges of parenting and the effects of poverty. Issues of immigration, acculturation, and language often complicate those associated with poverty. Health care disparity (limited access to health care services, varying standards of care, and ineffective health education) has an impact on intermediate and ultimate health and birth outcomes. Social isolation, less than a high school level education, poor employment skills and job options, and limited child care all add to the burden of life and to poor ultimate outcomes.

While a variety of scales have been available to assess family risk, until the LSP, there has not been a broad-based parent/child outcome tool available to track progress of high-risk, low-income parents and their young children ages 0–3 years. The LSP can measure change needed for the results-based accountability and utilization-focused evaluation type of outcomes required by funding sources and administrators (see Chapter 2). If supporting a parent's process toward a final positive outcome is the art and craft of home visitation, then measurement of incremental parent/child life skills progress is what is needed in order to document progress toward ultimate goals.

POVERTY AND POOR OUTCOMES

Families, and especially children living in poverty, have an impact on the health, education, welfare, justice, and psychosocial systems because of the long-term consequences and related costs associated with poverty. *According to the National Center for Children in Poverty (NCCP), almost one fifth of children in the U.S. live in poverty (18% in 2000), including 2.1 million children younger than age 3. These children face a greater likelihood of impaired development associated with impoverished environments.* Impaired developmental experiences and relationships affect infants' and toddlers' brain development, ability to form attachment relationships to a primary caretaker, and ability to regulate moods. These neurological and chemical responses can be permanent. Family stress affects the stress level of the baby and stress inhibits the parent's ability to create a nurturing environment (National Center for Children in Poverty, 2002). Children who live and grow in an impoverished family environment have a greater likelihood of experiencing poor nutrition, environmental toxin exposures, maternal depression, substance use, family violence, and child abuse/neglect. Each of these factors can inhibit typical development (Gavin & Lissy, 2000). Diminishing child care resources, poor quality care, and prohibitive costs for good child care services add another environmental risk. These factors all combine to increase the likelihood of unintended and profoundly negative outcomes to the family, to the child, and to society.

Even in light of the compelling data regarding the effects of poverty, home visitation programs constantly face challenges including

- maintaining or increasing funding and political support for the model
- identifying and utilizing the most effective interventions
- demonstrating positive parent/child outcomes and long-term cost effectiveness

Unlike most economically advanced countries, the United States does not fund universal home visitation services for new parents. The preventive home visitation services that do exist for identified high-risk families are frequently under-funded in most states and communities. The lack of adequate funding can be attributed in part to the fact that one-on-one home visitation services are expensive, and by the fact that the short- and long-term effects of programs are seldom seen by those who pay for the services. A study of the cost effectiveness of case management and home visitation done by the U.S. Department of Health and Human Services, Health Resources and Services Administration (HRSA) supports the short- and long-term benefits and probable cost effectiveness of positive home visitor relationships with vulnerable mothers and their children (Gavin & Lissy, 2000). It is difficult to imagine that visitation services are not cost effective given that the long-term costs of not providing them spread across so many service systems.

The service costs estimates for the six largest U.S. visitation programs run between $1,300 and $5,000 per family per year. One federally funded intensive intervention program, Early Head Start (EHS), has costs for one site estimated at $11,500 per family per year; costs may be lower, depending on labor costs for a given area (Gomby, 2003). Categorical funding streams and continuous under-funding have contributed to the inability of programs to demonstrate positive outcomes and cost effectiveness with solid evidence. This is particularly true when multiple funding sources are necessary in order to sustain a program. For example, one moderate-sized parent education program in a mid-sized California county that is an LSP pilot site survives because of, and in spite of, 17 different funding sources. Each funding source has different outcome requirements, and data and quarterly reports must be done separately for each funding cohort.

Although evaluation services are valuable, they constitute added expenses for programs that have to maximize service delivery to needy families. As a result, many programs do not conduct evaluations unless they are required to do so. Unfortunately, a formal evaluation is sometimes experienced as extra work, as a threat, or is considered an impediment to providing services, instead of being seen as an essential element for success. This may be related to the lack of utilization focused evaluation concepts or the lack of a common frame of reference between the program and the evaluator. The type and amount of data required from staff that is already required to manage large amounts of paperwork has a very real impact on whether a program welcomes evaluation. It is in this context that the LSP may be able to provide valuable and time-efficient outcome data for programs and in ways that will ultimately preserve home visitation services for low-income families.

CHAPTER OVERVIEWS

This book provides background material and instruction on the use of the LSP for individual assessment, for intervention and program planning, and for data analysis to capture caseload progress. The secondary purpose of this book is to describe the "best practice" factors that are most likely to produce significant positive change in high-risk families so that programs can determine what intervention changes they might want to incorporate in order to improve their effectiveness.

Chapter 2 summarizes the struggle over the last 25 years to describe the outcomes that are unique to the home visitation field. The executive summary of home visitation outcomes in *The Future of Children* report (Gomby and Culross, 1999), stated that only "modest" results should be anticipated from visitation programs. The report generated the need for programs to find or create tools that measured the outcomes that were actually occurring because of visitation work with families and to improve interventions.

Chapter 3 summarizes current thinking on what constitutes best practices for home visitation programs and what is likely to produce measurable and significant results.

Chapter 4 supplies important background information about the development and field-testing of the LSP, including the reliability and validity work. It also describes the purpose of the LSP and what it does and does not cover.

Chapter 5, Instructions for Using and Scoring the LSP, explains how to use the LSP within the context of a home visitation program. This chapter is the training manual for staff and is provided on a CD-ROM for on-site printing so that each visitor can have his or her own set of instructions for easy reference. Training of staff in use and scoring is required to ensure inter-reliability. The chapter contains instructions for completion of heading data, and gives criteria to determine a parent's score for each of the 43 scales.

Because the LSP is a summary of visitor information and perceptions about a parent and child, the use of other screening and assessment tools is expected and encouraged particularly for child developmental and maternal depression. The concept of a *target score* for each scale is introduced and examples given of how to use target scores to show outcome progress. Target scores are the behavior descriptions listed in the columns that are the acceptable or desirable outcomes. Confidentiality and issues related to the Health Insurance Portability and Accountability Act of 1996 (HIPAA) are also included.

Chapter 6 suggests how to use the individual parent's LSP in reflective supervision, for intervention planning, and for family-centered case plans. Instructions on how to compare sequential LSP scores and examples are provided. This chapter is also included on the compact disc to copy for staff training.

Chapter 7 is about program evaluation, process evaluation, and outcomes-based evaluation. It is written specifically for use by clinical program staff who need to understand and plan evaluation and who do not have evaluator training. The reasoning and methodology for doing evaluation of any program is outlined and the use of the LSP data discussed in detail with illustrations.

Chapter 8 describes some of the implementation steps and planning necessary to begin use of the LSP within a single site, a program with multiple sites, or a large state or national system.

At the end of the book, the **Appendix section** contains checklists and forms to be used with the LSP. A sample case, with forms filled in, is provided (Appendix F) to illustrate the LSP. Appendix A, the LSP instrument, as well as Appendix B (Abbreviations Used in the LSP), Appendix E (LSP Data Entry Form), and Appendix H (Cumulative LSP Score Sheet), are included on the accompanying CD-ROM, along with Chapter 5, Instructions for Using and Scoring the LSP.

TWO

The History of the Chase

The Elusive Outcome

• • • • • • • • • • • • • • • •

*The human condition: insidious prejudice, stultifying fear of
the unknown, contagious avoidance, beguiling distortion of
reality, awesomely selective perception, stupefying self-
deception, profane rationalization, massive avoidance of
truth—all marvels of evolution's selection of the fittest.
Evaluation is our collective effort to outwit these human
propensities . . . if we choose to use it.*

Halcome (Patton, 1997, p. 3)

• • • • • • • • • • • • • • • •

HISTORY OF HOME VISITATION DATA: DEMOGRAPHICS, OUTPUTS, AND OUTCOMES

Since the late 1800s, nurses and social workers laboring in poor neighborhoods have been a lifeline for families living in poverty (Sherwood, 2005). The social and societal conditions in the United States that have an impact on poverty and maternal/child health have grown more complex and more costly, and the funding for home visitation is more difficult to obtain. Child abuse prevention laws were strengthened and this created some mandated funding for social work for abuse intervention. Without similar legislative support, and except for some mandated roles such as communicable disease control, public health nursing is funded by county or city dollars that are quickly shrinking.

Since the early 1970s, the field of home visitation, once the exclusive function of publicly funded programs such as nursing and social services, has expanded. The expansion included a range of locally run independent visitation programs and national visitation programs with standards, training, and staffing components. In the early 1990s this expansion was based in part on the hope that home visitation was a promising interven-

7

tion and the untested belief that paraprofessionals were the most cost efficient and effective visitors.

Before his death in 1996, David Packard, chairman of the David and Lucile Packard Foundation, stated

> I have come to believe that this country's future is being seriously compromised by inadequate attention to the problems facing many of our children and their families. America is no longer the land of opportunity for many of our young people because we have not been giving enough attention to the problems of their early childhood. (as cited in Sherwood, 2005, p. 5)

The growth of home visitation programs has not kept up with the increased demand for services by families and their young children living in poverty. In addition, the effectiveness of the home visitation model has been seriously challenged by recent studies, as discussed later in this chapter.

Some of the factors influencing increasing need and service growth include

- Expanding numbers of immigrant families, cultures, and languages
- Increasing poverty, particularly young children and single-parent families
- Shrinking public and philanthropic funds, particularly at state and county levels
- Welfare reform and time limitations on Temporary Assistance for Needy Families (TANF) benefits
- Nursing shortages; increasing use of paraprofessionals
- Skyrocketing costs of medical and foster care
- Concepts of prevention and early intervention and brain development
- Cost containment and managed medical care
- Shifts in public health focus away from maternal/child health to communicable disease and environmental threats (HIV, toxins, terrorist threats)
- Increase in community-based organizations (CBO) and community-directed services
- Less governmental focus on the issues of women, infants, and children and on poverty and prevention relative to other issues

Demographics: Families Served by Home Visitation

Service to new immigrants has always been a part of home visitation in the United States, but the numbers and types of families arriving shifted since the early 1900s from those affected by slavery and emancipation to European immigrant families and then to immigrants from East Asian countries after the Vietnam War. This wave of immigrants began simultaneously with the arrival in large numbers of Hispanic immigrants from Mexico and Latin America. The move to understanding cultures and valuing diversity, led by dedicated African Americans and Latino Americans, resulted in a somewhat improved national consciousness regarding racial/ethnic discrimination and cultural competence has become a core value of strength-based visitation. In this context, visitation agencies dealing with an increasing variety of newly arrived families began to collect *demographic information* regarding the populations served.

The rising interest in cost containment added the need for programs to provide *output data* to funding sources to demonstrate the number of the required activities accomplished (e.g., number of parents served, number of visits completed).

> The decline in support for government programs was fueled by the widespread belief that such efforts were ineffective and wasteful . . . while the Great Society and War on Poverty programs of the 1960s had been founded on good intentions and high expectations, they came to be perceived as failures. (Patton, 1997, p. 12)

Patton goes on to say that "Poverty statistics—including the number of multigenerational welfare recipients and rates of homelessness, hard-core unemployment and underemployment—as well as urban degradation and increasing crime combine to raise questions about the effectiveness of services." So the field of home visitation began to think about collecting *outcomes* to demonstrate the worth and fundability of the programs.

With the publication of the 1999 Packard Foundation Report, *The Future of Children— Home Visiting: Recent Program Evaluations* (Gomby & Culross, 1999) the home visitation field had to face the grim realization that measurement of their outcomes activities had resulted in unimpressive results. This unique wake-up call by one of the most influential funding and research organizations in the nation resulted in serious demands by funding sources for programs to demonstrate *goal-related client outcomes* (Sherwood, 2005). This left the field with a serious question to define: "What are the outcomes for home visitation?" This was followed quickly by "Who defines them?" Funding sources? Evaluators? Programs? State and federal governments? Universities? "All of the above" appears to be the answer, and as with blind men describing the proverbial elephant, confusion has ensued. The telescopic point of focus on the ultimate national outcomes for home visitation is extremely important to programs but is not particularly helpful for the home visitor and the work that goes on in the living rooms, kitchens, or bedrooms of poor families. Knowing that the ultimate outcome or goal is improved infant mortality or skillful parenting is essential, but it is not how you get there. The ultimate outcomes do not measure the incremental steps, the parent skills, and the community resources necessary at the level where visitors practice and that are necessary to achieve the ultimate goals. Some of the confusion in outcomes measurement is the result of the focus on the too-distant ultimate outcome goals in the absence of well-defined intermediate parent/child outcomes and skills.

Meanwhile, at a time when the number of home visitors available scarcely addressed the population needing services, the Packard Foundation Report fueled a 20-year debate about whether nurses or ethnically matched paraprofessionals from the community demonstrated better family outcomes. The nursing model described by David Olds, which continues to produce the most convincing evidence of significant and diverse maternal/

child outcomes, did *not* show similar results by paraprofessionals, and in fact showed almost no significant outcomes in families visited by paraprofessionals (Olds, Henderson, & Kitzman, 1994; Olds, Kitzman, Cole, & Robinson, 1997; Olds et al., 2002).

Surprisingly, the data from the Olds study have not resulted in a massive windfall of funding for nursing visitation models in general, although the number of Nurse-Family Partnership (NFP) sites has expanded significantly to about 250 sites nationally. The research also did not diminish the growing number of paraprofessional models. However, it did set a gold standard for outcomes, for quality training, and for best practice interventions.

The challenge for any visitation program continues to be the demonstration of significant and multiple positive outcomes for the families served regardless of whether the program uses nursing or paraprofessional visitors, or whether it is a local community-based organization or national system. The large national systems are making progress with their evaluation studies and outcome data, but it has been slow, challenging work. This is not common knowledge for the non-system home visitation programs and hopefully will be something they begin to watch. Although the larger systems' leadership and evaluators talk among themselves regularly at, for example, the Home Visit Forum sponsored by the Harvard Family Research Project, the shared knowledge that trickles to non–system-linked services is very limited. Many locally run programs have not discovered ways to define and collect outcomes, except as funding or management requires. Moreover, without an outcome tool used across the variety of sites and programs, comparable outcome data for the entire range of home visitation services are not available.

Demographic data describe the characteristics of the population served, such as age, sex, income, and ethnicity. Although they are not outcome data, they can be linked to family outcomes and yield important information.

Families targeted for publicly funded home visitation programs generally receive some kind of public assistance, fall within the federal 200% of poverty guidelines, or have a serious health problem such as extreme prematurity or have a teen pregnancy. The poverty population in the United States is estimated at 35.8 million (12.5% of the population). Racial and ethnic minorities are overrepresented in this population, as are families with young children. The poverty rate for young children runs at about 18%, according to the Center for Children and Poverty. Visitation programs work to become expert in serving the new immigrants and ethnically diverse families in their communities. The annual Federal report on poverty and health coverage showed the number living in poverty, the "new poor," increased by 1.3 million and the uninsured increased by 1.4 million representing 15.6% of the population (U.S. Census Bureau, 2003).

Not all families living in poverty have the same abilities and resource utilization characteristics. There are different levels of life skills that are emerging from the data regarding low-income populations. Community programs are beginning to describe the needs of these families with more specificity, to distinguish between the types of intervention and services offered based on need, and to "triage" services when funding prohibits universal low-income visitation. Most visitation programs focus on maternal/child health, although some attempt to service fathers as well.

Some low-income women function well and are educated, but their life plans have been temporarily interrupted by an unplanned pregnancy. These women may have social support networks and an understanding of changing roles and expectations. They may obtain and apply information easily and independently access and benefit from prenatal care and pediatric services. However, research indicates that the national attendance in prepared childbirth education classes is about 20%–30% and is primarily composed of college-educated women in their first pregnancy (Thompson, 1990). Women in this group can continue their education independently.

Having a home visitor may increase the skills of low-income women and their capacity as parents and helps identify potential concerns early in the relationship; visitation services may be a nicety and not a necessity. In a less costly alternative model, higher functioning mothers may benefit from telephone case management with significant outcomes, as demonstrated in a hospital-based phone follow-up study carried out in California (De la Rocha, 2004). Other low-income mothers are lower functioning and poorly educated, with low literacy skills. They may be uncertain about what being a parent entails and may have limited knowledge of child health and development. They are unlikely to engage in independent learning. They may not understand instructions from health providers, identify or communicate needs, and be able to find community resources or use classes (Smith & Wollesen, 2004). These families are the ones who are most likely to benefit from home visitors. However, in order to manage pregnancy and parenthood safely, not all of this group may need visits by nurses. Well-trained paraprofessional visitors or teams of nurses and paraprofessionals *may* effectively support life skill information and change. Access to health care services alone is not enough to produce the desired health and parenting outcomes (Kogan et al., 1994).

The third poverty subgroup is the highest risk. These families have complicated social and medical issues such as substance abuse, violence, severe depression and mental illness, or cognitive delays. They are more likely to have medical complications, premature births, congenital birth problems, and poor parenting knowledge and skills and are at greater risk for child abuse or neglect. Research suggests that the highest risk group may benefit the most from visitation services. The group is complex enough to benefit from services from professional or licensed staff (nurses, social workers, or infant mental health therapists) or from a nurse-paraprofessional team. The bibliography of the David Olds research with first-time mothers is available from the National Center for Children, Families and Communities web site. His research indicates that the mothers who showed significant benefits from nurse visitation had the highest risks (Korfmacher, O'Brien, Hiatt, & Olds, 1999). Mothers with the most known risks generally make the best use of information provided (Kogan et al., 1994). The high-risk group generally needs the coordinated support of primary care and multiple community resources, including center-based services and child care, in order to produce good results. *Building School Readiness Through Home Visitation*, a report funded by the California First 5 Commission, recommended that home visiting services be embedded "in a system that employs multiple service strategies focused on both parents and children" and include consultation "with families regularly to make sure that the mix of services is appropriate" (Gomby, 2003).

There are communities and states where universal visitation for all live births exists, but they are few and unique. Communities that are able to provide visitation for all of their poverty-level or Medicaid-funded live births are nearly as rare. Universal home visitation after birth of a child should be a national goal. Better outcome data should help achieve this ideal.

Outcome Models: Utilization-Focused Evaluation, Results-Based Accountability, and Critical Pathways

Programs look for measurable outcomes and do evaluation either because they are interested in and see the value of evaluation or because it is required. In these days of tightened accountability and scarce resources, having clearly defined outcomes and a simple but comprehensive evaluation is essential. Two evaluation models address the reasons for outcomes and offer the most useful evaluation concepts and structures. The first model is *utilization-focused evaluation* (UFE; Patton, 1997), and the second is *results-based accountability* (RBA). The RBA model has been developed and simplified for programs by Mark Friedman (Friedman, 2000), and his work is particularly useful to programs that are conceptually new to outcome measurement. Programs can find a succinct and helpful summary of the UFE framework for program evaluation on the Centers for Disease Control and Prevention (CDC) web site (CDC, 1999).

   Reinventing Government (Osborne & Gaebler, 1992) emphasized the following concepts, which are reflected in the models described above:

- What gets measured gets done.

- If you do not measure results, you cannot tell success from failure.

- If you cannot see success, you cannot reward it.

- If you cannot reward success, you are probably rewarding failure.

- If you cannot see success, you cannot learn from it.

- If you cannot recognize failure, you cannot correct it.

- If you can demonstrate results, you can win public support. (cited in Patton, 1997, p. 14)

Utilization-Focused Evaluation

UFE is based on the premise "that evaluation ought to be useful" (Patton, 1997), and therefore evaluators should design their studies and data to be useful to the people and programs they are evaluating. It is a real world approach to understanding the impact of a program and includes the many factors that are deemed important to the stakeholders, managers, and line staff. Patton suggests using systematic inquiry and quality indicators that have been shown to measure what is important to the program; he also promotes honesty, respect, and responsibility toward those who are asking the questions (Patton, 1997). Using this premise, programs plan what they want to measure, usually in consultation with an evaluator. The concepts of UFE were incorporated into the design of the LSP.

Results-Based Accountability

RBA is similar to UFE in that the evaluation is focused on the desired results or outcomes. RBA holds "programs accountable not only for the performance of activities, but also for the results they achieve" (Weiss, 1998). RBA uses logic, reason, and realistic expectations to find real, meaningful, and realistic solutions to social problems (Friedman, 2003). The first step in RBA is defining what results are expected. Articulation of goals and objectives as well as specification of measurable indicators are the early steps in RBA efforts. Clearly articulated goals—or expected results—reflect the values identified in the plan for the program or intervention and are statements of the expected outcomes. Although goals are generally expressed in terms of the entire population, they can be specific to individual agencies or programs. Goals and objectives are often expressed within a specific period and in quantifiable terms. For a prenatal program, the desired results might be better birth outcomes. One example of a desired result is that "all mothers will be healthy and prepared for childbirth."

Objectives or outcomes are derived from the larger goals. They are statements of the short-term conditions needed to achieve the desired conditions. As with goals, they are expressed in terms of a time frame for the participants of a program. An example of an outcome linked to a goal for a perinatal program serving families for a 2-year period is that 95% of children younger than age 2 will be fully immunized. The LSP includes for each scale the acceptable or optimal scores for each scale; these scores are termed the *target range* for the scale.

Under RBA, the next step is to understand birth or child outcomes and how they manifest within a program or a community. Finding a way to measure a desired outcome starts with either literature on the subject or from some promising practice that is yet unproved. In planning program evaluation, it is important to know whom the program aims to serve (e.g., the demographics). How does the program define birth or child outcomes and how does the definition fit with the design of the program? Are there measures that can be used or adapted to define success or failure of the program? Often the process of defining goals and outcomes is repeated frequently as the planning and implementation evolve. Data collected to demonstrate program outcomes and the ultimate social or health outcomes (e.g., reduce child abuse, prevent preterm births, and lower infant mortality rates) have not yet focused on measuring the types of and changes in individual life skills at the parent/child outcome level. These intermediate parent/child outcomes, which are the focus of the LSP, are the missing pieces in the "how do we get there from here" continuum to the ultimate outcomes.

Neal Halfon and his team of researchers at the UCLA Center for Healthier Children, Families, and Communities approach defining outcomes from a public health perspective. This group has produced one of the most useful and thought-provoking studies of outcomes, the RAND document entitled the *California Health Report* (Halfon et al., 2000). It presented an updated conceptual model based on the 1974 work of Evans and Stoddart that described the complex interrelationship of structural factors, process indicators, and outcomes. In the *California Health Report,* Halfon described the Critical Pathway leading to the Ultimate Outcomes. The Critical Pathway refers to "the interlinked chain of structures, processes and outcomes":

- Structural Determinants (e.g., poverty, maternal education)
- Process Determinants (e.g., access to prenatal care, substance abuse)
- Intermediate Outcomes (e.g., low birth weight, drug-exposed infants)
- Ultimate Health Outcomes (e.g., infant mortality, developmental delay) (Halfon et al., 2000)

So where do the individual parent/child life skills outcomes fit in this model? Are parent life skills another process determinant? Are parent skills an unrecognized intermediate outcome? The answer to this lies partly in the perspective of the observer. The only possible answer for strength-based programs is that parent/child outcomes at the individual and caseload levels must be added to the pathway to outcomes. Without this addition to the flow that produces the ultimate outcomes, we fail to measure what visitors and parents do to achieve the ultimate outcomes or fail to notice their contribution to achieving the ultimate outcomes.

From the home visitation perspective, what is missing from the Critical Pathway model is the parents' contribution to the path to ultimate outcomes. The Critical Pathway model below describes where home visitation services and parent/child outcomes appear to fit in the continuum to one ultimate outcome. The pathway model has been modified to read:

> *Structural Determinants*—home visitation services available
> *Process Determinants*—family receives home visitation services
> *Intermediate Outcomes*—parent life skills outcomes (e.g., parent creates safe home environment; uses information and resources independently; avoids substance and tobacco use)
> *Ultimate Outcomes*—lower infant mortality

Another way to illustrate the home visitation pathway is seen in Figure 2.1.

IMPACT OF MATERNAL/CHILD HOME VISITATION STUDIES

The David and Lucile Packard Foundation Reports and Studies

David Packard was a man of vision. He was committed to a belief that public resources should be invested in programs wisely and should be based on scientific evidence. He wanted to use his Foundation to combine multidisciplinary research and grants in order to influence both practice and policy. As a result of his vision, the Packard Foundation developed the Center for the Future of Children and set about funding, collecting research, interpreting results, and publishing the findings for a broad range of child-related topics in *The Future of Children* series.

| HV services funded and available to low-income parents | Parent participates in HV, health care, and education services | Parent incorporates information, resources. Sets/achieves goals | Improved life skills and child health/ developmental outcomes | Cohort data for ultimate outcomes improve with time |

Figure 2.1. The home visitation pathway.

Home visitation was the focus of two *Future of Children* issues. The first was published in the winter of 1993, when home visitation was viewed as a highly promising intervention model. The second, *The Future of Children—Home Visiting: Recent Program Evaluations*, was published in 1999, and the research results it summarized were, with two exceptions, grim. This document summarized the results of outcome research for the six key home visiting models nationally. These were Hawaii's Healthy Start, Healthy Families America (HFA), the Nurse Home Visitation Program (now the NFP based on research by David Olds), Parents as Teachers (PAT), Home Instruction for Parents of Preschool Youngsters (HIPPY), and the Comprehensive Child Development Program (CCDP). The results are described in the executive summary as "varying widely." The report stated:

> Several models produced some benefits in parenting or in the prevention of child abuse and neglect on at least some measures. No model produced large or consistent benefits in child development or in the rates of health-related behaviors such as acquiring immunizations or well-baby checkups. (Gomby and Culross, 1999, p. 3)

The research failed to identify which parents would benefit most from what services, or which sites might succeed. Half of the planned visits were not completed, and the attrition rate ran between 20% and 67%. These data added to unimpressive outcomes for some studies. The Foundation staff concluded carefully that 1) results could not be generalized from one program to another, 2) changing human behavior is extremely hard, and 3) significant improvement in service delivery was needed if significant benefits were to be achieved.

The recommendations for improvement of home visitation services included the following (Gomby and Culross, 1999, p. 4):

1. Policymakers and practitioners should maintain modest expectations for home visitation services . . .

2. Existing programs should launch efforts to improve implementation and quality of service. . . .

3. Research should be crafted to help improve quality and implementation.

The 1999 *The Future of Children* research report was understandably not well received by many in the visitation field. Sherwood reported that Deborah Daro, who had performed the analysis for the HFA section of the report, commented after its release, "the assumptions had been that there was lots of positive stuff happening . . . but the tenor changed to . . . 'Here's a body of research that shows that none of this works'" (Sherwood, 2005, p. 10).

Nearly 10 years after the first report, the Foundation commissioned Kay Sherwood to conduct an impact case study to summarize what happened to the sites involved in the 1999 research report and to interview the staff. In 1996, Sherwood reported that the Foundation wanted "to be about learning, rather than just about accountability" and to "emphasize the goals of learning and increasing effectiveness—both for staff and grantees" (Sherwood, 2005, p. 15).

The Sherwood case study, *Home Visitation: A Case Study of Evaluation at the David and Lucile Packard Foundation,* was presented to The Evaluation Roundtable chaired by Michael Quinn Patton in Princeton in July 2002 (Sherwood, 2005). It summarized the political environment surrounding home visitation from 1993. It describes a time when the Center director was Richard Behrman, M.D., and Foundation staff stated, "we believe that research findings are promising enough to recommend that the use of home visitation should be further expanded and the evaluation of home visitation should be continued" (Gomby, Culross, & Behrman, 1993). A little earlier, the U.S. General Accounting Office issued a favorable report that called home visiting "a promising intervention for at-risk families" (GAO, 1990).

Sherwood recounts the intense soul-searching process of Foundation staff as the dismal results of the second round of research became evident. They asked themselves "Are we prepared to say that there is no evidence that early intervention, via home visiting, with pregnant and parenting teenagers is effective?" The research found that "home visiting can yield some important but modest benefits . . . there have been no studies of any program that relied solely on home visiting which have yielded large and/or long-term benefits for parents of children" (Sherwood, 2005, p. 17). Outside consultants were brought in to help with the decision regarding what to say about the data. One was Ann Segal, who worked with the U.S. Department of Health and Human Services, who is reported to have said, "I take away that the evaluation answer is right—there's nothing there. But these programs shouldn't be out there by themselves" (Sherwood, 2005, p. 17).

The decision to publish the findings resulted in the 1999 report. Deanna Gomby described the meeting at which the report was presented to visitation leaders as "fiery." Heather Weiss, who had been involved in home visit evaluation since the 1970s, has described the field as "having grown up by models without an infrastructure to have 'cross-model conversations'" and added that home visitation programs were "in need of infrastructure . . . to strengthen the models" (Sherwood, 2005, p. 18). Sherwood goes on to report the current responses by the programs regarding the impact. The consensus of the programs interviewed was that the anticipated devastation of home visitation programs did not happen.

One tangible result of the Packard report is the Home Visit Forum, housed at Harvard and chaired by Heather Weiss, to facilitate the cross-model conversations needed to strengthen programs. Another more recent and extremely valuable offshoot of the 1999 report is *Building School Readiness through Home Visitation,* a report commissioned by the California State First 5 Commission. It can be located on the commission web site (Gomby, 2003). Program practitioners will find it an essential and current resource on home visitation as it relates to school readiness outcomes.

The LSP is another effort at improving parent and program outcome data and cross-program knowledge. Its development was directly influenced by the impact of the 1999 Packard report on the thought process of one visitation practitioner.

Other Reports of Home Visitation Studies

The two most useful resources that summarize the various studies done to date regarding home visitation are found in *Cost Effectiveness of Case Management and Home Visiting* (Gavin & Lissy, 2000) and *Building School Readiness through Home Visitation* (Gomby, 2003). The *Cost Effectiveness Report* is available from the Health Resources and Service Administration (HRSA) web site. It provides a theoretical structure for case management by categorizing four types of interventions: instrumental support, informational support, appraisal support, and emotional support. The report suggests, "Before case management intervention, stressors directly impacted health behaviors; they now are first mediated by individual coping mechanisms" (Gavin & Lissy, 2000). The report includes a theoretical model of the relationship between social support via case management on improved maternal and child health. Programs may find this model useful in explaining how their services work in creating improved outcomes. It stated that most studies of home visitation have focused on intermediate outcomes. Intermediate outcomes are "outcomes that are not necessarily valued as endpoints themselves, but that are believed to lead to valued health and/or social outcomes (e.g., adequate prenatal or well-child care use, enrollment in social programs, vitamin use during pregnancy)" (Gavin & Lissy, 2000). They described intermediate maternal and infant outcomes, citing studies of short- and long-term outcomes. The report also describes the cost-effectiveness studies available.

The second resource, the *School Readiness Report,* is available from the California First 5 Commission web site (Gomby, 2003). The report reviews and updates studies from the main national systems and includes the findings of 17 meta-analyses and literature reviews done on home visitation as well as a bibliography. Gomby described the trend that has moved from just literature reviews to using meta-analysis in which statistical techniques are applied "to combine the results of similar studies to generate an estimate of the magnitude of the benefits produced by programs of similar types" (Gomby, 2003). The authors (Appelbaum & Sweet, 1999; Sweet & Appelbaum, 2004) of one of the meta-analyses of home visitation programs described in this report concluded that

- Effect sizes, while significant, are small for both child and parent outcomes. Their practical significance should be questioned.

- There is no evidence that the duration or intensity of intervention influences effect sizes.

- There are no consistent effects across outcome groups for target populations.

- No consistent effects were seen across outcome groups for primary goals.

The *School Readiness Report* summarized some of the randomized study results reported by several of programs or systems. For example, the Teenage Parent Home Visitor Services Demonstration conducted by Mathematica Policy Research, Inc., and the University of Pennsylvania showed that visited teens displayed improvement in time spent in education, increased economic well-being (higher earnings), and increased use of family planning (if discussed at visitation); had less job training and were employed less; and showed no change in educational attainment, Welfare and Medicaid use, and repeat births.

The EHS study conducted by Mathematica Policy Research, Inc., and Columbia University in conjunction with the EHS Research Consortium indicated that "center-based programs had beneficial effects on cognitive development and some . . . social development. Home-based programs had some effects on language development at age 2 but not 3, but no effects on cognitive development." There was no effect on parents' self-sufficiency, and small positive effects on parents' mental health. African Americans and white non-Hispanic families benefited most.

The NFP evaluations were conducted by Olds et al. (2002) in association with the Prevention Research Center for Family and Child Health at the University of Colorado and Cornell University. The results indicated that visited families had fewer live births and repeat pregnancies at 36 months of service; there were no differences in substance abuse, partner violence, quality of adult relationships, mental health scores, and social support, but less depression was seen at year 2; there was no difference in high school degree/employment; and there were no differences in home environment, mother–child interactions, nonviolent discipline, and parental stress (Gomby, 2003).

In conclusion, it appears that home visitation programs still need to evolve in terms of effective interventions and how to measure parent/child outcomes. Our hope is that the LSP will add significantly to the learning process and ultimately measure what, when, and how well parents change with the support of home visitation.

THREE

Maternal/Child
Home Visitation Best Practices

• • • • • • • • • • • • • •

It matters what a mother knows.

Sandra Smith, M.P.H., C.H.E.S. (2005, p. 2)

• • • • • • • • • • • • • • •

DEFINING CONCEPTS: BEST AND PROMISING PRACTICES

"Best practice" in home visitation programs implies a strategy or intervention that has been demonstrated to be effective by well-designed research. There is a direct and logical link between the measurement of outcomes and best practice methods. Programs wanting to produce good outcomes work continuously to identify and incorporate appropriate best practice methods for work with young families. Because the research required to demonstrate that something is a best practice takes time, commitment, and money, the term *promising practice* became part of the field's vocabulary. Promising practice implies that while not yet demonstrated with research, a strategy or model has a theoretical basis that suggests that good results are likely. Some promising practices become best practices and some are incorporated into program design without a research basis because they cost less or are simply the hot concept of the day. Programs are challenged to distinguish which practices are both theoretically sound and pragmatically useful to their particular model and population. To be truly promising, interventions should demonstrate a sound theoretical basis with concepts backed by current academic work or journal articles and preliminary data or early research results for similar populations.

BEST PRACTICE COMPONENTS OF HOME VISITATION

One comprehensive resource for information on home visitation best practice and cost-benefit studies is the *Cost Effectiveness of Case Management: A Review of Literature* (Gavin &

19

Lissy, 2000) available on the U.S. DHHS/Health Resources and Services Administration (HRSA) web site. Another resource is the Packard Foundation's *The Future of Children: Home Visiting* (Gomby & Culross, 1999). This article and the Future of Children series are available free on request. Other resources come from University linked web sites. The *Zero to Three* journal and ZERO TO THREE publications, represent the emerging edge of promising and best practices for young children and their families from a multidisciplinary perspective. The ZERO TO THREE publications are listed on the organization web site. Many publishers of children's resource books, and particularly Brookes Publishing, are committed to identifying and making the newest theories and resources available, and their catalogs become another way for programs to keep up with new research and promising practices. *The Home Visitor's Guidebook: Promoting Optimal Parent & Child Development* (Klass, 2003) is an example of the extremely diverse practical material available to support the development of home visitor knowledge and skills.

According to the Packard Foundation's *The Future of Children: Home Visiting* report (Gomby & Culross, 1999), the results of studies of the largest and best home visitation programs in the country "varied widely." The executive summary suggested that expectations for home visitation services should "be modest." Because of this report, many programs and nationwide visitation systems increasingly began to incorporate established best practices and to monitor program outcomes more rigorously. *Home Visiting: Reaching Babies and Families Where They Live* (Powers & Fenichel, 1999) succinctly reviewed 20 years of home visitation research, profiled 10 programs using visitation as a means of serving young families, and listed resources for programs.

In California, due to a windfall of tobacco tax revenue for services to young children from birth to 5 years old, the First 5: Children and Families State Commission sponsored an extensive home visitation report for public reference titled *Building School Readiness Through Home Visitation* (Gomby, 2003). Although not available in print, this extensive document is available to download from the First 5 web site. In this report, the author suggested which program characteristics are likely to produce high-quality home visitation outcomes, including

1. Clarity of program role and goals

2. Curriculum used matches program goals

3. Program adherence to program standards for:

    - Family engagement

    - Curriculum use

    - Staffing: training, retention, and supervision

    - Cultural competence and consonance

    - Services tailored to high-risk clients

4. Coordination of services within the community

5. Home visitation uses multiple intervention strategies for parents and children.

(With Gomby's permission, this summary has been turned into the Emerging Best Practice for Home Visitation Checklist [Smith & Wollesen, 2004] found in Appendix C.)

In addition to these program characteristics, there has been progressive clarity offered in literature and research on what program components and practices are essential for good outcomes. The remainder of this chapter will focus on these practices.

The California First 5 School Readiness Report (Gomby, 2003) just discussed contains a summary of home visitation research and an interesting list of the characteristics of the six largest visitation programs (Gomby, 2003). The programs reviewed are EHS, HFA, HIPPY, NFP, the Parent-Child Home Program (PCHP), and PAT. The report stated

> Most home visitation programs seek to create change by providing parents with (1) social support, (2) practical assistance, often in the form of case management that links families with other community services, and (3) education about parenting or child development. (Gomby, 2003)

The report went on to compare program differences across four areas: goals, intensity of services, staffing, and population served. The report stated that the following are goals that visitation programs are likely to share (Gomby, 2003):

- Enhance parenting skills
- Improve children's health
- Encourage early learning and development
- Prevent child abuse/neglect
- Enhance lives of parents and children

Examples given regarding the last goal—to enhance lives—include services aimed at decreasing family stress and maternal depression, decreasing social isolation, and increasing social supports; choosing longer intervals between childbirth and decreasing the number of subsequent births; increasing education and employment; decreasing welfare dependency; and improving family relationships and decreasing family violence (Gomby, 2003).

Not all home visitation programs provide the comprehensive services needed to address these goals. Some programs provide primarily parenting education and not comprehensive case management. However, most programs serving low-income families find that they cannot accomplish single-focus goals such as parent education without addressing the rest of the issues that interfere with a parent's ability to focus on the child. In high-risk communities, noncomprehensive educationally focused programs may be more of a funding, training, or marketing strategy than a functional reality. Program advocates need to clearly state to funders and other stakeholders that in order to produce significant and positive outcomes, home visitation services and parents must work in partnership to resolve the complex individual and societal problems encountered daily. To secure recognition of the importance of visitation and to ensure adequate funding, the field *must demonstrate improved outcomes* for more families and children produced by more programs than has been the case in the past.

Unfortunately, many home visitation programs have a long way to go to demonstrate that they actually affect core goals such as family use of preventive health services. The First 5 School Readiness Report, in summarizing the results of outcome research to date, indicated surprisingly mixed results and found that over half the studies reported very small or no effects. According to the report, "The strongest evidence for the benefits of home visiting programs lies in the domains of parenting behaviors, child safety and the prevention of child abuse and neglect" (Gomby, 2003). The modest visitation outcomes described often fail to live up to the results anticipated by the programs themselves. Positive change will require the program's willingness to collect and use data to work with other stakeholders to determine what can be done to improve systems and interventions, and then to look again at subsequent data.

Some of the specific intervention elements currently thought to influence positive outcomes include the following:

1. Services start early in pregnancy

2. Visits are frequent, continuing for several years

3. Staffing is stable

4. Services are relationship- and strengths-based

5. Staff receive high-quality training

6. Visitor caseloads are small

7. Evidence-based and literacy-appropriate curriculum is used

8. Reflective functioning is supported

9. Services are culturally attuned to families

10. Collaborative relationships exist with community service agencies.

Each characteristic listed above makes an important contribution to the intermediate parent/child outcomes. These characteristics will be described in detail.

Starting Pregnancy Services Early

Pregnancy can be the pivotal window of opportunity for early intervention and prevention of poor maternal/child outcomes and for breaking the locks of intergenerational poverty. Pregnancy is the time when the health of the mother and fetus can be significantly changed for the better. Examples of prevention opportunities include altering the causal risk factors linked to medical conditions such as tobacco use to premature births, vaginal infections to fetal demise and infant mortality, folic acid deficiencies to neural tube defects, and the effects of maternal drug and alcohol use on the infant. Dental care for the mother during pregnancy has been shown to prevent early childhood caries. Lead toxicity of a fetus is another prevention issue in some populations because of placental transmission from a mother's ingestion of lead from environmental factors and cultural practices.

Other prevention opportunities emerge after delivery. The encouragement of breast feeding is one of the earliest and best preventive opportunities available to visitation programs because many new mothers either never start or stop breast feeding shortly after discharge from the hospital. The benefits of breast feeding to mothers and babies are continually expanding and being substantiated by research. Breast feeding joins an already impressive list of documented prevention factors. These range from medical factors (immunizations, well-child examinations, early dental care, prevention of injury and ingestions), to infant mental health factors (bonding and attachment, regulation of states and moods, child abuse/neglect), to enhanced brain development factors (prevention and early identification of and intervention for environmental or medical developmental delays). The list of costly conditions that home visitors can prevent or positively affect by the information and support provided is truly impressive.

The two best windows of opportunity to offer pivotal information and support to young parents come early in pregnancy (first trimester) and in the first days after delivery. In early pregnancy and when caring for a newborn, parents are more vulnerable and thus have a greater need for supportive resources and are the most interested in learning how to safeguard the pregnancy and to care for the infant. These are times when love for their child can reduce isolation and parents can utilize resources for support outside the family system. This openness is particularly true for parents experiencing their first pregnancy. Programs that only provide services after delivery miss a major prevention opportunity. Programs that begin services later, after the first 2 years of life, miss a chance to influence bonding/attachment relationships and the massive surge of environmentally influenced synapse growth in the infant brain. Opportunities for preventive interventions continue to a lesser degree throughout the early parenting years and evolve as the child grows.

Some programs, although having many goals, have targeted specific prevention areas. For example, the National Healthy Start program is interested in preventing infant mortality and works collaboratively in communities to improve the many factors influencing mortality such as preterm delivery and low birth weight. HFA programs focus particularly on child abuse prevention. The NFP model targets both the development of maternal life skills and child abuse prevention.

Frequency of Visits and Length of Service

Best practice programs use a frequency of visits that ranges from weekly to twice per month. The EHS model schedules visits weekly and adds center-based socialization opportunities to lessen parental isolation, to provide experience with social play, and to provide the observation of good parenting from staff and other parents. The NFP program generally schedules visits twice per month, but visits occur weekly for 6 weeks at the start of service in early pregnancy and again after the birth of the first child. Some models, such as PAT, have a flexible curriculum that is divided into weekly, twice monthly, or monthly lessons, allowing visitors to better match family availability and preferences for the frequency of visits.

A recommended length of service for EHS is prenatal to 3 years and PAT is in two segments prenatal to 3 years and 3–5 years. The NFP requires that services start at less than 28 weeks of gestation and end at the child's second birthday. Other programs base visitation schedules on risk assessments, with the higher risk families receiving more frequent visits, and others such as public health nursing leave the length of service and frequency of visits up to the nurse.

The number of planned visits and the number of completed visits are seldom the same for any program. The national average for completed visits in any program regardless of the intended frequency is about 50% (Gomby & Culross, 1999). "While a precise minimum threshold is unknown, researchers have speculated that four visits or 3–6 months of service may be required for changes to occur" (Gomby & Culross, 1999). Programs may want to keep track of the attempted to completed visit ratio for the caseload or for individual visitors. Use of LSP heading data options to track the number of attempted and completed visits and the months of service periodically and at closure can provide programs with useful information about the relationship between significant outcomes and service intensity or "dose." The same data can be used to monitor the amount of caseload attrition. It is useful to know when clients are likely to leave services, whether they leave unchanged or with success in many areas, and *what* changes occur *when* across each of the LSP scales. It is important to capture the qualitative differences between parents who exit from service that are successful "graduations" with positive outcomes, and families who are lost to service with little or no positive effect.

Staff Stability

Gomby (2003) stated simply, "The success of home visiting depends upon the relationship between home visitor and parent." The quality of these pivotal relationships relate to the visitor's own personal characteristics; to the amount and quality of their education, orientation, and training; and to the visitor's field and life experiences. These relationships with families, when successful, are very intimate. They are about knowing, understanding, caring, and building trust. The visitor–parent relationship is the womb in which positive family change is created.

Lack of retention of skilled staff affects both the visitor–family trust relationship and parental outcomes. The national nursing shortage, the upward mobility of paraprofessional staff, and the tendency to pay low wages to nonlicensed visitors are key factors in staff attrition. Programs may show increased caseload attrition and lowered parent/child outcomes if the visitor–parent trust relationships are disrupted by frequent changes in visitors.

It is possible to have a parent transfer successfully from one visitor to another with careful planning and preparation, but a real risk remains that the transfer will fail and the parent will drop out. The higher the family's risk factors, the more likely the disruption of the parent–visitor relationship will cause an exit from service. Visitors with solid training and experience are generally able to establish or reestablish relationships more quickly and work more effectively with high-risk families.

Some interesting hybrid visitation models are using two types of visitors for the family, one a culturally matched paraprofessional and the other a nurse or social worker. These programs may want to monitor whether outcomes improve more in multiple-visitor caseloads than in caseloads with stable or single visitors. Acceptance of multiple sources of support is a higher skill than many high-risk and at-risk families show initially (LSP Scales 10 and 11).

Because of the importance of the caregiver–infant relationship in center-based infant programs such as EHS, program standards require that infant care providers remain stable for the same group of infants whenever possible. The NFP has found that the exception to increased attrition with change of nurse-visitor was when the nurse left due to her own maternity leave. Apparently, the family and child values underlying the nurse's absence made the change of nurse acceptable to the parents.

Relationship- and Strength-Based Services

Most, but not all, home visitation models have incorporated the empowering concepts of strengths-based relationships into their philosophy and interventions. This empowering style was borrowed from brief service and family therapy models such as solution-focused therapy (Berg, 1994) and from human self-efficacy (Bandura, 1986) and human ecology theories (Bronfenbrenner, 1979). Strengths concepts are based on the belief that people grow or heal faster as they become aware of and use their strengths. The strengths and solution models focus on using strengths and parent-identified solutions and not problems or recommendations by outsiders (O'Brien & Baca, 1997). Home visitors are taught to see the parents as the experts on their lives and their child; to notice what is right, not what is wrong; to point out strengths and successes; and to support parents in "learning to do" rather than doing something for them. Parents are encouraged to identify needs, goals, and plans of action and to carry them out successfully. This family-centered approach is quite unlike the one used by traditional medical and nursing models, in which the professional is the expert who diagnoses the patient's problem and prescribes the treatment or develops and carries out a nursing care plan for a relatively passive patient.

Strengths-based approaches are currently being enriched with another emerging recommended practice that involves the use of teaching strategies to support parents' reflective function skills (Slade, 2002). The concept of relationship-based interventions acknowledges the fact that the relationship with the visitor is as important as the content of curricula or interventions to produce positive outcomes. Relationship curricula for family service advocates such as *Empowerment Skills for Family Workers: A Worker Handbook* (Dean, 2000) and those taught by the National Resource Center for Family Centered Practice at the University of Iowa are available for sites that do not have their own materials or training resources. *The Babies Can't Wait* materials are a good example of relationship-based handbook and training, which is customized for programs working with infants and young families (Kimura, 1999, 2003). PAT, Head Start/Early Head Start (HS/EHS), Growing Great Kids (GGK), HFA, and the NFP, are other examples of programs committed to a strengths-based approach to families and whose training and parent education materials reflect this approach consistently. Programs that have not switched to a strengths approach should consider incorporating it before measuring outcomes because it is perhaps *the* most fundamental and effective means of supporting positive family change when combined with reflective function interventions.

Quality and Types of Staff Training

The training provided varies greatly between models. Most national visitation systems (EHS, HFA, PAT, and NFP) have strong standards that include required training, certification, site reviews, and/or recertification. Some systems leave training up to the individual sites believing that communities know best what is needed, but offer training resources and conferences. One example of sound certification requirements comes from PAT, in which basic training is 1 week for each age range certification (birth to 3 years and 3–5 years) and in which annual certification renewal is required. Training is often linked to parent education, interventions or child development curriculum, but visitation theory and skills extend well beyond parent education and child development. Other much needed training areas include strengths-based concepts and techniques, cultural competence, communication and listening skills, and management of high-risk or violent situations, mental illness, and drug use. Local programs not linked to the resources of larger systems often have the greatest challenge in locating, providing, and funding optimal training for staff. Programs funded on a fee-for-visit basis have fiscal reasons for keeping training and supervision time to a minimum. Stable and skilled staff, unbroken trust relationships, a strengths approach, and the quality and depth of training and supervision combine to have an impact on program effectiveness.

Low Caseload-to-Staff Ratios

Nationally, the size of home visitation caseloads varies greatly. Caseload ratios inflated by fiscal expediency or unrealistic expectations can anticipate poorer outcomes, and may not find measuring outcomes possible or practical. The HFA sites generally assign 10–15 families per visitor and EHS assigns 10 per family advocate. Public Health Nursing caseloads are often much higher, usually 40 families per nurse. The replication site requirements for the NFP state that nurses carry caseloads of no more than 25 families. Some hybrid case management models using teams of professional (nurse or social worker) and paraprofessional visitors have reported having teams carry over 100 families with mixed risk profiles in the caseloads. Some county programs are forced by funding or staffing shortages to triage caseloads and are only able to serve the highest risk situations. Others are attempting to serve all live births regardless of risk. There is an undefined but real "critical mass" relationship between caseload size and the curriculum, materials, data, and documentation paperwork required. Many program staff struggle with overwhelming paperwork and agency requirements for meetings, which negatively affect the time available for visits, quality of visits, and time available for reflection and lead to staff burnout, family attrition, and poor outcomes. Well-organized curriculum and stream-lined data and paper requirements will go a long way to support staff that support families. It is not a good idea to just add the LSP to an already overwhelming paper and data system. It would be better to streamline the system before using the LSP to measure out-comes, or the outcome data results and staff impact may be discouraging. However, maintaining the data necessary to monitor program effectiveness and attrition is impor-tant or visitation resources may be wasted due to poorer outcomes secondary to infre-quent contacts and parent–visitor relationships that lack closeness and content.

Evidence-Based Curriculum

To achieve positive parent/child outcomes, the regular use of evidenced-based curricu-lum is a key component. One of the cardinal features of programs such as the NFP and PAT is the use of updated evidence-based pregnancy and parenting curriculum. Both programs use research and evidence-based curriculum regularly in every visit and in response to parent interest and needs. Unfortunately, not all programs have been able to incorporate well-researched, comprehensive, culturally appropriate educational materi-als that are designed to match the stages and issues encountered at predictable times dur-ing pregnancy and early parenting. Programs not using this type of educational material regularly are likely to see poorer outcomes than programs that do. Health education research suggests that coverage of key health topics in pregnancy has a statistically sig-nificant effect on the related outcomes (Kogan et al., 1994). Examples of the key prena-tal topics used in the research-based pregnancy curriculum *Beginnings Guides* (Smith, 1998) include "eat a healthy diet, gain weight, take prenatal vitamins, do not drink alco-hol, do not do drugs, do not smoke, breastfeed." The key message research implications for home visitation are that programs should

- Be clear on the key messages delivered

- Provide curriculum that provides the accurate information

- Ensure that staff are trained to effectively use and reinforce the concepts

- Assess family outcomes to see if there was a significant impact

Outcomes will be improve measurably when program funding allows for materials used to move beyond dated photocopies and culturally inappropriate material. There are a number of philosophic and pragmatic barriers to incorporating a good curriculum. These include

- Failure to recognize that research-based curriculum is an essential ingredient in pro-ducing measurable positive outcomes

- Finding adequate and ongoing funding for educational materials

- Locating materials that are culturally appropriate and matched for family literacy

- Investment in training staff in the effective use of the materials

Resources for Curricula

Finding the best match in affordable curricula is a challenge, particularly for local programs that are not a part of larger systems. The search for an affordable curriculum has been made somewhat easier by several recent reference lists that log and compare various curriculums. Barbara Wasik, a professor at the University of North Carolina, has written and produced several valuable resources on staffing and training (Wasik, Sheaffer, Pohlman, & Baird, 1996; Wasik, Thompson, Sheaffer, & Herrmann, 1996). The Florida State University, Center for Prevention and Early Intervention Policy, under the direction of Mimi Graham, Ed.D., produced the *Infant–Toddler Curricula Comparison*. For years, under the guidance of Kathryn Barnard and colleagues at the University of Washington, School of Nursing, parent–infant relationship observation tools and resource materials have been available for parents on infant state and cues, such as the NCAST Teaching and Feeding Scales and the Keys to Caregiving materials (Barnard, 1978; Sumner & Spitz, 1994). The University of Wisconsin, UW-Extension, Family Living Programs, DHFS-Department of Public Health, lists a Comprehensive Home Visitation Programs for Families with Young Children Resource Guide on their web site. Some systems, such as EHS, provide programs with a resource list and trainers, giving EHS programs throughout the country access to some common materials such as those developed by the WestEd Center for Prevention and Early Intervention.

Evidence-based curriculum is continually evolving and improving. The good news is that as research changes, so do many of the curricula available. The bad news is that keeping staff and materials current is a challenge and is costly. Training requirements, bilingual materials, certification, and costs for use of specific curricula vary widely and change regularly. See Appendix L for a sampling of some of the high-quality curricula and/or training materials available at the time of publication.

Responsive Parent Education

Young pregnant women and new mothers have multiple needs for basic care and support. The philosophy of the program and intervention model often dictates whether the visitor provides pregnancy or parenting information, crisis referrals without taking time for pregnancy and parenting education, or comprehensive pregnancy and parenting education and needed referrals.

The latter model represents the current thinking on recommended practice/best outcomes. The establishment of the trust relationship between visitor and parent always takes precedence in the first few visits. It takes training, skill, and commitment by the visitor to be able to include educational materials in a chaotic or emotionally charged situation. The Olds NFP model holds that the inclusion of educational material in every visit sets up a strong statement about the importance of informed parenting, encourages self-efficacy and self-esteem, and improves some outcomes. The visits and the educational content may be the only thing in a young mother's life that *is* regular, that can be counted on, and as a result, the experience encourages trust and confidence.

Given the long list of educational content in most pregnancy and parenting curricula, visitors and supervisors are challenged to find ways to manage the materials for each visit for caseloads and for individual parents. The support provided to visitors varies from almost none (making photocopies before every visit and working out of cars instead of offices) to pre-made and sequentially organized materials for each family and for each planned visit. The availability of *topic indexes* for the curriculum used is one helpful means of knowing what subjects are included in the materials and their location. An alphabetical topic index allows a visitor to find the topics that a parent is interested in during or before a visit. This is responsive education and makes it more likely that a parent will utilize the information. A *documentation log* that lists the curriculum subjects in order of appearance in the curriculum can be used as checklists for individual client records to chart what materials have been covered and when. This type of log also allows the visitor to identify what materials were missed by either late enrollment or failed visits, so that parents can be caught up on important missing educational pieces. Best outcomes are more likely when a parent has internalized the concept of the importance of learning about pregnancy, about child development and about parenting. It is an important and basic parenting skill to know when information is needed and how to ask for information in other life situations.

Supporting Parents' Reflective Functioning

Reflective functioning theory linked to attachment was originally introduced in England in 1999 (Fonagy, 1999), and more recent research at the Yale Child Study Center suggests that reflective functioning skills are at the core of mothering (Slade, 2002). However, the parent education materials used by the NFP and the success of their program suggest that reflective functioning is much more and is at the core of life skills, including parenting. Support of maternal self-efficacy for life skills is one of the goals of the NFP model, and the parenting educational materials are coupled with regular use of "facilitators," or reflective questions for the mothers to complete. The subjects that are the focus of the questions run the gamut from relationships with family and spouse, to infant care and development, to the effects of smoking. The impact of these written reflective questions on parents is powerful. The questions trigger thoughtfulness and ownership of what young mothers know and believe, and the answers frequently result in an action plan or incorporation of a parenting concept.

The following working definition of reflective functioning was developed for the Beginnings Life Skill Development training materials: "Reflective Functioning is the capacity to think about and see the links between events, a person's behavior, feelings and knowledge, and to respond appropriately" (Smith & Wollesen, 2003). The use of reflective questions appears to be one of most powerful concepts and teaching strategies available for home visitors to use with parents to support parental reflective functioning skills.

Conceptually, it is important to notice that ideally four parallel reflective processes are set up. The first reflective dyad is the *parent using the visitor* to think out loud and collaboratively. The second is the *visitor using the supervisor* to think collaboratively about each family. Reflective questions are an essential skill in both dyads. A third parallel dyadic reflective process evolves in this early childhood world of home visits, as the mother teaches her toddler to think about limits and consequences as gross motor and language skills develop. Many parents did not develop strong reflective functioning skills in their own families, and a home visitor has the opportunity to affect the reflective functions of both the mother and toddler. Examples of some potentially unlearned reflective abilities (Smith & Wollesen, 2003) include a mother's ability to observe her own behavior and feelings, to link feelings to events usefully, to recognize the need for information or action, to weigh options, and to make plans thoughtfully. Reflective skills appear to have strong links to self-efficacy and ultimately to parental outcomes, and combined with supportive visitor relationships and curriculum may be the magical ingredient for creating significant change.

The fourth parallel reflective process is within the agency, where leadership is reflective and the organizational structure is collaborative, both within the organization and within the community. *Being in Charge: Reflective Leadership in Infant/Family Programs* describes reflection for new leaders (Parlakian & Seibel, 2001).

Cultural Consonance and Competence

As debates related to health care reform were voiced in the early to mid-1990s, cultural competence standards were developed in the state of California and other states as Medicaid services transitioned toward managed care. State and federal governments required health care providers to provide information and written materials in the primary language of the client. Some of these changes came in response to tragic and costly miscommunication between providers and consumers. An example of a tragic result is a case in which the prescription for medication written by a physician for a young Spanish-speaking woman written in English said "Take once a day," and she died after taking 11 pills per day (*once* means *eleven* in Spanish) instead of one pill per day. That type of error is a linguistic one. Cultural competence requires more; it requires knowledge of values, family relationships, cultural treatments and practices, and different beliefs regarding body functions, child rearing, spiritual beliefs, and gender or age roles. Cultural competence standards require a range of translation services that allow the consumer to both understand and consent to what is being prescribed.

However, cultural competence goes beyond language capacity and bilingual/bicultural staff. For communities where there are only a few ethnicities and languages, culturally consonant services and staffing can be relatively easily managed and maintained. In larger urban areas, as many as 60–70 ethnicities and languages may be represented in the low-income population served. This represents a massive cultural challenge to any service system.

The sheer numerical complexity of serving highly diverse populations expands regularly with each new wave of immigrants, particularly as they arrive from third world or war torn countries. Some immigrants come with subcultures and languages that are unique only to their small tribe and bear no resemblance to the dominant culture of their country of origin. Legal immigrants often arrive in the United States as a group and are located together with similar cultural groups to aid in transition and acculturation. This also allows transitional support and comfort in their new communities. These families often know that they will be living here permanently and may never return "home." Motivation for change, adaptation, and integration is very different for these families than it is for illegal immigrants who plan to be here briefly and return to their home country.

The arrival of new immigrants with their diverse cultures, customs, religions, and languages means that agencies serving them need to learn and record descriptions of these characteristics so that staff can be trained and sensitive to differences. But the ink will barely be dry when the programs will discover that the characteristics of the first generation are no longer true for the second generation and may no longer be recognizable by the third generation. It is wise never to assume that you know an individual's culture and beliefs. Ask. *Ask* to understand. Cultural competence is most powerful and respectful when it is individualized and not generalized.

Programs serving young families have a unique opportunity to help a diverse community value and understand its members. Examples of programs using their structures to support multiethnic understanding include the use of families in boards and advisory or planning groups, and parent activities such as the EHS "socializations."

Collaborative Community Stakeholders

Extending collaboration beyond the agency management level has been an important trend. There appear to be four types of collaborative efforts used by the home visitation model: interagency collaboration, inclusion of parents as advisors, use of cross-discipline consultants for staff, and collaboration between different home visitation programs.

Several of the larger visitation systems have formally incorporated community and parent collaboration in their standards and infrastructure. Other visitation programs have become collaborative out of experience and necessity. In some states, statutes such as those creating the First 5 Children and Families Commission have mandated local control of how the funds are awarded and have built structures supporting collaboration between funded programs. The wisdom reflected in these models points to the need for multiple views being woven together at a local level in order to identify local needs, create the changes in systems, and develop responsive resources. The groups have been able to carry out needs assessments, map resources, draft interagency consents for release of information, build trusted and responsive referral relationships and services, carry out political advocacy, and sometimes share funding and sites.

Some but not all programs have learned to include parents in their advisory boards and collaborative planning meetings. HS/EHS and the National Healthy Start organization are two strong examples of inclusiveness and collaboration. Their advisory boards and consortiums consist of representatives of community stakeholders, agencies, and parents. Program staff working in these visitation models are often graduates of the program. Measuring the effects of collaborative efforts on parents and children and at the community level is a challenge; often anecdotal or qualitative measures are what is available to document the value of collaboration. Programs resort to counting the number of agencies present at meetings or the number of referrals made by visitors as indicators of the success of collaboration.

The third form of collaboration is the use of multidiscipline consultants, often from other agencies, for regular one-on-one time with home visitors to discuss specific family or child situations. The consultants are usually nurses or infant mental health social workers or psychologists who come to the programs and may go on shared visits. Other communities have consultation available through the community's special education system or by medical teams for children with suspected or identified special needs.

The fourth type of emerging collaboration happens when the home visitation agencies in a county or community discover that they share common goals and common service populations. Some collaborative groups use interagency agreements to formalize mutual goals and to define each agency's role and responsibilities, including funding issues. To avoid duplication of services, ensure that family needs and services are well matched, and keep all visitation caseloads full, a group may create a common resource through which requests for home visitation may be screened and cases assigned for any of the community programs. Interagency education and training programs are another common example of sharing funds and resources. Some programs manage to share office space or apply for grants together or agree on which program will apply for specific funds.

In communities where all the visitation services use the LSP, creation of a common data bank may be possible to centralize the costs of data management. This requires agreements and protection of confidentiality by use of numerical case identifiers, or getting informed consent from parents. Other groups have agreed to use the LSP as a common outcome tool, with each agency maintaining its own data but meeting periodically to share and compare baseline and sequential aggregate data so that all of the programs can learn from the data. This can be a powerful way to use the LSP for needs assessment, planning, program improvement, and advocacy for visitation services. A collaborative planning tool such as "Better Together" (see Appendix D) can help to identify common interests basic to forming collaborative visitation planning groups (Singley & Wollesen, 2003).

Margaret Mead said, "Never doubt that a small group of thoughtful, committed citizens can change the world; indeed, it is the only thing that ever has™" (courtesy of the Institute for Intercultural Studies, Inc., New York). For programs to be effective, collaboration is essential. However, the greatest challenge may be in noticing what has changed and proving that it has changed significantly.

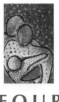

FOUR

Development and Field Testing of the LSP

PURPOSE, TARGET POPULATION, AND DEVELOPMENT

One purpose of the LSP is to describe the progressive outcomes of individual parents and children and of the caseloads served by home visitation programs. The young families enrolled in visitation programs usually are low-income households and have the various risk factors associated with poverty.

Most evaluation tools are developed in research settings located in universities or in private corporations specializing in field research consultation. The LSP was developed in the field primarily for clinical and outcome use and secondarily for use in research settings. It was written by Linda Wollesen as a distillation of more than 35 years of home visitation experience in public health nursing programs and was created in response to the need for a comprehensive outcome tool for home visitation services. The existing family outcome tools, the California Matrix, the Automated Assessment of Family Progress (AAFP), and the North Carolina Family Assessment Scale (NCAFS), focus on family outcomes rather than the individual parent and infant/toddler outcomes, which are needed by most home visitation programs (Endress, 2000; Kirk, 1998; NRCFCP, 1994). The AAFP, the Matrix, the nursing home visitation research of David Olds, and the home visitation articles edited by Deanna Gomby for the Packard Foundation became the main catalysts for the design of the LSP scales.

The thought process that was the basis for the content of the LSP consisted of four primary design components. The first component was *to define* which parent and child outcomes are unique to home visitation services versus which are the primary responsibilities of health care, child development, education, and/or other service programs. Among the community of care, there are many shared outcomes for healthy pregnancies and good child development, and the interventions by the various programs overlap in many cases. Home visitation services provide collaborative and supportive roles to the direct care providers and offer an array of unique approaches. The second component required in the design of the LSP was *to identify* what are basic parental life skills and to describe the range of progress or characteristics seen in each of these skill areas.

For the purposes of the LSP, a life skill is defined as a behavior, ability, attitude, or characteristic used to achieve and maintain a satisfying and healthy life, free from the negative affects of poverty. It includes the ability to

- Have nurturing relationships
- Provide for health care and healthy life styles
- Utilize resources and information
- Complete a basic education
- Have regular gainful employment
- Provide for basic needs (housing, transportation, nutrition)
- Raise children who have optimal health and development

A third design goal was to produce a tool to quantify outcomes and have high content validity and interrater reliability. The tool also needed to capture the sequential comparison of situational progress of individual parent–child dyads and for program caseloads. This chapter describes the reasoning behind each scale and what material is and is not covered in the LSP as a whole. An underlying premise of the LSP is that behavior is learned, relationships and life skills are learned, and progress can happen and be described and quantified.

Purpose of the LSP

The LSP has a number of clinical and outcome specific purposes:

- To profile service population characteristics, including an individual parent or child, a caseload, or a caseload subset
- To document baseline characteristics and quantify sequential change by comparing baseline profiles with ongoing and closing data
- To identify parent and child strengths, needs, and goals for thoughtful, collaborative planning
- To compare service populations enrolled in different programs within an agency, visitation system, or community
- To demonstrate long-term outcomes, accounting for variables such as service dose (months of service and number of visits, type of staff or service model)
- To provide an information resource for reflective supervision
- To identify life skills categories and types of clients showing the most and least progress
- To support outcome data analysis using multiple psychosocial and health-related variables

- To provide data and a perspective for program improvement, funding, community planning, and training

Target Population

The LSP targets at-risk and high-risk parents and their children from pregnancy to age 3 years who are living in poverty. The health, social services, justice system, and educational costs related to impoverished families are extremely expensive to our society. Unfortunately, the programs bearing the costs of preventive services usually are not the ones incurring the benefit of the costs saved. This makes funding for home visitation services a challenge.

In the now classic 1989 book, *Within Our Reach: Breaking the Cycle of Disadvantage,* Lisbeth B. Schorr describes "the high cost of rotten outcomes," defines risk factors associated with poverty, and makes a powerful case for reforming national policies. Unlike other advanced countries, the United States does not have the elimination of poverty as a goal, although some would argue that welfare reform was intended to do this (Schorr & Schorr, 1989). Inadequate funding for poverty prevention exists in spite of spiraling costs related to poverty-associated health care, child development, and early failure in school; welfare and foster care costs; and justice system, violence, and substance treatment.

The impressive outcomes of the research by Olds and associates and the cost–benefit study of the Olds and the Perry Preschool models by the RAND Corporation resulted in national acclaim for these models. Since then, the combined impact of the attacks of September 11, 2001, the depressed economy, and the costs of antiterrorism measures and war have combined to create funding cuts and cause programmatic changes even to well-established and effective programs. Funding shortfalls for foundations and governmental resources emphasize the challenge facing the field of home visitation to clearly describe complex skills that are needed by families in order to prevent "rotten" outcomes. A related challenge is to demonstrate how much positive family change is possible and to show which programs are effective in supporting the development of these skills. A common parent/child outcome tool and data bank, which spans programmatic boundaries, may contribute to the ability of the home visitation field to advocate effectively for funding for the services needed to eradicate poverty.

LSP Pilot Study Environment

The pilot study for the LSP was originally conducted in several community-based home visitation programs in one California county. The LSP is now used by a variety of programs in many states, including several of the nationally linked programs (HFA, National Healthy Start [NHS], PAT, EHS) and statewide systems.

Field testing and academic support from experts in evaluation and early childhood came after the initial development and as the result of other clinicians hearing about the LSP at conferences or from colleagues. Word spread among evaluators providing consultation to local programs through Federal or State grants such as EHS, Safe Schools, and First 5 of California. Valuable support came from ZERO TO THREE/National Center for Clinical Infant Programs, an organization that provided the LSP's author with a Fellowship in 2000–2002 that resulted in access to national experts. The collaborative thinking and ongoing dialogs, which developed between the LSP's author and the pilot sites using the LSP, resulted in valuable clarifications to the scales and training materials.

Field testing was conducted by each site or cluster of programs using separate databases that were designed in response to site-specific program goals, funding requirements, and technical ability. Each site had to develop its own database using Access (Microsoft Corporation) or SPSS (SPSS Inc.) software. Some sites were fortunate enough to have grant-linked evaluator assistance from private consultants or university-based research groups.

The LSP was written originally in 1998–1999 when the author was a supervising public health nurse with management and supervision responsibility for four home visitation programs run by the Monterey County (California) Public Health Department. The programs included public health nursing, a state-funded high-risk infant follow-up, an Adolescent Family Life Program (AFLP), and the NFP program. The latter was an approved replication site for the "best practice" model developed by David Olds and colleagues at the University of Colorado. The health department programs were joined under consultation agreements by other countywide visitation programs, which included PAT and a new EHS site. All of these programs participated in the pilot study for the LSP. They used a common database and had interagency agreements and informed parental consents. This collaborative effort gave a countywide snapshot of the baseline profiles of families being served by home visitation. The experience provided a population of about 800 families in the open caseloads for anonymous study as each program's data became available. Substantial grant-based funding was acquired by programs using the LSP for sequential outcome data. The analysis of some of the anonymous versions of LSP pilot database will be used to provide the examples of evaluation described in Chapter 7.

History of LSP Development and Testing

1998–1999

- LSP written with 37 scales
- Preliminary inter- and intrarater reliability estimated at 90% by Brad Richardson, Ph.D., lead evaluator for the National Resource Center for Family Centered Practice at the University of Iowa School of Social Work

1999

- LSP use and Access database piloted internally in Monterey County public health nursing and associated community programs

2000

- LSP expanded to 43 scales

- LSP used to demonstrate Monterey County NFP and PAT outcomes for California First 5 grants
- LSP training began for 11 other California programs, counties, and First 5 sites, and expanded to sites in Montana and Pennsylvania

2001–2002

- ZERO TO THREE National Fellowship awarded to the LSP's author, to refine and publish the LSP. Kathryn Barnard, Ph.D., R.N., was Board Member and mentor for the LSP.

2002–2003

- Content validity study carried out using 46 multiethnic expert reviewers representing nine disciplines and consisting of ZERO TO THREE Fellows, trainers from national home visitation programs, evaluators, and staff from sites using the LSP
- LSP instructions for use in reflective supervision completed in collaboration with Sandra Smith, M.P.H., C.H.E.S.; the work was funded by two ZERO TO THREE grants and incorporated into reflective function training and materials. The materials are linked to the *Beginnings Guides* curriculum, illustrated by Laurel Burch, and subsequently published in 2004 as a CD with training required for use.

2003–2004

- LSP database designed using MS Access XP Professional 2000 software and available for programs that do not wish to develop their own LSP software
- LSP data web site for data entry and analysis reports is being considered in collaboration with the University of Washington, Center for Health Education and Research (CHER), in Seattle. This will create easy access to sophisticated data analysis for individual home visitation programs or systems of programs. It is expected that the Access data entry screens currently used by most programs using the LSP will form the basis for entry into a web-based system. Plans are being made to transfer existing LSP data into the Web data banks to provide important continuity for programs. CHER at the University of Washington in Seattle is considering management of the Beginnings & Life Skills Progress trainings to ensure reliability and for related trainer trainings.

RELIABILITY AND VALIDITY TESTING

Definition of Reliability and Validity

It is important to understand the difference between validity and reliability. A valid instrument measures the constructs it says it is measuring in a clear and consistent way. The Weiss definition of validity is "the extent to which a measure captures the dimension of interest" (Weiss, 1998). Reliability means "the consistency or stability of a measure over repeated use" (Weiss, 1998). It is measured by the proportion between the true score variance and the total variance. This is called partial correlation and indicates the proportional relationship between item measurements.

Validity and item analysis are used to construct measurement scales, to improve existing scales, and to evaluate the reliability of scales already in use. Specifically, validity and item analysis aid in the design and evaluation of the scale that is made up of multiple individual measurements (e.g., different items, repeated measurements, or different measurement devices). The LSP has 43 different scales that measure different constructs. Some scales are related directly to each other and other scales are related indirectly or are related sequentially in time to each other. For example, a pregnant mother would not have an infant scale scored until after the birth of the baby. A mother with depression might show a high correlation score on the relationship with spouse scale.

Construct Validity

In order to understand the traditional definition of construct validity, it is first necessary to understand what a construct is. A construct is an attribute, proficiency, ability, or skill that occurs in human experience and is defined by established theory. For example, self-esteem is a measurable construct. It exists in theory and exists in people. Construct validity and reliability are important if you want to be able to say that the measurement tool consistently measures the same thing each time it is used. Specifically, it is important to know how consistent the results are for the 43 different items being assessed by the LSP in repeated uses.

The following is an example of the process that needs to occur to establish construct validity:

1. Establish what it is you want to measure within a series of phrases or easily understood concepts (also called *net of meaning*). For example, for a scale about self-esteem, this means having an understanding of what self-esteem means and how to measure it. The meaning of self-esteem is based on the literature, but it is not a static or constant expression.

2. Find and use established measures if they are available. If an established measure is not available in the form needed, make revisions to match your theory and needs starting with what is available. Continuing the example of self-esteem, there are established ways to measure self-esteem based on the literature, and measurements are found in existing tools. However, to measure change in self-esteem within a certain context, such as "parental confidence and sense of self-worth," adapt or change some of the existing measures to accommodate project needs.

3. If changes are made in the wording or text of the standardized measure, be able to explain why the change was made and re-test the wording changes to make sure that others easily understand it to ensure consistent use.

Each of the 43 scales or constructs in the LSP has gone through this process during the 3 years of its development. The validity is measured using *alpha scores*. An alpha score measures internal consistency of the average scores for each item at the time it is administered. Data from each year the test was administered were calculated, but total scores for the total years were not.

Table 4.1. Illustration of the different correlations between initial and ongoing at 12-months assessment done with families in two different programs using the LSP. The alpha scores range between 0.64 and 0.9852, which indicates acceptable to excellent.

	Alpha scores (Total sample size = 3,937 cases)	Program A (1,728 cases at 12 months)
Relationships (Scales 1–11)	0.9407	0.9223
Education (Scales 12–16)	0.7786	0.6447
Health and medical care (Scales 17–23)	0.8981	0.7994
Mental health/substance abuse and other risks (Scales 24–29)	0.9852	0.6874
Basic essentials (Scales 30–35)	0.9427	0.7248
Infant/toddler development (Scales 36–43)	0.9407	0.7791
Total: all items	0.9386	0.8145

Source: LSP pilot study data

The formula for calculating an alpha score is

$$\text{Alpha score } (\alpha) = (k \, / \, (k - 1)) \times [1 - \Sigma(s^2_i) \, / \, s^2_{sum}]$$

Where s^2_i indicates the variances for the k individual items, s^2_{sum} indicates the variance for the sum of all items. The closer α is to 1.0, the more reliable the test. An alpha score range of 0.60–0.75 is acceptable; 0.75 or greater is best.

Another way to calculate the alpha score is to use a statistical software package on your own collected data. Table 4.1 illustrates the alpha scores calculated on the total use of LSP data during a 3-year period and then scores calculated by two different programs.

Table 4.1 illustrates the different correlations between initial and ongoing at 12 months assessment done with families in two different programs using the LSP. The alpha scores range between 0.64 and 0.9852, which indicates acceptable to excellent.

Interrater or Interobserver Reliability

Another way to estimate validity and reliability is doing an *interrater reliability test*. Interrater or interobserver reliability testing determines the degree to which different raters/observers give consistent estimates of the same phenomena. Whenever people are conducting a part of the measurement procedure, reliable or consistent results can be a concern. People can be easily distracted and sometimes have a bias for or against what they are trying to measure. They get tired of doing repetitive tasks or they may daydream and sometimes misinterpret the data; or the person collecting the data may not want to do it so they fudge the results just to finish and return to more "important" work.

So how do we determine whether observers are being consistent in their observations? There are two major ways to estimate interrater reliability. Each person—called a rater—observes a family and assigns a score he or she believes most accurately represents the family. If the different raters do this independently, without speaking or consulting with each other, the percentage agreement between the raters can be calculated. For example, 100 observations were rated by two raters. For each observation, the rater could check a score of 1–5. On 86 of the 100 observations the raters checked the same score. In this case, the percentage agreement would be 86%. It is a crude measure, but it does give an idea of how much agreement exists.

A second way to measure interrater reliability is to give an example of a scenario that may have occurred during a home visit and ask two people to rate the scenario using the LSP. In the year 2000, five narratives were written based on case histories of program participants (Richardson, 2000). Twelve staff (11 nurses and 1 social worker) served as raters using the LSP. The staff completed assessments on the LSP score sheet, rating the clients described in the narratives using the 31 outcome categories of the LSP.

This early interrater reliability test found a 90% agreement on Scales 5–30 within acceptable ranges. However, Scales 12–19 did not achieve 90%. Recommendations for syntax change were made and the LSP was adapted, with the final reliability estimated at 90%.

During the developmental stages of the LSP, numerous interrater tests were performed to understand the content of the LSP scales and the results of the training. An official interrater reliability test in which two reviewers evaluated the same dyad at the same time was not done. However, in more than 3 years of development, it has become clear due to alpha Cronbach analysis of data that there is a range of agreement between 70% and 90% on how to score the 43 items of the LSP (De la Rocha, 2004). As programs using the LSP become available in which two visitors are involved with each family (usually one nurse and one paraprofessional), formal interrater reliability tests can be performed more easily.

Test-Retest Reliability

We estimate test-retest reliability when we administer the same test to the same (or a similar) sample on two different occasions. This approach assumes that there is no substantial change in the construct being measured between the two occasions. The amount of time allowed between measures is critical. We know that if the same thing is measured twice, the correlation between the two observations will depend in part on how much time elapses between the two measurements. The shorter the time gap, the higher the correlation; the longer the time gap, the lower the correlation. This occurs because the two observations are related over time—the closer in time, the more similar the factors that contribute to error. Because this correlation is the test-retest estimate of reliability, considerably different estimates may be obtained depending on the interval. For this reason, we recommend using the same person to administer the LSP at 6-month intervals.

Another way to measure internal consistency is to use mathematical equations to test the relationship between the different items on the LSP. This is accomplished by doing an interitem correlation between items designed to measure the same construct. First, compute the correlation between each pair of items. Using pilot data from one program, correlations were computed. The average interitem correlation score was 0.90, with the individual correlations between each scale ranging from 0.84 to 0.95.

INTERRATER RELIABILITY AND NEED FOR TRAINING

The original inter- and intrarater reliability study (Richardson, 2000) included a 4-hour training for staff in the use and scoring of the LSP. The training used an earlier version of the material now covered in Chapter 5. To ensure similar high inter- and intrarater reliability, programs should train staff thoroughly in the use of the LSP and provide each trainee with a set of Instructions for Use and Scoring (see Chapter 5) for easy reference. The training should review the material covered in the Instructions, including the completion of the heading information and the criteria for scores for *each* scale. Most programs will find that consistent scoring is reinforced when the same trainer provides consistent training. The trainer is usually a certified LSP trainer or a program supervisor who is on site or in regular contact with staff. When programs use the direct supervisor/ trainer for reflective supervision, and review each newly scored LSP with the visitor, good reliability (80th–90th percentiles) is very likely. Staff questions or confusion can be answered consistently and in a timely fashion in supervision sessions.

Two human factors can influence the accuracy of the information reflected in a scored LSP: whether a parent shares accurate information with the visitor, and the interview and observation experience of the visitor. The first is a trust and relationship issue between the visitor and the parent, and the second is a training and experience issue. A third influence on what information a parent shares is the privacy of the visit environment. Others present during the visit may prevent a parent from comfortably sharing information with the visitor. The ability to score the LSP consistently appears to be transdisciplinary, and visitors with nursing, social work, and parent education backgrounds as well as trained paraprofessionals are able to use the tool reliably if the above conditions have been met.

LSP CONTENT VALIDITY REVIEW PROCESS

Reviewers who voluntarily participated in the content validity review process were provided with a review page for each scale. Each scale's review page contained the scale, the instructions for the scale, and a section for comments. The purpose of the study was to determine whether the scales measure clearly and adequately what they state they measure. The comments were used to make final revisions to the scales as they appear in the LSP-43. All but four reviewers chose to review all the scales, with the number of comments ranging from 0 to 27. The average number was five comments per reviewer. All scales received at least one comment. These comments were presented to an Advisory Review Panel consisting of the following ZERO TO THREE Fellows:

- Patricia Brady, Ph.D., national trainer and consultant with Illinois Healthy Families America and adjunct professor at St. Xavier University.

- Mimi Graham, Ed.D., was a Head Start Director, Principal of the Mailman Center for Child Development at the University of Miami School of Medicine, and Education

Director of the National Infant Health and Development Program. She is currently Project Director of the FSU Center for Prevention and Early Intervention Policy.

- Teresa Jacobsen, Ph.D., is Associate Professor, School of Social Work, University of Illinois at Urbana-Champaign; she was Co-Director of the University of Illinois at Chicago Parenting Assessment Team and is the author of a soon to be published text on parenting problems of mothers with major psychiatric disorders.

- Walter Gilliam, Ph.D., psychologist and associate research scientist at the Yale Child Study Center specializing in evaluation of services for young children and their families.

- Sandra Smith, M.P.H., C.H.E.S., Health Education Specialist with the University of Washington, Center for Health Education and Research, clinical instructor in Health Services, and editor of the *Beginnings Guides* pregnancy and parenting curriculum.

The scale revisions were completed in October, 2003. The resulting LSP is the focus of this text.

DESCRIPTION OF LSP SCALES: DESIGN CONTENT AND LIMITATIONS

The Parent scales reflect five areas of life skills: relationships, education and related issues, health care use for parent and child, substance abuse and mental health concerns, and the ability to provide for basic needs.

The first goal of designing the LSP was to discover the important areas of functioning and to describe them simply. Conceptually, the logic is that there are shades of risk in any category of life skills that home visitors have intuitively recognized as reflective of relative risks. Although parent skills may not always progress from low to high exactly from one column to the next, there is consensus among visitors as to the direction of progress. For example, Scale 1, Relationship with Family/Extended Family, and Scale 2, Relationship with Boyfriend, Father of the Baby, or Spouse, are about the parental support network and relationship skills. There is a logical continuum of progress that goes from Violence (Column 1), to Separation (Column 2), to Verbal Conflict (Column 3), to Inconsistency or Indifference (Column 4), to Supportive Relationships (Column 5). As families learn more appropriate relationship skills, they may or may not go from violence to separation to verbal conflict, but there is a logical ranking of these relative behavioral stages from worse to better. The logic of the ordering of "separation" as a lower score than "verbal conflict" is that in the latter someone is there to potentially learn together to create a healthier family relationship, whereas in the former, the partner is not available to learn better ways of being together. Parents, when asked whether they thought having verbal fights was better or worse than ending the relationship, all stated that the end of the relationship was worse.

A second design goal was to record the current characteristics rather than to describe historical information. The LSP is scored in 6-month increments and does not capture events, characteristics, or skills that occur prior to the 6-month period being described. This means, for example, that if a parent was abused as a child, the LSP does not capture this important history. The LSP measures what is currently happening and the incremental changes from baseline measures.

The following section describes what each scale measures and does not measure and some of the logic in the scoring sequence and contents. It does not explain how to use or score the scales. Instructions for use can be found in Chapter 5.

Parent Scales

The scales that begin the LSP describe three general areas of relationships:

- Relationships with Family, Spouse, and Friends (Scales 1–3)
- Parenting Attitudes and Skills (Scales 4–8)
- Relationships with Services and Resources (Scales 9–11)

Relationships with Family, Spouse, and Friends (Scales 1–3)

1. **Relationship with Family/Extended Family** describes the family support relationship

2. **Relationship with Boyfriend, Father of the Baby (FOB), or Spouse** describes the quality of the primary male (or female) relationship

3. **Relationships with Friends/Peers** describes the parent's other supporting friendships or social isolation

The relationship scales (Scales 1–3 and 6) reflect similar gradations across the scores of 1–5. Violent relationships are always Column 1. This is true also for Discipline (Scale 6), in which a score of 1 indicates abuse and cases of medical neglect; Scale 6 has a relationship with Scales 20 and 21, Child Well Care and Child Sick Care, because of issues of medical neglect.

Parenting Skills (Scales 4–8)

This subsection includes the three primary parenting skills:

5. **Nurturing** is the bonding/attachment quality of the parent–child relationship

6. **Discipline** is the parental ability to teach a child appropriate behavior

7. **Support of Development** indicates the ability to encourage and optimize a child's development

In addition, there are secondary areas of assessment:

4. **Attitudes to Pregnancy** identifies a risk spectrum that reflects whether a child is wanted during pregnancy

8. **Safety** focuses on protection skills and provision of a safe environment. This scale was included as a parenting skill, because unintentional injury is one of the most costly categories of health care costs for low-income families.

Most home visitation programs use the work of Brazelton (1984) and Barnard (1978) on infant states and early communication cues, and the parent's ability to read and respond. Tools such as the Nursing Child Assessment Satellite Training (NCAST) Feeding Scales (currently known as the Parent–Child Interaction [PCI] Program) and NCAST's Keys to CaregivinG are extremely useful in noticing the behaviors described in the Nurturing scale (Scale 5). There is a relationship between Scale 5 and the Child Scales 40–42.

Parental Support of Development (Scale 7) has a direct relationship with the Child Scales 36–40 which measure infant/toddler development across the skill domains of Communication, Gross and Fine Motor, Problem Solving, and Personal-Social. The LSP does not screen development; it summarizes the results of developmental screening done using standardized screening tools such as the Ages & Stages Questionnaires®: A Parent-Completed, Child-Monitoring System (ASQ; Bricker et al., 1999), the Denver Developmental Screening Test–II (Denver II; Frankenburg et al., 1992), and other similar screening or assessment instruments.

Relationships with Supportive Resources (Scales 9–11)

   9. **Relationship with Home Visitor** is the ability to establish trust with a visitor

  10. **Use of Information** is the ability to incorporate new information

  11. **Use of Resources** is the ability to identify needs and use resources

If parents are unable to trust and use the visitor, it is unlikely whether they can effectively use any resources, and it is likely that this scale will be an indicator of the potential for progress across many other life skills. The ability to use outside resources and new information is one of the best indicators for success and can be used as case closure criteria if rationing of services is necessary (unless program service requirements prevent skill-based closures).

Education and Employment (Scales 12–16)

These scales include education and items closely related to education:

  12. **Language** indicates the ability of parents whose primary language is not English to show progress toward becoming fully bilingual

  13. **Less than 12th Grade Education** indicates the ability of teens to show progress toward high school graduation

  14. **Education** indicates the ability of adults to achieve high school graduation and *higher education or training*

  15. **Employment** shows employment status

  16. **Immigration** indicates immigration progress for non-U.S. citizens

In this country, a family's successful movement out of poverty depends on at least minimal high school education and employment in jobs that pay more than the minimum wage. The skills needed to achieve this include speaking and writing English, possessing a high school degree or the equivalent, and either U.S. citizenship or immigration status with permits that allow employment. There is a separate scale to describe Cognitive Ability (Scale 29) in the Mental Health section, which describes parents with either learning disabilities or developmental delays.

The Language scale (Scale 12) is *only* for parents for whom English was not their first language. The number of parents in a caseload whose first and primary language is English can be identified by use of the score of zero. The scale also allows programs to identify the percentage of parents in a caseload with no or low literacy in any language; examples of this type of immigrants include some Cambodian, Hmong, and Oaxican families. The number and percentage of fully bilingual persons or the progress to that skill can also be identified using this scale. Establishment of English language skills is often the first step on the ladder up the socioeconomic system for immigrant families planning to stay in the United States. The program support of the ability of immigrant parents to speak and read English may also be one of the primary ingredients needed for successful school readiness for their children. There is no scale that describes the literacy level of English-speaking parents or progress toward literacy in general, although indications of significant literacy problems will show in the Education and Cognitive Ability scales. One good functional resource for health literacy screening and developmental support ideas is found in the Beginnings Life Skill Development materials (Smith & Wollesen, 2004).

The two Education scales (Scales 13 and 14) provide a means to identify those parents with less than a high school education and the progress they are making, and those who have a high school or higher education and their progress. Scale 13 is most useful to programs interested in tracking the reenrollment and progress to graduation of teen parents or the progress of first, second, and third generation immigrants. A baby is a powerful motivation for change. It is possible for pregnant teens to progress from being high school dropouts to attending college and working within a 2–3-year service period, with adequate support from family and an effective home visitor.

Scale 15, Employment, is useful in tracking 1) the length of time a mother remains at home with an infant (a correlation is likely with the Child Care scale), 2) when different young parent populations choose (often from necessity) to go to work, and 3) whether income is at a subsistence level or better. The scale does not measure income (see Basic Essentials, Income, Scale 34). However, three scales contain markers for families with incomes within 200% of the Federal Poverty Level. (See Basic Essentials section, Scales 31, 33, and 34; parents using the Special Supplemental Nutrition Program for Women, Infants, and Children [WIC], Medicaid, or Temporary Assistance for Needy Families [TANF] can be identified by their scores.)

The final scale in the Education section, Immigration (Scale 16), was included in Education instead of the Basic Essentials section because of its close interrelationship with the other scales of Language, Education, and Employment. The upward mobility of families living in the United States who are from other countries has a direct relationship to their intent to stay or to return to their county of origin *and* to their ability to find good jobs. The socioeconomic trajectory for migrant families who move frequently or seasonally is significantly influenced by these moves. Correlations can be expected in the areas of health care utilization, education, and resource use and the family's ability to provide consistent developmental support for their infants. The rate of outcome progress is likely to be different for immigrant families, and programs may want to be able to describe the progress of specific ethnic groups or migrant families served in order to identify the difference in progress.

Health and Medical Care (Scales 17–23)

The Health and Medical Care scales include the following categories:

17. **Prenatal Care** describes the amount of prenatal care received

18. **Parent Sick Care** captures how care is used for illness

19. **Family Planning** describes use of family planning methods

20. **Child Well Care** describes how preventive health care is used

21. **Child Sick Care** describes how care is used for illness

22. **Child Dental Care** describes preventive dental care and treatment

23. **Child Immunizations** states the amount and types of immunizations obtained

Home visitation programs with strong medical outcome goals will notice the absence of the usual list of health and nutrition markers such as premature births, birth weight, gestational diabetes, hypertension, and anemia. Home visitation programs, including public health nursing, operate in supportive and educational roles to medical services for these medical outcomes. In establishing these scales, the questions became what exactly is the primary domain of home visitation programs and what is primarily the domain of medicine, and what are the parental skills and values that accomplish the medical indicators of a healthy pregnancy and a healthy child. The outcome markers chosen for the Health section describe access choices and appropriate utilization of the health care system for prenatal care, family planning, well and sick care, child dental care, and child immunizations. These scales do not describe whether quality of care or access issues exist in a community, although parental utilization patterns can strongly point to these issues being a factor, and qualitative parental surveys may be indicated.

Prenatal Care scale (Scale 17) is the only one of the Parent scales that cannot be used for fathers. It describes when the woman started prenatal care and whether she kept all of her appointments. Historically, programs and health research noted the trimester that care was begun. However, a more complete picture includes whether the appointments were kept and whether health recommendations were understood and carried out (see Scales 10 and 11 for other care-related variables). In addition, what obstacles (see Scales 31–33) had to be overcome by the mother to do this? Examples of underlying skills basic to any of the health scales is whether a parent has a calendar, is able to schedule an appointment, understands the importance of health care, and has the motivational and organizational skills to keep the appointment and to comprehend and follow health care instructions. These skills are not listed specifically in the scales but are fundamental to the outcomes listed in the scales.

This sequence is notable by the absence of a well-child care scale for parents. The Well Care scale was deleted from the original LSP because it did not meet preliminary reliability standards but also because parents living below the poverty level seldom have health insurance and thus do not often seek medical care. The use of preventive health care in any area other than family planning and prenatal care is seldom seen, nor is it encouraged by funding or primary health care resources. There is also no maternal dental care scale, despite the clear importance of prenatal dental care, because resources for prenatal dental care seldom exist in most communities. Two markers that are included are the use of the Emergency Room for health care, which is both an access and education issue, and whether a parent follows the recommended treatment recommendations (e.g., taking antibiotics as prescribed).

Programs (such as NHS) that need to identify the incidence of specific medical conditions can use the Medical Codes section of the parent and child heading information to do this in an automated way and to correlate those conditions with specific LSP scale outcomes. This scale can be scored for fathers as well, and the data can be sorted by the male/female identifiers in the heading information.

Family Planning (Scale 19) is used to track family planning method understanding, utilization, and access by either parent. It does not track whether a specific method or safe-sex precautions were used. It does not track the time interval between pregnancies, although that data could be obtained by comparing birth dates of subsequent children. This is not easily accomplished in most LSP data systems. It does not capture the incidence of sexually transmitted diseases or HIV/AIDS, although they can be identified using the medical condition categories. Some visitation programs that primarily provide parenting education and do not provide family planning information may choose not to score this scale, although this would be a lost intervention opportunity.

Child Well Care (Scale 20) describes the extent to which parents have obtained preventive well-child care according to the recommended periodicity. Immunizations, which occur in this well-child care context, have a separate scale (see Scale 23). In most states, the Child Health and Disability Prevention Program (CHDP) and the Medicaid-funded Early and Periodic Screening, Diagnosis and Treatment (EPSDT) provide funding for well-child care for children of low-income immigrants and children born in the United States. Information on financial eligibility and the recommended appointment periodicity are available from the programs. These programs usually pay for treatment of conditions discovered during a well-child examination if they are not medically eligible for other types of funding. The scale does not list medical conditions diagnosed or treated during these examinations.

Child Sick Care (Scale 21) identifies whether a parent seeks care for a sick child appropriately and follows treatment recommendations. This can apply to the care needed for common minor illnesses of childhood or those children with severe acute or chronic conditions. However, the parental care and effort required to manage a child's cold versus cancer are vastly different. Medical conditions for the child are not listed in the scale but in the optional Medical Codes section of the headings on Page 5.

Child Dental Care (Scale 22) is scored only after a child has begun teething, usually at about age 6 months. The outcomes for dental care involve variables that relate to the information and skill of the parent to obtain care and support dental health, but they also involve the availability of funding and dental resources. This scale is not able to capture whether a mother had preventive dental care during pregnancy, something that is now thought to be basic to prevention of early childhood caries due to bacteria transmitted to the fetus during pregnancy. Maternal access to dental care is still difficult to obtain in most communities. Low-cost or subsidized dental resources are usually more widely available and can be paid in some cases through CHDP/EPSDT when caries are identified on a well-child examination.

Child Immunizations (Scale 23) describes whether a child has completed the recommended immunizations for his or her age. It does not list the date or the specific immunizations but it is expected that home visitors will use the child's immunization record and compare it with the tables of recommended immunizations in order to score the scale. These immunization tables change regularly and staff need to obtain updated tables annually. The parental skills involved include understanding the importance of disease prevention by immunizing children, accessing the community resources for immunization and having the organizational skills to obtain them in a timely way, and having the ability to keep the records. There is also the skill of facing the feelings encountered about having to subject a loved infant to pain.

Mental Health and Substance Use/Abuse (Scales 24–29)

24. **Substance Use/Abuse** describes the extent of drug and alcohol use and/or abuse

25. **Tobacco Use** describes the extent of tobacco use or second-hand exposure

26. **Depression/Suicide** describes the degree of depression and its impact on functionality

27. **Mental Illness** describes the incidence and functional impact of mental illness

28. **Self-Esteem** looks at a spectrum of behaviors indicating self-esteem

29. **Cognitive Ability** describes the incidence and functional impact of developmental delays or learning disabilities

Substance Use/Abuse (Scale 24) is designed to describe the extent of use or abuse of alcohol and drugs during pregnancy and early parenting. It provides a means to quantify a spectrum of a recent drug use ranging from chronic multidrug abuse with addiction, to binge use without apparent addiction, to rare or experimental use, to the use of legal substances that are stopped during pregnancy, to no use at all. It does not name the substances or distinguish between use of drugs or alcohol, because both are hazardous to health and parenting. The scale instructions in Chapter 5 do provide a criteria list for suspected use for scoring purposes, but they do not provide diagnostic criteria for addiction or stages of recovery. There are other scales available, such as the *Diagnostic and Statistical Manual of Mental Disorders, Fourth Edition* (DSM-IV; APA, 1994) section on Substance Use Disorders, that can be used to screen for this. Scale 24 does allow for identification of a parent in recovery who is remaining clean and sober. For example, it is possible to distinguish between a woman on methadone and in ongoing recovery programs with "clean" tests versus a mother on methadone and in recovery with "dirty" tests. It does not describe what type of program a parent is participating in but can sequentially describe relapse history by comparison of sequential scores. This is also one of the scales in which a parent may not have revealed substance use in the first intake LSP, so use may show up in later data as trust grows or observable symptoms appear.

Programs that serve significant numbers of substance-using parents usually out of necessity have developed strong collaborative relationships with drug treatment programs and use them as training and case consultation resources. These programs also usually train staff to recognize the high likelihood that women using substances or in drug treatment programs may have a history of physical and/or sexual abuse and are at risk for posttraumatic stress disorder (PTSD), depression, and other personality disorders and for significant difficulty with parenting. The LSP can capture these additional diagnostic characteristics in Scale 26, Depression/Suicide; Scale 27, Mental Illness; and in the Parenting scales if programs run correlations on their data. It will not describe the historical background that has contributed to the conditions, such as rape, molestation, incest, abuse, or their own prenatal exposure to drugs or alcohol (fetal alcohol syndrome or effects [FAS or FAE]). Programs may run separate comparative LSP data on these very-high-risk subpopulations, because the support needed for significant progress and the length of time that recovery takes can lower the LSP data for the larger caseload. Use of the LSP in reflective supervision for individual substance-using parents will likely show the clusters of lower scores typical of substance use on the companion Mental Health Scales 26–29 (Depression, Mental Illness, Self-Esteem, and Cognitive Ability) and on the Parenting Scales 4–8. The Medical Codes area in the heading could be used to identify specific drugs used or stages of recovery from other substance scales. Because this is a parental scale, it can identify fetal drug exposure by implication based on parental use. Programs needing to capture confirmed substance or alcohol exposure for a child can use the Medical Codes area in the heading on Page 5.

Tobacco Use (Scale 25) accounts for both parental use and second-hand exposure to tobacco. It includes conceptually the use of any form of tobacco, although smoking is the most likely form of use. Because the use of tobacco can double the chance of premature births (Oser & Cohen, 2003), many programs and prenatal services provide specific anti-tobacco education materials in order to encourage cessation. A related issue is how to support parental communication skills when they need to ask family or other smokers living in the household to smoke outside. This scale is a good example of LSP data that are useful to programs targeting infant mortality and the prevention of premature births. These data can provide the community with a snapshot of tobacco use within the child-bearing community.

Depression (Scale 26) is an example of a mental illness that has a 10%–27% incidence (Gelfand, & Teti, 1990; Seifer & Dickstein, 1993; Stamp, Williams, & Crowther, 1996). Depression deserved a separate scale in order to capture the both the incidence of depression and the adequacy of a parent's coping skills and utilization of community resources which, when combined, make recovery possible. Because there are several valid screening instruments for depression (Edinburgh Post Partum Depression Scale, Beck Post-partum Depression Screening Scale, and Center for Epidemiological Studies-Depression

Scale [CES-D]) available for use by visitation programs, the focus of the LSP is to identify the incidence of depression and progress to recovery (Beck & Gable, 2002; Cox, Chapman, Murray, & Jones, 1996; Radloff, 1991). However, the LSP does not provide a
structure to screen or diagnose depression or the type of depression (PTSD, postpartum,
chronic, bipolar, and situational or environmentally induced). Because of some early LSP
pilot site data that show depression at less than 5% in caseloads, and from some recent
national system program data, it may be possible for programs to demonstrate prevention of situational depression as a program outcome. However, controlled research will
be needed to prove that prevention of depression in poor populations is possible. Further
study is needed to link reduced depression to effective parental empowerment and skill
development, and then to identify the interventions that may produce decreases in the
incidence of environmentally induced depression (DSM-IV; APA, 1994).

Some programs may need to run separate comparative data and correlations on
these high-risk subpopulations, because the support needed for significant progress and
the length of time that recovery takes can lower the LSP outcome data for the individuals and the caseload. Close monitoring of infant developmental outcomes and parenting
skills is recommended for both individual families and caseloads because of the potential
negative effect of maternal depression on parenting and child development, particularly
communication and attachment. The Medical Codes area in the heading could be used
to provide diagnostic categories of depression seen in the caseloads, and the data may
prove useful for collaborative planning with mental health services.

The Mental Illness scale (Scale 27) describes a parent with suspected or diagnosed
mental illness meeting diagnostic criteria described in the DSM-IV-TR. It describes whether
a parent is in effective treatment and the parent's ability to carry out activities of daily
living (ADL). The LSP does not name or diagnose a condition, and home visitors who
score positive findings for a parent on the LSP Mental Illness scale do not diagnose mental illness. However, when a visitor encounters parents exhibiting gross symptoms of
mental illness, it is possible to score the LSP based on valid suspicions. For example, a
parent reporting or exhibiting visual or auditory hallucinations is easily recognizable in
a home setting, and the program's staff would act quickly to ensure that treatment resources are available and used and that a child is safe. The existence of a major mental
illness creates an extremely challenging management problem for home visitation programs and their collaborative treatment partners. When used in court under a subpoena,
the LSP can help show for protective service, legal, and treatment purposes the extent of
the effects of parental mental illness on life skills and parenting. Other life skills scales are
likely to be lower and to show less change for the better depending on the effective control of the parent's mental illness, and safe parenting needs close monitoring. The *Diagnostic Classification of Mental Health and Developmental Disorders of Infancy and Early Childhood*
(Diagnostic Classification:0–3 [DC:0-3]) are extremely helpful to programs concerned
about infant mental health issues caused by parenting impaired by mental illness, and
the Parent–Infant Relationship Global Assessment Scale (PIRGAS) shown in the DC:0-3
is a good way to summarize this (Greenspan, Weider, et al., 1994). Unfortunately, many
communities do not have infant mental health treatment teams available for consulta-

tion, and for some areas, adult mental health services are only available or accessible via an emergency (911) call.

There is an old saying that success breeds success; in the case of parents, success breeds self-esteem (Scale 28). Visitation programs that use a strength-based intervention model, such as PAT and EHS, are keenly aware of the importance of recognizing strengths and supporting parental self-esteem. Because self-esteem appears to be one of the pivotal "magical" ingredients for successful parenting and life skills development, it was given a separate scale in the LSP. There appears to be a relationship, yet unproved, between the growth of parenting knowledge and skill and the parent's sense of this success, and their ability to believe they can change other areas of their lives. Self-esteem and self-efficacy theory suggests a number of components, and competence is one.

The LSP scales do not capture all of the elements that make up a person's sense of self, but they focus on the elements of competence, coping, expressed coping, defensiveness, initiative, and pride. A parent may not necessarily grow through the stages as listed on the scale, but he or she can still be seen to be progressing. There may be strong relationships between this scale and Scale 26, Depression.

Cognitive Ability (Scale 29), like Mental Illness (Scale 27), matches the degree of a parent's known or suspected delay or learning disability with their functional level to carry out ADL. The degree of parental cognitive delay seen in family environments by a home visitor is likely to be no lower than mild to moderate delay, because individuals with more severe disabilities are difficult to care for in a home setting as they age. Criteria for delays can be found in Chapter 5, Instructions for Use. This scale does not test parents for cognitive delays, intelligence, or learning disability. That is the task of education and support services for delayed individuals, and there are extensive diagnostic tools available for these experts. However, parents with cognitive delays or learning disabilities make up a small portion of most home visitation caseloads and, like those with mental illness, represent one of the greatest challenges. This scale was designed to identify parents with special developmental or educational needs and to track the amount of support needed and received in order to maximize functionality and successful parenting. The progress these parents show on other scales can be considerably slower, and child protective services are often involved. Syndromes that may have implications for genetically inherited conditions are another issue and further identification with parent and child medical codes linked to scale outcomes may be useful.

Basic Essentials (Scales 30–35)

30. **Housing** describes a parent's housing circumstances

31. **Food/Nutrition** describes the adequacy and type of nutritional needs and resources used

32. **Transportation** tells the primary type of transportation utilized

33. **Medical/Health Insurance** indicates the type of insurance coverage

34. **Income** refers to the adequacy of a parent's income

35. **Child Care** describes the type and frequency of child care used

The Housing scale (Scale 30) describes the parent's housing circumstances in a range from homelessness, shelters, and dangerously substandard conditions to independent renting or owning of a family apartment or home. The scale can discriminate the increasing number of parents who are forced by finances to live in multiple family environments. These living arrangements are crowded and affect the quality of life and relationships (Scales 1 and 2) and the quality of parenting (Scales 5–8). Scale 8, Safety, is one example that may have a high correlation with Housing. Unpleasant and crowded housing and lack of privacy appear to be the strongest motivators for parents to work toward a better life, and this can be used by visitors in goal-setting discussions with parents.

Home visitation programs support families in obtaining adequate food and nutrition by working closely with the WIC program as the primary food and nutrition resource nationally and with other emergency food resources in their communities. The home visitor role is usually one of information and referral, although many provide supplemental nutritional education for pregnant and parenting families. The Food/Nutrition scale (Scale 31) does not measure the sort of markers that health care providers or WIC would use, such as body mass index (BMI) and anemia tests, or obesity and diabetes tracking. It simply records whether a family is connected with services, and whether food resources are needed or adequate. This is based on the supportive role of home visitation for these issues. It is anticipated that programs will be tracking nutrition markers for children using growth charts for BMI tracking and head circumference to ensure that their perceptions of a family's nutritional status are accurate. The issues of obesity, Type II diabetes, and childhood obesity are currently of high national interest, and specific diagnostic conditions are not captured by this scale. Visitation programs that are a part of the effort to improve these issues may choose to track a parent's or child's specific nutrition-related medical conditions using numerical medical codes in the heading data. The use of the medical codes will not show in the data whether a specific condition changes for better or worse; however, if successfully treated it would show a score of 5.

The Transportation scale (Scale 32) measures a life skill that influences success in several other scales such as Health Care Utilization, Education, and Employment. Transportation varies in importance greatly in urban and rural settings. This scale tells what sort of transportation a parent uses. It does not measure whether public transportation is adequately available for use, nor does it measure political issues involved such as the impact of immigration law on a parent's ability to obtain a driver's license or insurance. Programs may be able to use the LSP data for their service population to lobby for adequate resources.

The Medical/Health Insurance scale (Scale 33) captures the range of health insurance coverage that pertains to the parent. There is no scale to capture the same issue for the child because coverage is typically available for low-income children for both well-child care and illnesses. The target range (see Chapters 5 and 6 regarding Target Range) suggested for this scale is any score from 2 to 5, meaning that a parent has some form of coverage paid by a third party, whether it is Medicaid or private insurance. Discrimination against people of color and poor people regarding quality health care and easy access is finally under serious study, although the impact of that data remains to be seen. Programs using SPSS software may want to run correlations between this scale and the health care utilization scales for parents for each of the scores 1–5 to measure effect of coverage on health care.

The Income scale (Scale 34) uses a pragmatic blend of income indicators, but it does not list the actual income level for the parent–child dyad. In that sense, the LSP is unlike the income eligibility scales used for eligibility determination by the poverty safety net programs like WIC or CHDP. This is based on the first author's experience in the field, which suggests that poverty-level parents, particularly women, often are unable to state accurately their actual income, making it difficult for field staff to obtain correct data. This scale will allow programs using SPSS to correlate income status with homelessness in the Housing scale. Using Microsoft Access, it is possible to identify the number and percentage of their service population that use either full-scope Medicaid or Pregnancy and Emergency coverage only. The latter tends to correlate to data found in the Immigration scale. Scores of 3 or 4 will have strong relationships with the Employment scale; however, this scale includes adequacy of the income available to meet basic needs. The adequacy of income to meet family needs is a relative concept, and for LSP purposes it is always based on the parent's perception of adequacy.

The Child Care scale (Scale 35) describes whether, how often, and what sort of child care is used. Programs can use it in conjunction with the education and employment scales to notice what happens to the infant when the parent becomes employed or returns to school. One parent education program that has been using the LSP for several years found parents delaying returning to work and using child care until the infant was 12–18 months old. The program has shown in its LSP data that the national economic downturn created an earlier need for employment and child care to 6 months of age. The earlier need for child care came at a time of preexisting shortages, as well as less child care subsidization and funding. This scale, unfortunately, does not measure the availability of child care resources. Programs may want to show child care utilization differences between the different cultures and ethnicities served by the program. This can be done by linking data from this scale to the racial and ethnic indicators in the heading.

Child Scales

Child Development (Scales 36–40)
These scales cover the domains of

36. **Communication:** language development and resource use

37. **Gross Motor:** large muscle ability and resource use

38. **Fine Motor:** skills using hands and fingers and resource use

39. **Problem Solving:** cognitive ability and resource use

40. **Personal-Social:** socialization skills and resource use

These scales are not a developmental screening or assessment test but they

- Summarize the results of developmental screening by domain
- Identify existent or emerging/regressing delays by domain
- Identify average or above average development based on screening or assessment by domain
- Identify the extent of use of needed special early intervention services

Programs can use these scales to show the number and percentage of the children served who have delays. For prevention programs, it is hoped that these percentages will be considerably lower due to the effects of interventions on environmental or parenting-related delays. More important, effective prevention and education programs should be able to show that their children show much higher percentages of average and above average development than would be anticipated for children at poverty level in their communities. It will, however, take creatively designed community-wide collaborative screening efforts or control studies to show this.

Emotional Development and Regulation (Scales 41–42)

41. Social-Emotional extends beyond Scale 40 to identify children with infant mental health issues and resource use, usually based on the Ages & Stages Questionnaires®: Social-Emotional: A Parent-Completed, Child-Monitoring System for Social-Emotional Behaviors (ASQ:SE; Squires et al., 2002)

42. Regulation describes a range of self-regulatory abilities

The Social-Emotional and Regulation scales (Scales 41 and 42) were designed to allow programs to identify infants and toddlers showing emerging infant mental health, sensorimotor, or regulatory needs. As with the Development scales, the Social-Emotional scale should be based on screening with other instruments such as ASQ (Bricker et al., 1999), ASQ:SE (Squires et al., 2002), NCAST (Sumner & Spitz, 1994), Bayley Scales of Infant Development–Second Edition (BSID-II; Bayley, 1993), NBAS (Brazelton, 1984), and Denver II (Frankenburg et al., 1992), to show if infant mental health services were obtained. These scales are not diagnostic but can show the number and percentage of infants in the service population that have affective or psychosocial needs. Emerging autism spectrum disorders identified in the caseloads would be seen as low scores in these scales.

Breast Feeding (Scale 43)

43. Breast Feeding was the last scale to be written and was included because of the ever-expanding list of benefits associated with breast feeding. It does not require a certified lactation expert to score it, because it simply focuses on the length of time a child was breast fed. This is minimal information on breast-feeding skills and motivation of parents. It was added to the Infant scales, rather than to the Parent scales, because of the benefits to the infant. Correlations with Scale 5, Nurturing, are anticipated. Data from this scale can be a good indicator of the collaborative effectiveness of community breast-feeding education resources on length of breast feeding and could demonstrate whether parents served by the visitation program breast feed longer than other families in the community.

GIFTS OF EXPERIENCE FROM PILOT SITES

From 1999 to the present, LSP pilot sites located in three agencies in Monterey County, CA, have been the birthing place for the development of LSP concepts and for the testing of databases. The programs involved represented a spectrum of service intervention, agency settings, and staffing types. The home visitation models were a comprehensive nursing best practice research replication site, a nationally respected parent education site, and a national visitation and center-based early intervention site. The agencies represented included public health, early childhood education, and county office of education/early intervention services. Staff reflected the range of home visitors seen elsewhere in the United States and included certified public health nurses with baccalaureate degrees, early childhood educators with baccalaureate or masters educational backgrounds, and newly trained paraprofessionals with high school and some community college education. The structure and interventions used by all three sites included

- Use of a strengths-based approach to work with families

- Use of extensive parent education curriculum

- Frequent visitation (weekly or twice per month)

- Capped caseloads of between 10 and 24 cases per home visitor

- Long service relationships with families (usually from pregnancy until the infant was 2–3 years old)

- Reflective supervision (weekly or monthly)

- Extensive staff training in curriculum use and interventions

It is not an accident that the program's shared characteristics match the characteristics of best practice visitation services listed in Chapter 3. The programs included an Olds NFP replication site in the Health Department, a certified PAT program located in an Adult School setting, and a new EHS program run by the County Office of Education. The sequential data available from these programs represent 1–3 years of experience with the LSP.

The three programs also enjoyed extremely functional collaborative planning and mutual support. The collaborative efforts included a noncompetitive approach to funding, shared dedication to the community and families, mutual appreciation of each other's service goals and delivery model, use of collaboratively planned interagency trainings, and use of the LSP to produce comparative interagency outcome data. The dedication of the management, supervisors, and staff to thoughtful use of the LSP and the data is responsible largely for the quality and usefulness of the information in this book. One example of the importance of this dedication is that experience with the pilots confirmed that the LSP could be used successfully and reliably by nurses, parent educators, and paraprofessional home visitors. The pilot experience also models exactly the sort of collaborative and conscious use of data for program (and LSP) improvement that is the hallmark of utilization-focused evaluation and what Patton refers to as "being Active-Reactive-Adaptive." Therefore, it comes as no real surprise that new sites interested in using the LSP frequently ask about whether it might be possible for other programs in their communities or systems to also use the LSP and create a common basis for community-wide planning and broadening impact. The specific areas of refinement that the pilots contributed to were

- Refinement of the wording use in the LSP scales by participation in the content validity study

- Use of the LSP as a part of the reflective supervision process

- Experimentation with the use of two MS Access 2000 databases designed for LSP data management and simple analysis

- Collaborative design and use of baseline and sequential LSP data transformed into useful reports for program funding sources and evaluators

- Discussions regarding program impact, including strengths and improvements needed, as demonstrated by the LSP data (informal formative evaluation)

- Use of LSP data for program improvement, funding, advocacy, and sustainability

REFLECTIVE SUPERVISION IN PILOT STUDIES

When the LSP was used as a basis for discussion when families opened to service, it helped the visitors in all three pilot settings to identify parent strengths and needs, helped them with goal-setting work with parents, and was useful in focusing interventions. One surprising outcome while using the LSP in reflective supervision sessions came from nurses who worked with extremely high-risk families: mitigation of staff burnout resulted from their ability to see positive change on the LSP scales which would otherwise have been missed in tragic or chaotic situations. One strong positive effect of the LSP is its facilitation of both "forest and tree" perspectives of a family's skills and living circumstances. A family's chaotic life, when described in scales with names and recognizable behaviors, becomes more manageable and improves with clearly planned interventions and recognizable progress. Programs that use the LSP in reflective supervision (see Chapter 6) can anticipate the rewards that come with improved perspective and will find that it helps to facilitate case management, reduce staff burnout (or what some therapists are calling *secondary trauma effects*), and increase the likelihood of positive parent/child outcomes.

FIVE

Instructions for Using and Scoring the LSP

The LSP is a summary that a home visitor uses to sort and organize information gathered from visits, screening tools, and observation of the family. The first four pages summarize a parent's skills in relationships, education and employment, health and medical care, mental health and substance use, and basic essentials. The fifth page focuses on the developmental and psychosocial characteristics of an infant or toddler. The LSP is not a developmental screening tool but instead gives a succinct summary of developmental screening results and, when delays are present, captures whether early intervention services are needed. It does not describe whether nutrition, education/early intervention services, or medical care is effective, because those outcomes are the primary responsibility of those disciplines. The focus of most home visitation services and of the LSP is on the growth of parental life skills needed for a good, healthy, and successful life; on parenting abilities; and on the child's cognitive, motor, psychosocial, and regulatory development.

USING THE LSP

Home visitation services play a unique and collaborative role in parent education, family needs identification, referral to community resources, and developmental screening. Because the relationship between the family and home visitor is intimate, based on trust, and dedicated to building strengths, the LSP was not designed to be used in an interview form with a list of questions for a parent to answer. If used that way it could interfere with establishing a trust relationship. It is intended to help a visitor reflect on complex family issues in a way that facilitates a clear understanding of family needs, strengths, and issues and results in more effective visitation services. The caseload data generated are useful for a variety of purposes: supervision, training, program planning, and demon-

---

Chapter 5 is included on the CD-ROM that accompanies this book.

strating outcomes for funding purposes. **Agencies using the LSP are responsible for its safe and confidential use and are responsible for the training and supervision of staff regarding high-risk and reportable situations such as child abuse, domestic abuse, suicide/depression, homicidal threats, and mental illness/ depression.**

Format

The LSP is generally printed as a five-page form, which takes a trained and experienced home visitor about 5 minutes to complete. Scoring consists of circling pertinent information listed in each of the scale columns and entering the resulting scores in the score column for later data entry. Some programs provide comprehensive support services and find that they will use all data from all of the scales in the LSP. Other programs have a more specific focus and only some LSP scales will be used to demonstrate targeted outcomes. **Each scale is scored separately,** and there is no total LSP score similar to an IQ. Programs can use all or just some scales.

The LSP is generally completed in the office or car after a visit and it is filed in the family or medical record. Use one LSP for each individual parent (pp. 1–4) and child (p. 5) served (e.g., if a single parent has two children, one parent form would be used and two infant scales would be completed). If both parents and more than one child are being served, keep copies of extra parent and child scales available. Because a completed LSP contains highly confidential information, it needs to be protected by all staff, specifically by the visitor, data clerk, and supervisor. The LSP, as with other program data, should be included on a signed informed parental consent form.

Frequency of Use

Most programs want to capture baseline date that shows the family characteristics at intake—before services have made a difference—and the progress over time. The first few home visits generally are needed to establish a trusting relationship, describe services, complete intake forms, and gather basic information about the parent(s) and child or children. An experienced visitor usually can gather enough information to complete the first LSP scales within the first two visits.

Waiting longer than the first two visits to do the initial LSP, programs run the risk of diluting later outcomes. Ongoing LSPs are usually completed every 6 months and at closure. If a parent's initial LSP is begun in pregnancy, it is recommended that the next ongoing LSP be delayed until the infant's can be done using a developmental screening tool such as the ASQ at age 4 or 6 months. This prevents doing two separate LSPs at different dates on the parent and child. Use of the LSP in 6-month increments allows programs to note not only how scoring changes over time but also when changes happen relative to the length of time in the program.

HEADING INFORMATION

The basic data in the heading at the top of the first page is needed to sort data into meaningful reports. LSP data usually are not the only data collected by programs. *All* of the data listed below are essential in order to produce accurate sequential data reports. Some programs have the mistaken idea that because the same data are collected in other places or systems, it is redundant to do so for the LSP. However, in the absence of certain LSP data, changes cannot be linked to any other categories, such as differences between changes seen in different ethnic groups. In one situation, because dose indicators were deleted, no comparison could be calculated between amount of service and change seen. Because it generally takes less than 5 minutes to complete or enter the entire form and because the LSP is only completed 2–3 times per year, the cost to enter *all* of the data is not prohibitive. It is important for program managers to understand conceptually the differences between simple numerical counts of some characteristics (e.g., age distribution) and multiple variable analyses, correlations, or relationship-table analyses.

Parent/Guardian Heading Data

Parent (top, Page 1) includes:

- Family record identification number

- Individual number (usually two digits)

- Web database identification number (if applicable)

- Client's name (last name and first name)

- Client date of birth (DOB; 6 digits)

- Sex

- Race and ethnicity (optional)

- Medical codes (optional)

- Type and dates of LSP: initial, ongoing (with number, e.g., 1, 2, 3), and closing

- Next LSP due: date

- Months of service

- Number of attempted visits

- Number of completed visits

- Home visitor (initials or number)

- Agency/program or site designator

Child Heading Data

Child (top, Page 5) includes:

- Family record/index number

- Individual number (usually two digits)

- Web ID number

- Child's name (last name and first name)

- Date of birth (DOB; 6 digits)

- Age (years/months)

- Type and dates of LSP: initial, ongoing (with number, e.g., 1, 2, 3), and closing

- Parent's months of service

This heading information allows an agency to sort data by age, sex, race/ethnicity, medical code, visitor, and program and to generate caseload reports by programs and by individual visitors depending on the software used for data management (see Chapter 7, Section 2).

Because the LSP is designed to be scored sequentially every 6 months, heading data include the type of the LSP being scored (e.g., Initial, Ongoing by number, and Closing). The information summarized on any LSP applies *only* to the 6-month period immediately preceding the LSP date. It does *not* capture historically significant information such as a parent's own history of physical or sexual abuse as a child. This serves to keep the LSP data focused on current behavior, attitudes, and skills. As a result, the LSP is able to capture progress and change. For example, if child abuse occurs and the child is placed and then returned to the parent who is now off drugs and learning to parent well, all of these changes can be captured by sequential scoring of the LSP.

A third type of heading information collected is the "dose" or amount of services received by the family. This refers to the months of service (MOS) and the number of attempted and completed visits. Without the dose of service contact being tracked, the sequential scale scores are nearly worthless and outcomes may be incorrectly assigned to program effects. Some programs are required to carry unavailable clients due to welfare reform requirements; thus it would be important to note how much or little progress is made for a client who has been open to service for 12 months but who had only two completed visits. Most programs only count face-to-face visits as completed visits, regardless of the place. Phone calls do not "count" for a visit on the LSP. In some cases in which families have been lost to follow-up and updated information is unavailable, the data will need to be closed and only data from the last LSP will be resubmitted under the closing date as the final score.

One of the most difficult factors to manage in home visitation programs is the issue of a parent who is unavailable for anticipated visits. Some "not-home" or "failed" visit rates reportedly run as high as 50%, which is costly for staff utilization and program costs and impact and is quite problematic if funding is based on completed visits (Gomby, 2003). Some critics of home visitation suggest that missed visits reflect the client's lack of value for the service, and for some families this may be true; however, this is a simplistic view because there are multiple causes for not-home visits. The reasons for failed visits vary depending on the stage of parental involvement with the visitor, the parent's organizational skills, the amount and type of family crisis and family support, the impact of education and information provided to the parent, and the parent's life skills or circumstances (e.g., use of a calendar or availability of a phone or transportation). Later, even parental success such as working and going to school can affect a parent's availability for visits. In addition to dose-related data, parental involvement is measured by Scale 9, Relationship with Home Visitor.

In most LSP databases, the heading data and scale scores for parents and infants are entered separately, linked only by the Family Record Number. The heading data at the top of the child's form (Page 5) are intentionally minimal. The parent's months of service are repeated on the child's form, including children for whom service began during the mother's pregnancy. The number of visits for the infant would be redundant information. The child's LSP status (Initial, Ongoing, or Closing) is tracked independent of the parent's status.

GENERAL SCORING INSTRUCTIONS

1. Each scale stands alone and is scored individually across a range of 0–5 points, using 0.5-point increments, as indicated by the number values across the top of the columns.

2. Behaviors or skills described in the columns that apply to an individual are circled, and the numbers are entered in the Score column. Either whole numbers (0–5) or decimals (e.g., 1.5, 2.5) are entered as scores. If some of a parent's or child's characteristics are circled in more than one column, a *split score* is the result—meaning that two or more columns have circled information in them. These split scores are averaged, using the column numbers and decimal points (e.g., 1.5, 2.5) that appear over the lines. This number will be the score that will be entered in the Score column (e.g., items circled in both Columns 1 and 2 would be scored as 1.5 in the Score column).

   Circled characteristics show strengths and needs at a glance and are useful for reflective supervision. Numerical scores are useful for data purposes.

3. Scores range on a continuum from Inadequate (1) to Competent (5), reflecting the characteristics, development, and/or learning curve of the parent or child. Assign a score of 1 for violent behaviors and reportable conditions such as child abuse or domestic violence that occurred in the last 6 months.

4. Zero (0 = NA) is used for scales with *No Answer*, that were *Not Asked* or *Not Applicable*. A zero score is preferred if a visitor is uncertain of an answer; the score can be changed on subsequent LSPs as information is available. However, frequent use of zeros may indicate that a visitor has training or supervision needs.

5. The LSP is specific to an individual parent or child (use one form per parent and child). There is no "family" score and there is no cumulative score for all of the scales, because each of the scales contains very different characteristics and the scores are

used for both clinical purposes and data analysis. For example, on Page 1, a mother who is a victim of domestic violence would score 1 on Scale 2, but if that is averaged with the other scales and all the other relationship scales have scores of 4 or 5, the score that indicates violence would be lost. Some evaluators will use an average of the mean scores of the larger measurement groupings (e.g., Relationships or Education) for statistical analysis rather than for clinical purposes.

6. Although the LSP was designed primarily for work with mothers, all of the LSP scales can be scored for fathers, with the exception of Scale 17, Prenatal Care.

7. Some LSP scales (e.g., Scale 1, Family/Extended Family; Scale 2, Boyfriend, Father of the Baby, or Spouse; and Scales 5–7, Nurturing, Discipline, and Support of Development) are more likely than others to have split scores. This allows the scores to reflect more than one relationship, such as parenting differences by a mother with both an infant and a 3-year-old. Any scale can have split scores.

8. Scores should apply only to skills, behaviors, or attitudes occurring currently or over the last 6 months. This interval captures changes and keeps the profile of parent skills and child development current.

9. Some scales are not always scored.

The following scales are not scored if the parent is pregnant and not parenting a child age birth to 3 years:

• Parent Scales 5–8

• Child Health Scales 20–23

• Scale 35, Child Care

• Infant/Toddler Scales 36–43

Scale 4, Attitudes to Pregnancy, is scored only during pregnancy and up to 1 month after delivery.

Scale 12, Language, is scored only for parents for whom English is a second language.

Scale 15, Employment, is not scored for teens unless they are employed.

Scale 16, Immigration, is scored only for parents who are not U.S. citizens by birth.

Scale 17, Prenatal Care, is not scored for fathers or for mothers if it has not been an issue within the past 6 months.

Scale 22, Child Dental Care, is scored only after an infant has teeth.

BASIC DATA INSTRUCTIONS

Family Record and Individual Identification Number

The Family Record Identification Number is the agency case number. Numbers for the family and individual are treated as two separate entries. This unique individual identifier allows for anonymous data reports, which can be separated by individual parent and child scores. Some programs find it useful to always designate a father as 01, a mother as 02, the oldest child 03, the next child 04, so that data can be identified clearly. A parent and a child or another child should never have the same individual number. Some programs are part of larger chart numbering systems and must use the designated coding system. Software should be able to handle either numeric or alphanumeric record identifiers, but it is essential that the individual code be used as a separate entry even if it is part of a larger case number. For example, "GON1247902" would become Family Record ID Number "GON12479" and Individual Number "02," if "02" was the individual client identifier.

Client Name

Consistent use of last name followed by first name is recommended for accurate, alphabetically listed data reports. If family score groupings are needed, family and individual numbers provide a way to sort these, because last names of family members seldom match. Middle names are not used because record and individual numbers are reliable unique identifiers. Programs will need to provide instructions to staff on handling culturally linked names, for example, Maria Guadalupe Gonzales, is Ma. Guadalupe Gonzales, a.k.a. "Lupe," so the instructions for LSP entry might be to use Guadalupe Gonzales as the first and last name. Inconsistent name entry makes for erroneously inflated caseloads and data reports.

Databases can and should be programmed to avoid duplicate entry based on case numbers and LSP dates. Even with safeguards, programmers, staff, and data clerks need to enter names consistently to ensure clean data and avoid errors.

Race and Ethnicity

This information is optional, because many programs either capture this demographic data in another database or no longer collect this information because of the growing number of multiethnic individuals. However, if programs want to link outcome data with race and ethnicity, such as programs monitoring disparity trends in access to care, these categories would need to be completed. Using the race or ethnicity list of choice, programs would assign a one- or two-digit code for each of the categories they want to track; staff would enter the applicable number on the line for Race or Ethnicity.

Medical Codes

Use of medical codes is also optional. Programs needing to track specific medical conditions for either parent or child can use either ICD-9 (National Center for Health Statistics, 2005), DSM-IV (APA, 1994), or DC:0-3 (Greenspan et al., 1994) codes or their own numeric code for the condition list of choice.

Type of LSP

Check one box to indicate which LSP is being done: Initial, Ongoing with *number* (e.g., Ongoing 1, 2), or Closing (whenever it occurs). This item is crucial and is required to measure sequential change for individuals or caseloads.

Date

The date entered is the date the LSP was done, not the scoring date. This will allow programs to have reports of LSPs done between specific dates, such as a funding or fiscal year, and for the useful "reminder lists" that indicate which clients have an ongoing LSP due next month. The date can also be used in a database to prevent duplicate LSP entries.

Months of Service

Enter the total number of *completed* months a parent has been open to service. This is important because outcomes have a relationship with length and frequency of service. The Initial LSP could show "0," "1," or "2" months of service depending on when the LSP was done.

Number of Attempted and Completed Visits

Enter the cumulative number of attempted and completed visits. Attempted visits are those that were scheduled and the visit made but the parent was not home at the appointed time. Visits that have been canceled and rescheduled do *not* count as attempted visits. Completed visits are face-to-face encounters, not necessarily done in the home, but phone visits are not counted as a completed visit.

Visitor Identification (ID)

Enter the home visitor's initials and/or number. Smaller agencies will find that it is easier to read and sort data if initials are used to identify staff. Larger agencies may need to use employee numbers. Visitor ID data allow for caseload reports to be generated by individual staff and for the next-LSP-due lists to be sorted by visitor.

Agency/Program

Enter the agency and/or program name (usually initials). In agencies with multiple programs, ensuring that a list of program initials are available for staff and clerks is useful so that entries will be consistent. Data can be "lost" in the computer when a new clerk has entered the program initials incorrectly and the report query uses the standard designation. In some communities where the LSP is used by all visitation programs and data go to a shared database, consistent program designators can allow for data comparison across multiple agencies. This can be done with or without a shared database. Shared databases require legal agreements and confidentiality precautions. For small, single-program agencies, only one program name is necessary.

Next LSP Due

Next LSP Due is a month/year date when the next 6-month LSP update is due. The date can be used to generate monthly reminder lists for visitors and supervisors. LSPs frequently cannot be done exactly when planned, due to family availability or crisis, but outstanding LSP lists are useful to staff and supervisors.

Data entry staff should be trained to *return any incomplete LSP to staff for completion* and to notify supervisors if they see unusual scoring errors or patterns being generated by an individual or group. For accurate data, clerks should never guess at the missing answer. Route slips with prewritten lists to check off items that are missing or incorrect and/or the use of a highlighter on the LSP are two strategies data clerks use to communicate what edits are needed. Some programs have a supervisor review every LSP submitted for data entry to avoid incorrect data entry. The latter is recommended.

SCALE SCORING INSTRUCTIONS

The information summarized applies ONLY to events, skills, and relationships that have *occurred within the last 6 months.*

PARENT SCALES

Relationships with Family, Spouse, and Friends (Scales 1–3)

This section describes the parent's primary support system, the parent's relationship/parenting skills with his or her child or children, and the parent's relationship with and ability to use the home visitor, information, and resources.

1. Family and/or Extended Family
The quality of support available to parents varies greatly and has serious implications for parental success and identity. Because the functional definition of family often includes extended family or in-laws, this item can be used to summarize relationships with either or both family types by circling which relationship is being described. Scale 1 describes the quality of family relationships and Scale 30 describes housing circumstances. The parent may or may not live with the family.

Column 1 reflects *physically violent and abusive* family relationships with overt hostility.

Column 2 indicates that there is a *loss of contact or physical separation* from the family, so that useful support is not available when needed. This includes both emotional estrangement and loss of contact due to immigration.

Column 3 describes relationships in which there is *verbal conflict or frequent arguments* but some tangible support is available for the parent and baby.

Column 4 captures families whose relationships offer *conditional or inconsistent support.* This includes situations in which the parent has physical support but not does not feel close to or cared for by the family.

Column 5 reflects a *loving, supportive* family.

2. Boyfriend, Father of the Baby (FOB), or Spouse

Circle boyfriend, FOB, or Spouse, and circle more than one, if applicable. Boyfriend implies an intimate sexual relationship with someone who is *not* the FOB. FOB is specific for a child or the pregnancy. Spouse applies to legal marriage or long-term common-law marriage relationships. Some young mothers may have relationships in all three categories within a 6-month period. This scale can be used for fathers by interpreting boyfriend to be Girlfriend (GF), and FOB to be Mother of the Baby (MOB).

If more than one relationship is applicable, it may result in split scores, meaning that items in more than one column are circled and averaged. Domestic violence is captured by a score of "1," by circling items in the first column. Reporting and referral for domestic violence should follow state law and agency protocol; the visitor should assess carefully the severity of continuing risk, parental depression and suicide risk, and the impact of observed violence on the child.

The logic for the ordering of scoring Column 2, Separated or no contact, as a lower score than Column 3, Conflicted relationship with limited support, is that the potential exists for working with a couple to support improvement in a relationship (e.g., teaching communication skills and anger management, effects on children), whereas there is no potential for improvement in ended relationships.

Column 1 captures *physically violent relationships* with domestic partners and is used for women with *multiple sexual partners.* One example is when the mother is uncertain of the child's paternity versus when the father is known. Women with multiple sex partners or violent relationships may have a history of physical or sexual abuse and may show symptoms of drug use, depression, and low self-esteem.

Column 2 indicates that the relationship with the significant man has *ended and contact is lost.* This includes those couples separated due to immigration issues. The partner is not present to support pregnancy or parenting or to create a family life.

Column 3 indicates that the couple has *frequent verbal fights,* but the relationship continues and there is some support for the mother and baby.

Column 4 indicates that the relationship is *stable with one partner* but lacks the quality of a truly loving and supportive commitment. FOB may have other sexual relationships. They may or may not live together. *Inconsistent support or conditional support* is scored here.

Column 5 indicates a *loving, committed, and mutually supportive couple* and includes traditional "spouse" or common-law marriage relationships in which caring and support are present.

3. Friends and Peers

This scale describes the parent's peer support network. In talking about their friends, most parents seem to give answers that fall in only one column. However, for clients in transition, such as when a parent leaves a gang or drug-using friends, or returns to school, split scores may occur. Social isolation due to immigration, rural circumstances, or chaotic lifestyles is common for low-income parents. As parents develop their goals, support networks, and parenting skills, isolation scores may also show positive change. Scores on this scale often improve after parents return to school or work or participate in parenting classes.

Column 1 includes *gang-linked relationships* in which drugs, sexual initiations, or violence is a characteristic; the violence influences the quality of the group identity and support. Score this column if the FOB is a gang member and is still involved with the mother.

Column 2 indicates *social isolation,* regardless of the cause.

Column 3 indicates that friendships are *brief and casual* and lack depth or permanence or involve frequent verbal fights, leaving the parent feeling lonely, unsure of support, or that she is without close friends.

Column 4 indicates that the parent can name *a few close friends* who are available to talk with and offer support.

Column 5 indicates that the parent has an identified *group of close or long-term friends* with whom to share life and have *as a support network.* The parent feels supported by friends.

Relationships with Children (Scales 4–8)

Scales 4–8 apply to how the parent relates to all of his or her children, not just the most recent infant. Split scores can be common because of different parenting skills for different ages and needs of the children. If a parent is in the first pregnancy, Scales 5–8 are scored "NA" or "0." If a child is in foster placement because of abuse or neglect, score the scales on the parent's characteristics over the past 6 months, and if the child is adopted, the case and chart would generally be closed and the final LSP scored.

4. Attitudes to Pregnancy

This scale can be scored for either mother or father. Check "NA" and score "0" if the parent or couple is not currently pregnant. This scale is only scored during pregnancy and up to 1 month after delivery, after which "NA" is used until there is another pregnancy. Low scores for this scale may indicate that the mother may need extra support to establish reciprocal attachment and nurturing after the baby is born. Low scores are common for some substance-abusing mothers, some very young teens, denied pregnancy situations, and some rape-linked pregnancies, and for some parents with developmental delays or mental illness. Scale 19 is a separate scale for Family Planning.

Column 1 indicates a truly unwanted pregnancy. A therapeutic abortion or adoption may be wanted or planned. The parent's attitude is primarily hostile or indifferent to the baby compared with Column 2 (e.g., unwanted versus unplanned).

Column 2 indicates an unplanned pregnancy, characterized by fearfulness or ambivalence. Alternatively, the pregnancy may be kept in response to expectations from self, family, the FOB, or peers.

Column 3 indicates that although the pregnancy was unplanned, it is accepted.

Column 4 indicates that the pregnancy was planned and accepted but the parent is unprepared.

Column 5 indicates that the pregnancy was planned and wanted, and the parent was/is prepared for the baby.

5. Nurturing

For parents with both an infant and other children, differences in nurturing abilities may result in split scores. For example, a woman in recovery who has several children currently in placement for abuse or neglect may show very different behavior with a new baby due to changes in her drug use. The split score average would reflect that her nurturing ability is changing or that there are differences in how she cares for different children. Screening tools such as the NCAST–Feeding Scale or the Family Infant Relationship Support Training (FIRST) can be used to pinpoint parent responsiveness to cues and nurturing skills with infants younger than 1 year old.

Column 1 is used to describe the rare parent who appears *unable to nurture or love;* these parents often fail to notice or respond to infant cues and avoid holding and caressing. Empathy is lacking. The parent may meet DSM-IV-TR diagnostic criteria for personality disorders or other mental illness.

Column 2 indicates that nurturing is affected by the mother's own *flatness, apathy, and seeming indifference.* These behaviors are often seen with depression or significant developmental delays. Further screening for depression or developmental delay may be needed.

Column 3 describes a parent who *confuses nurturing and responsiveness with "spoiling"* or who lacks information about appropriate and necessary nurturing but responds to the information with positive changes. *Responses are sometimes appropriate* to intense infant cues and the state transitions described in the Keys to Caregiving and NCAST materials.

Column 4 indicates that the parent–infant relationship shows some *visible evidence of reciprocal attachment/bonding,* but the parent's responses to the child are *inconsistent* and may be influenced by immaturity, stress, and coping ability.

Column 5 indicates that the parent *shows loving, nurturing responses* to even subtle cues; she or he touches, responds, holds, comforts, and delights in the child. Reciprocal connectedness is present.

6. Discipline

"NA" may be used and may be appropriate for young infants who are not mobile, unless inappropriate discipline is observed or reported; however, it is important to remember that most child abuse occurs to children younger than age 1 year. Split scores are needed if a spectrum of discipline is noted or if discipline varies inappropriately across children of different ages. **Physical punishment means the use of hitting, spanking, slapping, pinching, or shaking. Physical abuse should meet the current legal definitions and may be indicated by bruises or more severe physical damage.** Discipline tends to have roots in family experiences, environmental norms, and cultural practices. These practices may not match what is currently known to have positive effects on the infants involved and may be damaging to the child. Appropriate intervention includes culturally sensitive parental education. Scoring should reflect the scale criteria listed in the instructions and should not be influenced by the presence of cultural components.

If the visitor files a child abuse report on either parent, or if there has been a known report filed by anyone in the last 6 months, circle the items that apply and enter a score of "1," regardless of whether other parenting abilities are present. If children are or have been in foster placement within the last 6 months, score a "1." If the children are permanently placed without reunification options, or have been adopted, scores should only reflect the status in the past 6 months. Some programs may shift services to the adoptive parent and score that parent's ability on the LSP.

Column 1 identifies a parent who has a history of *reported or suspected child abuse/neglect* in the past 6 months.

Column 2 describes parenting characterized by *frequent criticism or verbal abuse* of child(ren) or who *use physical punishment* described above for children (birth to 3 years old) who are scored on the LSP.

Column 3 characterizes parents with a *mixed range of abilities,* who sometimes show *angry/critical discipline* and who also use some age-appropriate *teaching* discipline.

Column 4 indicates that parenting is *more benign, lacking in boundaries, and ineffective* than angry or critical. Limits are sometimes *inconsistent* or fail to teach appropriate behavior. The discipline style may be linked to parental issues such as depression or low self-esteem.

Column 5 describes a parent who *consciously seeks to use age-appropriate discipline* and sees it as a means of teaching appropriate behavior. The parent uses distraction, redirection, houseproofing, or, later with toddlers, short time-outs to teach; the parent explains expected behavior and praises appropriate behavior.

7. Support of Child Development

This scale involves parental values and behaviors that support a child's physical and cognitive development. Split scores may be necessary for parents with children of different ages and developmental needs. The scale also reflects the parent's receptiveness to learning and incorporating new information about development, which may be influenced by the culture and values of the extended family. Parental activities that support development are scored here as a separate issue from the child's actual development (see Scales 36–39), because developmental delays can occur from organic causes such genetic conditions or parental neglect. However, a combination of low child developmental scores *and* low parental developmental scores is strongly suggestive of environmental causes in the absence of other conditions. Developmental observations summarized on the LSP about parents and children should be based on standardized screening or assessment tools, such as the ASQ, Denver II, BSID-II, or NCAST–Teaching.

Column 1 indicates that the parent has *markedly inappropriate or unrealistic expectations* of the child and/or fails to provide for or has a *limited knowledge* of developmental needs. The parent lacks information and *resists or rejects information on development*. Attitudes may indicate the presence of an underlying mental illness or substance use or abuse.

Column 2 indicates that the parent shows *limited knowledge* of the child's need for developmental support and *fails to provide a developmentally supportive environment*. Parenting has *passive, unresponsive, and language-poor characteristics*. This is sometimes seen in very poor, overcrowded families with limited education.

Column 3 indicates that the parent lacks developmental information but *responds to information* by using some of the new ideas. The parent *provides a few age-appropriate toys* and is *open to new resources* and information.

Column 4 indicates that the parent actively *seeks information on development and applies the information* provided. The parent notices and comments on the child's development and new abilities and interests.

Column 5 indicates that the parent is *informed about the current and coming developmental stages,* incorporates information, and *anticipates developmental needs*. The parent uses resources like libraries, toy exchanges, parent education, or parent support groups. The parent enjoys and takes time to play with and read to the infant or toddler.

8. Safety

Protecting an infant or child from environmental harm requires both knowledge and action on the part of a parent. Accidents account for a large part of health care costs and may result in permanent damage to a child. If an infant or child has sustained permanent damage or required hospitalization due to an unintentional injury or ingestion in the past 6 months, circle items in Column 1, and regardless of other items circled in other columns, score the item as "1." A sudden infant death syndrome (SIDS) death, or near-SIDS after which recommended precautions such as "Back to Sleep" have *not* been used, would also be scored a "1." Parental safety skills are age specific and the safety needs change as a child grows; as a result, split scores may be needed. Home safety precautions may be complicated by living in shared, crowded housing or by cultural issues (e.g., lead exposure from folk medicines).

Column 1 is used for children who have been *hospitalized for treatment* of an unintentional injury and/or who have sustained *permanent damage* in the past 6 months.

Column 2 indicates that the child had *outpatient or emergency treatment* of an unintentional injury in the past 6 months but sustained *no permanent damage.*

Column 3 is used for children who have had *no recent history* of unintentional injury but whose *home and/or car is not safe* or childproofed.

Column 4 indicates that there is *no recent history* of unintentional injury but home is only *partially safe* or childproofed. Family has and uses a car seat and accepts safety information.

Column 5 indicates that *home and car are safe* and the child is protected. The parent teaches safety and adapts the *environment for safety as child's age changes.* The parent talks with the child about safety.

Relationships with Supportive Resources (Scales 9–11)

9. Relationship with Home Visitor

Often, progress is seen in the relationship with the home visitor as trust develops. Split scores can be used if needed. In a 6-month period, leaps forward (or backward) in trust may be noted. Setbacks can happen if a child abuse report is filed. Scale 9 is one indicator of a parent's ability to accept and effectively use outside resources, which is a basic life skill. Visitors have an opportunity to support parents in actively learning resource use in a way that is consistent with parental goals for themselves and their children, such as using classes, libraries, and health or vocational resources. The relationship with a home visitor may be the first trusting experience with resources or "strangers" from outside the family.

Column 1 indicates that a parent is *hostile, defensive, and avoids or refuses services.*

Column 2 indicates that a parent is very *guarded and not trusting;* he or she frequently *breaks appointments.*

Column 3 indicates that a parent *passively accepts information and visits* but shows little active participation. He or she keeps most appointments for visits but does not call or ask for assistance.

Column 4 describes a parent who *seeks and uses information* and the home visitor to meet needs. The parent *calls with questions and to ask for help* and calls to cancel and reschedule appointments.

Column 5 indicates that a parent is *open to visits, is welcoming* and trusting, and uses and enjoys the visits.

10. Use of Information

The ability to identify and use needed information from reliable resources is an important life skill that is learned from life and educational experiences. Some families are distrustful of health resources. Some have limited education or literacy, and making use of written information is difficult. Some rely heavily on family and friends for information that may sometimes be incorrect and may disregard information provided by health or educational resources, particularly when it is not culturally compatible. The ability to seek out and use new information may be one of the most important characteristics that can help free families from poverty.

Column 1 indicates that a parent *refuses information* from the home visitor or health care resources, such as physicians or clinic staff, nutritionists, and so forth.

Column 2 is scored when the parent *relies on inaccurate information from informal sources,* rather that seeking accurate information from reliable sources.

Column 3 indicates that a parent *passively accepts information* from the home visitor or health care resources.

Column 4 indicates that a parent *accepts and uses most of the information* provided by the home visitor or health care resources.

Column 5 indicates that a parent *actively asks for and uses information* from the home visitor and health care resources.

11. Use of Resources

The ability to identify family or individual needs, and to locate and access the resources likely to meet those needs, is a crucial skill that can be learned with experience, support, and positive reinforcement. The ability to use a calendar, a phone, or transportation may be a skill that needs to be taught in order for the parent to access resources effectively. Parental ability to use resources also may be complicated by language issues.

Column 1 describes a parent who is *hostile, distrustful, or fearful of using resources* or who generally *refuses resource referrals.*

Column 2 indicates a parent who *passively accepts referrals* but misses appointments or shows limited follow-up.

Column 3 indicates a parent who will *use resources if access is facilitated* or who sometimes keeps appointments. The ability to access resources independently is not yet established and may be complicated by lack of other resources such as transportation.

Column 4 is scored for the parent who can *identify needs with assistance,* who *accepts referrals* to meet the need, and who *keeps most appointments.*

Column 5 is used for a parent who can *identify needs independently,* who *seeks out and uses resources,* and who *keeps or reschedules appointments.*

Education and Employment (Scales 12–16)

This section, Scales 12–16, includes issues related to Language, Education (one scale more useful for teens and the second more useful for adults), Employment, and Immigration.

12. Language

This scale is scored ONLY for a parent whose primary language is not English. Use a "0" and check NA if the parent's first language is English *and* he or she is not bilingual in any combination of English and another language. Bilingualism may expand job or educational options. This scale can be used to measure the percentage of the caseload that has significant English as a Second Language (ESL) challenges, and the data can document the changes families make.

Column 1 is used for a parent who *does not speak English* and has *no or low literacy* in any language. A parent who is *preliterate in any language* may not have developed visual symbolization skills, making it difficult to teach a child the alphabet or to read. This parent may *need translators* or same-language staff for home visits or provider use.

Column 2 is used to score a parent who is *fluent and literate in his or her primary language.* This parent *needs translators.*

Column 3 indicates that a parent sees the need for learning English and is *taking English classes.* The parent has some usable verbal skills in English that would allow for entry-level employment. The parent *manages some conversations, bills, and applications without translation* or assistance in English.

Column 4 indicates a parent who continues English classes and/or has *some useful written English* capability. The parent can *manage most bills, applications, and written instructions in English.*

Column 5 is used for a non–English-speaking parent who has become *fully bilingual* or speaks multiple languages including English.

13. Less Than 12th Grade Education (Adolescents age < 19 years and some adults)

This scale is used for teens who, because of age, should still be enrolled in school. Some programs choose to use Scale 13 to track adults who are working toward a General Education Development (GED) diploma. The sequence reflects *enrollment, grade-level status, attendance, and type of diploma targeted.* Scale 14, Education, can give the total percentage of the caseload that has not graduated from high school in Column 1 when it is used for both teens and adults. Job skills programs are described in Scale 14, Education.

Column 1 describes students who are *not enrolled* in school or who have dropped out.

Column 2 captures students who are *enrolled* but who have *limited attendance* and who are *not at grade level* for their age.

Column 3 is used for students who are *enrolled and attending any program regularly* but who are *not at the expected grade* level. This includes those who had previously dropped out but returned to school.

Column 4 reflects students who are *enrolled in independent study or adult schools, attend regularly* as required, and are *at grade level.* Their goal is a GED diploma.

Column 5 is for students enrolled in and *regularly attending high school* (regular or alternative) who are *at grade level.* The goal is to graduate with a high school diploma.

14. Education (Adults and teens)

The Education scale is used for adults and teens to capture the percentage of the caseload that has less than a 12th grade education. In addition to scoring, it may be helpful to add written comments such as "10th gr. in Mexico." Scoring is based on actual educational accomplishments. High school graduation is necessary for employment in most jobs that are not agricultural or manual labor and thus have potential for job growth and stability.

Column 1 indicates that a parent has *completed less than 12th grade in any country.*

Column 2 indicates that a parent has *graduated from high school* or has a GED diploma.

Column 3 indicates that a parent is *enrolled or obtaining job training.*

Column 4 indicates that a parent *attends or has recently graduated with a 2-year degree from a community college.*

Column 5 indicates that a parent *attends or has recently graduated from a 4-year college program* and/or is studying for an advanced degree.

15. Employment

Checking "NA" and scoring "0" would be appropriate for younger parents for whom employment is not a goal; however, scoring is appropriate for teen parents who are working. "NA" would *not* be used for a parent who has chosen not to work in order to stay home with a young or sick infant, because the scale indicates skill or experience and type of employment for the past 6 months. Written comments would add perspective, such as "by choice," "cultural issue" or "on Workers Comp."

Column 1 is used for a parent with *no work experience or job skills* or who is unemployed. Column 1 is scored even if unemployment is by choice to parent an infant or because of cultural values (e.g., women not working outside the home).

Column 2 indicates a parent who has *occasional entry-level jobs or seasonal employment.*

Column 3 indicates a parent who has *stable employment in multiple and/or low-income jobs.*

Column 4 is scored for a parent who is *regularly employed* in a job with *adequate salary and benefits.*

Column 5 identifies a parent who is working in his or her *career of choice with a good salary and benefits* and options for promotion. These jobs are often linked to job training or college education. Individuals on maternity or paternity leave are scored here.

16. Immigration

This scale applies only to those parents who are immigrants and not U.S. citizens by birth. Check "NA" and score "0" for a parent who is a U.S. citizen by birth. The word "Migrant" appears in several columns because the frequency of moves for migrant families adds a layer of complexity and disruption of education and services. Circle "Migrant" when appropriate in the column that matches the parent's immigration status. For two-parent families, score only the primary parent who is the focus of this LSP; usually it is the mother.

Column 1 is used for the *undocumented, migrant parent, without a work permit or card,* who frequently or annually returns to the country of origin. Often for these families, immigration and citizenship is not a goal. Moving often disrupts the continuity of the child's health and medical care and educational opportunities.

Column 2 identifies a parent who is *legally here with a valid work permit or card*. The parent may be migrant or in the United States *less than 5 years*. He or she plans to return to country of origin to live.

Column 3 identifies a parent who is *legally here with a valid work permit or card*. The parent may be migrant or in the United States *more than 5 years*. He or she plans to live in the United States.

Column 4 identifies a parent who *has a work permit or card or who is "documented" with a temporary visa*. He or she is applying for citizenship and/or plans to live permanently in the United States.

Column 5 identifies a parent who has *U.S. citizen status*.

Health and Medical Care (Scales 17–23)

This section is divided into parent and child health care issues.

17. Maternal Prenatal Care

Check "NA" and use a score of "0" if the parent being scored is the father. This is the only scale that is not appropriate for use with males. As with other scales, behavior is indicated but use of health care also reflects attitudes; information; ability to access services, organizational skills, support network, transportation, phones, and culture. These factors may all need to be included in assessment for referral to prenatal care and for other support purposes. Prenatal care means medical care; prenatal dental care would be a secondary referral by the medical care provider and is not included for scoring (although dental care is certainly important, recommended and prenatal treatment can prevent caries in the infant).

Column 1 is used for the mother who had no prenatal care for *this* pregnancy. The reason care was not received should be indicated (e.g., drugs, denial, access barriers).

Column 2 is used if prenatal care started late, in the 2nd or 3rd trimester, and for mothers who only kept *some* of the appointments.

Column 3 is used when prenatal care was started late, in the 2nd or 3rd trimester, but *most* of the appointments were kept.

Column 4 is scored for mothers who started prenatal care early, in the 1st trimester, and kept most of the appointments.

Column 5 is used for those mothers who completed the pregnancy within the last 6 months, had *early (Score 4) care, and who also kept the postpartum* appointment. The postpartum appointment is considered the completion of maternal perinatal care. (See Scale 19, Family Planning; services often start at the postpartum appointment.)

18. Parent Sick Care

This scale targets knowledge and behaviors that lead to appropriate care and treatment, as opposed to the inappropriate use of care such as using emergency rooms for routine care. Use of medical care involves multiple external and personal variables, including access skills and payment resources (see Scale 33, Medical/Health Insurance).

Column 1 is used for a parent who has an acute and chronic medical condition that was *without* diagnosis and treatment in the past 6 months.

Column 2 is used for a parent who, for whatever combination of reasons, seeks medical care *late* and who has become very ill before seeking care. The home is not a "medical home" and the family may use the emergency room for care of nonemergent conditions.

Column 3 is scored for a parent who seeks care in a timely way inconsistently and who fails to follow through with the treatment recommended, such as not taking medication as prescribed. The family uses multiple providers or medical home.

Column 4 describes a parent who seeks care appropriately, follows treatment as prescribed, and has a stable medical home. However, a healthy, preventive lifestyle has not yet been established and chronic conditions may be present.

Column 5 is used when a parent seeks care appropriately to cure or control medical conditions and makes lifestyle changes to maintain a healthy lifestyle. He or she has a stable medical home.

19. Family Planning

This scale focuses on current family planning use during the past 6 months. If the woman is pregnant, check "NA" and score "0." Written comments such as "method failure," "HIV risk" or "history of 4 abortions" are useful to target needs for intervention. The words "history of sexually transmitted disease" and "therapeutic abortion" apply only to the previous 6 months. Use of a "morning after" pill would be scored in Column 3. A permanent method of family planning would score in Column 5, signaling completion of birth control as a parent need, although the need for protection against sexually transmitted diseases (STDs) might continue. This scale can be scored if the client is male.

Column 1 indicates that the parent has *not used* a family planning method and is not trying to get pregnant. The parent may lack information needed to use an effective method or may lack life skills to prevent unplanned pregnancies. Unplanned pregnancies within the last 6 months are scored in Column 1.

Column 2 indicates that use of a family planning method, such as a condom, has only happened on *rare* occasions.

Column 3 indicates that the parent *inconsistently* and intermittently uses a family planning method.

Column 4 is used for parents who *regularly* use a family planning method to prevent pregnancy.

Column 5 indicates that parents *voluntarily plan to space* their children and regularly use a family planning method and STD protection. Parents who are planning a pregnancy and trying to get pregnant are scored here, as are those who have chosen a permanent birth control method at the end of intentional childbearing.

20. Child Well Care (Preventive Care)

This scale may need split scores if there are multiple children in the home and the use of well-child health care is different for each child. Lack of well-child care, while less than optimal, is not considered reportable neglect in most locations. Follow agency policy and state reporting laws.

Column 1 is used for children who have *never* had well-child or preventive health care. This is most frequently seen in new immigrants.

Column 2 is used for children who have *seldom* had well-child care or for whom well-child care stopped after early infancy visits.

Column 3 is used for children who still have an *occasional* well-child visit but who do not meet periodicity recommendations.

Column 4 indicates that children have planned annual well-child visits. Scores of 4 and 5 are both good scores. An annual examination takes less parental effort than the multiple examinations needed by younger infants.

Column 5 is used for children who have regular planned periodic visits for well-child purposes, such as the recommended CHDP examination schedule, and have not yet reached the age for annual examinations.

21. Child Sick Care

"Medical Neglect" should be circled and the scale scored as a "1" if a child abuse report has been filed for neglect in the past 6 months or if there has been a *failure to thrive* diagnosis for nonorganic causes and neglect is the conclusion of the physicians. Low scores will need further clarification and sometimes a psychological diagnosis to determine which factors contribute to a parent's ability to obtain proper care (e.g., depression, mental illness, or cognitive delays). Scores in Columns 4 and 5 are both good scores. Column 5 is intended to describe the difference between the effort needed and importance of regular care for a significant or chronic illness such as cancer, cerebral palsy, or a heart condition. A score of 5 can indicate the number of children with serious illnesses who are receiving the care they need. Because home visitation services are not responsible for medical diagnosis and treatment, the LSP does not use the ICD-9 diagnostic codes. Special databases would be needed to link LSP characteristics with the extensive categories and conditions listed in the ICD-9.

Column 1 is used to identify medical neglect and situations in which a child has received *no diagnosis or treatment* for acute or chronic medical conditions.

Column 2 identifies a child who *receives diagnosis and treatment only when very ill* or for whom the emergency room is the usual source of care.

Column 3 reflects a child who receives timely care for illness but who has inconsistent follow-up on treatment or return appointments.

Column 4 reflects a child who receives both timely treatment for *minor illnesses* and recommended follow-up.

Column 5 is scored for a child with a significant *acute or chronic medical condition,* for whom either control of the condition is maintained or cure achieved. A child receiving hospice care for impending death is scored here as well, because he or she is receiving the care needed.

22. Child Dental Care

Check "NA" and score "0" if the child is an only child and has no teeth. If there are several children with varying dental care needs, split scores will be required. Prevention of early childhood caries (ECC) or "baby bottle mouth" by prenatal maternal dental care and use of water only in bottles for sleep, if at all, would rate a 5. Inadequate funding and availability of dental care is a barrier to good dental health nationally.

Column 1 is used for toddlers with *serious ECC,* who have poor dental hygiene and no dental or preventive care.

Column 2 is used for children who have *some ECC,* inadequate dental hygiene, and no dental care.

Column 3 is scored for late treatment of ECC, but there is an established dental home and some dental hygiene.

Column 4 includes timely treatment of caries and some preventive care by a dentist and parents. Use Column 4 if an infant's age is less than the customary start of preventive dental care, about age 2 years, and if the parent brushes the child's teeth daily.

Column 5 reflects regular preventive care and daily oral hygiene by parent and timely treatment of early disease.

23. Child Immunizations

Split scores may apply for multiple children, because younger children are more likely to have complete immunizations (IZ) than those older than age 2 years. The difference between Column 3 and Column 4 is subtle. Column 3 suggests that immunizations were begun and stopped without active plans to continue. Column 4 implies a short delay, with return appointments planned or scheduled. Delay recommended by a physician due to an illness is an example of the latter. Most health departments issue updated lists of recommended immunization and schedules annually and offer low- or no-cost immunization clinics.

Column 1 is for a child who has had *no immunizations,* including a child whose parents refuse them because of alternative health or religious beliefs.

Column 2 is for families who have lost the records or for children whose immunization history is uncertain, such as immunizations given in another country without adequate documentation of the type of vaccine used.

Column 3 is for immunizations which were begun but are incomplete for age.

Column 4 indicates that immunizations are planned or scheduled but are overdue.

Column 5 reflects immunizations that are complete and current for a child's age.

Mental Health and Substance Use/Abuse (Scales 24–29)

Substance use (drugs and/or alcohol) and depression are both found in the DSM-IV, which categorizes mental illness for clinical purposes; however, because these conditions are so prevalent in low-income populations, and because they each have specific treatment implications, they have been given separate LSP scales. It is recommended that programs serving this population have copies of the DSM-IV available for reference for diagnostic criteria for mental illness and addiction. Studies of maternal depression incidence in low-income populations suggest rates of between 10% and 40%.

24. Substance Use/Abuse

This scale applies to the use or abuse of drugs and/or alcohol during the past 6 months. If a client has a history of drug use or abuse, the Depression and Self-Esteem scales may be important to assess carefully because the three are often related, as is a history of rape, molestation, incest, or sexual abuse. Drug use may be a part of PTSD. The DSM-IV defines substance dependence and stages of recovery or "remission" and offers a useful perspective for collaborative support to parents in treatment.

Column 1 identifies parents who have a chronic and continuing history of drug addiction and/or alcohol abuse. Use the following criteria:

- Behavioral reasons for suspicion of use (e.g., slurred speech, disorientation or aggression, unsteady gait, alcohol breath)

- Client self-report

- Known history of arrest, incarceration, or treatment for drugs or alcohol

- Positive toxicology or tests during pregnancy or birth

- Suspected or diagnosed fetal alcohol syndrome (FAS) or fetal alcohol effects (FAE)

- Infant withdrawal symptoms and self-regulation problems

For clients who have no history and none of the above criteria applies, circle "no use" in Column 5 and do not use "NA" and a score of "0." This scale allows for repeated regression and recovery to be documented.

Column 2 indicates intermittent or episodic heavy use or binging but without apparent addiction. These parents are at great risk of becoming addicted or progressing to more or "harder" drugs.

Column 3 describes parents with *occasional or experimental use of illegal substances,* or those who are "clean" and participating in a recovery program (e.g., methadone treatment, Narcotics Anonymous, Alcoholics Anonymous). This may include parents participating in court-ordered treatment or treatment as a condition for the return of a child from foster care. These parents may be motivated to change. A methadone client with "clean" tests scores in Column 3, whereas someone in treatment who tests positive for other drugs would score in Column 1.

Column 4 indicates a client who describes a recent history (within the past 6 months) *of light "social" use of legal substances* (e.g., alcohol). This includes women who stopped any use during a current pregnancy.

Column 5 indicates a parent with *no reported or observed use/abuse of drugs or alcohol* within the past 6 months.

25. Tobacco Use

As with other scales, this scale applies to current use of tobacco products within the past 6 months, and "smoking" includes the use of any tobacco products. Use of marijuana or other drug-laced cigarettes would be scored on Scale 24. Smoking is a major cause of premature births. For multifamily households or work environments, reducing exposure to second-hand smoke can be a difficult educational challenge.

Column 1 is used for chain-smoking or equivalent nicotine exposure from smokeless tobacco products with use or second-hand exposure, more than two packs per day.

Column 2 applies to those who smoke less than two packs per day or who have some second-hand tobacco smoke exposure at home or at work.

Column 3 describes the parent who continues smoking while pregnant but decreases the number of cigarettes or second-hand exposure. It can also refer to parents who, after delivery, protect the child from smoke exposure.

Column 4 indicates the parent who stops completely while pregnant or for whom there is no close second-hand exposure.

Column 5 describes the parent who has never smoked or been closely exposed to second-hand smoke.

26. Depression/Suicide

The incidence of depression in perinatal clients is estimated at between 10% and 40%, with the higher percentages more common in studies of poverty-level women. Intervention with clients who are depressed should always include assessment for suicide risk and referral for treatment when needed. Screening scales to assess depression (Edinburgh Postnatal Depression Scale, Beck Depression Inventory, and CES-D) are available, and depression is described in the DSM-IV-TR. The LSP Depression scale includes clients with postpartum depression, chronic depression with or without a history of PTSD, and situational or environmental depression. A diagnosis of bipolar disorder and related mood disorders should be scored under Scale 27, Mental Illness. If the parent has been so severely depressed that he or she was hospitalized within the past 6 months, or if there is a dual mental health diagnosis, the severity of illness would also show in scores on Scale 27. The activities of daily living (ADL), which consist of the ability to manage food, clothes, hygiene, bills, and so forth, are often affected by depression, mental illness, and cognitive ability, as is the ability to parent well and to perceive self and life (reflective function).

Column 1 indicates a parent who has a *history of reoccurring or chronic depression with suicide attempts*. These parents have severe difficulty carrying out ordinary ADL and parenting, and they lack perception into the extent of their illness or its effects on their child or family life.

Column 2 applies to people who *report recurrent or chronic depression* but who deny having suicidal thoughts or attempts. They have moderate problems with ADL and parenting, but they have some perspective and awareness of it being a problem for them and their family.

Column 3 indicates a parent with *recent postpartum depression or current situational depression* (e.g., unhappy about life or relationships). ADL, parenting, and awareness are only somewhat affected. These parents may or may not have had treatment.

Column 4 accounts for a parent who *manages or controls depression,* including those who use mental health or counseling services and/or medication and have gained good control, so that ADL, parenting, and insight are adequate.

Column 5 is reserved for a parent who is *not depressed* or who has successfully recovered before the past 6 months. This includes a happy, content, or optimistic parent who has not been depressed.

27. Mental Illness

This scale refers to mental illness as listed in the DSM-IV-TR. It excludes depression as defined above but includes those hospitalized for depression and those with more complex conditions that have depression as one component, such as bipolar disorder.

Column 1 is for a parent with *severe symptoms* of psychosis or other types of mental illness, *with or without diagnosis,* treatment, or medication. These parents have severe difficulty managing ADL and parenting, and insight into the extent or effects of their illness is not evident.

Column 2 is for clients with *symptoms of mental illness, who have been diagnosed but treatment is inconsistent or ineffective.* They have moderate problems with ability to carry out ADL, to parent, or to demonstrate insight into the extent or effects of their illness.

Column 3 indicates that *symptoms of mental illness are under control, and diagnosis and treatment are established.* These parents are under enough control that ADL, parenting, and insight are only somewhat affected.

Column 4 indicates mental illness that is due to situational causes. Illness tends to be short-term and treatment is effective. ADL, parenting, and insight are adequate.

Column 5 indicates parents with no history or symptoms of mental illness.

28. Self-Esteem

The scores on Scale 26, Depression/Suicide, and this scale will often be very similar. Self-esteem is learned in a social and family context as children, and it is rooted in perceptions of ourselves and our worth and abilities relative to others.

The low side of the self-esteem scale involves lack of goals that are acted on, generalized inertia or fear of trying something, and depression. Defensive behaviors that are coping mechanisms, but are not helpful to progress in life, are also likely. Recognition and support that is given in such a way that the person perceives his or her strengths, abilities, and goals can be used to revive self-esteem and accounts for much of the progress seen in families served by strengths-based programs.

Column 1 identifies a parent who shows poor self-esteem by being self-critical and expecting criticism from others. He or she has difficulty initiating action, particularly in new situations. This parent usually appears or reports being depressed.

Column 2 is for a parent who is not openly self-critical and who is able to cope but lacks confidence; he or she may have a flat affect or fearfulness and may have limited initiative for trying new skills.

Column 3 identifies a parent who shows poor self-esteem by living shrouded in defensiveness and irritability. The blame is directed outward toward others or as excuses for him or herself in a way that seems on the surface to be protection from self-criticism. The parent may initiate new things but may give up easily.

Column 4 can be used to describe the parent who is gaining in confidence and skills, and who is beginning to actively initiate new skills. This parent tends to be shy when praised but can recognize his or her own competence, and emerging self-confidence is visible.

Column 5 is for the parent who expresses confidence in his or her skills and ability to learn and who expresses pride in achievements and successes.

29. Cognitive Ability

This scale offers a structure in which to identify a parent with developmental delays (DD) or learning disabilities (LD). Cognitive delays, called *mental retardation* in the DSM-IV, are classified as Mild (IQ = 50–70), Moderate (IQ = 35–50), Severe (IQ = 20–35), and Profound (IQ < 20). Most parents with cognitive disabilities who are enrolled in community visitation programs will be in the Mild range and may not be able to read or tell time. As with mental illness and because of an underlying condition, parents with cognitive disabilities may show limited or slower life skills progress. Program intervention focuses on obtaining adequate support rather than a cure and is usually undertaken in collaboration with social services and programs serving individuals with developmental disabilities. Immigration and language issues add another layer of complexity for home visitors. For the parent with a delay, noting whether the parent is able to read, tell time, use good judgment, and respond appropriately to a baby's cues will be extremely important for the child's welfare. Nurturing responsiveness should be indicated on Scale 5 (Nurturing).

LDs are also classified in the DSM-IV, although they are managed primarily by educational interventions, and these parents have a much higher life skills potential with adequate educational support. Obtaining educational and psychological testing records, if available, may prove extremely helpful in adapting parenting materials and obtaining support services.

Column 1 is used when a *DD (Mild to Moderate with IQ < 70) is suspected* but when there has been *no known diagnosis or support services are not in place*. The ability to carry out normal ADL, parenting, and judgment are significantly impaired.

Column 2 indicates a parent who has been *diagnosed with a DD but has adequate educational or special services support*. The degree to which ADL, parenting, and judgment are *impaired is moderate* but is mitigated by the support available.

Column 3 is for parents with more *functional levels of DD or LD, who have some problems with ADL, parenting, and judgment* but are able to cope with some support from a spouse or family.

Column 4 indicates that the *cognitive ability to carry out ADL, parenting, and judgment is adequate* without support. The parent has received special education or learning services. Markers such as ability to work, drive, shop, and pay bills independently are present.

Column 5 is used for a parent who, because of the abilities observed, such as reading or high school graduation, *demonstrates average or above average cognitive abilities*. He or she is competent with ADL.

Basic Essentials (Scales 30–35)

This section deals with the parent's abilities to provide for the basic needs in life. It contains what are perhaps the most concrete areas of life skills. They are directly influenced by the abilities reflected in LSP Section 2, Education, and Section 3, Mental Health, and by the supportive relationships described in Scales 1 and 2 found in Section 1.

30. Housing
Housing is one of the basic areas that is essential to quality of life and sometimes makes the impact of poverty graphically visible. Frequent moves, chaotic lives, overcrowding, squalor, and homelessness mean that little time or energy is available to be directed to other needs and often to children's needs. As the economy worsens, home visitors frequently encounter overcrowded, multifamily housing. Poor housing can be a strong motivation for improving life skills.

Column 1 is used to indicate *homeless* families. Use this column for home environments that are so *substandard* that some basic utilities are missing or so poor as to be dangerous and require reporting to environmental health services. Homes that are *so dirty that the children are endangered* are scored here.

Column 2 indicates the parent with *unstable housing who moves frequently* (e.g., family moved more than once in the last 6 months).

Column 3 is used for low-income families that share *rental space with strangers or friends, or for a teen in a foster home*. If there are also frequent moves, split scores with Column 2 may be needed.

Column 4 indicates parents who are able to *live with families or extended family* or in-laws. Overcrowding may be an issue, but this is usually a more stable and supportive environment than that scored in Column 3.

Column 5 can be used for the family who *rents or owns its own apartment or home.*

31. Food/Nutrition

This scale focuses on the parent's ability to obtain and provide adequate food and nutrition. Many factors, including culture and immigration issues or information, may influence a parent's eligibility for services and ability to provide food adequately. This scale does not measure the quality of the nutrition of the individual parent or child and does not address food-related conditions such as diabetes, obesity, or anorexia. Codes for these conditions can be listed in the medical code field found in the heading.

Column 1 indicates families who *run out of food* and must rely on charity or food banks for emergency food. Hunger exists as a real threat for these families.

Column 2 indicates that the family has *inadequate food resources but has food;* the concern is about the amount or quality.

Column 3 indicates families that *use nutritional resources for low-income families,* such as WIC, food stamps, or other similar services.

Column 4 is scored if the family income allows for *adequate amount and quality of food.* This is frequently seen in extended families that share housing and resources.

Column 5 is scored if family income provides for optimal food and nutrition.

32. Transportation

This is a key scale that affects the parent's ability to access other needed services. The ability to use public transportation, have a driver's license, obtain car insurance, and drive or have access to a car usually needs to be assessed in order to support a parent's skill development. There is a significant difference in the use and value of public transportation versus private cars in large urban versus rural settings. In some urban environments, use of public transportation (Column 2) may be a good permanent answer to transportation needs.

Column 1 identifies families who have *no transportation resources.*

Column 2 identifies families who *use public transportation.*

Column 3 identifies whether a parent has *access to a car or can ride with others,* including a spouse.

Column 4 indicates that the family *has a car and the client (not just the spouse) has a license.* Immigration may influence licensure.

Column 5 identifies that the parent *has a car and license and drives.*

33. Medical/Health Insurance

This scale refers to the health coverage for the parent being scored, not the child or family. Some families, particularly undocumented immigrants, may have different coverage for different members. Most low-income children are eligible for federally or state-funded health care coverage. Medical insurance or publicly funded health care programs vary greatly between states and communities. The names of publicly funded health care programs vary between states and communities.

Column 1 indicates that the parent has *no health care coverage* and is unable to afford care.

Column 2 is used if the parent *has government-funded coverage for pregnancy or emergency only and does not have coverage for routine health care.* This is seen most frequently in low-income immigrant families.

Column 3 is used for low-income families who are eligible for and *have full scope Medicaid* with or without a monthly Share-of-Cost (SOC).

Column 4 indicates a parent who has a state-*subsidized insurance program,* with or without a partial pay plan or copayment.

Column 5 indicates that a parent has *private insurance* (privately or job-linked) with or without copayments.

34. Income

This scale refers to the income of the parent being scored, not the family. For clients who are pregnant teens living at home or unemployed, dependent women, the score would be based on the parent's or the supporting FOB's income, until they have TANF, child support, or income from employment. "Low income" refers to parents whose income qualifies for the 200% of FPL, a scale that is adjusted annually and is available through social service or CHDP programs. "None" is usually an infrequent temporary crisis but should be used if that has been the case in the last 6 months. Because these conditions change quickly, a split score may be needed. This may be seen with homelessness in Scale 30, Housing. Income from illegal activities such as drug sales or prostitution is not counted.

Column 1 reflects that the parent has *no source of income.*

Column 2 identifies a parent receiving *TANF, SDI, or child support.*

Column 3 is used for a *low-income, employed* parent. It can reflect seasonal employment and includes families who meet 200% for FPL criteria (e.g., family is eligible for the WIC or CHDP program).

Column 4 indicates that parents are *employed with a moderate income* and are able to meet expenses most of the time.

Column 5 reflects that the parent is receiving an *adequate salary* for the area's cost of living.

35. Child Care

Check "NA" and score "0" if the woman is pregnant. This scale reflects the reality that for these economic times, most low-income families need both parents working in order to survive and be independent. As a result, finding good child care becomes a life skill. It is not intended to devalue the importance of a mother staying home with her infant.

Because of research on infant brain development, the quality of the child care environment is extremely important. Many extended family environments that are secure and nurturing lack adequate stimulation for good brain development, and the quality in other child care resources varies greatly. Providing information on how to select good child care and local resources can help young families make good choices.

Column 1 is used for parents with *no child care or who have not yet used it.*

Column 2 indicates that *multiple people or places are used for occasional child care* with *unsafe or poorly supervised environments* that create *unstable caretaking relationships* for the child.

Column 3 is scored when parents prefer to use a caring friend or relative where the environment is *stable and safe but offers limited developmental support.*

Column 4 is used for care environments, both *homes and centers, that are used regularly and provide both the love and stimulation* needed by young children.

Column 5 reflects use of a *high-quality child care center* that intentionally provides the best in child care. These centers have *low staff-to-child ratios, have nurturing and well-trained staff, and provide toys and activities for cognitive, physical, and social development.*

CHILD SCALES

Child Development (Scales 36–40)

The LSP child scales summarize developmental data gathered from visit observations, parental report, and use of standardized screening tools such as the ASQ, ASQ:SE, or Denver II. Scales 36–40 match the order of the ASQ to facilitate translation of developmental domain scored to the LSP, and Scale 41 can be based on information from the ASQ:SE. Because the ASQ is based on parent observation, it is consistent with strengths-based home visitation services and facilitates parents' interest in and knowledge of their child's development. Some programs use both the ASQ and ASQ:SE; others choose to use the ASQ:SE only when scores on the Personal-Social questions of the ASQ suggest that more information is needed. Some programs also use The FIRST, for neurologically immature babies and their parents, or the DC:0-3.

Mandated Early Intervention

Under federal educational law (Individuals with Disabilities Education Act [IDEA] Amendments of 1997 [PL 105-17], Part C), all states must provide early intervention/education for infants with delays. Specific criteria for eligibility exist in all states (e.g., 25% delay in two areas of development or 50% delay in one area of development).

There is confusion about *screening* versus *assessment* in some home visitation programs, and the terms should not be used interchangeably. Screening refers to the identification of children who need further diagnosis or formal assessment of developmental or psychosocial characteristics. Screening tools (e.g., ASQ, Denver II) are different from assessment tools (e.g., BSID-II) and functional development assessments (e.g., The Ounce of Prevention Scale [The Ounce Scale]; Meisels et al., 2003). Formal assessments are the legal responsibility of the educational programs providing early intervention services and generally are done by a multidisciplinary team as part of the individualized education program (IEP).

Because of the growing body of evidence showing that children with special needs and their parents benefit from a more individualized and functionally based approach to developmental screening, assessment and intervention are needed. Over the next few years there may be a shift by early intervention services to the use of functionally based tools and approaches. The Ounce is one such example. Work by Greenspan, Lourie, and Weider has resulted in the Functional Developmental Growth Chart and Questionnaire (Greenspan, DeGangi, & Wieder, 2001; Greenspan & Weider, 2000), which lists developmental behaviors by age in months. It is significantly different from and more comprehensive than previous scales. These essential developmental behaviors include focusing and attention, engaging in relationships, purposeful interaction, problem solving, use of ideas (words and symbols to convey intent or feelings), and logical bridges between ideas.

The LSP child scales are useful for programs that screen children for special developmental needs. The child scales are not designed to provide a formal or functional assessment of children likely to be eligible for special developmental intervention services. However, early intervention services can use the LSP scales to track parental life skills development and to summarize program participation, and in many cases the infants progress into an average range of development for age.

LSP scales are primarily for use with children from ages 6 months to 3 years, although the developmental Scales 36–40 can be used for preschoolers ages 3–5 years depending on the upper limits of the screening tool used. For preschool use, enrollment in early intervention would be translated to mean special education if delays are identified. **(Reminder: use one LSP Page 5 per individual child.)**

The LSP does not provide information regarding the range of medical, developmental, psychosocial, affective, or regulatory conditions that may be found in infants, premature infants, toddlers, and preschool-age children. The most common are cerebral palsy, global delays due to birth anoxia, developmental delays related to parenting, congenital genetic and neurological conditions, vision and hearing problems, autism spectrum disorders, regulation and attention difficulties, aphasia, and sensory-motor problems.

LSP caseload data can be used to summarize the number and percentage of children with developmental delays meeting early intervention criteria (score of 1–3) or emerging or improving delays (score of 3.5) and with average (score of 4–4.5) or above-average development (score of 5). These data may prove useful to early interventionists and county offices of education for program planning regarding site and staffing needs.

Child Scale Terminology

Early intervention (EI) services are generally delivered through either local school districts or county offices of education. States and communities each have different names for the required IDEA program, and home visitors are generally familiar with the program name used in their community that provides mandated early intervention services.

Adjusted age (AA) or *chronological age* (CA) is circled to indicate whether prematurity was a factor considered in the screening. **AA is used up until age 2 years if an infant was premature.** Screening tests give instructions on how to calculate the AA.

Child Development (Scales 36–40)

Use the following interpretation from the screening tools used (e.g., ASQ or Denver II):

Columns 1–3. Circle and score Columns 1–3 to indicate a child who has IDEA-eligible delays, which means the child has scores in the shaded "cut-off" section (25th percentile on the ASQ or passes less than the 25th percentile of items in the relevant domain on the Denver II for CA or AA, *and* meets Early Start Criteria of one domain at 50% of AA or CA, or two domains at 25% of AA or CA).

Columns 3–4. If a child shows *emerging or improving delays* that are not severe enough to meet early intervention criteria, use a score of 3.5.

Column 4. This score reflects *average or age-appropriate development* and indicates that a child scores above the cut-off score on the ASQ or has passed most items on the Denver II for the domain skills touched by the CA or AA age line. A few cautions or fails on the Denver II can be included.

Column 5. This is for a child who is showing *advanced or above average development,* meaning that the sixth question in the ASQ domain section was checked "Yes" or the child scored at the 60th percentile (1 standard deviation above the mean). On the Denver II, the child scored above 50% on the domain items.

Emotional Development and Regulation (Scales 41 and 42)

41. Social-Emotional

This scale is designed to reflect those infants who, when screened on instruments like the ASQ:SE, are found to be in need of the support and intervention offered by infant mental health (IMH) specialists. The field of infant mental health is emerging and services for infants and toddlers are not always available in many locations. As with the other developmental LSP scales, this scale reflects both the need for infant mental health services and whether the child is receiving needed services.

42. Regulation

This scale reflects emerging self-regulatory characteristics of a child that aid or interfere with development, exploration, and relationships. This can be scored based on parental report, visitor observation, and/or use of an age-appropriate screening tool.

Column 1 is used for the *irritable, hard to console, or extremely active* infant or toddler who sends unclear cues, is unresponsive to parenting, and demonstrates characteristics of poor self-regulation and/or self-comforting. Toddlers with emerging attention deficit disorder (ADD) or attention-deficit/hyperactivity disorder (ADHD) are scored here.

Column 2 is used for infants with *flat affect or significant passivity.* They show little exploration of their environment, do not seek comfort or share "conversations," or seem not to enjoy toys or objects around them. Some neurologically immature infants may "shut down" in response to sensory overload.

Column 3 indicates children who are *anxious, withdrawn, or clingy*. They show some play and some *limited exploration*. They are very dependent on parents for regulation.

Column 4 is used for a child with average regulation abilities, with quiet or changeable moods, who explores and returns to share or seek comfort from a parent.

Column 5 is for the "easy," happy, well-regulated infant who is easily consoled or redirected in play to another object. The child shows secure parental connection, explores actively, and shares delight.

In the book *From Neurons to Neighborhoods* (Shonkoff & Phillips, 2000), the authors state, "the growth of self-regulation is a cornerstone for early childhood development that cuts across all domains of behavior," and one chapter is dedicated to this subject. Children who show behaviors described in Columns 1–3 may need help making the transition from a coregulation relationship with their parent to functional self-regulation.

The ZERO TO THREE's DC:0-3 (Greenspan et al., 1994) provides valuable reference material for clinicians and health professionals for the screening, referral, and treatment of infants. Infants who are likely to have regulation problems will often have neurologically immature bodies, will have been exposed to substances, or live in marginal or violent home environments. Parents with infants with regulatory issues frequently need special support. Regulatory parent/infant support is described in *Individualized Developmental Care for the Very Low Birth Weight Preterm Infant* (Als et al., 1994) and in the Family Infant Relationship Support Training tool known as FIRST (Browne et al., 1999). There is also a variety of excellent texts regarding sensory integration, and many communities have access to occupational and physical therapists with skills in this area of practice, although funding for treatment may be harder to identify. Hospitals, primary care, and home visitation programs are the pivotal resources available to support parents' learning about infant states, cues, and how to help babies develop self-regulation skills.

Children are born with some temperament characteristics (Thomas & Chess, 1997). The definition of temperament now most commonly accepted is "biologically rooted individual differences in behavior tendencies that are present in early life and are relatively stable across various kinds of situations and over the course of time" (Bates, 1989). However, a young child's genetically based temperament characteristics and regulatory behavior can be influenced to various degrees by several factors. These include "brain processes, family environment, culture, nutrition, biomedical conditions, and toxic substances" (Wachs, 2004). Learned behaviors can be changed and neurological synapses grown, and behaviors that have organic causes can be influenced. In some biomedical situations, such as phenylketonuria (PKU) or cardiac conditions, which can be treated, or in the case of neurological immaturity second to pre-term birth, delays can be mitigated by adapted care and appropriate environmental supports. Supporting a parent's skill, confidence, and success with the infant is as important to the baby's self-regulatory outcome as a timely referral for special services is for developmental delays.

Breast Feeding (Scale 43)

43. Breast Feeding

This scale is intended to be applicable to infants from birth to 3 years, to capture the length of time a baby has been breast-fed. Score "0" if the infant's age is *older* than 6 months and they were *never breast-fed at any time*. Use Columns 1–4 for infants whose age is younger than 6 months.

Column 1 is scored if the infant's age is younger than 6 months and if the infant was never breast-fed or was breast-fed less than 2 weeks.

Column 2 is used for infants older than 6 months who were breast-fed, including expressed, for less than 1 month (2 weeks to 1 month).

Column 3 is used for infants younger than 6 months old who were breast-fed, including expressed, for 1–3 months.

Column 4 includes infants younger than 6 months old who were breast-fed/expressed, with or without supplementation, for 3–6 months,

Column 5 is for infants older than 6 months who were breast-fed with some supplementation for more than 6 months.

Resources to educate parents regarding value of breast feeding, to support the mother's decision process, and to provide expert consultation if problems arise can be found in most communities in prenatal care and WIC programs, and other breast-feeding groups such as La Leche League.

SIX

Reflective Supervision Using the LSP

• • • • • • • • • • • • • • • •

Reflection means stepping back from the immediate, intense experience of hands-on work and taking time to wonder what the experience really means…Through reflection, we can examine our thoughts and feelings about the experience and identify the interventions that best meet the family's goals for self-sufficiency, growth and development.

Rebecca Parlakian (2001a, p. 2)

• • • • • • • • • • • • • • • •

There is a growing list of information, research, and training materials about reflective supervision, and most of the strengths-based home visitation programs have begun using the model as a means of supporting the staff who are directly involved with families. Rebecca Shahmoon-Shanok (1992) calls reflective supervision "a relationship for learning" in the title of her training materials. As with caseload size and frequency of visits with families, there is a wide variation in the frequency of reflective supervision and the content and reflective usefulness of the relationship. The best practice NFP model encourages weekly sessions of about an hour as a standard of practice. For supervision to take place this frequently requires the commitment of the visitor and supervisor as well as concrete support from the program and agency. Some other models are only able to manage monthly sessions and use peer supervision in groups rather than one-on-one sessions (Pawl, 2004). Both models have important advantages, but trust, frequency, and collaborative reflection are crucial elements. In many public health nursing and social service models, supervision has been more of an update for the supervisor than a time when the nurse can think about where she is going with a family and plan strategies and resources. The following material is a summary of how supervision is different when its focus is reflection, and how the LSP can be used to maintain a unique big picture of parent and child progress over time.

VISITOR'S GOALS FOR REFLECTIVE SUPERVISION

The goals of the home visitor with regard to reflective supervision are

- To obtain personal support for the heartbreak and frustration encountered in difficult family situations and heavy caseloads. The underlying belief is "how I feel is important and I need support, too."

- To notice and celebrate effective interventions, family progress, and successes

- To actively use the supervisor to think out loud and to reflect about specific families with an experienced and supportive person. Collaborative thinking brings unique perspectives.

- To obtain expert information and views and maintain a positive relationship

- To plan strategies and interventions, identify resources, and plan reflective questions for use with parents on subsequent visits to help focus their reflection on important issues or blind spots

- To use awareness of successes or disappointments to improve skills and performance and to promote the habit of useful self-awareness

- To prevent burnout and watch for personal blind spots that diminish effectiveness; to share feelings and learn by insight, self-nurturing, and self-observation

SUPERVISOR'S GOALS FOR REFLECTIVE SUPERVISION

The goals of the supervisor with regard to reflective supervision are

- To provide support to each individual staff member

- To reflect and validate the strengths and unique assets of each person

- To build and maintain a strong, trusting, and positive relationship with staff

- To listen actively to family and staff issues

- To let the staff member take the lead in prioritization of the session

- To support collaborative and individual reflective thinking

- To support intervention planning and design reflective questions for use with individual parents

- To provide expert knowledge, guidance, resources, and direction when necessary

- To encourage self-assessment and professional growth

- To notice and celebrate family progress

- To prevent burnout; to help maintain perspective and monitor blind spots

- To identify training and orientation needs and program service issues

REFLECTIVE SUPERVISION CHARACTERISTICS

Supervision is most powerful when it is

Regular
Frequent
Collaborative
Prioritized
Reflective

Regular means that a specific time is set aside and is given top priority; it can be counted on to happen as planned. This makes a powerful value statement on the importance of support and reflection. Home visitors know that they are as important as what they do and that they can count on time for their own support and thoughtful reflection.

Frequent is as often as a program can afford in terms of staffing and revenue generation issues. Weekly supervision is ideal. If supervision is truly reflective, it will influence both staff retention and client outcomes.

Collaborative supervision reflects a shared vision and commitment to the importance of the work being done. It is a conscious agreement to work together mutually using the relationship for the goals specified previously.

Prioritized focus of supervision (e.g., which families, situations, and topics are discussed) is the primary responsibility of the individual visitor and the secondary responsibility of the visitor–supervisor dyad. It generally includes discussion of newly enrolled families, high-risk and reportable or dangerous family situations (e.g., domestic violence, child abuse, drug use, and depression/suicide issues), success and progress, emerging problems, and needed resources. Also important for the heart of the visitor and for maintaining positive perspectives is discussion of closures and transfers. Most supervision dyads also choose a regular ongoing review of all open families. The LSP review in supervision will be one way to structure the task of keeping family strengths and needs updated for new and continuing families and for those who are nearing completion or who were lost to services prematurely.

Reflective suggests that together the visitor and supervisor consider each session as an opportunity to learn by insight, self-observation, reflection, and support. It is a time to discuss feelings about families and work experiences as well as to debrief staff about or to plan specific interventions. The term *reflective* signifies taking time to focus on program content and processes as well as the quality of relationships with families. One of the most important components of reflective supervision is acknowledging strengths—specifically, to note what is effective and done well by the family, the visitor, the dyad, and the program. Success and recognition of success build satisfaction. It is equally important to discuss emerging family goals, needs, and blind spots, or needs that are seen as hopeless, and to plan intervention options that are likely to be effective and useful to the parent.

One of the underlying concepts of utilization-focused evaluation (Patton, 1997) is that an outcome tool should *be useful to the people who use it.* LSP data are by design a means to track program outcomes, but the individual LSP is equally useful to home visitors and supervisors. Reflective supervision using the LSP is a powerful way to review periodically and summarize quickly each individual parent's strengths, needs, and progress and to review the child's developmental and attachment characteristics. The broad categories of skills or characteristics that the LSP focuses on are

- Relationships
- Education/employment
- Maternal and child health care
- Mental health/substance abuse
- Basic essentials
- Child development and attachment

These categories and the individual scales offer a quick "forest and tree" perspective for a visitor to use to describe a parent and child in a supervision session. Many times, important patterns of growth or otherwise unnoticed changes become visible as the LSP is discussed. Staff using each newly scored LSP for supervision will find that it enhances their ability to notice strengths and needs and to see parent and child progress. In most programs, this periodic review means that an LSP is reviewed regularly: initially on opening a family (within the first two visits), then every 6 months with each subsequent LSP, and *at closure* whenever that happens. It is a time to shift the focus to all areas of parental skill and not just to the crisis or primary issue of the moment. These review sessions become another powerful way to listen to or see a family. Taking time to notice progress also can be an antidote for visitor burnout.

For visitation programs in which both a professional and a paraprofessional make up a service team for each family, the LSP provides a format to develop common language and criteria for discussing strengths, needs, progress, intervention, and goals. Reflective supervision sessions for the service dyad when an LSP is discussed may be a valuable addition to enhanced teamwork. Because the number of families served by dyads is often greater than the usual caseload, use of the LSP twice per year for reflective dyad supervision may be a workable option.

When assessing a new family or talking about them in reflective supervision, a visitor can also use the visual at-a-glance pattern of circled scores for each scale to summarize *strengths, needs, and goals:*

Scores of 4–5 indicate *strengths*

Scores of 1–2 suggest *needs* or *dangerous conditions*

A score of 3 suggests areas still in progress or needing work to reach *goals* or target score range

Progress shows as movement up the scale toward a higher or target score; regression or increasing need is indicated by a lower score. The needs identified on the LSP may or may not be one of the parent's goals, and these unrecognized needs may constitute "blind spots." Goals are what the parent states are their short- and long-term plans, hopes, and dreams. The teamwork with the parent begins with parental goals, not program-identified goals, but includes raising issues the parent has not yet identified as a need (e.g., family planning, return to school, parenting information). The only circumstance in which visitor goals override parent goals is when urgent health or reportable safety issues such as depression, domestic violence, or child abuse/neglect exist and must be addressed immediately.

USE OF THE INITIAL LSP FOR REFLECTIVE SUPERVISION

Reflective questions for the supervision thought process at intake might include some of the following:

- Does this parent notice and take pride in his or her strengths?

- How can you encourage awareness of and pride in his or her strengths?

- What needs and goals does the parent identify now?

- What plans, information, resources, or skills does the parent need to achieve his or her goals?

- What supports are available to the parent?

- How is your relationship with the parent? The family? Is there trust, and how do you know?

- Can you see other needs that you are concerned about which are not a parent priority now? What do you want to do about them?

- Are child welfare, violence, or health issues involved that cannot wait to be addressed?

- Can the issue wait and is information or reflection needed for the parent *to want* to add them to the goal list?

- Does this parent have experience setting goals or is it a skill to be learned?

- What skills does the parent have that can be used to build other skills? For example, what is needed to schedule an appointment for the child for a health examination? A calendar? A car? A health care provider? Health coverage?

- What reflective questions are you thinking of for this family for the next visit? Write down the issues they address and the reflective questions you might use.

USE OF THE ONGOING LSP FOR REFLECTIVE SUPERVISION

Reflective questions for ongoing supervision might include questions such as

- Comparing the previous LSP (particularly the initial baseline) with this one, what is changing?

- Which scales show higher scores, indicating progress?
- Are any scales scored lower, suggesting increasing needs or emerging risks?
- How have the strengths, needs, and goals changed?
- Have earlier goals been accomplished or progress made?
- Has self-esteem increased as a result? How does it show?
- What goals, needs, or skills is the parent working on now?
- What information or support is needed?
- How are you feeling about this parent and this child?
- How is your relationship with this family?
- In what ways have you been effective and what do you plan to do next?
- What reflective questions are you thinking of for this family for the next visit? Write down the issues and the reflective questions you might use.

USE OF THE CLOSING LSP FOR REFLECTIVE SUPERVISION

Reflective questions for supervision regarding closure might include

- Comparing the initial LSP with the closing LSP, what changed?
- How much progress was made?
- Did the parent "graduate" successfully or leave while there were still significant needs?
- Was the closure planned or unexpected and were you able to say goodbye?
- What worked? What didn't work, and is there something you would do differently?
- How are you feeling?
- What have you learned?
- If you had one wish for this family, what would it be?

The above questions are suggestions; reflective supervision dyads will make up thoughtful questions as they gain experience with reflective supervision using the LSP.

USE OF THE CUMULATIVE LSP SCORE SHEET

One easy way to maintain perspective on each individual parent's and child's changes with each subsequent LSP is to use a cumulative score sheet similar to the sample (see Appendix H). This sheet is used to record the score (0–5) for each scale as sequential LSPs are completed. It becomes a summary of progress at a glance. Although a cumulative score sheet can be automated and updates printed for the visitor or supervisor as a new LSP is entered into the database, the exercise of a visitor writing the scores in by hand would make it more likely that they would notice and reflect on changes and needs for intervention planning purposes. In either case, keeping a copy of the cumulative score sheet in the family record on top of the completed LSPs will keep the summary handy for review. One additional option is for the visitor to highlight the scores for each scale that fall in the target range (see target-range LSP, Appendix J). The highlights make visible the progress into adequate or competent skill levels.

SEVEN

Using the LSP
for Evaluation Purposes

• • • • • • • • • • • • • • • • •

*Go placidly amid the noise and haste, and remember what
peace there may be in avoiding options. . . . if you merely
want to believe that the universe is unfolding as it should,
avoid evaluation, for it tests reality. Evaluation threatens
complacency and undermines the oblivion of fatalistic
inertia. In undisturbed oblivion may lie happiness, but
therein resides neither knowledge or effectiveness.*

Halcome's Indesiderata (Patton, 1997, p. 116)

• • • • • • • • • • • • • • • • •

The LSP is an assessment tool that also measures change. Measuring change in knowledge, attitude, or behavior is at the core of research and evaluation. Change can be measured at the individual, caseload, and program levels using the LSP. The way in which the LSP measures change at the individual level is described in more detail in previous chapters. This chapter describes ways to use LSP data to evaluate

- The impact of the home visitation program on individual families

- Changes in caseload intervention or focus

- Single and multiple program evaluations using the LSP data

There are two sections to this chapter. The first section describes the elements of program evaluation and illustrates one method in using LSP data for evaluation purposes. It describes basic information on what to consider when doing a program evaluation for programs that do not have a third-party evaluator. The second section gives examples of how to use different software programs to collect data and conduct analyses. The second section offers additional ways to use data for evaluation purposes.

SECTION 1: USING THE LSP FOR PROGRAM EVALUATION

There are three parallel levels of change involved in using the LSP for program evaluation. The first level of change is seen in the behaviors and skills of the parents and children being served by the home visitation program. Individual mother–child relationships and parenting/life skills are measured using the LSP's 43 separate scales. Each of these 43 scales measures a different concept or behavior that can be observed, scored, and measured. As subsequent LSPs are done, it is possible to capture and measure the changes that are occurring within the family. Did family dynamics change for the better or for the worse? Are the positive changes closer to the target range or are there still unmet needs and undeveloped skills that require continued education and intervention?

The second level of change is within the caseload of the professional. When a professional has a caseload of 10–25 families, it is important to know the characteristics of the families being followed and to understand commonalities and differences. This information is used to focus the interventions, to aid in finding different resources within the community, and to monitor how the case manager is accomplishing his or her tasks. Using the LSP can help determine whether more home visits are needed for families and if there are specific issues that should be addressed. If the caseload is primarily teen mothers, the caseload will have a different focus from a caseload of older mothers. If any families that are not having problems are being maintained in the caseload, consider closing those cases. Are there areas in which the case manager could use additional training or supervision? These issues can be seen by analyzing the data at the caseload level.

The third level is using LSP data to evaluate a single home visitation program. Is the program making a difference in the lives of families being served by the program? What aspects of the program address change in family situations or behaviors? Are the changes based on expected outcomes or are there secondary effects not identified previously? As the LSP measures change in the families, it is also used to show the success of the program. The LSP data may imply that the interventions are successful and no program change is necessary or that they are unsuccessful and program change is needed.

Home visitation programs often differ in their focus on specific populations. For example, if the program is a prenatal program then the evaluation focus would be on the change in attaining early prenatal care and improved birth outcomes. If the program provides services only during the postnatal period, then the focus is more on the maternal–child relationship and child development. If the program targets the postpartum period and focuses primarily on mothers of young children who are leaving jail or prison, then the program focus would be in child abuse prevention, basic parenting skills, improved family dynamics, or harm reduction related to substance abuse behaviors. The LSP scales span the range of focus represented by these examples and can facilitate program impact studies in a wide variety of settings.

The fourth level of change is change within a system of programs, which may or not be related but they use the same measures for reporting. These programs may coexist within the same agency, community, or county system, or they may be in the same state or national program. For example, if an administrator wants to see an increase in the number of young parents attaining higher levels of education, the LSP can be used to track trends in this population being served by the multiple programs using one or more of the outcome scales related to education. Home visitation programs may use different curricula but have common goals for families. LSP data can be used to test the effectiveness of the curricula in working with diverse populations using different intervention models.

Program Evaluation Primer

Understanding program evaluation does not have to be challenging. Many programs have been evaluated successfully with or without an external evaluator and complex data analysis. Some aspects of program evaluation are technical but many are intuitive. A nationally recognized program evaluator states, "The only limitation for data or information is the ingenuity and imagination of the evaluator" (Weiss, 1998). Successful program evaluation entails knowing how to ask the questions and how to find the answers given the information available.

This evaluation primer details the steps to follow when planning a program evaluation. Each step of the process is described and each builds on the previous step until a full picture is presented. The information on why do it, how to start, how to design a study using the LSP, and what to do with the data once it is collected is detailed in this chapter.

What Is Program Evaluation and Why Should It Be Done?

Carol Weiss gives a number of reasons why a program should be evaluated. One is that an evaluation is required by a funder to show how well the program is meeting its goals. The initial funding period requires that a progress report or evaluation findings be presented as a condition for continued funding. The belief that a good program works and meets its goals without evaluative data or data for a progress report is risky. Narratives and anecdotal stories can help in retaining funding; however, there are no guarantees. Many wonderful programs that did a great job in meeting goals lost funding with or without supporting data. The economic and political environments always affect funding streams for health and social programs. Still, lack of data that support the effectiveness of the intervention increases the likelihood of funds being curtailed or cut completely.

Another reason for program evaluation includes understanding what strategies or methods are best employed in reaching at-risk families and children and making a real, meaningful difference in their lives. In the current climate, resources are scarce; therefore, using evidence-based practice is imperative because it demonstrates what works and what does not work in different populations and within different cultural contexts. Is the intervention worthwhile for families or is there something else that will work better? Is the program worth continued funding? A well-planned evaluation can answer some of these questions.

Program evaluation is a systematic process of gathering information and data about a program and analyzing all of the information intuitively. An evaluation plan details what is expected from the program intervention and how the information will be collected. The evaluation plan describes program inputs, curricula, specific goals, objectives, and expected outcomes. An essential element to the plan is a description of what data are needed and how the data will be collected. On the other side, an evaluation report should describe what was accomplished and how the intervention affected the lives of families and children.

Data are useful for both program accountability and sustainability. They are also necessary to show what is and what is not working. Programs want to use "promising practices" or "recommended practice models" in service delivery to maximize the outcomes they hope to achieve. They also want to maximize the scarce dollars available for services. The desire to continuously improve program quality, the need to find and sustain funding, and the sense that what was done has made a difference in the lives of young families all drive the need for quality program evaluation.

How to Start a Program Evaluation Process

This section describes how to start the program evaluation process for a simple single-site program. The range of skills required to begin the evaluation process varies greatly between in-house evaluators who are responsive to the administration and caught up in the internal politics of the agency, and external evaluators who may or may not understand what the program has actually accomplished. Issues to discuss when starting the evaluation process using the LSP include the following:

- A progress or final report is required for a funding source(s), and program staff do not know what information to gather or how to write a report.

- There is no internal evaluator, but information on whether the program is meeting its goals is needed for quality improvement.

- A program manager or an external evaluator wants specific information on how to use LSP data for program evaluation.

To begin the program evaluation process, the first step is to determine the expected outcomes of the program. The second step is to identify existing sources of data or information related to the program. Are there intake forms that can be used? Is there other information about the program that can affect success? What are the sources of data or information, and are they electronic or only on paper? The third step is to design a study using a variety of methods.

Elements of a Study Design

What are the desired short, intermediate, and long-term outcomes expected from the home visitation intervention? Are the outcomes written down and followed, or are they implied or just assumed? Clearly stated, realistic outcomes can help in measuring the effect of the program or intervention. When defining outcomes, the following questions should be asked:

- What are the intended outcomes? What are the markers of success for the program? Is there an expected amount of change for the group as a whole, such as improved pregnancy outcomes? Can they be stated clearly and concisely?

- What does the home visitation program do that leads to the expected outcomes? What is the intervention, and what is known about it? Is it based on a "promising practice" or an "evidence-based practice"? Is it a social experiment based on existing literature? Is there an established curriculum and why did the program choose this curriculum? What did other evaluators find when they evaluated a program that used this curriculum?

- What are unintended or unanticipated outcomes or circumstances that may occur? Are there unintended outcomes—such as improved employment opportunities for the father of the baby or moving out of the area for a better job—that are not being captured in the data?

Sources of Data

Many sources of data are used when conducting a program evaluation. The most common sources of data come from

- Written or electronic intake forms; the LSP assessment tool; and other assessment tools that measure specific strengths or problems (such as specific tools for postpartum depression, infant developmental progress, infant–parent interactions, pre/posttests, consumer satisfaction surveys)

- One-on-one staff supervision with cumulative notes collected electronically

- Other program records

- Secondary data to supplement specific program data (e.g., immunization rates, use of well-child visits, fertility rates, low birth weight births, and premature births)

Measurable Program Characteristics

Types of activities or interventions: Identify the range of activities being performed by the program, such as home visitation and parenting classes. Is there a planned clinical approach or curriculum?

Types of staff: Professionals, trained staff, paraprofessionals, peers, volunteers

Frequency of service: Daily, weekly, or monthly (e.g., dose or intensity that can be measured as the number of home visits, and the number of encounters that are not home visits)

Duration of service: 1 week, 1 month, 6 months with aftercare, 1 year after birth, 3 years after birth

Start of services: After 28 weeks of gestation, during the last trimester, after birth, or only during the early postpartum period

Integrity of service: Is there a method to collect important information disclosed after the initial assessment that differs from the first assessment, such as symptoms of domestic violence in the relationship, substance abuse problems, or symptoms of depression?

Quality of service: For example, the actual length of time the service continued, the number of no-shows for appointments, the number of refusals captured in the data

Program stability: Has the program existed long enough to become institutionalized or is it still a pilot project?

Other Static Data Elements

Program size: The number of clients expected to be served

Structure: Nonprofit organization, public health or private service center, parenting program, or Early Head Start program

Annual budget and budget trends: Are there planned cutbacks this year that may affect the program?

Age of program since established: New, 1–3 years, 4–7 years

Program classification: Is it considered a mandated service or safety-net provider?

Rate of staff turnover: Low, medium, or high

Descriptive Information

- What is the target population?

- **Number of families in the program at a given time:** Does it fluctuate? Is there a waiting list?

- **Demographics:** Mothers, fathers, and children (e.g., age, date of birth, sex, education, employment, number and ages of other children; relationship of the newborn or toddler to those who care for him or her, race/ethnicity, language(s) spoken at home, home location by Zip code, census track, school district catchments area)

Many of the previously stated elements might be collected already as part of the intake process. Whether there is an evaluator, the previous description of a program evaluation offers a framework for getting started. Adding the LSP to the mix offers a set of outcomes that can be used alone or in conjunction with the other program components to understand how a program meets or fails to meet its goals.

Evaluation Design

The design of the evaluation is dependent on the outcomes expected from the intervention and the kind of information needed for reporting. The program strategy or purpose, the parent education curriculum, and the stated goals of the program drive the design. A program evaluation design can be simple or complex depending on the need for the information gathered. A simple design would look like a pre- and posttest. When using the LSP, a simple design would be to compare the initial scores to the closure scores on relevant scales for families served by the program. This kind of comparison can lead to bias and misinterpretation of the results, but it can provide some interesting evaluative information.

A more complicated evaluation design is a cohort study or a case-control study. A cohort study looks at a specific group of individuals that meet specific criteria. An example of this would be the state and federally funded Black Infant Health programs that target African American pregnant mothers in order to reduce low birth weight babies. The cohort is African American women of childbearing age who are pregnant during the time of the intervention and enrolled in the program. The cohort is studied over a period of time, looking for specific changes in the number of babies born to African American mothers with low birth weight. This only yields information about those enrolled and biases the final report.

A case-control study design separates people who receive a specific intervention from those who do not receive it and compares the results from both groups. The assumption is that people who receive the intervention will have better outcomes than those who do not. The criteria for each group are spelled out early in the design process. For example, a study may comprise a group of 100 African American mothers from one town or area who receive the Black Infant Health intervention of 10 home visits during and after pregnancy, compared with a group of 100 African American mothers from another town who do not receive any home visitation during the perinatal period. The groups are comparable but the intervention is not. The study allows comparison of the outcomes from both groups.

Another type of study design is random assignment of eligible mothers into an intervention group and a comparison group. Random assignment is considered the most scientifically rigorous but is also the most problematic for most programs. Most program interventions are not large enough for random assignment, and many programs do not want to assign families randomly into treatment or nontreatment groups because of ethical reasons. If the goal is to improve the lives of young children and their families, being assigned into a nontreatment group or a lesser treatment group is often deemed unethical. One way around this ethical dilemma is to use families from a waiting list, if there is one. Using this method, families who need services will receive them at a later date, and there will be a comparison group available.

Types of Evaluation

There are two types of program evaluation: *process* (or *formative*) and *summative* evaluation. A process or formative evaluation helps a program understand itself; more specifically, it is used to understand the different elements of the program and how they contribute, mediate, or hinder reaching the expected goals. A summative evaluation looks at outcomes, trends, or changes in the long term. What changes were expected, and were the outcomes or goals met or not met within a specified time period? If the goals were not met completely, what percentage of change did occur and is it acceptable?

As an example, a program that focuses on early intervention with pregnant teens may have a primary goal to decrease premature births. A process evaluation would measure the change in attitudes toward pregnancy and birth from teen mothers who are engaged in the program compared with the time before they were enrolled in the program. A summative outcome would look at the rates of premature births for the program population and compare them to the overall rate of teen premature births within the community during the intervention period.

Another more clearly stated process outcome might be to increase first trimester prenatal care for teenage mothers, rather than to decrease infant mortality or reduce premature births. The first goal of increasing first trimester prenatal care is measurable and attributable to the intervention, whereas with the other goals—decrease premature births or infant mortality—it may be more difficult to attribute the change to the intervention. A process evaluation looks at what is reasonable and meaningful to the program in the short term and starts there. Adjustments can be made during the course of the program to make it more realistic and meaningful.

Summative evaluation is focused on more specific outcomes than is a process evaluation. Defining specific outcomes becomes important to do early in the intervention. Summative outcomes should reflect what is reasonable to accomplish by a program within a specified period. The time period is usually the length of time the program is funded, a fiscal year or a calendar year. It is important to have data that measure what was chosen as a primary outcome and have confidence in its accurate measurement.

A summative evaluation, for example, might show an improvement in social support for new mothers. Social support is a concept that is measured by the relationship scales in the LSP. Relationships with family, friends, spouse/partners, or father of the baby and a relationship with the home visitor are assessed in Scales 1–11. If a program has a goal of increasing social support, then all of these scales can be used to measure this program outcome by looking at program-specific scores on these scales over a period of 6 months or 1 year. Did the program show an improvement in the families served by this program? Other specific outcomes can be used to show the end results of the program's intervention.

Comparing initial scores with ongoing or closure scores on certain measures can yield summative information for the program when comparing the scores for all individuals enrolled in the program. The comparison shows that there was change in parental attitudes and behaviors on certain scales. It is also possible to compare outcomes between different time periods. Comparing Time 1 to Time 2 for a group of families receiving a series of home visits and measuring the distance to the target scores for that group is relevant and meaningful to program evaluation.

One important factor to remember is that clusters of LSP scales are affected at different times within the perinatal period. When evaluating a program that serves only pregnant mothers, pay special attention to the scales that could affect birth outcomes, such as the use of tobacco (Scale 25) or illegal drugs (Scale 24), a history or symptoms of mental disorders (Scale 26 or 27), the attitudes to pregnancy (Scale 4), and the trimester when prenatal care began (Scales 17–19).

For programs that only work with first-time mothers, focus on parenting skills, relationship, and infant development scales has greater relevance. If the program serves women both during and after pregnancy, then focus on the scales appropriate to the groups of mothers in the different stages.

Examples of How to Use LSP Data

The following examples illustrate one way to use LSP data to measure change within a family, within a caseload, and within a program for program evaluation. The examples are based on fictitious data derived from the pilot study. The interpretations are suggestive only. Figure 7.1 illustrates scores for one family. Figure 7.2 illustrates how to use the data in program management. Figure 7.3 illustrates the use of data for caseload evaluation. Figure 7.4 describes how scores from program specific data can be used to show change within a program over time and then between different programs. The first eight scales were used for all of these examples. This was done for consistency purposes and does not reflect the only scales that can be combined for assessment and evaluation.

Score		Scale	1	1.5	2	2.5	3	3.5	Target range 4	4.5	5
1	2.5	Family/Extended Family		2.5					1.5 from target range		2.5 from optimal target range
2	3	Boyfriend, FOB, or Spouse					3		1.0 from target range		2.0 from optimal target range
3	2.5	Friends/Peers		2.5					1.5 from target range		2.5 from optimal target range
4	1.5	Attitudes to Current Pregnancy	1.5						2.5 from target range		3.5 from optimal target range
5	2.5	Nurturing		2.5					1.5 from target range		2.5 from optimal target range
6	1.5	Discipline	1.5						2.5 from target range		3.5 from optimal target range
7	1.5	Support of Development	1.5						2.5 from target range		3.5 from optimal target range
8	2.5	Safety		2.5					1.5 from target range		2.5 from optimal target range

Figure 7.1. An example of scoring the LSP for family change with Maria, a teenage mother. Shaded columns indicate target range for acceptable scores.

Use of Initial Data for Case Management and Reflective Supervision

I. Total score on Relationship Scales 1–3 = 8.0 out of a possible score of 15.

Interpretation

* None of the scales is within the target range.
* A score of 8 is 3 points below the lower target range (4 × 3 = 12) and 6.5 from the highest target range (5 × 3 = 15).
* The score closest to the target range is Scale 2—Relationship with Boyfriend, FOB, or Spouse/Partner. This is a strength of the mother rather than a risk or deficit.
* The lower scores are with other family and friends that indicate a lack of social support and a possible issue to address during the next home visit.

Therefore, supportive relationship skills may be an area of focus for the home visitor at the next visit. Which relationships on which to focus can be refined further based on the area of most need.

II. Total score for Scales 4–8 on Relationships with Child(ren) = 9.5 out of a possible score of 25.

Interpretation

- None of the parent–child relationship (Scales 5–8) scores is within the target range.

- The total score is 11.5 points from the lower target range ($4 \times 5 = 20$) and 15.5 from the highest target range ($5 \times 5 = 25$).

- Such low scores on the infant–parent relationship reflect a need to address all areas of this relationship during the intervention planning.

- One of the greatest risks in this family is child abuse or neglect.

Therefore, child development, realistic expectations, child safety, and discipline are important areas on which to focus at the next visit.

Score		Scale	0	1	1.5	2	2.5	3	3.5	4	4.5	5
										Target range		
1	4	Family/Extended Family								4		1.0 from optimal target range
2	3.5	Boyfriend, FOB, or Spouse							3.5	0.5 from target		1.5 from optimal target range
3	5	Friends/Peers										5
4	5	Attitudes to Current Pregnancy										5
5	3.5	Nurturing							3.5	0.5 from target		1.5 from optimal target range
6	4	Discipline								4		1 from optimal target range
7	4	Support of Development								4		1 from optimal target range
8	5	Safety										5

Figure 7.2.   An example of scoring the LSP for family change with Susie, a 24-year-old first-time mother in a program for new mothers associated with hospital discharge planning. Shaded columns indicate target range for acceptable scores.

I. Total score for Scales 1–3 on Relationships = 12.5 out of a possible score of 15.

Interpretation

- All of the scales are within the target range but there is room for improvement.

- This score exceeds the lower target range of 12 but is 2.5 points from the optimal target range of 15.

- The mother has good social support and relationships with family and friends. No intervention is needed unless she later discloses that there are problems with intimidation and control that may be associated with domestic violence in her current relationship.

Therefore, it can be concluded that her strength is relationships with family and friends who can support her newly emerging role as a mother.

II. Total score for Scales 4–8 on Relationships with Child(ren) = 21.5 out of a possible score of 25.

Interpretation

- This score is within the target range and indicates that the mother has a good understanding of her postpartum experience and child development.

- The home visitor would continue to support these strengths and provide information about emerging developmental changes of her child.

Use of Data for Caseload Process Evaluation

Caseload scores are based on the initial use of the LSP in a Teenage Mothers Program (total 10 mothers).

	Scale	Average or mean scores, range 1–5			Target range	
1	Family/Extended Family		2.76		1.24 from target range	2.24 from optimal target range
2	Boyfriend, FOB, or Spouse		2.9		1.1 from target range	2.1 from optimal target range
3	Friends/Peers			3.2	0.8 from target range	1.8 from optimal target range
4	Attitudes to Current Pregnancy		2.9		1.1 from target range	2.1 from optimal target range
5	Nurturing			3.5	0.5 from target range	1.5 from optimal target range
6	Discipline	1.9			2.1 from target range	3.1 from optimal target range
7	Support of Development			3.2	0.8 from target range	1.8 from optimal target range
8	Safety		2.3		1.7 from target range	2.7 from optimal target range

Figure 7.3. Use of LSP data for caseload process evaluation. Caseload scores based on initial use of LSP in a teenage mothers program. Sum scores from all 10 mothers for each scale and divide by 10 to get average or mean scores.

Average score for Scale 1 is 2.76 for 10 teenage mothers.

Average score for Scale 2 is 2.9 for 10 teenage mothers.

Average score for Scale 3 is 3.2 for 10 teenage mothers.

Average score for Scale 4 is 2.9 for 10 teenage mothers.

Average score for Scale 5 is 3.5 for 10 teenage mothers.

Average score for Scale 6 is 1.9 for 10 teenage mothers.

Average score for Scale 7 is 3.2 for 10 teenage mothers.

Average score for Scale 8 is 2.3 for 10 teenage mothers.

Interpretation (Process Evaluation)

- None of the scores is within the target range, and discipline is the lowest average score.

- These girls have some peer support, little family support, and little support from the father of the baby.

- Most of the pregnancies are unplanned and acceptance of the pregnancy is ambivalent.

- The girls had some concerns about their pregnancy, which is not unusual for teenage mothers.

- These teen mothers are nurturing but do not know enough about child discipline and could benefit from more information about child development and age-appropriate discipline.

Conclusion

These findings lead the case manager to focus his or her attention on self-perception for mothers who are pregnant, appropriate child discipline, and child development.

Scale	1. Average scores at initial	2. From target*	3. Average scores 12 months	4. Average scores at closure	5. From target*	6. Difference in means scores, initial to closure	7. % change
1 Family/ Extended Family	2.45	2.55	2.7	4.2	0.8	1.75	+58%
2 Boyfriend, FOB, or Spouse	2.5	1.5	2.5	2.0	2.0	−0.5	−25%
3 Friends/Peers	3.15	1.85	3.8	4.9	0.1	1.75	+62.5%
4 Attitudes to Current Pregnancy	2.97	2.03	3.15	3.45	1.55	0.48	+86%
5 Nurturing	3.12	1.88	3.45	4.56	0.44	1.44	+68%
6 Discipline	1.95	3.05	2.45	4.5	0.5	2.55	+43%
7 Support of Development	2.11	2.89	3.5	4.3	0.7	2.19	+49%
8 Safety	3.1	1.9	3.9	4.6	0.4	1.5	+67%
Total scores	21.35	18.65**	25.45	32.51	6.49	11.16	+78.6%

Figure 7.4.   Data based on program participation (cases opened and closed) during fiscal year 2002–2003. (Note: months of service or number of visits is not calculated here, but it could be included in the analysis.) Total number of mothers = 200. Sum the scores from all 200 mothers for each scale and divide by 10 to get average or mean scores. Average (mean) scores for all mothers are added together then divided by 200 (or the number of clients being considered). Percent change is calculated by taking the closing score (Column 4) minus the initial score (Column 1) to get the difference in mean scores (Column 6); then the difference in scores (Column 6) divided by the closing score (Column 4) yields percent change (Column 7). Range for totals is 8 × 5 = 40. Range of scores is 1–5. A core of 5 is the high end of the target score.

Interpretation (Outcome Evaluation)

This example is based on the eight relationship scales, not on all 43 scales. The first column indicates what the average scores were during the first assessment. The second column shows the distance from the mean score at intake. In other words, this is the amount of change that is needed on each scale to move this group of mothers into an acceptable range of social support. It can become the goal of the intervention to move this score toward that target range. Column 3 indicates the scores based on an assessment done at 12 months after the initial assessment. It is clear that progress has been made in increasing social support and decreasing the negative behaviors that were present at intake to the program. Column 4 indicates the average scores taken at closure. The time may vary between families as they progressed out of the program. These scores show significant progress toward the target range. In fact, many of them have moved into the target range. Column 5 shows the amount of progress made. Column 6 shows the amount of difference between the initial administration of the LSP and the closure LSP based on average scores. Column 7 indicates the percent change from the initial LSP to closure administration of the LSP.

The greatest change occurred on Scale 4, Attitudes to Pregnancy (86%), and Scale 5, Nurturing (68%). The ability to communicate, maintain relationships, and form a stronger relationship with the baby during pregnancy has long-term positive effects on child development. The change in Scale 6, Discipline, is also important to note. Teenage mothers often lack information on how to educate and discipline their young children. Exposure to the program curriculum that focuses on child discipline improved those skills and subsequently lowered the risk of child abuse and neglect. These mothers understood and practiced appropriate discipline with their children.

The shaded line at the bottom indicates the summed score for all eight scales. It represents the summed average scores for each column. The far right cell shows the overall improvement for each of these scales for the total population served. It also indicates a 78.6% improvement for the program participants overall, which is considerable given the slow process of change.

Comparing One or More Programs

After program-specific data are analyzed, a comparison between programs is possible from looking at the average scores, the change toward the target range for each scale or set of scales, and then the overall change. Did one program do better than another in reaching its goals? What factors contributed to the improvements? Did one program have more families with higher risk factors such as mental health disorders, substance abuse, or family violence? How are the families similar or different in each of the programs? Was a smaller or larger change expected? These questions can be answered by completing a chart similar to the one in Figure 7.4 for each program and then performing an intuitive comparison. It is also possible to perform a more complex statistical comparison using a statistical software program. This type of analysis is described below.

Further Analysis

The description of changes depends on the information the program has captured using the LSP and any other intake information. The LSP headings include ethnicity, age, and diagnosis. Doing a cross-tabulation or a pivot table (using spreadsheet program software) allows for analysis that is more complex. This multivariate analysis allows the exploration of the differences in change among different ethnic groups or among families with different diagnoses such as gestational diabetes, failure to thrive, congenital health conditions, premature births, and so forth.

In addition, program-specific change can be seen by looking at the number of staff and the number of families seen. How many home visits were done by each staff member, and on average how many home visits did each family receive in a specific period? Has one part of the program worked better than another and if so, why? Does a team work with high-risk families that have mental health or substance abuse problems? If so, the changes on certain scales may be less dramatic than for lower risk families. At this step of the process, the inputs and results from program efforts start to make sense. The scores can increase on one scale more or less than expected, or they may not change as expected. This information drives change within the focus of the program.

At this stage, an additional step may be to calculate the costs of providing services and the results of the services to families. A full-blown cost effectiveness analysis is possible if staff has the expertise to create the model and make the economic calculations, but there is a simpler way. If it is important to show the direct and indirect costs of providing the program from the program budget, it is possible to do a simple cost effectiveness estimate. Direct costs are staff salaries, benefits, and supervision. Indirect costs are rent, utilities, supplies, and basic overhead for operating the program. If these costs are totaled and the number of home visits are summed and then divided, an estimate of the cost for each home visit is calculated. Multiply that cost by the average number of home visits each family receives and the cost of providing services to a family is more evident. All of this information can go into a report that describes the program activities, the results, the estimated costs, and the value of providing the service to families.

More on Interpretation

A problem inherent in interpretation of data is that if one of a program's stated goals is prevention of problems, and problems are prevented, the data do not change. This does not necessarily mean that the problem has not improved. Conditions did not worsen, the status quo remained consistent, and problem behaviors were prevented. Scores on some of the scales may start within the target range and remain there throughout the period of the intervention. One somewhat befuddled evaluator moaned, "But you can't show that you've done anything unless you show improvement." Scores within the target range for child discipline, childhood immunizations, and child development scales that remain consistently high indicate success in keeping the childhood development on target. Prevention programs are thrilled when the scores start high and stay high. The child is developing on target, the immunizations are being received on schedule, and the mother is learning age-appropriate discipline measures. For a program that works with high-risk parents who historically have problems in these areas, consistency is a sign of success.

A second consideration in interpreting the LSP data is that the child development scales may not show improvement for children who are born with special health needs or congenital defects that may impede development. These kinds of developmental delays may not be preventable and, therefore, programs need to take care in explaining this phenomenon. Infants with environmentally caused delays due to inadequate or abusive parenting can be identified early in the family interactions with the home visitor and this will be reflected in parenting scale scores. Support for changes in parental behaviors can prevent further delays. These children might also be eligible for early intervention programs within the community or be removed from the home by child protective services for foster placement. Programs need to explain the variations between the scores and expectations in relation to the program's efforts.

Some scales will not show improvement until the second pregnancy. For example, in the early prenatal care or use of family planning scales, the second pregnancy may show greater improvement within a program that focuses on postpartum mothers. If the mother has already delivered the child then the score for entry into prenatal care will not be a good way to reflect the success or failure of the program to encourage early entry into care.

SECTION 2: DATABASE DEVELOPMENT

Using Software Programs for LSP Data Collection and Analysis

The simplest and most easily available data management tool for LSP data is a relational database such as Microsoft (MS) Access 2000–2004, a statistical software program such as SPSS, or a spreadsheet program such as MS Excel. MS Access is a common relational database. A relational database has interrelated tables linked by a key field or variable. The key variable or field is usually a unique family number that is either sequential or coded into the system. It is a readily available software program and is simpler to use than many statistical software packages. Some programs using older versions of Access will need to upgrade to the 2000 version to use some of the improvements available in later versions. Earlier Access versions are not compatible with the MS 2000 or XP operating systems.

A statistical software package such as SPSS offers more flexibility but requires more training and skill. It offers opportunities to conduct more complex analysis than a relational database, but complex analysis may not always be needed. A simple spreadsheet software program works for some analyses but has limitations for very complex and ongoing studies. Still, many programs use spreadsheet software programs for program evaluation and find them to be satisfactory. Success with any software depends on the skills of the people who are entering and analyzing the data.

Database Design Issues

If MS Access 2000 is used to create the entry fields and to customize the data reports, staff should plan on at least 4–6 weeks of programming work to create the database. If a recent version of MS Access is not a part of the program's existing software, the purchase cost will need to be added to the budget. For some programs, upgrading software may mean updating hardware as well.

If MS Access is used, it will take about 4 weeks or 160 hours of program design, including time to pilot the software and for program revisions and retesting. Design time estimates are

20–60 hours for basic design or relational tables, queries, and reports

40–80 hours for more advanced development

20–40 hours for pilot testing the software for ease of use and refinements

Caution is warranted in choosing a programmer. Many programmers cannot appreciate the nuances requested by visitation programs in the course of software application design. Some remarkable programming mistakes have been made, even with very explicit instructions. Programs would be wise to allow an additional week or 2 of time for testing new data programs with a small batch of data (1–20 LSPs). This test is to catch errors in logic, calculation, and design and to allow for redesign time. One laughable example of a design error occurred when a "Reminder Report" for the next LSP due was programmed for the pilots. The designers programmed monthly reminders for the entire caseload, but without alphabetical sort or printouts sorted by visitor's caseloads. The same software program, as first written, printed a reminder for each mother and each baby on a separate page for the entire caseload. For the average program that would be about 250 pages for each report, which is not very useful on a monthly basis!

Incorporating the LSP into a Program

Thoughtful planning is needed to introduce the LSP into a caseload. The decision to start using the LSP in an existing program as an assessment and outcome tool should include the following:

1. For all new cases, do an initial LSP and then the ongoing and closure LSPs.

2. For all ongoing cases, designate the first ongoing LSP as a Time 1 and then subsequent assessments as Time 2, 3, and so forth; only new cases would have initial LSPs.

When the LSP is incorporated into existing caseloads, the cleanest model is to assess only newly enrolled families. This works with programs where family turnover is high and enrollment is relatively short. However, for programs in which families are retained for 3 years and there is a low attrition rate, or pressure exists to demonstrate immediate results, the decision may be more difficult. Alternatively, if a program has an existing caseload, a decision may be made to simply start doing LSPs on both new and open cases as of a specified date (e.g., the start of a fiscal year).

The benefit is that the tool is implemented more consistently if every family is scored regardless of time in the program; however, some cases in the database will not have an initial LSP for comparison. In this situation, the ongoing LSP scores would still show changes in the Percentage in Target Range reports, just not when compared with baseline. Caseload attrition will catch up so that all families will eventually have an intake LSP, but in the interim the data are affected. The sample reports shown later in this section come from a program that began LSP use with an all-new caseload. The numbers reflect the caseload build, with the fewest cases having been in the program for the longest time but showing the greatest program effects.

For a new program, whether part of an existing program or a new venture, it is easiest to begin LSP with newly enrolled parents. All families will have intake LSPs to compare with ongoing and closing LSPs.

Describing the Amount of Service

Time measurements in LSP reports are usually expressed as months of service (MOS). How the dose of service received is described and calculated from the information in the

Heading section of the LSP. The heading data include both MOS and Number of Attempted (missed) Visits and Completed Visits. Programs can decide whether to use one measure, both measures (MOS and completed visits), or a formula created by dividing the number of visits by MOS. The pilots only used the months of service as the measure in the database. Using a formula would provide a more accurate dose picture for all reports. The length of service in home visitation programs runs from weeks to years, contact frequency varies from weekly to monthly, and the national "missed visit" ratio shows a completion rate of about 50% (Gomby, 2003).

What Do You Want To Know?

The first step in building an evaluation data system for the LSP is to

1. Look at data that have already been collected by the program in existing databases

2. Identify data that are unique to the LSP and need to be captured

3. Decide which LSP heading characteristics should link to LSP scale outcomes

Most programs are embedded within systems of existing agency programs and are part of a network. Many systems have existing methods to collect, store, and analyze program data. Most programs will collect basic demographic characteristics such as name, address, phone number, gender, and age of participants. The method by which this information is collected and stored is an important first step to managing data. Ascertain what kind of system is in place, what software is being used, and if adaptations can be made to the existing system to capture data from the LSP. Is Information Technology (IT) available to help with programming and technical support? Are the LSP data collected within the existing system or do they have to be collected and entered separately? Is the hardware available to the program capable of standing alone outside of the network or does it have to be connected? If it can stand alone, does the hardware have the capacity (memory and hard drive space) and software programs to accommodate a separate database? How secure are the data? Will the data be safe from unauthorized access and is there a standard back up process to protect the data from loss once it is entered? These are all important questions to ask before the creation of the LSP database.

The second step in building an evaluation data system for the LSP is to identify what data fields are needed. If the program targets pregnant mothers, then only the scales related to pregnancy, relationships, use of services, and risk factors would be captured. For a prenatal and postpartum program, all scales could be used, but at different times. If the program targets specifically mothers with children from birth through age 3 years, then the prenatal scales would not be used unless the mother became pregnant again during the service period. Setting up the database with these issues in mind helps with understanding the results of the analysis. In order to plan for the necessary information, program managers and staff need to become familiar with the content of each scale. The Cumulative Score Sheet (see Appendix H) will help to identify which scales are important to monitor. The Data Report Planning Tool (see Appendix K) indicates data that can be extracted from each LSP scale.

To decide which LSP heading characteristics are needed to link to outcomes, it is necessary to know what other demographic data are being collected separate from the

LSP and what LSP heading data are needed. If the program already captures race, ethnicity, language, education, and maternal age, LSP outcomes should link to these items but these data need not be collected again. Is it important to know whether the baseline and outcome profiles for African American mothers are different from the Latina or Native American mothers? The outcomes for substance using mothers or mothers with HIV may be different from the rest of the population served. The progress toward change may vary for new immigrants versus mothers born in the United States; teen mothers versus older mothers; primiparas versus multiparas; and mothers versus fathers as primary caregivers. The simplest report looks at the range of scores for the entire caseload.

Calculating Baseline Scores for a Caseload

Data from each initial or baseline LSP form the basis for comparative scores for the caseload. A number of basic decisions must be made. The first is how to calculate a caseload. In order to have a large baseline sample, it is suggested that the number of Initial LSPs be cumulative and not capped off at an arbitrary point in time such as the end of a funding cycle. For comparative purposes, all the subsequent LSPs are compared with the baseline score captured at baseline. The number, as in $N = 256$, represents the number of initial LSPs done in a caseload. For the LSP pilots, the N value was stated at the top of the written summary report. The initial LSP, done for a parent at the start of service, forms the baseline profile for the caseload. It is the best picture of parent skills or risks during entry into the program.

To capture outcome progress over time, it is necessary to compare these three measures as either

1. Intake/Baseline LSPs to Ongoing LSPs at X months of service

2. Intake/Baseline LSPs to Closure LSPs at X months of service

A sample of suggested reports is provided below. There are five suggested reports: Number, Percentage, Percentage in Target Range, Initial to Closure at X Months of Service, and Caseload Management Reports.

Suggested Reports

Using a relational database established for the LSP data for the pilot programs, five different types of reports were designed:

- Number of individuals assessed and scored in each scale

- Percentage of individuals assessed and scored in each scale or within certain categories, such as Spanish speakers

- Percentage in Target Range: percentage assessed who score within the target range for each time period measured for each scale

- Intake to closure at X months of service

- Caseload management: lists open and closed cases, by visitor or LSP due

Each LSP scale has a separate column for scale scores, with values from 0 to 5 in 0.5 increments. The Number Report includes a range that includes the value zero. The zero in the Number Report allows managers to monitor the number of times a scale is not scored. At times, staff did not score a particular scale because they were uncomfortable with the content. For example, a zero in Scale 19, Family Planning, for a postpartum mother suggests supervision and training needs. At other times the zero has another meaning. In Scale 4, Attitudes to Pregnancy, the number scored in Columns 1–5 indicates the number of pregnant women in the caseload at intake and at any other measure, and the zero means the number of individuals who are parenting and not pregnant at the time. Similarly, for Scale 12, Language, the number of zeros indicates the number of parents in the caseload who were native English speakers; this value should not change.

Number Report

The Number Report (see Table 7.1) shows the distribution of the number of parents who were given scores in each column across the 0–5 scoring range. One Number Report should be generated for each scale in the LSP, and parent scales should be separate from infant scales to avoid duplication of results. When the parent scales are not separate from the infant scales before calculating the reports, the numbers are inflated to look as if there are almost twice as many families.

The Number Report is used when interpreting the Percentage reports. If the percentage scoring in the desirable target range for a particular scale is high, for example 98%–100%, this looks impressive if the number of parents is 150. If that same percentage is based on a sample of 10 parents, however, the low number makes the percentage less useful for interpretation.

Table 7.1. Number report for Scale 23, Child Immunizations

Scale	N	0	1	1.5	2	2.5	3	3.5	4	4.5	5
Initial	202	46	1	0	1	0	2	1	6	10	135
0–11 months	77	5	0	0	0	0	1	0	2	9	60
12–17 months	15	1	0	0	0	0	0	1	0	2	11
18–23 months											
24–30 months											

Percentage Report

The Percentage Report (see Table 7.2) shows the full range of percent of parents' LSP scores and is important for describing characteristics of the caseload that may not show in the Target Range Report. For the Percentage Report, if the zero column is not deleted, the percentages are skewed negatively and interpreted incorrectly. In calculating the Percentage Report, first delete the zeros or the percentages will be inaccurate. For example, if there are 25 zeros for a scale, and 75 scores 1–5, the zeros would account for 25% of the total. If those 25 zeros are deleted, then the range of percentages across scores 1–5 show clearly and form the basis for 100% of the scores.

Table 7.2. Percentage report for Scale 23, Child Immunizations

Scale	N	0	1	1.5	2	2.5	3	3.5	4	4.5	5
Initial	202	NA	1%	0	1%	0	1%	1%	4%	6%	87%
0–11 months	77	NA	0	0	0	0	1%	0	3%	12%	83%
12–17 months	15	NA	0	0	0	0	0	7%		14%	79%
18–23 months											
24–30 months											

Several scales yield information that cannot be obtained unless the number and percentages are calculated. Examples of this are the percentages of speakers of English as a primary Language, speakers of Spanish, and speakers who are bilingual. In other scales, valuable information can be identified, such as the number of abused children, the number and percentage of depressed mothers, and the number and percentage of mothers in either TANF or WIC programs.

The Percentage in Target Range Report

The Percentage in the Target Range Report (see Table 7.3) shows the number and percentage of parents scoring in the Target Range. The Target Range is an "adequate to optimal" score for any scale. A percentage of parents who were given scores within the target range at each time period establish the goals for each of the scales. In other words, if only 10% of a caseload was found to be in the target range at the baseline and then this figure rose to 15% at the second assessment period, there would be a 5% increase above baseline in the number of parents who improved.

The Target Range varies for each scale, although most are scores of 4–5. The target ranges are shown visually as highlights on the LSP with target scores (see Appendix J). The target scores also appear as the numbers following the scale name on the blank Cumulative Score Sheet (see Appendix H).

Table 7.3. Target range report for Scale 23, Child Immunizations

Targets	Intake	0–11 months	12–17 months	18–23 months	24–30 months
Number	151	71	13		
Percent (%)	97	99	93		

Intake to Closure Report

The Intake, or Baseline, to Closure Report (see Table 7.4) compares baseline target scores with those at closure at various lengths of service. This report is another example of program experience that drives software programmer's design logic. Program managers know that simply adding the scores for all closing cases does not produce accurate and meaningful results. Closure outcomes for parents who drop out of a program after only two or four visits are likely to show scores that are vastly different from those of parents who remain in the program for regular visits over years of service. As a result, a separate report is needed to show the outcome distribution based on different lengths of service.

The Intake to Closure Report should have time samples that are different from the Number and Percentage Reports. An example of a measurement range is 0–3 months,

4–6 months, 7–12 months, 13–18 months, 19–23 months, and 24–36 months. This will be influenced by program decisions on the length of time expected for engagement. Pilot studies showed varying rates of attrition and refill of a caseload. The parents with early departures from the program generally showed lower LSP scores and had complex and chaotic lives. Positive outcomes could occur in the 1–6-month range; however, the greatest change in outcomes occurred when parents left the program at around 12 months, even though the program goal was to engage parents for 24 months. This report can help programs see the characteristics of parents who leave early and those who are "successes" and the speed at which success can occur. The LSP scores can be used to help define successful closure criteria for programs when triage closures are necessary.

Table 7.4.   Intake to Closure report for Scale 23, Child Immunizations

Targets	Intake	0–3 months	4–6 months	7–12 months	13–18 months	19–23 months	24–36 months
Number	151	3	9	7	2		
Percent (%)	97	100	100	100	100		

Case Management Reports

Two particularly useful caseload reports can be used for case management. The Open Caseload Report, printed alphabetically for the entire open caseload, allows the case manager to track his or her progress with each family. A report that lists the names, birthdays, or parents and children of each family gives a snapshot of the caseload. This report can be run monthly or quarterly depending on the size of the caseload and the program. The Reminder Report calculates when the next LSP is due based on the first date of service for each month. It gives the case manager a list of families who require a second or third LSP. The Reminder Report is a useful way to make sure the LSPs are done within the specified time period.

Each data run would then consist of 43 pages of reports. The raw data reports are useful to program managers to understand caseload and staff scoring patterns, but they are not useful as printed for public use for advocacy and sustainability. To be useful these MS Access reports need to be "translated" into understandable text descriptions of the sequential outcomes for each scale.

This evaluation discussion is a primer for programs that are new to evaluation and for more experienced programs on some methods of analysis of LSP data as part of program evaluation. Because evaluation of this level of parent/child outcomes is in its infancy, significant learning will be necessary as programs and systems begin collecting LSP data and seeing the progress resulting from their interventions to support parent skills.

The understanding of the impact of best practice and the ability to see which practice components are most effective will gradually emerge in the data and the cross-program discussions that ensue. . . . if we manage this data wisely.
Asking questions about impact . . . that's evaluation.

Gathering data . . . that's evaluation.
Making judgments . . . that's evaluation.
Facilitating use . . . that's evaluation.
Putting all those pieces together in a meaningful whole that tells people something
they want to know and can use about a matter of importance.
Now, that's *really* evaluation!
Halcome (Patton, 1997, p. 371)

EIGHT

Integrating the LSP
into Sites and Systems

• • • • • • • • • • • • • • • •

*The question "Does it work?" lies at the crux
of all program evaluation.*

Gilliam & Leiter, 2003, p. 7

• • • • • • • • • • • • • • • •

INCORPORATION PLAN OVERVIEW

To ensure that the LSP accomplishes what a program needs it to accomplish, an implementation plan that is well thought out is good insurance. To be effective, the planning process should begin *before* the initial training and LSP use.

In addition to the following reflective questions about specific aspects of implementation, programs may find it helpful to reference *Evaluating Early Childhood Programs: Improving Quality and Informing Policy* (Gilliam & Leiter, 2003). This article is a basic primer for program evaluation with key concepts defined, an evaluation checklist, and a sample logic model.

The size of the program significantly influences the ease of fit and planning required in order to incorporate the LSP into the program. Integration issues are far simpler for a small single site than for a national system or sites within a state or national system. Some programs will use the LSP for clinical purposes only, whereas others will use the LSP for both clinical and data purposes. Some programs will want to start with clinical use and later begin using the LSP for data. Some sites, particularly those linked with universities, may want data for formal research purposes. However, these stages of incorporation apply to all sites:

1. Decide whether the LSP fits program needs and interests, and identify the funding needed to institutionalize the LSP.

2. Train staff, supervisors, and data management personnel in use and scoring.

3. Identify trainers who will provide ongoing training for new staff and maintenance for continuing staff.

4. Determine how the LSP fits into the existing documentation, data collection, reflective supervision, and clinical practice.

5. Plan how to develop a new LSP data system versus coordination with or incorporation into an existing data system.

6. Plan how to use the data to create useful reports for funding, program improvement, and collaborative community planning or pan-system planning.

DOES THE LSP FIT PROGRAM NEEDS?

Because data provided by the LSP focus on parent/child outcomes, many of the data are new and not redundant. However, programs using other risk-screening tools such as the Family Stress Scale or Kempe Child Abuse Risk Scale may see some overlapping information (Abidin, 1995; Schmidt & Carroll, 1978). Generally, these screening forms have not been turned into sequential databases and are used for clinical purposes. Programs usually want to keep their existing screening tools and use them to provide information summarized in the LSP, but other sites find the information redundant and opt to simply use the LSP. However, adding the LSP raises questions such as

- Does the LSP provide data that are new, redundant, or more complete than data from other forms?

- Does the LSP provide data that we want/need to be collecting? What is the purpose?

- How will staff feel about use of the LSP? Clinically? For data?

- Will use be voluntary or mandatory?

- How often will the LSP be used? Every 6 months as recommended? More frequently? In coordination with scheduled IFSPs?

- Will existing informed client consent forms be adequate? Will HIPAA requirements need to be met or human subjects reviews completed?

WHAT ARE THE TRAINING NEEDS?

If the LSP will be used for clinical purposes only, training of staff in use and scoring will be needed, but training with a certified trainer is recommended if the LSP is being used for data purposes. Programs will need to decide whether to use a certified LSP trainer, find funding to certify their own trainers, or simply train their own staff. Information about site training and costs, the certification of trainers, and lists of certified trainers by state and systems will be available on the LSP web site. Training questions to be answered include:

- Who will do the initial training? What are the training and implementation costs for materials? For data?

- When is the best time to train the trainers? To train staff?

- What is the staff attrition rate, and how can the training of new staff be accomplished in a timely and reliable way?

- How will supervision follow up on appropriate use of the LSP with each visitor after training? Will a supervisor review and discuss each LSP with the visitor for clinical and data purposes? Has the process for supervisory review been described in writing to facilitate implementation?

- What are the training needs for data entry and technical assistance staff?

- What are staff training needs with regard to how the LSP fits with existing forms?

- Are training or instructions needed for primary and back-up clerks who supply and/or copy forms?

HOW DOES THE LSP FIT WITH FORMS AND SCREENING TOOLS?

Any program considering the LSP already has some type of intake, screening, history, or risk assessment forms. Most have individual or family charts that include progress notes of some kind. Some use automated charting. Many use individual or family service plans or goal sheets periodically. Sometimes these are completed with the parent's participation or as part of a program or nursing care plan. Program forms, although the bane of most home visitors, are important and necessary. They provide the conceptual structure and flow for providing service, gathering information, and charting high-risk situations for which the record may be subpoenaed as evidence. The questions of integration into the forms system are important:

- What forms do we use now and how does the LSP fit with them? Are some data redundant and can they be deleted, or is the redundancy a necessity?

- Is there a logical order for forms (e.g., history or intake forms) to flow into the LSP, and which forms (e.g., ISPs or goal forms) are facilitated by information in the LSP?

The Healthy Family America–Indiana (HFA-I) sites that are using the LSP have incorporated their form flow into the basic LSP training to ensure that the staff understands how the LSP fits into the existing documentation and clinical practice. Some HFA-I core and advanced trainers are certified LSP trainers. The training describes the HFA-I forms used, specifically the assessment forms, the Infant/Toddler HOME, the NCAST Difficult Life Circumstances, the NCAST Community Life Skills, and the Family Stress Checklist (Hawaii FSC). The training structures the discussion regarding how information from these forms is used to complete the LSP scales. The summary created by the LSP helps to formulate the ISP on a quarterly basis. A similar incorporation process should occur in any site or system, whether large or small.

Some programs, particularly nursing models, have taken short-cuts to documenting the information and forms that were used with a particular parent. These lengthy but helpful logs list all the curriculum topics or materials in the order in which they are generally used for pregnancy and parenting visits. The logs also list the program forms that are due for completion at the times they are due, and include the next LSP. In the log, staff check off, date, and/or initial when a topic has been covered, material given, or forms completed. This prevents recording routine material in long-hand or automated progress notes and expedites the charting process. It also highlights information the parent has received or missed. Some programs have created their own documentation logs, and some use the ones provided in curricula such as the Beginnings Life Skill Development.

The role of the supervisor appears to be one of the most important components of successful integration. The role includes using the LSP in reflective supervision and for quality assurance for the accuracy and reliability of the data. If LSPs are sent directly to a data entry clerk instead of first going to a supervisor, the clerk's judgment, understanding, and attention to detail may not be adequate to catch errors. The results may be incomplete, inaccurate, or "dirty" data. From the beginning, if the supervisor reviews every LSP for clinical content and intervention planning with the visitor, the clinical interventions are likely to be more effective and the data submitted more reliable. The ongoing orientation of new staff can be done by the supervisor and may provide new staff with a better view of how the LSP fits into forms and interventions than if training is done by someone outside the program. If a supervisor is not a certified trainer, it will be important to use a certified LSP trainer if the LSP is being used for data.

HOW DOES THE LSP FIT WITH THE DATA MANAGEMENT SYSTEM?

Adding the LSP to an existing data system can be relatively simple or extremely complex. The simplest incorporation involves the purchase and use of the preformatted LSP data entry and report application (currently using MS Office Professional-XP and the XP operating system). It is available through the LSP web site.

In this case, the LSP data entered and the data reports generated are completely independent of any other data systems used by the site. The LSP data in the MS Access XP application migrate with relative ease to more sophisticated systems such as SPSS. Evaluators use the more sophisticated systems for correlations and alpha tests for reliability and to calculate whether the amount of change is statistically significant. The other data collected by programs generally continue independently and have no direct data relationship with the LSP.

For sites that have multiple offices or are part of state or community-wide systems, in the model described above each site can manage its own data and/or forward the data to a central location via CD, through a web-based system, or as written reports. The other option is for each site to complete individual data entry forms (see Appendix E) and to send them to a central site for data entry and report generation.

More complex systems currently using an Access database for all their data and needing to incorporate the LSP data into their existing system will require technical assistance. Programs that plan to design or adapt their own databases need to ensure that the design costs are within the program's budget and that programmers understand the reports needed. Data systems that cannot provide relational data reports are not useful for the LSP.

HOW WILL LSP DATA BE USED FOR REPORTS?

Programs can use the LSP data for a large variety of purposes. Some types of reports may be obvious and immediately needed, and other reports may evolve gradually as programs or funding requirements shift focus. Some questions regarding data reports are

- Will the LSP be used for sequential data to capture improvement? If so, for what or whom will the data be used and what do they require?

- When will data reports be needed and will they be done on a routine schedule? Annually? Quarterly? What are the various purposes for which data reports will be needed? What are the required budget and grant timelines? Can these reports be run at any time by special request?

- What manager will be responsible for writing the summary reports from the data reports and reviewing them for accuracy? Who will be responsible for presenting the reports to management, funding sources, staff, and the community?

- What management team will be responsible for using the data reports for program improvement or planning? How will staff be included in the discussion regarding outcome data and planning?

- Will LSP data be used for formal research proposals or participating in the research of other institutions? For journal articles?

- Will program staff manage the data or will outside services (statistician, evaluator, epidemiologist, or university) be required? What orientation will be needed for the outside evaluator to do an appropriate and useful analysis of the data?

The July 2003 *Zero To Three* journal, *Evaluating Infant–Family Programs*, is dedicated to evaluation of programs serving young children. As with other issues, excellent resource references are listed. Two resources may be particularly helpful: The *Pathways to Outcomes* web site directed by Lisbeth B. Schorr in partnership with the Annie E. Casey Foundation, and *Planning for Success: Mapping Goals, Services and Outcomes for Program Improvement* which is located on the Ounce of Prevention web site in conjunction with the Robert Wood Johnson Foundation. The *Zero To Three* journal on evaluation ends with an article called, *From Program Evaluation to Persuasive Reports* (Smith & Brown-Clark, 2003), which includes a useful tool to check reports for brevity, clarity, picturesque language, and accuracy.

Together, with thoughtful work and sound evaluation, perhaps we can do what Isabel Allende suggests: "We can change the world in half a generation by raising the children differently" (Seattle, 1995, Northwest International Women's Conference).

REFERENCES

Abidin, R. (1995). *Parental Stress Index–Third Edition.* Lutz, FL: Psychological Assessment Resources.

Als, H., Lawhon, G., Duffy, F., McAnulty, G., Gibes-Grossman, R., & Blickman, J. (1994). Individualized developmental care for the very low birth weight preterm infant. *Journal of the American Medical Association, 272*(11), 853–1578.

American Psychiatric Association. (1994). *Diagnostic and statistical manual of mental disorders* (4th ed.). Washington, DC: Author.

Appelbaum, M., & Sweet, M. (1999). *Is home visiting an effective strategy?* Workshop presentation University of California, San Diego, copies available from mappelbaum@ucsd.edu

Bailey, K.D. (1994). *Methods of social research* (4th ed.). New York: The Free Press.

Bandura, A. (1986). *Social foundations of thought and action: A social cognitive theory.* Englewood Cliffs, NJ: Prentice Hall.

Barnard, K. (1978). NCAST: Nursing Child Assessment Satellite Training Learning Resource manual. Seattle: University of Washington.

Bates, J.E. (1989). Concepts and measures of temperament. In G.A. Kohnstamm, J.E. Bates, & M.K. Rothbart (Eds.), *Temperament in childhood* (pp. 3–26). New York: John Wiley & Sons.

Bates, J., & Wachs, T. (Eds.). (1994). *Temperament: Individual differences and the interface of biology and behavior.* Washington DC: American Psychological Association.

Bayley, N. (1993). *Bayley Scales of Infant Development—II.* San Antonio, TX: Harcourt Assessment.

Beck, C., & Gable, R. (2002). *Postpartum Depression Screening Scale.* Los Angeles: Western Psychological Services.

Berg, I. (1994). *Family based services: A solution-focused approach.* New York: W.W. Norton.

Brazelton, T.B. (1984). *Neonatal Behavioral Assessment Scale–Second Edition* (NBAS). Philadelphia: J.B. Lippincott.

Bricker, D., Squires, J., Mounts, L., Potter, L., Nickel, R., Twombly, E., & Farrell, J. (1999). *Ages & Stages Questionnaires® (ASQ).* Baltimore: Paul H. Brookes Publishing Co.

Briggs-Gowan, M., Carter, M., Irwin, S., Wachtel, K., & Ciccehetti, D. (2004). The Brief Infant-Toddler Social and Emotional Assessment: Screening for Social-Emotional Problems and Delays in Competence (BITSEA). *Journal of Pediatric Psychology, 29*(2), 143–155.

Bronfenbrenner, U. (1979). *The ecology of human development.* Cambridge, MA: Harvard University Press.

Bronfenbrenner, U. (1992). *The ecology of human development: Experiments by nature and design.* Cambridge, MA: Harvard University Press.

Browne, J., MacLeod, A., & Smith-Sharp, S. (1999). *Family Infant Relationship Support Training Program (FIRST).* Denver, CO: The Children's Hospital Association Center for Family and Infant Interaction.

Centers for Disease Control and Prevention (CDC). (1999, September 17). Framework for program evaluation in public health. *MMWR Morbidity and Mortality Weekly Report, 48*(RR-11), 1–40.

Cox, J.L., Chapman, G., Murray, D., & Jones, P. (1996). Validation of the Edinburgh Postnatal Depression Scale (EPDS) in non-postnatal women. *Journal of Affect Disorders, 39,* 185–189.

Dean, C. (2000). Empowerment skills for family workers—A worker handbook. The comprehensive curriculum of the New York State Family Development Credential, Cornell Empowering Families Project, 2000, Cornell Distribution Center, Cornell University.

De la Rocha, O., Rolon, I., & Mintzer, C. (2004). Bridges for newborns: An evaluation of the pilot program for Bridges II, January 2003–2004; http://www.ccfc.ca.gov

Early Head Start (EHS) data: Making a difference in the lives of infants, toddlers and families: The impact of Early Head Start. Administration for Children and Families, Child Outcomes Research and Evaluation office at http://www.acf.hhs.gov/programs/opre/

Emde, R.N., Bingham, R.D., & Harmon, R.J. (1993). Classification and the diagnostic process in infancy. In C.H. Zeanah, Jr. (Ed.), *Handbook of infant mental health*. New York: Guilford.

Endress, J. (2000). *Family development matrix.* Institute for Community Collaborative Studies, Monterey Bay, CA: California State University. http://hhspp.csumb.edu/community/commsites.htm

Evans, R.G., & Stoddart, G.L. (1994). Producing health, consuming health care. In R.G. Evans, M.L. Barer, & T.R. Marmor (Eds.), *Why are some people healthy and others not? The determinants of health of populations* (pp. 29–64). New York: Aldine DeGruyter.

Fenichel, E. (Ed.). (1992). *Learning through supervision and mentorship to support the development of infants, toddlers and their families: A source book.* Washington, DC: ZERO TO THREE: National Center for Infants, Toddlers and Families.

Fonagy, P. (1999). *Transgenerational consistencies of attachment: A new theory.* Paper to the Development and Psychoanalytic Discussion Group, American Psychoanalytic Association Meeting, Washington DC, online at http://psychematters.com/papers/fonagy2.htm

Fonagy, P., & Target, M. (1997). Attachment and reflective function: Their role in self-organization. *Development and Psychology, 9,* 677–699.

Frankenburg, W., & Dodds, J. (1975). *Denver Developmental Screening Test–Revised.* Denver: DDM, Inc.

Frankenburg, W.K., Dodds, J.B., Archer, P., Bresnick, B., Maschka, P., Edelman, N., & Shapiro, H. (1992). *Denver II* (2nd ed.). Denver: DDM. Inc.

Friedman, M. (2000). *Results based accountability for Proposition 10 commissions: A planning guide.* Los Angeles: UCLA Center for Healthier Children, Families and Communities.

Friedman, M. (2003, March). What works: Policy brief for families and children's services:

Use of results based accountability. Retrieved from http://www.resultsaccountability.com

Gavin, N., & Lissy, K. (2000). *Cost effectiveness of case management and home visiting: A review of the literature.* Washington, DC: U.S. Department of Health and Human Services, Maternal and Child Health Bureau, Health Resources and Services Administration (HRSA), http://mchb.hrsa.gov/

Gelfand, D., & Teti, D. (1990). The effects of maternal depression on children. *Clinical Psychology Review, 10,* 262–272.

Gilkerson, L., & Shahmoon-Shanok, R. (1999). Relationships for growth: Cultivating reflective practice in infant, toddler, and preschool programs. In J.D. Osofsky & H.E. Fitzgerald (Eds.), *WAIMH handbook of infant mental health, Vol. 2. Early intervention, evaluation and assessment* (pp. 3–32). New York, John Wiley & Sons.

Gilliam, W., & Leiter, V. (2003). Evaluating early childhood programs: Improving quality and informing policy. *Zero To Three, 25*(6), 6–13.

Glascoe, F., Martin, E., & Humphrey, S. (1990, October). A comparative review of developmental screening tests. Child Development Center, Department of Pediatrics, Vanderbilt University. *Pediatrics, 86,* 547–554.

Gomby, D., Culross, P., & Behrman, R.E. (Eds.). (1993). *The future of children: Home visitation.* The David and Lucille Packard Foundation, Vol. 3, No. 33. Out of print; available at http://www.futureofchildren.org

Gomby, D., & Culross, P. (Eds.). (1999). *The future of children—Home visiting: Recent program evaluations.* The David and Lucile Packard Foundation, retrieved from http://www.futureofchildren.org

Gomby, D. (2003). *Building school readiness through home visitation,* funded by the California First 5 Commission and available from http://www.ccfc.ca.gov

Greenspan, S., DeGangi, G., & Wieder, S. (2001). *The Functional Emotional Assessment Scale (FEAS) for infancy and early childhood: Clinical and research applications.* Bethesda, MD: Interdisciplinary Council for Development and Learning Disorders.

Greenspan, S.I., & Meisels, S. (1994). Toward a new vision for the developmental assessment of infants and young children. *Zero To Three, 14*(6), 1–8.

Greenspan, S.I., & Weider, S. (2000). The assessment and diagnosis of infant disorders: Developmental level, individual differences, and relationship-based interactions. In J.D. Osofsky & H.E. Fitzgerald (Eds.), *WAIMH handbook of infant mental health: Vol. 2. Early intervention, evaluation, and assessment* (pp. 203–237). New York: John Wiley & Sons.

Greenspan, S.I., Weider, S., and the ZERO TO THREE Diagnostic Classification Task Force. (1994). *Diagnostic classification of mental health and developmental disorders of infancy and early childhood (DC:0-3).* Washington, DC: ZERO TO THREE: National Center for Infants, Toddlers and Families.

Halfon, N., Ebener, P., Sastry, N., Wyn, R., Ahn, P., Hernandez, J., & Wong, D. (2000). *California health report.* UCLA Center for Healthier Children, Families and Communities. Santa Monica, CA: Rand.

Jacobsen, T. (2004). Clinical assessment & treatment of parenting problems in mothers with major psychiatric disorders. In M. Gopfert, J. Webster, & M. Seeman (Eds.), *Parental psychiatric disorders: Distressed parents & their families.* Melbourne, Australia: Cambridge University Press.

Karoly, L., Kilburn, R., Bigelow, J., Caulkins, J., & Chiesa, J. (2001). *Assessing costs and benefits of early childhood intervention programs: Overview and application to Starting Early, Starting Smart.* Santa Monica, CA: Rand.

Kimura, L. (1999). *Babies can't wait: Relationship-based home visiting.* Woodland, CA: BCW Publishing.

Kimura, L. (2003). *Relationship-based training for early Head Start home visitors: A workbook.* Woodland, CA: BCW Publishing.

Kirk, R.S. (1998). Building quality assurance and outcome measures into managed care. In R. Alsop & A. Winterstein (Eds.), *Proceedings of the third annual roundtable on managed care in child welfare* (pp. 85–90). Englewood, CO: American Humane Association Press.

Klass, C. (2003). *The home visitor's guidebook.* Baltimore: Paul H. Brookes Publishing Co.

Kogan, M., Alexander, G., Kotelchuck, M., Nagey, D., & Jack, B. (1994). Comparing mother's reports on the content of prenatal care received with recommended national guidelines for care. *Public Health Reports, 109*(5), 637–645.

Korfmacher, J., O'Brien, R., Hiatt, S., & Olds, D. (1999). Differences in program implementation between nurses and paraprofessionals providing home visits during pregnancy and infancy: A randomized trial. *American Journal of Public Health, 89*(12), 1847–1851.

Lally, J.R. (2002). The Program for Infant/Toddler Caregivers (PITC): A relationship-based curriculum. WestED/PITC in collaboration with the California Department of Education. Available at http://www.pitc.org

Landy, S. (2000). Assessing the risks and strengths of infants and families in community-based programs. In J.D. Osofsky & H.E. Fitzgerald (Eds.), *WAIMH handbook of infant mental health: Vol. 2. Early intervention, evaluation, and assessment* (pp. 335–375). New York: John Wiley & Sons.

Lynch, E.W. (1996). Assessing infants: Child and family issues and approaches. In M.J. Hanson (Ed.), *Atypical infant development.* Austin, TX: PRO-ED.

McDonough, S.C. (2000). Preparing infant mental health personnel for the twenty-first century practice. In J.D. Osofsky & H.E. Fitzgerald (Eds.), *WAIMH handbook of infant mental health: Vol. 2. Early intervention, evaluation, and assessment* (pp. 535–546). New York: John Wiley & Sons.

McLennan, J.D., & Kotelchuck, M. (2000). Parental prevention practices for young children in the context of maternal depression. *Pediatrics 105,* 1090–1095.

Meisels, S. (1996). Charting the continuum of assessment and intervention. In S.J. Meisels & E. Fenichel (Eds.), *New visions for the developmental assessment of infants and young children.* Washington, DC: ZERO TO THREE: National Center for Infants, Toddlers and Families.

Meisels, S., Marsden, D., Dombro, A., Weston, D., & Jewkes, A. (2003). *The Ounce scale.* New York: Pearson Early Learning.

Minde, K. (2000). The assessment of infants and toddlers with medical conditions and their families. In J.D. Osofsky & H.E. Fitzgerald

(Eds.), *WAIMH handbook of infant mental health: Vol. 2. Early intervention, evaluation, and assessment* (pp. 81–117). New York: John Wiley & Sons.

Murray, L., & Carothers, A.D. (1990). The validation of the Edinburgh Post-natal Depression Scale on a community sample. *British Journal of Psychiatry, 157,* 288–290.

National Center for Children, Families, and Communities (NCCFC) and NFP data available from http://www.nursefamilypartnership .org. Research publications include NFP information and bibliography of Olds related article under the Prevention Research Center for Family and Child Health, University of CO Pediatric Dept.

National Center for Children in Poverty. (2002, March). *Early childhood poverty: A statistical profile.* Mailman School of Public Health, Columbia University. www.nccp.org

National Resource Center for Family Centered Practice. (1994). *Family centered services: A handbook for practitioners.* University of Iowa, School of Social Work, http://www.Uiowa .edu/~nrcfcp

National Center for Health Statistics (NCHS). (2005). International Classification of Diseases–9th edition (ICD-9). Medical Management Institute.

O'Brien, R., & Baca, R.P. (1997). Application of solution focused interventions to nurse home visitation for pregnant women and parents of young children. *Journal of Community Psychology, 25*(1), 47–57.

Olds, D.L., Henderson, C.R., Jr., & Kitzman, H. (1994). Does prenatal and infancy nurse home visitation have enduring effects on qualities of parental caregiving and child health at 25 to 50 months of life? *Pediatrics, 1,* 89–98.

Olds, D., Kitzman, H., Cole, R., & Robinson, J. (1997). Theoretical foundations of a program of home visitation for pregnant women and parents of young children. *Journal of Community Psychology, 25*(1), 9–25.

Olds, D.L., Robinson, J., O'Brien, R., Luckey, D.W., Pettitt, L.M., Henderson, C.R., Jr., Ng, R.K., Sheff, K.L., Korfmacher, J., Hiatt, S., & Talmi, A. (2002). Home visiting by paraprofessionals and by nurses: A randomized, controlled trial. *Pediatrics, 110*(3), 486–496.

Osborne, D., & Gaebler, T. (1992). *Reinventing government: How the entrepreneurial spirit is transforming the public sector from schoolhouse to statehouse, city hall to the Pentagon.* Reading, MA: Addison-Wesley.

Oser, C., & Cohen, J. (2003). *America's babies, The ZERO TO THREE Policy Center data book.* Washington, DC: ZERO TO THREE: National Center for Infants, Toddlers and Families.

Parke, M. (2004). *Who are "fragile families" and what do we know about them?* Center for Law and Social Policy (CLASP), Brief #4. Publication # 04-01. Wahsington, DC: CLASP. Available at http://www.clasp.org/publications.php ?id=6&type=2

Parlakian, R. (2001a). *Look, listen, and learn: Reflective supervision and relationship-based work.* Washington, DC: ZERO TO THREE: National Center for Infants, Toddlers and Families.

Parlakian, R. (2001b). *The power of questions: Building quality relationships with infants and families.* Washington, DC: ZERO TO THREE: National Center for Infants, Toddlers and Families.

Parlakian, R., & Seibel N. (2001). *Being in charge: Reflective leadership in infant/family programs.* Washington, DC: ZERO TO THREE: National Center for Clinical Infant Programs.

Patton, M.Q. (1997). *Utilization-focused evaluation* (3rd ed.). Newbury Park, CA: Sage Publications.

Pawl, J. (2004, July). Consultation to the EHS consultants. *Zero To Three, 24*(6), 33–38.

Powers, S., & Fenichel, E. (1999). *Home visiting: Reaching babies and families where they live.* Washington, DC: ZERO TO THREE: National Center for Infants, Toddlers and Families.

Radloff, L. (1991). The use of the Center for Epidemiological Studies Depression Scale (CES-D) in Adolescents and Young Adults. *Journal of Youth and Adolescence, 20*(2), 149–166.

Richardson, B. (2000). *Preliminary reliability study of the Life Skill Progression,* unpublished, University of Iowa, School of Social Work, National Resource Center for Family Centered Practice-evaluator.

Rudolf, L. (1977). CES-D: A self-report depression scale for research in the general population. *Applied Psychological Measurements, 1*(3), 385–501.

Schmidt, B., & Carroll, C. (1978). *The Kempe Family Stress Inventory (KFSI)*. Denver: Authors, www.kempecenter.org

Schorr, L.B., & Schorr, D. (1989). *Within our reach: Breaking the cycle of disadvantage*. New York: Anchor Books.

Seifer, R., & Dickstein, S. (1993). Parental mental illness and infant development. In C.H. Zeanah, Jr. (Ed.), *Handbook of infant mental health*. New York: Guilford.

Shaddish, W.R., Cook, T.D., & Leviton, L.C. (1991). *Foundations of program evaluation: Theories of practice*. Newbury Park, CA: Sage Publications.

Shahmoon-Shanok, R. (1992). The supervisory relationship: Integrator, resource, and guide. In E. Fenichel (Ed.), *Learning through supervision and mentorship to support the development of infants, toddlers and their families: A source book* (pp. 37–41). Washington, DC: ZERO TO THREE: National Center for Infants, Toddlers and Families.

Sherwood, K. (2005, Spring). Packard Foundation home visitation case study. In M.Q. Patton & P. Patrizi (Eds.), *New directions in evaluation. Teaching evaluation using the case method:* San Francisco: Jossey-Bass.

Shonkoff, J., & Phillips, D. (Eds.). (2000). *From neurons to neighborhoods: The science of early childhood development*. Work of the Committee on Integrating the Science of Early Childhood Development of the National Research Council and the Institute of Medicine, National Academies Press or ZERO TO THREE: National Center for Infants, Toddlers and Families.

Singley, C., & Wollesen, L. (2003, April). *Better together: Community collaboration*. Unpublished presentation, Parents as Teachers national conference, St. Louis, MO.

Slade, A. (2002, June/July). Keeping the baby in mind: A critical factor in perinatal mental health. *Zero To Three, 22*(6), 10–16.

Smith, S. (1998). Information giving: Effects on birth outcomes and patient satisfaction. *The International Electronic Journal of Health Education, 3,* 135–145. University of Washington Center for Health Education Research, available at http://www.uwcher.org

Smith, S. (2005). *Essential beginnings pregnancy guide*. Seattle: Practice Development, Inc.

Smith, S., & Brown-Clark, J. (2003). From program evaluation to persuasive reports. *Zero To Three, 25*(6), 51–52.

Smith, S., & Wollesen, L. (2003). Adapted with permission from Gomby, Deanna S., Building School Readiness Through Home Visitation (January 2003), report for the First 5 of California Children and Families Commission.

Smith, S., & Wollesen, L. (2004). *Beginnings Life Skill Development Curriculum: Home visitor handbook*. Seattle: Practice Development Inc.

Solchaney, J. (2001). *Promoting maternal mental health during pregnancy: Theory, assessment and intervention*. Seattle: NCAST, University of Washington.

Sommerville, G. (2002). Program description for media by Public Private Ventures for the Nurse-Family Partnership and National Center for Children, Families, and Communities, available at http://www.nursefamilypartnership.org

Spitz, R. (1946). Anaclitic depression: An inquiry into the genesis of psychiatric conditions in early childhood. *The Psychoanalytic Study of the Child, 2,* 53–74.

Squires, J., Bricker, D., Twombly, E., Yockelson, S., Schoen Davis, M., & Kim, Y. (2002). *Ages & Stages Questionnaires®: Social-Emotional (ASQ:SE). A parent-completed, child-monitoring system for social-emotional behaviors*. Baltimore: Paul H. Brookes Publishing Co.

Stamp, G., Williams, A., & Crowther, C. (1996). Predicting postnatal depression among pregnant women. *Birth, 23*(4), 218–212.

Sumner, G., & Spitz, A. (1994). NCAST caregiver/parent-child interaction feeding manual. University of Washington, School of Nursing. Seattle: NCAST Publications.

Sweet, M., & Appelbaum, M. (2004). Is home visiting an effective strategy? A meta-analytic review of home visiting for families with young children. *Child Development, 75*(5), 1435–1456.

Thomas, A., & Chess, S. (1997). *Temperament and development*. New York: Brunner-Mazel.

Thompson, J. (1990). Chapter title. In I.R. Merkatz & J. Thompson (Eds.), *New perspectives on prenatal care* (p. 550). New York: Elsevier.

U.S. Census Bureau News Press Release 8/26/2004. 2003 Census. Retrieved from http://www.census.gov

U.S. Department of Health and Human Services. (n.d.). *Healthy People 2010.* Office of Disease Prevention and Health Promotion, www .healthypeople.gov

U.S. General Accounting Office. (1990). *Home visiting: A promising early intervention service delivery strategy,* 10/2/1990, HE9401262. Washington, DC: Author.

Wachs, T.D. (2004). Temperament and development: The role of context in a biologically based system. *Zero to Three, 24*(4), 12–21.

Wagner, M., Graham, M., & Chiricos, C. (2001) *Infant-toddler curricula comparison.* Tallahassee: Florida State University Center for Prevention & Early Intervention Policy, retrieved from http://www.epeip.fus.edu

Wasik, B.H. (1993). Staffing issues for home visiting programs. *The Future of Children, 3*(3), 140–157.

Wasik, B.H., Sheaffer, L.G., Pohlman, C. & Baird, T. (1996). *A guide to written training materials for home visitors.* Chapel Hill, NC: The Center for Home Visiting, University of North Carolina at Chapel Hill.

Wasik, B.H., Thompson, A., Sheaffer, L.G., & Herrmann, S. (1996). A guide to audio visual training materials for home visitors. Chapel Hill, NC: The Center for Home Visiting, University of North Carolina at Chapel Hill.

Weiss, C.H. (1998). *Evaluation.* Englewood Cliffs, NJ: Prentice Hall.

Zeanah, C.H. (2000). *Handbook of infant mental health.* New York: Guilford.

Zeanah, C.H., Boris, N.W., & Scheeringa, M.S. (1997). Psychopathology in infancy. *Journal of Child Psychology and Psychiatry, 38,* 81–99.

Life Skills Progression™ (LSP) Instrument

Also available on the CD-ROM that accompanies this book.

THE LIFE SKILLS PROGRESSION (LSP)

Family record ID # _____   Indiv. # _____   ☐ Initial _____ / _____ / _____   Months of service _____

Web ID # _____   ☐ Ongoing # _____ / _____ / _____   No. attempted visits _____   No. completed visits _____

Client name _____   ☐ Closing _____ / _____ / _____   Home visitor _____

(last name, first name)   Next LSP due _____ / _____ / _____   Agency/program _____

Client DOB _____ / _____ / _____   ☐ Female ☐ Male   Race _____   Ethnicity _____   Medical codes _____

Item	Score	Areas of Life Skill Development	0 Low — 1	1.5 — 2	2.5 — 3	3.5 — 4	4.5 — 5 High
RELATIONSHIPS WITH FAMILY AND FRIENDS							
1		**Family/ Extended Family**	Hostile, violent, or physically abusive family relationships	Separated. No contact. Not available for support	Conflicted, critical, or verbal abuse; frequent arguments. Reluctant support or in crisis	Inconsistent or conditional support. Emotionally distant but available	Very supportive. Mutually nurturing family relationships
2		**Boyfriend, FOB, or Spouse**	Hostile, violent, or physically abusive; multiple partners or uncertain paternity	Separated. No contact. Not available for support	Conflicted, critical, or verbal abuse; frequent arguments. Reluctant support or in crisis	Inconsistent or conditional support. Emotionally distant but available	Very supportive. Loving, committed (unmarried, married, or common law)
3		**Friends/Peers**	Hostile, violent, or high-risk friends; friends gang linked	Very few or no friends. Socially isolated and lonely	Conflicted, casual, or brief friendships. Some crisis support from friends	A few close friends who can be counted on for support	Many close friends. Extensive support network
RELATIONSHIPS WITH CHILD(REN)							
4		**Attitudes to Pregnancy**	Unplanned and unwanted. Abortion or adoption plan	Unplanned, ambivalent, fearful. Coerced to keep child	Unplanned and accepted	Planned but unprepared	Planned, prepared, welcomed
5		**Nurturing**	Hostile, unable to nurture, bond, or love child; very limited responsiveness	Indifference, apathy, depression, or DD impair nurturing	Lacks information/modeling of love. Afraid nurturing "spoils." Marginal connectedness	Bonded; loves, responds inconsistently. Some reciprocal connections	Loving, responsive, praises; regulates child well. Reciprocal connections
6		**Discipline**	Has shown reportable levels of physical abuse or severe neglect	Uses physical punishment. Frequent criticism; verbal abuse	Mixture of impatient/ critical and appropriate discipline	Inconsistent limits. Ineffective boundaries. Teaches desired behavior effectively sometimes	Uses age-appropriate discipline. Teaches, guides, and directs behavior effectively
7		**Support of Development**	Poor knowledge of child development. Unrealistic expectations. Ignores or refuses information	Little knowledge of child development. Limited interest in development. Passive parental role	Open to child development information. Provides some toys, books, and play for age	Applies child development ideas. Interested in child's development skills, interests, and play	Anticipates child development changes. Uses appropriate toys/books; plays and reads with child daily

RELATIONSHIPS

Instructions: *Complete on primary parent and infant/toddlers < 3 yrs at intake, every 6 months, and at closure. Circle applicable scale categories and enter numerical score. Send to data clerk and file original in chart.*

Life Skills Progression™ (LSP): An Outcome and Intervention Planning Instrument for Use with Families at Risk by L. Wollesen and K. Peifer.

THE LIFE SKILLS PROGRESSION (LSP)

Family record ID # _____   Indiv. # _____   **Parent Scale** *Page 2*

Item	Score	0 Low	1	1.5	2	2.5	3	3.5	4	4.5	5 High
	RELATIONSHIPS WITH CHILD(REN) *CONT.*										
8	Safety		Child hospitalized for Tx of unintentional injury. Has permanent damage		Outpatient/ER Tx of unintentional injury to child. No permanent damage		No unintentional injury to child. Home/car unsafe; not childproofed		No unintentional injury to child. Home partially safe. Uses car seat. Uses information		Child protected, no injury. Home/car safe. Teaches safety. Seeks/uses information for age
	RELATIONSHIPS WITH SUPPORTIVE RESOURCES										
9	Relationship with Home Visitor		Hostile, defensive. Refuses HV services		Guarded, distrustful. Frequent broken appointments		Passively accepts information and visits. Forgets some appointments		Seeks/uses information. Calls for help or to cancel appointments		Trusts; welcomes visits; asks for information; keeps appointments
10	Use of Information		Refuses information from HV or HC		Uses inaccurate information from informal sources		Passively accepts some information from HV and HC		Accepts/uses most information from HV or HC		Actively seeks/uses information from HV, HC, and other sources
11	Use of Resources		Resource needs unrecognized. Community resources not used or refused; hostile		Resource needs unrecognized. Limited use when assisted by others. Misses most appointments		Accepts help to identify needs; uses resources when assisted by others. Keeps some appointments		Identifies needs. Uses resources with little assistance. Keeps most appointments		Identifies needs. Uses resources independently. Keeps or reschedules appointments
	EDUCATION & EMPLOYMENT										
12	Language (for non-English speaking only)		Low/no literacy in any language		Literate in primary language. Some verbal English skills		Takes ESL classes. Verbal ESL established		Takes ESL classes. Written ESL established		Fully bilingual
13	<12th Grade Education		Not enrolled		Enrolled, limited attendance any program. Not at grade level		Enrolled, attends regularly any program. Not at grade level		Attends regularly; at grade level. Adult school or independent study. Goal: GED	Attends regularly at grade level. HS/Alt HS Goal: HSD	
14	Education		<12th grade education in any country		Has graduated with GED or HSD		Attends and/or graduated job/tech training		Attends and/or graduated community college		Attends and/or graduated college or grad school
15	Employment		Unemployed, unskilled, or no work experience		Occasional, seasonal, or multiple entry level jobs		Stable employment in low-income job		Stable employment with adequate salary and benefits		Career of choice with potential good salary and benefits
16	Immigration		Undocumented. No permit/card. Frequent moves/trips disrupt services, work, or education		Has work permit/card. In U.S. < 5 years. Migrant. Plans return to country of origin		Has work permit/card. In U.S. > 5 years. Migrant. Plans to live in U.S.		Has work permit/card or temporary visa. Applying for citizenship		Obtained U.S. citizenship
	HEALTH & MEDICAL CARE										
17	Prenatal Care		No prenatal care	Care starts 2nd–3rd trimester. Keeps some appointments		Care starts 2nd–3rd trimester. Keeps most appointments		Care starts 1st trimester. Keeps most appointments	Keeps postpartum appointments	

Side labels: RELATIONSHIPS (items 8–11); EDUCATION (items 12–17)

Life Skills Progression™ (LSP): An Outcome and Intervention Planning Instrument for Use with Families at Risk by L. Wollesen and K. Peifer.

THE LIFE SKILLS PROGRESSION (LSP)

Family record ID # _____   Indiv. # _____   **Parent Scale** *Page 3*

HEALTH & MEDICAL CARE CONT.

Item	Score	Low 0	1	1.5	2	2.5	3	3.5	4	4.5	5 High
18	Parent Sick Care		Acute/chronic conditions go without Dx/Tx. No medical home	Seeks care only when very ill. Uses ER for care. No medical home		Seeks care inconsistently; inconsistent Tx follow-up. Unstable medical home			Seeks care appropriately. Follows Tx recommended. Has medical home		Seeks care appropriately. Cure or control obtained. Has medical home
19	Family Planning		No FP method used. Lacks information about FP	FP method use rare. Limited understanding of FP		Occasional use of FP methods. Some understanding of FP			Regular use of FP methods. Good understanding of FP		Regular use of FP methods. Plans/spaces pregnancies
20	Child Well Care		None; no medical home	Seldom; no medical home		Occasional appointments. Unstable medical home			Has annual exam only. Has stable medical home		Keeps regular CHDP/ well-child appointments with same provider
21	Child Sick Care		Medical neglect. No Dx/Tx for acute or chronic conditions	Has care only when very ill. Uses ER for care		Timely care for minor illness but inconsistent Tx f/u			Timely care of minor illness. Follows Tx recommended		Obtains optimal care/ control for acute or chronic conditions
22	Child Dental Care		No dental home or care with serious ECC. Poor hygiene	No dental home or care with some ECC and inadequate Tx/hygiene		Has dental home and hygiene but late Tx of ECC			Has dental home. Some preventive care/timely Tx		Has dental home. Regular preventive care and timely Tx
23	Child Immunizations		None or refused	IZ history uncertain. Records lost		IZ begun, but no return appointment			IZ delayed, has return appointment		Complete or up-to-date IZ

MENTAL HEALTH & SUBSTANCE USE/ABUSE

Item	Score	Low 0	1	1.5	2	2.5	3	3.5	4	4.5	5 High
24	Substance Use/ Abuse (drugs and/ or alcohol)		Chronic Hx drug and/or alcohol abuse with addiction	Drug/alcohol binge or intermittent use, without apparent addiction		Rare or experimental use of drugs or clean; in recovery group or Tx program			Occasional use of legal substances; stops if pregnant		No Hx or current use/abuse
25	Tobacco Use		Chain smokes; >2 packs/ day; uses smokeless; heavy second-hand exposure	Non-chain use or some second-hand exposure		Decreases amount when pregnant. Controls second-hand exposure			No use or second-hand exposure in past 6 months or current pregnancy		None or never
26	Depression/Suicide		Recurrent chronic depression with suicidal attempts/thoughts. Severe problem with ADL, parenting, and insight/perception	Recurrent chronic depress on without suicidal attempts/thoughts. Moderate problem with ADL, parenting, and insight/perception		Recent postpartum or situational depression. Some problem with ADL, parenting, and insight/ perception			Manages or controls depression with Tx and/or medications or has recovered. Adequate ADL, parenting, and insight/perception		Not depressed; optimistic
27	Mental Illness		Severe symptoms of MI with/without Dx/Tx/medications). Severe problem with ADL, parenting, and insight/self-perception	Symptoms of MI. Diagnosed but Tx inconsistent or ineffective. Moderate problem with ADL, parenting, and insight perception		Symptoms under control. Diagnosed and in Tx. Some problem with ADL, parenting, and insight/self-perception			Situational or short-term MI. Recovered without relapse. Adequate ADL, parenting, and insight/ self-perception		No observed mental illness

Side labels: HEALTH & MEDICAL CARE / MENTAL HEALTH

THE LIFE SKILLS PROGRESSION (LSP)

Family record ID # _____ Indiv. # _____ **Parent Scale** *Page 4*

MENTAL HEALTH & SUBSTANCE ABUSE CONT.

Item	Score	0 Low	1	1.5	2	2.5	3	3.5	4	4.5	5 High
28	Self-Esteem		Poor; self-critical. Anticipates criticism from others. Rarely initiates; avoids trying new skills			Copes sometimes but with limited confidence and flat affect. Limited initiative for learning new skills		Irritable/defensive. Makes excuses, blames others. Initiates/starts using new skills but gives up easily		Beginning to actively initiate. Develops skills and recognizes own competence. Emerging confidence visible	Confident in skill and ability to learn. Expresses pride in achievements and successes
29	Cognitive Ability		Suspected mild-moderate DD. No Dx or support services. Severe problem with ADL, parenting, and judgment		Diagnosed DD or LD; has education and/or support services. Moderate problem with ADL, parenting, and judgment		Diagnosed or suspected mild DD/LD. Needs some support by others. Some problem with ADL, parenting, and judgment		Suspected or known special education or LD. Support by others not needed. Adequate ADL, parenting, and judgment	Average or above average cognitive ability. Competent ADL	

BASIC ESSENTIALS

Item	Score	0 Low	1	1.5	2	2.5	3	3.5	4	4.5	5 High
30	Housing		Homeless, in shelter, or extremely substandard place		Unstable/inadequate, crowded housing with frequent moves		Stable rental. Lives with strangers or friends		Lives with family/extended family (own or FOBs). Shares expenses	Rents/owns apartment or house	
31	Food/Nutrition		Relies on emergency food banks/charity; runs out of food		Inadequate or unavailable resources. Worried about amount/quality of food		Regularly uses government resources; WIC and/or food stamps	Low family income provides adequate amount/quality of food			Income provides optimal amount and quality of food
32	Transportation		None or inadequate resources, or unable to use resources		Uses public transport		Some access to shared car. Rides with others; no license	Has own license/drives. Borrows car		Has own car and drives with license and insurance	
33	Medical/Health Insurance		None/unable to afford care or coverage		Medicaid for pregnancy or emergency only		Medicaid full-scope benefits with or without Share of Cost	State-subsidized or partial-pay coverage		Private insurance with or without co-pay for self/others	
34	Income		None or illegal income only		TANF and/or child support; SDI		Employed with low income. Seasonal or 200% FPL	Employed with moderate income; meets expenses most of time		Adequate salary	
35	Child Care		None used yet or no resources available		Multiple sources. Occasional use. Unsafe or inadequate environment		Uses caring friend/relative with safe/stable environment, but limited developmental support	Uses caring friend/relative with safe/stable environment and good developmental support			High-quality child care center with safe environment and good developmental support

MENTAL HEALTH · *BASIC ESSENTIALS*

Life Skills Progression™ (LSP): An Outcome and Intervention Planning Instrument for Use with Families at Risk by L. Wollesen and K. Peifer.

THE LIFE SKILLS PROGRESSION (LSP)

Family record ID # _____ Indiv. # _____ Parent's months of service _____

Web ID # _____

Child's name _____
(last name, first name)

DOB checkboxes: □ Female □ Male   Age __/__ (years/months)   □ Initial __/__/__   □ Ongoing # __/__/__   □ Closing __/__/__

Child's DOB __/__/__ (years/months)   Medical codes _____

CHILD DEVELOPMENT

Item	Score	Areas of Life Skill Development	0 Low	1	1.5	2	2.5	3	3.5	4	4.5	5 High
		INFANT/TODDLER DEVELOPMENT (4 MONTHS–3 YEARS)										
36		Communication*		Below AA/CA and EI criteria. Referred to EI. Not enrolled or attending		Delays; meets EI criteria. Referred; enrolled. Sometimes attends		Delays; meets EI criteria. Referred; enrolled. Attends regularly	No delays. Average development for AA or CA		Above average development for AA or CA	
37		Gross Motor*		Below AA/CA and EI criteria. Referred to EI. Not enrolled or attending		Delays; meets EI criteria. Referred; enrolled. Sometimes attends		Delays; meets EI criteria. Referred; enrolled. Attends regularly	No delays. Average development for AA or CA		Above average development for AA or CA	
38		Fine Motor*		Below AA/CA and EI criteria. Referred to EI. Not enrolled or attending		Delays; meets EI criteria. Referred; enrolled. Sometimes attends		Delays; meets EI criteria. Referred; enrolled. Attends regularly	No delays. Average development for AA or CA		Above average development for AA or CA	
39		Problem Solving*		Below AA/CA and EI criteria. Referred to EI. Not enrolled or attending		Delays; meets EI criteria. Referred; enrolled. Sometimes attends		Delays; meets EI criteria. Referred; enrolled. Attends regularly	No delays. Average development for AA or CA		Above average development for AA or CA	
40		Personal-Social*		Below AA/CA and EI criteria. Referred to EI. Not enrolled or attending		Delays; meets EI criteria. Referred; enrolled. Sometimes attends		Delays; meets EI criteria. Referred; enrolled. Attends regularly	No delays. Average development for AA or CA		Above average development for AA or CA	
41		Social-Emotional**		Shows signs of neurological or environment-linked concerns. No IMH services		Shows signs of neurological or environment-linked concerns. Referred to or court ordered IMH. Limited participation		Shows signs of neurological or environment-linked concerns. Regular participation in IMH with positive results	No signs of neurological or environment-linked concerns requiring referral to IMH		Responsive, social, alert; communicates needs/feelings. Emotionally connected to parent	
42		Regulation		Irritable; hard to console or poor self-regulation. Cues unclear. Non- or overly responsive to environment		Passive/flat affect; little exploration. Does not seek comfort or share delight often		Anxious, withdrawn, clingy. Relies on coregulation. Limited self-regulation, exploration, and play	Quiet or changeable moods; seeks comfort and uses self-regulation, exploration, and play		Happy, content; easily consoled. Well connected to parent. Explores, plays, shares delight	
43		Breast Feeding	Not breast-fed or breast-fed < 2 weeks		Breast-fed/expressed < 1 month		Breast-fed/expressed for 1–3 months		Breast-fed/expressed 3–6 months, with or without supplement		Breast-fed/expressed > 6 months with some supplement	

* **Rating should be based on a developmental screening or assessment (e.g., ASQ, Denver II, Bayley, BRIGANCE) or ** on a social-emotional screening (ASQ:SE).**

Instructions: *Complete on primary parent and infant/toddlers < 3 yrs at intake, every 6 months, end at closure. Circle applicable scale categories and enter numerical score. Send to data clerk and file original in chart.*

Life Skills Progression™ (LSP): An Outcome and Intervention Planning Instrument for Use with Families at Risk by L. Wollesen and K. Peifer.

Abbreviations Used in the Life Skills Progression™ (LSP)

AA	adjusted age. Developmental expectations are adjusted due to amount of prematurity by the time between birth and anticipated due date.		FP	family planning
			FPL	Federal Poverty Level
			f/u	follow-up
ADL	activities of daily living		GED	General Education Development degree (high school equivalency diploma)
adv	advanced			
alc	alcohol		HC	health care
ASQ	Ages & Stages Questionnaires®		HS	high school
ASQ:SE	Ages & Stages Questionnaires®: Social-Emotional		HSD	high school diploma
			IIV	home visit (a service delivery method used by home visitation programs)
BF	boyfriend			
CA	chronological age. The actual age of the child, usually expressed as years, months, days			
			Hx	history (i.e., medical history and physical examination)
CHDP	Child Health and Disability Prevention		ID	identification
			IMH	infant mental health
DD	developmental delay		ISP	individualized service plan
Denver II	Denver Developmental Screening Test–II		IZ	immunization(s)
			LD	learning disability
dev	development, developmental		Medicaid	Federal and state health insurance program
DOB	date of birth			
Dx	diagnosis		MI	mental illness
ECC	early childhood caries		NA	not applicable, not asked, or not available
EI	early intervention. IDEA: legally required special education for infants birth to 3 years with DD			
			No.	number
			occ	occasional
env	environment		outpt	outpatient
ER	emergency room		PHN	public health nurse
ESL	English as a Second Language		pks	packs (of cigarettes)
FAE	fetal alcohol effects		PNC	prenatal care
FAS	fetal alcohol syndrome		PP	postpartum
FOB	father of the baby		Rx	prescription (for medication)

SDI	state disability insurance	+Tox	Positive toxicology. Mother or child tested positive for drugs at birth or during pregnancy
SOC	Share of Cost. The amount some families must pay per month to be eligible for Medicaid coverage.		
		Tx	treatment
SS	Social Security	Vol	voluntarily
STD	sexually transmitted disease	WIC	Special Supplemental Nutrition Program for Women, Infants, and Children (a subsidized food program)
TANF	Temporary Assistance for Needy Families		

APPENDIX C

Emerging Best Practice for Home Visitation Checklist

This checklist and reflective questions guide self-assessment of program quality.

❑ **Program goals are clearly defined**

Can you clearly state your program's goals in a sentence or two?
For example: At its essence, our program:

- ❑ Promotes healthy first pregnancies in low income women by.........
- ❑ Promotes parenting skills in families with children under age 3 years by.....
- ❑ Promotes family economic self-sufficiency by........
- ❑ Helps families find stable housing by..........

What good outcomes are NOT your goals? To whom do you refer families for assistance in those areas?

❑ **Curriculum matches your program goals**

Curriculum guides how home visitors translate program goals into action. Programs produce benefits in those outcomes on which home visitors focus.

How well does the curriculum you use match your goals?

What is the primary area of focus in your curriculum? Is it the same as your program's primary focus?

Which parts of the curriculum are considered to be of core importance to the program? How are home visitors focusing on those parts?

❑ **Maintain program quality standards**

Curriculum and materials

How well does the curriculum fit your clients?

Are materials attractive, easy to understand and use, acceptable, persuasive? How do you know?

Family engagement

In what ways do you enroll families?

How do you retain families in your program?

How do you maintain enthusiastic, active family involvement during home visits? In recommended activities between visits? In program improvement?

Staffing: training, retention, supervision

Home visitors are the program.

How confident do home visitors feel in their ability to affect program goals? Do they feel supported?

Do they fully understand and endorse the curriculum? Do they deliver it as intended?

Is protected time for reflective supervision built into the program?

How and for how long are you able to retain well-trained staff?

Cultural consonance

Does staff speak the language of client families?

Does staff understand and value clients' cultural views and practices regarding parenting, health, and roles of women?

Services tailored to high-risk clients

How do you accommodate very high-risk families?

How confident do home visitors feel in their ability to recognize and address domestic violence, child abuse, maternal and child mental health problems, substance abuse?

How do you know when you are in over your heads?

Who do you collaborate with or refer families to when they have exceptional needs?

❑ **Collaborate and coordinate services within service area**

Referrals

How do you locate new families?

How do you avoid overlapping services with other programs?

Messages

How do you describe your services to families? To referral sources?

What are the key messages that your program and other local programs promote? Are you reinforcing the same messages?

Training

How do you collaborate with other programs for staff training?

Who decides on training content?

How do you train staff to work collaboratively with other programs?

❑ **Monitoring to guide practice and support quality improvement**

How do you know when you are successful?

Do staff receive regular feedback regarding effectiveness, parent satisfaction?

What are the ways you get feedback from parents? From staff? From other programs?

How do you use the feedback? How does feedback affect program design?

❑ **Home visiting is one of several strategies to achieve goals**

What center-based or group activities do you offer for individuals or families who do not enjoy home visits?

How and where does your home visiting program fit in the array of services available to families in your community? (medical, social, mental health, high-quality child care, education, employment, ESL, literacy)

Source: Gomby, 2003.

APPENDIX D

"Better Together"

Home Visitation Community Collaboration
Planning Worksheet

1. WHY work together?

*   How many families with young children would benefit from parent education and home visiting in your service area? Pregnant? Parenting?

*   What is the number of low income births in your area per year?

*   How many children enroll in kindergarten in your area per year?

*   How many families and how many children do you currently serve per year?

*   For how long a service period?

*   What is the attrition rate and pattern in number of visits or months of service?

*   How many families are you not able to serve in your program? (live birth rate less families served; factoring in length of service)

*   How many are on the waiting list and how long do they wait?

*   Why partner with other home visitation programs?

*   Who else in your service area is doing similar home visit or parent education services within the same target group?

Life Skills Progression™ (LSP): An Outcome and Intervention Planning Instrument for Use with Families at Risk
by L. Wollesen and K. Peifer.

145

- How are the other visitation services similar or different from yours? Staffing? Training? Funding? Curriculum? Service setting? Supervision? Professional training or consultation? Type of agency?

- What do you have in common with the other visitation services?

- How do you relate to each other now? Shared vision? Common goals? Collaboration? Universal visitation? Funding competition and cost effectiveness? Avoiding duplication of services? Collaboration versus competition for client referrals?

- Do you have a common visitation intake resource? Are you able to match client need to the different visitation service models? Are you able to keep all caseloads full? Are you able to maintain a waiting list for nonurgent families?

- List the current funding sources for each of the visitation services listed above, including your agency.

- Is sustainability for any of the programs an immediate issue? How can the group help sustain a service in jeopardy?

- What are new, potential, or emerging funding sources?

2. **WHAT?**
   - Describe your vision of home visitation community collaboration. What does it look like?
     Functions
     Funding
     Facilities
     Outcome tool and data management
     Training
     Partners
     Consultants
     Benefits of collaboration

   - Shared interagency referral clearinghouse?

   - Creative funding for collaborative programs? (e.g., EHS, public health nursing, teen programs, early intervention [IDEA-C]) What funding sources have similar targets?

   - What things or system changes are on your wish list?

- What "out of the box" changes would you make?

- Who could your partners be? Would they expand or improve services? Benefits of collaboration? Drawbacks?

- What could you learn from each other's models and materials?

- What types of data do you each collect now? What types do you want or need? Is it comparable across the agencies? How is it shared or used now?

- If your program(s) were successful, how would success be demonstrated?

3. HOW?
- List the steps you might take to organize and maintain a home visitation collaborative:

LSP Data Entry Form

Also available on the CD-ROM that accompanies this book.

LSP Data Entry Form

PARENT

Family record ID # _____ Indiv. # _____

Web ID # _____ DOB ____/____/____

Last name _____ First name _____

❑ Male ❑ Female   Race/Ethnicity _____

Medical codes _____ _____ _____ _____ _____

❑ Initial LSP ____/____/____   ❑ Ongoing LSP ____/____/____   ❑ Closing LSP ____/____/____

Date next LSP due ____/____/____

No. months of service _____   No. attempted visits _____   No. completed visits _____

Home visitor _____ Agency _____

Scale	Score	Scale	Score	Scale	Score
1. Family/extended family		13. Educ. < 12 yrs		25. Tobacco use	
2. BF, FOB, spouse		14. Education		26. Depression/suicide	
3. Friends/peers		15. Employment		27. Mental illness	
4. Attitudes to pregnancy		16. Immigration		28. Self-esteem	
5. Nurturing		17. Prenatal care		29. Cognitive ability	
6. Discipline		18. Parent sick care		30. Housing	
7. Support of development		19. Family planning		31. Food/nutrition	
8. Safety		20. Child well care		32. Transportation	
9. Relationship w/HV		21. Child sick care		33. Medical/health insurance	
10. Use of information		22. Child dental care		34. Income	
11. Use of resources		23. Child immunizations		35. Child care	
12. Language		24. Substance use/abuse			

CHILD

Family record ID # _____ Indiv. # _____

Web ID # _____ DOB ____/____/____

Last name _____ First name _____

Medical codes _____ _____ _____ _____ _____

❑ Initial LSP ____/____/____   ❑ Ongoing LSP ____/____/____   ❑ Closing LSP ____/____/____

Scale	Score	Scale	Score	Scale	Score
36. Communication		39. Problem solving		42. Regulation	
37. Gross motor		40. Personal-social		43. Breast feeding	
38. Fine motor		41. Social-emotional			

Sample Scored
LSP Instrument

"Selene and Jason"

THE LIFE SKILLS PROGRESSION (LSP) — Parent Scale Page 1

Family record ID # __GON46971__   Indiv. # __01__   ☐ Initial __/__/__   Months of service __10__

Web ID # _____   ☒ Ongoing # __2__   __03/25/04__   No. attempted visits __26__   No. completed visits __10__

Client name __Gonzales, Selene__   ☐ Closing __/__/__   Home visitor __CM__
(last name, first name)

Client DOB __02/05/89__   ☒ Female ☐ Male   Race __1__   Next LSP due __09/25/04__   Agency/program __FTM__   Ethnicity __2__   Medical codes __6,14__

Item	Score	Areas of Life Skill Development	0 Low	1	1.5	2	2.5	3	3.5	4	4.5	5	High
		RELATIONSHIPS WITH FAMILY AND FRIENDS											
1	2.5	Family/Extended Family		Hostile, violent, or physically abusive family relationships		Separated. No contact. Not available for support mo		Conflicted, critical, or verbal abuse; frequent arguments. Reluctant support or in crisis fa		Inconsistent or conditional support. Emotionally distant but available		Very supportive. Mutually nurturing family relationships	
2	3	Boyfriend, FOB, or Spouse		Hostile, violent, or physically abusive; multiple partners or uncertain paternity		Separated. No contact. Not available for support		Conflicted, critical, or verbal abuse; frequent arguments. Reluctant support or in crisis		Inconsistent or conditional support. Emotionally distant but available		Very supportive. Loving, committed (unmarried, married, or common law)	
3	2	Friends/Peers		Hostile, violent, or high-risk friends; friends gang linked		Very few or no friends. Socially isolated and lonely		Conflicted, casual, or brief friendships. Some crisis support from friends		A few close friends who can be counted on for support		Many close friends. Extensive support network	
		RELATIONSHIPS WITH CHILD(REN)											
4	0	Attitudes to Pregnancy	√	Unplanned and unwanted. Abortion or adoption plan		Unplanned, ambivalent, fearful. Coerced to keep child		Unplanned and accepted		Planned but unprepared		Planned, prepared, welcomed	
5	3.5	Nurturing		Hostile, unable to nurture, bond, or love child; very limited responsiveness		Indifference, apathy, depression, or DD impair nurturing		Lacks information/modeling of love. Afraid nurturing "spoils." Marginal connectedness		Bonded; loves, responds inconsistently. Some reciprocal connections		Loving, responsive, praises; regulates child well. Reciprocal connections	
6	3	Discipline		Has shown reportable levels of physical abuse or severe neglect		Uses physical punishment. Frequent criticism; verbal abuse		Mixture of impatient/ critical and appropriate discipline		Inconsistent limits. Ineffective boundaries. Teaches desired behavior effectively sometimes		Uses age-appropriate discipline. Teaches, guides, and directs behavior effectively	
7	2.5	Support of Development		Poor knowledge of child development. Unrealistic expectations. Ignores or refuses information		Little knowledge of child development. Limited interest in development. Passive parental role		Open to child development information. Provides some toys, books, and play for age		Applies child development ideas. Interested in child's development skills, interests, and play		Anticipates child development changes. Uses appropriate toys/books; plays and reads with child daily	

RELATIONSHIPS

Instructions: Complete on primary parent and infant/toddlers < 3 yrs at intake, every 6 months, and at closure. Circle applicable scale categories and enter numerical score. Send to data clerk and file original in chart.

Life Skills Progression™ (LSP): An Outcome and Intervention Planning Instrument for Use with Families at Risk by L. Wollesen and K. Peifer.

THE LIFE SKILLS PROGRESSION (LSP)

Family record ID # GON46971 Indiv. # O1 **Parent Scale** *Page 2*

Item	Score	Indicator	0 Low	1	1.5	2	2.5	3	3.5	4	4.5	5 High
		RELATIONSHIPS WITH CHILD(REN) *CONT.*										
8	3	Safety		Child hospitalized for Tx of unintentional injury. Has permanent damage		Outpatient/ER Tx of unintentional injury to child. No permanent damage		No unintentional injury to child. Home unsafe; not childproofed *(circled)*		No unintentional injury to child. Home partially safe. Uses car seat. Uses information		Child protected, no injury. Home/car safe. Teaches safety. Seeks/uses information for age
		RELATIONSHIPS WITH SUPPORTIVE RESOURCES										
9	3	Relationship with Home Visitor		Hostile, defensive. Refuses HV services		Guarded, distrustful. Frequent broken appointments		Passively accepts information and visits. Forgets some appointments *(circled)*		Seeks/uses information. Calls for help or to cancel appointments		Trusts; welcomes visits; asks for information; keeps appointments
10	3	Use of Information		Refuses information from HV or HC		Uses inaccurate information from informal sources		Passively accepts some information from HV and HC *(circled)*		Accepts/uses most information from HV or HC		Actively seeks/uses information from HV, HC, and other sources
11	2.5	Use of Resources		Resource needs unrecognized. Community resources not used or refused; hostile		Resource needs unrecognized. Limited use when assisted by others. Misses most appointments *(circled)*		Accepts help to identify needs; uses resources when assisted by others. Keeps some appointments *(circled)*		Identifies needs. Uses resources with little assistance. Keeps most appointments		Identifies needs. Uses resources independently. Keeps or reschedules appointments
		EDUCATION & EMPLOYMENT										
12	5	Language (for non-English speaking only)		Low/no literacy in any language		Literate in primary language. Some verbal English skills		Takes ESL classes. Verbal ESL established		Takes ESL classes. Written ESL established		Fully bilingual *(circled)*
13	1	<12th Grade Education	Not enrolled *(circled)*			Enrolled, limited attendance any program. Not at grade level		Enrolled, attends regularly any program. Not at grade level		Attends regularly; at grade level. Adult school or independent study. Goal: GED		Attends regularly at grade level. HS/Alt HS Goal: HSD
14	1	Education		<12th grade education in any country *(circled)*		Has graduated with GED or HSD		Attends and/or graduated job/tech training		Attends and/or graduated community college		Attends and/or graduated college or grad school
15	0	Employment		Unemployed, unskilled, or no work experience ✓		Occasional, seasonal, or multiple entry level jobs		Stable employment in low-income job		Stable employment with adequate salary and benefits		Career of choice with potential good salary and benefits
16	0	Immigration — Born in U.S.		Undocumented. No permit/card. Frequent moves/trips disrupt services, work, or education ✓		Has work permit/card. In U.S. < 5 years. Migrant. Plans return to country of origin		Has work permit/card. In U.S. > 5 years. Migrant. Plans to live in U.S.		Has work permit/card or temporary visa. Applying for citizenship		Obtained U.S. citizenship
		HEALTH & MEDICAL CARE										
17	4	Prenatal Care	No prenatal care			Care starts 2nd–3rd trimester. Keeps some appointments		Care starts 2nd–3rd trimester. Keeps most appointments *(circled)*		Care starts in 1st trimester. Keeps most appointments		Keeps postpartum appointments *(circled)*

Side labels: RELATIONSHIPS / EDUCATION

THE LIFE SKILLS PROGRESSION (LSP)

Family record ID # GON46971   Indiv. # O1   **Parent Scale** *Page 3*

HEALTH & MEDICAL CARE

Item	Score	0 / Low / 1	1.5 / 2	2.5 / 3	3.5 / 4	4.5 / 5 / High
18 — Parent Sick Care	3	Acute/chronic conditions go without Dx/Tx. No medical home	Seeks care only when very ill. Uses ER for care. No medical home	*(circled)* Seeks care inconsistently; inconsistent Tx follow-up. Unstable medical home	Seeks care appropriately. Follows Tx recommended. Has medical home	Seeks care appropriately. Cure or control obtained. Has medical home
19 — Family Planning	3	No FP method used. Lacks information about FP	FP method use rare. Limited understanding of FP	*(circled)* Occasional use of FP methods. Some understanding of FP	Regular use of FP methods. Good understanding of FP	Regular use of FP methods. Plans/spaces pregnancies
20 — Child Well Care	5	None; no medical home	Seldom; no medical home	Occasional appointments. Unstable medical home	Has annual exam only. Has stable medical home	*(circled)* Keeps regular CHDP/well-child appointments with same provider
21 — Child Sick Care	3	Medical neglect. No Dx/Tx for acute or chronic conditions	Has care only when very ill. Uses ER for care	*(circled)* Timely care for minor illness but inconsistent Tx f/u	Timely care of minor illness. Follows Tx recommended	Obtains optimal care/control for acute or chronic conditions
22 — Child Dental Care *(no teeth)*	0	No dental home or care with serious ECC. Poor hygiene	No dental home or care with some ECC and inadequate Tx/hygiene	Has dental home and hygiene but late Tx of ECC	Has dental home. Some preventive care/timely Tx	Has dental home. Regular preventive care and timely Tx
23 — Child Immunizations	4	None or refused ✓	IZ history uncertain. Records lost	IZ begun, but no return appointment	*(circled)* IZ delayed, has return appointment	Complete or up-to-date IZ

MENTAL HEALTH & SUBSTANCE USE/ABUSE

Item	Score	0 / Low / 1	1.5 / 2	2.5 / 3	3.5 / 4	4.5 / 5 / High
24 — Substance Use/Abuse (drugs and/or alcohol)	5	Chronic Hx drug and/or alcohol abuse with addiction	Drug/alcohol binge or intermittent use, without apparent addiction	Rare or experimental use of drugs or clean; in recovery group or Tx program	Occasional use of legal substances; stops if pregnant	*(circled)* No Hx or current use/abuse — *spouse uses meth*
25 — Tobacco Use	5	Chain smokes; >2 packs/day; uses smokeless; Heavy second-hand exposure	Non-chain use or some second-hand exposure	Decreases amount when pregnant. Controls second-hand exposure	No use or second-hand exposure in past 6 months or current pregnancy	*(circled)* None or never
26 — Depression/Suicide	2	Recurrent chronic depression with suicidal attempts/thoughts. Severe problem with ADL, parenting, and insight/perception	*(circled)* Recurrent chronic depression without suicidal attempts/thoughts; Moderate problem with ADL, parenting, and insight/perception	Recent postpartum or situational depression. Some problem with ADL, parenting, and insight/perception	Manages or controls depression with Tx and/or medications or has recovered. Adequate ADL, parenting, and insight/perception	Not depressed; optimistic
27 — Mental Illness	5	Severe symptoms of MI with/without Dx/Tx/medications). Severe problem with ADL, parenting, and insight/self-perception	Symptoms of MI. Diagnosed but Tx inconsistent or ineffective. Moderate problem with ADL, parenting, and insight/self-perception	Symptoms under control. Diagnosed and in Tx. Some problem with ADL, parenting, and insight/self-perception	Situational or short-term MI. Recovered without relapse. Adequate ADL, parenting, and insight/self-perception	*(circled)* No observed mental illness

Life Skills Progression™ (LSP): An Outcome and Intervention Planning Instrument for Use with Families at Risk by L. Wollesen and K. Peifer.

THE LIFE SKILLS PROGRESSION (LSP)

Family record ID # GON46971   Indiv. # 01   **Parent Scale** *Page 4*

Item	Score	Category	0 Low	1	1.5	2	2.5	3	3.5	4	4.5	5 — High
		MENTAL HEALTH & SUBSTANCE ABUSE CONT.										
28	2	Self-Esteem	Poor; self-critical. Anticipates criticism from others. Rarely initiates; avoids trying new skills			(Copes sometimes but with limited confidence and flat affect. Limited initiative for learning new skills)		Irritable/defensive. Makes excuses, blames others. Initiates/starts using new skills but gives up easily		Beginning to actively initiate. Develops skills and recognizes own competence. Emerging confidence visible		Confident in skill and ability to learn. Expresses pride in achievements and successes
29	5	Cognitive Ability		Suspected mild-moderate DD. No Dx or support services. Severe problem with ADL, parenting, and judgment		Diagnosed DD or LD; has education and/or support services. Moderate problem with ADL, parenting, and judgment	Diagnosed or suspected mild DD/LD. Needs some support by others. Some problem with ADL, parenting, and judgment		Suspected or known special education or LD. Support by others not needed. Adequate ADL, parenting, and judgment		(Average or above average cognitive ability. Competent ADL)	
		BASIC ESSENTIALS										
30	4	Housing	Homeless, in shelter, or extremely substandard place			Unstable/inadequate, crowded housing with frequent moves		Stable rental. Lives with strangers or friends	(Lives with family (extended family own or FOBs). Shares expenses)			Rents/owns apartment or house
31	3.5	Food/Nutrition	Relies on emergency food banks/charity; runs out of food			Inadequate or unavailable resources. Worried about amount/quality of food		(Regularly uses government resources; WIC and/or food stamps)		Low family income provides adequate amount/quality of food *father helps*		Income provides optimal amount and quality of food
32	2.5	Transportation	None or inadequate resources, or unable to use resources			(Uses public transport)		(Some access to shared car. Rides with others; no license)	Has own license/drives. Borrows car		Has own car and drives with license and insurance	
33	3	Medical/Health Insurance	None/unable to afford care or coverage			Medicaid for pregnancy or emergency only		(Medicaid full-scope benefits with or without Share of Cost)		State-subsidized or partial-pay coverage	Private insurance with or without co-pay for self/others	
34	2	Income	None or illegal income only		(TANF and/or child support; SDI)			Employed with low income. Seasonal or 200% FPL		Employed with moderate income; meets expenses most of time		Adequate salary
35	1	Child Care	(None used yet or no resources available)			Multiple sources. Occasional use. Unsafe or inadequate environment		Uses caring friend/relative with safe/stable environment, but limited developmental support	Uses caring friend/relative with safe/stable environment and good developmental support			High-quality child care center with safe environment and good developmental support

MENTAL HEALTH — BASIC ESSENTIALS

THE LIFE SKILLS PROGRESSION (LSP)

Child Scale *Page 5*

Family record ID # __GON46971__   Indiv. # __02__   ☐ Initial __/__/__   Parent's months of service __10__

Web ID # ____

☒ Ongoing # __2__ 03/25/04

Child's name __Gonzales, Jason__   ☐ Closing __/__/__
(last name, first name)

Child's DOB __10/20/03__ ☐ Female ☒ Male Age __0/6__ (years/months)   Medical codes __5__

CHILD DEVELOPMENT

INFANT/TODDLER DEVELOPMENT (4 MONTHS–3 YEARS)

Item	Score	Areas of Life Skill Development	0 Low	1	1.5	2	2.5	3	3.5	4	4.5	5 High
36	4	Communication*		Below AA/CA and EI criteria. Referred to EI. Not enrolled or attending		Delays; meets EI criteria. Referred; enrolled. Sometimes attends		Delays; meets EI criteria. Referred; enrolled. Attends regularly	No delays. Average development for AA or CA		Above average development for AA or CA
37	4	Gross Motor*		Below AA/CA and EI criteria. Referred to EI. Not enrolled or attending		Delays; meets EI criteria. Referred; enrolled. Sometimes attends		Delays; meets EI criteria. Referred; enrolled. Attends regularly	No delays. Average development for AA or CA		Above average development for AA or CA
38	4	Fine Motor*		Below AA/CA and EI criteria. Referred to EI. Not enrolled or attending		Delays; meets EI criteria. Referred; enrolled. Sometimes attends		Delays; meets EI criteria. Referred; enrolled. Attends regularly	No delays. Average development for AA or CA		Above average development for AA or CA
39	4	Problem Solving*		Below AA/CA and EI criteria. Referred to EI. Not enrolled or attending		Delays; meets EI criteria. Referred; enrolled. Sometimes attends		Delays; meets EI criteria. Referred; enrolled. Attends regularly	No delays. Average development for AA or CA		Above average development for AA or CA
40	4	Personal-Social*		Below AA/CA and EI criteria. Referred to EI. Not enrolled or attending		Delays; meets EI criteria. Referred; enrolled. Sometimes attends		Delays; meets EI criteria. Referred; enrolled. Attends regularly	No delays. Average development for AA or CA		Above average development for AA or CA
41	0	Social-Emotional** ASQ:SE not done	✓ Shows signs of neurological or environment-linked concerns. No IMH services		Shows signs of neurological or environment-linked concerns. Referred to or court ordered IMH. Limited participation		Shows signs of neurological or environment-linked concerns. Regular participation in IMH with positive results		No signs of neurological or environment-linked concerns requiring referral to IMH		Responsive, social, alert; communicates needs/feelings. Emotionally connected to parent
42	4	Regulation		Irritable; hard to console or poor self-regulation. Cues unclear. Non- or overly responsive to environment		Passive/flat affect; little exploration. Does not seek comfort or share delight often		Anxious, withdrawn, clingy. Relies on coregulation. Limited self-regulation, exploration, and play		Quiet or changeable moods; seeks comfort and uses self-regulation, exploration, and play		Happy, content; easily consoled. Well connected to parent. Explores, plays, shares delight
43	3	Breast Feeding		Not breast-fed or breast-fed < 2 weeks		Breast-fed/expressed < 1 month		Breast-fed/expressed for 1–3 months		Breast-fed/expressed 3–6 months, with or without supplement		Breast-fed/expressed > 6 months with some supplement

* **Rating should be based on a developmental screening or assessment (e.g., ASQ, Denver II, Bayley, BRIGANCE) or ** on a social-emotional screening (ASQ:SE).**
Instructions: Complete on primary parent and infant/toddlers < 3 yrs at intake, every 6 months, and at closure. Circle applicable scale categories and enter numerical score. Send to data clerk and file original in chart.

Life Skills Progression™ (LSP): An Outcome and Intervention Planning Instrument for Use with Families at Risk by L. Wollesen and K. Peifer.
Copyright © 2006 Paul H. Brookes Publishing Co., Inc. All rights reserved.

Selene & Jason's Story

as told with the Life Skills Progression™ (LSP)

PARENT SCALES: RELATIONSHIPS (SCALES 1–11)

Relationships with Family/Friends

1. **With family/extended family**
   Selene, age 15, is the mother of Jason, age 6 months. Her relationship with her family is difficult for her. She has not seen her mother for several years and doesn't know how to contact her. She lives with her father, who is hard working and provides financial support but drinks heavily. When drunk, he is mean, angry, and critical of Selene. (LSP score 2.5)

2. **With boyfriend, FOB, spouse**
   Selene, although legally a child, with her father's approval recently married her boyfriend. He is 19 and is working in a gas station to try to earn money for an apartment of their own. He lives with his parents. They are struggling to stay together as a couple and they fight a lot (not physically), especially when he uses methamphetamines. (LSP score 3)

3. **With friends/peers**
   Selene reports that since she dropped out of school a couple of years ago, she doesn't have any friends or close relatives. She wishes her mother-in-law was nicer, because she has no women to turn to for help. (LSP score 2)

Relationships with Children

4. **Attitudes to pregnancy**
   Her pregnancy came as a surprise and she felt ambivalent about the baby for months. Selene was very scared to tell her father. (LSP score 0; scale not applicable because baby > 1 month old)

5. **Nurturing**
   Since Jason was born she has fallen in love with her son and wants to be a good mother. She picks up on his cues easily and responds when he cries most of the time. She says she is afraid to spoil him if she holds him too much. (LSP score 3.5)

6. **Discipline**
   Selene gets frustrated easily now that the baby is more active, and she frequently responds angrily. Jason goes to her for comfort and looks to share discoveries with her, but he seems frightened when she yells at him. She hasn't hit him because she does not want to be like her mom. (LSP score 3)

7. **Development**
   Because she had no good role models or information about parenting and development, she is just beginning to learn how important it is to play with and read to Jason. After 10 months of service, she is beginning to use some of the information and ideas her visitor has given her about how to help Jason learn about his world. (LSP score 2.5)

8. **Safety**
   The house she lives in belongs to her father, and although Jason has never been seriously hurt, the house has not been made safe for an active baby. Safety and development are two areas that home visit information has focused on recently. (LSP score 3)

Relationships with Supportive Resources

9. **With home visitor**
   Selene's trust in her visitor has grown steadily. She is still very shy and quiet about accepting information. She is home for most of the scheduled visits. Her visitor feels that Selene is still learning to ask for help and hasn't yet called her visitor when there is a problem. (LSP score 3)

10. **Use of information**
    For Selene to use the information given to her, the visitor has learned that she usually can't follow instructions unless she is able to actually try it while the visitor is present. She doesn't read things by herself. (LSP score 3)

11. **Use of resources**
    When needs and appointments have come up, such as WIC and medical care, Selene is usually not organized well enough to keep appointments unless someone takes her. She is just learning how to call to schedule appointments (LSP score 2.5)

PARENT SCALES: EDUCATION AND EMPLOYMENT (SCALES 12–16)

12. **Language**
    Selene is fully fluent in English; she uses her birth language of Spanish at home. Her reading ability is not at grade level. Although she doesn't like to read, she is able to read newspapers and most of the materials brought by the visitor. (LSP score 5)

13. **Less than 12th grade education**
    Selene dropped out of school in 9th grade and although she is thinking about trying to go back to school, she has not yet enrolled. (LSP score 1)

14. **Education**
    Her education level is < 12th grade. (LSP score 1)

15. **Employment**
    Selene is a young teen, is not employed, and has not held a job. She wants to be a beautician. (LSP score 1)

16. **Immigration**
    Selene was born in the U.S. to parents who are undocumented. (LSP score 0/not applicable)

PARENT SCALES: HEALTH AND MEDICAL CARE (SCALES 17–23)

17. Prenatal care

Selene did not go for prenatal care until her second trimester and missed appointments frequently, but she did keep her postpartum appointment with the help of her visitor. (LSP score 4)

18. Parent sick care

When Selene is sick she has gone for care in a timely way if her father takes her. However, often she has not taken the medication correctly, particularly antibiotics, which she stops taking as soon as she feels better. (LSP score 3)

19. Family planning

She began "depo" after delivery but because she didn't like how she felt, she stopped. Her husband uses condoms sometimes. (LSP score 3)

20. Child well care

She has made sure that she takes Jason for his well-child exams regularly and has not missed one of his appointments, but she has to ask for transportation from either her husband or father. (LSP score 5)

21. Child sick care

She takes Jason to the doctor as soon as she recognizes that he is sick, but she sometimes forgets to finish up his medication as directed. (LSP score 3)

22. Child dental care

Although Jason is chewing on everything, he has no teeth yet. (LSP score 0)

23. Child immunizations

Jason's immunizations had been up to date for age until he got ill and they were postponed by the MD. He has an appointment to get them. (LSP score 4)

PARENT SCALES: MENTAL HEALTH AND SUBSTANCE USE/ABUSE (SCALES 24–29)

24. Substance use/abuse: drugs and alcohol

Selene says she has never used drugs although her husband does. (LSP score 5)

25. Tobacco use

Selene does not smoke and neither does her father. (LSP score 5)

26. Depression/suicide

Although she has never been treated, Selene says she has felt sad most of her life. She denies feeling suicidal and doesn't think she wants to see anyone about it. (LSP score 2)

27. Mental illness

Selene has no apparent reported symptoms or history of mental illness, other than feeling depressed. (LSP score 5)

28. Self-esteem

The visitor initially thought Selene was just shy, but after hearing about her life with her parents, feelings of failure in school, and lack of confidence, she is concerned about her self-esteem and is working to build her confidence as a mother. (LSP score 2)

29. Cognitive ability
Because of her grade level, lack of a special education history, current reading ability, and the way she quickly understands new things once she tries them, the visitor feels that Selene's cognitive ability is probably at least average. The help she needs from others has to do with limitation due to age and experience. (LSP score 5)

PARENT SCALES: BASIC ESSENTIALS (SCALES 30–35)

30. Housing
Selene lives with her father. (LSP score 4)

31. Food/nutrition
Selene uses WIC, but her father helps with food costs, too. Her nutrition is adequate. (LSP score 3.5)

32. Transportation
Selene does not drive because of her age. She uses the bus or relies on her father or husband. Her husband is just now getting a car. (LSP score 2.5)

33. Medical/health insurance
Selene and Jason both have Medicaid without a Share of Cost. (LSP score 3)

34. Income
Selene and Jason both receive TANF/cash aid. (LSP score 2)

35. Child care
No child care has been used yet. If Selene returns to high school, child care will be available. Her mother-in-law might be another option. (LSP score 1)

INFANT SCALES (SCALES 36–43)

36. Communication
Jason scored in the average range for his chronological age on the ASQ at 4 and 6 months. (LSP score 4)

37. Gross motor
Jason scored in the average range for his chronological age on the ASQ at 4 and 6 months. (LSP score 4)

38. Fine motor
Jason scored in the average range for his chronological age on the ASQ at 4 and 6 months. (LSP score 4)

39. Problem solving
Jason scored in the average range for his chronological age on the ASQ at 4 and 6 months. (LSP score 4)

40. Personal-social
Jason scored in the average range for his chronological age on the ASQ at 4 and 6 months. (LSP score 4)

41. Social-emotional
(Not scored; ASQ:SE not done)

42. Regulation
Jason is a quiet, watchful, and sometimes fearful child, particularly if either his mother or grandfather is loud and angry. He can be reassured and consoled. At 6 months he is actively exploring the house and looks to share discoveries with his mom. (LSP score 4)

43. Breast feeding
Jason was breastfed for 3 months (LSP score 3)

Cumulative LSP
Score Sheet

Also available on the CD-ROM that accompanies this book.

Life Skills Progression Cumulative Score Sheet

Parent name _____ Child name _____

Parent scales with target range	Initial score 0–5	6-mo score 0–5	12-mo score 0–5	18-mo score 0–5	24-mo score 0–5	30-mo score 0–5	36-mo score 0–5
RELATIONSHIPS							
1. Family　　4–5							
2. Boyfriend, FOB, or spouse　4–5							
3. Friends/peers　4–5							
4. Attitudes to pregnancy　4–5							
5. Nurturing　4–5							
6. Discipline　4–5							
7. Development　4–5							
8. Safety　4–5							
9. Home visitor　4–5							
10. Use of information　4–5							
11. Use of resources　4–5							
EDUCATION							
12. Language　3–5							
13. <12 yr education　3–5							
14. Education　2–5							
15. Employment　2–5							
16. Immigration　2–5							
HEALTH/MEDICAL CARE							
17. Prenatal care　4–5							
18. Parent sick care　4–5							
19. Family planning　4–5							
20. Child well care　4–5							
21. Child sick care　4–5							
22. Child dental care　4–5							
23. Child immunizations　4–5							

Parent scales with target range		Initial score 0–5	6-mo score 0–5	12-mo score 0–5	18-mo score 0–5	24-mo score 0–5	30-mo score 0–5	36-mo score 0–5
MENTAL HEALTH AND SUBSTANCE USE/ABUSE								
24. Substance use/abuse	3–5							
25. Tobacco use	3–5							
26. Depression/suicide	4–5							
27. Mental illness	3–5							
28. Self-esteem	3–5							
29. Cognitive ability	3–5							
BASIC ESSENTIALS								
30. Housing	3–5							
31. Food/nutrition	3–5							
32. Transportation	3–5							
33. Medical/health insurance	2–5							
34. Income	3–5							
35. Child care	3–5							
CHILD SCALES Name:								
36. Communication	3–5							
37. Gross motor	3–5							
38. Fine motor	3–5							
39. Problem solving	3–5							
40. Personal-social	3–5							
41. Social-emotional	3–5							
42. Regulation	4–5							
43. Breast feeding	4–5							

Sample Cumulative
LSP Score Sheet

"Selene and Jason"

Life Skills Progression Cumulative Score Sheet

Parent name Sample case: S.G.   Child name J.G.

Parent scales with target range		Initial score 0–5	6-mo score 0–5	12-mo score 0–5	18-mo score 0–5	24-mo score 0–5	30-mo score 0–5	36-mo score 0–5
RELATIONSHIPS								
1. Family	4–5	2.5	2.5	2.5				
2. Boyfriend, FOB, or spouse	4–5	3	3	3.5				
3. Friends/peers	4–5	2	2	3				
4. Attitudes to pregnancy	4–5	3	0	0				
5. Nurturing	4–5	0	3.5	4				
6. Discipline	4–5	0	3	4				
7. Development	4–5	0	2.5	3				
8. Safety	4–5	0	3	2				
9. Home visitor	4–5	2	3	3.5				
10. Use of information	4–5	3	3	3				
11. Use of resources	4–5	2	2.5	3				
EDUCATION								
12. Language	3–5	5	5	5				
13. <12 yr education	3 5	1	1	3				
14. Education	2–5	1	1	1				
15. Employment	2–5	1	1	1				
16. Immigration	2–5	0	0	0				
HEALTH/MEDICAL CARE								
17. Prenatal care	4–5	3	4	0				
18. Parent sick care	4–5	3	3	3				
19. Family planning	4–5	3	3	4				
20. Child well care	4–5	0	5	5				
21. Child sick care	4–5	0	3	4				
22. Child dental care	4–5	0	0	4				
23. Child immunizations	4–5	0	4	5				

Parent scales with target range	Initial score 0–5	6-mo score 0–5	12-mo score 0–5	18-mo score 0–5	24-mo score 0–5	30-mo score 0–5	36-mo score 0–5
MENTAL HEALTH AND SUBSTANCE USE/ABUSE							
24. Substance use/abuse 3–5	5	5	5				
25. Tobacco use 3–5	5	5	5				
26. Depression/suicide 4–5	3	2	3				
27. Mental illness 3–5	5	5	5				
28. Self-esteem 3–5	2	2	4				
29. Cognitive ability 3–5	5	5	5				
BASIC ESSENTIALS							
30. Housing 3–5	4	4	5				
31. Food/nutrition 3–5	2	3.5	3				
32. Transportation 3–5	2.5	2.5	2.5				
33. Medical/health insurance 2–5	3	3	3				
34. Income 3–5	3	2	3				
35. Child care 3–5	0	1	3				
CHILD SCALES Name: J.G.							
36. Communication 3–5	0	4	4				
37. Gross motor 3–5	0	4	4				
38. Fine motor 3–5	0	4	4				
39. Problem solving 3–5	0	4	4				
40. Personal-social 3–5	0	4	4				
41. Social-emotional 3–5	0	0	0				
42. Regulation 4–5	0	4	4				
43. Breast feeding 4–5	0	3	4				

APPENDIX J

LSP Instrument
with Target Scores Shaded

THE LIFE SKILLS PROGRESSION (LSP)

Parent Scale *Page 1*

Family record ID # _____ Indiv. # _____ ☐ Initial __/__/__ Months of service _____

Web ID # _____ ☐ Ongoing # __/__/__ No. attempted visits _____ No. completed visits _____

Client name _____ ☐ Closing __/__/__ Home visitor _____
(last name, first name)

Next LSP due __/__/__ Agency/program _____

Client DOB __/__/__ ☐ Female ☐ Male Race _____ Ethnicity _____ Medical codes _____

Item	Score	Areas of Life Skill Development	0 Low	1	1.5	2	2.5	3	3.5	4	4.5	5 High
RELATIONSHIPS WITH FAMILY AND FRIENDS												
1		Family/ Extended Family		Hostile, violent, or physically abusive family relationships		Separatec. No contact. Not available for support		Conflicted, critical, or verbal abuse; frequent arguments. Reluctant support or in crisis		Inconsistent or conditional support. Emotionally distant but available		Very supportive. Mutually nurturing family relationships
2		Boyfriend, FOB, or Spouse		Hostile, violent, or physically abusive; multiple partners or uncertain paternity		Separated. No contact. Not available for support		Conflicted, critical, or verbal abuse; frequent arguments. Reluctant support or in crisis		Inconsistent or conditional support. Emotionally distant but available		Very supportive. Loving, committed (unmarried, married, or common law)
3		Friends/Peers		Hostile, violent, or high-risk friends; friends gang linked		Very few or no friends. Socially isolated and lonely		Conflicted, casual, or brief friendships. Some crisis support from friends		A few close friends who can be counted on for support		Many close friends. Extensive support network
RELATIONSHIPS WITH CHILD(REN)												
4		Attitudes to Pregnancy		Unplanned and unwanted. Abortion or adoption plan		Unplanned, ambivalent, fearful. Coerced to keep child		Unplanned and accepted		Planned but unprepared		Planned, prepared, welcomed
5		Nurturing		Hostile, unable to nurture, bond, or love child; very limited responsiveness		Indifference, apathy, depression, or DD impair nurturing		Lacks information/modeling of love. Afraid nurturing "spoils." Marginal connectedness		Bonded; loves, responds inconsistently. Some reciprocal connections		Loving, responsive, praises; regulates child well. Reciprocal connections
6		Discipline		Has shown reportable levels of physical abuse or severe neglect		Uses physical punishment. Frequent criticism; verbal abuse		Mixture of impatient/ critical and appropriate discipline		Inconsistent limits. Ineffective boundaries. Teaches desired behavior effectively sometimes		Uses age-appropriate discipline. Teaches, guides, and directs behavior effectively
7		Support of Development		Poor knowledge of child development. Unrealistic expectations. Ignores or refuses information		Little knowledge of child development. Limited interest in development. Passive parental role		Open to child development information. Provides some toys, books, and play for age		Applies child development ideas. Interested in child's development skills, interests, and play		Anticipates child development changes. Uses appropriate toys/books; plays and reads with child daily

*(Left margin, vertical: **RELATIONSHIPS**)*

Instructions: *Complete on primary parent and infant/toddlers < 3 yrs at intake, every 6 months, and at closure. Circle applicable scale categories and enter numerical score. Send to data clerk and file original in chart.*

THE LIFE SKILLS PROGRESSION (LSP)

Item	Score	0 Low	1	1.5	2	2.5	3	3.5	4	4.5	5 High
RELATIONSHIPS WITH CHILD(REN) *CONT.*											
8	Safety		Child hospitalized for Tx of unintentional injury. Has permanent damage		Outpatient/ER Tx of unintentional injury to child. No permanent damage		No unintentional injury to child. Home/car unsafe; not childproofed		No unintentional injury to child. Home partially safe. Uses car seat. Uses information		Child protected, no injury. Home/car safe. Teaches safety. Seeks/uses information for age
RELATIONSHIPS WITH SUPPORTIVE RESOURCES											
9	Relationship with Home Visitor		Hostile, defensive. Refuses HV services		Guarded, distrustful. Frequent broken appointments		Passively accepts information and visits. Forgets some appointments		Seeks/uses information. Calls for help or to cancel appointments	Trusts; welcomes visits; asks for information; keeps appointments	
10	Use of Information		Refuses information from HV or HC		Uses inaccurate information from informal sources		Passively accepts some information from HV and HC		Accepts/uses most information from HV or HC	Actively seeks/uses information from HV, HC, and other sources	
11	Use of Resources		Resource needs unrecognized. Community resources not used or refused; hostile		Resource needs unrecognized. Limited use when assisted by others. Misses most appointments		Accepts help to identify needs; uses resources when assisted by others. Keeps some appointments		Identifies needs. Uses resources with little assistance. Keeps most appointments	Identifies needs. Uses resources independently. Keeps or reschedules appointments	
EDUCATION & EMPLOYMENT											
12	Language (for non-English speaking only)		Low/no literacy in any language		Literate in primary language. Some verbal English skills		Takes ESL classes. Verbal ESL established		Takes ESL classes. Written ESL established	Fully bilingual	
13	<12th Grade Education	Not enrolled			Enrolled, limited attendance any program. Not at grade level		Enrolled, attends regularly any program. Not at grade level		Attends regularly; at grade level. Adult school or independent study. Goal: GED	Attends regularly at grade level. HS/Alt HS Goal: HSD	
14	Education				<12th grade education in any country	Has graduated with GED or HSD		Attends and/or graduated job/tech training	Attends and/or graduated community college	Attends and/or graduated college or grad school	
15	Employment	Unemployed, unskilled, or no work experience			Occasional, seasonal, or multiple entry level jobs		Stable employment in low-income job		Stable employment with adequate salary and benefits	Career of choice with potential good salary and benefits	
16	Immigration	Undocumented. No permit/card. Frequent moves/trips disrupt services, work, or education			Has work permit/card. In U.S. < 5 years. Migrant. Plans return to country of origin	Has work permit/card. In U.S. > 5 years. Migrant. Plans to live in U.S.			Has work permit/card or temporary visa. Applying for citizenship	Obtained U.S. citizenship	
HEALTH & MEDICAL CARE											
17	Prenatal Care	No prenatal care		Care starts 2nd–3rd trimester. Keeps some appointments		Care starts 2nd–3rd trimester. Keeps most appointments			Care starts in 1st trimester. Keeps most appointments	Keeps postpartum appointments	

Side labels: RELATIONSHIPS · EDUCATION

Life Skills Progression™ (LSP): An Outcome and Intervention Planning Instrument for Use with Families at Risk by L. Wollesen and K. Peifer.

THE LIFE SKILLS PROGRESSION (LSP)

Family record ID # _____ Indiv. # _____ **Parent Scale** *Page 3*

HEALTH & MEDICAL CARE

HEALTH & MEDICAL CARE CONT.

Item	Score	0 Low	1	1.5	2	2.5	3	3.5	4	4.5	5 High
18	Parent Sick Care		Acute/chronic conditions go without Dx/Tx. No medical home	Seeks care only when very ill. Uses ER for care. No medical home		Seeks care inconsistently; inconsistent Tx follow-up. Unstable medical home		Seeks care appropriately. Follows Tx recommended. Has medical home		Seeks care appropriately. Cure or control obtained. Has medical home	
19	Family Planning		No FP method used. Lacks information about FP	FP method use rare. Limited understanding of FP		Occasional use of FP methods. Some understanding of FP		Regular use of FP methods. Good understanding of FP		Regular use of FP methods. Plans/spaces pregnancies	
20	Child Well Care		None; no medical home	Seldom; no medical home		Occasional appointments. Unstable medical home		Has annual exam only. Has stable medical home		Keeps regular CHDP/ well-child appointments with same provider	
21	Child Sick Care		Medical neglect. No Dx/Tx for acute or chronic conditions	Has care only when very ill. Uses ER for care		Timely care for minor illness but inconsistent Tx f/u		Timely care of minor illness. Follows Tx recommended		Obtains optimal care/ control for acute or chronic conditions	
22	Child Dental Care		No dental home or care with serious ECC. Poor hygiene	No dental home or care with some ECC and inadequate Tx/hygiene		Has dental home and hygiene but late Tx of ECC		Has dental home. Some preventive care/timely Tx		Has dental home. Regular preventive care and timely Tx	
23	Child Immunizations		None or refused	IZ history uncertain. Records lost		IZ begun, but no return appointment		IZ delayed, has return appointment		Complete or up-to-date IZ	

MENTAL HEALTH

MENTAL HEALTH & SUBSTANCE USE/ABUSE

Item	Score	0 Low	1	1.5	2	2.5	3	3.5	4	4.5	5 High
24	Substance Use/ Abuse (drugs and/ or alcohol)		Chronic Hx drug and/or alcohol abuse with addiction	Drug/alcohol binge or intermittent use, without apparent addiction		Rare or experimental use of drugs or clean; in recovery group or Tx program		Occasional use of legal substances; stops if pregnant		No Hx or current use/abuse	
25	Tobacco Use		Chain smokes; >2 packs/ day; uses smokeless; heavy second-hand exposure	Non-chain use or some second-hand exposure		Decreases amount when pregnant. Controls second-hand exposure		No use or second-hand exposure in past 6 months or current pregnancy		None or never	
26	Depression/Suicide		Recurrent chronic depression with suicidal attempts/thoughts. Severe problem with ADL, parenting, and insight/perception	Recurrent chronic depression without suicidal attempts/thoughts; Moderate problem with ADL, parenting, and insight/perception		Recent postpartum or situational depression. Some problem with ADL, parenting, and insight/ perception		Manages or controls depression with Tx and/or medications or has recovered. Adequate ADL, parenting, and insight/perception		Not depressed; optimistic	
27	Mental Illness		Severe symptoms of MI with/without Dx/Tx/medications). Severe problem with ADL, parenting, and insight/self-perception	Symptoms of MI. Diagnosed but Tx inconsistent or ineffective. Moderate problem with ADL, parenting, and insight/self-perception		Symptoms under control. Diagnosed and in Tx. Some problem with ADL, parenting, and insight/self-perception		Situational or short-term MI. Recovered without relapse. Adequate ADL, parenting, and insight/ self-perception		No observed mental illness	

THE LIFE SKILLS PROGRESSION (LSP) Family record ID # _____ Indiv. # _____ Parent Scale *Page 4*

Item	Score	0 Low	1	1.5	2	2.5	3	3.5	4	4.5	5 High
MENTAL HEALTH & SUBSTANCE ABUSE CONT.											
28	Self-Esteem		Poor; self-critical. Anticipates criticism from others. Rarely initiates; avoids trying new skills			Copes sometimes but with limited confidence and flat affect. Limited initiative for learning new skills		Irritable/defensive. Makes excuses, blames others. Initiates/starts using new skills but gives up easily		Beginning to actively initiate. Develops skills and recognizes own competence. Emerging confidence visible		Confident in skill and ability to learn. Expresses pride in achievements and successes
29	Cognitive Ability		Suspected mild-moderate DD. No Dx or support services. Severe problem with ADL, parenting, and judgment		Diagnosed DD or LD; has education and/or support services. Moderate problem with ADL, parenting, and judgment		Diagnosed or suspected mild DD/LD. Needs some support by others. Some problem with ADL, parenting, and judgment		Suspected or known special education or LD. Support by others not needed. Adequate ADL, parenting, and judgment	Average or above average cognitive ability. Competent ADL	
BASIC ESSENTIALS											
30	Housing		Homeless, in shelter, or extremely substandard place		Unstable/inadequate, crowded housing with frequent moves		Stable rental. Lives with strangers or friends	Lives with family/extended family (own or FOBs). Shares expenses		Rents/owns apartment or house	
31	Food/Nutrition		Relies on emergency food banks/charity; runs out of food		Inadequate or unavailable resources. Worried about amount/quality of food		Regularly uses government resources; WIC and/or food stamps	Low family income provides adequate amount/quality of food		Income provides optimal amount and quality of food	
32	Transportation		None or inadequate resources, or unable to use resources		Uses public transport		Some access to shared car. Rides with others; no license	Has own license/drives. Borrows car		Has own car and drives with license and insurance	
33	Medical/Health Insurance		None/unable to afford care or coverage		Medicaid for pregnancy or emergency only		Medicaid full-scope benefits with or without Share of Cost	State-subsidized or partial-pay coverage		Private insurance with or without co-pay for self/others	
34	Income		None or illegal income only		TANF and/or child support; SDI		Employed with low income. Seasonal or 200% FPL	Employed with moderate income; meets expenses most of time		Adequate salary	
35	Child Care		None used yet or no resources available		Multiple sources. Occasional use. Unsafe or inadequate environment		Uses caring friend/relative with safe/stable environment, but limited developmental support	Uses caring friend/relative with safe/stable environment and good developmental support		High-quality child care center with safe environment and good developmental support	

MENTAL HEALTH / **BASIC ESSENTIALS**

Life Skills Progression™ (LSP): An Outcome and Intervention Planning Instrument for Use with Families at Risk by L. Wollesen and K. Peifer.

THE LIFE SKILLS PROGRESSION (LSP)

Family record ID # _____ Indiv. # _____ ☐ Initial __/__/__ Parent's months of service _____

Web ID # _____ ☐ Ongoing # __/__/__

Child's name _____ ☐ Closing __/__/__
(last name, first name)

Child's DOB __/__/__ ☐ Female ☐ Male Age __/__ (years/months) Medical codes _____

CHILD DEVELOPMENT

INFANT/TODDLER DEVELOPMENT (4 MONTHS–3 YEARS)

Item	Score	0 Low / 1	1.5 / 2 / 2.5	3	3.5 / 4	4.5 / 5 High
36		**Communication*** — Below AA/CA and EI criteria. Referred to EI. Not enrolled or attending	Delays; meets EI criteria. Referred; enrolled. Sometimes attends	Delays; meets EI criteria. Referred; enrolled. Attends regularly	No delays. Average development for AA or CA	Above average development for AA or CA
37		**Gross Motor*** — Below AA/CA and EI criteria. Referred to EI. Not enrolled or attending	Delays; meets EI criteria. Referred; enrolled. Sometimes attends	Delays; meets EI criteria. Referred; enrolled. Attends regularly	No delays. Average development for AA or CA	Above average development for AA or CA
38		**Fine Motor*** — Below AA/CA and EI criteria. Referred to EI. Not enrolled or attending	Delays; meets EI criteria. Referred; enrolled. Sometimes attends	Delays; meets EI criteria. Referred; enrolled. Attends regularly	No delays. Average development for AA or CA	Above average development for AA or CA
39		**Problem Solving*** — Below AA/CA and EI criteria. Referred to EI. Not enrolled or attending	Delays; meets EI criteria. Referred; enrolled. Sometimes attends	Delays; meets EI criteria. Referred; enrolled. Attends regularly	No delays. Average development for AA or CA	Above average development for AA or CA
40		**Personal-Social*** — Below AA/CA and EI criteria. Referred to EI. Not enrolled or attending	Delays; meets EI criteria. Referred; enrolled. Sometimes attends	Delays; meets EI criteria. Referred; enrolled. Attends regularly	No delays. Average development for AA or CA	Above average development for AA or CA
41		**Social-Emotional**** — Shows signs of neurological or environment-linked concerns. No IMH services	Shows signs of neurological or environment-linked concerns. Referred to or court ordered IMH. Limited participation	Shows signs of neurological or environment-linked concerns. Regular participation in IMH with positive results	No signs of neurological or environment-linked concerns requiring referral to IMH	Responsive, social, alert; communicates needs/feelings. Emotionally connected to parent
42		**Regulation** — Irritable; hard to console or poor self-regulation. Cues unclear. Non- or overly responsive to environment	Passive/flat affect; little exploration. Does not seek comfort or share delight often	Anxious, withdrawn, clingy. Relies on coregulation. Limited self-regulation, exploration, and play	Quiet or changeable moods; seeks comfort and uses self-regulation, exploration, and play	Happy, content; easily consoled. Well connected to parent. Explores, plays, shares delight
43		**Breast Feeding** — Not breast-fed or breast-fed < 2 weeks	Breast-fed/expressed < 1 month	Breast-fed/expressed for 1–3 months	Breast-fed/expressed 3–6 months, with or without supplement	Breast-fed/expressed > 6 months with some supplement

* **Rating should be based on** a developmental screening or assessment (e.g., ASQ, Denver II, Bayley, BRIGANCE) or ** on a social-emotional screening (ASQ:SE).
Instructions: Complete on primary parent and infant/toddlers < 3 yrs at intake, every 6 months, and at closure. Circle applicable scale categories and enter numerical score. Send to data clerk and file original in chart.

Life Skills Progression™ *(LSP): An Outcome and Intervention Planning Instrument for Use with Families at Risk* by L. Wollesen and K. Peifer.

APPENDIX K

LSP Data Report Planning Tool

LSP Data Report Planning Tool

Check data options desired for each scale.   **Use chart to locate applicable scores in database.**

X	Scale data options	0	1	1.5	2	2.5	3	3.5	4	4.5	5
	RELATIONSHIPS										
	1. Family/Extended Family										
	# not scored for this scale	X									
	# % w family violence		X	X							
	# % separated from family of origin				X	X					
	# % w hostile family relationships						X	X			
	# % in target range								X	X	X
	2. BF, FOB, Spouse										
	# not scored for this scale	X									
	# % w domestic violence		X	X							
	# % separated BF/FOB/spouse				X	X					
	# % w hostile relationship						X	X			
	# % in target range								X	X	X
	3. Friends/Peers										
	# not scored for this scale	X									
	# % w violent or gang relationships		X	X							
	# % w social isolation issues				X	X	X	X			
	# % in target range								X	X	X
	4. Attitudes to Pregnancy										
	# not scored for this scale (= # not pregnant in caseload)	X									
	# % unplanned pregnancies		X	X	X	X	X	X			
	# % planned pregnancies								X	X	X
	# % planned/prepared pregnancies										X
	# % in target range								X	X	X
	5. Nurturing										
	# not scored for this scale	X									
	# % w impaired nurturing		X	X	X	X	X	X			
	# % in target range								X	X	X
	6. Discipline										
	# not scored for this scale	X									
	# % with reported child abuse		X	X							
	# % using harsh discipline				X	X					
	# % in target range								X	X	X
	7. Support of Development										
	# not scored for this scale	X									
	# % in target range								X	X	X

X	Scale data options	0	1	1.5	2	2.5	3	3.5	4	4.5	5
	8. Safety										
	# not scored for this scale										
	# % treated inpatient or ER		X	X	X	X					
	# % in target range								X	X	X
	9. Home Visitor										
	# not scored for this scale	X									
	# % refused services		X	X							
	# % w frequent broken appointment				X	X					
	# % in target range								X	X	X
	10. Use of Information										
	# not scored for this scale	X									
	# % refused services		X	X							
	# % in target range								X	X	X
	11. Use of Resources										
	# not scored for this scale	X									
	# % refused services		X	X							
	# % in target range								X	X	X
	EDUCATION										
	12. Language										
	# not scored for this scale	X									
	# % English primary language	X									
	# % w no/low literacy any language		X	X							
	# % English as Second Language		X	X	X	X	X	X	X	X	X
	# % studying ESL						X	X	X	X	
	# % fully bilingual										X
	# % in target range						X	X	X	X	X
	13. < 12th Grade Education										
	# not scored for this scale	X									
	# % not enrolled		X	X							
	# % in target range						X	X	X	X	X
	14. Education										
	# not scored for this scale	X									
	# % < 12th grade educ any country		X	X							
	# % attend or have HS diploma				X	X					
	# % in or graduated college								X	X	X
	# % in target range				X	X	X	X	X	X	X
	15. Employment										
	# not scored for this scale	X									

X	Scale data options	0	1	1.5	2	2.5	3	3.5	4	4.5	5
	# % unemployed		X	X							
	# % employed				X	X	X	X	X	X	X
	# % in target range				X	X	X	X	X	X	X
	16. Immigration										
	# not scored for this scale	X									
	# % U.S. citizens by birth	X									
	# % undocumented w/o permits		X	X							
	# % immigrant w work permits				X	X	X	X	X		
	# % immigrant obtained citizenship									X	X
	# % in target range				X	X	X	X	X	X	X
	HEALTH & MEDICAL CARE										
	17. Prenatal Care										
	# not scored for this scale	X									
	# % w no PNC		X	X							
	# % w late PNC				X	X	X	X			
	# % in target range								X	X	X
	18. Parent Sick Care										
	# not scored for this scale	X									
	# % w no or unstable med home		X	X	X	X	X	X			
	# % in target range								X	X	X
	19. Family Planning										
	# not scored for this scale	X									
	# % w no to occasional FP method		X	X	X	X	X	X			
	# % in target range								X	X	X
	20. Child Well Care										
	# not scored for this scale	X									
	# % w no or unstable med home		X	X	X	X	X	X			
	# % in target range								X	X	X
	21. Child Sick Care										
	# not scored for this scale	X									
	# % w medical neglect		X	X							
	# % w no or unstable med home		X	X	X	X	X	X			
	# % in target range								X	X	X
	22. Child Dental Care										
	# not scored for this scale	X									
	# % w no or inadequate dental care		X	X	X	X	X	X			
	# % in target range								X	X	X

X	Scale data options	0	1	1.5	2	2.5	3	3.5	4	4.5	5
	23. Child Immunizations										
	# not scored for this scale	X									
	# % w no or inadequate IZs		X	X	X	X	X	X			
	# % in target range								X	X	X
	MENTAL HEALTH AND SUBSTANCE USE/ABUSE										
	24. Substance Use/Abuse										
	# not scored for this scale	X									
	# % w chronic use w addiction		X	X							
	# % w any use past 6 months		X	X	X	X	X	X	X	X	
	# % without drug/alcohol use										X
	# % in target range						X	X	X	X	X
	25. Tobacco										
	# not scored for this scale	X									
	# % w use or exposure		X	X	X	X	X	X			
	# % w/o use/exposure this pregnancy								X	X	X
	# % in target range						X	X	X	X	X
	26. Depression/Suicide										
	# not scored for this scale	X									
	# % w depression not controlled		X	X	X	X	X	X			
	# % without depression										X
	# % in target range								X	X	X
	27. Mental Illness										
	# not scored for this scale	X									
	# % w MI not well controlled		X	X	X	X	X	X			
	# % without MI										X
	# % in target range						X	X	X	X	X
	28. Self-Esteem										
	# not scored for this scale	X									
	# % in target range						X	X	X	X	X
	29. Cognitive Ability										
	# not scored for this scale	X									
	# % w DD or LD		X	X	X	X	X	X	X	X	
	# % in target range						X	X	X	X	X
	BASIC ESSENTIALS										
	30. Housing										
	# not scored for this scale	X									
	# % homeless		X	X							

X	Scale data options	0	1	1.5	2	2.5	3	3.5	4	4.5	5
	# % unstable housing/frequent moves				X	X					
	# % in target range						X	X	X	X	X
	31. Food/Nutrition										
	# not scored for this scale	X									
	# % w inadequate food resources		X	X	X	X					
	# % using WIC/food stamps						X	X			
	# % in target range						X	X	X	X	X
	32. Transportation										
	# not scored for this scale	X									
	# % without transportation		X	X							
	# % using public transport				X	X					
	# % in target range						X	X	X	X	X
	33. Health Insurance										
	# not scored for this scale	X									
	# % without coverage		X	X							
	# % with pregnancy/ER Medicaid				X	X					
	# % with full-scope Medicaid						X	X			
	# % with subsidized insurance								X	X	
	# % with private insurance										X
	# % in target range				X	X	X	X	X	X	X
	34. Income										
	# not scored for this scale	X									
	# % with no or illegal income only		X	X							
	# % with TANF, child support or SDI only				X	X					
	# % at or under 200% FPL	X	X	X	X	X	X	X			
	# % in target range						X	X	X	X	X
	35. Child Care										
	# not scored for this scale	X									
	# % none or not used		X	X							
	# % inadequate/unsafe child care				X	X					
	# % in quality center care										X
	# % in care w friend/relative						X	X	X	X	
	# % in target range						X	X	X	X	X
	CHILD SCALES										
	36–40. Communication, Gross Motor, Fine Motor, Problem Solving, Personal-Social										
	# not scored for this scale	X									
	# % w EI eligible delays		X	X	X	X	X				

X	Scale data options	0	1	1.5	2	2.5	3	3.5	4	4.5	5
	36–40. Communication, Gross Motor, Fine Motor, Problem Solving, Personal-Social (continued)										
	# % w EI delays, good attendance						X				
	# % w emerging/regressing delays							X			
	# % w average development								X	X	
	# % w above average development										X
	# % in target range						X	X	X	X	X
	41. Social-Emotional										
	# not scored for this scale	X									
	# % w signs of neuro or env concerns		X	X	X	X	X	X			
	# % in target range								X	X	X
	42. Regulation										
	# not scored for this scale	X									
	# % w inadequate regulation		X	X	X	X	X	X			
	# % in target range								X	X	X
	43. Breast Feeding										
	# not scored for this scale	X									
	# % not breast-fed		X	X							
	# % breast-fed < 3 mo		X	X	X	X	X	X			
	# % in target range								X	X	X

APPENDIX L

Resources

Ages & Stages Questionnaires® (ASQ)—A Parent-Completed Child-Monitoring System, Second Edition, by Diane Bricker, Ph.D., & Jane Squires, Ph.D., with assistance from Linda Mounts, M.A., LaWanda Potter, M.S., Robert Nickel, M.D., Elizabeth Twombly, M.S., and Jane Farrell, M.S.

Ages & Stages Questionnaires®: Social-Emotional (ASQ:SE)—A Parent-Completed Child-Monitoring System for Social-Emotional Behaviors, by Jane Squires, Ph.D., Diane Bricker, Ph.D., & Elizabeth Twombly, M.S., with assistance from Suzanne Yockelson, Maura Schoen Davis, & Younghee Kim

Paul H. Brookes Publishing Co.
http://www.brookespublishing.com

Automated Assessment of Family Progress (AAFP) (1998–2001)
http://www.uiowa.edu/~nrcfcp/new/matrix.html

Baby Basics Program/Book
http://www.whatoexpectnext.org

Beginnings Guides: pregnancy/parenting, birth to 3 years curricula
http://www.BeginningsGuides.com
Beginnings Life Skill Development (see Smith & Wollesen, 2003): 1-day training materials
Life Skills Progression: outcome tool, 1-day training
http://www.BeginningsGuides.com/LSP

The Brazelton Institute
http://www.brazelton-institute.com

Bright Futures: National Center for Education in Maternal and Child Health
Parent and health education materials
http://brightfutures.org

California Children & Families Commission
http://www.ccfc.ca.gov

Center for Health Education and Research (CHER)
University of Washington School of Medicine and School of Public Health and Community Medicine
http://www.depts.washington.edu/CHERweb/index.html

Center for Home Visiting
University of North Carolina at Chapel Hill
http://www.unc.edu/~uncchv

Center for Law and Social Policy (CLASP)
http://www.clasp.org

Denver Developmental Screening Test, Second Edition (Denver II)
Denver Developmental Materials, Inc.
http://www.denverii.com

Early Head Start
http://www.acf.hhs.gov/programs/opre/

Family Infant Relationship Support Training
    (FIRST)
http://www.jfkpartners.org/first.asp

Future of Children
The Packard Foundation article *Future of Children: Home Visitation* (see Gomby, 1999) and
    the Future of Children series are available
    free upon request
http://www.futureofchildren.org

Grants Alert for nonprofit organizations
http://www.GrantsAlert.com/edicatopm.cfm

Growing Great Kids
Parenting, child, and staff development
    modules/handouts; 5-day training
http://www.greatkidsinc.org

Healthy Families America (HFA)
http://www.healthyfamiliesamerica.org

*The Home Visitor's Guidebook: Promoting Optimal
    Parent & Child Development* (see Klass, 2003)
    is an example of the extremely diverse practical material available to support the development of home visitor knowledge and
    skills.
Paul H. Brookes Publishing Co.
http://www.brookespublishing.com/

International Classification of Diseases, Ninth
    Edition (ICD-9)
    http://www.cdc.gov/nchs/icd9.html

National Center for Children in Poverty
    (NCCP)
Mailman School of Public Health, Columbia
    University, New York, NY
http://www.nccp.org

National Resource Center for Family Centered
    Practice
University of Iowa, School of Social Work,
    National Healthy Start Association (NHSA)
http://www.Uiowa.edu/~nrcfcp
http://www.healthystartassos.org
    http://www.mchlibrary.info/databases/about
    HSNRrefcoll.html

NCAST Teaching and Feeding Scales (see Sumner & Spitz, 1994)
Other NCAST Assessments:
Community Life Skills Scale (CLSS)
Difficult Life Circumstances Scale (DLC)
Keys to CaregivinG and Network Survey
http://www.ncast.org/contact.asp

Nurse-Family Partnership (NFP; see Olds):
    bibliography available from http://
    nursefamilypartnership.org

Ounce of Prevention Fund
The Ounce Scale
http://www.ounceofprevention.org

Parents as Teachers (PAT)
Born to Learn: staff manuals, parenting handouts/curricula 0–3 years, 3–5 years, special
    needs, and teens; training/certification per
    person and site
http://www.patnc.org

Partners for a Healthy Baby
Pregnancy/parent education handbook/handouts, 5-day training
http://www.cpeip.fsu.edu

Partners in Parenting Education (P.I.P.E)
Staff handbook/parent handouts, 2-day training
http://www.howtoreadyourbaby.com

Pathways to Outcomes (see Schorr & Schorr
    [1989])
http://www.PathwaysToOutcomes.org

Program for Infant/Toddler Caregivers (PITC;
    see Lally [2002])
http://www.pitc.org

Psychological Assessment Resources, Inc.
http://www.parinc.com

Rand Corporation
Child policy documents available online
http://www.rand.org

U.S. DHHS/Health Resources and Services
    Administration (HRSA)

Cost Effectiveness of Case Management: A Review of Literature (see Gavin & Lissy, 2000) is available from
http://www.mchb.hrsa.gov/

U.S. Government Accountability Office (GAO)
http://www.GAO.gov

U.S. Government Census
http://www.census.gov

WestED: Center for Prevention and Early Intervention
http://www.wested.org/cpei

ZERO TO THREE: National Center for Infants, Toddlers and Families
Zero To Three journal and publications on reflective questions and reflective supervision
http://www.zerotothree.org

Index

Page numbers followed by *f* indicate figures; those followed by *t* indicate tables.

A LEVEL
FRENCH

02'

William B Barratt
Former Senior Lecturer at a college of Higher Education

Advisors:

Mike Buckby
Senior Research Fellow, Language Teaching Centre, York

Eileen Verlarde
Senior Chief Examiner, A-Level, NEAB

First published 1992
Revised 1996
Reprinted 1993, 1994, 1997, 1998

Letts Educational
Aldine House
Aldine Place
London W12 8AW
0181 740 2266

Text © William B Barratt 1992, 1996

Typeset by Jordan Publishing Design

Design and illustrations © BPP (Letts Educational) Ltd 1996

British Library Cataloguing in Publication Data
A CIP record for this book is available from the British Library

ISBN 1 85758 396 5

Printed and bound in Great Britain by WM Print, Walsall WS2 9NE

Letts Educational is the trading name of BPP (Letts Educational) Ltd

CONTENTS

PREFACE

I would like to thank Mike Buckby, Senior Research Fellow at the Language Teaching Centre York, and Eileen Verlarde, Senior Chief Examiner for A-Level for NEAB, for much valuable advice during the planning stages of this book, for reading the text and for their many helpful suggestions. I am also grateful for the encouragement and advice of Hélène Burrows, Diane Fletcher and Andy Dobson who tried out a great deal of the material with their students at Halesowen College and Worcester Sixth Form College. I would also like to thank students in my own classes who have contributed their thoughts on ways of learning and what kind of material they find most beneficial. I am grateful too to Jean-Louis Drommi and Guillemette Belleteste for their close scrutiny of the French text and their comments. Lastly I would like to thank the editorial staff of Letts Educational for their encouragement and the friendly working relationship fostered over a number of years.

ACKNOWLEDGEMENTS

The author and publishers are grateful to the following for permission to reproduce their extracts and photographs.

Text
p 108 'The calming of the waters' (Marc 4, 5) from *L'Alliance Biblique Universelle* translation of the Bible, reprinted by permission of the Société Biblique Française;
p 138 'Les médias disent vrai?' (avril 1990) reproduced by permission of *Phosphore*;
p 141 'Circuit de la drogue dans le monde' (août 1990) reproduced by permission of *Phosphore*;
p 141 'Les Européens sont-ils de bons conducteurs?' (août 1990) reproduced by permission of *Phosphore*.
p 197 'Qu'est-ce qui est tendre...' (août 1990) reprinted by permission of *Nice-Matin*;
p 201 'Le Sida — Fléau des années 90' (1 août 1990) reproduced by permission of *Modes et Travaux*;
p 209 'Deux élèves japonais enterrés vivants' (23 juillet 1990) reproduced by permission of Nice-Matin;
p 215 'Les dames du crime' (août 1990) reprinted by permission of *Modes et Travaux*;
p 216 'L'Aventure en Amérique' (août 1990) reproduced by permission of *Modes et Travaux*;
p 219 'Que faire en cas d'incendie' (8 septembre 1990) reproduced by permission of *50,000,000 de consommateurs*, published by the Institut National de la Consommation;
p 219 'Hold-up' (août 1990) reproduced by permission of *Le Dauphiné Libéré – Vaucluse-Matin*;
p 222 'Une crèche bilingue dès septembre, à Coulogne' (15 août 1990) reprinted by permission of *Littoral Nord*;
p 230 'Allerte à l'ovni sur l'autoroute Paris-Lille' from *Ça m'intéresse* No 175, September 1995
p 231 'La valeur de la famille en France' from *Ça m'intéresse*, April 1995

Photographs
p 133 The Hulton Picture Company
p 139 Ian Thraves

STARTING POINTS

In this section:

How to use this book
   The structure of the book
   GCSE and A/AS-level compared

A-level examination objectives
   Listening
   Speaking
   Reading and writing
   Grammar, structures and vocabulary
   The AS-level examination and modular syllabuses
   Language-learning strategies
   Vocabulary
   Quality of language
   The four skill areas
   Coursework and how to tackle it
   Literature and background studies
   A plan of action

The examination

Syllabus checklists and examination paper analysis
   Associated Examining Board
   University of Cambridge Local Examinations Syndicate
   University of London Examinations and Assessment Council
   Northern Examinations Assessment Board
   Northern Ireland Council for the Curriculum, Examinations and
      Assessment
   University of Oxford Delegacy of Local Examinations
   Oxford and Cambridge Schools Examination Board
   Scottish Examinations Board
   Welsh Joint Education Committee

HOW TO USE THIS BOOK

The material in this book has been designed to exemplify and practise the kinds of language task required by the Examination Boards for French at A and AS-Level. The book also provides a bridge for the wide gap that exists between GCSE and A (or AS-Level) French. It has also been devised with the needs of the self-learner in mind. The material as a whole has been devised to represent many of the recurring themes and aspects of contemporary society required at A and AS-Level. Students will benefit therefore from working through as much of this as they can. Students will also find it beneficial if they can work with another person for many of the tasks. Not only is this more enjoyable but you will learn a great deal from each other. Now read through the following sections.

THE STRUCTURE OF THE BOOK

The sections on aims and objectives give an overall picture of what is needed in order to build upon knowledge already acquired for GCSE French.

The section on how to study deals with the ways in which you can consolidate and extend competence in the four language skills. This is followed by advice on how to organise your work and how to prepare for the examination.

A summary of each Examination Board's requirements is given on pages 15–24. The summaries give a brief description of the tasks required in each paper or module together with the time and marks allocated. They should be read in conjunction with the detailed syllabus for your particular Board, of which you should get a copy.

The unit on dictionaries provides an introduction to, and practice in, using larger dictionaries than you may have been accustomed to previously. The units on vocabulary and gender provide a framework upon which you can build in order to extend your store and knowledge of words and accuracy in using them.

The grammar chapter gives practical explanations and examples of the main points required to fill the gaps and extend what you have already acquired. Each unit is followed by exercises, with answers at the end of the chapter. You can work through this chapter systematically or dip into the parts you need. This chapter is derived from a long acquaintance with what is really essential in grammatical knowledge and where students need most help.

The unit on oral work sets out the features common to most oral examinations and provides advice and a good deal of practice material. This unit should be studied in conjunction with the next one on pronunciation.

The listening unit gives practical advice on how to deal with this part of the Examination.

The chapter on reading and writing skills deals with specific tasks. They are accompanied by examples from the Examining Boards' papers and model answers. This is followed by practice exercises and advice on how to improve each skill. You will benefit from working through all the units here since many of the skills complement each other.

The literature chapter provides an introduction to this subject for newcomers. There are model answers and advice on writing answers to questions.

The coursework chapter provides advice, guidance and some ideas for the themes of topic work.

The verb table (appendix 1) should be used as a reference tool but also as a learning aid by photocopying and blanking out sections to be filled in as a check on learning.

Appendix 2 contains a number of useful sources of further information that should complement much of the previous material.

GCSE AND A/AS LEVEL COMPARED

The broad aims of studying French at A-Level are very similar to those at GCSE Level. The main differences lie in the breadth and depth of knowledge expected and the flexibility with which you can use this knowledge. The extension of your competence in French is closely linked with increasing maturity. By speaking and listening to the language, by reading and writing it, you will be able to increase your knowledge of the world and society, discover and discuss the opinions of others and develop your own viewpoint and outlook. Study of a language becomes just as much a tool as it is a target. The A-Level Examination will test your ability to handle ideas as well as your ability to speak, understand, read and write French.

One important difference between studying French at GCSE and A-Level is the responsibility put upon you as learner. You cannot be told or shown everything you need in order to pass the A-Level Examination. There will inevitably be an element of the unexpected. You will have to develop your own habits for studying and apply these consistently so that you take charge of your own learning and create learning opportunities for yourself. Guidance and help with this task will be found in this book.

A typical description of some of the aims of an A-Level syllabus in French might be the following:

1 To develop the candidates' intellectual and critical faculties by encouraging the acquisition and development of

- awareness of the use of language,
- an imaginative and creative approach to language,
- learning strategies and study skills,
- awareness and understanding of themselves, of other individuals and contemporary society.

2 To enable the candidates to attain sufficient command of language skills in order to

- communicate easily and with confidence in French-speaking environments,
- understand and appreciate spoken and written French from a variety of sources and in registers including colloquial, informative and literary,
- seek and convey information, report and express ideas and feelings in various modes such as conversation, discussion, personal and analytical writing.

3 To form a sound base of language and learning skills required for further study (of French and other languages) and continuing use in work and leisure.

4 To encourage first-hand contact with the contemporary culture and civilisation of France or French-speaking communities through, for example,

- exchange of letters, cassettes or magazines, etc.,
- where possible travel and residence.

5 To further the candidates' appreciation of language by helping them to understand contemporary culture and civilisation (both British and French) from the viewpoint of the respective peoples.

6 To foster interest in the views of French-speaking people on current issues.

You will see from the above that study of French at A-Level is as much about extending you as a person as it is about acquiring knowledge.

Increasing your confidence and competence in using a foreign language has an immediate and valuable practical purpose in everyday life. Despite the growth of English as a worldwide language, you can only really get to know and understand people from another country and their way of life, whether for it is for pleasure or for commercial purposes, by communicating with them in their own language.

A-LEVEL EXAMINATION OBJECTIVES

Just as at GCSE level the A-Level examination objectives are based upon the four skills of speaking, listening, reading and writing. These skills often go together and complement each other so that listening, reading and writing may be combined in a single module or paper.

Listening

The main differences in objectives for listening skills at A-Level relate to the ability to pick out relevant ideas as well as facts; to summarise or extract the main points of what you have heard. You will hear a greater variety of speakers and kinds of interchange than at GCSE level and some of the spoken passages will be longer. They will be taken from a variety of authentic sources such as recorded news items, telephone messages, announcements, talks and discussions. Some questions may be framed in English but the majority will be in French. Other ways of testing comprehension include non-verbal responses, summary, gap-filling, transcribing parts of what you have heard, listing points mentioned in sequence or writing a letter or report.

Speaking

Objectives for spoken French at A-Level are really an expansion of the skills expected at GCSE. A typical description of what is required at GCSE level might be: "to seek and provide information, to take part in conversational interchange, to express opinions in French in a range of situations within the candidates' own experience". At A-Level you will be expected to "extract more detailed information by following up initial questions" or to "marshall ideas in order to persuade" to "counter the opinions of another person" or "present orally the substance of an English or French text". The important differences therefore at A-Level are being able to pick out and manipulate ideas, making use of the spoken language for a greater variety of purposes and often taking the initiative yourself and explaining how and why. There is also much more unpredictability at A-Level. Topics are no longer closely defined. You will have the chance though of talking about something that interests you and that you have prepared. Role-play, general conversation and talking around a prepared topic figure in the oral examination of most Boards. The oral exam tends to be a little longer at A-Level, from 15 to 30 minutes, depending on the Examination Board.

Reading and writing

There are some important differences in objectives for reading and writing at A-Level: you may be required to translate from and into French and you will do more writing in French of various kinds. The written element in French normally counts for more in the overall weighting of marks.

Passages are usually taken from from magazines, newspapers and other contemporary sources. Comprehension questions are mostly in French but may be in English, depending on the Board. You may be required to summarise a passage or part of one in French or English. You may have to translate selected extracts into English or give a brief résumé or paraphrase in French. The emphasis is again on being able to deal with ideas and opinions as well as factual items. Some Boards have longer passsages for translation into English or French. Retranslation – that is translating into French a short passage in English based closely on what you have just read – is also a task required by some Boards.

Writing in French can take the form of an essay presenting points for and against a certain issue or a composition of a more imaginative kind. Writing letters or reports in French is required by some Boards. There is also the possibility with most Boards of an extended piece of writing in French on a selected subject done in your own time and presented as coursework.

Studying French literary texts, or books on certain aspects of French life and culture, are also features of most A-Level syllabuses. In both cases you are required to read texts in French and answer questions about them in French. Wide reading of this kind comes as a bit of a shock after GCSE but if thoroughly done it has a beneficial effect on your competence in writing and understanding French. You will be able to extend your vocabulary, meet and develop new ideas and use the language you have thus acquired in essay and composition work.

Grammar, structures and vocabulary

The grammar and structures required for Higher Level GCSE form the basis for what you need at A-Level with two important considerations. Firstly, many of the points of grammar that formerly you only needed to recognise, certain pronouns and tenses for example, will now be required for active use in writing and speaking. Secondly, the range of grammatical items will need to be extended. This is particularly the case with verbs and tenses . You will have to extend the range of verbs you are familiar with in the present tense and also make some additions to tense, mood and voice. The subjunctive, for example, is not required by some Boards at GCSE level or only the present subjunctive by others. You will need to use both the present and the perfect subjunctive as well as recognise its other two tenses.

Most GCSE Examination Boards publish a defined content of their syllabus which lists grammar, structures, vocabulary and expressions as well as functions and notions of language required for their examination. *Send off for your copy.* It is an extremely useful document for A-Level students as a check list, a quick reference and a learning aid. You will get something of a boost when you find out how much you already know! Defined content syllabuses are pretty indigestible for all but the most gifted GCSE students but they become more easy to assimilate as you grow in confidence and all the bits and pieces of French you have acquired settle down.

Needless to say that the vocabulary needed for A-Level is far broader than for GCSE and no definitive list can be made. It is important to acquire the habit of keeping a vocabulary book right from the start. Many words are going to be more for productive use, others you will need just to understand. More will be said about this in the section on how to to study.

The AS-Level examination and modular syllabuses

The AS-Level examination is meant to be a natural extension of the skills acquired at GCSE Level for those students who have obtained grade C or above and wish to continue their study of the language during their sixth form course. The attainment level is identical with that of A-Level but the content is half that of an A-Level syllabus and should require half the contact time. The broad aims and examination objectives are therefore similar to those already outlined. An AS-Level course is meant to extend over two years. The reduced content of the syllabus is reflected in fewer items in each examination paper and consequently a shorter examination time. Writing in French is now required for AS-Level by most Boards. Marks are usually assigned equally to the skills of listening, reading, writing and speaking. The listening, reading, writing and speaking parts of the AS exam are usually identical with all or part of the A-Level examination.

Modular syllabuses are now available with three of the Examination Boards. This means that you can take some modules at certain times during a four year period instead of taking all of them in one final examination. 30% of the total examination must however still be by external terminal examination. Each module carries at least 15% of the subject weighting and is of full A-Level standard whether examined early or late. You can retake modules to obtain a better result but the last result of the terminal examination must count whether or not it is the best one. Modules passed have a shelf life of four years. Consult the syllabus for your Board for full details.

Modular syllabuses create a certain amount of flexibility. You could for example obtain modules for an AS-Level and convert this later into an A-Level. You could continue studies after leaving school or college to improve or add to your modules. Intensive courses might become available. If you have spent a longish period in France you might feel most confident in taking an oral module fairly soon after your return.

In practice, however, many students would probably prefer to take most of their modules towards the end of the normal 21 months course. The four language skills are difficult to acquire separately. They complement each other and you get better at all of them over a period.

LANGUAGE-LEARNING STRATEGIES

Gaining competence in a foreign language often appears a slow process. It is difficult to see how far you have come because there is no accurate way of measuring the distance in the short term. This is partly because of the maturation factor in language learning. It seems that we have to allow time for the brain to order and assimilate what has been fed into it before it can be retrieved and used as language. This is probably true of all attempts to assimilate knowledge but it appears more obvious with foreign language learning. This is perhaps because knowing a foreign language involves several skills, often needed at once and also because language is mostly unpredictable. We can never be sure of what we are going to hear or read any more than we can know beforehand what we will say or write. One thing is certain: it is important to be consistent and persistent in your learning habits: a little at a time over a long period is better than hectic bursts of activity.

Another effect that you might notice is the impression of reaching a plateau or threshold in your learning and the feeling that you can't get any further. This pause effect is quite normal and connected with the maturation factor already mentioned. You *will* move off, but imperceptibly at first.

Using a foreign language is a skill and skills have to be practised otherwise they fade or 'stiffen up'. The phrase often heard on older people's lips, "My French/German/Spanish is a bit rusty" is very evocative of this phenomenon. It helps a great deal therefore if you set yourself targets and procedures for study: learning so many words a week; devoting a set amount of time to each of the language skills; reading through and adding to your literature or grammar notes; consulting books of criticism; reading background or topic material.

It helps enormously if you can work with a friend, particularly one following the same course. One obvious advantage is being able to practise your oral skills together. But you will also be able to plug the gaps in each other's knowledge. Grammar points often seem clearer when explained by someone on the same level as yourself. If you both come to a dead stop on the same point it probably needs clearing up with the whole class and will give your teacher something to focus on. You can also test each other's vocabulary.

If no learning companion is at hand, finding someone you can teach basic conversational French to can be quite helpful. Having to explain things to someone else sharpens up your own understanding and grasp of language.

Vocabulary

The number of words you know the meanings of and can use or recognise is one of the most important keys to success in learning a foreign language. It is vital that you acquire word learning habits right from the beginning. Be curious about words and how they are used. The English language has been highly influenced by French in former years and very many words share similarities of spelling and meaning as well as divergences. The French language has also undergone fertilisation from English in the past. This process is still ongoing and often the subject of much controversy in France.

Get used to writing down new words and their meanings and set aside time to learn them. More will be said about this aspect in the following sections. Some Boards allow the use of dictionaries in all or some parts of the Examination. The main purpose of having a dictionary available in the Examination is to check the meaning or spelling of the *occasional* word. *It cannot be a substitute for learning vocabulary during the whole of your course.*

QUALITY OF LANGUAGE

It is now a requirement that quality of English language is assessed at GCE A and AS-level. This will be applied particularly where continuous prose is used in an examination answer. If your Board requires you to write continuous prose – for example in a literature question – make sure that:

❶ You write in complete sentences that convey meaning clearly.

❷ Punctuation – capital letters, full stops, commas, semi colons and colons – are used properly (for example when referring to the title of a book, play or poem this should be either underlined or put in inverted commas).

❸ Spelling is correct.

Most of these details also apply when you are doing a French to English translation or answering a comprehension question in English.

THE FOUR SKILL AREAS

Listening

This is possibly the most neglected skill and the one that can be most obviously deficient to Examiners marking papers. If French is used a lot in the classroom for all the activities that don't specifically need English your exposure to spoken French will be increased. Some time will no doubt be devoted to listening to taped material in the classroom. You will need nevertheless to create your own opportunities for practising listening skills at other times.

You have immediate access to French voices by tuning to either side of BBC 4 on long wave. There are at least three radio stations that can be received in Britain. France-Inter the national station on 160 kHz, and Europe 1, a commercial station on 180 kHz, will give you the best reception, depending on what part of the country you live in. Radio Luxemburg is on 230 kHz. You can listen casually, just letting the language flow over you or you can make a point each day of listening to something specific. If you have never listened to French announcers before you will probably be alarmed at the speed of their speech. This is particularly the case with news bulletins and weather forecasts because the news reader is using a printed text that he or she has to fit into a given time. Speed of delivery does vary however and it is partly a case of tuning in your ear. Other items like interviews and discussions are at a slower pace. France-Inter for example, has a "What the papers say" slot between morning news bulletins and a series of relaxed interviews with people from all walks of life during the morning and at the end of the afternoon. Advertisements on the commercial stations as well as the government directed ones on France-Inter, are also worth listening to.

By recording ten minutes of a programme you can listen to it as many times as you like. Try with the beginning of a news bulletin that lists the main items first or with part of an interview. You will find it easier if at first you just try to listen out for words that you can understand. You probably won't be able to understand every word, nor is it essential to do so. Later you can listen for content and try making a list of the items talked about. Select a shorter section and try writing down words or phrases that you can catch. Have a dictionary at hand. Each time you listen you should be able to fill in a bit more. As you get better at this try making a transcript of a short section. Take the tape and specific problems to your teacher for explanation.

There are commercially produced tapes available, often accompanied by a transcript of the tape. Cassettes Radio France publish a catalogue of tapes taken from their programmes. The newspaper *Authentik* (*l'Authentique en Français*, published 5 times a year in Dublin produces a tape with transcript and exercises. *La Vie Outre-Manche*, a magazine for francophiles, appears monthly and has an accompanying tape of readings from its articles (see Appendix 2).

There are several useful things you can do once you have a tape with a transcript.

❶ Try listening several times to the tape while following the printed version with your eye. If you have not done this before you will be surprised by the way words merge or seem swallowed because of linking, use of liaisons, stress and intonation patterns.

❷ Make a few photocopies of the transcript. With Tippex block out every seventh or so word. Listen again and see if you can fit in the words in your mind, or write them in. You could also select verbs, nouns or adjectives for blocking out.

❸ You could also try reading the text over the taped voice, with the volume turned low. This helps to practise intonation and stress patterns.

Another source of taped material are the BBC schools programmes. They offer a wide range of live interviews designed for different levels and are accompanied by a booklet. It is often helpful to select a level below the one you are doing. This has the effect of reinforcing what you perhaps only partly remember.

You could try your local library. They often have tapes and videos that accompany courses. Your local university or polytechnic is sure to have a language laboratory and might allow you to use it and their tape library. Exchanging live recorded tapes with a French school or friends in France is another possibility.

Watching French films with subtitles on television can be very helpful. Satellite TV and video recording bring a further range of possibilities. Again, news, interviews and discussions are good starting points. Commercials, documentaries, soap opera series, films that you have already seen and are dubbed in French (where do you think the word "dubbed" comes from?) are relaxing ways of listening. There are usually current series of language programmes on TV for older learners. Try the beginners' courses. You will be surprised how much you know and how much you will re-learn or reinforce.

Speaking

There are two aspects to this skill: practising saying or reading French to get your tongue round words and to perfect a smooth flow; practising responding to a spoken cue and reacting to a spoken situation.

Working with a tape is the best way of practising pronunciation on your own. The voice-over already mentioned is one way. A taped text with gaps in for you to repeat or anticipate what is said is a mechanical but useful exercise. This also works well in a language laboratory because you are 'closer' to the sound of your own voice wearing earphones. A way of simulating a language laboratory at home is the following: you need two tape recorders. Play the recorded tape on one of them, set the other to record. You can then try reading aloud the transcript at the same time as it is being played. When you play both tapes back from the same point you will be able to compare your intonation and pronunciation with that of the recorded tape. Another possibility is to use the pause button on the first recorder to stop the tape after a short sentence or phrase. You then repeat the sentence or phrase which is recorded on the second machine. When you play back from the same point you will hear the French voice followed by your own and be able to compare the two.

It is possible to do basic role-plays on your own by imagining the other person and just reacting to the English cues. Some people use their pets as stand-ins to create the illusion of talking to someone. You can also rehearse situations in your head while travelling in the bus or train. Internal rehearsal is something we might at times do in English and is a well-known feature of day-dreaming. Try some day-dreaming in French. Research has shown that successful language learners are in-the-head rehearsers.

As well as role-plays, explaining some aspect of life in your own country is something that you can do in your head by taking subjects like opening times of banks, pubs, post offices, the meanings of abbreviations such MOT, PYO, VAT, how cricket is played, what happens on Christmas day and so on. Short news items from newspapers fulfill the same function.

You can record one part of a role-play on tape leaving a gap for your response, perhaps with a response added as a further reinforcement. If you work through a tape several times you will begin to memorise the dialogue and be able to retrieve phrases that can be used in other situations.

Taking turns to play the parts with a friend is better still, since you will tend to learn from one another. You could try using some of the higher level GCSE role-plays to begin with. Put some play-acting into this activity. It helps to make the situation more convincing as well as more enjoyable.

Most role-plays centre on (a) giving or asking for information or (b) on resolving a situation or problem. A simple way of practising role-plays with a friend, is to have two cards, one with the cues in English and the other with full responses in French (the part normally played by an examiner). The roles can then be exchanged. Another way is to have both roles labelled A and B fully written out in French and English alternately on two cards or on a sheet that folds down the middle. You then have the possibility of either just reading the French or of playing the role from the English version. This method can be a bit restrictive since there is often an element of the unexpected in A-Level role-plays but it can boost confidence in the early stages. You may be contradicted, challenged to prove something, have to apologise or deal with the displeasure or seeming indifference of your role-play opposite.

Your opportunities for speaking and listening to French can be increased by joining a local *Cercle français* or other French club, using your French Assistant(e), joining an evening class. There are also many intensive language days and courses all over the country, many are organised by ALL (The Association for Language Learning, see Appendix 2) others by local universities, or colleges of further education. There are also many *Stages d'été* in France as well as the possibility of finding part-time employment there. The Service Culturel of the French Institute will provide a full list of courses and the Central Bureau for Educational visits and Exchanges has information about jobs and other activities.

It should be possible in the very near future to practise your spoken French by a live link-up with French speakers through the computer network. You will be able to contact a fellow student in France and arrange and have say half an hour's conversation in French in exchange for half an hour in English.

Reading and writing

You will be required to do more writing in French at A-Level than you did for GCSE and of the four skills, writing has slightly more marks assigned to it in the examination. The writing section of the exam will test your ability to produce French with a minimum of spelling and grammatical errors and to express and order your ideas clearly. Marks are given for both accuracy and expression, so both are important. You will need to check your written French for mistakes in a routine way and establish a system for checking spelling, gender, agreement and tense (see page 171 for specific guidance). This is particularly important with coursework in French since this will not be corrected for you by your teacher before being sent to the Examination Board for marking.

Apart from the written tasks you do as assignments there are other ways in which you can practise writing French with a practical purpose.

Firstly by corresponding regularly with with a pen-friend. When deciding on a correspondent you might like to bear in mind that French is a language used by people every day in many other parts of the world apart from France: in Canada, large parts of the African continent, Madagascar and islands in the Indian ocean, in some of the Carribean and South Pacific islands (e.g. Tahiti), as well as in parts of Switzerland, in Belgium, Luxemburg and the Lebanon. You can now find and communicate with a pen-friend via the Internet.

You could also write letters to France to gather information for your topic work or to pursue interests or hobbies that will almost certainly be represented by clubs or organisations in France. It is also worth contacting your local Chamber of Commerce or LX centre (government sponsored Language and Export Centres, see Appendix 2) to discover what firms in your area are doing business with France or French speaking countries and who might find your services helpful.

The reading you do for A-Level covers a wide range of texts. If you choose a literary option you will be dealing with plays and novels. Non-literary options will introduce you to various aspects of French life and culture. Topics in language work are explored through newspaper and magazine articles, brochures, surveys, market reports and cover aspects issues and concerns of everyday life.

There are three kinds of reading process that you might need: Skimming – reading quickly through a text to find out what it is about; scanning – to find particular information; reading closely to extract full detail.

In practice scanning and skimming go together, particularly in the early part of your sixth form course. You need a lot of practice before you can do them efficiently. You will complain at first that you are always having to read carefully because you find it difficult to come to grips with the meanings of words and phrasing of sentences at the same time. It is worth bearing in mind not every word necessarily counts in a text and it is sometimes better to skip over obstacles rather than keep coming to a dead halt.

You will get quite a bit of practice from the reading you do in class and from set texts. You will also have to read using your own initiative in connection with any topic work you do. This might involve regular dips into magazines and newspapers as well as into books where you are looking for relevant passages or details.

You should also try to be as wide ranging as possible in what you read in French. Bilingual texts of all kinds, labels, instructions and directions for installation, holiday and tourist brochures are now commonplace. See what your local tourist bureau has to offer in French. You can improve your reading skills and enlarge and consolidate your skills by actively looking our for this kind of material.

Your place of study will probably subscribe to magazines and newspapers. The *Authentik* publication already referred to has a good range of articles from the French press. The French monthly magazine for 16 to 18-year-olds, *Phosphore* is an excellent publication, informative, relevant to this age group and written in a language you will be able to understand.

Some popular magazines, especially in the feminine press, are now available in French and English. Examples are: *Cosmopolitan*, *Anna* (a German publication, but appears in French and English), *Elle* and *Marie-Claire*. These magazines nearly all produce a different version for the British market. *Anna* however has a certain number of articles and adverts that are the same or similar in both languages. Having both versions gives you the possibility of comparing language but also of scanning or skimming and checking with the English version or of trying translations both ways yourself. In the case of different version it is interesting and enlightening to compare the choice of material chosen for the respective countries. Two monthly French magazines *Ça m'intéresse* and *Réponse à tout* provide a lot of interesting information about nature and ecology, scientific research, and many aspects of French life and society. They could be useful for topic work but also for just dipping into. Persuade your school or college to subscribe to them.

Check what your local library, college or polytechnic has to offer. Many English detective stories as well as other novels have been translated into French. Try dipping into some that you are already familiar with in English. You should also find helpful the bilingual texts in the series *Les langues pour tous* published in France by Presse Pocket. The latter are often taken from the classics of English literature and are intended for French students studying English. If you are also doing English Literature at A-Level you might find a translation of one of your set texts and you might *faire d'une pierre deux coups*!

The computer Internet system offers a growing number of opportunities for accessing all kinds of information. Through the French Embassy's "France la carte" you can have access to France Télécom's online information system, Télétel with its 17 000 services including the latest news, tourism and travel as well as scientific, environmental and business databases. British Telecom's education network Campus 2 000 offers further online teaching services.

The ability to read and understand French more and more easily has positive advantages. It enables you to pursue and develop your hobbies and interests through the medium of French. Whether you are keen on fishing, windsurfing, stamp-collecting or environmental issues there will be plenty of organisations in France who you can get in touch with and whose publications or magazines you can acquire or access through the computer network.

Coursework and how to tackle it

If your Board has a coursework option as part of the examination make sure you find out what the requirements are as soon as possible when you begin your A-Level studies. Coursework has the advantage of allowing you to research and write about something that interests you and do this in your own time. Find out how many pieces of work are needed and the dates for submission which are normally at the end of May in the first and second years of your course. These dates can sound a long way off in September but it is important to start thinking about a theme and a title as soon as possible. It will take time to find out what sort of information or material you are going to need and to accumulate it.

Literature and background studies

Nearly all Boards have an examination based on literary texts or on background studies. You can usually opt to answer questions on just one of these areas or a combination of both.

Answers are normally in French. Background studies are concerned with various aspects of French historical, cultural and social life and you study a theme or a topic through books and articles in French. Literature is studied through reading novels, plays, short stories or poetry mainly by 19th and 20th century French authors. You will be expected to show a good factual knowledge of your books or topics and, more importantly, show that you are able to use this to illustrate, explain, justify or support a point of view.

Whether you choose to study a topic or a literary text it is essential to begin your reading as soon as possible. This can be a daunting task at first since you will only have been used to reading quite short texts for GCSE. It helps if you begin your reading with texts in a more conversational style but there is no short cut to getting better at reading French texts. You can only do it through practice. The more you do the easier it will become. One thing is certain, literature and background studies will greatly improve your performance in the skills not only of reading and understanding, but also of speaking and writing French. More advice will be given in the chapters on literature and coursework.

A PLAN OF ACTION

On pages 15–24 you will find syllabus check lists and paper analysis. Make sure you read carefully the detailed syllabus for your particular Board. *Get hold of a copy!* Detailed syllabuses often give marking schemes which will give you a clearer idea of what examiners are looking for. Some Boards publish specimen papers with answers and marking schemes. They also publish from time to time Examiners' reports for a particular year's examination. These reports are also valuable because they give a detailed breakdown of how each paper was tackled, why marks were lost by some candidates but also why others scored highly. Your school or college should have copies of specimen papers and Examiners' reports.

Your work will be more purposeful and effective if you can get yourself organised from the beginning. You could start with a loose-leaf folder and some dividers. Main divisions will be language, grammar, literature, topic, vocabulary. These can then be further subdivided where necessary.

- **Language** should be divided into the main skills tested by your particular Examination Board. Start with writing in French. Include here notes from class discussions on various topics, useful phrases and vocabulary and any copies of texts used. Also add, over the period of your course, assignments, essays or other pieces of work and themes for essays that might figure in the Examination. If you work out model answers to the latter, reduce these to a series of headings so that they will be easier to memorise.

  Under language you could also include sections for: translation both ways, paraphrase, cloze exercises, summary, reading comprehension and any exercises you have done.

- **Listening** should include a note of the theme of passages that you heard plus your written answers, noting any words, the sound of which you found difficult . Also include a note of any weekly listening practice done by yourself and what it was about.

- **Grammar.** This section should contain notes on explanations done in class, with examples, and any exercises you have done.

- **Literature.** This section would include your summary of the action and characters for each text, notes on the author and his or her background, either from classwork or your own research, as well as essays done and possible themes for further questions. You might also include *brief* quotations that usefully illustrate particular points.

- **Topic.** Here you should include your outlines for possible themes of research and the sources consulted and any notes on these as well as copies of texts or visual material.

- **Vocabulary.** You might want to include this section within topics or you may prefer to keep a separate book for this purpose. Whichever you choose, have some way of dividing words from their meanings so that you can cover up one side for learning purposes. You might want to list words under themes. For example: pollution, health, poverty, population, transport, education, war, racial problems, national characteristics. This depends on the requirements of your Board. You may wish to list words under the headings of: people, emotions, things, ideas. Make a distinction, for learning purposes, between active and passive words, that is between those you are going to need to use, and those which only need to be recognised. It is helpful to put *un* or *une* in front of each word so that you can memorise the gender at the same time and to give plural or feminine forms if these are irregular.

Using your system

Once you have got a system working it makes it easier to file material regularly. When you do this think about the best place to put each piece of work. This will make you read through what is already there. Make a regular habit of looking through sections of your file, but don't just be content with reading through. When looking at the material on essays for example, ask yourself how would I say this..., or what's the word for... Look these up and add them. Also add any other articles you come across that deal with similar or related themes and underline useful words or expressions in them.

When you have accumulated several pieces of written French in the form of exercises, start listing the kinds of mistakes you have been making, e.g. label them T. for tense, Gen. for gender, Gr. for grammar, V. for vocabulary, A. for agreement, S. for spelling. In this way you will discover where you tend to make most mistakes and be able to take effective action.

This process will sometimes refer you back to the grammar section. You may have to look the point up in this book or elsewhere. Try to find exercises to practise the point and discuss it with a teacher or friend.

If retranslation or translation into French is one of the skills needed, make a list of reoccuring structure words like: *yet*, *ago*, *according to*, *because of*, *thanks to* and so on. Also make a list of grammar points that reoccur in cloze exercises. In the literature section go over essays done and improve them with the help of the teacher's corrections and then reduce these to note form for memorisation and revision purposes. Note the weak points in your essays: retelling the story to no purpose, not discussing the real question, not using references to the text to support your arguments, so that you can improve on these.

Make a regular habit of learning vocabulary, and enlist the help of a friend to test you if possible. If you highlight words that cause difficulty you will automatically re-read these every time you look down a column. Explore and add further vocabulary by investigating different themes.

Revision

If you have been doing as suggested above on a regular basis you will have been doing the kind or revision necessary for effective language learning. You will feel less inclined to try and cram every thing into the few weeks before the exam. Part of the secret is making effective use of time available during your course. Set yourself a target of a number of hours per week – say 20 – which will include doing work set as well. Keep a log over a couple of weeks and treat yourself to time off when you have achieved your target. Those 45 or so minutes while you are waiting for tea, for example, can soon add up and swell your total.

Examiners are always drawing attention to lack of basic knowledge of vocabulary and grammar. One excellent way of dealing with this is to get hold of a detailed GCSE syllabus and to read through the lists of language tasks, communication strategies and vocabulary by topic areas – the one available from The Northern Examination and Assessment Board (NEAB) is a good example. You will find that you know a lot of it but you will also find blank spots and things that you half know. Doing this will plug the gaps and reinforce what you are already familiar with.

Well before the actual exam, say two months, work out a revision timetable. Make a list of priorities based on how long ago you did something and on the kinds of mistakes you are tending to repeat. Go through these systematically with the most distant and most persistent faults first, ticking off what you have covered on a wall chart. In the run up to the exam you should only be dealing with minor or very persistent stumbling blocks.

Do not concentrate on a particular area the day before the exam. Take time off to do something completely different.

THE EXAMINATION

You should already be familiar with the format and layout of each paper for your particular Board. Depending on the Board, some or all of the instructions will be in French. You should also be familiar with the French wording of questions from practice with your teacher. Bear in mind the total length of time for the whole paper and allocate roughly how long you can spend on each part. Read through each part carefully, paying especial attention to the instructions when there are choices or options available and highlighting them.

During the exam it helps to increase your liquid intake to combat loss through perspiration. Increasing the amount of sugar and carbohydrate you eat also helps to compensate for lower blood sugar levels and that empty feeling in your stomach that is commonly experienced at these times.

Oral

On the day of the oral exam make sure you arrive in plenty of time. Make a conscious effort to think in French and hold conversations with yourself or with a friend in the time before. Most examiners make a point of meeting and briefing all the candidates before the exam to set them at their ease. If there is a preparation period before the exam, divide up the time, allowing enough to prepare each part of the test. In the exam try to work *with* the examiner. You will make his or her task easier and he or she will grateful and reward you accordingly. Remember that the oral is marked positively. You will score marks for what you can do, not have them deducted for mistakes.

Listening

Where individual cassette tapes are available read through the questions for each section before listening to the tape. They will give you a framework for what you are about to hear. Do not spend too long listening again and again to one particular part of the tape. You will score more marks by giving equal attention to all parts of the paper. This is particularly important when part of the paper consists of reading and or writing tasks that might take longer than the listening part. Always be guided by the mark allocation for the relative value of each task.

Where a single tape is played to all candidates, follow the instructions with your eye as they are repeated by the tape. There is normally a short pause before each extract is heard, giving you enough time to read through the questions or tasks. The latter will give you an outline for what you are about to hear, so do read through them all.

Literature or topic

In literature or topic papers read through *all* the questions. Don't just pick the first one you think you can answer.

Read each word in the question and underline or highlight key words. Ask yourself "What is this question asking me to do?"

Beware of plunging right away into questions that seem a bit like ones you have done before. You can probably use some of the original material but you might have to change the emphasis or order of things.

Questions usually have more than one part. Make sure you give sufficient attention to each part.

Spend 5–10 minutes planning out your answer. Make sure it has a clear structure. This will impress the examiner more than anything, even if you have made mistakes in the French.

After each paragraph ask yourself "Have I justified or explained the points I am making?", "Have I backed up my points through reference to the text or specific information?"

Reading and writing

Where passages in French are involved, read these several times. You are bound to meet words you do not understand. Don't panic at this. Some of these might come to you later or you might only need to work out an approximate meaning which will become clearer after several readings. You might not need to know the full meaning of some of them at all! If you highlight the words you don't know, it is helpful when a retranslation follows. By searching through the highlighted items you might be able to guess at a word you need. If a dictionary is permitted use it only to check meanings of words that are essential to the question.

Note. Avoid using red or green for your underlining. Examiners use these colours for marking and re-marking.

Allocate enough time to do each part of the paper. If you have only a short time left at the end with one question to do, spend time on this, in note form if necessary, rather than on polishing up the ones you have already done. You can get no marks for a question if you have written nothing and the ones you have done will not compensate enough. It is important to look at the number of marks alloted to each question. It gives you an idea of how much detail is needed and a guide to how much time it is profitable to spend on that question. Obviously it is foolish to spend a lot of time on a question that has only 5 marks when an essay, for example, has 35.

Do not waste time copying out an answer again. Make sure you spend enough time planning at the beginning; write on alternate lines so that you have space to insert corrections when you check through what you have written.

Leave time for corrections at the end. Make sure you have underlined titles, used inverted commas where required, check spelling and punctuation. Apply a language accuracy check to your written French (see page 171).

Here are two common complaints from examiners. Do not write alternatives above or below the line, leaving the final choice to the examiner. He or she will always mark the first thing that you have written so cross out what is not required. When you are asked to state the number of words used, be accurate and honest. There is usually a penalty for too few or sometimes for too many words. If in doubt, the examiner will count them and you will only have caused irritation.

Presentation is important. With thought and careful planning it should be possible to produce answers that do not have too many crossings out. You will impress an examiner more if your script is easy to read.

SYLLABUS CHECKLISTS AND PAPER ANALYSIS

* Monolingual dictionaries allowed
** Bilingual dictionaries allowed

ASSOCIATED EXAMINING BOARD
A-level and AS-level

Paper number	Duration	% of marks		Covered in Unit
		A level	AS level	
1 Listening, reading and writing	1½ hours	30%	60%	3.3, 4.1, 4.2
2 Reading and writing	2½ hours	30%	–	4.1, 4.2, 4.2, 4.3, 4.4
3 Topics	2½ hours	20%	–	4.1, 5.1
4 Coursework	–	20%	–	6.1, 6.2
5 Oral	20 minutes	20%	40%	3.1
6 Oral	20 minutes	20%	40%	3.1

A-level candidates sit 4 papers: 1, 2, 3 *or* 4, 5 *or* 6.
AS-level candidates sit 2 papers: 1 and 5 *or* 6.

Paper analysis

Paper 1 Listening, reading and writing
Part 1   Listening: 3–4 short items: summary, rank ordering, questions and answers in French, gap filling, true/false statements, completion and correction of sentences.
Part 2   Listening: one longer passage, linked in theme to parts 3 and 4. Questions and answers in English
Part 3   Reading: one passage 200 words, tasks as in part 1, questions in French
Part 4   Writing in French: 100 words, letter, short article, report related to parts 3 and 4

Paper 2 Reading and writing
Part 1   Four to five short passages, tasks as in Paper 1, part 1, in French
Part 2   One longer passage, questions and answers in French; translation of section into English.
Part 3   250 words in French in response to stimulus material, choice from 2 sets of material

Paper 3 Topics
Two essays of 350 words in French, from one of two questions on each of topics studied. 5 topics areas.

Paper 4 Coursework
Four written pieces in French of 700–1000 words, two pieces on each of two topics studied, one piece an in-depth study, the other creative.

Paper 5 Oral   20 minutes (20 minute preparation time)
Section (i) Discussion of stimulus material provided during 20 minute preparation period, choice from set of two
Section (ii) Discussion of material chosen and prepared by candidate
Section (iii) General conversation (A-level only)

Paper 6 Oral   20 minutes (20 minute preparation time)
As in paper 5 but conducted and assessed by centre

UNIVERSITY OF CAMBRIDGE LOCAL EXAMINATIONS SYNDICATE

A-level and AS-level

Paper number	Duration	% of marks		Covered in Unit
		A level	AS level	
Component 1 Speaking	20 minutes	25%	40%	3.1
Component 2 Listening	1 hour	20%	20%	3.3
Component 3 Reading and writing	2½ hours	25%	40%	4.1, 4.2, 4.4
Component 4 Essay in French	1½ hours	10%	–	4.1
Component 5 Coursework	–	20%	20%	6.1, 6.2
Component 6 Texts/Thematic studies	2½ hours	20%	–	5.2
Component 55 Coursework	–	10%	–	6.1, 6.2
Component 66 Texts/Thematic studies	1¼ hours	10%	–	5.2
Component 33 Reading	1 hour	–	20%	4.2

A-level candidates sit 5 or 6 papers: components 1, 2, 3, 4 and *either* 5 *or* 6, *or* 55 and 66.
AS-level candidates sit 3 or 4 papers: components 1, 2 and *either* 3 *or* 33 and 5

Paper analysis

Component 1 Speaking
i) Introduction (3 minutes 5%) and discussion of topic (7–8 minutes 10%) chosen by candidate
ii) General conversation (8–9 minutes 10%)

Component 2 Listening (individual cassette)
Section 1, Part A, a number of short items with variety of exercises: gapped transcript, questions in French, non-verbal responses, e.g. true/false statements, grid filling, etc. Part B, one longer item with questions and answers in French.
Section 2 (A-level only), one longer item with questions and answers in English.

Component 3 Reading and writing
Two French texts, related themes. Tasks: Section 1, non-verbal responses, recognition, manipulation, questions in English. Section 2, comprehension and interpretation tested through questions in French. Summary and comparison of issues raised in both texts tested through a writing task of not more than 140 words in French. Section 3 (A-level only), one English text related to contemporary English society for explanation to a French speaker through questions and answers in French. A guided composition in French drawn from elements of the passage.

Component 4 Essay in French
One essay 250–400 words in French. Six topics areas preset in February of the examination year with one question on each in the Exam.

Component 5 Coursework
Submission of a file of coursework in French totalling 2 000 words approximately.
The total 2 000 words to be made up of either two short pieces of 500 words each and one long piece of 1 000 words or two pieces of 1 000 words. Up to 1 000 words may be based on material studied by the whole class. The remaining 1 000 words must reflect the candidate's own interests.

Component 6 Texts/Thematic studies
Two essays in French chosen from either or both of two sections. Section 1, literary texts, two questions on each of five texts. One question consisting of a context passage followed by questions in French. Section 2, thematic studies. A choice of four themes with three questions on each. Candidates must refer in detail to one named text and to additional material studied.

Component 55 Coursework (1 piece 1 000 words or 2 pieces 500 words)

Component 66 Texts/Thematic studies
(1 question from either texts or thematic studies section)

UNIVERSITY OF LONDON EXAMINATIONS AND ASSESSMENT COUNCIL
A-level and AS-level

Paper number	Duration	% of marks		Covered in Unit
		A level	AS level	
Module 1 Listening*	1 hour	15%	30%	3.3
Module 2 Reading and writing*	1½ hours	15%	30%	4.1, 4.2, 4.4
Module 3 Oral	15 minutes	20%	40%	3.1
Module 4 Oral extension	10 minutes	15%	–	3.1
Module 5 Topics and texts*	2½ hours	20%	–	5.1, 5.2, 6.1, 6.2
Module 6 Writing in registers*	1¼ hours	15%	–	4.1

A-level candidates sit 6 papers: modules 1, 2, 3, 4, 5 and 6.
AS-level candidates sit 3 papers: modules 1, 2 and 3.

Paper analysis

Module 1: Listening
(Individual cassettes)
Questions and answers in French and English; also non-verbal responses

Module 2: Reading and writing
Questions and answers in French and English; non-verbal; continuous writing in French

Module 3: Oral
Discussion of topic chosen by candidate. Assessed by Teacher or External Examiner

Module 4: Oral extension
either **paper 1 General conversation**

or **paper 2 Interpreting** between a French and a non-French speaker

Module 5: Topics and texts

either **paper 1 Essay in French** two essays in French on *either* two topics *or* two texts *or* one topic and one text

or **paper 2 Coursework** extended writing in French on free choice of subject (2 pieces of 1000 words each)

Module 6 Writing in registers
One piece in French from one of three sections a) Creative writing b) Discursive essay c) Work-related assignment

NORTHERN EXAMINATIONS ASSESSMENT BOARD
A-level

Paper number	Duration	% of marks		Covered in Unit
		A level	AS level	
1 Coursework/Culture and Society	–	20%	–	5.1, 5.2, 6.1, 6.2
2 Reading and writing	3 hours	40%	–	4.1, 4.2, 4.3, 4.4, 4.5
3 Listening	1 hour	20%	–	3.3
4 Speaking	15 minutes	20%	–	3.1

A-level candidates sit all 4 papers. NB Paper 1 is *either* coursework *or* a written paper on Culture and Society.

Paper analysis

Paper 1 *Either* internal assessment of coursework

or written paper Culture and Society

Coursework
2 essays totalling approximately 2000 words each based on the study of one work of fiction or non-fiction or one book-based essay plus one based on personal research equivalent in scope to a second book.

Culture and Society
Three sections. Three questions to be answered with a maximum of two from one section.
Section A Questions in French on prescribed literary texts, mainly 20th century.
Section B Questions in English on prescribed literary texts from the 17th century to the present day.
Section C Questions in French on prescribed background topics.

Paper 2 Reading and writing test
Two texts in French of approximately 600–700 words. A variety of language comprehension exercises which will always include i) questions in French ii) translation of an extract from text into English iii) translation of about 80 words from English into French based on one or both the texts iv) a free composition with a choice of letter, narrative, dialogue, discursive, imaginative or descriptive theme.

Paper 3 Listening test
One longer and a number of shorter items. A variety of comprehension questions: questions and answers in English, summary, multiple choice questions, transcription from tape, finding French equivalent from tape of English phrase.

Paper 4 Speaking
20 minutes preparation time for i) role-play ii) reporting task: explanation in French of short English text iii) conversation which could include discussion of books read or films seen by or topics studied by candidate. The former may be drawn from material studied for other parts of the examination.

NORTHERN EXAMINATIONS ASSESSMENT BOARD
AS-level

Paper number	Duration	% of marks		Covered in Unit
		A level	AS level	
Speaking	15 minutes	–	40%	3.1
1 Listening comprehension	1 hour	–	30%	3.3
2 Reading comprehension	2 hours	–	30%	4.2

AS-level candidates sit all 3 papers.

Paper analysis

Speaking
20 minutes preparation time for i) role-play ii) reporting task: explanation in French of short English text iii) conversation which could include discussion of books read or films seen by or topics studied by candidate. The former may be drawn from material studied for other parts of the examination.

Paper 1 Listening comprehension
One longer and a number of shorter items. A variety of comprehension questions: questions and answers in English, summary, multiple choice questions, transcription from tape, finding French equivalent from tape of English phrase.

Paper 2 Reading comprehension
A number of shorter and longer texts. Questions designed to test general and detailed understanding. Questions in English or French, answers in English only.

NORTHERN IRELAND COUNCIL FOR THE CURRICULUM, EXAMINATIONS AND ASSESSMENT
A-level and AS-level

Paper number	Duration	% of marks		Covered in Unit
		A level	AS level	
1 Oral**	15–20 minutes	20%	40%	3.1
2 Listening and Reading	45 minutes	20%	40%	3.3, 4.1, 4.2
3 Reading and Responding	1 hour	10%	20%	4.1, 4.2
4 Writing	2½ hours	30%	–	4.1, 4.3
5 Writing for Vocational Contexts	2½ hours	30%	–	–
6 Literature/Civilisation	2½ hours	20%	–	5.2, 5.3, 5.4
7 Coursework	–	20%	–	6.1, 6.2

A-level candidates sit 5 papers: 1, 2, 3, 4 *or* 5, 6 *or* 7.
AS-level candidates sit 3 papers: 1, 2 and 3.

Paper analysis

Paper 1 Oral
i) Discussion of stimulus material provided in 20 minute preparation time, choice of 1/3
ii) General conversation.

Paper 2 Listening and Reading
Listening comprehension plus mixed-skill exercises in English and French.

Paper 3 Reading and Responding
Reading comprehension plus mixed-skill exercises in French.

Paper 4 Writing
Letter/personal response, plus translation into French, plus translation into English.

Paper 5 Writing for Vocational Contexts
Mixed skill exercises based on stimulus material, e.g. business letter, report or summary from stimuli in French.

Paper 6 Literature/Civilisation
Choice of any two questions to be answered in French.

Paper 7 Coursework
Two extended essays in French of not more than 2000 words in total. Chosen project will form one element of discussion in the general conversation in the Oral Examination.

UNIVERSITY OF OXFORD DELEGACY OF LOCAL EXAMINATIONS

A-level and AS-level

Paper number	Duration	% of marks		Covered in Unit
		A level	AS level	
Unit 1 Work and leisure*	2 hours	25%	50%	3.3, 4.1, 4.2 4.3, 4.4
Unit 2 Contemporary society*	2½ hours	30%	–	3.3, 4.1, 4.2 4.4
Unit 3 Terminal oral*	15 minutes	15%	25%	3.1
Unit 4 Terminal oral*	15 minutes	15%	25%	3.1
Unit 5 Coursework oral*	15 minutes	15%	–	3.1
Unit 6 Coursework*	–	15%	–	5.1, 5.2, 6.1, 6.2
Unit 7 Topic essay*	1½ hours	15%	–	5.1, 5.2

A-level candidates sit 1 of 3 options:
Option A: units 1, 2, 3, 4 and 6
Option B: units 1, 2, 3, 4 and 7
Option C: units 1, 2, 3, 5 and 7
AS-level candidates sit units 1, 3 and 4.

All units are available for modular assessment. This means that after initial registration candidates may take and accumulate units over a period of up to four years (see syllabus for full details).

Paper analysis

Unit 1 Work and leisure
Reading: true/false statements, gap-filling, translation into English of short extract, short summaries, notes. *Listening:* questions in English. *Writing:* letter, report.

Unit 2 Contemporary Society
Reading: matching sentence halves, paraphrase. *Listening:* short summaries, details in French, questions in French, true/false statements, gap-filling. *Writing:* letter.

Unit 3 Terminal oral
Discussion of topic chosen by candidate.

Unit 4 Terminal oral
Extended role-play, ½ hour preparation time

Unit 5 Coursework oral
Sample of tasks during final year, e.g. pair work; role-play; group discussion

Unit 6 Coursework
Writing 1 piece 1000–1200 words or 2 pieces each of 500–700 words in French on literary or non-literary theme

Unit 7 Topic essay
One essay in French, 450–500 words, on literary or non-literary theme

OXFORD AND CAMBRIDGE SCHOOLS EXAMINATIONS BOARD
A-level and AS-level

Paper number	Duration	% of marks[†]		Covered in Unit
		A level	AS level	
Module 1 Listening and speaking I*	1 hour			3.1, 3.3
Module 2 Listening and speaking II*	1 hour			3.1, 3.3
Module 3 Responsive reading I*	1½ hours			4.1, 4.2, 4.3
Module 4 Responsive reading II*	1½ hours			4.2, 4.3, 4.4
Module 5 Writing	2 hours			4.1, 4.3
Module 6 Literature and civilisation*	2½ hours			5.1, 5.2

[†]each module totals 100%

A-level candidates sit all modules.

AS-level candidates sit modules 1, 2 and 3.

All modules are available for modular assessment. This means that after initial registration candidates may take and accumulate modules over a period of up to four years (see syllabus for full details).

Paper analysis

Module 1: Listening and speaking I

Part 1, listening comprehension (individual cassettes) ¾ hour
Questions and answers in French; some non-verbal

Part 2, oral test ¼ hour
Negotiating, role play, choice 1/2, discussion, material chosen in advance from one of three

Module 2: Listening and speaking II

Part 1, listening comprehension (audio, individual cassettes) ¾ hour
As in Module 1 but longer and more complex answers

Part 2, oral test Task: discussion of topic chosen by candidate ¼ hour

Module 3: Responsive reading I

Part 1, comprehension: 1 passage 400 words, 10–12 questions and answers in French. Translation into English of short passage

Part 2, letter or short report (linked to passage above) 140–150 words in French

Module 4: Responsive reading II

Part 1, comprehension one or several passages, questions and answers in French, explanations, comments

Part 2, translation into English, 1 passage 150 words

Module 5: Writing (any 2 of 4)

Part 1, guided writing 250 words in French

Part 2, translation into French 1 passage 200 words

Part 3, free composition I one discursive or argumentative essay in French

Part 4, free composition II one descriptive or argumentative essay in French

Module 6: Literature and civilisation
3 answers in French chosen from either or both parts.

Part 1, literary texts (10–12) (one context, two general questions on each text)

Part 2, civilisation and society (two questions on each of four themes)

SCOTTISH EXAMINATIONS BOARD
Higher grade

Paper number	Duration	Higher Grade	Covered in Unit
1 Reading	1¾ hours	90 marks	4.2, 4.3, 4.4
2 Listening and writing**	1 hour	30 marks	3.3, 4.1
3 Essay*	1¼ hours	40 marks	4.1, 4.2
4 Cloze test	30 minutes	20 marks	4.4
5 Speaking	15 minutes	90 marks	3.1

Higher Grade candidates take all 5 papers.

Paper analysis

Paper 1 Reading
Two passages in French of not more than 1000–1200 words. Questions in English; multiple choice translation of phrases from the text, the best of three to be chosen; translation of short extract without support.

Paper 2 Listening/writing
Section A, give substance in French of 1½–2 minute recording in note form using outline supplied. Section B, write 100–120 words in French expressing views on topic of the tape recording.

Paper 3 Essay
One essay in French of 200–250 words in the form of a letter, dialogue or continuous prose in response to a reading stimulus.

Paper 4 Cloze test
i) Text with ten gaps for completion, choice of three words per gap.
ii) Gapped text to be completed unaided (dictionaries not allowed).

Paper 5 Speaking
i)   Introduction of topic by candidate 10 marks
ii) Discussion of topic with teacher 50 marks
iii) Discussion of book read by candidate 30 marks.

WELSH JOINT EDUCATION COMMITTEE
A-level and AS-level

Paper number	Duration	% of marks		Covered in Unit
		A level	AS level	
A1 Reading comprehension	2½ hours	20%	60 marks	4.2, 4.3
A2 Written French**	3 hours	20%	–	4.1, 4.3, 4.4
A3 Listening comprehension	1 hour	20%	60 marks	3.3
A4 Oral**	15–20 minutes	20%	–	3.1
A5 Literature	2½ hours	20%	–	5.1, 5.2
A6 Extended language**	1½ hours	20%	–	3.1, 5.1, 5.2, 6.1, 6.2
A7 School-based project	–	20%	–	6.1, 6.2
Reading comprehension	1½ hours	–	30 marks	4.2, 4.3
Oral test (a)	10 minutes	–	30 marks	3.1
Oral test (b)**	15–20 minutes	–	60 marks	3.1

A-level candidates take 5 papers: A1, A2, A3, A4 and *either* A5 *or* A6 *or* A7.
AS-level candidates have a choice of two options:
Option 1 = A3, A1 and oral test (a).
Option 2 - A3, Reading comprehension and oral test (b).

Paper analysis

A1 Reading comprehension
2–3 short passages, 1 longer. Questions and answers in English; translation into English/Welsh of part(s) of texts.

A2 Written French
1 short letter 150 words; 1 essay 250 words choice from discursive, analytical, explanatory, descriptive. Either summary in French, 150 words, of English/Welsh text or translation into French of English/Welsh text of 120 words or short report based on statistical material provided in English/Welsh/French.

A3 Listening Comprehension
Short dialogues and news items; one longer interview or talk. Questions and answers in French.

A4 Oral
a) 1 short role-play b) Conversation c) Discussion of one issue related to one of prescribed topics chosen by candidate. ** during preparation period only.

A5 Literature
One context/commentary question answered in English/Welsh. 2 essays each on a different set text. This option also includes a teacher-assessed element of two best essays/commentaries in English/Welsh during upper sixth year.

A6 Extended language
Two essays in French 120-150 words, one on each set text. 3 questions set per text. An oral exposé followed by discussion with external examiner. This option also includes a teacher-assessed element of two oral exposés or two short essays in French on set texts or a mixture of both.

A7 School-based project work
1500 words approximately on an approved subject during upper sixth year. It may consist of one piece or 2-3 shorter pieces on related topics.

Oral Test
a) Conversation about self b) Discussion of one issue related to one of prescribed topics chosen by candidate.

Reading comprehension
2–3 short passages, 1 longer. Questions and answers in English; questions on visual/verbal stimulus

Oral test
a) 1 short role-play b) Conversation c) Discussion of one issue related to one of prescribed topics chosen by candidate. ** during preparation period only.

A-LEVEL FRENCH

In this section:

VOCABULARY

Units in this chapter

1.1 *Dictionaries*
1.2 *Common word patterns*
1.3 *Gender*

1.1 DICTIONARIES

A good dictionary is an essential tool for all language learners. It is worth spending some time and money over your choice. You will need it during language lessons, when working on your own and (depending on the Examination Board), during the exam itself. It is important that you are familiar with using your copy and what it can do for you. Some Boards specify a monolingual dictionary, that is a French–French one as used by native speakers. Others allow the use of a bilingual dictionary (i.e. a French–English, English–French one). Both types of dictionary are useful and ideally you should have both. You can also now obtain French dictionaries on CD-ROM. This would give you all the advantages of rapid searching and quick access.

The very small pocket dictionary that you probably had for GCSE has a very limited use at A-Level. When considering buying a larger dictionary check when it was printed or last revised. Dictionaries very quickly get out of date.

A reliable bilingual dictionary will help with everything you need including translation from English into French. A monolingual one lacks an English–French section but has many other advantages. It will help you to think more in the language since meanings are explained in French. It will help you to write more accurate and appropriate French because you will often be able to use or adapt phrases, descriptions and definitions from the text of the dictionary. It will also give you synonyms and perhaps antonyms (opposites) which are helpful in paraphrasing tasks.

Dictionaries

Collins-Robert English–French, French–English Dictionary 2nd edition 1995 (bilingual)
Concise French Dictionary 1993 Larousse (bilingual)
Dictionnaire du Français 1980 Larousse (monolingual)
Petit Larousse Illustré 1992 Larousse.   Dictionary and encyclopedia (monolingual)
Oxford Hachette French Dictionary on CD-ROM 1995 Oxford
Larousse Thesaurus 2nd edition 1994

CONTENTS OF A DICTIONARY

Preface or Introduction – Avant-propos

This is usually contained in the first few pages. It explains the theory behind the selection of words, their meanings, and the conventions of spelling/ordering of words adopted by the compilers of the dictionary. An explanation of the abbreviations used is often included here also. This section can be very helpful in getting you to know how to use the dictionary.

List of abbreviations – Abbréviations

These are the abbreviations used in the text of the dictionary itself. They may be included in the introduction. The more important ones will be dealt with below. Some dictionaries also have under the heading of 'abbreviations' a list of acronyms, *sigles* in French. More recently, published dictionaries have omitted this kind of list since it gets out of date rapidly. Instead they include the more common acronyms, like HLM (*habitation à loyer modéré)*, within the text of the dictionary itself. You need to be familiar with many of the French acronyms in everyday use.

Phonetic guide to pronunciation – *Système phonétique et transcription*

In table form, this lists the vowels and consonants with their phonetic symbols in square brackets [ ] and examples of pronunciation. A monolingual dictionary might also give the range of spellings that can represent each sound. This can be useful, for example for 'sorting out' the spellings for the four nasal sounds in French. A bilingual dictionary will also have a corresponding section for the sounds of English.

Grammar section

Most dictionaries have a complete list of regular and irregular verbs. Bilingual ones sometimes have a grammar outline. Monolingual dictionaries usually just have a verb list but often deal with some grammatical usage in the text. For example, under the entry *dans* you could find a summary and comparison of the various uses of *dans* and *en* meaning 'in'. Monolingual dictionaries sometimes have lists of prefixes and suffixes used in the construction of words. From these you can see patterns for turning verbs into nouns, nouns into adjectives and for changing the sense of a verb by a prefix. This is a helpful back-up to the Vocabulary and Common Patterns sections of this book.

USING A DICTIONARY

French–English section

The main working part of a dictionary is the alphabetical list of words. To be able to use the dictionary quickly and efficiently you need to know the layout and conventions of this section.

Usually, words are listed together with their plurals or the feminine form if these are irregular or, in some bilingual dictionaries, with the parts of a verb. With verbs some dictionaries refer you by number to an irregular verb list. Next, in square brackets, there is a phonetic transcription of the sound of the word. For example:

cheval, -aux [ʃ(ə)val, o] *faux, fausse* [fo, fos]

Grammatical abbreviations

This is followed by a grammatical abbreviation telling you what part of speech the word is. You will need to be familiar with the following:

English	French
a. – adjective	adj. – *adjectif*
adv. – adverb	adv. – *adverbe*
{n. – noun	n. – *nom* } one or
{s. – substantive	s. – *substantif* } other is used
v.tr.– verb transitive	v.tr.– *verbe transitif*
v.i. – verb intransitive	v.i. – *verbe intransitif*
v. – verb	v. – *verbe*
f.– feminine	f. – *féminin*

m. – masculine   m.– *masculin*
pl. – plural   pl. – *pluriel*

Definitions

Following the abbreviation for the part of speech, there is either a definition of the word, if it is a monolingual dictionary, or an English equivalent in a bilingual one. When definitions are very numerous, they may be divided under Roman numerals (I, II, III etc.) or under numbers (1, 2, 3, etc.). These may again be subdivided under either letters or figures. It saves time when there are many meanings to skim through the main divisions for the most appropriate context for the word you are looking up. Do not just select the first meaning you see on the page. Words with a smaller number of entries are usually just numbered 1, 2, 3, etc. and are much easier to scan. Don't forget that equivalent words given in a dictionary are only approximations and are not necessarily the precise word needed for what you are translating (see section on translation).

Not finding a word

It is helpful initially, if you know from the context whether the word is a noun, adjective or verb. However, if you cannot find it listed, it is possibly the plural of a noun/adjective or, even more likely, the past participle/past historic tense of a verb. In this case, you will have to look through infinitives that start with the first three letters of the word. Failing this consult a list of irregular verbs. Don't forget all the compounds of irregular verbs! Check if there is a prefix to the verb. If the word starts with '*re*' it might just be the prefix of a common verb like *faire* (e.g. *refaire* – to remake, re-do; the past historic of which is *je refis, il refit, ils refirent* etc.).

Using the English–French section

Consulting this section to find the right word is a more hazardous process. There are obvious snags to translating word for word. You will most often want to use the English–French section when doing a translation from English to French. Try to resist this temptation when writing an essay, a letter or a report in French. You will derive more benefit and write more accurately if you get used to using a monolingual dictionary.

If you do have to consult the English–French section, the guidelines mentioned previously should still be followed. In addition:

● Check the meaning in the French–English section. You should get back to the same word.

● Look at the examples given of the word in use. These will give you a better feel for the meaning and you might be able to use or adapt the example phrase. Consulting a monolingual dictionary will give you a further check on the word.

● Look at any abbreviations that follow the word: (v.) is vulgar (pop. – *populaire* in French); (fam.) means the word is familiar, (*fam. familier* in French); (sl.) means slang (arg. – *argot* in French); (pej.) means pejorative or insulting (*péj.* in French). The Collins–Robert dictionary has a grading system of asterisks (from one to three) indicating the degree of offensiveness or familiarity of a word. You should exercise great care in the use of such words. Most of them will rarely be suitable for most of the writing tasks at A-Level. Other abbreviations might indicate technical, medical, scientific usage and so on. Make sure that the word you are choosing is not too technical or restricted for the context.

● Take great care when dealing with English verbs followed by a preposition. The latter can change the meaning of a verb completely. Take the verb 'to run' as an example. French *courir* might be a suitable equivalent in some cases: I ran to catch the bus – *j'ai couru pour attraper l'autobus*, but sentences like 'my car ran into a tree', 'the police ran him in', 'I ran into him yesterday' will all require different verbs in French. A verb like 'run' has a large number of entries, with several sub-sections. When there are a number of prepositional uses listed, it is worth remembering these are listed *alphabetically* by preposition. This can save time when skimming.

Exercices

1 Vérifiez la prononciation des mots suivants. Soulignez les mots de même prononciation.
- (a) vert, verre, vers
- (b) pour, pur, peur
- (c) sûr, sur, sœur
- (d) fait, fée, fête
- (e) désert, dessert, des serres
- (f) foie, foi, fois
- (g) volet, voler, volée
- (h) veille, vieille, viol
- (i) thon, ton, temps
- (j) feindre, fendre, fondre

2 Parmi les mots suivants lesquels riment l'un avec l'autre.
- (a) rhum, rhume, somme
- (b) alcool, sol, colle
- (c) femme, madame, thème
- (d) dent, dans, dont

3 Vérifiez dans un dictionnaire la prononciation des mots suivants:

solennel	le Christ
évidemment	album
condamner	Adam
baptême	Degas
Jésus Christ	équateur

4 (i) Vérifiez le genre des mots suivants
(ii) Employez-les dans une phrase pour en faire ressortir la signification.

tour	poste
mort	poêle
mode	voile
critique	Champagne
vase	champagne

5 Check the meanings of the following which contain particular uses of common verbs. What would you write down in French and English as a reminder of the phrase? (e.g. en vouloir à quelqu'un?)
- (a) Ah! Ce prof, il m'agaçait continuellement, *il m'en voulait,* hein.
- (b) Quand il nous a vus, *il s'est sauvé.*
- (c) *Je tiens* beaucoup à vous voir ce soir.
- (d) Cet ouvre-boîte, je ne sais pas comment *m'en servir.*
- (e) On peut *se passer* d'eau durant trois jours mais on peut *se passer de* nourriture durant trois semaines.
- (f) Ah, *je m'en doutais* qu'il le ferait!
- (g) *Il s'est privé* de cigarettes pour toute une semaine.
- (h) Pour le physique *il tient* de son père.
- (i) Est-ce que vous *croyez* en Dieu?
- (j) *Il ne croit plus au* Père Noël
- (k) Ce nouveau prof, *qu'en pensez-vous?*
- (l) Depuis qu'elle est partie *je pense* souvent à elle.

6 Vérifiez l'accord de l'adjectif dans les exemples suivants:

une chemise *bleu marine*
un corsage *mauve*
une jupe *bleu clair*
des chaussettes *marron*
de l'eau *frais*
une tranche *épais*

7 Vérifiez le sens des phrases qui suivent:

(a) Son doigt avait été sectionné
(b) Il aimait regarder cette dame à la dérobée
(c) J'ai trouvé une bague de diamant
(d) On va déguster ces huîtres
(e) Il va rester définitivement en France
(f) Il faut observer les convenances
(g) Au café j'ai demandé une blonde
(h) Les étudiants donnent souvent des leçons particulières
(i) Où est-ce qu'il a suivi sa formation?
(j) J'ai suivi avec intérêt l'exposé de cette jeune Suédoise
(k) Je ne me suis pas rendu compte des difficultés qu'il m'avait signalées
(l) C'est une jeune fille très sensible
(m) C'est un garçon très sérieux
(n) Il m'a eu. Il m'a joué un sale tour
(o) J'ai un chien dressé pour chercher les truffes
(p) Il faut que je me recycle

Anecdote: The following ingenious translation was offered in the old GCE exam for the French phrase, *Il était assis au fond de la pièce à l'ombre* – 'He was fond enough of his bit in the dark.' How do you think the candidate arrived at this interpretation? What better translation could you find?

8 Même jeu. Trouvez un mot français pour le mot anglais en italique

(a) What are *his motives*?
(b) An *experienced* journalist
(c) A *demonstration* in front of the town hall
(d) A *disaster area*
(e) A *sensible* idea
(f) He's *going on a course* in Lyon
(g) *I draw* my money on Fridays
(h) It gives me *vertigo*
(i) I have nothing to say *on this issue*
(j) I've always kept a *diary*
(k) How do you hope to become a *photographer* if you haven't got a *camera*?

9 Trouvez un verbe ou une phrase pour traduire les mots en italiques:

(a) *Carry* straight on
(b) The coach *carries* 30 passengers
(c) The plan is difficult to *carry out*
(d) I was *carried away* with excitement
(e) I've *run out* of sugar
(f) I *ran into* him in the supermarket
(g) He was *run over* by a lorry
(h) Don't *run away* with the idea that you can *run* this place

(i) Is the engine *running*?

(j) He is *running* as town councillor

(k) I'll *look after* you

(l) I'll *look into* it

(m) I'll *look in* tomorrow

(n) She *looks sad*

(o) *I look up to* him

(p) She's a *good-looker*

(q) It *looks like* rain

10 Traduisez en anglais le passage suivant en faisant ressortir:

(a) un style plutôt familier;

(b) un style soigné.

Marc était au restaurant avec son amie/son flirt/sa poule Annie. Ils avaient bien mangé/bouffé/s'étaient bien nourris et Annie avait consommé/avalé/bu deux bouteilles de gros rouge/pinard/vin de table. Elle était maintenant complètement paf/ivre/soûle et, soudain, elle a commencé à gueuler/hurler/parler très fort. Enfin le restaurateur leur a demandé de partir/décamper/ficher le camp. Ils ont trouvé ça rigolo/marrant/amusant.

11 Comment ça s'écrit en français et en anglais?

Vérifiez l'orthographe des mots suivants en soulignant les mots anglais:

example – exemple

character – caractère

miroir – mirror

adresse – address

apartment – appartement

utensil – ustensile

crystal – cristal

alcool – alcohol

eccentric – excentrique

millionnaire – millionaire

contrat – contract

agression – aggression

12 Inventifs

Il y a quelques centaines de mots composés en français. Ils s'appellent des inventifs. Une grande partie de ceux-ci sont composés d'un verbe et d'un nom. Par exemple *un tire-bouchon, un porte-monnaie, un essuie-mains*. Elargissez votre vocabulaire en choisissant ci-dessous dans la première liste un verbe et ensuite un nom qui convient dans la deuxième liste. Attention, un verbe peut s'associer à plusieurs noms. La plupart des inventifs de ce type s'écrivent avec un tiret mais quelquefois ils forment un seul mot. Ils sont aussi presque tous du genre masculin. Vérifiez la signification et le genre des mots à l'aide d'un dictionnaire. Attention, ne pas fabriquer des noms trop inventifs!

1	**2**
pare – porte – coupe – casse – garde – cache – chasse – gratte – essuie – passe – lève – ouvre – cure – lance – chauffe – presse – tourne	– croûte – partout – robe – brise – boîte – papier – vis – ciel – feuille – eau – nez – noisettes – pierres – chasse – fou – citron – pipe – cou – parole – pieds – tête – bonheur – voix – neige – vélos – temps – bébé – œil – monnaie – fenêtre – tôt/tard – sexe

1.2 COMMON WORD PATTERNS

Learning words and their meanings is an ongoing process. We continue to meet words in English that we haven't seen or heard before. Some of these are committed to memory straight away, others are forgotten completely. Some will look familiar when you meet them again but you can't quite remember what they mean. You may find concrete words (i.e. words standing for objects) easier to memorize because you have a picture in your mind to go with them. Abstract words (i.e. ones standing for an idea) are often more difficult to store in your mind. They are best remembered when associated with a word you already know.

Broadly speaking, words in English and in foreign languages fall into three categories: **active words** (i.e. words you can understand straight away and use in writing and speaking); **passive words** (i.e. ones that you can recognize when you see or hear them but that you cannot retrieve instantly from your memory store); and **deducible words** (i.e. that you can work out the meaning of because of what you already know of the language). There is probably a gradual movement of words from the third category towards the first category, depending on how often you use or meet them. The gradual assimilation process in language learning already mentioned also plays its part.

RECORDING AND LEARNING VOCABULARY

It is essential to have a vocabulary book in which you write down new words as you meet them. Write in two columns (one for the word and one for its meanings) so that you can cover up one side of the page and try to recall one and the other. Be selective in what you write down. Some words are more commonly used than others. Keep one half of the book for words that you may only need to recognize, the other for words that you are more likely to need to use. This decision is not always easy to make on your own. Your teacher is the best guide. It helps to write a short phrase illustrating the meaning, particularly with abstract or idiomatic uses. For example:

> *que de* – what a lot of
> *Que de bruit!* – What a lot of noise!

It is helpful to put *un* or *une* in front of nouns so that you learn the gender at the same time. You could also try writing masculine words in blue and feminine ones in red. You also need to note any irregularities in plurals or feminine endings and with verbs the group it belongs to together with the past participle, if this is odd. Write clearly because your visual impression is a part of the memorizing process. Record words on a regular basis and also read through your vocabulary book often, preferably getting a friend to test you. If you highlight words that you have difficulty with, every time you read through your vocabulary book your eye will be caught by these and you will be doing a bit of automatic revision.

How do we remember French words and what they mean? Some are easy because they look just like the English word and have roughly the same meaning. These are called **cognates**. Others are deceptive because they look like the English word but have a very different meaning. The term *faux amis* – 'false friends' has been coined for these (*French False Friends*, C W E Kirk-Greene, Routledge and Kegan Paul). Other words contain a clue within them. If for example you already know the word *chaud* you might guess that *chaleureux* has got something to do with it. Some words you will remember because of some peculiarity or funny association. The word *poubelle* – dustbin, is one of these and *quincaillerie* – ironmonger's shop, sounds a bit like its meaning. *Caoutchouc*, meaning the substance 'rubber', is not as easily forgotten as its spelling! You might even remember some words because of where you have written them on the page! One thing is certain: the more words you learn, the more you will be able to recognize and guess at others.

Here are some more strategies for learning vocabulary:

Opposites

Learning words as pairs of opposites can also be effective. You may find both words in the same text but more often you will have to look one of them up. A monolingual dictionary is useful for this purpose. You will soon find that there are often several possibilities for the opposite of a word. Adjectives have the widest range; verbs and nouns fewer possibilities. Here are some examples you are likely to meet.

Adjectives

bon – mauvais, meilleur – pire, vrai – faux, dur – tendre/mou, pareil – différent, naturel – artificiel, absurde – logique, modéré – excessif, raisonnable – exagéré, courageux – lâche, faible – fort, supérieur – inférieur.

Nouns

espoir – désespoir, puissance – faiblesse, vérité – mensonge, augmentation – réduction, hausse – baisse, patronat – ouvriers, cadres – exécutants, le bien – le mal, les riches – les pauvres, les nantis – les démunis (the haves and have nots).

Verbs

Perdre – trouver, se rappeler – oublier – augmenter – diminuer, avancer – reculer, conserver – jeter, parler – se taire, économiser – gaspiller

Adverbs

Mal – bien, plus – moins, peu – beaucoup.

Check the meanings of the above if you don't recognize them. Check the feminine forms of the adjectives (and the genders of the nouns). Find a phrase to use them in.

Word families

Grouping words around a theme, or building word families, can also be a helpful memorizing process. There is some evidence to suggest that we store words in our own language in fields or areas of meaning (*Words in the Mind*, J Aitchison, Blackwell). Therefore, it would seem sensible to use this existing pattern to create word families in another language. For example, words to do with politics:

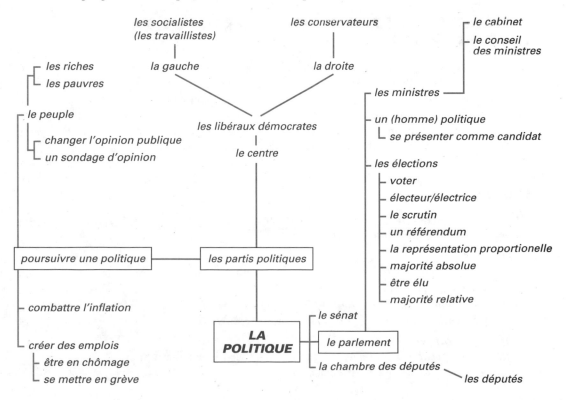

The previous example is a fairly detailed one. You might find that a simplified version works better for you. You could also try colour-coding parts of your diagram.

Another variation of family grouping is synonym building. This can help you to think of alternative words to use instead of always sticking to the same word or expression. (*See also* pages 212–213.)

Adjective 'size'

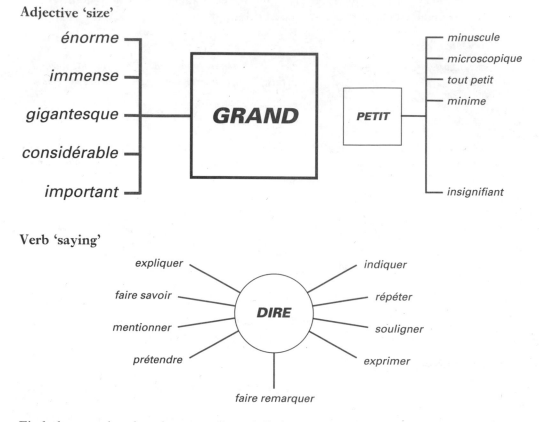

Verb 'saying'

Find phrases using these in a monolingual dictionary. A useful reference book: *Dictionnaire Bordas des synonymes et antonymes*, Bordas, 1988.

COMMON PATTERNS OF WORDS IN FRENCH AND ENGLISH

Knowing and recognizing patterns of words in French, and their similarities with English ones, can be a great help in vocabulary building and give you access to more words. It gives you a big advantage in reading comprehension because you can work out meanings more easily. It helps in writing because you can deduce and generate words yourself. It also helps with paraphrase and language exercises, helping you to manipulate words with greater facility. The beginnings and endings of words (i.e. the prefixes and suffixes) are the keys to this skill.

Prefixes

❶ Prefix: *'ré-'*, *'re-'*, or *'r-'* This changes the meaning of many verbs to 'again', 'once more' or 'back'. Here are some examples:

voir – revoir:
J'espère la revoir cet été – I hope to see her again this summer

s'insérer – se réinsérer:
Après cinq années en prison il est difficile de se réinsérer dans la société
After 5 years in prison it is difficult to readapt to social life

appeler – rappeler:
Je ne me rappelle plus son nom – I can't remember his name any more
Rappelle-moi demain – Call me back tomorrow

avoir – ravoir:
Est-ce que je peux ravoir mon livre? – Can I have my book back?

② **Prefix: '*de-*' or '*dé-*'** This has the same value as the 'un-' prefix in English but also of 'de-' and 'dis-'.

Déboutonnez votre chemise – Unbutton your shirt
J'ai vite défait le paquet – I quickly undid the parcel
La Lozère est un département très dépeuplé – The Lozère is a very depopulated 'département'
Il faut désarmer tous les pays du monde – We must disarm all the countries of the world

Sometimes the *de*-prefix makes up a pair of opposites (e.g. *faire – défaire*, 'do up' – 'undo' *attacher – détacher*, 'attach' – 'detach'). Or it can give a new meaning to a word (e.g. *détourner un avion* – 'hijack a plane').

③ **Prefix: '*in-*' and also '*ir-*' and '*il-*'** These are the equivalents of English 'un-', 'in-' and 'non-'.
Here are some examples of '*in-*':
égal – inégal, equal – unequal
cassable – incassable, breakable – unbreakable
capable – incapable, capable – incapable
attendu – inattendu, expected – unexpected
connu – inconnu, known – unknown
direct – indirect, direct – indirect
visible – invisible, visible – invisible

Note
'*in*' + vowel is pronounced as '*ine*' (as in '*mine*', '*fine*')
'*in*' + consonant is pronounced as '*in*' (as in '*vin*', '*pin*')

Here are some examples of '*ir-*' and '*il-*':
réel – irréel, real – unreal
légal – illégal, legal – illegal
logique – illogique, logical – illogical
régulier – irrégulier, regular – irregular

④ **Prefix: '*mal-*'** The equivalent of English 'dis-', 'un-' and 'mis-':
honnête – malhonnête, honest – dishonest
heureux – malheureux, happy – unhappy
des enfants maltraités – ill-treated children

Note also *content – mécontent, se fier à – se méfier de* (mistrust)

⑤ **Prefix: '*pre-*'** Equivalent of English 'for-', 'pre-'. Here are some examples:
Il est impossible de prédire l'heure de son arrivée – forecast, foretell
On n'avait pas prévu toutes les difficultés – We hadn't foreseen all the difficulties
Un préjugé c'est une opinion préconçue – Prejudice is a preconceived opinion

⑥ **Prefixes: '*sur-*' and '*sous-*'** These work just like the English 'under-', 'over-':
la surproduction
les régions surpeuplées
les pays sous-développés

Note also
souligner – underline, stress
Un film russe avec sous-titres – A Russian film with subtitles

⑦ **Prefix: '*mi-*'** Equivalent of half, part. Here are some examples:
la mi-temps dans un match – half-time
s'arrêter à mi-chemin – half-way
répondre à mi-voix – in a low voice, whisper
les yeux mi-clos – half-closed eyes

Suffixes

1 **Suffix: '-tion'** There are a large number of words in French and English with this suffix. Many have more or less the same meaning. They are **all feminine gender words**. For example:

situation – position – compétition – variation – intention – contradiction

Others don't have exactly the same spelling or suffix in English:
traduction – translation
punition – punishment
réparation – repairs

Others have different meanings to the word they look like in English:
manifestation – demonstration
formation – training
revendication – claim, demand
Les revendications des manifestants étaient légitimes. Ils demandaient une augmentation de salaire – The claims of the demonstrators were well-founded. They were asking for a wage increase.

2 **Suffix: '-té' and '-tié'** Roughly the equivalents of '-ty' in English but also of '-ness' and '-ship'. For example:
beau – beauté
solidaire – solidarité
égal – égalité
pauvre – pauvreté
libre – liberté
sain – santé
gai – gaieté
ami – amitié
propre – propreté

Note
(a) *propriété* means property
(b) words with the *'-té'*, *'-tié'* suffixes, of abstract meaning, are all **feminine**

3 **Suffix: '-eur'** This comprises a large group of words to do with size, colour, human and abstract qualities. They are mostly of feminine gender. They have no single corresponding suffix in English. For example:
blanc – blancheur
grand – grandeur
chaud – chaleur
haut – hauteur
rouge – rougeur
profond – profondeur
la couleur – une odeur

Note
le bonheur – happiness
le malheur – unhappiness
un honneur – an honour

Also in *'-eur'* there are a large number of words denoting occupations and professions, mainly of masculine gender:
un employeur
un professeur
un producteur (films, industry)
un metteur en scène (producer, theatre)
un réalisateur (producer, television)

Look up the section on gender for the **feminine** equivalents of these.

4 **Suffix: '*-er*'** This is another common suffix denoting occupation, often the equivalent of '-er' in English. For example:
épicier
policier
banquier
hôtelier
cuisinier
fermier

5 **Suffix: '*-able*'** This makes a verb into an adjective. Here are some examples:
faire – faisable
imaginer – imaginable
manger – mangeable
laver – lavable
réparer – réparable
trouver – trouvable (introuvable)

Note
potable – drinkable
eau potable – drinking water

6 **Suffix: '*-ette*'** This ending indicates a smaller version of something and is always feminine.
For example:
un cigare – une cigarette
une fille – une fillette
une tarte – une tartelette
une fourche (gardening) – *une fourchette* (eating)
un banc – une banquette (seat in train, car)

Note
un banquet – banquet (ceremonial dinner)

7 **Suffix: '*-eux*' '*-ieux*'** These suffixes are equivalent to the English '-ous'. Here are some examples:
mystérieux
courageux
sérieux
dangereux
furieux
contagieux
précieux
montagneux
religieux

8 **Suffix: '*-aire*'** This is the English '-ar' and '-ary':
populaire
un salaire
vulgaire
nécessaire
une secrétaire
extraordinaire
élémentaire
primaire
un anniversaire
un millionnaire

9 **Suffix: '*-que*'** This is the English '-c', '-ck', '-cal', and '-k':
automatique
classique
une attaque

une remarque
économique
logique
une banque
plastique
romantique
tragique
une brique
physique

⑩ Suffix: '-er' These verbs in French are '-ate' verbs in English:
faciliter
exagérer
imiter
compliquer
faciliter
abdiquer
améliorer
compenser

⑪ Suffix: '-e' This ending in French is the consonant ending (no '-e')in English:
le calme
modeste
une insulte
un adulte
moderne
une lampe
le pilote
rapide
une plante

⑫ Suffix: '-ant' This present participle ending in French is the '-ing' in English:
charmant
choquant
dégoûtant
intéressant
préoccupant (worrying)
provocant
amusant
insultant
brillant

⑬ Suffix: '-ment' This adverbial ending in French is the '-ly' in English:
absolument
rarement
sûrement
généralement
gravement
énormément
sincèrement
complètement
immédiatement

Note (*see also* page 104)
évident – évidemment
constant – constamment
récent – récemment
fréquent – fréquemment

Look up words you do not recognise and write a phrase using them.

Near cognates

These are words that come from the same root in both languages but have acquired a French or an English 'look' as the case may be:

❶ French *'gu-'*, English 'w-' (a small group):
la guerre
Guillaume (*le prénom*)
une guêpe – wasp
guetter – keep watch, look out
un guerrier – warrior

❷ Initial *'e-'* in French, initial 's' in English:
école
étable
étage (*d'un bâtiment*)
étudiant
étrangler
estomac
étranger
état
épeler – spell

The French word might be a bit 'buried' in the English one. Can you work out what the following mean?
regarder le petit écran
Il fait si chaud! On va étouffer ici
une carte à grande échelle
Marie-Antoinette est morte sur l'échafaud
l'écureuil est un animal très agile.

❸ *'-êt'*, *'-ât'*, *'ôt'* in French, '-est', '-aste', 'ost' in English:
une bête
une tempête
un hôte
la crête (*d'une montagne*)
la pâte (*dentifrice*)
la hâte
le mât (*d'un bateau*)
une fête

Having pointed out a number of parallels between French and English words, the following stumbling blocks should be noted:

❹ Nouns
un psychologue – psychologist
un scientifique – scientist
un sociologue – sociologist
un psychiatre – psychiatrist
un photographe – photographer
un homme politique – politician
un géographe – geographer

❺ Adjectives
pessimiste – pessimistic
optimiste – optimistic
évocateur – evocative
réaliste – realistic
bénéfique – beneficial
bénévole (*un groupe bénévole*) – voluntary group
conservateur (*le parti politique*) – conservative
le parti travailliste – the Labour party

⑥ Attention aux faux amis suivants:

faire *un stage* = do a course of training (usually connected with your job or profession. But 'to go on the stage' = commencer à faire du théâtre, devenir acteur/actrice.

il *prétend* savoir jouer de la guitare = he claims he can play the guitar.

But 'to pretend to do something' = faire semblant de faire quelque chose.

avoir une licence = have a university degree. But 'to have a driving licence' = avoir le permis de conduire.

Also 'être *licencié* ' = to be made redundant.

la location de vélos = bike hire. But 'I can't locate the hotel on this map' = Je n'arrive pas à trouver/repérer l'hôtel sur cette carte.

une manifestation sur la grande place = a demonstration on the main square. But 'I will demonstrate how it works' = je vais vous montrer/expliquer comment cela fonctionne.

une voiture *d'occasion* = a second hand car. 'I drive occasionally' = de temps en temps je conduis/je prends le volant.

Assister à un match = to be at the match and 'il y avait une grande *assistance*' = there was a big audience. 'Assister' can mean to assist but more in the sense of 'looking after', 'caring for', e.g. assister les pauvres and l'Assistance publique = health and social security services.

A very useful book that deals with lookalike words and gives useful information about France is: P. Thody and H. Evans, *Faux amis and keys words A Dictionary Guide to French Language, Culture and Society through Lookalikes and Confusables*, Paperback edition 1995.

Exercices

1 Cherchez dans la partie encadrée le contraire des adjectifs suivants:

grand	premier	vrai	mauvais	fort	sec
bon	sale	faible	tendre	ancien	propre
dur	pauvre	long	petit	vieux	court
sage	privé	doux	méchant	riche	intelligent
nouveau	jeune	stupide	dernier	faux	public

2 Dites la même chose d'une façon différente. Par exemple:
Ce n'est pas correct – C'est incorrect
Il n'est pas content – Il est mécontent
(a) Il n'est pas honnête
(b) Cette marque n'est pas connue en France
(c) Cette occasion n'est pas ordinaire
(d) Cette date n'est pas possible
(e) Il n'est pas heureux
(f) Cette information n'est pas utile
(g) Ce rendez-vous n'est pas convenable
(h) Je ne suis pas optimiste
(i) Cette viande n'est pas tendre
(j) Ce n'est pas bon marché

3 Complétez ces phrases:
le bonheur et le
en hiver et en
grand-père et
en bas et en

entrer et
le pour et le
le chaud et le
le matin et l(e)
mon neveu et ma
jour et
faire et
une photo en noir et
le bien et le
le début et la
frère et
arriver et
question de vie ou de
pile ou

4 Dites le contraire sans employer le négatif:
  (a) Je regarde peu la télévision
  (b) Je vais quelquefois à Paris
  (c) C'est loin d'ici
  (d) J'adore les frites
  (e) Il fait déjà jour
  (f) A la fin de l'après-midi
  (g) Cette eau est pure
  (h) Au premier étage
  (i) Le chef est de mauvaise humeur
  (j) Cette fourchette est propre

5 Without using a dictionary, make a collection of French words ending in '-tion' and -ion that have the same spelling as their English counterparts. Find at least one for as many letters as possible of the alphabet. You can leave out B, K, W, X, Y and Z. Score double marks for H, J, U. Do this with a friend or make it a team game and compare your lists afterwards. Score nought for getting the same word as the other team. Check the meanings in a dictionary.

6 Do the same thing with words that end in '-ty' in English and '-té' in French (e.g. *éternité* – eternity, *rapidité* – rapidity).

7 Repeat the same activity, this time with '-er' verbs that closely resemble English verbs (e.g. *danser* – dance, *changer* – change, *avancer* – advance).

8 'Le chat de ma tante' Use one of two phrases: *Le chat de ma tante est adorable/ bilingue/charmant* or *Ma tante a un chat adorable/bilingue/charmant* (the second one practises position of adjectives) and work through the alphabet. You can leave out very difficult letters. This works well as a team game. You must be ready to justify the adjective used (e.g. *le chat de ma tante est affecté parce qu'il prend toujours ses repas dans la salle à manger*).

9 Other variations on this are: *Le chat de ma tante sait* + verb (e.g. **arranger** *les fleurs*); or + adverb (e.g. *Le chat de ma tante chante* **affreusement**).

10 Combien des appareils cités ci-dessous est-ce que vous possédez dans votre maison? Faites trois listes:
  (a) Ceux qui sont indispensables
  (b) Ceux qui sont assez utiles
  (c) Comparez votre liste avec celle de votre voisin

Un adoucisseur d'eau, un aspirateur, une cafetière électrique, un congélateur, un couteau électrique, une cuisinière électrique, une essoreuse, un fer à coiffer, un fer à repasser, un flash électronique, une perceuse électrique, une friteuse électrique, un gaufrier, un grille-pain automatique, une hotte de cuisine, une huche à pain, un lave-vaisselle, une machine à coudre, une machine à éplucher les pommes de terre, une machine à tricoter, un mixer à main, un moulin à café électrique, un pèse-personne, un radio-réveil, un rasoir électrique, un réfrigérateur, une rôtissoire électrique, une tondeuse à gazon, une trancheuse électrique, une tronçonneuse, un four à micro-ondes, un sèche-linge, un magnétoscope, une caméra vidéo, un lecteur de disques compacts à laser, un micro-ordinateur, une chaîne hi-fi, un lave-linge, une baignoire à remous, un traitement de texte, une imprimante.

1.3   GENDER

Knowing whether a noun is masculine or feminine in French, is one of the more difficult things to acquire for someone who has not learned the language from an early age. Gender has no real connection with sex. Nouns simply fall into one of two groups in French. Some languages have a third group called neuter nouns. There is no logic to these divisions. In English we lost these distinctions a long time ago. However, we still tend to think of ships and countries as feminine. You would say 'Britain and her (or possibly 'its') sovereignty', but never 'his' sovereignty. There are some gender oddities in French:

(a) *Pierre est **une** personne que je connais très bien* (*Personne* is always feminine).

(b) *Mon père a été **la** victime d'une attaque*

(c) *Il n'est pas **la** dupe de tout le monde*

(d) *Mme Cresson était **le** premier Premier ministre féminin*

(e) *Un soldat* usually performs the duty of *une sentinelle*

The best way to remember gender is to learn it with the noun; by putting *le* or *la*, *un* or *une* into your memory with the word or by combining the noun with an adjective when you learn it. (e.g. *de l'eau chaude.*) The next best thing is is to make up some basic rules together with the most common exceptions.

BASIC RULES

Gender by meaning

Feminine	Exceptions
❶ Names of countries and rivers ending in a mute '-*e*' *la Pologne, la Russie, la Loire*	*le Mexique, le Rhône*
❷ Most abstract nouns: *la peur, la foi* (faith), *la douleur*	*le courage, le vice*
❸ Names of females: *une nièce, une grand-mère, une chatte, une chienne*	*un ange* – angel, *un témoin* – witness, are always masculine Also *écrivain, auteur, médecin, professeur* etc., which have been traditionally male occupations

	Masculine	Feminine

4 Names of countries and rivers not ending
in mute '*-e*':
le Brésil
le Canada
le Cher (river)
le Loir (river)

5 Names of trees, minerals, and metals:

	Masculine	Feminine
	le chêne – oak	*la bauxite*
	le pin	
	le sable	
	le charbon – coal	
	le cuivre – copper	

6 Seasons, months, days of week, points of compass, and decimal weights and measures:
le printemps
le mois de janvier
le lundi
le nord
un kilo
un gramme

Gender by derivation

	Masculine	Feminine

1 Words and expressions not originally nouns:
un oui
un non
un pourboire
le savoir-faire
un devoir

2 Nouns from verbs not ending in mute '*-e*':

Nouns from verbs ending in
mute '*-e*':

Masculine	Feminine
un refus	*la marche*
un emploi	*la visite*
le choix	*la chasse*
un espoir	

3 Compound nouns made up of two nouns take the gender of the first noun. The great
majority of these are masculine:

But

Masculine	Feminine
un chou-fleur	*une basse-cour* – back yard
un chef-d'œuvre	*une porte-fenêtre* – French window

4 Compound words made up of verb + noun. These are all masculine and there are
many of them:
un tourne-vis
un tire-bouchon
un pare-soleil – sun-visor
un parapluie – works on the same principle, as does *un parachute*.
The verb is *parer* to 'ward off', 'protect from'

Gender by ending

1 All words with the suffix '*-tion*' are **feminine**. There are very many of these:
une installation
la composition
la position
etc.

❷ Nearly all words ending in '-*té*', and '-*tié*' are **feminine** if they are abstract in meaning:

une amitié
la santé,
la propriété
la capacité
etc.
These are numerous.
Exception: *le traité*

❸ Nearly all words ending in '-*eur*' are **feminine** if **abstract** (do not refer to an object):

la couleur
la froideur
la grosseur
la profondeur

Exceptions

un honneur
le bonheur
le malheur

Gender pairs

Masculine	Feminine
❶ '-*eur*' (role or occupation)	'-*euse*, '-*trice*'
un acteur	*une actrice*
un chanteur	*une chanteuse*
un instituteur	*une institutrice*
un inspecteur	*une inspectrice*
un vendeur	*une vendeuse*
❷ '-*er*', '-*ier*'	'-*ère*', '-*ière*'
le plancher	*la lumière*
le papier	*la misère* – poverty
un fermier	*une fermière*

Exceptions

le caractère	
le mystère	*la mer*

Masculine	Feminine
❸ '-*eau*', '-*il*'	'-*elle*', '-*ille*'
le chapeau	*une chapelle*
le bateau	*une rondelle* – slice
un château	*une fille*
un fil (de coton)	
le cil – eyelash	

Exceptions

	une eau
	la peau – skin

Masculine	Feminine
❹ '-*t*'	'-*tte*', '-*te*'
le mot	*la patte* – paw
le pot	*la pâte*
le chocolat	*une allumette*
le sujet	*la crête*
le but	*la planète*
une capote	
une anecdote	

Exceptions

un vote	*la forêt*
le pilote	*la dent*
un antidote	*la plupart*
	la part

5 '-c'

le lac
le bac – ferry or exam
un flic
un choc

'-che'

la tâche – task, job
la cloche

Exceptions

le manche – handle
un reproche – reproach, blame

6 '-age' (as a suffix)
le village
le courage
un reportage

'-age' (not a suffix)
la cage
la rage
la page

Exception

un âge

7 '-oir'
le miroir
un mouchoir
un couloir – corridor

'-oire'
la gloire
une histoire

Exceptions

un laboratoire
un observatoire,
le conservatoire
un ivoire – ivory

8 '-é'
le dé – dice
le marché
la matinée

-ée'
une journée
une année

Exceptions

le lycée
le musée

9 '-on'
un bâton
le son
le béton – concrete
le ton
un ballon

-onne'
une couronne
une consonne

10 '-acle', '-ecle'
un miracle
un obstacle

***

Exception

un cercle

une débâcle – disaster, rout

11 '-ège'
le piège – trap
un collège
le cortège

***

12 '-ème'
le poème
le thème
le problème

***

Exception

la crème

⑬ *'-o'*   ***
le numéro
un zéro
un écho

⑭ *'-ou'*   ***
un caillou – pebble
un fou
un trou
un chou

⑮ ***   *'-esse'*
la paresse
une ivresse – drunkenness
la messe – mass, religious service
une masse – weight

⑯ ***   *'-ie'*
la maladie
une colonie
une tragédie
la folie

Exceptions

un incendie
le génie – genius, spirit

⑰ ***   *-ine'*
la colline
une mine
la cantine

⑱ ***   *'-une'*
la fortune
la rancune – grudge, rancour

⑲ ***   *'-ure'*
la nature
une voiture
la couture – dressmaking

⑳ ***   *-ance', '-anse'*
la vengeance
la chance
la danse

㉑ ***   *'-ence', '-ense'*
la prudence
la défense
la décence

Exception

le silence

㉒ *'-isme'*   ***
le communisme
le socialisme
le réalisme
le romantisme

The above guidelines to gender are designed as **basic reference points**. The main endings have been covered together with those exceptions it is felt you are likely to meet. You should note other exceptions as you come across them.

Words that change their meaning according to gender

There are about a hundred of these in French, of which you are likely to meet only a small number. Some common words are included but very often the other word in the pair is fairly rare. For example, I learned many years ago that *la mousse* means 'moss' but that *le mousse* means 'cabin boy'. It wasn't until recently that I read in a northern French newspaper '*Le mousse perdu d'un bateau dans la Manche*'. I don't think I had ever come across the word before in print let alone in spoken French. Here are some of the commonest of these words. It is worth remembering that even if you get the gender wrong it would hardly be noticed in speech and in most cases the context makes the meaning clear enough.

Masculine	Feminine
le livre – book	*la livre* – pound (money, weight)
le tour (de France) – round trip	*la Tour Eiffel* – tower
le mode d'emploi (pour les médicaments)	*la mode (pour les vêtements)*
un poste de télévision	*la poste où on achète des timbres etc.*
un critique (la personne dont le métier est de critiquer les livres, films etc.)	*une critique c'est le livre ou l'article dans lequel on écrit ses jugements*
un mémoire (une note ou un rapport sur q.c.)	*la mémoire (la faculté de se rappeler i.e. On a une bonne ou une mauvaise mémoire)*
un somme (petit sommeil)	*la somme (qu'il faut payer)*
le vase (dans lequel on met des fleurs)	*la vase (ce qui se trouve souvent au fond des lacs ou rivières)* – mud, silt
le physique – physical appearance	*la physique* – physics
le voile – veil *(Les Musulmanes le portent)*	*la voile* – sail
le poêle – stove	*la poêle* – frying pan

GRAMMAR

Units in this chapter

As already mentioned in the section on aims, the grammar that you learned for GCSE should provide a sound basis for what you need at A and AS-Level with two important considerations: (a) many grammar points, only needed previously to be recognised and understood for reading and listening, now come into active use for speaking and writing; (b) the range of grammatical considerations needs to be expanded and in some cases extended, particularly with verbs.

The knowledge and understanding of grammar that you gained for GCSE was probably restricted by the use you needed to make of it. A lot of language was needed for transactional purposes. For example, the *je, tu* and *vous* parts of the verb were used more frequently in speaking and writing than *nous, il* and *elle*. The plural forms *ils* and *elles* were needed even less. Similarly your use of the imperfect may have been restricted to *j'étais* and *j'avais*, even though you had learned the other parts. The part of the conditional you used most was probably *je voudrais*. The result of this is that the overall picture you have of French grammar is bitty and uneven.

For A-Level, you need to have a good basic framework of grammar so that you know the main parts and their names and can fit the new rules that you come across into an overall pattern.

The grammar section that follows is **not** intended to be a complete grammar of the French language. The aim is to provide a description and an explanation for learning and reference of the main grammatical features that need to be understood and put into use at A and AS-Level. Broad rules and guidelines will be given; not necessarily all the exceptions and oddities. You will find these in a complete grammar reference book. Good books to consult are:

H Farrar, *A French Reference Grammar, 2nd edition*, 1973 OUP

L Byrne and E Churchill *A Comprehensive French Grammar*, Revised edition Blackwell 1993
Thalia Marriot and Mireille Ribière *Help Yourself to French Grammar*, Longmans 1990
P Rogers and J Long *La Grammaire en Clair*, Nelson Harrap 1983

The most conspicuous area with probable gaps in knowledge is the verb: this comes first. The verb is the main working part of a sentence. Getting it right earns you more credit and makes the rest of the sentence fall into place more readily.

Tense

Getting an 'overall picture' of the system of tenses is an important part of learning languages. Once acquired for one language it can be applied to learning other ones. Tense is to do with time. There are three basic aspects of time, common to all languages: past, present and future. These are exemplified in the former Soviet slogan 'Lenin lived; Lenin lives; Lenin will live.' Even if the prediction does not fulfil itself the slogan covers the full range of time.

You can then make adjustments to the way you look at past time: actions that began in the past or were completed in the past (the perfect tense in French) in contrast to actions that were continuous or repeated themselves (the imperfect tense). If you take a step further back into the past, before something else happened, the pluperfect is used. Similarly, referring to the future, you can make a prediction that someone will have done something (before something else) and the future perfect is used. 'Will', put into reported speech, becomes 'would' (he said he would arrive early) and the conditional or future in the past is needed.

2.1   PRESENT TENSE

Use

The present tense is used in French as it is in English except that:
(a) French has only one present tense form where English has three:
   (i) *Je trouve mon travail difficile* – I find my work difficult
                  – I am finding my work difficult
                  – I do find my work difficult
(b) French uses a present tense where English has a perfect continuous tense for an action started in the past but still happening now:
   (i) *Il habite Birmingham depuis dix ans* – He has been living in Birmingham for ten years
   (ii) *Je t'attends ici depuis une heure* – I've been waiting for you here for an hour

This present tense is usually signalled by *depuis* but *il y a* and *voici* can also introduce the same idea:
   (iii) *Il y a un an maintenant que je travaille là-bas* – I've been working there for a year now
   (iv) *Voici trente minutes que je t'attends!* – I've been waiting for you for half an hour!

The question 'How long have you/has he/she been...' is usually introduced by *Depuis combien de temps* or *Depuis quand*.

If you take a step back into the past with this continuous idea, you get in English: 'She said she **had been** waiting for me for an hour'

In French you need a continuous past tense, so the **imperfect** is used:
Elle a dit qu'elle m'attendait depuis une heure.

Formation

The present tense is usually encountered early in a French course because the present seems a logical place to start. Unfortunately the present tense in French is the most complicated in terms of irregularities. Many of these irregular verbs are amongst the most frequently used in the language. It is helpful to divide the present tense into two groups: regular and irregular.

REGULAR VERBS

These fall into three groups according to the ending of the infinitive (this is the part you find when you look up a verb in the dictionary).

❶ *'-er'* **verbs** The biggest group, containing about 90 per cent of the verbs in the language. All verbs in *'-er'* belong here.

je chante	*nous chantons*
tu chantes	*vous chantez*
il chante	*ils chantent*
elle chante	*elles chantent*

❷ *'-ir'* **verbs** These make up about 350 verbs. **Note** there are several commonly used verbs in *'-ir'* which are irregular (e.g. *venir; ouvrir; dormir* etc. — *see* verb list, page 253).

je ralentis	*nous ralentissons*
tu ralentis	*vous ralentissez*
il ralentit	*ils ralentissent*
elle ralentit	*elles ralentissent*

❸ *'-re'* **verbs** Again there are a number of common irregular verbs in *'-re'* that do not belong to this group (e.g. *boire; lire; naître* — *see* verb list).

je descends	*nous descendons*
tu descends	*vous descendez*
il descend	*ils descendent*
elle descend	*elles descendent*

Spelling and pronunciation

There are two main difficulties with the present tense: knowing which letters are pronounced and which are silent. The following should be noted about the three regular groups:

(a) All persons of the singular sound the same –

   je descends, tu descends , il descend (final *'-ds'* or *'-d'* are silent)

(b) The final *'-ent'*, the third person plural, is not pronounced –

   il parle and *ils parlent* sound the same

You can tell the third person singular from third person plural in verbs beginning with a vowel or silent *'h'*, because of the liaison or slur in the latter;

elle arrive but *elles arrivent* and *il habite* but *ils habitent* — the *'s'* sounds like a *'z'*

Some deviations in the regular verbs

Again it is a question of spelling and pronunciation. The endings remain regular but the rest of the verb changes slightly.

(a) **Double *'t'* and *'l'*,** e.g. *jeter* – to throw and *projeter* – to project:

Je jette	*Vous jetez*
Tu jettes	*Nous jetons*
Il jette	*Ils jettent*
Elle jette	*Elles jettent*

The example above shows a double consonant before a silent ending. *Jette* rhymes with *fillette*. In *jetons and jetez* the *'e'* sounds like the *'e'* in *'le'*.

   With *appeler* and *rappeler*, double the *'l'* in the same way. The pronunciation of *'e'* follows the same pattern.

(b) **Verbs with an *'e'* syllable before the *'-er'* ending,** e.g. *lever, répéter, amener, espérer, acheter* etc. change the sound of the *'e'* by adding or changing an accent.

J'achète	*Nous achetons*	*Je répète*	*Nous répétons*
Tu achètes	*Vous achetez*	*Tu répètes*	*Vous répétez*
Il achète	*Ils achètent*	*Il répète*	*Ils répètent*
Elle achète	*Elles achètent*	*Elle répète*	*Elles répètent*

You will notice that the accent changes, appears or disappears, according to whether the ending is silent or not. Can you see a similarity of pattern with the previous group?

(c) **Verbs in '-oyer', '-uyer',** e.g. *envoyer, employer, essuyer, ennuyer,* all change '*y*' to '*i*' before a silent ending:

J'envoie but *Vous envoyez*
Il essuie but *Vous essuyez*

(d) **Verbs in '-ger',** like *changer, arranger, manger,* all have an extra '*e*' before the first person plural ending:

Nous arrangeons

(e) **Verbs in '-cer'** have a cedilla beneath the '*c*' in the same place:

Nous avançons

The rule here is that before '*a*', '*o*' or '*u*', '*c*' and '*g*' are pronounced as a hard '*c*' as in *Calais* and '*g*' as in *gare* so an '*e*' or cedilla needs to be added to keep the soft '*s*' or '*zh*' sound. An '*e*' or '*i*' would make the following '*c*' or '*g*' soft anyway. So you only get cedillas before '*a*', '*o*' or '*u*' if the '*c*' has to remain soft. For example:

Mâcon (en Bourgogne) but *un maçon (un homme qui construit des bâtiments avec des briques)*

IRREGULAR VERBS

You could start to give rules about the peculiarities of the present tense of irregular verbs. For example, **four** have a third person plural ending in '*-ont*': *Ils ont (avoir)*; *Ils sont (être)*; *Ils font (faire)*; and *Ils vont (aller)* — **three** have a second person plural in '*-es*': *Vous dites*; *Vous faites*; *Vous êtes.*

This soon gets complicated, however, and bogged down with exceptions. The only way to get to grips with them is to learn them by saying them over to yourself using a verb table. If you photocopy a table where, for example, the present tense is written out in full, you can blank out selected parts of verbs, photocopy them and then try writing in the missing parts.

It is useful to know that the 14 most commonly used French verbs are the following:
être avoir faire pouvoir voir dire aller savoir vouloir venir devoir donner falloir prendre
You will see that they are all irregular except '*donner*'. It is important to know not only their present tense but also their other tenses.

Another helpful fact to remember is that, having learned to say and spell the present tense of, say, *mettre* – put or place, all the compound verbs (those formed by adding a prefix) become accessible to you. For example: *promettre* – promise, *permettre* – permit, *admettre* – admit, *soumettre* – submit, *transmettre* –transmit, *commettre* – commit.

Compound verbs are often fairly close in appearance to English verbs with a similar meaning. (What does *compromettre* mean? — *Ce scandale va compromettre cet homme politique.)* This extension of learning one verb also applies to all the other tenses that you will meet.

Exercices

1 Traduisez en français:
(a) Do you watch television every night?
(b) Do you do your homework while you are watching television?
(c) Are you waiting for the six o'clock train?
(d) No, I'm waiting for my friend
(e) Is he working in London?
(f) I am thinking of her while I write this letter
(g) Is he going to come with us?
(h) Does he speak Russian?
(i) I am writing to thank you for the present
(j) What are you doing this evening?

2 Traduisez:

    (a) Depuis combien de temps est-ce qu'il habite Bruxelles?

    (b) Ça fait deux semaines que je reçois des coups de téléphone mystérieux

    (c) Cela fait deux ans que nous nous écrivons

    (d) Depuis quand est-ce qu'il la connaît?

    (e) Voici deux mois que j'attends une lettre

3 Traduisez:

    (a) How long have you been waiting for me?

    (b) I've been here since six o'clock

    (c) They have been writing to one another for years

    (d) She has been in England for years

    (e) That makes five years I have known you

2.2 PERFECT TENSE

Use

This is probably the most frequently used tense in French after the present. 'Perfect' means 'finished', so this tense is used for actions completed in the past. English verbs have three ways of indicating this idea:

> You found your bag!
>
> You have found your bag
>
> You did find your bag

In French, *Vous avez trouvé votre sac* would be used for all of these. The French name *passé composé* means that it is a made up verb with two parts: *avoir* — the auxiliary verb — and the past participle, just like the English 'have found'. Most verbs in French form their perfect tense with *avoir*, the rest with *être*. You need to know two things then to form the perfect tense:

(a) Is it an *avoir* or an *être* verb?

(b) What is the past participle?

Formation

Avoir or *être*

(a) Most verbs take avoir:

> *Vous avez commencé?*
> *Ils ont trouvé l'adresse.*

(b) About 16 verbs, very frequently used, take *être* to form the perfect tense:

aller	—	*venir*
arriver	—	*partir*
monter	—	*descendre*
entrer	—	*sortir*
mourir	—	*naître*
tomber	—	*rester*
devenir	—	*revenir*
rentrer	—	*retourner*

So *je suis arrivé* can mean 'I have arrived' and *elle est partie* 'she has left'. These verbs are best remembered as pairs of opposites as shown above. There are 'about' 16 because by prefixing '*re-*' to many of them their number increases. For example, *remonter* – to go back up/go up again.

These verbs belong to such a group, not because of some conspiracy on the part of the French to make their language diffficult for foreigners, but because they are all 'intransitive' when used with *être* – that is they can't have a direct object. You can't 'go something or someone' or 'fall something or someone' (*see also* pages 55 and 78).

A few of them however can be used with a direct object (transitively) in which case they do take *avoir* and undergo a slight change of meaning:

(i) *J'ai monté vos valises, monsieur* – I've taken your suitcases up

(ii) *Le voleur a sorti un revolver* – The thief got out a gun

(iii) *J'ai rentré les chaises du jardin* – I've taken in the chairs from the garden

Descendre and *retourner* can also be used like this.

c) All reflexive verbs take *être* to form the perfect tense. The reflexive pronoun is kept with all the persons:

(i) *Je me suis levé à 6 heures* – I got up at six o'clock

(ii) *Nous nous sommes promenés jusqu'à 10 heures* – We walked until ten o'clock

(iii) *Vous vous êtes bien amusés?* – Did you have a good time?

PAST PARTICIPLES

It is essential to know this part of the verb. It should be memorized together with the infinitive as a group. The following outline rules are useful:

(a) All '*-er*' verbs have a past participle ending in '*é* '. This sounds identical with the infinitive ending '*-er*', so beware when writing!

(b) Regular '*-re*' and '*-ir*' verbs have a past participle ending in '*-u*' and '*-i*' respectively. The trouble is remembering which are the regular '*-re*' and '*-ir*' verbs.

(c) All the other past participles have to be learned. There are certain patterns:

pouvoir – *pu*
savoir – *su*
devoir – *dû*
recevoir – *reçu*
vouloir – *voulu*
falloir – *fallu*
pleuvoir – *plu*

Unfortunately, others are 'non-conformist':

(i) *souffrir J'ai souffert le martyre pour apprendre ces verbes* –
I went through agonies to learn these verbs

(ii) *lire Il a beaucoup lu* – He has read a lot

(iii) *courir J'ai couru partout pour trouver ce vin* –
I've been all over the place to find this wine

(iv) *croire Elle ne m'a pas cru* – She didn't believe me

Learning the past participles requires an effort. Try working backwards by copying out 20 to 30 past participles and then see if you can write down the infinitive beside each one. Remember that having learned one it might give the pattern for several compounds:

ouvrir – *ouvert*
offrir – *offert*
couvrir – *couvert*

It is also helpful to say the English past participle in your mind when you are learning:

offert – offered
couvert – covered

Exercices

1 Try hanging the 16 *être* verbs in the following acrostic:

A   A   D   D   E   M   M   N   P   R   R   R   S   T   V
R
R
I
V
E
R

2 La famille de Jean-Paul est nombreuse mais ce soir il est resté seul dans le salon. Où sont ses parents, ses sœurs Marie-Claude, Sandrine, Claudette et Alice, son frère Albert et le chat?

    Voici des notes pour vous aider:

    Maman – montée dans sa chambre – papa descendu dans la cave – Alice pas encore rentrée– Sandrine allée à la discothèque – Albert pas revenu depuis ce matin – Claudette sortie avec ses amis – Marie-Claude rentrée à 6h, restée 5 minutes, repartie – la chatte tombée de la fenêtre, morte

    Jouez le rôle de Jean-Paul. Qu'est-ce qu'il s'est dit?
    Exemple: Maman est montée dans sa chambre. Papa…

3 Traduisez
    (a) Has he left?
    (b) Did he stay a long time?
    (c) He went up to his room
    (d) He hasn't gone out
    (e) Did he arrive on time?
    (f) I got back late
    (g) He fell over outside the café
    (h) I have returned the books
    (i) My friends have returned
    (j) I have brought down your luggage
    (k) He got out a pen
    (l) I was born in Scotland

4 Role-play: Pour faire le rôle de M. Camembert, préparez des réponses détaillées; pour le rôle du policier préparez vos questions.

    Au commissariat, M. Camembert fait sa déposition. Voici les notes qu'il a préparées:

    levé 6h – descendu – pris un café – sorti de la maison – entré dans un tabac – arrivé à la gare, pris le train de 7h15 – descendu à la gare St Lazare – arrivé au bureau – monté au 5e – resté toute la journée

The police officer also wants the following details: the precise times of the above actions, did he get dressed or washed even? Did he eat nothing? What did he buy in the tabac? Did anyone see him go into the office building? What did he do at lunchtime? Did he leave the office during the day?

5 (i) Il a conduit (from conduire) means 'conducted', 'led', 'driven'. Can you find French cognates for the verbs on page 31?

    reduced –
    seduced –
    introduced –

produced –

deduced –

constructed –

(ii) Also, find the French for 'translated' and 'destroyed'. 'Well cooked' is bien cuit. What is the infinitive of this verb?

2.3 PAST PARTICIPLE AGREEMENT

Rules

1 The 16 or so *être* verbs all agree with the subject of the verb. The suffixes '-*e*', '-*s*' or '-*es*' may need to appear on the end of the past participle:

(i)   *Elle est partie*

(ii) *Marie et son amie sont arrivées*

(iii) *Ils sont revenus*

A woman writing a letter would have to put *Je suis allée au théâtre hier soir*. Since the past participles of nearly all these verbs end in a vowel you cannot hear the agreement. The exception is *mourir*:

(iv) *Colette, la romancière, est morte en 1954*

2 All the other verbs agree if there is a direct object and it comes before the verb. This is easy to spot if the direct object is a pronoun since it will come just before the verb anyway:

(i)   *Ta sœur? Oui, je l'ai vue tout à l'heure*

(ii) *Je les ai trouvées délicieuses, les pêches de son jardin*

But the agreement can be more easily overlooked if the direct object is a noun further away from the following verb:

(iii) *Les pêches que j'ai achetées ce matin sont très bonnes*

(iv) *Quels copains a-t-il vus là-bas?*

(v)   *Voici les cartes postales que Jean et Marie m'ont envoyées*

If you still have difficulty in deciding what the object is and whether it is direct or indirect try the following formula: ask yourself 'who' or 'what' after the verb. So in the last two sentences for example: 'Saw who?' — 'friends'. 'Sent what?' — 'Postcards'. Conversely asking yourself 'who' or 'what' before the verb will give you the subject.

3 Direct or indirect? The simplest explanation is to say that an indirect object has a preposition (nearly always 'to') in front of it in English. So you would ask yourself 'to whom?' or 'to what?' after the verb to get the indirect object. There is no agreement with an indirect object so *lui* 'to him/her' and *leur* 'to them' do not agree:

(i)   *Ta mère? Oui, je lui ai déjà parlé*

4 Reflexive verbs follow the rule already given. The past participle will agree if the reflexive pronoun is a direct object.

(i)   *Elle s'est levée* – She got who up? Herself. *Se* is a preceding direct object.

(ii) *Ils se sont habillés* – They dressed who? Themselves. *Se* is again a preceding direct object

The following cases need special care with agreements however:

(iii) *Elle s'est coupée* – She cut **herself**

Se is a preceding direct object so the past participle agrees but...

(iv) *Elle s'est coupé la jambe* – She cut her leg

Cut what? Her leg. The direct object follows the verb in this case. The word *se* here means literally 'to herself' so is indirect.

(v)   *Nous nous sommes écrit tous les jours* – We wrote to each other every day

(vi) *Elles se sont parlé souvent* – They often spoke to one another

In both these examples there is no agreement since the reflexive pronouns are indirect objects, the equivalent in English of 'to each other/one another'.

(vii) *Elles se sont posé toutes sortes de questions* –
They asked each other all sorts of questions

(viii) *Elle s'est demandé pourquoi* – She wondered (asked herself) why

(ix) *Ils se sont montré leurs cadeaux* – They showed each other their presents

No agreement here because, in French, you pose questions 'to someone', 'ask to someone' and 'show to someone'. The reflexive pronouns are all indirect here and not like the English verb construction.

Since you cannot, in most cases, hear a past participle agreement (except for the few verbs and their compounds that end in a consonant like *écrit, mis, conduit*) making this agreement is purely a written convention. The French have to learn the rules for doing this at school and it does cause them some difficulty. Only very careful speakers would say:

(x) *Les lettres que j'ai mises sur la table* – The letters that I put on the table

5 There is never any agreement with the pronoun *en* meaning 'some, 'any', or 'of them'.
(i) *Ses lettres? Oui, j'en ai gardé beaucoup* – His letters? Yes, I've kept many of them

6 The past participle of an impersonal verb never agrees (an impersonal verb is one introduced by *il* meaning not 'he', in this case, but 'it' or 'there' in English). Examples likely to occur are:
(i) *La chaleur qu'il a fait cet été* – The heatwave we have had this summer
(ii) *Les efforts qu'il m'a fallu* – The effort it cost me
(iii) *Les problèmes qu'il y a eu cette année* – The problems there have been this year

Exercice

Faites accorder le participe passé, s'il le faut:
(a) Ils sont arrivé
(b) Mes deux sœurs sont parti
(c) Marie-Antoinette est mort en 1793
(d) Ma montre, où est-ce que je l'ai laissé?
(e) Je les ai trouvé sans difficulté
(f) Les poires que j'ai acheté hier ne sont pas mûres
(g) Elle s'est baigné dans la mer
(h) Marie a couché son petit frère et puis elle s'est couché
(i) Nous avons descendu nos bagages
(j) Quelles valises avez-vous descendu?
(k) Ils sont descendu, vos frères?
(l) Elles se sont regardé un moment puis se sont embrassé
(m) Elle s'est gratté la tête
(n) Ils se sont donné rendez-vous pour le lendemain
(o) Des escargots? Ah, j'en ai trouvé de beaux après la pluie

2.4 WORD ORDER

NB: this unit refers to word order of negatives and object pronouns with the perfect tense.

Rules

The negatives: *ne... pas, ne... personne, ne... rien, ne... jamais*

The object pronouns:

me	*le*	*lui*	*y*	*en*
te	*la*	*leur*		
se	*les*			
nous				
vous				

These grammatical items are usually encountered before you start using the perfect tense. You then have the problem of knowing where to fit them in with the two parts of the perfect tense. The three rules you have probably learned about the position of the pronouns with the perfect tense are:

❶ For *ne... pas, ne... rien, ne... jamais, avoir* or *être* go in between the two words:
- (i) *J'ai regardé la télé* – I watched television
- (ii) *Je n'ai pas regardé la télé* – I did not watch television
  Note that in *ne... personne* phrases, *personne* always comes after the past participle because of its length:
- (iii) *Je n'ai vu personne* – I saw no one

❷ Pronouns come before *avoir* or *être*.

❸ If there are two pronouns they come in the same order as the above table. For example:
- (i) *Je ne les lui ai pas donnés* – I did not give them to him

These rules work quite well when you are writing but are impossible to apply on the spot when speaking. A good way of helping to acquire mastery of these rules is to practise manipulating certain combinations of negatives and object pronouns with the perfect tense. Start with a basic question sentence in the perfect tense that you might actually want to ask:
- (ii) *Vous avez vu mes clefs?* – Have you seen my keys?

and answer yourself first in the positive, next in the negative:
- (iii) *Oui, je les ai vues* and *non, je ne les ai pas vues*

Exercice

Essayez les questions:

(a) Vous avez trouvé mon sac?
    (i) Oui, je...   (ii) Non, je...

(b) Vous lui avez donné l'adresse?
    (i) Oui, je la lui ai donnée   (ii) Non, je...

(c) Il vous a donné son adresse?
    (i) Oui, il...   (ii) Non, il...

(d) Ces pêches, vous les avez achetées hier?
    (i) Oui, je...   (ii) Non, je...

(e) Je ne... achetées, on me... données

(f) J'ai écrit deux fois à ma correspondante
Je lui ai écrit deux fois
    (i) Je... envoyé une longue lettre
    (ii) Je ne... envoyé de carte postale

2.5   IMPERFECT TENSE

Use

❶ 'Imperfect' means unfinished, so this tense is used to describe an action that was continuous in the past. Its nearest equivalent in English is 'was' or 'were' doing something. The use of the imperfect tense for continuous action in the past is, in many ways, in direct contrast to the perfect tense (used for completed action). You often find them used together in the same sentence:

(i) *Je prenais une douche quand mon voisin m'a téléphoné* –
I was taking a shower when my neighbour rang me

(ii) *J'ai trouvé la clef sous une chaise quand je nettoyais le salon* –
I found the key under a chair when I was cleaning the lounge

You will often find that you have to decide between a perfect and an imperfect, particularly when translating from English into French or when answering questions on a passage in French.

2 The imperfect is also used for something that happened frequently or habitually in the past:

(i) *Tous les soirs il buvait un grand verre de cognac avant de se coucher*

English conveys this idea by 'used to' or 'would drink'. The simple past tense might also be used in English 'every evening he drank'. In sentences like this, there is usually an adverbial expression like *toujours*, *souvent*, *tous les soirs* or *quelquefois* that makes the habitual meaning clear.

3 The third use of the imperfect is closely connected with **1** above. It is used for description or to convey the idea of the state of something in the past:

(i) *Sa maison se trouvait à mi-hauteur sur la montagne* –
His house was/stood half-way up the mountain

(ii) *De ses fenêtres on avait une vue splendide sur tout le paysage* –
From his windows you had a superb view over the whole countryside

The description of the world at the beginning of the book of Genesis illustrates this descriptive use very well.

(iii) '*La terre* **était** *comme un grand vide, l'obscurité* **couvrait** *l'océan primitif et le souffle de Dieu* **agitait** *la surface de l'eau...*'

4 You have to be careful when translating 'was' and 'were' into French to distinguish between an imperfect and a perfect sense to the action:

(i) *J'ai été triste quand il m'a téléphoné* – *Son coup de téléphone m'a rendu triste*

(ii) *J'étais triste quand il m'a téléphoné* – *J'étais déjà d'une humeur triste au moment où il a téléphoné*

This 'was/were' problem also occurs with *il y a*. Compare the following:

(iii) *Il y avait souvent des accidents à cet endroit mais hier matin il y a eu un accident fatal*

Thus, 'was' and 'were' are not always translated by the imperfect tense. (*See also* the passive, page 50.) Compare also the following:

(iv) *J'avais une idée de son nom mais je ne pouvais pas me le rappeler*

(v) *J'ai eu l'idée de le chercher dans l'annuaire*

In the first sentence, the idea **was present in the mind for some time** but in the second **it came suddenly**.

To sum up then, the imperfect is used:

(a) To say what was happening.

(b) What used to happen.

(c) Describe how things were or appeared to be in the past.

(d) You need to distinguish between a completed and a continuous action in the past. Care is needed when dealing with 'was' and 'were'.

Formation

Go to the first person plural present tense and remove the '*-ons*' ending. Add the following endings for the imperfect tense:

-ais	*-ions*
-ais	*-iez*
-ait	*-aient*

Ralentir – to slow down (*nous ralentissons*)
 Je ralentissais *Nous ralentissions*
 Tu ralentissais *Vous ralentissiez*
 il ralentissait *Ils ralentissaient*
This works for nearly all verbs, regular or irregular.

Note

(a) The imperfect of *être* is:
 J'étais   *Nous étions*
 Tu étais   *Vous étiez*
 Il était   *Ils étaient*

(b) Verbs ending in '*-ger*' and '*-cer*' need an '*e*' before the '*g*' and a cedilla under the '*c*' if the following vowel would otherwise make them soft (*see* present tense, page 51). Examples:

 Je commençais *Nous commencions* *J'arrangeais* *Nous arrangions*
 Tu commençais *Vous commenciez* *Tu arrangeais* *Vous arrangiez*
 Il commençait *Ils commençaient* *Il arrangeait* *Ils arrangeaient*

You will notice that in two cases, the first and second persons plural, the '*i*' always makes the respective consonant soft. (*See also* appendix 1, page 253.)

(c) The imperfect endings '*-ais*', '*-ait*' and '*-aient*' all sound the same. French primary-school children do lots of dictation practice to get this point home!

Exercices

1 Comblez les blancs dans le texte suivant:

> Dimanche à 10 heures j'ét__ dans ma chambre avec mon frère. Mon père et notre voisin ét__ dans le garage. Ils essay__ de réparer notre voiture qui ét__ en panne. Maman ét__ dans le salon. Elle tricot__. Mon frère et moi jou__ aux échecs.

2 Répondez à ces questions en disant la vérité:
 (a) Que faisiez-vous dimanche dernier à 9 heures?
 (b) Et à 11 heures?
 (c) Que faisiez-vous hier soir à 8 heures?
 (d) Où habitiez-vous quand vous aviez cinq ans?
 (e) Est-ce qu'il pleuvait ce matin quand vous êtes sorti? Sinon, quel temps faisait-il?
 (f) Hier, vous portiez un chemisier blanc, un tricot vert et une jupe grise? Sinon, qu'est-ce que vous portiez?

3 Traduisez en français:
 (a) She usually woke at 6.00 and stayed in bed till 7.00
 (b) This morning however she got up at 7.30 and left the house at 8.00
 (c) While we were watching television last night someone stole my bike
 (d) I dreamt about a strange school where all the teachers wore blue-jeans and smoked in class. There were no lessons in the afternoon. We all played games and went home at 4.00
 (e) When my father went fishing he usually got up very early and came back late without any fish. Last Sunday though he came back with a large trout
 (f) 'I caught it myself' he said. We didn't believe him!
 (g) I was having a shower when you rang
 (h) When I was young I listened to the radio a lot
 (i) When my grandfather was young there was no television
 (j) What did people do in the evenings in those days?

4 Le récit suivant est tiré du Nouveau Testament où il est intitulé 'Jésus apaise les eaux'. Connaissez-vous son titre en anglais? Pour combler les blancs, trouvez le verbe qui convient le mieux dans la liste qui suit.

Notez

Dans la version originale le passé simple (voyez plus loin) est utilisé au lieu du passé composé.

> Le soir de ce même jour, Jésus __ à ses disciples 'Passons de l'autre côté du lac'. Ils ont quitté la foule; les disciples __ Jésus dans la barque où il __. D'autres barques encore __ près de lui. Et voilà qu'un vent violent __ à souffler, les vagues __ dans la barque de sorte que, déjà , elle __ d'eau. Jésus __ à l'arrière du bateau et __ la tête appuyée sur un coussin. Ses disciples l'__ alors et lui __, 'Maître, nous allons mourir. Cela ne te fait-il rien?' Jésus __, il __ sévèrement au vent et __ à l'eau du lac: Silence! Calme-toi! Alors le vent __ et __ un grand calme. Puis Jésus __ aux disciples, 'Pourquoi avez-vous peur? N'avez-vous pas encore de foi?'
>
> Mais ils __ très effrayés et ils __ les uns aux autres:
>
> 'Qui est donc cet homme, pour que même le vent et l'eau du lac lui obéissent?'

dormait – était – a dit – il y a eu – ont emmené – se sont dit – étaient – s'est mis – est tombé – s'est réveillé – ont dit – a dit – a parlé – se remplissait – se trouvait –se jetaient – ont réveillé – étaient – a dit

2.6 PAST HISTORIC TENSE

This tense is not used in spoken French. You will meet it in works of fiction and non-fiction and in articles in newspapers and magazines. Because it is not acquired naturally, it has to be learned in school by native speakers of French. You need to be able to recognize it as a past tense.

You may be required to use it when translating into French passages written in a literary style or possibly in other kinds of writing. You should check with your teacher what is required by your particular Examining Board.

Use

The past historic is the direct equivalent in use of the perfect tense except for the fact that it is never spoken. In writing, choice between the two tenses depends on the literary style. The past historic is becoming less popular at the moment with some French writers. You cannot mix the two tenses in the same piece of writing. However, since the past historic is never spoken, when direct speech is given in a piece of writing — what someone actually said — the perfect tense must be used. Here is an example from an imaginary story:

> *Bernard **entra** dans le salon et **s'assit** en face de Thérèse.*
>
> *'Qu'est-ce que **tu as fait** hier soir? **Tu es sortie** sans manger et **tu es revenue** vers 6 heures ce matin.'*
>
> *Elle ne **répondit** rien et **continua** à regarder fixement le feu.*

This tense is called *le passé simple* in French because it doesn't need another verb like *avoir* or *être* to form it. The verb itself changes. You can compare it in this respect to the simple past of some verbs in English: 'she sings' becomes 'she sang'; 'I see' becomes 'I saw'.

The English term 'past historic' is to do with the fact that this tense is used principally to relate the events in a story: *une histoire*.

Formation

1 '-er' verbs

All verbs ending in '-er' in the infinitive form the past historic in the same way. Remove the '-er' and add the following endings:

-ai	*-âmes*
-as	*-âtes*
-a	*-èrent*

J'allai	*Nous allâmes*
Tu allas	*Vous allâtes*
Il alla	*Ils allèrent*

2 Regular '-ir' and '-re' verbs (e.g. *ralentir, faiblir, descendre* and *rendre*) have the following endings:

-is	*-îmes*
-is	*-îtes*
-it	*-irent*

Je faiblis	*Nous faiblîmes*
Tu faiblis	*Vous faiblîtes*
Il faiblit	*Ils faiblirent*

3 Many verbs in '-oir', but not all of them, have the following endings:

-us	*-ûmes*
-us	*-ûtes*
-ut	*-urent*

Je voulus	*Nous voulûmes*
Tu voulus	*Vous voulûtes*
Il voulut	*Ils voulurent*

But this time you don't always just add the endings instead of the '-oir':

savoir – Je sus; boire – Je bus; pouvoir; Je pus; avoir – J'eus

Do you notice a similarity between the past participle and the past historic? In fact, the past participle is a good guide to the past historic of many, **but not all**, irregular verbs. One common verb you can't do this with is *voir*:

Je vis	*Nous vîmes*
Tu vis	*Vous vîtes*
Il vit	*Ils virent*

and also of course *revoir* and *prévoir*!

Note

(a) The final '-ent' is not pronounced if you have to read a passage aloud.

(b) There is always a circumflex accent over the '-a', '-i' or '-u' of the first and second persons plural.

4 There are a number of exceptions to rules **2** and **3** above. Sometimes the past participle is a guide; sometimes it is not. Note the following:

(a) *écrire, décrire* (to describe), *s'inscrire* (to sign up, get enrolled) and others, add an extra syllable:

    (i) *Il écrivit*   *Ils écrivirent*

Similarly *conduire* (and also *séduire*– seduce, *réduire* – reduce, *traduire* – translate and others) add another syllable too.

    (ii) *Il conduisit*   *Ils réduisirent*

(b) There is a group of verbs in '-eindre' and '-aindre' (e.g. *craindre* – fear, *peindre* – paint, *éteindre* – extinguish, put out). These all have a '-gn' in the past historic:

    Il éteignit   *Ils peignirent*
    Il craignit   *Ils craignirent*

(c) Some verbs just have to be learned:

    Etre   *Il fut*   *Nous fûmes* (nothing to do with *fumer* – to smoke!)

Faire	Il fit	Nous fîmes
Naître	Il naquit	Nous naquîmes

Note also *venir* and *tenir*:

Je vins	Nous vînmes
Tu vins	Vous vîntes
Il vint	Ils vinrent
Je tins	Nous tînmes
Tu tins	Vous tîntes
Il tint	Ils tinrent

Don't forget *retenir* – retain, *se souvenir* – remember, *maintenir* – maintain, *convenir* – agree, and others.

Note also the following which may be a puzzle when you first meet them:

Mettre	– *Je mis*
Prendre	– *Je pris*
Mourir	– *Il mourut*
Vivre	– *Il vécut*
Lire	– *Il lut*
Se taire	– *Il se tut* (not from *tuer* – to kill!)

Exercice

Trouvez l'infinitif et la signification des phrases suivantes:

les pompiers éteignirent le feu – ils purent le comprendre – nous fûmes bientôt dehors – il dut payer une amende – il produisit ses papiers – ils s'inscrivirent aux cours du soir – la grippe le retint au lit – les résultats surprirent le prof – ils revinrent au week-end – il but le verre d'un trait – à ce moment il sut la vérité – il fallut attendre un peu – le matin il plut – il maintint longtemps sa situation – son raisonnement me convainquit – il se tut un instant puis il rit – ils nous dirent bonjour – nous fumâmes deux cigarettes avant de nous coucher

2.7 PLUPERFECT TENSE

The perfect tense is used to say what has happened in the past; the pluperfect goes one step further back and says what **had** happened (before something else). For example:
(i)   *Elle dit* (present) *qu'elle m'a souvent vu* (past) *au supermarché*
(ii) *Elle a dit* (past) *qu'elle m'avait souvent vu* (further back in past) *au supermarché*
(iii) *Je ne l'ai pas vue. Elle était déjà sortie*

You can reverse the order of these two statements:
(iv) *Elle était déjà sortie. Je ne l'ai pas vue*

Due to the tenses it is still clear which event came first.

Use

The most frequent use of the pluperfect is in reported speech (i.e. when relating something someone said, did or saw etc.). For example:
(i)   **Actual statement** *Je ne suis pas sorti hier soir. J'ai regardé la télé jusqu'à 11 heures. J'ai bu un verre de lait et puis je me suis couché à 11h15.*
(ii) **Reported statement** *Il a dit qu'il n'était pas sorti hier soir, qu'il avait regardé la télé jusqu'à 11 heures, qu'il avait bu un verre de lait et qu'il s'était couché à 11h15.*

The use of 'had' in English usually signals a pluperfect in French. However, English is not so particular and 'had' can often be left out: 'he asked me what time I arrived'.

In French this would have to be:

(iii) *Il m'a demandé à quelle heure j'étais arrivé*

Similarly:

(iv) *Elle m'a montré l'endroit où l'accident s'était produit* –
      She showed me the spot where the accident happened (or had happened)

If you rely on thinking in English, you could miss the need for the pluperfect in such cases.

Note The phrase 'had been doing' in English, as a continuous unfinished action in the past, is translated by an imperfect tense (see page 49).

Formation

Like the perfect tense, the pluperfect is made up of two parts: *avoir* or *être* + the past participle. However, this time you need the **imperfect** of *avoir* or *être*.

J'avais vu	*Nous avions vu*
Tu avais vu	*Vous aviez vu*
Il avait vu	*Ils avaient vu*
Elle avait vu	*Elles avaient vu*

J'étais sorti(e)	*Nous étions sorti(e)s*
Tu étais sorti(e)	*Vous étiez sorti(e)(s)*
Il était sorti	*Ils étaient sortis*
Elle était sortie	*Elles étaient sorties*

Je m'étais levé(e)	*Nous nous étions levé(e)s*
Tu t'étais levé(e)	*Vous vous étiez levé(e)(s)*
Il s'était levé	*Ils s'étaient levés*
Elle s'était levée	*Elles s'étaient levées*

Note

(a) The choice of *avoir* or *être* depends on the same rules as for the 16 verbs and reflexive verbs
    (*see* above)

(b) The past participle agrees if necesssary (*see* above)

(c) The negatives, *ne... pas*, *ne... rien* etc., go in exactly the same positions as with the perfect tense

Exercices

1 (a) Voici la déclaration de M. XX. Mettez les verbes au plus-que-parfait.

Je suis descendu à l'hôtel Splendide. J'y suis arrivé vers 7 heures. J'ai mangé à l'hôtel. Après je suis sorti me promener. J'ai marché pendant une heure. Puis je suis revenu à l'hôtel. Dans le bar j'ai rencontré un ancien collègue. Nous avons bu quelques verres ensemble. Je me suis couché vers 11h45.

(b) Même exercice, mais commencez avec 'Il a dit que...':

2 Traduisez (des verbes avec être):
(a) I had arrived late so I went to bed early
(b) When the bus stopped he got out
(c) She had left early in order not to miss the train
(d) They had presented themselves at the police station
(e) I didn't know that she had got married

3 Traduisez (pronoms + expressions négatives):
   (a) I hadn't seen her since Saturday
   (b) He had said nothing to me
   (c) They hadn't found anyone there
   (d) Had he already talked to you about it?
   (e) My sisters had never visited Paris

4 Traduisez:
   (a) He says that he has never travelled by plane
   (b) He said that he had never travelled by plane
   (c) I found I hadn't understood what he said
   (d) She said she telephoned last week
   (e) I am sure the letter has arrived
   (f) I was sure the letter had arrived
   (g) 'I have never seen this man,' she said
   (h) He remembered he saw Fifi at the bank
   (i) He said he had never seen the man
   (j) I couldn't find the letter he sent me

5 Read the following 'fait divers':

INCENDIAIRE

Lunéville: Un mineur de 13 ans a été interpellé samedi par les policiers de Lunéville (Meurthe et Moselle) et a reconnu être l'auteur d'incendies, au cours de la semaine passée, dans des immeubles HLM de la ville. L'adolescent avait mis le feu à des poubelles. Quatre personnes, dont un bébé, avaient été légèrement intoxiquées au cours de ces incendies. Remis à ses parents, il sera présenté au juge des enfants.

Six incidents are referred to:
   (i) Four people and baby affected by fumes
   (ii) Confessed to being responsible
   (iii) Minor questioned by police
   (iv) He will appear in court
   (v) Returned to parents
   (vi) Set fire to dustbins

   (a) Number these in the order in which they occured.
   (b) At what point in time does the report start?
   (c) Explain why some verbs are in the pluperfect.

6 Lisez le fait divers suivant. Soulignez et marquez les verbes au passé composé et au plus-que-parfait. Quatre événements sont mentionnés, deux sont récents, deux datent du 18e siècle. Savez-vous les distinguer?

SUR LES TRACES DE DE SAUSSURE. GENEVE – MONT BLANC EN MOINS DE 24 HEURES

Chamonix: Il y a quelques jours, deux Haut-Savoyards – Pierre Cusin et Thierry Gazin – ont battu le record Chamonix: Mont Blanc et retour en moins de 8 heures. Ces deux spécialistes de cross en montagne avaient voulu saluer ainsi à leur manière le bicentenaire de l'ascension du Mont Blanc. Devant cette brillante réussite, ils ont décidé de ne pas en rester là. Avec Christophe Gotti du CAF* d'Annecy, ils ont décidé de refaire l'itinéraire du savant genevois, Horace Benedict De Saussure. Celui-ci, bien avant, avait réussi la conquête du Mont Blanc dont il fut l'instigateur. Il était allé de Genève à Chamonix à pied, puis bien plus tard, en 1787, avait gravi le Mont Blanc, avec Jacques Balmont, dans des conditions que l'on imagine il y a 199 ans.

   Le trio sportif est donc parti pour Genève hier soir pour remonter toute la vallée de l'Arve en courant.

   * Club Alpin Français

Anecdote

Si vous croyez que le plus-que-parfait est difficile pour les Anglais, les Français ont quelquefois des problèmes avec le 'had had' dans notre langue. Par exemple:

Had he had time he would have come – S'il avait eu le temps il serait venu

Mais considérez le cas en anglais du prof qui en corrigeant la composition de John, souligne son 'had' et écrit au dessus 'had had':

The teacher, where John had had 'had', had 'had had'!

2.8 PAST ANTERIOR TENSE

This tense is only found in books written in formal style. It is never used in spoken French. You don't need to learn how to use it, but you may need to recognize it for translation and understanding purposes.

Use

Virtually the only use is after the following conjunctions, when one action immediately follows another. The other verb in the sentence is then always in the past historic: *dès que, aussitôt que, du moment que, à peine... que, quand, lorsque.*

For example:

(i) *Dès que son ami fut revenu il lui apprit la nouvelle –*
As soon as his friend had returned he told him the news

(ii) *A peine eut-il terminé son discours qu'il tomba mort –*
Scarcely had he finished his speech when he dropped dead

Formation

The past historic of *avoir* or *être* + past participle of the verb.

2.9 FUTURE TENSE

There are two ways of indicating future time in French: using the verb *aller* followed by the infinitive of the verb:

(i) *Qu'est-ce que nous allons faire ce soir?* – What are we going to do this evening?
Using the future tense of the verb:

(ii) *Est-ce qu'il fera beau demain?* – Will it be fine tomorrow?

There is a slight difference in implication between these two uses. The future with *aller* implies partly the immediate future but also a relationship between the present moment and a future event:

(iii) *Qu'est-ce que nous allons faire ce soir? Et qu'est-ce que nous ferons demain?*

The implication is that the present situation has got something to do with this evening's plans but that tomorrow stands on its own as it were. If this sounds a bit complex don't worry too much. *Aller* + infinitive will serve in most circumstances where you can't remember the correct future tense.

Use

The future tense is used in much the same way in French as it is in English: to refer to future time. The main difference is that English doesn't always use a future when future time is implied.

(i) *Quand il arrivera dites-lui d'attendre* – When he **arrives** tell him to wait

(ii) *Je serai là aussitôt que je serai prêt* – I'll be there as soon as I **am** ready

You will see that English uses a **present** but French uses a **future** tense.

The one major exception to this is after *si* meaning 'if' in French:

(iii) *S'il arrive, dites-lui d'attendre* – If he comes, tell him to wait

(iv) *Je viendrai si je suis prêt* – I'll come if I'm ready

The most straightforward rule that works with *si* is the following: after *si* (meaning "if") always use the same tense that is used in English. In the above examples, it is the present tense but the rule should also work for the other tenses considered below.

Formation

1 Regular verbs

Add the following endings to the infinitive (with '*-re*' verbs, remove the final '*-e*' first)

-ai	*-ons*
-as	*-ez*
-a	*-ont*

Réussir	*Je réussirai*	*Nous réussirons*
	Tu réussiras	*Vous réussirez*
	Il réussira	*Ils réussiront*
Apprendre	*J'apprendrai*	*Nous apprendrons*
	Tu apprendras	*Vous apprendrez*
	Il apprendra	*Ils apprendront*
Retourner	*Je retournerai*	*Nous retournerons*
	Tu retourneras	*Vous retournerez*
	Il retournera	*Ils retourneront*

2 Irregular verbs

The endings are the same but the inside part of the verb changes, sometimes substantially. These verbs have to be learned separately. They are nearly all commonly used verbs.

Voir	*Je verrai*	*Nous verrons*
	Tu verras	*Vous verrez*
	Il verra	*Ils verront*
Faire	*Je ferai*	*Nous ferons*
	Tu feras	*Vous ferez*
	Il fera	*Ils feront*
Aller	*J'irai*	*Nous irons*
	Tu iras	*Vous irez*
	Il ira	*Ils iront*

Look up the future tense of the following if you are not sure of them:

être – avoir – envoyer – venir/tenir – pouvoir – savoir – vouloir – courir – mourir – devoir – recevoir – falloir – pleuvoir

Note the '*r*' sound just before the ending is the signal of a future tense being used when you hear spoken French.

2.10 CONDITIONAL TENSE

This tense may not have been pointed out to you during your preparation for GCSE. You would have used it without knowing it in such phrases as *je voudrais, j'aimerais* – I would like/love, and *Est-ce que je pourrais?* – Could I?

Use

The conditional is used in two ways:

1 To express a condition attached to a statement:
  (i) *J'irais la voir si j'avais le temps* – I would go and see her if I had the time

2 To put the future in the past (not so daft as it sounds!):
  (i) *Il dit qu'il arrivera tard* – He says he will arrive late (said now)
  (ii) *Il a dit qu'il arriverait tard* – He said he would arrive late (reporting what he said)

  Note Be careful to distinguish between 'would' in English that means 'used to' and needs an imperfect tense in French, and the 'would' that has a condition attached to it or is simply 'will' in the past.

3 The conditional is also used to express an allegation or an unsubstantiated fact:
  (i) *D'après les journaux, il y aurait des centaines de morts* –
      The newspapers claim that hundreds are dead
  (ii) *Selon certains observateurs on serait au bord d'une guerre* –
      Some observers think we are on the brink of war

  This use is **very common** today in newspapers and broadcasts.

4 Another use, closely connected to the last one, is to express a possibility or a supposition:
  (i) *Serait-il malade?* – Might he possibly be ill?
  (ii) *Y aurait-il quelque explication rationnelle de ce phénomène?* –

  Could there be some rational explanation for this phenomenon?

Formation

The imperfect endings are put on to the future stem (i.e. instead of the future endings you use the imperfect ones):

-ais	*-ions*
-ais	*-iez*
-ait	*-aient*

Venir	*Je viendrais*	*Nous viendrions*
	Tu viendrais	*Vous viendriez*
	Il viendrait	*Ils viendraient*
Arriver	*J'arriverais*	*Nous arriverions*
	Tu arriverais	*Vous arriveriez*
	Il arriverait	*Ils arriveraient*

Note
(a) The first person singular is pronounced almost exactly like the first person of the future tense.
(b) As with the imperfect tense '*-ais*', '*-ait*', and '*-aient*' all sound the same.

2.11 FUTURE PERFECT TENSE

This tense needs to be included in this group of 'future-type' tenses, as well as the conditional perfect tense (overleaf). As well as saying what someone 'will do' you can say what they 'will have' done; as well what they 'would do', what they 'would have' done.

Use

It is used in the same way as English 'will have':
  (i) *Il aura déjà reçu ma lettre* – He will have already received my letter

(ii) *A 6 heures elles seront arrivées là-bas* – By six they will have arrived there

Note English does not always use 'will have' when a future is implied:

(iii) *Téléphone-moi dès que tu auras reçu sa lettre* – Phone me as soon as you have received his letter

Compare this with the future tense example given above. You will find this use particularly after *quand, dès que* and *aussitôt que*.

Formation

The future perfect is formed from the future of *avoir* or *être* + the past participle.

Recevoir
    J'aurai reçu   *Nous aurons reçu*
    Tu auras reçu   *Vous aurez reçu*
    Il aura reçu   *Ils auront reçu*

Arriver
    Je serai arrivé(e)   *Nous serons arrivé(e)s*
    Tu seras arrivé(e)   *Vous serez arrivé(e)(s)*
    Il sera arrivé   *Ils seront arrivés*
    Elle sera arrivée   *Elles seront arrivées*

2.12 CONDITIONAL PERFECT TENSE

Use

It is used in the same way as the English 'would have':

(i) *Il m'aurait entendu si j'avais crié un peu plus fort* –
He would have heard me if I had shouted a bit louder

(ii) *Je ne serais pas parti si tôt si j'avais su que le train aurait du retard* –
I wouldn't have left so early if I had known that the train would be late

You will note that, in the examples for both these tenses, the future perfect is followed by a perfect tense and the conditional perfect by a pluperfect. This is a common combination of the tenses.

Note The conditional perfect is also used to express an allegation or a statement that cannot be vouched for, just like the conditional above.

(iii) *Le voleur aurait pénétré dans le bâtiment par une fenêtre laissée ouverte* –
It is thought that the thief got into the building through a window left open

(iv) *Vous auriez donc vu, de vos yeux vu, le rhinocéros se promener en flânant dans les rues de la ville?* – You are supposed to have seen then, with your own eyes, the rhinoceros strolling through streets of the town?

Formation

The conditional perfect is formed from the conditional of *avoir* or *être* + the past participle:

Trouver
    J'aurais trouvé   *Nous aurions trouvé*
    Tu aurais trouvé   *Vous auriez trouvé*
    Il aurait trouvé   *Ils auraient trouvé*

Partir
    Je serais parti(e)   *Nous serions parti(e)s*
    Tu serais parti(e)   *Vous seriez parti(e)(s)*
    Il serait parti   *Ils seraient partis*
    Elle serait partie   *Elles seraient parties*

Tenses after *si*

It has already been noted that when the future is implied in French a future or a future perfect tense must be used, except after *si* where it means 'if'. *Si* can also mean 'if/whether':

(i) *Je ne sais pas si je le verrai ce soir* – I don't know if/whether I will see him tonight
A future type tense is used after *si* that can mean 'whether'. As already pointed out, the simplest rule to follow after *si* is to use the same tense that is used in English.

(ii) *S'il arrive, dites-lui d'attendre* – If he comes, tell him to wait
A present tense is used in English so a present tense is used in French. However, in these examples:

(iii) *Je me demande s'il viendra* – I wonder if he will come
(Future tense in English after 'if', so same in French.)

(iv) *Je lui ai demandé si elle aimerait sortir avec moi* –
I asked her if she would like to go out with me
(Conditional in English so the same in French.)

This rule with *si* can usually be relied upon.

Note The simple past in English is translated by the **imperfect** in French:

(v) *Si je savais son adresse je lui écrirais* – If I **knew** his address I would write to him

Exercices (for future perfect and conditional perfect tense)

1 Traduisez en français:
   (a) He will find the letter
   (b) He would have found the letter (if he had looked in the cupboard)
   (c) He will have found the letter
   (d) He would find the letter (if he looked in the cupboard)
   (e) Shall I go out with him tonight?
   (f) I would have gone out with him tonight
   (g) I would go out with her (if I had some money)
   (h) He will already have gone out

2 Les verbes suivants sont au futur. Trouvez:
   (a) L'infinitif de chaque verbe
   (b) Le conditionnel (à la même personne)
   (c) Le futur antérieur
   (d) Le conditionnel passé
   Exemple, il retiendra:
   (a) retenir
   (b) il retiendrait
   (c) il aura retenu
   (d) il aurait retenu
      ils feront – ils seront – je verrai – nous aurons – il pourra – il aura – il pleuvra – nous enverrons – il mourra – il faudra – ils jetteront – il vaudra

3 Traduisez en français:
   (a) When you see him give him this
   (b) If you see him give him this
   (c) As soon as I have finished I'll telephone you
   (d) If I had enough money I would like to travel
   (e) What are we going to do this evening?
   (f) What would we do without television?
   (g) I am sure he would have told you that
   (h) If we had been there we would have seen him
   (i) I asked her whether she would like to come with me to Greece
   (j) I don't know if she would come

4 (a) Traduisez en anglais.
  (b) Transposez au passé en commençant par 'C'était la veille du grand départ...'

C'est la veille du grand départ. Bientôt Marie-Claude va faire ses valises car elle va partir demain matin à 5 heures. Demain soir elle sera à Cannes. Elle aura passé dix heures dans le train et aussitôt qu'elle aura mangé elle ira se coucher à l'hôtel. On lui a dit que, de sa fenêtre, elle pourra voir la mer dès qu'il fera jour.

5 Traduisez en français:
  (a) If I see him, I'll give him this. If he asks me who gave it to me, I'll tell him the truth.
  (b) When I see him, I'll give him this. When he asks who gave it to me I'll tell him the truth.

6 Traduisez en anglais:

Deux cents militants kurdes ont manifesté hier à Paris et ont occupé le premier étage de la Tour Eiffel. Selon leurs responsables, deux d'entre leurs compatriotes seraient morts récemment des suites de mauvais traitements dans les prisons turques, et plusieurs autres seraient actuellement dans un état critique.

7 Dans l'extrait suivant quels détails sont établis et lesquels sont supposés?

Hier matin, sur un parking à Chateaudun, un homme a reçu plusieurs coups de couteau d'une jeune fille mineure, apparemment son amie. Ce serait un témoin qui aurait alerté la police. La victime dont l'identité n'est pas encore connue, a été transportée dans un état grave à l'hôpital. Il aurait notamment le poumon perforé. Quant à la jeune fille, elle se serait constituée prisonnière vers 4h 15 à la gendarmerie de Poulains.

2.13 SUBJUNCTIVE MOOD

Use

The subjunctive is a mood of the verb. There are three moods:

(a) **indicative**, used most of the time for stating facts where there is no uncertainty in the mind of the speaker

(b) **subjunctive**, for stating ideas, possibilities and wishes which might not necessarily happen

(c) **imperative**, for giving orders and commands

The subjunctive has virtually disappeared from English. For example, do you say, 'If I **were** you I wouldn't do that' or 'If I **was** you I wouldn't do that'? The '**were**' here is used to state a possibility. You would still probably say 'May he **succeed** in his plans' but you might say instead 'I hope he **succeeds** in his plans'. 'I were' and 'he succeed' are both remnants of the subjunctive in English.

In French, the subjunctive in the present tense (and to some extent the perfect tense) is very much alive and used in the spoken language. The imperfect and the pluperfect subjunctives are confined to the written language and then most often to the third person singular.

You will need to be able to use the present and perfect subjunctives in essays and translations into French and to recognize the other two tenses when you meet them in texts.

Formation

1 Present tense

Regular verbs

Take the third person plural present tense, remove the '*-ent*' and add the endings:

-e	*-ions*
-es	*-iez*
-e	*-ent*

ils finissent	*Que je finisse*	*Que nous finissions*
	Que tu finisses	*Que vous finissiez*
	Qu'il finisse	*Qu'ils finissent*

ils changent	*Que je change*	*Que nous changions*
	Que tu changes	*Que vous changiez*
	Qu'il change	*Qu'ils changent*

Ils entendent	*Que j'entende*	*Que nous entendions*
	Que tu entendes	*Que vous entendiez*
	Qu'il entende	*Qu'ils entendent*

Note Since the subjunctive always has *que* before it it is a good idea to learn it in this way. French schoolchildren learn it like this.

Irregular verbs

The following verbs have almost the same endings as above but the inside part changes. They are all very commonly used and should be learned:

Que je sois	*Que nous soyons*
Que tu sois	*Que vous soyez*
Qu'il soit	*Qu'ils soient*

Que j'aie	*Que nous ayons*
Que tu aies	*Que vous ayez*
Qu'il ait	*Qu'ils aient*

Que je fasse	*Que nous fassions*
Que tu fasses	*Que vous fassiez*
Qu'il fasse	*Qu'ils fassent*

Que j'aille	*Que nous allions*
Que tu ailles	*Que vous alliez*
Qu'il aille	*Qu'ils aillent*

Que je puisse	*Que nous puissions*
Que tu puisses	*Que vous puissiez*
Qu'il puisse	*Qu'ils puissent*

Que je sache	*Que nous sachions*
Que tu saches	*Que vous sachiez*
Qu'il sache	*Qu'ils sachent*

Que je veuille	*Que nous voulions*
Que tu veuilles	*Que vous vouliez*
Qu'il veuille	*Qu'ils veuillent*

You should be able to tell which verbs these come from.

2 Perfect subjunctive

This is the present subjunctive of *être* or *avoir* + the past participle:

Que j'aie fini	*Que nous ayons fini*
Que tu aies fini	*Que vous ayez fini*
Qu'il ait fini	*Qu'ils aient fini*

Que je sois resté(e)	*Que nous soyons resté(e)s*
Que tu sois resté(e)	*Que vous soyez resté(e)(s)*

Qu'il soit resté   *Qu'ils soient restés*
Qu'elle soit restée   *Qu'elles soient restées*

❸ Imperfect subjunctive

You will only meet this tense in written French where it is confined, almost entirely, to the third person singular. In everyday spoken French, when a past subjunctive is needed, the perfect subjunctive is used instead. The third person singular of the imperfect subjunctive bears a close resemblance to the past historic.

Note Even though the imperfect subjunctive is hardly used any more in speech (in casual conversation) it does give the speaker an unusual importance; people would stop to listen. Here are some examples:

il fut (past historic)   *il arriva* (past historic)   *il attendit* (past historic)
qu'il fût (imperfect   *qu'il arrivât* (imperfect   *qu'il attendît* (imperfect
subjunctive)   subjunctive)   subjunctive)

The endings are as follows:

-sse	*-ssions*
-sses	*-ssiez*
-ût	*-ssent*

Que je fusse	*Que nous fussions*
Que tu fusses	*Que vous fussiez*
Qu'il fût	*Qu'ils fussent*

All you have to remember is to put the vowel from the past historic '-a', '-u' or '-i' before the double '-ss' and to put a circumflex before the '-t' of the third person singular. The imperfect subjunctive translates just like an ordinary past tense. French children have to learn about this tense in school.

❹ The pluperfect subjunctive

This is formed from the imperfect subjunctive of *avoir* or *être* + the past participle.
(i) *Bien qu'il ne fût jamais allé en France il parlait très bien le français –*
Although he had never been to France he spoke French very well

It is used in the subjunctive clause when the meaning is clearly 'had'. It only occurs in 'literary-style' written French. You are unlikely to need to use it. The following special uses of it however, could be confusing in a translation:

Used instead of a conditional perfect:
(i) *Il eût mieux fait de rester chez lui – il aurait mieux fait de rester chez lui –*
It would have been better for him to stay at home
(ii) *Il aimait rester au lit le matin, ne fût-ce que pour dix minutes –*
He liked staying in bed in the morning, even if it were only for 10 minutes

If you are studying seventeenth or eighteenth century texts you will come across lots of examples of the above uses.

Using the pluperfect subjunctive as though it were a conditional perfect (see (i) above) is also fairly common today in 'literary-style' French.

Basic rules

After certain conjunctions:

❶ Saying **'although'**– *quoique, bien que:*

(i) *Bien que ce ne soit pas toujours le cas –* Although it isn't always the case

❷ Saying **'so that, in order that'** – *pour que, afin que:*

Parlez plus haut pour qu'il puisse vous entendre – Speak louder so that he can hear you

❸ Saying **'before, until', 'without'** – *avant que, jusqu'à ce que, sans que*:

(i) *Il nous faut attendre jusqu'à ce qu'elle soit prête –* We must wait until she is ready
(ii) *Dites-le-lui avant qu'il ne le sache par ma lettre –*
Tell him it before he finds out from my letter

(iii) *Je suis entré dans la chambre sans qu'elle m'ait entendu* –
I entered the room without her hearing me

Note

(a) An infinitive construction is preferred when the subject of both clauses is the same:
Il est parti avant de lire ma lettre – **He** left and **he** didn't read my letter

(b) The phrase *après que*, referring to events that have already taken place does not need a subjunctive. Can you explain why?

(c) Also *avant de* is sometimes easier to use than *jusqu'à ce que*:
Je vais travailler avant d'aller à l'université – I am going to work until I go to university

❹ Saying 'provided that', 'on condition that' – *pourvu que, à condition que*:

Je le ferai à condition qu'elle ne me le reproche pas –
I'll do it provided that she doesn't reproach me for it

❺ Saying 'unless' – *à moins que*:

(i) *A moins qu'on ne prenne vite des mesures importantes l'atmosphère de notre planète sera complètement dégradée* – Unless serious measures are taken quickly the atmosphere of our planet will be totally ruined

❻ Saying 'so that', 'in such a way that'– when intention rather than result is implied:

(i) *Il faut imposer des amendes très sévères de sorte que les industriels soient obligés d'arrêter la pollution* – Severe fines must be imposed so that industrialists are forced to stop pollution

But

(ii) *La loi a été si vigoureusement appliquée que personne n'ose plus l'enfreindre* – The law has been so rigorously applied that no one dares break it any more

❼ Saying 'whoever', 'however', 'wherever', 'whatever', 'whether'. These are best learned in phrases that could be used or adapted for essays:

(i) *Quel qu'il soit je ne le laisserai pas entrer* – Whoever he is I shan't let him in

(ii) *Aussi désagréable que soit la tâche, il faut la faire* –
However disagreeable the task is, it must be done

(iii) *Où (quelque part) qu'on aille dans notre pays, on voit les mêmes problèmes* –
Wherever you go in our country, you see the same problems

(iv) *Quoi qu'il arrive, il faut continuer la lutte* –
Whatever happens, we must continue the struggle

Note Take care not to confuse *quoique* 'although' with *quoi que* 'whatever':

(v) *Que ce soit pendant ma vie ou pendant celle de mes enfants...* –
Whether it's during my lifetime or that of my children...

(vi) *Quels que soient vos vrais sentiments il vaut mieux ne pas les révéler tout de suite* –
Whatever your real feelings are it's best not to show them straight away

❽ **Giving a command**

Que + subjunctive can be used as a command form in 'careful-style' French:

(i) *Qu'il parte tout de suite et qu'il ne revienne pas avant 6 heures* –
Let him leave immediately and not return before six o'clock

After certain verbs

❶ **After verbs that, generally speaking, convey an emotional attitude:**

Wishing; wanting; desiring; requesting; regretting; feeling sorry/pleased/surprised; demanding; commanding etc.

(i) *Je suis très content que tu sois venu* – I am very pleased that you have come

(ii) *Il est surpris que j'aie accepté son invitation* – He is surprised that I accepted her invitation

(iii) *Je veux que vous fassiez cela demain* – I want you to do that tomorrow

(iv) *Nous regrettons qu'elle ne soit pas là* – We are sorry that she is not there

(v) *Il demande que j'y aille tout de suite* – He is asking that I go there immediately

(vi) *Je m'étonne qu'il ait fait cela* – I am astonished that he did that

Note

These sentences are made up of two parts (clauses): a main clause and a subsidiary clause. The subjunctive always comes in the subsidiary clause and is always introduced by *que* (*see* the conjunctions above). If the tense in the subsidiary clause is a present tense in English, then a present subjunctive is needed in spoken French; if it's a past tense, then a perfect subjunctive is required. In 'careful-style' written French, an imperfect or pluperfect subjunctive might occur (*see* below). Most Examining Boards will accept a present subjunctive (in a translation or essay) where an imperfect is preferable.

2 **After verbs expressing fear:**

(i) *J'ai peur qu'il ne fasse quelque erreur* – I am afraid of him making some mistake

(ii) *Nous craignons qu'il ne soit réélu comme Premier ministre* –
We are afraid that he might get re-elected as Prime Minister

(iii) *Vous avez peur qu'il ne soit pas réélu?* – You are afraid of him not being re-elected?

Note The *ne*, in the first two examples, occurs when **both** clauses are in the affirmative. When the subjunctive clause is in the negative *ne...pas* is used as normal. *A moins que* (*see* **5** on page 73) has a similar *ne* and behaves in the same way.

3 **Verbs expressing personal opinion:**

I think, believe, hope, am sure/am certain, say etc. A subjunctive is required after these verbs only when they are in the negative or used interrogatively. Here are some examples:

(i) *Je crois qu'il a parfaitement raison* – I think/believe he is quite right

(ii) *Il est sûr qu'elle ne le fera pas* – He is sure that she will not do it

but:

(iii) *Je ne crois pas qu'il ait parfaitement raison* – I don't think that he is quite right

(iv) *Est-il sûr qu'elle ne le fasse pas?* – Is he sure that she won't do it?

Here are some other examples:

(v) *Je ne dis pas que cela soit vrai* – I don't say that that is true

(vi) *Croyez-vous qu'ils disent toujours la vérité* – Do you think that they always tell the truth?

(vii) *J'espère qu'elle reviendra* – I hope that she will come back

Note: the verb *espérer* (to hope), used affirmatively, expresses more certainty than 'hope' in English and only requires a subjunctive when used as a question or negatively (Compare with *probable* below.)

4 **Impersonal verbs: most common examples**

(i) *Il faut que* – It is necessary that

(ii) *Il se peut que* – It may be that

(iii) *Il importe que* – It is important that

(iv) *Il est regrettable que* – It is regrettable that

(v) *Il est possible/impossible que* – it is possible/impossible that

(vi) *Il est improbable/peu probable que* – it is improbable/not very probable that

(vii) *Il semble que* –It seems that

(viii)*Il est douteux que* – it is doubtful that

Note

(ix) *Il est probable que vous comprenez*

(x) *Il est certain que vous comprenez*

(xi) *Il me semble que vous comprenez*

They all express a degree of certainty that does not require a subjunctive.

5 **Subjunctive versus indicative:**

The use of a subjunctive can depend on whether the statement or idea expressed is a personal opinion or an established fact:

(i) *C'est la plus grande carotte qu'on ait jamais vue* (in the opinion of the speaker)

(ii) *C'est la plus grande carotte qu'on a jamais récoltée*
(this one is in the Guinness book of records)

(iii) *L'Antarctique est la dernière région du monde où l'homme n'a pas détruit la nature* (speaker is sure and wants to convince his audience)

(iv) *L'Antarctique est la dernière région du monde où l'homme n'ait pas détruit la nature* (speaker gives this as his own opinion)

(v) *Je cherche un petit coin à la campagne où je puisse vivre tranquillement* (a wish unfulfilled)

(vi) *J'ai trouvé un petit coin à la campagne où je peux vivre tranquillement* (a wish fulfilled)

You can also say, avoiding the subjunctive:

(vii) *Je cherche un coin pour vivre tranquillement*

Exercices

1 Traduisez les bouts de phrases suivants:
   (a) So that he understands
   (b) Although we know
   (c) Unless he comes
   (d) You must go there (il faut)
   (e) Provided he does it
   (f) Before he leaves
   (g) Let him leave and not come back!
   (h) Whatever he says
   (i) Whatever your reasons are
   (j) It may be that the government is right
   (k) Without him knowing
   (l) Until they learn
   (m) Although they do not understand
   (n) Although they have understood
   (o) Provided that she has finished

2 Traduisez:
   (a) I think you are right
   (b) Do you think they are right?
   (c) I am afraid that it is too late
   (d) It is possible that the situation is too serious
   (e) It is probable that he is taking the necessary measures
   (f) It is not likely that he is taking the necessary measures
   (g) I am sorry that you do not agree with me
   (h) I am surprised that they have done that
   (i) Do you think the government is following the right policy?
   (j) I hope this information is correct
   (k) I am pleased that he did that
   (l) Do you think that is true?
   (m) I do not think that is possible
   (n) It is regrettable that he took this decision
   (o) I am afraid that I might make a mistake

3 Traduisez:
   (a) Vous eussiez mieux fait de venir me voir tout de suite
   (b) Quelles que soient vos raisons je ne peux pas approuver cette action
   (c) Quoi que vous fassiez, n'écoutez pas ses excuses
   (d) Je cherche quelqu'un qui puisse m'aider aujourd'hui
   (e) J'ai déjà trouvé quelqu'un qui pourra m'aider demain
   (f) Quelque difficile que vous trouviez ce travail, il faut que vous fassiez de votre mieux

(g) Je vais voyager avant de commencer mes études à l'université
(h) Que vous trouviez ou non quelqu'un pour faire ce travail, cela m'est égal
(i) J'ai peur qu'elle ne soit déjà partie
(j) Il faut que vous vous reposiez un peu, ne fût-ce que quinze minutes

2.14 MODAL VERBS

May, must, might, ought, could, should, would

These modal verbs are best learned in an example together with the meaning:
  (i)   *Pouvons-nous entrer?* – May we come in?
  (ii) *Il se peut que cela soit vrai*
        Il est possible que cela soit vrai } – That may be true
  (iii) *Cela pourrait être vrai* – That could/might be true
  (iv) *Vous pourriez le faire ce soir* – You could do it this evening
  (v)   *Vous auriez pu le faire sans moi* – You could have done it without me
  (vi) *Je dois le faire ce soir*
        Il faut que je le fasse ce soir } – I must/have to do it this evening
  (vii) *J'ai dû le faire hier soir* – I had to do it last night
  (viii)*Mon parapluie? J'ai dû le laisser chez moi* – I must have left it at home
  (ix) *Elle devait venir à 6 heures* – She was to come at six
  (x)   *Vous ne devriez pas l'aider à faire ses devoirs* – You shouldn't help him with his homework
  (xi) *Vous devriez vous reposer un peu* – You ought to/should rest a little
  (xii) *Vous n'auriez pas dû le faire sans moi* – You shouldn't have done it without me
  (xiii)*Il ne voulait pas le faire sans moi* – He wouldn't do it without me (he was unwilling)*
  (xiv)*Je voudrais vous aider* – I would like to help you

Note also:
(a) *Vous risquez de vous rompre le cou* – You **might** break your neck
(b) *"would" needs special care when translating. Distinguish between: (i) 'would' (a conditional, 'he would do it' if he could); (ii) 'would' (willing to); (iii) 'would' (used to, imperfect tense).

Can you?

  (i)   *Vous savez jouer du piano?* – Can you play the piano? (have you learned?)
  (ii) *Vous savez nager?* – Can you swim? (do you know how to?)
  (iii) *Pouvez-vous nager? (habillé de ce manteau)* – Are you capable of swimming? (with that coat on)

Knowing people/places/facts
(a) Being **acquainted** with people or places is expressed by *connaître*.
(b) Knowing **facts, having knowledge** is expressed by *savoir* (savvy).
  (i)   *Vous savez où se trouve Apt? Oui, dans le Midi. C'est une ville que je connais très bien.*

Exercice

1 Traduisez:
    (a) I must have left it at home
    (b) You shouldn't be afraid
    (c) You ought not to have paid
    (d) Could you lend me 10 francs?

(e) I must work harder
(f) Will you come this evening?
(g) Will she be there?
(h) Do you know what the capital of Estonia is?
(i) Before the war I knew Tallin very well
(j) Can you do it before this evening?

2.15 THE PASSIVE VOICE

Use and formation

Having dealt with the **mood** of the verb (*see* page 70) one further aspect needs to be considered: the **voice**. There are two main voices: **active** and **passive**. Consider the two following statements:

(i) *Fifi m'embrasse* – Fifi kisses me
(ii) *Je suis embrassé par Fifi* – I am kissed by Fifi

The first uses the verb actively; the subject 'Fifi' is doing the action to the object 'me'. The second uses the verb passively so that the object receives the action and comes first in the sentence while 'the doer' (or agent) comes last. Note that the passive in French is a direct translation of the English 'I am kissed', *je suis embrassé*, and the agent is indicated by *par*. You should now be able to work out what the following would be in French (cover up the right-hand column before checking your answer):

(i) Fifi is kissed by me	*Fifi est embrassée par moi*
(ii) I shall be kissed by Fifi	*Je serai embrassé par Fifi*
(iii) I have been kissed by Fifi	*J'ai été embrassé par Fifi*
(iv) I was kissed by Fifi (once)	*J'ai été embrassé par Fifi*
(v) I was kissed by Fifi (all the time)	*J'étais embrassé par Fifi*
(vi) I had been kissed by Fifi	*J'avais été embrassé par Fifi*
(vii) I would be kissed by Fifi (if she liked me)	*Je serais embrassé par Fifi*
(viii) I would have been kissed by Fifi	*J'aurais été embrassé par Fifi*
(ix) Fifi would have been kissed by me	*Fifi aurait été embrassée par moi*
(x) Fifi had been kissed by me	*Fifi avait été embrassée par moi*

Note The past participle in the passive always agrees with the subject. All the tenses of the active voice are possible in the passive and usually follow the English model word for word. Care has to be taken though with 'was'. Does it mean a single action or a repeated or habitual one? (*See also* imperfect tense, pages 57–58.)

Now try using the verb actively in the above sentences. The first one is done for you. Cover up the the section below which gives the answers.

(i) *Fifi est embrassée par moi* – *J'embrasse Fifi*
(ii) *Fifi m'embrassera*
(iii) *Fifi m'a embrassé*
(iv) *Fifi m'a embrassé*
(v) *Fifi m'embrassait*
(vi) *Fifi m'avait embrassé*
(vii) *Fifi m'embrasserait*
(viii) *Fifi m'aurait embrassé*
(ix) *J'aurais embrassé Fifi*
(x) *J'avais embrassé Fifi*

In theory any French verb that is transitive (takes a direct object) can be used in the passive voice. In practice however the passive is more often than not avoided. There are three ways of doing this:

● By using *on* (as a subject)
● By using a reflexive verb

● By using the verb actively (if possible)

You have to avoid the passive with intransitive verbs in French (those that take an indirect object).

❶ **Using *on* as a subject** You can say in English 'I was told to wait'. But in French you tell 'to' someone – *dire à quelqu'un*, so you would have to say something like 'to me was told to wait'. To avoid this difficulty you say instead:

(i)   *On m'a dit d'attendre* – I was told to wait (literally 'one told me to wait')
(ii) *On m'a montré un siège* – I was shown a seat
(iii) *On leur a demandé de s'asseoir* – They were asked to sit down
(iv) *On m'a donné un programme* – I was given a programme

❷ **Using a reflexive verb** You could in theory say:

(i)   *Je suis bien intéressé par les films japonais* – I am very interested in Japanese films
In practice you would say:
(ii) *Je m'intéresse beaucoup aux films japonais*
Here are some other examples:
(iii) *Le français se parle beaucoup dans les pays africains* –
      French is spoken a lot in African countries
(iv) *Cela se fait rarement ici* – That is done rarely here
(v)   *Il s'est fait beaucoup de mal en exprimant cette opinion* –
      He has done himself a lot of harm in expressing that opinion
(vi) *Cela se trouve partout en Europe* – It is found everywhere in Europe
(vii) *Cet appareil photo se vend maintenant dans tous les magasins* (or *Cet appareil photo est en vente dans tous les magasins*) – This camera is being sold now in all the shops

❸ **Using the verb actively** Try the sentence 'I was given this idea by my sister' (if you start with *j'ai été donné* it starts to mean you were given *away*). So *Ma sœur m'a donné cette idée*. Here are some other examples:

(i)   *Mon prof m'a dit de ne pas travailler si dur* – I was told by my teacher not to work so hard
(ii) *Son refus m'a surpris* – I was surprised by his refusal
In the latter example you could say *J'ai été surpris par son refus* but the active form gives a livelier style.

The past participles of some verbs can behave more like adjectives than active parts of verbs. Here are some examples:

(i)   *Le magasin est ouvert de 8 à 18 heures*
(ii) *J'étais embarrassé par ses visites*
(iii) *Mon ami était respecté de tout le monde*
(iv) *Vous serez accompagné d'un policier*
(v)   *La pièce était éclairée par une seule ampoule*
In these cases the passive (more like verb 'to be' + adjective) is more appropriate.

In the present tense some verbs differ in meaning according to whether they are used actively or passively. Compare:

(i)   *la porte est ouverte* and *la porte s'ouvre*
(ii) *les pêches sont vendues au marché* and *les pêches se vendent 2F le kilo*
(iii) *elle est habillée* and *elle s'habille*

Exercices

1   Traduisez en utilisant le passif:
    (a) He was invited by a friend
    (b) You will be noticed by the police
    (c) The thief was arrested by a fireman
    (d) A solution had been found

  (e) The secrets were revealed
  (f) The theory of relativity was proposed by Einstein
  (g) He is known by everyone
  (h) This model is sold everywhere
  (i) My plans will be accomplished one day
  (j) The general would have been run over (*écraser*) by a tank

2 Même exercice en évitant le passif:

3 Traduisez:
  (a) He will not be re-elected (*réélu*) next time
  (b) I was ordered not to move (*ne pas bouger*)
  (c) We were not told the truth
  (d) We were asked not to wait
  (e) The advert is seen everywhere
  (f) He is thought to be very clever
  (g) That is not done here
  (h) I was forgiven by my sister
  (i) The face of the earth has been changed by man
  (j) The skin is burned by too much sun
  (k) The door opens slowly, a hand is seen in the opening (*dans l'embrasure*), a strange cry is heard!
  (l) The doors of the TGV open when the train stops
  (m) The doors are not open before the train stops

2.16   PRESENT PARTICIPLE

Use

The present participle in French is used in the following ways:

❶ Like a verb ending in '-ing' (in English):
  (i) *Criant et gesticulant, la foule d'ouvriers s'est avancée vers le palais* –
      Shouting and waving their arms the crowd of workers advanced towards the palace
  (ii) *Rentrant chez moi très tard et réfléchissant à tous ces problèmes je me sentais triste* –
      Returning home late and reflecting upon all these problems I felt sad

Note The participle in '-ing' is used fairly loosely in English. In French it **always** implies an action(s) going on at the same time as the main verb. For example:
  (iii) *Assis derrière son bureau il avait l'air très important* –
      Sitting behind his desk he looked very important

If you started with *'S'asseyant à son pupitre'* this would mean 'as he was sitting down he looked important'. Similarly:
  (iv) *Caché derrière la porte il pouvait tout voir* –
      Hiding behind the door he could see everything
  (v) *Couché sur son lit* – Lying on his bed
  (vi) *Agenouillé devant le feu* – Kneeling in front of the fire

❷ Like an adjective
  (i) *un livre intéressant* – an interesting book
  (ii) *une histoire émouvante* – a touching story
  (iii) *une dame charmante* – a charming lady
  (iv) *un visage souriant* – a smiling face

Note Unlike the verbal use above, the participle agrees here just like an adjective.

3 After the preposition '*en*' to mean one of three things:

(a) '**By doing something**'
  (i) *En écoutant tous les matins France-Inter, j'ai appris à comprendre le français quand on le parle vite* – By listening to France-Inter every morning, I learned to understand French spoken quickly
  (ii) *Le voleur a réussi à casser la fenêtre en se servant de son coude* – By using his elbow the thief managed to break the window

Note After verbs expressing the idea of beginning and finishing (*commencer, finir, débuter, terminer, achever*), 'by doing something' is expressed by *par* + infinitive:
  (iii) *Il a commencé par m'expliquer la vraie situation* – He began by explaining the real situation
  (iv) *Il a fini par nier ce qu'il avait dit* – He finished by denying what he had said

In all other cases 'by doing something' will be rendered by *en* + present participle

(b) '**While doing something**'
  (i) *Je préfère travailler en écoutant de la musique* – I prefer to work while listening to music
  (ii) *En revenant de la banque j'ai vu un accident* – While on my way back from the bank I saw an accident

(c) '**Upon/on doing something**'
  (i) *En entrant dans la pièce j'ai vu que tout était en désordre* – Upon entering the room I found that everything was in disarray
  (ii) *En le voyant sortir un revolver j'ai su qu'il allait peut-être me tuer* – On seeing him draw a gun I realized that he was perhaps going to kill me

Note The present participle is used in many cases in English where it is not used in French.
  (iii) before leaving – *avant de partir*
  (iv) without saying goodbye – *sans dire au revoir*
  (v) after seeing him – *après l'avoir vu*
  (vi) instead of working – *au lieu de travailler*

The golden rule with these examples is that **after a preposition you need an infinitive**.

(d) '**Having done something**' followed by a consequence:
  (i) *Ayant reçu sa lettre, je savais ce qu'il comptait faire* – Having received his letter I knew what he expected to do
  (ii) *Son amie n'étant pas revenue il est parti sans elle* – His girl friend not having returned he set off without her

Note *avoir* or *être* is required according to the verb.

(e) '**After having done something**', what happened next:
  (i) *Après avoir essayé de lui téléphoner plusieurs fois j'ai enfin réussi à le joindre* – After having tried several times...
  (ii) *Après m'être couché de bonne heure j'ai été réveillé par un grand bruit* – After having gone to bed early...
  (iii) *Après être resté deux jours là-bas il m'a fallu revenir chez moi* – After having stayed there two days...

Note You could also say in English 'Having tried...', 'Having gone to bed...' or 'After trying...' etc.

Formation

This is formed by removing '*-ons*' from the first plural present tense and adding '*-ant*' which is phonetically similar. '*-ant*' is the equivalent in English of '*-ing*'. There are three present participles that cannot be obtained in this way: *ayant*, 'having'; *étant*, 'being'; *sachant*, 'knowing'.

Exercices

1 Traduisez:
   (a) By working at weekends and by saving money (*faire des économies*) they were eventually able to buy a house
   (b) I did it while watching television
   (c) She was sitting in front of the fire with the cat lying on her lap (*sur les genoux*)
   (d) Having arrived late I missed the first act
   (e) After locking and bolting (*verrouiller*) the door I went to bed
   (f) Before leaving check (*vérifiez*) that you have closed all the windows
   (g) He found on arriving that the other guests had already started the meal
   (h) Begin by learning the irregular verbs
   (i) You can't get rid of (*se débarrasser de*) your rubbish by dumping it in the street.
   (j) Waving her hands and motioning to me she managed to attract my attention
   (k) A charming lady with a smiling face
   (l) I like playing the guitar, watching football on television and going out with my mates

2 Traduisez. Dans ces exemples vous trouverez que l'emploi de '-ing' en anglais ne correspond pas avec le '-ant' en français:
   (a) Il aime beaucoup la pêche et la chasse et il adore faire de la voile
   (b) Voir c'est croire
   (c) Toute la maison a besoin d'être nettoyée
   (d) Je vous remercie de me l'avoir rappelé
   (e) Les femmes ont la réputation d'être de bonnes conductrices
   (f) Dans *l'Avare* de Molière, Maître Jacques est puni pour avoir dit la vérité
   (g) Une machine à coudre; une salle à manger; une leçon d'équitation; une leçon de conduite; une auto-école
   (h) Oui, je le vois qui s'approche. Il court très vite, il fait des signes de la main et il crie

2.17 *FAIRE* AND THE INFINITIVE

Consider the difference between the following:
   J'ai réparé mon vélo and *J'ai fait réparer mon vélo au magasin*
In the first example you did the work yourself; in the second you got it repaired (had it repaired) by someone else. '*Faire* + infinitive' is used to convey this idea in French. This combination is used a great deal to express a variety of ideas where English often uses a different verb.
   Can you work out what the following mean?
   (i)   *Le ministre des transports a fait construire une route de contournement pour notre ville*
   (ii)   *Le prof essaie de faire travailler ses élèves*
   (iii) *Maman m'a fait manger tout ce qui restait sur mon assiette*
   (iv)   *Je n'aime pas tellement ce pull, mes parents me l'ont fait acheter*
   (v)   *S'il conduit aussi vite que ça, il se tuera ou il se fera arrêter par la police*
   (vi)   *Servez-vous je vous en prie; je fais servir Jean d'abord parce qu'il est le plus petit*
   (vii) *Faites entrer ces messieurs; faites venir le médecin*
   (viii) *Vous portez cette lettre à la poste? Faites-la porter par un de vos élèves**
   (ix)   *Il a fait sécher ses vêtements devant le feu***
   (x)   *Faites taire ces élèves, ils font trop de bruit***

Note
* Get one of your pupils to take it: you have to say in French *par un de vos élèves* to make it clear which is the direct and which the indirect object.

** If pronouns are used with *faire* + infinitive the pronoun goes before *faire*. So, in (ix) and (x) above *Je les ai fait sécher devant le feu* and *Je les ai fait taire* but the past participle does not agree.

You can say in English 'I boiled some water' but in French you have to say *J'ai fait bouillir de l'eau* since you don't really do the boiling yourself! This also applies to other cooking processes:

(i) *Faites cuire dans de l'eau bouillante pendant trois minutes*
(ii) *Faites griller le pain des deux côtés*
(iii) *Faites fondre du beurre dans une casserole*
(iv) *Faites frire dans du beurre*
(v) *Faites rôtir ce poulet pendant deux heures*

The verbs *voir*, *entendre*, *sentir* and *laisser* are also often combined with another verb in the infinitive in a similar way. For example:

(vi) *Je le vois venir* – I can see him coming
(vii) *Je l'entends sonner* – I can hear him ringing
(viii) *Je sentais mes cheveux se hérisser* – I felt my hair standing on end
(ix) *Laissez-les se battre* – Let them fight
(x) *Laissez passer cette dame* – Let the lady through
(xi) *Je l'ai entendu dire cela à son ami* – I heard him tell his friend that
(xii) *J'ai été triste de la voir nous quitter si tôt* – I was sad to see her leave us so early

Exercice

Traduisez:

(a) Send for his father
(b) Don't leave him waiting on the doorstep, show him in
(c) Grill for ten minutes
(d) I've had a house built in the country
(e) Get him to eat something
(f) He got some cakes brought from the pâtisserie
(g) Let him speak
(h) Keep those dogs quiet!
(i) The thief got caught the next day
(j) I got my sister to do this homework

2.18 VERBS TAKING PREPOSITIONS

Some verbs do not need a preposition to link with the following verb. For example:

(i) *Savez-vous nager?*
(ii) *J'aime faire du ski*
(iii) *Voulez-vous sortir ce soir?*
(iv) *J'espère aller à l'université l'année prochaine*
(v) *Il n'ose pas prendre une décision*
(vi) *Il faut faire quelque chose*

Many verbs do need a preposition however. The main choice is nearly always between *à* or *de*. The following essential ones have to be learned, preferably in a meaningful combination with a following verb or noun.

❶ Verb + *à*

(i)   *aider à faire ses devoirs*

(ii)   *s'attendre à réussir*

(iii) *consentir à venir*

(iv)   *se décider à partir*

(v)   *forcer à le faire*

(vi)   *inviter à venir*

(vii) *obliger à payer*

(viii) *réussir à le persuader*

(ix)   *apprendre à parler*

(x)   *commencer à pleuvoir*

(xi)   *continuer à écrire*

(xii) *encourager à continuer*

(xiii) *hésiter à prendre une décision*

(xiv) *se mettre à discuter*

(xv)   *persister à se plaindre*

❷ Verb + *de*

(i)   *je suis chargé de lui parler* (have the job of)

(ii)   *cesser de pleuvoir*

(iii) *défendre de traverser la rue*

(iv)   *essayer de le persuader*

(v)   *faire semblant de consentir*

(vi)   *finir de faire des excuses*

(vii) *offrir de payer*

(viii) *oublier de le faire*

(ix)   *décider de lui parler*

(x)   *refuser d'accepter*

(xi)   *remercier de son offre*

(xii) *demander de le faire*

(xiii) *empêcher de faire quelque chose*

(xiv) *je vous félicite de votre succès*

(xv)   *menacer de dire la vérité*

(xvi) *ordonner de venir*

(xvii) *permettre de l'accompagner*

(xviii) *regretter de ne pas pouvoir venir*

(xix) *je vous excuse d'être en retard*

Many verbs require the preposition *à* before an indirect object. In the following examples make a note of the preposition used in English. It is not always 'to'. For example: *Il a acheté un vélo à mon frère.*

(i)   *J'ai conseillé à mon ami de dire la vérité*

(ii)   *Emprunter de l'argent à votre oncle*

(iii) *Est-ce qu'on peut se fier à cette personne?*

(iv)   *Il faut obéir à ses parents*

(v)   *Ordonner aux soldats de tirer*

(vi)   *Il plaît beaucoup à cette fille*

(vii) *Prêter ce roman à mon frère*

(viii) *Raconter des histoires à sa grand-mère*

(ix)   *J'ai réfléchi à ce que j'avais fait*

(x)   *Il volait aux riches pour donner...*

(xi)   *Il a ri de moi* (he laughed at me)

(xii) *Il a dissimulé sa faute à son père*

(xiii) *Il a livré le secret à sa sœur*

(xiv) *Envoyer une carte à ses parents*

(xv)   *Montrez ça au prof*

(xvi) *Offrir sa place à une vieille dame*

(xvii) *Je pense souvent à elle*

(xviii) *Prendre l'argent aux riches pour le donner...*

(xix) *Promettre au prof de le faire*

(xx) *Répondre tout de suite à sa lettre*

(xxi) *Il ressemble beaucoup à James Dean*

(xxii) *Enseigner le russe à sa grand-mère* (teach one's grandmother Russian)

Some other words, mainly adjectives and nouns, also require prepositions before a following infinitive. Here are some examples:

❶ *à*

(i) *Je suis prêt à vous aider* – I am ready to help you

(ii) *J'ai beaucoup à faire* – I have a lot to do

(iii) *Le dernier à arriver* – The last to arrive

(iv) *Le premier à parler* – The first to speak

(v) *Je n'ai rien à dire* – I have nothing to say

(vi) *J'ai quelque chose à dire* – I have something to say

(vii) *Maison à vendre* – House for sale

❷ *de*

(i) *Je suis heureux/triste/étonné/surpris/content de vous voir* –
I am happy/sad/astonished/surprised/content to see you

(ii) *Je suis obligé de lui parler* – I am obliged to talk to him

(iii) *J'ai la permission de lui parler* – I have permission to speak to him

(iv) *J'ai l'occasion de lui parler* – I have the chance to speak to him

(v) *Je n'ai pas le droit de lui parler* – I haven't the right to speak to him

Note

(a) A few verbs have *de* before an object

(i) *Il s'est approché de moi* – He came up to me

(ii) *Cela dépend des circonstances* –That depends on the circumstances

(iii) *Je vous remercie de votre lettre* – I thank you for your letter

(iv) *Il ne faut pas se moquer du Premier ministre* –
You mustn't make fun of the Prime Minister

(v) *Je ne me souviens pas de son nom* – I don't remember his name

(vi) *Il jouit (from jouir) d'une grande réputation* – He enjoys a great reputation

(vii) *Il sait jouer de la guitare* – He can play the guitar

(viii) *Se servir d'un tourne-vis pour ouvrir la boîte* –
To use a screwdriver to open the tin

(b) The following verbs have a preposition in English but none in French:

(i) *J'ai payé les verres cassés* – I paid **for** the broken glasses

(ii) *J'ai sonné et j'ai demandé Marianne* – I rang and asked **for** Marianne

(iii) *J'ai regardé ma montre* – I looked **at** my watch

(iv) *J'attends mon ami* – I'm waiting **for** my friend

(v) *Je cherche mes clefs* – I'm looking **for** my keys

(c) Notice the *à* and *de* construction with the following:

(i) *Il a demandé à Jean de le faire*

(ii) *Il a promis à Jean de le faire*

(iii) *Il a permis à Jean de le faire*

(iv) *Il a dit à Jean de le faire*

(v) *Il a ordonné à Jean de le faire*

(d) Take care with the following phrases which can cause difficulty:

(i) *En vouloir à quelqu'un à cause de quelque chose* – To hold something against someone

(ii) *Il m'en veut à cause de mon succès* –
He bears me a grudge because of my success

(iii) *Ne m'en voulez pas, hein* – Don't hold it against me, eh

(iv) *Il tient beaucoup à réussir dans ce projet (tenir à faire quelque chose)* –
He's very keen on succeeding in this plan

(v) *Il tient de son père (tenir de)* – He takes after his father

(vi) *se passer de quelque chose* – To do without something

(vii) *On peut se passer de nourriture pendant deux semaines, mais on ne peut pas se passer d'eau* – You can do without food for two weeks but you can't do without water

Se douter de quelque chose – to suspect something

(viii) *Il est marié? Je ne m'en suis jamais douté* – He's married? I never guessed/suspected it

(ix) *C'est lui qui a fait le coup? Ah, je m'en doutais!* – He was the one responsible? I thought as much!

Douter de – to doubt something

(x) *Je doute que ce soit lui qui ait fait cela.* – I doubt if it was him that did that (*see* subjunctive, page 47)

Se tromper de quelque chose – to make a mistake about something

(xi) *Je me suis trompé d'appartement* – I got the wrong flat

Servir à + verb

(xii) *Ce torchon sert à nettoyer le tableau* – This cloth is used to clean the board

Servir de +noun

(xiii) *Son mouchoir lui sert de torchon* – His handkerchief serves as a rag

Se servir de

(xiv) *Je me suis servi de mon mouchoir pour nettoyer mes souliers* – I used my handkerchief to clean my shoes

Penser à 'think about' and ***penser de*** 'think of' are frequently confused

(xv) *Que pensez-vous de sa nouvelle petite amie?* – What do you think of his new girlfriend?

(xvi) *Elle pense souvent à son amie tuée pendant la guerre* – She often thinks of her friend killed in the war

(xvii) *Il a manqué son train* – He missed his train

(xviii) *Il me manque deux cents francs* – I'm missing 200 francs (200 francs short)

(xix) *Ses amis lui manquent* – He misses his friends

(xx) *Il manque de respect* – He lacks (does not show) respect

(e) The following examples of unexpected use of prepositions are often pointed out:

(i) *Quelqu'un a bu dans ce verre* – Someone has been drinking **out of** this glass

(ii) *Elle a pris un verre dans le placard* – She took a glass **from out of** the cupboard

(iii) *Il a pris les bijoux sur le comptoir* – He took the jewels from (off) the counter

(iv) *Il nous faudra tous boire à la même bouteille* – We'll all have to drink **from** the same bottle

Exercices

1 Traduisez:
   (a) He agreed to come and see me
   (b) I hesitated to say anything
   (c) I invited him to visit me
   (d) I congratulated her on her success
   (e) I forgot to write
   (f) He refused to accept
   (g) I refused to accept
   (h) I tried to persuade them
   (i) They offered to pay
   (j) He bought the car from my father
   (k) He borrowed the money from his sister
   (l) Can you trust politicians?
   (m) You must laugh at their behaviour
   (n) I must rob a bank to pay for my holiday
   (o) I am always the last to know

2 Traduisez:
   (a) You have nothing to say?
   (b) Everything depends on his decision
   (c) You must pay for the damage
   (d) Who are you waiting for?
   (e) Tell your cousin to bring his sister
   (f) I rang the wrong number
   (g) I haven't had a chance to talk to her
   (h) He was using his sleeve to clean the board
   (i) I promised my teacher to work harder next year
   (j) I was forbidden to use my handkerchief to clean my shoes with
   (k) What do you think of him?
   (l) Do you often think about her?
   (m) Are you short of anything?
   (n) I miss France!
   (o) Can you play the piano?

3 Traduisez en anglais:
   (a) On pourrait bien se passer de télévision
   (b) Il est toujours en prison? Je m'en doutais
   (c) Je tiens beaucoup à visiter la Corse cette année
   (d) Il m'en voulait de ce que je lui avais fait
   (e) A quoi ça sert?
   (f) Nous n'allons pas tous boire dans le même verre, j'espère

2.19 ARTICLES

Note Almost as many mistakes are made in exam papers with the articles in French as with the verbs.

The definite article: *le, la* and *les*

(*See also* gender, pages 42–47)

(a) The definite article is used in much the same way in French as in English to particularize a noun. Here are some examples:
   (i) *Vous voyez le garçon là-bas?* – You see **the** boy over there?
   (ii) *Fermez les fenêtres* – Close **the** windows

(b) It is also used to **generalize** a noun where, in English, this is done by **leaving out** the article:
   (i) *Vous préférez le thé ou le café?* Do you prefer tea or coffee?
   (ii) *Les chats sont plus intelligents que les chiens* – Cats are more intelligent than dogs

(c) The article is also used in French before countries, provinces, continents and **languages** where often it is left out in English:
   (i) *La Lituanie, l'Estonie et la Lettonie se sont liberées de la Russie* –
      Lithuania, Estonia and Latvia won their independence from Russia
   (ii) *La Bretagne se trouve dans l'ouest de la France* – Brittany is in the west of France
   (iii) *Elle parle bien le français, l'espagnol et le portugais* –
      She speaks French, Spanish and Portugese well

   Note also the following:
   (iv) *le soir, l'après–midi, le matin* – in the evening(s), in the afternoon(s) etc.
   (v) *lundi* – on Monday but *le lundi, le mardi* – on Mondays, Tuesdays
   (vi) *La semaine dernière, l'année prochaine* – last week, next year

(d) *De* combines with *le, la* and *les* to form the partitive articles *du, de la, des* and *de l'*, having the meanings in English of 'some' and 'any'. Here are some examples:

(i) *Vous avez **du** vin blanc? Non mais j'ai **du** cidre* –
Have you any white wine? No, but I've got some cider

Often no article at all is needed in English. For example:

(ii) *Qu'est-ce qu'il vous faut? **De l'argent? Des provisions? De l'eau?*** –
What do you need ? Money? Provisions? Water?

Note After *ne... pas* the partitives *du, de la, de l'* and *des* all change to *de*. Here are some examples:

(iii) *J'ai **de l'argent** mais je n'ai pas **de** provisions et je n'ai pas **d'**eau*

(iv) *Vous n'avez pas **de** pêches blanches aujourd'hui? Non, mais j'en ai des jaunes*

(v) *Vous avez **du** temps? Non, je n'ai pas **de** temps*

(e) Partitives *de l'* and *des* are replaced by prepositional *d'* before *autre(s)*. It is best to just learn likely combinations such as:

(i) *Vous avez **d'**autres amis?* – Do you have other friends?

(ii) *Vous avez **d'**autres idées?* – Do you have other ideas?

(iii) *D'autres personnes vous diront le contraire* – Other people will say the opposite

(iv) *Certains prétendront que notre climat n'est pas en train de changer, d'autres maintiendront le contraire* – Some claim that our climate is not changing, others maintain the opposite

(f) *De l'* and *des* are possible however when the meaning is clearly 'of the'. Here is an example:

(i) *Je n'ai pas visité la maison **des** autres garçons de ma classe* –
I haven't visited the houses **of the** other boys of my class.

(g) *De* should be used instead of partitive *des* with an adjective before a plural noun, as below

(i) *de grands enfants* but *des enfants indisciplinés*

(ii) *ce sont de petites erreurs* but *ce sont des erreurs considérables*

(iii) *de jeunes adolescents* but *des adolescents maltraités*

There are some exceptions to this rule however; some combinations of adjective and noun are felt to be so common that they go naturally together with *des* in front of them. These include:

(v) *des petits pois*

(vi) *des jeunes filles*

(vii) *des grands groupes*

(viii) *des jeunes gens*

(ix) *des grands-pères*

(h) *De* is used after expressions of quantity. Here are some examples:

(i) *beaucoup de problèmes*

(ii) *trop de travail*

(iii) *combien d'argent?*

(iv) *un verre de vin*

(v) *peu de gens*

(vi) *un plein d'essence* (a full tank)

(vii) *une bouteille d'eau*

(viii) *une semaine de pluie*

(ix) *rempli de vin* (filled with wine)

(x) *un bon nombre de personnes*

Note

Again, where the real meaning is 'of the', *du, de la, de l'* and *des* are possible. For example:

(xi) *Beaucoup **des** enfants ici sont malheureux* – A lot **of the** children here are unhappy

(xii) *Donnez-moi un verre **du** vin que vous m'avez offert hier* – Give me a glass **of the** wine that you offered me yesterday

In the latter phrase, you could also say:...*de ce vin que vous m'avez offert hier*.

(i) After *la plupart* and *bien* as expressions of quantity *du, de la, de l'* and *des* are required. For example:

(i) *La plupart **des** invités n'étaient pas venus* – Most of the guests had not come

(ii) *J'ai couru bien **des** risques* – I ran a lot of risks

Note 'many of them' is *beaucoup d'entre eux*.

(j) *De* is needed in French after *quelqu'un, quelque chose, personne, rien, quoi* where there is nothing in English. For example:
   (i) *rien d'intéressant* – nothing interesting
   (ii) *quelqu'un d'important* – someone important
   (iii) *Personne de blessé?* – Anyone injured?
   (iv) *Il n'y a eu personne de blessé* – There was no one injured
   (v) *Quoi de neuf?* – What's new?

The indefinite article: *un, une* and *des*

There are fewer things to point out about the indefinite article. It is used in much the same way in French as in English with a few phrases which need to be learned:
Note the following:
   (i) *J'ai mal à la gorge* – I have **a** sore throat
   (ii) *Quelle grande maison!* – What **a** big house!
   (iii) *10F la livre* – 10 francs **a** pound
   (iv) *Mon père est dentiste, ma mère est médecin* – My father is a dentist, my mother is a doctor
In the last example, the definite article is usually left out when stating someone's profession. If you add an adjective to the statement however, the article reappears:
   (v) *Sartre était **un** philosophe célèbre*

Exercice

Traduisez:
   (a) I like football, swimming and basketball
   (b) Pass me the salt please
   (c) Whales (baleines) are still hunted by the Japanese
   (d) Elephants will soon be an endangered species (une espèce en voie de disparition)
   (e) Garlic is an important ingredient in Provençal cooking
   (f) I would like a bottle of water, a kilo of peaches and a tin of the beans that you recommended
   (g) My brother wants to become a doctor – he's full of strange ideas
   (h) Many doctors believe that jogging is dangerous for health
   (i) Most of the people that I have met don't go to church on Sundays
   (j) On Saturday nights I do the cooking
   (k) Many people had arrived late, others hadn't bothered to come
   (l) Last week; next year; in the evening; on Mondays
   (m) There was no wind but plenty of rain
   (n) We haven't got any bananas or peaches
   (o) France is nearly two and a half times bigger than England
   (p) What do we need for the picnic – ham, bread, butter, lettuce, wine or orange juice, peaches and cheese.

2.20 OBJECT PRONOUNS

me	*le*	*lui*	*y*	*en*
te	*la*	*leur*		
se	*les*			
nous				
vous				

The object pronouns are best remembered in this form. They always go in this order **in front of** the verb.

Note

(a) The **first** column pronouns are **direct** or **indirect** and have the following meanings:
'me' or 'to me'; 'you' or 'to you' ; 'himself, herself, oneself' or 'to himself, to herself, to oneself'; 'us' or 'to us'; and 'you' or 'to you'.

(b) The **second** column ones are **direct only** and mean:
'it' (masculine), 'him'; 'her', 'it' (feminine); 'them' (people or things).

(c) The **third** column are **indirect only** and mean:
'to him'; 'to her'; and 'to them' (people).

(d) *Y* means 'there' or 'to it'

(e) *En* means 'some', 'any' and 'of it'

Rules

To get the pronouns right make sure that

❶ They go before the verb, or the auxiliary verb (*avoir* or *être*)

❷ ...in the above order

❸ You know whether a pronoun is direct or indirect, 'to' might not be used in English
 (i) *Je **lui** ai envoyé la lettre hier* – I sent **him** the letter yesterday
Take special care with verbs that take an indirect object in French but a direct one in English. For example
 (ii) *Je lui réponds* – I answer him
 (iii) *Je lui dis* – I tell her
 (iv) *Je lui demande* – I ask him
 (v) *Il lui promet* – He promises her
 (vi) *Elle lui téléphone* – She telephones him

Note

(a) Pronouns replace nouns; *y* replaces *à* + noun. Here are some examples:
 (i) *Vous allez souvent à Biarritz? Oui, j'y vais tous les ans*
 (ii) *Vous pensez souvent à votre vie ensemble? Non, je n'y pense pas souvent*
 (iii) *Je réfléchis à cette question , oui, j'y réfléchis beaucoup!*

(b) *En* replaces *de* + noun. For example:
 (i) *Vous avez des croissants? J'en ai quelques-uns. Il vous en faut combien?*
 (ii) *J'ai besoin d'argent. J'en ai plus besoin que vous*
 (iii) *Il se moque de cette idée, oui, il s'en moque*

(c) With a negative imperative (telling someone not to do something) the pronouns follow all the above rules. For example:
 (i) *Ne le lui donnez pas* – Don't give it to him
 (ii) *Ne lui répondez pas* – Don't answer her/him
 (iii) *N'y allez pas!* – Don't go there!
 (iv) *Ne vous couchez pas par terre* – Don't lie on the ground
With a **positive imperative** they come **after** the verb, **direct before indirect** joined by hyphens.

(d) *Me* and *te* change to *moi* and *toi* if they come in final position.
For example, from the above phrases:
 (i) *Donnez-le-lui!*
 (ii) *Répondez-lui!*
 (iii) *Allez-y!*
 (iv) *Couchez-vous par terre!*
 (v) *Assieds-toi !*
 (vi) *Envoyez-le-moi* but *Donnez-m'en une douzaine*
General note You must learn the basic rules of position and meaning of the pronouns

with the tenses of verbs. You are less likely to need to use them with imperatives however unless you are writing dialogue or direct speech.

The object pronouns are best practised in their different combinations with verbs so that order and position become fixed in your mind (*see* word order, pages 56–57).

Exercices

1 (a) Suivez le modèle:
Me le donnez-vous? Oui, je vous le donne
Me les donnez-vous? Oui, je…
Me les prêtez-vous? Oui, je…
Allez-vous me les envoyer? Oui, je vais…
Allez-vous m'en envoyer? Oui,
Allez-vous le lui présenter? Oui,

(b) Reprenez les mêmes exemples en commençant la réponse par 'non':

2 (a) Suivez le modèle:
Est-ce que vous allez souvent en France? Oui, j'y vais souvent.
Est-ce que vous allez maintenant au café? Oui, …tout de suite
Est-ce qu'il s'intéresse beaucoup à la mécanique? Oui,
Est-ce que vous réfléchissez beaucoup à ce problème? Oui,
Est-ce que vous pensez souvent à ce temps-là? Oui,

(b) Reprenez le même exercice en répondant 'non':

3 (a) Suivez le modèle:
Avez-vous des places? Oui, j'en ai quelques-unes
Est-ce qu'il reste des places? Oui, il…
Avez-vous besoin de ces brochures? Oui,
Vous a-t-il parlé de son accident? Oui, il
Des pêches? Combien… voulez-vous?/Il… faut combien?

(b) Reprenez en répondant 'non':

4 A frequent criticism by examiners is that, when writing French, candidates tend to repeat nouns instead of using pronouns in their place. In the following exercises, replace nouns by object (or subject) pronouns wherever possible:

(a) Les brochures? J'ai envoyé les brochures à mon ami la semaine dernière.

(b) Mon rapport? J'ai déjà présenté mon rapport au comité.

(c) Mon télex à M. Dupont? J'ai déjà envoyé le télex à M. Dupont ce matin. Quoi, M. Dupont n'a pas encore reçu mon télex? M. Dupont aurait dû recevoir mon télex.

(d) Téléphonez à M. Dupont et dites à M.Dupont que j'ai bien envoyé un télex à M. Dupont et que M.Dupont devrait recevoir bientôt ce télex.

(e) 'Mon projet? Vous voulez que je vous explique mon projet? Bon, je vais vous expliquer mon projet.'
'M. Dupont?'
'Ah, oui, j'ai déjà expliqué à M. Dupont mon projet. M. Dupont était très content de mon projet.'

5 Traduisez:
(a) I have already sent them to him
(b) Send him it. He needs it straight away
(c) Telephone her and tell her that I will talk to her about it later
(d) Possibilities? Yes, there are several of them. Let's examine them
(e) He sent you them last week

(f) He didn't send you them last week?

(g) I am sure I told him to send you them.

6 The imperatives are best practised in set phrases, both positive and negative. Give the contrary command in each case. For example: Donnez-le-moi – ne me le donnez pas.

    (a) (i) Donnez-les-moi!

        (ii) Envoyez-les-lui!

        (iii) Expliquez-les-nous!

        (iv) Répondez-lui tout de suite!

        (v) Parlez-lui-en!

    (b) (i) Ne le lui dites pas!

        (ii) Ne me l'envoyez pas!

        (iii) Ne lui en parlez pas!

        (iv) Ne m'en donnez pas beaucoup!

        (v) Ne vous asseyez pas là! (la peinture y est fraîche)

2.21 EMPHATIC PRONOUNS

moi	*nous*
toi	*vous*
lui	*eux*
elle	*elles*

Use

1 **To stress the subject in a sentence or phrase.**

(i) *Toi, tu es bête* – **You** are stupid

(ii) *Lui, il ne comprend rien* – **He** doesn't understand a thing

(iii) *Elles, qu'est-ce qu'elles en savent?* – What do **they** know about it?

Spoken English stresses the subject in these examples by emphasizing the word 'you'. This cannot be done in French.

Note that *lui* as an emphatic pronoun means 'him' or 'he'.

2 **After prepositions**

(i) *avec moi*

(ii) *à côté d'elle*

(iii) *derrière nous*

(iv) *sans eux*

(v) *venez avec elle*

(vi) *c'est mon idée à moi* (its **my** idea)

3 **With a preposition after the verb**

Where there is no *le, la* or *les* as an object in front of the verb.

You can say:

(i) *Je vous la présenterai* – I'll introduce her to you

But you cannot say;

(ii) *Je vous lui présenterai* – I'll introduce you to her (or is it **her to you?**)

To avoid this ambiguity, you say:

(iii) *Je vous présenterai à elle* (you to her)

Here are some other examples:

(iv) *Je pense à elle tout le temps*

(v) *Il a besoin d'elle*

(vi) *Il est content de moi*

(vii) *Elle est fière de lui* – She is proud of him

(viii) *Je ne me fie pas à lui* – I don't trust him

(ix) *Il se moque de moi* – He's poking fun at me

④ **After** *c'est* **and** *c'était*
  (i) *C'est lui qui a tort*
  (ii) *C'était moi le gagnant* – I was the winner
  (iii) *Qui est là? C'est elle*

⑤ **After** *ni... ni*
  (i) *Ni lui ni elle ne savaient la vérité* – Neither he nor she knew the truth
  (ii) *Ni moi ni lui ne nous attendions à une telle réponse* –
       Neither he nor I were expecting such a reply

⑥ **With** *-même(s)*
  (i) *moi-même* – myself
  (ii) *lui-même* – himself
  (iii) *eux-mêmes* – themselves

Exercice

Traduisez:
(a) Repeat after me
(b) In front of her; behind him; with us
(c) They don't understand
(d) What does he think about it?
(e) Neither she nor I knew the answer
(f) I need him
(g) They are afraid of her
(h) I made it myself
(i) What does he think of us?
(j) I am ashamed of you

2.22   RELATIVE PRONOUNS

Qui

This means 'who', 'which' or 'that' as **subject** to the verb and is usually found joining two clauses together.
  (i) *C'est un mot qui n'est pas français* – It's a word that/which is not French
  (ii) *Vous voyez l'homme qui porte un chapeau?* – You see the man (who is) wearing a hat?

Que or qu'

These mean 'whom', 'who', 'which' or 'that' as **object** to the verb. For example:
  (i) *Voici le pull que j'ai acheté* – Here is the jumper (that/which) I bought
  (ii) *La propriété que j'ai achetée en France* – The property (that/which) I bought in France
  (iii) *Une fille que j'ai rencontrée pendant les vacances* – A girl (that/who/whom) I met in the holidays.

You will see from the brackets used above that in English you can leave out the relative pronoun. You **cannot** do this in French.

Note

(a) *Qui* never loses its final vowel before a word beginning with a vowel.
    If you are not sure about subject and object, the simplest rule of thumb (to decide

whether *qui* or *que* is needed) is to use *que* when the verb already has a subject, and *qui* when there is no subject. Between *que/qu'* and the verb there will be a subject pronoun (*il, elle, nous, vous* etc.) or a noun. Between *qui* and the verb there will be either an object pronoun or nothing at all. For example:

(i)   *Le vélo que j'ai acheté*
(ii) *Le vélo que mes parents ont acheté*
(iii) *Le vélo qui est dans le garage*
(iv) *Le vélo qui se trouve dans le garage*

(b) The subject can sometimes come after the verb in French so that the above rule won't work. For example: *L'instrument que mon frère utilisait, était un vieux trombone* is more easily expressed as

(i)   *L'instrument qu'utilisait mon frère était un vieux trombone*

This avoids the two verbs of each clause coming together.

Ce qui and ce que/ce qu'

Where 'which' means 'that which', translate it by *ce qui* or *ce qu(e)*. *Ce qui* and *ce que* refer to ideas already mentioned (or about to be stated). The choice of *qui* or *que* depends on the subject/object relationship as above. Here are some examples:

(i)   *Je ne comprends jamais ce qu'il dit* – I never understand what he is saying
(ii) *Il n'a pas expliqué ce qui était arrivé* – He didn't explain what had happened
(iii) *Ce que je ne comprends pas c'est pourquoi il a fait cela* –
      What I don't understand is why he did that
(iv) *Ce qui m'intéresse dans cette affaire c'est le rôle du Premier ministre* –
      What interests me in this affair is the part played by the Prime Minister

Another way of looking at *ce qui* and *ce que* is to regard them as the end bit of the interrogative phrases *qu'est-ce que* and *qu'est-ce qui*:

(v)   *Qu'est-ce qu'il a dit? Je n'ai pas entendu ce qu'il a dit* – I didn't hear what he said
(vi) *Qu'est-ce qui l'intéresse? Je ne sais pas ce qui l'intéresse* – I don't know what interests him

Note

(a) The form *tout ce que/qui* means 'everything that' or 'all that':

(i)   *Tout ce que je peux vous dire c'est que...* – All I can tell you is that...
(ii) *On aurait pu prédire tout ce qui était arrivé* –
      You could have predicted everything that had happened

(b) *Ce dont* means literally 'that of which' and is found in a clause depending on a verb that takes the preposition *de*:

(i)   *Je ne me rappelle pas ce dont il a parlé* – I don't remember what he talked about

Lequel, laquelle, lesquels and lesquelles

These mean 'which' and only refer to things. They are used in the following ways:

❶ To ask a question

(i)   *J'ai un vin blanc sec et un demi-sec. Lequel préférez-vous?* – Which (one) do you prefer?
(ii) *J'ai des pêches blanches et des jaunes. Lesquelles prenez-vous?* – Which (ones) are you having?

Note *Lequel* is the pronoun to the adjective *quel*. For example:
(iii) *Quel vin préférez-vous?*

❷ With a preposition:

(i)   *L'église devant laquelle se trouve une petite place* – The church in front of which is a little square
(ii) *Le train dans lequel il avait voyagé* – The train in which he had travelled
(iii) *La compagnie pour laquelle je travaille* – The company for which I work

Note That in the last two examples you can also say in English:
'The train he had travelled in' and 'The company I work for'.

Qui is used when referring to people in similar phrases except after *parmi* (among, amongst) and *entre* (between):

(iv) *L'ami avec qui j'ai voyagé* – The friend I travelled with

(v) *L'homme pour qui je travaille* – The man I work for

(vi) *Les spectateurs parmi lesquels était un inspecteur de police* –
The spectators amongst whom was a police inspector

De combines with *lequel* etc. to give the following:
duquel, de laquelle, desquels and *desquelles.*

Similarly, *à* combines with *lequel* to give:
auquel, à laquelle, auxquels and *auxquelles.*

They have the meanings respectively of 'of which' and 'to which' and agree with the noun to which they refer. Although you can say *L'école à laquelle je vais* it is preferable to say *L'école où je vais* and *Le village où j'habite* instead of *Le village dans lequel j'habite.*

Dont means 'of which', 'of whom', 'whose' and can refer to people as well as things. It always refers back to the noun immediately before it. *Duquel* and *de qui* also have the same meanings, but *dont* is always used instead unless there is any ambiguity:

(vii) *Le livre dont je parle est français* – The book I am talking about is French

(viii) *Ce monsieur dont j'ai oublié le nom* – The man whose name I have forgotten

(ix) *Il m'a montré la voiture dont deux des vitres étaient cassées* – He showed me the car of which two of the windows were broken

But

(x) *Ce monsieur avec les deux chiens dont je vous ai parlé* (you talked about the dogs)

(xi) *Ce monsieur avec les deux chiens de qui je vous ai parlé* (you talked about the man)

Note *Dont* cannot be used to ask a question. Other forms are used instead:

(xii) *De qui parlez-vous?* – Who are you talking about?

(xiii) *De quels chiens parlez-vous?* – Which dogs are you talking about?

(xiv) *A qui est ce livre?* – Whose book is this?

2.23 INTERROGATIVES

'What' as a question

1 *Qu'est-ce que* or *Que* begin the question '**what**'. For example:

(i) *Qu'est-ce qu'il a répondu?/ Qu'a-t-il répondu?* – What answer did he give?

(ii) *Qu'est-ce qu'on joue/ Que joue-t-on ce soir au théâtre?* – What's on at the theatre this evening?

Note If you start with *que* you turn subject and verb the other way round.

Qu'est-ce qui also means '**what**' but as **subject** to the verb. For example:

(i) *Qu'est-ce qui se passe/ Qu'est-ce qui arrive ?* – What's happening?

These can also be expressed as *Que se passe-t-il?* and *Qu'arrive-t-il?*

2 *Quoi* is used in '**what**' question phrases like 'with what?', 'in what?' etc.

(i) *Avec quoi est-ce qu'il a ouvert la porte? Il n'avait pas de clé* – What did he open the door with?

(ii) *A quoi pense-t-il?* – What is he thinking of (*see* penser à/de, page 85)

(iii) *Dans quoi allons-nous mettre nos achats?* – What are we going to put our shopping in?

Note The preposition in English is often detached from the word 'what':

(iv) *Je vais à Londres demain. Pour quoi faire?* – I'm going to London tomorrow. To do what?

'Who' as a question

Qui, qui est-ce qui, qui est-ce que all ask the question 'who?'. Here are some examples:
  (i)   *Qui est venu? Qui est-ce qui est venu?* – Who has come?
  (ii) *Qui cherchez-vous? Qui est-ce que vous cherchez?* – Who are you looking for?

Exercices

1 Traduisez:
  (a) I know she is right
  (b) I think he will arrive late
  (c) I don't know what he is going to say
  (d) What will you tell him?
  (e) Which of these two wines do you prefer?
  (f) There's the house I talked to you about
  (g) There's the tree under which we sat and on which we carved our names
  (h) What I don't understand is that he never has any money
  (i) Which politician are you talking about?
  (j) You don't know the difficulties we have had
  (k) What is interestng is the fact that he has denied all responsibility
  (l) Among these problems which is the most serious?
  (m) Who left the door open?
  (n) It's a programme that starts tonight and that you mustn't miss
  (o) Whose shoes are these?

2 Dans l'extrait suivant remplacez les blancs par le relatif qui manque:

LES MAUVAIS EFFETS DU SOLEIL

Chaque année, les services d'urgence récupèrent des touristes inconscients, _____ se sont laissé aller sous notre soleil sans penser _____ il n'avait rien à voir avec celui du bord des plages anglaises. On ignore le fait _____ le sable réfléchit 20% des radiations et l'eau 10% et _____ la quantité d'UVB est maximale entre 11 heures et 14 heures. _____ on ignore surtout, c'est _____ les effets du soleil sont cumulatifs. Voici _____ m'a expliqué un chef de service de dermatologie, 'Tout s'additionne. Je vois parfois des patients _____ me disent _____ depuis deux ou trois ans, ils ont nettement diminué leurs expositions au soleil. Mais tout _____ ils ont emmagasiné il y a 10 ou 20 ans est enregistré'.

2.24 DEMONSTRATIVE ADJECTIVES AND PRONOUNS

NB: this unit also includes indefinite adjectives and pronouns.

Demonstrative adjectives

Ce, cet, cette and ces

These are the equivalent of 'this' or 'that' in English. (*Cet* is only used before masculine singular nouns beginning with a vowel or an '*h*' not pronounced. e.g. cet homme, cet hôtel, cet incident)

The suffixes '*-ci*' or '*-là*' can be added to the noun following *ce, cet, cette* or *ces* to mean specifically 'this' or 'that' but it then becomes emphatic so you only use it when stressing something. For example:

(i) *Que voulez-vous que je lise? Cet article-ci ou cet article-là?*

Demonstrative pronouns

1 Celui, celle, ceux and celles

These look a bit like the adjective *ce* + a combination of the strong form pronouns (*see* page 91). Three things can be added to *celui, celle, ceux* and *celles*.

(a) '*-ci*' or '*-là*'
(i) *celui-ci, celle-ci, ceux-ci, celles-ci*
(ii) *celui-là, celle-là', ceux-là', celles-là'*

These have the meanings 'this one', 'this', 'these ones', 'these' and 'that one', 'that', 'those ones' and 'those'. Here are some examples:

(iii) *J'hésite entre ces deux tricots, celui-ci est très joli mais celui-là en cachemire est plus chic* – I can't decide between these two jumpers, this one is very pretty but this one is made of cashmere and is smarter

(iv) *Quelles pêches préférez-vous? Celles-ci ou celles-là* – Which peaches do you prefer? These or those

(b) *De*

De indicates belonging to someone and is the equivalent of 's and s' in English:

(i) *Voici notre système pour les brosses à dent, pour ne pas se tromper: celle de ma mère est bleue, celle de mon père est rouge, celle de mon petit frère est verte* – ...my mother's is blue, my father's is red and my little brother's is green

(c) *Que, qu'* and *qui*

These mean: 'the one that/which' 'those that/which' and 'the ones that/which' respectively. Here are some examples:

(i) *Donnez-moi encore de ces pêches blanches. Celles que j'ai achetées hier étaient délicieuses* – Give some more of those white peaches. The ones I bought yesterday were delicious

(ii) *Ceux qui arriveront en retard ne seront pas admis* – Those arriving late will not be admitted

(d) The pronoun can exist by itself in a sentence:

(i) *Tous ceux ayant le même âge* – All those of the same age

(ii) *Cette marque est celle recommandée à la télévision* – This brand is the one recommended on television

(e) The pronoun can also be followed by *dont*, like *ce* above:

(i) *Tu vois cette fille aux cheveux blonds là-bas? C'est celle dont je t'ai parlé* – She's the one I told you about

Note This is a common use in written French:

(ii) *Mes filles, Marie-Claire et Sandrine, sont très différentes de caractère: celle-ci est bavarde et oisive et celle-là est taciturne et travailleuse* – My daughters Marie-Claire and Sandrine have very different characters: the latter is quiet and hard-working the former is lazy and a chatterbox

Can you work out why *celle-là* should mean 'the former' and *celle-ci* 'the latter'?

2 Cela, (ça), ceci

These mean 'that' and 'this' respectively and are **indefinite** demonstrative pronouns. *Ça* is the abbreviated form of *cela* and is much used in colloquial French:

(i) *C'est formidable, ça!* – That's wonderful!

(ii) *Ça, où l'as-tu acheté?* –Where did you buy that?

(iii) *Ça alors!* – You don't say!

(iv) *Ça, je ne le crois pas* – I don't think so at all

It should be replaced by cela when you write French except when you are writing colloquial dialogue.

Ça and *ceci* refer to facts or statements previously mentioned or about to be, and also to things. They have no gender. Here are some examples:

 (i) *Faire le trajet en moins de six heures? Ça, c'est pas possible* – Do the journey in less than six hours? That's not possible

 (ii) *Est-ce que ça vous gêne si je fume?* – Does it bother you if I smoke?

 (iii) *Deux comme ça (en indiquant des gâteaux)* – Two like that

 (iv) *Retenez bien ceci: l'argent ne fait pas le bonheur* – Always remember this: money doesn't bring happiness.

Ça can also be added to single words to give a bit more weight to them:

 (v) *Je ne suis pas sorti samedi soir. Tiens, pourquoi ça?* – I didn't go out on Saturday night. Really, why was that?

You will also find: *Où ça? Quand ça? Comment ça?*

Exercice

1   Traduisez:

 (a) Which jumper would you like? This one is pretty but that one will be warmer

 (b) Cotton ones are easier to wash but woollen ones don't crease (*se froisser*)

 (c) This summer; this year; this time; this weather; these mosquitoes (*moustiques*)!

 (d) That's really annoying that is!

 (e) My car's broken down. I've borrowed my brother's

 (f) Which peaches would you like ? These are 6F a kilo and those are 8,50F

 (g) Natural resources must be conserved. That is very important

 (h) Which box do you want? The one on the kitchen table

 (i) These solutions are difficult to apply (*appliquer, mettre en œuvre*). Let's examine the ones proposed by M. Dupont

 (j) That's the last straw (*le comble*)! Those ideas are ridiculous

Other common indefinite adjectives and pronouns

On

This subject pronoun is much more widely used in French than its English equivalent 'one'. Always singular, it can mean: 'we'; 'you'; 'they'; or 'people'. What meanings would you give to 'on' in the following?

 (i) *On a bien mangé dans ce restaurant*

 (ii) *On ne fait pas ça ici!*

 (iii) *On vous a dit d'attendre*

 (iv) *On dit que la maison est hantée*

 (v) *On était plus honnête quand j'étais jeune*

 (vi) *On ne me fait pas comme ça, hein!*

(*see also* passive, page 78)

Quelque(s)

The adjective *quelque(s)* means 'a few' or 'some'. For example:

 (i) *J'ai eu quelque difficulté à resoudre ce problème* – I had a little difficulty in resolving this problem

 (ii) *Quelques centaines de personnes ont été blessées* – A few hundred people were hurt

 (iii) *J'ai quelques idées* – I have a few ideas

Quelqu'un

A pronoun meaning 'some one' or 'somebody'. For example:

 (i) *Quelqu'un a volé mon argent* – Some one has stolen my money

 (ii) *Je connais quelqu'un qui aurait pu le faire* – I know somebody who could have done it

Note These phrases are also important:
- (iii) *N'importe qui* – anyone (no matter who)
- (iv) *N'importe qui aurait pu le faire* – Anyone could have done it

Quelques-uns, quelques-unes

Pronouns having the meanings 'some' and 'a few' and refer back to nouns. For example:
- (i) *Quelles belles pêches! Achetons-en quelques-unes* – Let's buy a few
- (ii) *Quelques-uns de mes amis ont déjà leur permis de conduire* – Some of my friends have already passed their driving test
- (iii) *Quelques-unes de ses amies sont belges* – Some of his/her friends are Belgian

Quelque chose and autre chose

These mean 'something' and 'something else' respectively. Here are some examples:
- (i) *Vous connaissez quelque chose au sujet de cette affaire?* – Do you know something about this business
- (ii) *Non, pas grand-chose* – No, not much
- (iii) *Vous n'avez pas autre chose à faire?* – Haven't you got something else to do?

Plusieurs and certains

These mean 'several' and 'certain' respectively. The adjective *plusieurs* is often confused with the adjective *quelques* (*see* above):
- (i) *Il y a plusieurs années* – **Several** years ago
- (ii) *Il y a quelques années* – A **few** years ago

Note also Some other phrases:
- (iii) *plusieurs fois* – several times
- (iv) *quelquefois* – sometimes

Plusieurs can also work as a pronoun:
- (v) *Il était là. Plusieurs l'ont vu* – He was there. Several people saw him

Compare this with:
- (vi) *Certains affirment qu'ils l'ont vu* – Certain/some people are sure they saw him.

Chaque, chacun

These mean 'each' and 'each one' respectively. *Chaque* is the adjective and is always followed by a noun:
- (i) *Chaque personne avait apporté son déjeuner* – Each person had brought their lunch
- (ii) *Tous mes amis sont venus. Chacun m'a apporté un cadeau* – All my friends came. Each one brought me a present

Tout, toute, tous and toutes

This is the **adjective** meaning 'all', 'every' 'the whole'. For example:
- (i) *tous les jours* – every day
- (ii) *tous mes amis* – all my friends
- (iii) *toute la ville* – the whole town

Note The masculine plural form *tous*.

Tout is also a pronoun meaning 'everything' and 'all':
- (iii) *Tout n'est pas perdu* – All is not lost
- (iv) *Je crois tout ce qu'il m'a dit* – I believe everything he has told me.

Tous is also a pronoun meaning 'everyone' (the 's' is pronounced):
- (v) *Ils étaient tous là* – They were all there
- (vi) *Tous étaient venus* – They had all come

(If 'they' are all feminine, you would of course say – *Elles étaient toutes venues*.)

Note *Tout* occurs in numerous expressions like:
- (vii) *tout de suite* – immediately
- (viii) *tout à coup* – suddenly
- (ix) *tout de même* – all the same
- (x) *tout à fait* – completely

It never has an '*e*' on the end in these cases.

Tel, telle, tels and telles

These are mainly used as adjectives:

    (i)   *Une telle réponse est inacceptable* – Such a reply is unacceptable

    (ii) *Un tel homme mérite d'être puni* – Such a man deserves to be punished

Note The order of words in French is different. For example, *pareil/pareille* can often be substituted for *tel*:

    (i)   *Avez-vous jamais entendu une pareille idée?*– Have you ever heard of such an idea?

You can also use the adverb *tellement* where *si* doesn't fit, in phrases like:

    (ii) *J'étais tellement en colère* – I was so angry

    (iii) *Il avait tellement besoin de cet argent* – He needed the money so much

    (iv) *Il aime tellement cette fille* – He loves that girl so much

Exercice

2 Traduisez:

    (a) People say that money doesn't bring happiness. I can't accept such an idea

    (b) I spent the evening with a few friends

    (c) Some of his best friends had come to say good-bye

    (d) That happened some years ago

    (e) I have some idea of what you mean

    (f) Did you do anything interesting at Bognor? Not much

    (g) Each time I saw him he looked different

    (h) In Ionesco's play, each character eventually turns into a rhinoceros

    (i) There were several girls in the photo. Each one was wearing a white dress

    (j) All the efforts I have made are useless

    (k) They had all arrived too early

    (l) Everything is possible if you feel that people have confidence in you

2.25 *C'EST* AND *IL EST*

Rules

The following guidelines should help to decide which to use.

❶ *Il* (or *elle*) is always used when 'it' refers back to a particular noun or person:

    (i)   *Faites attention à **mon chien**, il est méchant*

    (ii) *Tu as vu **sa sœur**? Elle est chouette, hein?*

    (iii) ***Mon verre**, où est-ce que je l'ai mis? Il est là*

❷ *Il est* introduces an idea not made clear until the end of the statement. It is often found in the following type of phrase: *il est* + adjective + *de* + infinitive. Here are some examples:

    (i)   *Il est difficile de trouver quelqu'un qui parle russe*

    (ii) *Il est dangereux de s'aventurer dans le lit de cette rivière*

    (iii) *Il est impossible de tout savoir*

    (iv) *Il est facile de trouver un bon restaurant en France*

Note In spoken French, *c'est* tends to be used instead of *il est* in the above construction. You should keep to *il est* in written French.

❸ *C'est* is used to refer to an idea already made clear. For example, in the above sentences another speaker would add, if he or she agreed:

    (i)   *Oui, c'est difficile*

(ii) *Oui, c'est dangereux*

(iii) *Oui, c'est impossible*

(iv) *Oui, c'est facile*

Other examples are:

(v) *Il viendra? Oui, c'est probable* ('it' here means 'the fact that he will come')

(vi) *J'ai couru 10 kilomètres sans être fatigué. Vraiment, c'est formidable ça.*

4 *Il* (or *elle*) *est* is used, when saying what someone is like or does:

(i) *Vous voyez mon frère sur la photo? Oui, il est grand*

(ii) *Je vous présente mon ami Jean-Paul. Il est ingénieur. Et sa femme Colette, elle est dentiste.*

However if you qualify the individual by adding an adjective, *c'est* is used:

(iii) *C'est un grand garçon votre frère!*

(iv) *Je vous présente M. Moulin, c'est notre dentiste*

(v) *Vous connaissez M. Rodez? Il paraît que c'est un scientifique distingué*

A rule sometimes given for the last example is: use *il est* when an adjective or noun follows; *c'est* when adjective as well as noun follows.

5 **Emphasis** *C'est* is used to lay particular emphasis on a part of a sentence or phrase. For example, take the sentence:

Marie m'a prêté sa jupe. Various parts could be emphasized as follows:

(i) *C'est Marie qui m'a prêté cette jupe (Marie et pas une autre)*

(ii) *Cette jupe, c'est qu' elle me l'a prêtée (pas donnée)*

(iii) *C'est à moi que Marie a prêté la jupe (pas à ma sœur)*

(iv) *C'est cette jupe que Marie m'a prêtée (et pas une autre jupe)*

(v) *C'est une jupe que Marie m'a prêtée (et pas une robe)*

Note In these examples the tonic accent would also fall on the word being emphasized. How would the same parts of the sentence be stressed in English: (i) in speech (ii) in print?

Exercice

Comblez les blancs dans les phrases suivantes avec il est, c'est, elle est, ils sont, elles sont.

(a) Qui a fait ça? _____ mon père

(b) Je vous présente ma tante _____ institutrice

(c) _____ formidable l'Angleterre a gagné au Parc des Princes!

(d) On peut maintenant traverser la Manche par le tunnel. _____ incroyable! Mais _____ impossible de faire cela dans sa voiture.

(e) Ma sœur? _____ au Brésil

(f) Mes deux sœurs rient et bavardent tout le temps. _____ bêtes

(g) _____ inspecteur de police. _____ un inspecteur bien connu en France.

(h) Les croissants? _____ sur la table dans la cuisine, n'est-ce pas?

2.26 POSSESSIVE ADJECTIVES AND PRONOUNS

Possessive adjectives should be familiar to you as the following:

mon, ma, mes – my   *ton, ta, tes* – your (singular)   *son, sa, ses* – his or her

notre, notre, nos – our   *votre, votre, vos* – your (plural)   *leur, leur, leurs* – their

They must agree with the noun they refer to. The commonest mistake is to assume that *sa* means 'her', *son* means 'his' and *ses* means 'their'. But:

(i)   *son père* – his or her father
(ii) *sa mère* – his or her mother
(iii) *ses parents* – his or her parents (or relations)
(iv) *leur père* – their father
(v)   *leurs parents* – their parents

Possessive pronouns are as follows:

le mien	*le tien*	*le sien*	*le nôtre*	*le vôtre*	*le leur*
la mienne	*la tienne*	*la sienne*	*la nôtre*	*la vôtre*	*la leur*
les miens	*les tiens*	*les siens*	*les nôtres*	*les vôtres*	*les leurs*
les miennes	*les tiennes*	*les siennes*	*les nôtres*	*les vôtres*	*les leurs*
mine	yours	his or hers	ours	yours	theirs

They have to agree with the noun they refer to:
(i)   *Cette valise, c'est la vôtre? Oui, c'est la mienne.*
(ii) *Cette voiture, c'est la sienne?* (Its/his/hers)

You can also indicate possession by using the strong form pronouns (*moi, toi, elle, lui* etc.) with *c'est*. For example:
(iv) *Cette valise, c'est à vous? Oui, c'est à moi*
(v)   *Cette voiture, c'est à elle?*

Note In the last example, it is possible in this way to make it clear whom you are referring to.

Exercice

Traduisez:
(a) Her son, his sister, his mother, his (female) cousin, their parents
(b) Is this book his? No, it's hers
(c) She arrived with their friends and he came with his
(d) Which book is his?
(e) Whose is this?
(f) Mine (socks) are grey, his are blue
(g) It's not mine (car), it's theirs

2.27   ADJECTIVES

Adjectives agree with the nouns they describe in the following ways:

❶ Add an '*-e*' for the feminine singular, '*-es*' for feminine plural and '*-s*' for masculine plural.
For example:
(i)   *Une petite ville*
(ii) *Un petit village*
(iii) *Des petites villes*
(iv) *Des petits villages*

The effect of adding '*-e*' to an adjective ending in a consonant is to make the final consonant sounded where before it was silent. It is important when reading and speaking to observe this sound change.

❷ Adjectives already ending in '*-e*' stay the same:
(i)   *Un jeune garçon*
(ii) *Une jeune fille*

❸ Many adjectives in common use behave in slightly different ways. The following patterns need to be learned:

(a) Masculine plurals –

    (i)   Adjectives ending in '-al' have '-aux' in the masculine plural:
        les routes nationales but *les plans nationaux*

    (ii) A few adjectives in '-eau' have '-eaux' in the masculine plural:
        les nouvelles publications but *les nouveaux journaux*

    (iii) Adjectives already ending in '-s' or '-x' in the masculine singular stay the same:
        les jours les plus **heureux** *de la vie*

(b) Feminine singulars –

	masculine singular	feminine singular
(i) '-el'/'-elle'	*un parc naturel*	*une ressource naturelle*
(ii) '-eil'/'-eille'	*un exemple pareil*	*une idée pareille*
(iii) '-er'/'-ère'	*le Premier ministre*	*la première séance*
(iv) '-eur'/'-euse'	*un homme menteur*	*une fille menteuse*
(v) '-f'/'-ive'	*un marché actif*	*la vie active (working life)*
(vi) '-ien'/'-ienne'	*un vin italien*	*la cuisine italienne*
(vii) '-x'/'-euse'	*un ami heureux*	*une vie heureuse*

The following don't have a regular pattern and they are best remembered in an example:

adjective	masculine singular	feminine singular
bas/basse	*un ton trop bas*	*la marée basse*
blanc/blanche	*un vin blanc*	*faire nuit blanche* (not to sleep a wink)
bon /bonne	*un bon exemple*	*une bonne idée*
bref/brève	*un bref discours*	*une brève explication*
complet/complète	*un dossier complet*	*une collection complète*
doux/douce	*un temps doux*	*une voix douce*
faux/fausse	*un faux billet*	*une fausse idée*
favori/favorite	*mon sport favori*	*ma matière favorite*
frais/fraîche	*un matin frais*	*une boisson fraîche* (cool)
gentil/gentille	*il est gentil*	*elle est gentille*
long/longue	*un long voyage*	*une longue journée*
meilleur/meilleure	*mon meilleur ami*	*une meilleure solution*
public/publique	*l'ordre public*	*de notoriété publique* (common knowledge)
sec/sèche	*un temps sec*	*une serviette sèche*

Position of adjectives

The general rule is that most adjectives come after the noun. However, the following commonly used ones usually come before:

autre	*grand*	*meilleur*	*bon*
*beau**	*gros* (fem. *grosse*)		*nouveau**
chaque	*jeune*	*plusieurs*	*petit*
court	*joli*	*quelque*	*faux* (fem. *fausse*)
bref (fem. *brève*)		*mauvais*	*vieux** (fem. *vieille*)
gentil	*méchant*	*vilain* (ugly, nasty)	*long* (fem. *longue*)
premier (fem. *première*)		*dernier* (fem. *dernière*)	

* These adjectives have an additional masculine singular form that is only used before a noun beginning with a vowel or a silent "h" (compare ce, cet. See page 96)
Examples:

    (i)   un bel endroit
    (ii) un vieil ami
    (iii) un nouvel hôtel
    (iv) un adolescent français
    (v) un jeune adolescent

(vi) un adolescent heureux
(vii) chaque adolescent
(viii) une fille française
(ix) une jeune fille
(x) une fille heureuse
(xi) une jolie fille

Note *Des* in front of an adjective before a plural noun usually changes to *de*. For example:

(xii) *de jeunes adolescents* (*see* partitive, page 87)

Adjectives can also be combined:

(i) *les jeunes adolescents français*
(ii) *les jeunes filles heureuses*

Two adjectives following a noun are always joined with *et*.

(i) *un jeune adolescent travailleur et heureux*

Exercices

1 Traduisez:
(a) Natural resources
(b) A good idea
(c) Low tide
(d) A cool morning
(e) A mild winter
(f) A soft voice
(g) A long day
(h) A new solution
(i) An untruthful girl
(j) A complete collection
(k) A false idea
(l) There were several pretty young French girls at the party
(m) The working population
(n) Some old friends; an old friend (male)
(o) Parisian life
(p) A few new French publications
(q) Small Italian towns
(r) A brief explanation
(s) A public place
(t) A public square

2 Some adjectives change their meaning according to whether they precede or follow the noun. Here are some of the most frequently used ones. Check their meanings with the help of a dictionary.
(a) De Gaulle était un grand homme; c'était aussi un homme grand
(b) Ce millionnaire est un pauvre homme, mais il n'est pas un homme pauvre
(c) Mon ancienne école est une école ancienne
(d) L'année dernière c'était 1995 mais 1999 sera la dernière année du siècle.
(e) Ma propre maison; j'aime habiter une maison propre
(f) Un certain homme; trouvez un homme certain
(g) Ma chère femme a acheté un manteau cher
(h) Je suis né le même jour que vous; il est tombé malade le jour même de son arrivée
(i) Il a une nouvelle voiture. C'est un modèle nouveau?
(j) Le seul Chinois que je connaisse; seuls les Chinois savent le faire
(k) Encore un verre? Je t'apporte un nouveau verre? Voilà un nouveau verre tout neuf
(l) Je le lui dirai la prochaine fois que je le verrai, ce sera peut-être la semaine prochaine

2.28   ADVERBS

❶ Most adverbs are formed by adding '*-ment*' to the feminine of the adjective. For example:
- (i) *lent, lente, lentement* – slowly
- (ii) *heureux, heureuse, heureusement* – happily, fortunately

❷ A small group of adjectives in '*-ent*' and '*-ant*' (**not** *lent* above) form their adverbs in '*-emment*' and '*-amment*' respectively. The most frequently met with are:
- (i) *abondant, abondamment*
- (ii) *constant, constamment*
- (iii) *courant, couramment*
- (iv) *évident, évidemment*
- (v) *récent, récemment*
- (vi) *violent, violemment*

Note '*-emment*' is always pronounced '*-amment*'.

❸ Here are some adverbs which may cause difficulty:
- (i) *profond, profondément*
- (ii) *énorme, énormément*
- (iii) *précis, précisément*
- (iv) *aveugle, aveuglément*
- (v) *bref, brièvement*
- (vi) *gentil, gentiment*

❹ The following adjectives having irregular adverbs:
- (i) *bon, meilleur*
- (ii) *mauvais, pire*
- (iii) *petit, peu*
- (iv) *bien, mieux*
- (v) *mal, pis*

Make sure you can distinguish an adjectival use from an adverbial one: adjectives describe or refer to nouns, objects or things; adverbs describe how the verb is carried out. For example:
- (vi) *Ecrivez en bon français* – Write in good French *(bon* describes the kind of French)
- (vii) *Il parle bien le français* – He speaks French well *(bien* describes how the speaking is done)

Similarly:
- (viii) *Il a peu mangé* and *il a pris un petit repas*

The words *meilleur* (adjective) and *mieux* (adverb, both with the meanings 'better' and 'best' are frequently confused. Also, *mauvais* (adjective) meaning bad, and *mal* (adverb) meaning badly, can cause problems:
- (ix) *Mon meilleur ami* – My best friend
- (x) *Ce dictionnaire est meilleur que celui-là* – This dictionary is better than that one
- (xi) *Il parle mieux le français que moi* – He speaks French better than I do
- (xii) *Faites de votre mieux* – Do your best
- (xiii) *J'ai mal dormi; j'ai fait un mauvais rêve* – I slept badly; I had a bad dream

2.29   COMPARISONS

Both adjectives and adverbs can be used in comparisons. Here are some examples:
- (i) *Brigitte est plus jolie que Sylvie mais Sylvie est plus intelligente que Brigitte* (adjective)
- (ii) *Sylvie parle mieux le français que Brigitte* (adverb)

Note also the following comparative phrases:
  (i)   *Il travaille **autant** que moi* – He works **as much as** I do
  (ii) *Il se sentait **de plus en plus** fatigué* – He was becoming **more and more** tired
  (iii) ***Plus** on travaille **plus** on se sent fatigué* – **The more** you work **the more** tired you become
  (iv) *J'ai **de moins en moins** envie de travailler* – I feel **less and less** like working
  (v)   ***Moins** on travaille, **moins** on a envie de travailler* – **The less** you work **the less** you feel like working

Exercice

Traduisez:
(a) A former colleague
(b) She alone can do it
(c) Evidently he can speak Russian as well as you
(d) He has bought another house. Is it a new one?
(e) The very day that he arrived
(f) These letters arrived on the same day
(g) I was deeply moved (ému)
(h) The last time I saw her she was wearing brand new shoes
(i) Would you like another cup? (two possibilities)
(j) I met him recently
(k) Put some clean socks on
(l) The more he explained the less I understood
(m) She can draw better than me
(n) It's not a bad car but the engine is running badly at the moment
(o) They don't go out very much, just a little walk now and again
(p) Are you feeling better?
(q) It's getting more and more difficult to find a good programme on television
(r) Which programme do you like watching best?
(s) They all believe blindly in progress
(t) Britain is not the least polluted country in the world

2.30 ANSWERS TO GRAMMAR EXERCISES

PRESENT TENSE

1 (a) Est-ce que vous regardez (tu regardes) la télévision tous les soirs?
   (b) Est-ce que vous faites (tu fais) tes devoirs en regardant la télé/pendant que vous regardez (tu regardes) la télé?
   (c) Est-ce que vous attendez (tu attends) le train de six heures?
   (d) Non. J'attends mon ami.
   (e) Il travaille à Londres?/Est-ce qu'il travaille à Londres?
   (f) Je pense à elle pendant que j'écris cette lettre.
   (g) Il va venir avec nous/Il vient avec nous?
   (h) Est-ce qu'il parle russe?
   (i) Je vous écris pour vous (te) remercier pour le (du) cadeau.
   (j) Qu'est-ce que vous faites (tu fais) ce soir?

2 (a) How long has he been living in Brussels?
    (b) For two weeks I've been getting strange telephone calls.
    (c) We have been writing to each other for two years.
    (d) How long has he known her?
    (e) I've been waiting for a letter for two months

3 (a) Depuis combien de temps est-ce que vous m'attendez?/ tu m'attends?
    (b) Je suis ici depuis 6 heures.
    (c) Voici/Il y a des années qu'ils s'écrivent?/ Ils s'écrivent depuis des années.
    (d) Elle est en Angleterre depuis des années/ Ça fait des années qu'elle est ici en Angleterre.
    (e) Ça fait cinq ans que je vous (te) connais.

PERFECT TENSE

1 16 être verbs

```
A  A  D  D  E  M  M  N  P  R  R  R  S  T  V
R  L  E  E  N  O  O  A  A  E  E  E  O  O  E
R  L  S  V  T  N  U  I  R  T  S  N  R  M  N
I  E  C  E  R  T  R  T  T  O  T  T  B  I
V  R  E  N  E  E  I  R  I  U  E  R  I  E  R
E     N  I  R  R  R  E  R  R     R  E
R     D  R                 N        R
          E                 E
                            R
```

2 Alors maman est montée dans sa chambre et papa est descendu dans la cave. Ma sœur Alice n'est pas encore rentrée. Sandrine est allée à la discothèque. Mon frère Albert est sorti ce matin et il n'est pas encore revenu. Claudette est sortie avec ses amis. Marie-Claude est rentrée à 6 heures, elle est restée 5 minutes puis elle est repartie. La chatte est tombée de la fenêtre, elle est morte, je crois!

3 (a) Est-il parti?
    (b) Il est resté longtemps?
    (c) Il est monté dans sa chambre.
    (d) Il n'est pas sorti.
    (e) Il est arrivé à l'heure?
    (f) Je suis rentré(e)/ retourné(e)/ revenu(e) tard.
    (g) Il est tombé devant le café.
    (h) J'ai rendu les livres.
    (i) Mes amis sont revenus/rentrés.
    (j) J'ai descendu vos bagages.
    (k) Il a sorti un stylo.
    (l) Je suis né(e) en Ecosse.

4 Role-play

M. Camembert: Eh bien, je me suis levé à six heures, je suis descendu, j'ai pris un café et puis je suis sorti de la maison. Je suis entré dans le tabac du coin. Je suis arrivé à la gare et j'ai pris le train de 7h15. Je suis descendu à la gare St Lazare. Je suis arrivé à mon bureau et je suis monté au 5ème étage. J'y suis resté toute la journée.

L'agent: Vous ne vous êtes pas lavé? Vous ne vous êtes pas habillé? Vous n'avez rien mangé? A quelle heure êtes-vous sorti? Au tabac, qu'est-ce que vous avez acheté? Qui vous a vu entrer dans l'immeuble où se trouve votre bureau? Qu'est-ce que vous avez fait pendant le déjeuner? Vous n'êtes pas sorti pendant la journée?

5 (i) réduit, séduit, introduit, produit, déduit, construit
    (ii) traduit, détruit, bien cuit (verbe 'cuire')

PAST PARTICIPLE AGREEMENT

(a) Ils sont arrivés.
(b) Mes deux sœurs sont parties.
(c) Marie-Antoinette est morte en 1793.
(d) Ma montre, où est-ce que je l'ai laissée?
(e) Je les ai trouvé(e)s sans difficulté.
(f) Les poires que j'ai achetées hier ne sont pas mûres.
(g) Elle s'est baignée dans la mer.
(h) Marie a couché son petit frère, puis elle s'est couchée.
(i) Nous avons descendu nos bagages.
(j) Quelles valises avez-vous descendues?
(k) Ils sont descendus, vos frères?
(l) Elles se sont regardées un moment puis se sont embrassées.
(m) Elle s'est gratté la tête.
(n) Ils se sont donné rendez-vous pour le lendemain.
(o) Des escargots? Ah, j'en ai trouvé de beaux après la pluie.

WORD ORDER OF NEGATIVES AND OBJECT PRONOUNS WITH THE PERFECT TENSE

(a) Oui, je l'ai trouvé/ Non, je ne l'ai pas trouvé.
(b) Non, je ne la lui ai pas donnée.
(c) Oui, il me l'a donnée/ Non, il ne me l'a pas donnée.
(d) Oui, je les ai achetées hier/ Non, je ne les ai pas achetées hier.
(e) Je ne les ai pas achetées, on me les a données.
(f) Je lui ai envoyé une longue lettre. Je ne lui ai pas envoyé de carte postale.

IMPERFECT TENSE

1 Dimanche à 10 heures j'étais dans ma chambre avec mon frère. Mon frère et notre voisin étaient dans le garage. Ils essayaient de réparer notre voiture qui était en panne. Maman était dans le salon. Elle tricotait. Mon frère et moi jouions aux échecs.

2 (a) J'étais au lit. Je lisais.
    (b) Je faisais mes devoirs.
    (c) Je regardais la télé.
    (d) J'habitais Walsall.
    (e) Il ne pleuvait pas. Il neigeait et il faisait du vent.
    (f) Non, je portais un pantalon gris, une chemise bleue et un tricot bleu.

3 (a) Elle se réveillait d'habitude à 6 heures et elle restait au lit jusqu'à 7 heures.
    (b) Pourtant ce matin elle s'est levée à 7h30 et elle a quitté (elle est sortie de) la maison à 8 heures..
    (c) Pendant que nous regardions/qu'on regardait la télévision hier soir quelqu'un a volé mon vélo.
    (d) J'ai rêvé d'une drôle d'école où tous les profs portaient des blue-jeans et fumaient en classe. Il n'y avait pas de leçons l'après-midi. Tout le monde faisait du sport et rentrait à la maison à 4 heures.
    (e) Quand mon père allait à la pêche, il se levait normalement très tôt le matin et rentrait tard le soir bredouille (sans poissons). Cependant dimanche dernier, il est revenu avec une grande truite.
    (f) 'Je l'ai attrapée moi-même', a-t-il déclaré. Nous ne l'avons pas cru.
    (g) J'étais sous la douche/je me douchais quand vous avez téléphoné.

(h) Quand j'étais jeune j'écoutais beaucoup la radio.

(i) Quand mon grand-père était jeune, il n'y avait pas de télévision.

(j) Qu'est-ce que les gens faisaient le soir à cette époque-là?

4 The calming of the waters

Le soir de ce même jour, Jésus a dit à ses disciples, 'Passons de l'autre côté du lac'.

Ils ont quitté la foule; les disciples ont emmené Jésus dans la barque où il se trouvait. D'autres barques encore étaient près de lui. Et voilà qu'un vent violent s'est mis à souffler, les vagues se jetaient dans la barque, de sorte que, déjà, elle se remplissait d'eau. Jésus était à l'arrière du bateau et dormait, la tête appuyée contre un coussin. Ses disciples l'ont réveillé et lui ont dit,

'Maître, nous allons mourir. Cela ne te fait-il rien?'

Jésus s'est réveillé, il a parlé sévèrement au vent et a dit à l'eau du lac, 'Silence! Calme-toi!'

Alors le vent est tombé et il y a eu un grand calme. Puis Jésus a dit aux disciples,

'Pourquoi avez-vous peur? N'avez-vous pas encore de foi?'

Mais ils étaient très effrayés et ils se sont dit les uns aux autres,

'Qui est donc cet homme, pour que même le vent et l'eau du lac lui obéissent?'

Marc 4,5 (Traduction de *l'Alliance Biblique Universelle*, 1988)

PAST HISTORIC TENSE

éteindre – The firemen put out the fire.

pouvoir – They could/were able to understand.

être – We were soon outside.

devoir – He had to pay a fine.

produire – He produced his papers.

s'inscrire –They signed on for evening classes.

retenir – The flu kept him in bed.

surprendre – The results surprised the teacher.

revenir –They came back at the weekend.

boire – he emptied/drank the glass in one go.

savoir – at that moment he knew the truth.

falloir – it was necessary to wait for a bit.

pleuvoir – in the morning it rained.

maintenir – he kept his job for a long time.

convaincre – his explanation/reasoning convinced me.

se taire, rire – he remained silent/said nothing for a moment then burst out laughing.

fumer – we smoked two cigarettes before going to bed.

PLUPERFECT TENSE

1 La déclaration de M. XX:

(a) J'étais descendu à l'hôtel Splendide. J'y étais arrivé vers 7 heures. J'avais mangé à l'hôtel. Après j'étais sorti me promener. J'avais marché pendant une heure. Puis j'étais revenu à l'hôtel. Dans le bar j'avais rencontré un ancien collègue. Nous avions bu quelques verres ensemble. Je m'étais couché vers 11h45.

(b) Il a dit qu'il était descendu à l'hôtel Splendide, qu'il y était arrivé vers 7 heures et qu'il avait mangé à l'hôtel; il a ajouté qu'après il était sorti se promener et qu'il avait marché pendant une heure; ensuite qu'il était revenu à l'hôtel et que, dans le bar, il avait rencontré un ancien collègue. Puis, il a déclaré qu'ils avaient bu quelques verres ensemble. Enfin, il a affirmé qu'il s'était couché vers 11h45.

2 (a) J'étais arrivé tard donc je me suis couché tôt.
   (b) Quand le bus s'est arrêté il est descendu.
   (c) Elle était partie de bonne heure pour ne pas manquer le train.
   (d) Ils s'étaient présentés au commissariat.
   (e) Je ne savais pas qu'elle s'était mariée.

3 (a) Je ne l'avais pas vue depuis samedi.
   (b) Il ne m'avait rien dit.
   (c) Ils n'y avaient trouvé personne.
   (d) Il vous en avait déjà parlé?
   (e) Mes sœurs n'avaient jamais visité Paris.

4 (a) Il dit qu'il n'a jamais voyagé en avion.
   (b) Il a dit qu'il n'avait jamais voyagé en avion.
   (c) J'ai trouvé que je n'avais pas compris ce qu'il avait dit.
   (d) Elle a dit qu'elle avait téléphoné la semaine dernière.
   (e) Je suis sûr que la lettre est arrivée.
   (f) J'étais sûr que la lettre était arrivée.
   (g) 'Je n'ai jamais vu cet homme' a-t-elle dit.
   (h) Il s'est rappelé qu'il a vu Fifi à la banque.
   (i) Il a dit qu'il n'avait jamais vu cet homme.
   (j) Je ne pouvais pas trouver la lettre qu'il m'avait envoyée.

5 (a) Incendiaire: (vi), (i), (iii), (ii), (v), (iv)
   (b) Following being questioned by police.
   (c) At this point in the account we go back to the events before this.

6 Sur les traces de De Saussure

   Chamonix: Il y a quelques jours, deux Haut-Savoyards — Pierre Cusin et Thierry Gazin — ont battu(pc) le record Chamonix–Mont-Blanc et retour en moins de 8 heures. Ces deux spécialistes des cross en montagne avaient voulu(pp) saluer ainsi à leur manière le bicentenaire de l'ascension du Mont-Blanc. Devant cette brillante réussite ils ont décidé(pc) de ne pas en rester là. Avec Christophe Gotti du CAF d'Annecy ils ont décidé(pc) de refaire l'itinéraire du savant genevois, Horace Benedict De Saussure. Celui-ci bien avant avait réussi (pp) la conquête du Mont-Blanc dont il fut l'instigateur. Il était allé(pp) de Genève à Chamonix à pied, puis bien plus tard, en 1787, avait gravi(pp) le Mont-Blanc avec Jacques Balmont dans des conditions que l'on imagine il y a 199 ans.

   Le trio sportif est donc parti pour Genève hier soir pour remonter toute la vallée de l'Arve en courant.

   Les quatre événements sont:
   (i) Trajet à pied Genève-Chamonix par De Saussure.
   (ii) Même trajet, en courant, par P Cusin, T Gazin et C Gotti.
   (iii) Ascension du Mont-Blanc par De Saussure en 1787.
   (iv) Ascension du Mont-Blanc par P Cusin et T Gazin, aller et retour en courant en moins de huit heures.

CONDITIONAL AND FUTURE TENSES

1 (a) Il trouvera la lettre.
   (b) Il aurait trouvé la lettre (s'il avait jeté un coup d'œil dans le placard).
   (c) Il aura trouvé la lettre.
   (d) Il trouverait la lettre (s'il jetait un coup d'œil dans le placard).
   (e) Est-ce que je sortirai avec lui ce soir?
   (f) Je serais sortie avec lui ce soir.
   (g) Je sortirais avec elle(si j'avais de l'argent)
   (h) Il sera déjà sorti.

2 (a) (i) faire (ii) ils feraient (iii) ils auront fait (iv) ils auraient fait
(b) (i) être (ii) ils seraient (iii) ils auront été (iv) ils auraient été
(c) (i) voir (ii) je verrais (iii) j' aurai vu (iv) j' aurais vu
(d) (i) avoir (ii) nous aurions (iii) nous aurons eu (iv) nous aurions eu
(e) (i) pouvoir (ii) il pourrait (iii) il aura pu (iv) il aurait pu
(f) (i) avoir (ii) il aurait (iii) il aura eu (iv) il aurait eu
(g) (i) pleuvoir (ii) il pleuvrait (iii) il aura plu (iv) il aurait plu
(h) (i) envoyer (ii) nous enverrions (iii) nous aurons envoyé (iv) nous aurions envoyé
(i) (i) mourir (ii) il mourrait (iii) il sera mort (iv) il serait mort
(j) (i) falloir (ii) il faudrait (iii) il aura fallu (iv) il aurait fallu
(k) (i) jeter (ii) ils jetteraient (iii) ils auront jeté (iv) ils auraient jeté
(l) (i) valoir (ii) il vaudrait (iii) il aura valu (iv) il aurait valu

3 (a) Quand vous le verrez donnez-lui ceci.
(b) Si vous le voyez donnez-lui ceci.
(c) Aussitôt que j'aurai fini je vous téléphonerai.
(d) Si j'avais suffisamment d'argent j'aimerais voyager.
(e) Qu'est-ce que nous allons faire ce soir?
(f) Que ferions-nous sans la télé?
(g) Je suis sûr qu'il vous aurait dit cela.
(h) Si nous avions été là nous l'aurions vu.
(i) Je lui ai demandé si elle voudrait venir avec moi en Grèce.
(j) Je ne sais pas si elle voudrait venir (be willing to come).

4 (a) It's the day before the big day when she sets off. Soon Marie-Claude will be packing her cases because she is setting off tomorrow morning at 5.00. Tomorrow evening she will be in Cannes. She will have spent ten hours in the train and, as soon as she has eaten, she will go to bed at the hotel. She has been told that, from her window, she will be able to see the sea as soon as it gets light.
(b) C'était la veille du grand départ. Bientôt Marie-Claude allait faire ses valises car elle allait partir demain matin à 5 heures. Demain soir elle serait à Cannes. Elle aurait passé dix heures dans le train et aussitôt qu'elle aurait mangé elle irait se coucher à l'hôtel. On lui avait dit que de sa fenêtre elle pourrait voir la mer dès qu'il ferait jour.

5 (a) Si je le vois, je lui donnerai ceci. S'il me demande qui me l'a donné, je lui dirai la vérité.
(b) Quand je le verrai je lui donnerai ceci. Quand il me demandera qui me l'a donné, je lui dirai la vérité.

6 Two hundred militant Kurds demonstrated yesterday in Paris and occupied the first floor of the Eiffel Tower. According to their leaders, two of their fellow countrymen have allegedly died recently after being badly treated in Turkish prisons and several others are said to be in a critical condition.

7 Established facts: man received several stab wounds; his identity not known; taken to hospital in serious condition.
   Alleged events: a witness to the crime alerted the police; suffering from perforated lung; the young girl gave herself up.

SUBJUNCTIVE

1 (a) Pour qu'il comprenne.
(b) Quoique nous sachions.
(c) A moins qu'il ne vienne.
(d) Il faut que tu y ailles/vous y alliez.

(e) Pourvu qu'il le fasse.
(f) Avant qu'il ne parte (avant son départ).
(g) Qu'il parte et qu'il ne revienne pas!
(h) Quoi qu'il dise.
(i) Quelles que soient vos raisons.
(j) Il se peut que le gouvernement ait raison.
(k) Sans qu'il le sache.
(l) Jusqu'à ce qu'ils apprennent.
(m) Bien qu'ils ne comprennent pas.
(n) Bien qu'ils aient compris.
(o) Pourvu qu'elle ait fini.

2 (a) Je pense que vous avez raison.
(b) Pensez-vous qu'ils aient raison?
(c) J'ai peur qu'il ne soit trop tard.
(d) Il est possible que la situation soit trop préoccupante.
(e) Il est probable qu'il prend les mesures nécessaires.
(f) Il est peu probable qu'il prenne les mesures nécessaires.
(g) Je regrette que vous ne soyez pas de mon avis/d'accord avec moi/que vous ne partagiez pas mon opinion.
(h) Je suis surpris qu'ils aient fait cela.
(i) Pensez-vous que le gouvernement suive la bonne politique.
(j) J'espère que ces renseignements sont corrects.
(k) Je suis content qu'il ait fait cela.
(l) Pensez-vous que cela soit vrai?
(m) Je ne crois pas que cela soit possible.
(n) Il est regrettable qu'il ait pris cette décision.
(o) J'ai peur que je ne fasse quelque erreur/de faire une erreur.

3 (a) You would have done better to have come and seen me straight away.
(b) Whatever your reasons might be I cannot approve this action.
(c) Whatever you do, do not listen to his excuses.
(d) I am looking for someone to help me today.
(e) I have already found someone who can help me tomorrow.
(f) However difficult you find this work you must do your best.
(g) I am going to travel before beginning my studies at university.
(h) Whether you find someone or not to do this work, it's all the same to me.
(i) I am afraid that she may have already left.
(j) You must take a little rest even if it's only for fifteen minutes.

MODAL VERBS

(a) J'ai dû le laisser à la maison.
(b) Vous ne devriez pas/Tu ne devrais pas avoir peur.
(c) Vous n'auriez pas /Tu n'aurais pas dû payer.
(d) Pourriez-vous/pourrais-tu me prêter 10 francs/balles?
(e) Je dois travailler plus dur.
(f) Voulez-vous venir ce soir?
(g) Est-ce qu'elle sera là?
(h) Savez-vous quelle est la capitale de l'Estonie?
(i) Avant la guerre je connaissais très bien Tallin (la capitale de l'Estonie).
(j) Est-ce que vous pouvez/tu peux le faire avant ce soir?

PASSIVE

1 (a) Il a été invité par un ami.
(b) Vous serez remarqué par la police.

(c) Le voleur a été arrêté par un pompier.
(d) Une solution a été trouvée.
(e) Les secrets ont été révélés.
(f) La théorie de la relativité a été proposée par Einstein.
(g) Il est connu de tout le monde.
(h) Ce modèle est vendu partout.
(i) Un jour, mes projets seront réalisés.
(j) Le général aurait été écrasé par un tank.*

2 (a) Un ami m'a invité.
(b) La police vous remarquera.
(c) Un pompier a arrêté le voleur.
(d) On a trouvé une solution.
(e) Les secrets se sont révélés (on a révélé les secrets).
(f) Einstein a proposé la théorie de la relativité.
(g) Tout le monde le connaît.
(h) Ce modèle se vend partout/ on vend ce modèle partout.
(i) Un jour, je réaliserai mes projets.
(j) Un tank aurait écrasé le général.*
*Both these sentences could also mean – is supposed /alleged to have been run over by a tank
(See conditional, pages 66–67)

3 (a) Il ne sera pas réélu la prochaine fois.
(b) On m'a ordonné de ne pas bouger.
(c) On ne nous a pas dit la vérité.
(d) On nous a demandé de ne pas attendre.
(e) Cette réclame se voit partout.
(f) On pense qu'il est très intelligent/on le croit très intelligent.
(g) Cela ne se fait pas ici/On ne fait pas ça ici.
(h) Ma sœur m'a pardonné.
(i) La face du monde a été changée par l'homme/L'homme a changé la face du monde.
(j) Trop de soleil brûle la peau./ La peau est brûlée par trop de soleil.
(k) La porte s'ouvre lentement, une main apparaît dans l'embrasure, un cri bizarre se fait entendre/on voit la porte s'ouvrir lentement, on voit une main dans l'embrasure, on entend un cri bizarre.
(l) Les portes du TGV s'ouvrent quand le train s'arrête
(m) Les portes ne sont pas ouvertes quand le train s'arrête.

PRESENT PARTICIPLE

1 (a) En travaillant pendant le week-end et en faisant des économies ils ont finalement réussi à acheter une maison.
(b) Je l'ai fait en regardant la télévision.
(c) Elle était assise devant le feu, le chat sur les genoux.
(d) Etant arrivé en retard, j'ai manqué le premier acte.
(e) Après avoir fermé la porte à clef et mis le verrou je me suis couché.
(f) Avant de partir vérifiez que vous ayez(si vous avez) fermé toutes les fenêtres.
(g) En arrivant il a constaté que les autres invités avaient déjà commencé le repas.
(h) Commencez par apprendre les verbes irréguliers.
(i) On ne peut pas se débarrasser de ses ordures en les laissant dans la rue.
(j) En gesticulant et en me faisant des signes elle a réussi à attirer mon attention.
(k) Une dame charmante au visage souriant.
(l) J'aime jouer de la guitare, regarder les matchs de football à la télévision et sortir avec mes copains.

2 (a) He likes fishing and hunting a lot and he loves sailing.
(b) Seeing is believing.
(c) The whole house needs cleaning.
(d) Thank you for reminding me about it.
(e) Women are reputed to be good drivers.
(f) In Molière's L'Avare, Maître Jacques is punished for telling the truth.
(g) A sowing machine; a dining room; a riding lesson; a driving lesson; a driving school.
(h) Yes, I can see him coming. He is running very fast, he is waving and shouting.

GETTING THINGS DONE: *FAIRE* AND THE INFINITIVE

(a) Faites venir son père.
(b) Ne le faites pas attendre sur le seuil, faites-le entrer.
(c) Faites griller pendant dix minutes.
(d) J'ai fait construire une maison à la campagne.
(e) Faites-lui manger quelque chose.
(f) Il a fait apporter des gâteaux de la pâtisserie.
(g) Laissez-le parler.
(h) Faites taire ces chiens!
(i) Le voleur s'est fait arrêter/attraper le lendemain.
(j) J'ai fait faire ces devoirs par ma sœur.

VERBS TAKING PREPOSITIONS

1 (a) Il a accepté de venir me voir.
(b) J'ai hésité à dire quoi que ce soit.
(c) Je l'ai invité à me rendre visite.
(d) Je l'ai félicitée de son succès.
(e) J'ai oublié d'écrire.
(f) Il a refusé d'accepter.
(g) J'ai refusé d'accepter.
(h) J'ai essayé de les persuader.
(i) Ils ont proposé de payer.
(j) Il a acheté la voiture à mon père.
(k) Il a emprunté l'argent à sa sœur.
(l) Est-ce qu'on peut se fier aux hommes politiques?
(m) Il faut rire de leur conduite.
(n) Il me faut voler une banque pour payer mes vacances.
(o) Je suis toujours le dernier à savoir.

2 (a) Vous n'avez rien à dire?
(b) Tout dépend de sa décision.
(c) Vous devez payer les dégâts.
(d) Qui attendez-vous?
(e) Dites à votre cousin d'amener sa sœur.
(f) Je me suis trompé de numéro/ j'ai fait le mauvais numéro.
(g) Je n'ai pas eu l'occasion de lui parler.
(h) Il s'est servi de sa manche pour nettoyer le tableau.
(i) J'ai promis à mon prof de travailler plus dur l'année prochaine.
(j) On m'a défendu de me servir de mon mouchoir pour nettoyer mes souliers.
(k) Que pensez-vous de lui?
(l) Vous pensez souvent à elle?
(m) Il vous manque quelque chose?
(n) La France me manque!
(o) Savez-vous jouer du piano?

3 (a) You could easily do without television.
(b) He is still in prison? I thought as much.
(c) I am very keen on visiting Corsica this year.
(d) He bore me a grudge for what I did to him.
(e) What is it used for/ what use is it?
(f) We are not all going to drink out of the same glass, I hope.

ARTICLES

(a) J'aime le football, la natation et le basket.
(b) Voulez-vous me passer le sel s'il vous plaît.
(c) Les Japonais chassent toujours les baleines.
(d) L'éléphant sera bientôt une espèce en voie de disparition.
(e) L'ail est un ingrédient important de la cuisine provençale.
(f) Je voudrais une bouteille d'eau, un kilo de pêches et une boîte des (de ces) haricots que vous avez recommandés.
(g) Mon frère veut devenir médecin — il est plein d'idées bizarres.
(h) Beaucoup de docteurs croient que le jogging est mauvais pour la santé.
(i) La plupart des gens que j'ai rencontrés ne vont pas à l'église le dimanche.
(j) Le samedi soir c'est moi qui fait la cuisine.
(k) Beaucoup de gens étaient arrivés en retard, d'autres n'avaient pas pris la peine de venir.
(l) La semaine dernière; l'année prochaine; le soir; le lundi.
(m) Il n'y avait pas de vent mais beaucoup de pluie.
(n) Nous n'avons ni bananes ni pêches.
(o) La France est presque deux fois et demie plus grande que l'Angleterre.
(p) Qu'est-ce qu'il nous faut pour le pique-nique – du jambon, du pain, de la salade, du vin ou du jus d'orange, des pêches et du fromage.

OBJECT PRONOUNS

1 (a) Oui, je vous les donne.
Oui, je vous les prête.
Oui, je vais vous les envoyer.
Oui, je vais vous en envoyer.
Oui, je vais le lui présenter.
(b) Non, je ne vous les donne pas.
Non, je ne vous les prête pas.
Non, je ne vais pas vous les envoyer.
Non, je ne vais pas vous en envoyer.
Non, je ne vais pas le lui présenter.

2 (a) Oui, j'y vais tout de suite.
Oui, il s'y intéresse beaucoup.
Oui, j'y réfléchis beaucoup.
Oui, j'y pense souvent.
(b) Non, je n'y vais pas tout de suite.
Non, il ne s'y intéresse pas beaucoup.
Non, je n'y réfléchis pas beaucoup.
Non, je n'y pense pas souvent.

3 (a) Oui, il en reste.
Oui, j'en ai besoin.
Oui, il m'en a parlé.
Combien en voulez-vous?
Il vous en faut combien?

    (b) Non, il n'en reste pas.
          Non, je n'en ai pas besoin.
          Non, il ne m'en a pas parlé
          Je n'en veux pas/Il ne m'en faut pas.

4 (a) Les brochures? Je les lui ai envoyées la semaine dernière.
    (b) Mon rapport? Je le leur ai déjà présenté.
    (c) Mon télex à M. Dupont? Je le lui ai déjà envoyé ce matin. Quoi, il ne l'a pas encore reçu? Il aurait dû le recevoir.
    (d) Téléphonez-lui et dites-lui que je le lui ai bien envoyé et qu'il devrait bientôt le recevoir.
    (e) Mon projet? Vous voulez que je vous l'explique? Bon, je vais vous l'expliquer. M. Dupont? Je le lui ai déjà expliqué. Il en était très content.

5 (a) Je les lui ai déjà envoyé(e)s.
    (b) Envoyez-le-lui. Il en a besoin tout de suite.
    (c) Téléphonez-lui et dites-lui que je lui en parlerai plus tard.
    (d) Des possibilités? Oui, il y en a plusieurs. Examinons-les.
    (e) Il vous les a envoyé(e)s la semaine dernière.
    (f) Il ne vous les a pas envoyé(e)s la semaine dernière?
    (g) Je suis sûr que je lui ai dit de vous les envoyer.

6 (a) (i)   Ne me les donnez pas.
          (ii) Ne les lui envoyez pas.
          (iii) Ne nous les expliquez pas.
          (iv) Ne lui répondez pas tout de suite.
          (v) Ne lui en parlez pas.
    (b) (i)   Dites-le-lui.
          (ii) Envoyez-le-moi.
          (iii) Parlez-lui-en.
          (iv) Donnez-m'en beaucoup.
          (v) Asseyez-vous là, la peinture y est fraîche!

EMPHATIC PRONOUNS

(a) Répétez après moi.
(b) Devant elle; derrière lui; avec nous.
(c) Eux, ils ne comprennent pas.
(d) Lui, qu'est-ce qu'il en pense?
(e) Ni elle ni moi ne savions la réponse.
(f) J'ai besoin de lui.
(g) Ils ont peur d'elle.
(h) Je l'ai fait moi-même.
(i) Que pense-t-il de nous?
(j) J'ai honte de vous.

RELATIVE AND INTERROGATIVE PRONOUNS

1 (a) Je sais qu'elle a raison.
    (b) Je pense qu'il arrivera tard.
    (c) Je ne sais pas ce qu'il va dire.
    (d) Qu'est-ce que vous lui direz?
    (e) Lequel de ces deux vins préférez-vous?
    (f) Voilà la maison dont je vous ai parlé.
    (g) Voilà l'arbre sous lequel nous nous sommes assis et sur lequel nous avons gravé nos noms.
    (h) Ce que je ne comprends pas c'est qu'il n'a jamais d'argent.

(i) De quel homme politique est-ce que vous parlez?

(j) Vous ne savez pas les difficultés que nous avons eues.

(k) Ce qui est intéressant, c'est qu'il a nié toute responsabilité.

(l) Parmi ces problèmes lequel est le plus préoccupant?

(m) Qui a laissé la porte ouverte?

(n) C'est un programme qui commence ce soir et que vous ne devez pas manquer.

(o) Elles sont à qui ces chaussures?

2 Les mauvais effets du soleil

Chaque année, les services d'urgence récupèrent des touristes inconscients, **qui** se sont laissé aller sous notre soleil sans penser **qu**'il n'avait rien à voir avec celui du bord des plages anglaises. On ignore le fait **que** le sable réfléchit 20% des radiations et l'eau 10% et **que** la quantité d'UVB est maximale entre 11 heures et 14 heures. **Ce qu**'on ignore surtout, c'est **que** les effets du soleil sont cumulatifs. Voici **ce que** m'a expliqué un chef de service de dermatologie: 'Tout s'additionne. Je vois parfois des patients **qui** me disent **que** depuis deux ou trois ans, ils ont nettement diminué leurs expositions au soleil. Mais tout **ce qu**'ils ont emmagasiné il y a 10 ou 20 ans est enregistré.'

DEMONSTRATIVE ADJECTIVES AND PRONOUNS

1 (a) Quel tricot préférez-vous? Celui-ci est joli mais celui-là sera plus chaud.

(b) Ceux en coton sont plus faciles à laver mais ceux en laine ne se froissent pas.

(c) Cet été; cette année; cette fois; ce temps; ces moustiques.

(d) Ça, c'est vraiment embêtant.

(e) Ma voiture est en panne. J'ai emprunté celle de mon frère.

(f) Quelles pêches préférez-vous? Celles-ci sont à 6F le kilo, et celles-là sont à 8F,50.

(g) Il faut conserver nos ressources naturelles; cela est très important.

(h) Quelle boîte voulez-vous? Celle qui est sur la table de la cuisine.

(i) Ces solutions sont difficiles à mettre en œuvre. Examinons celles proposées par Dupont.

(j) Ça, c'est le comble! Ces idées-là sont ridicules.

OTHER INDEFINITE ADJECTIVES AND PRONOUNS

2 (a) On dit que l'argent ne fait pas le bonheur. Je ne peux pas accepter une telle idée.

(b) J'ai passé la soirée avec quelques amis.

(c) Quelques-uns de ses meilleurs amis étaient venus lui dire au revoir.

(d) Cela s'est passé il y a plusieurs années.

(e) Je vois/comprends ce que vous voulez dire.

(f) Vous avez fait quelque chose d'intéressant à Bognor? Pas grand-chose.

(g) Chaque fois que je le voyais il avait l'air différent.

(h) Dans la pièce de Ionesco tous les personnages, sauf le héro Bérenger, se changent finalement en rhinocéros.

(i) Il y avait plusieurs jeunes filles sur la photo. Chacune portait une robe blanche.

(j) Tous les efforts que j'ai faits sont inutiles.

(k) Ils étaient tous arrivés trop tôt.

(l) Tout est possible si vous croyez que les gens ont confiance en vous.

C'EST AND *IL EST*

(a) Qui a fait ça? C'est mon père.

(b) Je vous présente ma tante. Elle est institutrice.

(c) C'est formidable, l'Angleterre a gagné au Parc des Princes!

(d) On peut maintenant traverser la Manche par le tunnel. C'est incroyable! Mais il est impossible de faire cela dans sa voiture.

(e) Ma sœur? Elle est au Brésil.
(f) Mes deux sœurs rient et bavardent tout le temps. Elles sont bêtes.
(g) Il est inspecteur de police. C'est un inspecteur bien connu en France.
(h) Les croissants? Ils sont sur la table dans la cuisine, n'est-ce pas?

POSSESSIVE ADJECTIVES AND PRONOUNS

(a) Son fils, sa sœur, sa mère, sa cousine, leurs parents.
(b) Ce livre, est-il à lui?/C'est à lui, ce livre? Non, c'est le sien/à elle.
(c) Elle est arrivée avec leurs amis et il est venu avec les siens/avec ses amis à lui.
(d) Quel livre est à lui/est le sien?
(e) C'est à qui ceci?
(f) Les miennes sont grises et les siennes sont bleues.
(g) Elle n'est pas à moi, elle est à eux/ ce n'est pas la mienne, c'est la leur.

ADJECTIVES

1 (a) Des ressources naturelles.
   (b) Une bonne idée.
   (c) La marée basse.
   (d) Un matin frais.
   (e) Un hiver doux.
   (f) Une voix douce.
   (g) Une longue journée.
   (h) Une nouvelle solution.
   (i) Une fille menteuse.
   (j) Une collection complète.
   (k) Une fausse idée.
   (l) Il y avait plusieurs jolies filles françaises à la boum.
   (m) La population ouvrière.
   (n) De vieux amis; Un vieil ami.
   (o) La vie parisienne.
   (p) Quelques nouvelles publications françaises.
   (q) De petites villes italiennes.
   (r) Une explication brève.
   (s) Un lieu public.
   (t) Une place publique.

2 Change of meaning tasks
   (a) De Gaulle was a great man; he was also a tall man.
   (b) You feel sorry for that millionaire but he is not poor.
   (c) The school I used to go to is a very old one.
   (d) Last year was 1995 but 1999 will be the last year of the century.
   (e) My own house; I like to live in a clean house.
   (f) A certain man; find me a man I can rely on.
   (g) My dear wife has bought an expensive coat.
   (h) I was born on the same day as you; he fell ill the very day he arrived.
   (i) He has another car. It's a new model.
   (j) The only Chinese man that I know; only the Chinese know how to do it.
   (k) Another glass (to drink)? I'll bring you a fresh glass. Here's one that has never been used.
   (l) I'll tell him the next time I see him, perhaps that will be next week.

ADVERBS AND COMPARISONS

(a) Un ancien collègue.
(b) Elle est la seule qui puisse le faire.

(c) Evidemment il parle le russe aussi bien que vous.

(d) Il a encore acheté une maison. C'est une maison neuve?

(e) Le jour même de son arrivée.

(f) Ces lettres sont arrivées le même jour.

(g) J'ai été profondément ému.

(h) La dernière fois que je l'ai vue elle portait des chaussures neuves.

(i) Vous voulez encore une tasse (another drink)? Vous voulez une autre tasse (another cup – this one is cracked)?

(j) Je l'ai rencontré récemment.

(k) Mettez des chaussettes propres.

(l) Plus il a expliqué, moins j'ai compris.

(m) Elle sait mieux dessiner que moi.

(n) Ce n'est pas une mauvaise voiture mais le moteur ne marche pas bien/marche mal à présent.

(o) Ils ne sortent pas souvent, une petite promenade de temps en temps.

(p) Vous vous sentez mieux?

(q) Il devient de plus en plus difficile de trouver un bon programme à la télévision.

(r) Quel programme aimez-vous le mieux regarder?

(s) Ils croient tous aveuglément au progrès.

(t) La Grande-Bretagne n'est pas le pays le moins pollué du monde.

CHAPTER 3

ORAL AND AURAL TASKS

Units in this chapter

3.1 THE ORAL EXAMINATION

Contents
- Role-play
- Reporting tasks
- Study extracts
- Talking about a prepared topic
- Ensuring success in the oral examination

Depending on the Board, the oral examination carries from 20% to 25% of the total marks at A-Level and from 30% to 40% at AS-Level. It is, therefore, an important part of your work at A and AS-Level.

The oral test lasts 15–20 minutes with most Boards, or up to 30 minutes in the case of the Oxford and Oxford and Cambridge Boards. Some Boards provide the option of continuous assessment instead of, or combined with, a final oral test. This means that you can be tested orally at certain stages of your A-Level course or as a complete module.

Nearly all oral tests consist of some or all of three groups of tasks:

1. **Role-play** This involves getting information, resolving a problem or expressing opinions. The tasks are usually outlined in French, but may be in English depending on the Board.

2. **Reporting tasks or discussion of material provided** Reporting task material is in French but may be in English, depending on the Board. Discussion may be based on a prepared topic, on a book or film, on a passage to be studied before the Examination or on a research area or personal experience. Depending on the Board, discussion may be related to, or exclusive of topics prepared for the written paper. Check your Board's regulations carefully.

3. **General conversation**

Note You should check the following points about your oral:
(a) How long the test lasts

(b) How long the preparation time is. Some Boards give you a few days to prepare printed material for discussion when the latter is quite lengthy. Other Boards allow only about 20 minutes on the day of the test. The material is usually shorter in this case

(c) Whether dictionaries are allowed

(d) Whether or not you are allowed to make notes and refer to these during the test

(e) The tasks you will be required to carry out and what proportion of the test they represent

You should find all these details in the syllabus for your Board. You should also find a description of what skills the oral test is supposed to test and some indication of how marks are awarded.

Obtain from your library or send for copies of past oral papers. It can be helpful to get these from other Boards other than the one you are doing, particularly for role-playing tasks, in order to broaden the range of situations you might meet.

You should also try to obtain a copy of recent Examiners' reports. This will give you a clearer guide to what is expected of candidates.

ROLE-PLAY

This task often comes first. Instructions are given in the form of a brief, which sets the scene and tells you what role you are going to play, and a task that gives you the information needed to play the role. It is important to do all the things you are asked to do in the task description. If these are not itemized, it is a good idea to underline and number each bit so that you work through them systematically. Jot down a phrase or a few words in numbered order to help you with each part. You will not have time, and neither is it a good idea, to write out everything you want to say. There is usually more than one way of saying things. The main thing is to communicate the information. Once you get into the swing of things, you will find yourself reacting more naturally and all you have to do is keep an eye on the items in the task.

Most role-play situations call for a bit of play acting. You may have to appear forceful or persistent, you may have to apologize, you may have to object to something, show surprise or even concern. Enter into the spirit of the situation and don't be intimidated by the Examiner. He or she will find their task much easier if they can provoke some reaction from you. During the brief exchange of the role-play, a change in attitude often takes place: somebody is convinced, reassured or conciliated; it usually ends on a friendly note. Keep all this in mind.

Exercices

The following exercises have a brief and a task description modelled on those you are likely to meet in an exam. This is followed by a series of phrases that the other person might use. You would not have access to these in an examination. They are provided here to help you practise the roles with another person. Some Examining Boards provide suggestions of this kind for the Examiner's use; (he or she will have worked out a series of possibilities in any case). They are not meant to represent the only things that might be said. There is always a great deal of room for invention and flexibility. Work with a partner and study one of the roles; take it in turns to play each one. Do not just try and translate the information in the task description. Try and add bits of natural language. A possible version of the first role-play is done for you as an example of this.

EXAMPLE 1

Candidate's brief You are spending a year at Grenoble University and have been asked to lead a group of French school children, 14–16 years old, who are spending a few days in the Isère region. They are being accomodated in the *cité universitaire*. They are not happy with things and a spokesperson comes to complain.

Task You counter all their complaints with excuses or explanations:
- The rooms are small because this is student accomodation not a hotel
- It isn't costing them very much
- You admit that the meals aren't very good but you will see what can be done
- If funds allow, you could all eat out at least once
- The weather is not your fault — it is to be expected in mountains
- Excursions were recommended to you but you will consult whole group about next ones
- You are not empowered to give refunds
- Anyway, two days is hardly long enough to form an opinion
- If the group go home on their own account they will have to pay own fare
- Not fair to you, your first experience of this kind of thing in France
- Reiterate that you will do your best
- End on a friendly note saying that the weather forecast for the next few days is a lot better

Spokesman's brief You will complain strongly on behalf of the whole group. You have a fairly long list of complaints (you can enlarge on the above). You are gradually persuaded by the group leader and end on a friendly note. You begin the exchange. The following are possible things to say. Try to fill them out as much as possible:
- *Je viens vous parler parce qu'on n'est pas content, hein*
- *D'abord les chambres sont trop petites. On ne peut pas se réunir*
- *Les repas au réfectoire sont dégoûtants. Tout est froid, il n'y pas de choix*
- *Manger en ville, c'est cher*
- *On ne peut pas aller tout le temps manger en ville*
- *Il fait mauvais temps, il pleut sans cesse depuis deux jours*
- *Les excursions ne sont pas formidables — deux fois au musée!*
- *On voudrait que le voyage soit remboursé*
- *Il y en a beaucoup qui voudraient repartir chez eux*
- *Qu'est-ce que vous allez faire?*

Possible full exchange

Spokesperson Je viens vous voir, monsieur pour vous dire que nous ne sommes pas contents du séjour, vous savez.

Leader Ah bon, qu'est-ce qu'il y a? Qu'est-ce qui ne va pas?

S Euh, d'abord les chambres sont trop petites. On ne peut pas se réunir.

L Mais, ici c'est une cité universitaire, vous savez, pas un hôtel. C'est pour cela que le prix est si raisonnable.

S Et les repas au réfectoire sont dégoûtants. C'est toujours froid et il n'y a pas de choix. Et si on va manger en ville, ça revient cher.

L Pour les repas, je suis d'accord. C'est pas formidable. Je vais voir ce qu'on peut faire. On pourrait peut-être manger au moins une fois en ville, s'il nous reste de l'argent.

S Et puis il fait un sale temps depuis deux jours maintenant, il pleut sans cesse.

L Ecoutez, là vous allez un peu fort, hein. Ce n'est pas ma faute s'il pleut! Je ne peux rien au temps! Et puis à la montagne c'est souvent comme ça.

S Et les excursions, c'est pas formidable, hein? Deux fois au musée!

L On me les avait recommandés, mais... Ecoutez, je vais consulter le groupe pour la prochaine fois, hein?

S Il y en a qui voudraient qu'on les rembourse.

L Mais vous savez, je n'ai pas le droit de faire ça. Et puis il ne faut pas juger en deux jours. On est ici pour une semaine.

S Il faut dire que certains parlent de repartir chez eux.

L Bon, alors, ils faut qu'ils paient leur voyage. Je ne peux pas leur fournir un billet. Et ce n'est pas juste, pour moi. Vous savez, c'est la première fois que je fais ce travail.

S Bon, d'accord, je vais leur raconter ça et ce que vous avez dit.

L Dites-leur aussi que la météo prédit le retour du beau temps pour demain.

You will note that:
(a) Small details have been added
(b) Words like *écoutez, vous savez, bon, d'accord, mais* and *n'est ce pas* have also been added
(c) The words *hein* and *euh* appear; they are a trifle inelegant but it suits the style of a conversation between two young people]

EXAMPLE 2

Candidate's brief and task You are staying with the parents of your correspondant(e). Having heard about the famous cave paintings at Lascaux*, you try to persuade the father/mother to take you, and the family, by car to see them. For a variety of reasons they are not keen on going (e.g. already been, can't see real paintings anyway, too crowded on a Sunday, too far to drive, children car-sick/might misbehave, how about a day at the seaside instead?). You counter all these arguments as convincingly as possible and you end by persuading him/her because you might not have this opportunity again.

> *les peintures dans les grottes de Lascaux*

Parent's brief The candidate begins the exchange. You start off by being quite against the idea. You gradually change your opinion because your visitor is being particularly persuasive. Here are some phrases you might use:

- *On y est déjà allé*
- *C'est pas la peine, on ne voit pas les véritables peintures. La grotte est fermée au public**
- *Il y aura du monde dimanche*
- *C'est loin, hein. On en aura pour deux heures en voiture*
- *Vous savez, les enfants sont insupportables en la voiture*
- *Ils sont souvent malades*
- *On pourrait bien aller à la plage dimanche, non?*
- *Peut-être que vous avez raison — on ne voit pas ça en Angleterre.*
- *Bien, je suis persuadé(e)/Vous m'avez convaincu(e) Il faut que vous vous occupiez des enfants*
- *Ce sera votre faute s'ils ne sont pas sages*

> * *Mais on a recréé la grotte et les peintures dans une exposition appelée 'Lascaux II'*

Possible beginnings:
(a) On m'a parlé hier des peintures préhistoriques dans les grottes de Lascaux. Il paraît que c'est formidable. On pourrait y aller en voiture, non…
(b) Vous pourriez nous y emmener tous en voiture, dimanche?
(c) Je voudrais bien y aller. Serait-il possible d'y aller en voiture?
(d) On pourrait faire une excursion en voiture

EXAMPLE 3

Candidate's brief You arrive at a small railway station in the middle of France at 7.00 p.m., expecting to catch an overnight train to Montélimar where some friends are to pick you up by car at the station and give you a lift to Nice. They are expecting you to arrive at 10.00 a.m and have arranged to wait for one hour only. The syndicat has given you times of trains. You have just enough money for a ticket since all the banks were closed today for the 15 August.

Task
- Ask for a single ticket, platform and time of train
- Express surprise and dismay when told the time of the next train to Montélimar
- Ask the attendant to double check
- Can he suggest an alternative route or a way out of the problem?
- All his suggestions won't work because of the money situation, your friends can't be contacted etc.

- Stress the fact that they will not wait
- Accept his final suggestions with thanks and ask where you could stay the night

Note The idea of surprise might be expressed by '*Mais... je ne comprends pas/Non, ce n'est pas vrai.... J'avais bien noté l'heure du train/vous êtes sûr/vous ne vous êtes pas trompé*';
and dismay by '*c'est embêtant/c'est incroyable/il y a une erreur, non?*'

Attendant's brief You begin the exchange. You are rather annoyed at first and dismissive of this person's problem but you gradually begin to feel a bit sorry for them. You realize that your initial suggestions won't work. Then you hit on a good idea. Here are some possible phrases and responses:

- *Bonsoir monsieur/madame, vous désirez?*
- *Ça fait 240 francs*
- *Quai numéro deux, départ demain matin à 5 heures 15*
- *Arrivée à Montélimar à 11h27*
- *C'est écrit ici, hein, noir sur blanc!*
- *Ah non, il n'y pas d'autre train*
- *Alors, vous avez un vrai problème*
- *Je suis désolé, mais je ne peux rien faire*
- *Ecoutez, vous pourriez passer la nuit à l'hôtel et revenir demain pour prendre le train*
- *Ou bien téléphonez à vos amis pour leur dire que vous serez en retard*
- *Bon, je vois bien que c'est embêtant pour vous*
- *Eh bien écoutez, je vais téléphoner à la gare de Montélimar et laisser un message pour dire à vos amis de vous attendre. Ils ont quelle voiture ?*
- *Vous pouvez rester ici dans la salle d'attente*

EXAMPLE 4

Candidate's brief and task You are staying with a French family and giving English lessons to two boys aged 12 and 14. In return for this you are given your keep and spending money. You are becoming unhappy about the behaviour and attitude of your pupils. You ask to speak to the father about the matter.

Problems are the following:

- They arrive late or one of them is absent
- They don't do the work you have set them
- They don't pay attention and keep talking to one another; one of them is always making jokes
- Their friends keep phoning them or calling for them
- Be prepared to explain the methods you have been using — role-plays, games, reading texts, asking questions etc
- Ask the father if he will support you* by insisting on proper behaviour, regular attendance, (the hours of which you will both agree), and that they do their preparation
  * *Est-ce que je peux compter sur vous pour qu'ils fassent leur travail?*
- Also, you are embarrassed** to ask, but you have not yet received any spending money as agreed
  ** *Ça m'ennuie un peu de vous le dire, mais...*

Father's brief You appear surprised at first because you hadn't realized what was happening. You would like to know all the complaints. You would also like to make sure that your sons are not just bored or that the work is too difficult or too easy. Agree to a certain number of hours of lessons per day and to keeping an eye on the boys' work. Suggest an excursion with the family at the weekend. You apologize profusely about the non-payment of pocket money. It had slipped your mind! Here are some possible phrases and responses:

- *Vous voulez me voir, je crois*
- *Tiens! je ne savais pas ça*
- *Je n'étais pas au courant. Cela me surprend*

- *C'est parce que je ne suis pas ici pendant la journée*
- *Je vais m' occuper de ça, je vous assure*
- *Pouvez-vous me dire exactement ce que vous faites avec eux comme travail?*
- *Quelles méthodes est-ce que vous employez?*
- *Ce n'est pas un peu trop difficile/facile pour eux?*
- *Ils s'ennuient un peu, hein?*
- *Alors, c'est convenu, ... heures par jour le matin/l'après-midi, plus... heures de préparation*
- *Je vais surveiller ça, n'ayez pas peur!*
- *Ce week-end, nous pensons faire une excursion au bord de la mer. Est-ce que ça vous ferait plaisir de nous accompagner?*
- *C'est parfait*
- *Ah ça ! je n'y avais pas pensé. Je suis vraiment désolé. Vous auriez dû m'en parler plus tôt. Ne vous gênez pas une autre fois, hein*

EXAMPLE 5

Candidate's brief You are staying on a French campsite together with quite a few English families. The latter are not happy about a number of things on the site. Because you speak French better than they do, they ask you to voice their complaints to the owner of the site.

Task
Be polite but firm*. The owner will have an excuse or explanation for everything
- Say who you are and why you have come
- The toilets and showers are dirty and not cleaned often enough
- Some of the drains are blocked
- Some of the electrical fittings — plug sockets (les prises) — are loose (détachées) and dangerous
- There is no supervision at the swimming pool
- There is a lot of noise after 10.00 o'clock, particularly from the disco
- Point out the dangers and risks of all this — health, safety, risks to children, older people can't sleep etc.
- The owner seems unconvinced until you threaten to complain** at the Mairie
- End by obtaining an assurance that certain things will be put right

> *Je vous assure que je n'exagère pas*
> *Je dois insister pour qu'on fasse quelque chose*
> *Je suis obligé de vous signaler*
> *Je regrette de vous dire que...*
> *Je répète, ce n'est pas une exagération*
> *Ce n'est pas raisonnable, voyons...*
> *Vous ne trouvez pas que j'ai raison?*
> ** *Je serais obligé(e) de porter plainte...*

Owner's brief You give the impression that you do not take the person's complaints very seriously — you have had problems with British campers before! You can find an excuse or an explanation for all the complaints. You begin the exchange:
- *Je crois que vous voulez me voir*
- *Ah bon. Il me manque du personnel en ce moment, il y en a qui sont malades*
- *Il est difficile de trouver des remplaçants à présent*
- *Avec 2 000 campeurs, vous savez...*
- *L'électricien est en vacances. Les éboueurs sont en grève*
- *On n'a jamais eu d'accident dans la piscine*
- *Ils exagèrent un peu vos Anglais, non?/ Ce sont toujours les Anglais qui se plaignent!*
- *C'est un camping ici, on n'est pas à Colditz, hein!*
- *Après 10 heures il y a toujours un peu de bruit*
- *Il n'y pas de musique tous les soirs*
- *Vous n'allez pas porter plainte pour un rien!*

- *Que voulez-vous que je fasse?*
- *Bon, d'accord, je ferai nettoyer les toilettes/enlever les poubelles*
- *Je téléphonerai à un autre électricien*

EXAMPLE 6

Candidate's brief You are staying in Paris and the day before yesterday at about 5.00 p.m, you took a raincoat to the dry cleaners. You now find that you have lost the ticket. You go to the shop to collect your coat without being able to show the ticket.

Task

Explain to the assistant what has happened and apologize*:
- Be prepared to describe the raincoat (e.g. colour, size, style) and say when you brought it in
- Doesn't the gentleman remember you, he served you?
- The first coat he brings is the wrong one. Yours is a light blue, with a belt
- Say you are sorry for the inconvenience you are causing him**
- Be pleased*** when he brings the right coat, and thank him
- You are staying at the Hôtel Continental, rue Victor Hugo. You have your passport with you
- Ask how much you owe, thank the assistant again and take your leave

    * *Je vous prie de m'excuser/je regrette, mais... or Je suis désolé(e) mais...*
    ** *Je m'excuse de vous déranger, monsieur/madame*
    *** *C'est formidable, vous l'avez trouvé!*

Assistant's brief You are at first not very willing to cooperate and complain about customers always losing their tickets. You ask the candidate when the coat was left, a description (colour, size, style, with or without belt). You bring the wrong coat first and are not very pleased. Before handing over the right one ask where the person is staying and for some means of identification. Here are some possible phrases:
- *Mais vous savez c'est ce qu'ils disent tous! On perd tout le temps son billet*
- *Quand est-ce que vous l'avez laissé?*
- *Ah, non je ne me souviens pas de vous — je ne suis pas un ordinateur, moi!*
- *Décrivez-moi un peu votre imper, je vais tâcher de le retrouver*
- *Ce n'est pas le bon?*
- *Oh, il y en a des dizaines comme ça!*
- *Voilà, c'est bien le vôtre?*
- *Vous avez une pièce d'identité, une adresse à Paris?*
- *Ça fait 45 francs*
- *De rien, à votre service monsieur*

EXAMPLE 7

Candidate's brief Some friends have arranged to give you a lift on their way through Paris by car. You arrange to meet them very early in the morning near one of the slip roads to the périphérique. You have been waiting some time when you are approached by a policeman.

Task

Your passport is at the bottom of your rucksack:
- Explain that identity cards are not required in Britain
- Explain what you are doing there, when you expect your friends to arrive etc.
- Be prepared to answer other questions about where you are heading for, who your friends are, what sort of car they have etc.
- A small packet in your rucksack contains some English cheese — a present for the family you are going to stay with
- The policeman is eventually convinced but you express dissatisfaction* with the way you have been treated

*   *Je trouve votre attitude/conduite un peu impolie*
    Ce n'est pas poli, hein, de parler aux gens comme ça
    Ce n'est pas une manière de se conduire avec les visiteurs étrangers!

Policeman's brief   You are very suspicious of this person whom you have been watching for some time. The area is notorious for drug dealing. You are only slowly convinced of the person's innocence. You are genuinely baffled by the need to import cheese into France:

*   *Contrôle d'identité, vos papiers s'il vous plaît*
*   *Mais où sont-ils alors?*
*   *Désolé, mais il faut que je voie ça*
*   *Qu'est-ce que vous faites ici?*
*   *Elle me paraît un peu bizarre, votre explication*
*   *Comment vérifier ça?*
*   *Qui sont vos amis? Et leur voiture?*
*   *Je vous surveille depuis un bon moment*
*   *Il y a des trafiquants de drogue dans ce quartier, hein*
*   *Ce paquet, qu'est-ce que c'est?*
*   *Vous apportez du fromage en France! Ça c'est le comble!*
*   *Bon, euh, ça a l'air d'aller. Vous pouvez partir*
*   *Ecoutez! ce n'est pas ma faute, je fais mon boulot/travail, c'est tout*

Practice exam questions

1   This Board allows the use of a dictionary during the 15 minute preparation time for the role-play. You are not allowed to take notes into the interview room. You have 15 minutes in which to prepare this task. Do not try to write a full version of your role. There isn't time and it is not advisable because the exchange will seem less realistic. Instead, say over in your mind/or aloud each part of the task. Look up essential words as you go and jot these down together with key words for each part. Do this as many times as possible during the 15 minutes. Try to enter into the spirit of the situation and imagine that you *are* talking to a friend who is keen to advise you.

It is helpful if you can practise this role-play with a friend. A possible version of the Examiner's part is given below. Take turns to read through the whole role-play aloud. Then try doing the candidate's part with just the English brief in front of you.

Brief

You are staying with a French friend in a small village near Rennes. Down the road, there is a farm cottage for sale with some land. Your friend tries to persuade your father and mother that this would be an excellent investment as a second home. They are not convinced. You discuss the issues with your friend on behalf of your parents.

Task

*   Find out precise details of the property from your friend (e.g. number of rooms, price, how long it's been for sale). You need to discover whether the price is negotiable.
*   You are concerned about the state of the property market in France. What will happen to interest rates? Are there not large tax bills to be paid on second homes? What about other costs (e.g. solicitor, registration)?
    – Your friend reassures you on these matters – you are quite interested but still have some reservations.
*   Say you have heard that English people are not well accepted in these parts. Suggest possible reasons why this should be so (e.g. they don't speak French, they cause house prices to rise).
    – Apparently the locals are delighted to welcome 'les Anglais' around there!
*   You think that this is probably because they are the only people brave enough to

take on the repairs required to these old cottages! Say you are worried about how to get estimates from all the craftsmen, since you have seen that there is much to be done (e.g. works to the roof, extensive re-decorating).
– There is no problem with this. Your friend will help with everything. He/She is very keen for you to consider this thoroughly.

● You agree as a family to think about it seriously. After all, it would be nice to have a holiday home in France.

Oxford and Cambridge

Candidate's part

● *Est-ce que tu pourrais me donner des détails plus précis. Combien de pièces y a-t-il dans la maison/La maison a combien de pièces? Depuis combien de temps est-elle en vente?/Ça fait longtemps qu'elle est en vente? Quel est le prix?/On demande combien? On peut négocier le prix?/Tu penses qu'on pourrait négocier le prix?*

● *Tu sais, le marché immobilier en France est très difficile en ce moment. On ne sait jamais, le taux d'intérêt pourrait monter/il y aura peut-être une augmentation des taux d'intérêt. Et les taxes pour les maisons secondaires sont considérables, non? Et puis il y a d'autres frais n'est-ce pas, le notaire, l'enregistrement, les taxes locales etc.*

● *Et puis on m'a dit que les Anglais n'étaient pas très bien accueillis dans la région. C'est parce que la plupart des Anglais ne parlent pas français. Ils font monter le prix des maisons.*

● *C'est peut-être parce que ce sont seuls les Anglais qui ont le courage de réparer ces vieilles maisons délabrées. Et puis je ne sais pas me débrouiller pour obtenir des devis pour les travaux – il y a tellement de réparations à faire – le toit, les murs, la peinture.*

● *Bon, écoute je crois que nous allons réfléchir et discuter de la situation. Ce serait après tout merveilleux d'avoir une maison en France, surtout en Bretagne.*

Examiner's part

● *Il y a huit pièces. Une grande salle de séjour, une cuisine et trois chambres en haut. Elle est en vente depuis quelques mois seulement. Le prix est de 18 000 francs. Je connais bien M. Jacques le propriétaire et je crois qu'il accepterait un peu moins.*

● *Oui, le marché immobilier est difficile à présent, tu as raison. Je ne pense pas que les taux d'intérêt vont beaucoup changer. Pour les taxes, elles ne sont pas excessives et les frais supplémentaires non plus. On se débrouillera.*

● *Non, ce n'est pas vrai. Les Anglais sont très bien accueillis par ici dans la région, tu sais, pour des raisons économiques/cela rapporte de l'argent. En plus les Bretons aiment beaucoup les Anglais.*

● *Pour les réparations, aucun problème. Mon père a des amis qui travaillent dans le bâtiment. Nous pourrions nous charger de tout cela. Il faut y réfléchir sérieusement, hein? C'est une occasion. Il faut que tu essaies de convaincre ton père. Ce serait chouette d'avoir une maison en France.*

2 Here is another example from the same Board, this time with only the examiner's part.

Brief

You are a courier for a French travel company which specialises in luxury tours for British tourists in the Loire Valley. You arrive at a four star hotel which is featured in your company's brochure as offering 'outstanding cuisine in the most elegant surroundings'. Your company uses the hotel regularly for its package tours but this is your first visit with a 'luxury class' group. There is a problem.

Task

● You explain to the manager/manageress that you have discovered that your group is scheduled to eat in a conference room above the main restaurant. However, your guests' itinerary advertises that they are due to 'sample the gastronomy of the best restaurant in the region'. It is not acceptable therefore for them to eat '2nd class', as it were.

    – The manager/manageress explains that all travel groups eat in the conference room; otherwise there would not be enough room for private guests.

- You are very sympathetic to his/her problems but this is a very expensive tour and, as tour leader, it is your responsibility to act in the best interests of your clients. Explain to him/her your reasons for requiring preferential treatment (e.g. type of clientele, details in your brochure). You must persuade him/her that you are a special case.

    – He/She seems unconcerned and repeats to you the hotel rules.

- You are not to be beaten. Remind him/her how much trade your travel company does with the hotel (e.g. winter breaks, wine-tasting weekends).

    – He/She apologises for the situation, obviously moved by your arguments, but sees no solution.

- Suggest ways of taking pressure off the restaurant (e.g. stagger the arrival of your guests and eat before or after the restaurant's busiest time). Flatter him/her on the service and standards of cuisine. Surely their excellent staff can cope! Come to some arrangement.

    – He/She agrees that this is a good idea and asks whether it will satisfy your clients?

Respond appropriately.

Oxford and Cambridge

Examiner's part

- Il est normal pour tous les groupes touristiques de manger dans la salle de conférence. Autrement il n'y aurait pas assez de place pour les autres clients. On y est très bien, et on y sert les mêmes repas que dans le restaurant. La cuisine est très soignée.
- Mais je vous ai expliqué que si tous les clients mangeaient en bas dans le restaurant il n'y aurait pas assez de place. La salle de conférence est très élégante, avec de belles vues sur la rivière.
- La situation est regrettable. Je suis désolé mais je ne vois pas de solution.
- Oui, on pourrait peut-être décaler les heures des repas. Vos clients seraient-ils contents de venir un peu en avance ou même de manger plus tard?

3 Some Examination Boards present the situation and task in French with additional material in English relevant to the rôle you are going to play. Here is an example from the UODLE Board. You have 30 minutes in which to prepare the material. You are allowed a monolingual dictionary and you can take notes into the Examination. Having the situation and task in French is useful in providing some of the vocabulary needed. You can use the dictionary to check meanings in the French but you will obviously not be able to look up the French for an English word. Make brief notes writing down words or phrases. Do not write out a whole text.

Brief

Vous travaillez pour une compagnie aérienne britannique au stand d'informations à Heathrow, Londres. L'examinateur joue le rôle d'un professeur français responsable d'un group d'élèves âgés de 13 ans qui viennent de faire leur premier séjour en Grande-Bretagne. Ils ont fait un échange et ont été accueillis dans des familles anglaises.

    Il est six heures du soir. Le groupe est arrivé à l'aéroport pour le vol du retour. En y arrivant, ils apprennent que l'aéroport est fermé pour cause de brouillard. Aucun départ n'est prévu avant le lendemain matin.

Task

Le professeur responsable du groupe se presente au stand d'informations et vous demande de lui expliquer la situation. Pendant votre conversation vous devrez lui demander:

- *la destination du groupe*
- *l'heure et le numéro du vol*
- *le nombre de personnes dans le groupe*

Le professeur est évidemment très ennuyé de la situation et vous devrez discuter avec lui/elle des diverses possibilités, par exemple:

- *retourner dans les familles d'accueil pour la nuit et prendre le premier vol le lendemain matin*
- *passer la nuit dans les salles d'attente de l'aéroport et prendre un vol le lendemain matin*
- *réserver des chambres dans un hôtel à l'aéroport*
- *prendre le train et le ferryboat et demander un remboursement à l'assurance*

Sur la feuille ci-jointe vous trouverez quelques indications qui pourraient vous aider a régler les problèmes du groupe. Discutez de la situation avec le professeur et essayez de trouver la meilleure solution possible dans ces circonstances difficiles.

Il faudra vous montrer le plus serviable possible envers vos clients. Votre compagnie vous permettra de faire certaines concessions de votre gré (par exemple des repas gratuits, l'utilisation du téléphone) et de rembourser les billets d'avion non-utilisés. Cependant vous ne pouvez pas les loger gratuitement pour la nuit, puisque des centaines de passagers se trouvent dans la même situation.

HEATHROW AIRPORT

Shopping

Heathrow Airport Limited offers passengers well-known, branded shops, and high quality goods together with a well-publicised guarantee of value. By encouraging well-known high street shops like Austin Reed, Jaeger, Bally, Boots the Chemist and Olympus Sports to trade at the airport, Heathrow Airport Limited ensures that passengers are familiar with standards of quality and pricing.

Eating

In line with Heathrow's global policy to improve customer service, competing high street catering companies have been encouraged to run airport restaurants and bars. Heathrow Airport Limited believes this gives customers greater confidence in value for money and the quality of food and drink available. In 1991 famous name brands including Burger King, Upper Crust, Garfunkels, Harry Ramsdens, Tap and Spile and Haagen Dazs opened branches at Heathrow. In December 1992, McDonalds opened for business in Terminal 4.

Hotel information and reservations

There are Hotel Reservations desks in the arrivals hall of each terminal. They can book a wide selection of hotels, from basic youth hostels to luxury hotels.

Airport Hotels

Prices are per person	Our rating	Parking	Mon–Thurs		Fri–Sun	
			Twin	Single	Twin	Single
Arlington	★★		24.75	48.00	19.75	39.50
		15 nights inc	30.00	56.00	29.00	54.00
Ibis	★★	£3.50 per day	25.25	49.50	20.75	41.00
Ambassador	★★★		25.50	51.00	20.50	41.00
		8 nights inc	30.00	60.00	25.00	50.00
Novotel	★★★	8 nights free	34.75	67.00	28.00	49.00
Jul/Aug/Dec/Jan			29.00	54.00	28.00	49.00
Master Robert	★★★		32.00	63.00	28.00	53.00
		15 nights inc	35.00	68.00	28.00	53.00
Excelsior	★★★★		35.50	71.00	30.00	59.00
Jul/Aug/Dec/Jan/Apr			34.00	68.00	29.00	58.00
		15 nights inc	42.00	84.00	36.50	73.00
Crown Club Supplement			12.50	25.00	7.50	15.00

Entertaining Children

While there are presently no dedicated 'play areas' in the terminals at Heathrow, there are video game machines distributed around the terminals which are very popular with the younger visitors to the airport.

The spectators' viewing area, on the roof of Terminal 2, is also a good place to entertain children. They can enjoy an aerial view of airport activity and visit the area's cafeteria and shop. The viewing area can be reached by Clifton Road, next to Terminal 2. Admission is free.

Public Transport

Heathrow airport is very well served by public transport. The London Underground offers direct services into central London.

Examples of average journey times from Heathrow to:

Piccadilly Circus	47 minutes
King's Cross	55 minutes
Liverpool Street	61 minutes

Trains run every 5 minutes at peak times and every 9 minutes at off peak times and at weekends.

Flight times

Depart London	Arrive Paris
0630	0735
0725	0830
0845	1050
0915	1120

Train departures

Via Newhaven/Dieppe

Depart London Victoria Station	Arrive Paris
2140	0701

Oxford

Below is the part the Examiner might play. Work out your part and practise this with a friend. This role-play is a fairly long one and ten minutes are allocated in the exam. Take it step by step and do not be tempted to give a lot of information in one go. Use the information in English where you think it is appropriate. Select the cheapest hotel for example, offer a free meal in the new McDonalds, explain how to get to Victoria Station, explain what entertainments there are for children.

- *Est-ce que vous pouvez m'expliquer ce qui se passe?*
- *Ça c'est très embêtant, c'est très ennuyeux. Je suis ici avec un groupe de dix jeunes de treize ans. Leurs parents attendent leur arrivée à Paris ce soir. Ils ne savent pas ce qui se passe.*
- *Retourner dans leurs familles en Angleterre? Ce serait possible pour ceux qui habitent à Londres mais les autres familles sont loin d'ici. En tout cas il va être difficile de contacter toutes les familles et il n'est pas sûr qu'elles seront d'accord.*
- *Mais ces enfants ont besoin de dormir. Ils ont voyagé la journée. Ils sont fatigués.*
- *Je ne pourrais pas les surveiller toute la nuit.*
- *Ils vont s'ennuyer. Il n'y a rien à faire dans la salle d'attente.*

- *Et ils auront faim. Il faut qu'ils mangent quelque chose.*
- *Qui payera? Je n'ai pas prévu cette éventualité dans mon budget.*
- *Le premier vol est à quelle heure demain matin?*
- *Mais tous ces hôtels sont très chers, n'est-ce pas? Et puis comment savoir s'il y a assez de chambres?*
- *Et en plus il y a la question d'argent. Je n'en ai pas suffisamment.*
- *Est-ce qu'il y a un vol plus tard demain matin?*
- *Prendre le train? Mais il part à quelle heure? Et pour la traversée de la Manche? Il faudra passer la nuit à voyager? A quelle heure le train arrive-t-il à Paris?*
- *Comment on arrive à la gare Victoria?*
- *Est-ce que les billets d'avion peuvent être remboursés pour qu'on puisse prendre le train et le ferry?*
- *Bon, on va passer la nuit à l'hôtel. Je ne vois pas d'autre solution. Mais c'est très embêtant.*
- *Comment réserver des chambres pour tout le monde?*
- *Je crois que la compagnie devrait payer tous ces frais imprévus.*
- *Payer le repas du soir c'est quelque chose.*
- *Comment faire pour prévenir le plus vite possible les parents qui attendent à Paris?*

4 Here is another example, this time from WJEC. This is a fairly short role-play that will probably take about three minutes. You have 15 minutes preparation time and are allowed the use of a dictionary.

Brief

Au cours de vos études vous préparez un dossier sur le tourisme dans une certaine région de la France. Pour savoir ce que pensent les habitants de la région vous faites un stage dans une petite ville touristique dans l'intention de leur poser des questions. Dans une rue de cette ville vous abordez un(e) passant(e). L'examinateur (ou l'examinatrice) jouera le rôle du (de la) passant(e).

Task

- *Demandez-lui poliment s'il (ou elle) est prêt(e) à répondre à quelques questions.*
- *Demandez-lui s'il (ou elle) est de la région ou s'il (ou elle) est touriste.*
- *Expliquez ce que vous faites.*
- *Posez des questions pour savoir ce qu'elle pense des aspects suivants du tourisme dans cette ville et sa région:*
  Son importance
  Les problèmes posés
  Les attitudes des gens du pays
  Les attitudes des touristes
  S'il (ou elle) est pour ou contre
- *Remerciez-le (ou la) poliment d'avoir répondu à vos questions.*

Here is the part that might be played by the Examiner. Try working out your questions and play the parts with a friend:

- *Oui, je veux bien/Oui, avec plaisir.*
- *Je suis de la région. Je suis né(e) ici.*
- *Ça c'est très intéressant.*
- *Le tourisme, c'est assez important pour nous. C'est surtout une région agricole. Il y a peu d'industries et pas mal de chômage.*
- *Les problèmes? Ils ne sont pas graves, hein. Il y a plus de circulation en été. Il est difficile quelquefois de garer sa voiture en ville.*
- *Les touristes en général sont contents. La région leur plaît beaucoup, la montagne est très belle il y a des tas de choses à découvrir ici.*
- *Moi, je n'ai rien contre. Ça fait marcher les affaires, surtout en été. Et puis la ville est plus animée.*
- *Je vous en prie.*

REPORTING TASKS

The basis for this task in real life is having to explain to a French person, who does not read or understand English, the main points of a short piece of English text. The latter may be: a travel brochure; a newspaper item; an advertisement or other piece of publicity; or an account in English of something seen or witnessed. The latter may be accompanied by diagrams (e.g. in the case of an accident). The Examiner usually stays silent during this process.

Examination strategy

Marks are usually given for conveying a number of points (roughly 10 to 12, depending on the Board) and for quality of language and pronunciation. It is important therefore, when preparing, to underline the points you think are the main ones and to cover all these in your explanation. You will be given credit if you include them all, even though you may make some mistakes in French.

Conveying the information is partly a matter of knowing the vocabulary. Don't try to just translate the English. Sort out the points to be made first and jot down a word or a phrase in French to go with each one. Do not panic when you find words you do not know the exact French for. You will often find you can use a paraphrase or other words to get the meaning across. If you have been practising saying things in different ways, as already suggested, you will be more into the swing of this (*see* paraphrase, pages 212–213).

Note

(a) Here are some actual examples of references that managed to get the meaning across even though the French word was not exactly the right one:

the brain (*cerveau*) – 'Cette chose entre les deux oreilles' – 'la tête'
the man posted at the door (*le service de sécurité*) – 'l'homme à la porte/ qui surveillait la porte'
triggered an alarm (*a fait sonner l'alarme*) – 'Une cloche s'est mise à sonner'
exotic foods (*nourriture exotique*) – 'produits de différents pays/ de tous les pays du monde' nourritures rares/ recherchées'
shop assistant (*la serveuse*) – 'la femme dans le magasin/ qui servait/ derrière le comptoir'
the boot of a car (*le coffre*) – 'le derrière (l'arrière) de la voiture' – 'la boîte de la voiture'
7-day free trial guarantee (*essai gratuit pour 7 jours*) – 'on peut l'essayer pendant 7 jours, sans payer'

(b) Here is an example of a candidate's brief, with the points in bold type and some examples of what you might say:

> You are looking **through the window** of your hotel room in Paris when you witness a raid on the bank opposite. Your attention is drawn by the **noise of breaking glass**. You see **two men emerge** through the glass door of the bank. **One of them is holding a gun**. They are **both masked** and are **wearing rucksacks** on their backs. **One is taller** than the other and **seems** as though he is hurt. They charge across the pavement **knocking over an old lady**, one gets on to a **motorbike** the other, the **taller one, gets into a waiting car**, a **Mercedes**, you think. It all **happens in a flash**.

Imagine you are describing what you saw to the police. You could use the past tense in your description but you could also use the 'vivid present'. Make sure though that you are consistent and stick to whichever one you started with:

> J'étais dans ma chambre à l'hôtel et je regardais par la fenêtre. Soudain, j'ai entendu un grand bruit de verre qui se cassait et j'ai vu deux hommes sortir de la banque en face. Un des hommes tenait un revolver à la main. Ils étaient tous les deux masqués et avaient des sacs à dos. Un des hommes était plus grand que l'autre et semblait blessé. En sortant de la banque, ils ont heurté une vieille dame qui est tombée par terre. Un des hommes est monté sur une moto et l'autre, le plus grand, a sauté dans une voiture qui attendait. C'était une Mercedes, je crois. Tout cela s'est passé très, très vite.

(c) If you had used the present tense you could have started:

Je suis dans ma chambre à l'hôtel, je regarde par la fenêtre et soudain j'entends un bruit...

Study technique

1 You can practise this skill by taking any short news or publicity item, from the day's television or radio programmes, imagining that you have to tell a French person about them. By selecting items from as broad a range of sources as possible, and by sometimes working with a dictionary, you will broaden your vocabulary and experience of different areas of knowledge. You could also try making up in English short accounts of incidents witnessed as above. Shoplifting, break-ins, accidents and confrontations of various kinds are all likely material. It is more fun if you can work with a friend and have a bilingual dictionary handy. Try explaining a short item to your work companion who will take notes in English. If you do one item each, you can check back afterwards with the original to see how many details are correct and give each other a mark out of 10. If this activity is accompanied by asking in French, about things not quite understood, you will also be doing further valuable oral practice.

2 Although figures only sometimes occur in this kind of task, by including a few from time to time you can get valuable practice both in saying and understanding them.

Exercices

Here are some examples to be getting on with. You will have to cover up one half if you are working with a friend:

1 Est-ce que vous croyez aux coincidences?

Le Président Lincoln et le Président Kennedy ont été tous les deux assassinés. Voici quelques détails bizarres concernant leur vie et leur mort:

A (a) Lincoln's secretary was named Kennedy and Kennedy's secretary was named Lincoln

    (b) Lincoln was elected president in 1860 and Kennedy was elected* president in 1960

    (c) The wives of the two men, Mary Lincoln and Jackie Kennedy, both had children who died while their husbands were living in the White House

(d) Two of Lincoln's sons were named Edward and Robert. Edward died at the age of three whilst Robert lived on. Two of Kennedy's brothers were called Robert and Edward. Robert was assassinated whilst Edward lived on

(e) Both presidents were with their wives, and both were shot in the head**. They both died on a Friday

* élu

** reçu une balle dans la tête

B (a) Lincoln's assassin, John Wilkes Booth, and Kennedy's alleged assassin*, Lee Harvey Oswald, were both Southerners in their twenties

(b) Booth shot Lincoln while he was sitting in a theatre, then hid in a warehouse** Kennedy was shot from a warehouse; Oswald was found hiding in a theatre

(c) Booth and Oswald were both killed before they could be brought to court***

(d) Abraham Lincoln was succeeded by Andrew Johnson, born in 1808. John Kennedy was succeeeded by Lyndon Johnson, born in 1908. Both Johnsons had been senators before becoming president

(e) The names Lincoln and Kennedy each contain 7 letters, Andrew Johnson and Lyndon Johnson each have 13 letters, and John Wilkes Booth and Lee Harvey Oswald each have 15 letters

* prétendu assassin

** un entrepôt

*** avant d'être amené devant les tribunaux

2 Voici une comparaison entre les possibilités offertes par deux stations de sports d'hiver:

A Le massif de Ben Nevis (en Ecosse)   B St Moritz (en Suisse)

FACT FILE

- Ski pass £62 for six days in high season, £48 low season. Under 16's and over 60's, £42 high, £32 low
- Ski Packages, Midweek five-day packages, £100, which cover ski pass, tuition and ski hire and four hours' instruction daily
- Ski School: Six days, four hours daily, £50; two hours £33. Also individual tuition, £17 hourly. Also snowboarding, Telemark and ski touring
- Cross-country. Some high-altitude trails are available
- For non-skiers: Extensive walking trails, mountain biking, tennis, golf, fishing, swimming pool, gymnasium and cinema, all in Fort William
- Bed space: 70 hotels in the Fort William area with around 10,000 beds. Also self-catering chalets and some rooms in private homes
- Medical facilities: first-aid both at top and bottom of gondola station, full-time paramedic ski patrol. Hospital in Fort William
- How to get there: By air to Glasgow, Edinburgh or Inverness, then by road or train to Fort William (overnight sleeper from London)
- Information: Great Britain (0397 705825)

FACT FILE

- Ski Pass: Oberengadiner includes all lifts, swimming pool and public transport in area. 204 Swiss Francs for six days (low season 150). Children free up to six, then SF150. Beginners' Nursery lifts included in ski-school fee. Also points system available
- Ski School: Morning and/or afternoon classes available, SF182 for six days. Children up to 12 SF148. Individual tuition available, SF70 per hour. Also, ski touring, mono and surf
- Cross-country: Extensive (160km) for all levels. Also, floodlit track at Bad.
- For non-skiers: sleigh and toboggan runs, Cresta Run, horse riding, polo tournaments, golf on frozen lake, 120km of cleared paths. Also, pools, saunas, tennis, squash, English language cinema, shopping
- Bed space: 12,500, half of which is in hotels, rest in apartments
- Medical facilities: Doctors, dentists and fracture clinic in resort: Hospital at Samedan (6km)
- How to get there: Zurich airport, then either flight to Samedan, or road transfer (4 hours) or train, from anywhere in Europe, station in resort
- Information: Switzerland (82) 33147

Quelques mots et expressions

haute/basse saison – vacances de neige à prix forfaitaire – chalets indépendants – quelques chambres d'hôte – téléski pour débutants – leçons particulières – clinique sur place en cas de fracture

3 Cette semaine dans l'histoire du monde:

A Du 23 au 28 mars 1991

B Du 15 au 22 février 1991

THIS WEEK IN HISTORY

March 23, 1919: Benito Mussolini founded the Fascist Party in Italy.
March 23, 1956: Pakistan became a republic.
March 24, 1603: After the death of Queen Elizabeth I, the crowns of England and Scotland were joined under James VI of Scotland, who was to be known as James I of Great Britain.
March 24, 1848: Charles Albert, King of Sardinia, declared war on Austria.
March 24, 1972: The British government announced direct rule in Northern Ireland.
March 25, 1807: The slave trade was abolished in Britain.
March 25, 1815: Britain, Austria, Prussia and Russia formed a new alliance against Napoleon I of France.
March 25, 1924: King George II of Greece was deposed and a republic proclaimed.
March 25, 1957: The Treaty of Rome was signed by France, West Germany, Italy and the Benelux countries to establish the European Economic Community.
March 25, 1975: King Faisal of Saudi Arabia was assassinated in Riyadh by his mentally ill nephew.
March 26, 1953: Dr Jonas Salk announced the successful testing of a vaccine against polio.
March 27, 1802: Britain signs the peace of Amiens with Napoleon of France.
March 28, 1854: Britain and France declare war on Russia.
March 28, 1898: Germany passed an act allowing for a substantial expansion of its navy.
March 28, 1939: Madrid surrendered to General Francisco Franco, bringing to an end the Spanish Civil War.

THIS WEEK IN HISTORY

February 15, 1933: Giuseppe Zingara attempted to assassinate President Franklin Roosevelt in Miami.
February 16, 1937: Nylon, developed under the direction of Dr Wallace Carothers, was patented.
February 17, 1670: France and Bavaria signed a defensive alliance.
February 17, 1863: The International Red Cross was founded in Geneva.
February 17, 1934: King Albert I of Belgium was killed in a climbing accident.
February 18, 1965: The Gambia became an independent state within the British Commonwealth.
February 18, 1988: Boris Yeltsin was ousted from the ruling Communist Party Politburo.
February 19, 1803: The Act of Mediation restored independence to the Swiss cantons.
February 19, 1945: American troops landed on the island of Iwo Jima.
February 19, 1976: Iceland broke off relations with Britain over a fishing dispute.
February 20, 1437: James I of Scotland was murdered in Perth.
February 21, 1613: Michael Romanov was elected Czar of Russia.
February 21, 1916: The Battle of Verdun began in France during the First World War.
February 21, 1965: American militant black leader Malcolm X was murdered in New York.
February 22, 1828: Persia, and Russia signed the Treaty of Turkmanchai in which Persia ceded part of Armenia to Russia.
February 22, 1967: President Sukarno of Indonesia surrendered rule to General Suharto

Quelques mots et expressions

A *l'autorité directe – le commerce des esclaves – un traité – la paix – capituler*
B *breveté (patented) – expulsé du parti – rompu les relations diplomatiques – céder une partie de – capituler*

4 Les résultats de deux sondages:

A *Avez-vous confiance dans la police?*

DO YOU TRUST THE POLICE FORCE?

The Belgians are the greatest sceptics in Europe, according to the confidence they express in society's institutions. The police, the military and the legal professions are all held in rock-bottom esteem. Less than half said that they had confidence in the police (*see* chart right) compared to 70 per cent for Europe as a whole, and less than a third trusted lawyers or soldiers. In Denmark, the police are extremely popular, with nine out of ten people expressing their confidence. The Portuguese seem almost complacent: a full three-quarters express confidence in the police and armed forces, and about 60 per cent have faith in the legal system and the media. Even the advertising industry is seen as relatively trustworthy, scoring a 40 per cent confidence-rating. The British reserve special hatred for their media: only 14 per cent hold confidence in the industry.

Country	%
DENMARK	93%
NORWAY	81%
PORTUGAL	75%
IRELAND	74%
GERMANY	74%
UNITED KINGDOM	73%
FRANCE	69%
AUSTRIA	54%
SPAIN	52%
GREECE	52%
BELGIUM	43%

% respondents answering yes

Quelques expressions utiles

les gens les plus méfiants de l'Europe – l'armée, les hommes de loi – un tiers se méfiait des militaires – presque tout à fait satisfait – la loi et les médias – l'industrie publicitaire – mériter sa confiance – détester les médias

B *Seriez-vous prêt à retourner un objet perdu?*

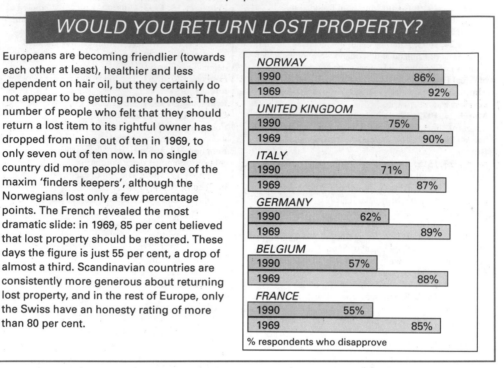

WOULD YOU RETURN LOST PROPERTY?

Europeans are becoming friendlier (towards each other at least), healthier and less dependent on hair oil, but they certainly do not appear to be getting more honest. The number of people who felt that they should return a lost item to its rightful owner has dropped from nine out of ten in 1969, to only seven out of ten now. In no single country did more people disapprove of the maxim 'finders keepers', although the Norwegians lost only a few percentage points. The French revealed the most dramatic slide: in 1969, 85 per cent believed that lost property should be restored. These days the figure is just 55 per cent, a drop of almost a third. Scandinavian countries are consistently more generous about returning lost property, and in the rest of Europe, only the Swiss have an honesty rating of more than 80 per cent.

NORWAY	
1990	86%
1969	92%

UNITED KINGDOM	
1990	75%
1969	90%

ITALY	
1990	71%
1969	87%

GERMANY	
1990	62%
1969	89%

BELGIUM	
1990	57%
1969	88%

FRANCE	
1990	55%
1969	85%

% respondents who disapprove

Quelques expressions utiles

deviennent plus amical l'un envers l'autre – être en meilleure santé/ se porter mieux – la lotion pour les cheveux/capillaire – retourner à son propriétaire – approuver la maxime 'celui qui le trouve, le garde' – le plus grand changement se révèle chez les Français – les Scandinaves se montrent les plus généreux – un taux d'honnêteté supérieur à…

5 Deux publicités

A *Stainsbury's fait du pain français*

Stainsbury's have been baking french bread for many years.

But now, cooling down in our larger stores, you'll also find French bread with a capital 'F'. Because although Stainsbury's bake it, it's actually made in France.

With French flour, French yeast, French water and, dare we say it, French *savoir faire*. The dough is made in Lyon. We then ship it over to England and bake it in our in-store bakeries.

The bread that comes out is as French as any boulangerie could bake it. It has a light, airy texture, with a crisp 'eggshell' crust. And oh, the flavour!

(Close your eyes and you could be in a pavement café on Boulevard St. Germain.)

As well as the classic white baguette, we also bake a selection of other French breads and pastries.

You'll find *baguettes de campagne* (a brown version made with sour dough), *pain de campagne* (a short, cob-shaped loaf) and *petit pain boule* (small, but perfectly formed roll).

And if you want to know where the expression 'melt in the mouth' comes from, just try our butter croissants.

Like all Stainsbury's bakery products, our traditional French bread is freshly baked every day. Or perhaps we should say Frenchly baked every day.

Quelques mots et expressions

Depuis plusieurs années – du vrai pain français – Stainsbury's le fait cuire mais il est fait en France – la farine, la levure, l'eau sont françaises – la pâte – transporté – cuit sur place – le véritable pain français – léger et croustillant – et son arôme! – imaginez-vous – avec la baguette classique – baguette et pains de campagne et des petits pains – nos croissants fondent dans la bouche – comme tous nos produits boulangers – cuit tout frais tous les jours

B   Arrêtez cette habitude dégoûtante. Arrêtez de fumer immédiatement!

Quelques mots et expressions

réussi pour des milliers de personnes – perdre l'habitude au bout de 5 jours – risque pour la santé – faire disparaître le besoin – sans douleur – grâce à ce traitement révolutionnaire développé aux Etats Unis – avaler un comprimé – supprimer votre désir de nicotine – l'odeur et le goût des cigarettes deviennent désagreables – regardez les statistiques – chaque cigarette raccourcit votre vie de cinq minutes et demie – une des causes principales des incendies – le succès est garanti ou vous serez remboursé

STUDY EXTRACTS

Study extracts usually take the form of passages, or other printed material, in French that you have to explain the gist of, expand on and/or answer questions about. You may have to select one from several and prepare this just before the oral exam or you may be given the material a week or so beforehand. Check the regulations of your particular Board.

You will need the skills of skimming, scanning and summary already referred to in the section on summary (*see* page 206). Read the material several times and underline the main points, paying particular attention to the beginnings of paragraphs for the main ideas. The important thing in the exam, with this kind of material, is for you to take charge and be ready to tell the Examiner about it. Try to 'stand back' from the material and think of it as a whole rather than attempting to just read out bits of it. Be prepared to say what it is and what it is about. The title might not necessarily do this for you. For example:

- *C'est un article/ une publicité/ une annonce/ une brochure/ un extrait/ un dépliant qui concerne* _____ */ qui traite de* _____

- *Dans cet article/ cette brochure il s'agit de* _____ */ il est question de* _____

Then go on to give the main points. The following formula may be appropriate:

- *D'abord on signale que... puis on explique que... ensuite on cite l'exemple de... enfin on tire la conclusion que...*

The material is often chosen for its contemporary interest; issues for debate or disagreement may be raised. You should decide on what stance (or attitude) you are going to adopt beforehand and have a reason (or an example) that you can quote to back up your opinion. Don't forget that you do not have to tell the absolute truth, though if it is something you feel strongly about, you will find it easier to say why. It is also worth remembering that the Examiner is not there to test your knowledge or judge your opinion. He or she just wants to find out if you can express your views convincingly in French and defend or support them with evidence. You may even be able to turn the situation around a bit and ask the Examiner for his or her views! For example the following may be appropriate:

Moi, je suis d'avis que...
A mon avis on a raison/ tort de dire que...
Je ne suis pas tout à fait convaincu que...
Ce qui est certain, c'est que...
Ce que je ne comprends pas, c'est que...
Ce qui est surprenant, c'est que...
Cela me surprend que ...
C'est un scandale! C'est une honte! C'est la faute du gouvernement/ des hommes politiques...
On devrait faire quelque chose...
Il faut qu'on fasse quelque chose...
C'est une exagération de dire que...
C'est une situation/ un problème préoccupant(e)/ qui concerne tous les pays du monde

If you are going to say something like *Oui, c'est intéressant*, always be ready to add a reason or an example.

Illustrative questions and answers

Short study extract

1 Les médias disent-ils vrai?
   Enquête réalisée du 1er au 15 septembre, auprès d'un échantillon de 2500 lecteurs de *Phosphore*, âgés de 14 à 18 ans

LES MÉDIAS DISENT VRAI			
En général, à propos des nouvelles qui sont diffusées dans les médias, est-ce que vous vous dites...			
	Presse (100%)	*Radio (100%)*	*TV (100%)*
Les choses se sont passées vraiment comme le média les raconte	8%	12%	19%
Les choses se sont passées à peu près comme le média les raconte	64%	66%	53%
Il y a sans doute pas mal de différence entre la façon dont les choses se sont passées et la façon dont le média les raconte	27%	21%	26%
Les choses ne se sont vraisemblablement pas passées du tout comme le média les raconte	1%	1%	2%

Possible answers

Ce tableau présente les résultats d'un sondage auprès des lecteurs d'un journal pour jeunes. Le but de l'enquête est de savoir s'ils croient ce qu'ils lisent dans les journaux, ce qu'ils entendent à la radio et ce qu'ils voient à la télé.

or

Dans ce tableau, on essaie de montrer ce que les jeunes pensent des informations présentées dans les journaux, à la radio, à la télévision: y croient-ils ou non?

On voit bien qu'en général ils pensent que les médias racontent plus ou moins la vérité, 64% à 53% le disent. Mais, ils croient moins la télé que les journaux.

Pour ceux qui croient absolument aux nouvelles racontées par les médias, c'est la télévision qui arrive en tête. On a peut-être plus tendance à croire ce qu'on voit.

Peu de jeunes croient que les médias ne racontent pas du tout la vérité.

Note Possible follow-up questions might be:
Pour savoir les nouvelles de la journée que faites-vous?
Pour vous, lequel des médias est le plus sûr? Pourquoi?
Quelles informations préférez-vous à la télé, à la radio? Et pourquoi?
Quel journal est-ce que vous préférez et pourquoi?

Longer study extract

ANIMAUX DE COMPAGNIE
LES AIMONS-NOUS VRAIMENT?

Trente millions d'animaux de compagnie pour cinquante-cinq millions de Français! Notre pays est le premier en Europe, et au monde, à porter un intérêt aussi grand à près de dix millions de chiens, sept millions de chats, neuf millions d'oiseaux, cinq millions de poissons, lapins, tortues, souris et cochons d'Inde ... Voilà les Anglais, les Allemands et même les Américains largement distancés. Pourtant ... combien de chiens neurasthéniques restent enfermés et seuls toute la journée? Combien sont mal nourris, et même maltraités? Combien d'abandonnés, chaque été? Le nombre faramineux de nos amis à quatre pattes reflète-t-il l'amour ou l'égoïsme?

Peut-être l'avez-vous déjà rencontré, à Paris, dans le métro, du côté de la Chaussée-d'Antin. Il joue de l'orgue de Barbarie. Près de lui, trois boules de poils. Sur l'orgue, une chatte tigrée lovée dans un petit panier. A sa droite, une noire: à sa gauche, une grise frisottée. Sa musique chante la nostalgie, le bonheur. Le joueur d'orgue est né allemand. Il a choisi notre pays parce que, dit-il, 'c'est celui de La Fontaine et de ses fables pleines d'animaux.' Le poète ne fut pas le seul à les chanter: les animaux emplissent notre patrimoine culturel: de Goupil le renard à la chèvre de Monsieur Seguin sans oublier le Chat botté, plus qu'aucune autre littérature au monde, la nôtre glorifie le règne animal. Pour nos concitoyens, ce sujet allume souvent les passions. Témoin Fabien Gruhier, journaliste au Nouvel Observateur, qui, en février 1982, fut submergé par une masse de courrier — autant d'insultes que de félicitations — pour avoir fustigé la saleté canine des rues de Paris...

Les Français cohabitent de plus en plus avec les bêtes. Mais pourquoi? 'Nous avons besoin des animaux', assure le docteur Michel Klein.

Selon Guy Quéinnec, professeur d'élevage et d'économie à l'école vétérinaire de

139

Toulouse, il existe trois conceptions: l'école éthologique, l'école utilitariste, l'école psychiatrique.

Pour l'école éthologique, posséder un chien est un critère d'affectivité sociale: aimer les chiens, c'est aimer les autres. Exemple, cet amour total, l'histoire soudaine entre un homme et un animal. Victor, artiste peintre, est un colosse: un double mètre, bon vivant. Il y a quelques mois, il aperçoit un garagiste en train de battre une jeune chienne qui se traîne avec peine. Victor menace le propriétaire: 'Salopard, je vous achète cette bête. Si vous refusez de me la vendre, je casse tout chez vous!' Depuis, Oona, plus douce qu'un agneau, est heureuse enfin et ne quitte plus son nouveau maître.

QUEL AMOUR?

L'école utilitariste estime que l'on possède un chien pour qu'il rende service: soit pour chasse, ou pour garder la maison. C'est surtout le cas en zone rurale. Ainsi, tous les ans, peu avant l'ouverture de la chasse, les demandes d'adoption augmentent dans les refuges de la S.P.A. 'C'est courant, explique-t-on là-bas: on vient chercher un chien, on s'en occupe, on le flatte, on le nourrit bien, pendant toute cette période. Puis une fois la chasse interdite on le laisse errer.' Parfois, on le garde, mais dans quelles conditions!

L'école psychiatrique, elle, pense que le chien aide à résoudre les difficultés personnelles du maître, problèmes de communication ou de maturité: à travers le chien ou le chat il recherche un éternel enfant ou une soumission qui puisse le gratifier.

Les bienfaits de la fréquentation quotidienne avec un animal de compagnie ne sont, c'est vrai, plus à démontrer. Les psychologues le savent: les enfants qui ont la responsabilité d'animaux sont plus équilibrés que les autres. Aussi, de plus en plus souvent, l'animal est-il présent à l'école. C'est un outil pédagogique qui initie l'enfant aux phénomènes de la vie. Le petit écolier apprend à soigner, à nourrir, à aimer les animaux et il en retire un bénéfice inestimable.

ULEAC

Answer plan

You will notice that this passage has a fairly clear structure; an opening paragraph deals with the French obsession with pets in comparison to other nations and raises some issues. Then some examples are given of this obsession. Next, reasons are given for this behaviour. There are three main ones. The concluding paragraph ends on a positive note. Here are some questions that an Examiner might ask:

(a) On the article

De quoi s'agit-il dans cet extrait?/Quel est le sujet de cet article?

Quelle différence est-ce qu'on remarque entre la France et les autres pays en ce qui concerne animaux de compagnie?

Quel est l'autre aspect de cette situation?

Quelles sont les trois raisons pour avoir un animal?

Que disent enfin les psychologues à ce sujet?

(b) Arising from it:

Avez -vous un animal à la maison et pourquoi le gardez-vous?/Pourquoi n'avez-vous pas d'animal?

Quels sont les avantages d'avoir un chat/un chien/un cheval etc?

Quels problèmes existent actuellement avec les gens et leurs animaux?

Si vous étiez au pouvoir que feriez-vous pour combattre ces problèmes?

Devrait-on avoir un permis pour posséder un chien?

Est-ce qu'on devrait proscrire certaines races de chien féroces ou dangereuses?

Note All these questions require a longer answer than just oui or non. Always be prepared to answer the 'why' part of the question, particularly when a tired Examiner has left it out!

Exercices

Here are some examples to work on. Try explaining the gist to a friend. He or she will need to cover up one of the pieces while you do this. Check the details and figures afterwards:

1 (a) Le circuit de la drogue dans le monde

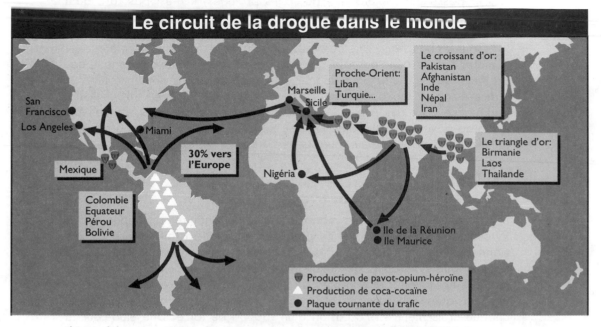

(b) La drogue en France — la consommation de l'héroïne

LA DROGUE EN FRANCE

Usagers: 150 000 environ (dont 2/3 d'héroïnomanes). Décès par overdose: environ 300 (uniquement les décès portés à la connaissance de la police).

Population atteinte: à 88% masculine. Age: 21-25 ans: 41%. 16-20 ans: 30%. 26-30 ans: 18%. 31-35 ans: 6,2%. 36-40 ans: 1,8%

La consommation d'héroïne (nombre de consommateurs)

Espagne	entre 80 000 et 120 000
Italie	80 000
France	80 000
Pays-Bas	20 000
RFA	12 300
Suisse	10 000
Autriche	3 000

(Source: *La Face cachée de l'économie mondiale* de Jean-François Couvral et Nicole Pless, chez Hatier)

2 Les Européens, sont-ils de bons conducteurs?
(a) Le gentleman conducteur

Le gentleman conducteur

Les automobilistes britanniques jouent fair-play, dans l'ensemble ils respectent davantage les règles du jeu routier que nous. La répression implacable, la lutte très sévère contre l'alcool au volant et le permis à points, qui est retiré automatiquement après un certain nombre d'infractions, ne suffisent pas à expliquer les scores plus qu'honorables de nos voisins d'outre-Manche au hit-parade de la sécurité: deux fois moins de tués qu'en France. Non, les racines sont certainement plus profondes. La courtoisie comme le flegme british influent sur le comportement du conducteur anglais: il s'arrête automatiquement pour laisser passer les piétons aux passages protégés, il n'est pas rare qu'il remercie d'un sourire et d'un geste de la main l'automobiliste qui le laisse passer et il n'encombre pas la voie de droite (celle des dépassements).

Dans les bouchons, il ne perd pas son sang-froid. S'il bout de colère (c'est humain), il ne le laisse pas transparaître: pas de coup de klaxon vengeur, pas de malin qui se faufile pour gagner deux ou trois places dans une file. Un indice éclairant du rapport qu'entretient l'automobiliste avec son véhicule: l'ambiance cosy des publicités des constructeurs britanniques. La caméra s'attarde davantage sur l'élégance du tableau de bord en bois brun et le moelleux des sièges de cuir, que sur les performances du moteur.

(b) Les Latins

Vous avez dit audace?

Il y a indiscutablement une manière latine de conduire. Les Alpes ou les Pyrénées passées, les règles ne paraissent plus tout à fait les mêmes. Les panneaux de limitation de vitesse paraissent moins retenir l'attention de l'automobiliste, les coups de klaxon intempestifs vous rappellent à l'ordre à la moindre hésitation. On a le pied sur l'accélérateur dès que le feu passe au vert, pas question de traîner! La loi, c'est souvent la loi du plus audacieux et chaque croisement est l'occasion d'un rapport de force. Une étude sur la traversée d'un carrefour simulée sur écran-vidéo a démontré que la perception du risque n'était pas la même chez un Allemand que chez un Espagnol, ce dernier étant nettement plus casse-cou. Etonnant, non?

TALKING ABOUT A PREPARED TOPIC

A theme

This will usually be something you have been preparing for some time. Check carefully whether you are allowed to bring illustrative material to the exam and whether notes are permitted.

You will be allowed to give an introduction to your chosen subject but do not just recite a piece learned off by heart and sit back expecting the Examiner to be wildly excited about your subject and to ask all the questions. Take the initiative. First, say briefly what your subject is, why you are interested in it and how you went about the research. It helps if you then have just **three main** aspects that you can keep in your mind. By the time you have covered these, the Examiner will have had time to relax a little and questions will have occured to him or her. They will also be impressed by the way you have organized the material!

Be prepared for open questions (**not** yes/no). Always have a reason or an example to back up what you are saying. Be prepared to respond to questions of the following kind:

Que feriez-vous si...?

Qu'est-ce que vous pensez de...?

Comment expliquez-vous cette attitude?

Que feriez-vous si vous étiez au pouvoir/ Premier ministre?

Quels remèdes apporter à cette situation?

Qu'est-ce qu'on peut faire? Quelle solution proposez-vous?

Ne trouvez-vous pas que le gouvernement est...?

Que pensez-vous des gens qui disent...?

Pourquoi dites-vous que...?

A book or film

Essentially, this will be something you have chosen yourself and, whether you liked it or not, you should have something to say about it. You may be allowed to talk a little about the story but the Examiner will soon get on to other aspects. Be prepared to answer questions of the following kind:

Quel est le thème principal de ce livre (it is a good idea to have a category for the book: *c'est un roman/ d'aventure/policier/ de science fiction*)
C'est une histoire d'un/une...
Ce sont les aventures de...
Il y a plusieurs meurtres...
Cela se passe à notre époque/au 19e siècle
C'est une aventure imaginaire/véritable
C'est raconté par l'auteur
Il/elle raconte ses expériences de...
Pourquoi l'avez-vous choisi?
Pourquoi l'avez-vous/ne l'avez-vous pas aimé?
Vous regrettez de l'avoir choisi? Pourquoi?
Quelle impression vous a fait ce livre/film?
Quel personnage vous a le plus frappé? (if you have found X or Y *sympathique* be prepared to say why)
Quel est le personnage-clef? (make sure you distinguish between *un personnage* — a character and *leur caractère* — their personality/character).
Quels moments/épisodes sont les plus mémorables/passionnants pour vous?
Est-ce qu'il y a un message/une morale dans ce livre/film?
Selon vous, le sujet est-il important/sérieux/léger?
En le lisant/regardant est-ce que vous avez appris quelque chose?
Pourquoi l'auteur a-t-il écrit ce livre/tourné ce film?

General conversation

This aspect is found with all the Examining Boards. In theory it could be about almost anything but the following areas are favourite ones:

1 Future plans for study and career

2 Your hobbies and pastimes

3 Your school/college and what you think of it

4 Visits to France and your impressions of French life and people, making appropriate comparisons with life here. (You will probably have found the French *sympathiques,* but do be prepared to say why and what other qualities they possess! *See* list, literature chapter, page 242)

5 Contemporary problems or issues that concern you and your ideas for overcoming them

6 Any events that are occupying national or world attention at that time

Make sure you have run through all these possibilities and either asked yourself appropriate questions or worked through them with a friend.

Questions leading into these themes

1 *Qu'est-ce que vous allez faire l'année prochaine?*
Vous avez l'intention de continuer vos études l'année prochaine?
Quels sont vos plans pour l'avenir?
Qu'est-ce que vous comptez faire dans la vie?
Pourquoi voulez-vous devenir_____?

2 *Que faites-vous pendant vos loisirs?*
Le sport, c'est important pour vous?

Pourquoi? D'où vient cet intérêt pour _____?
Regarder la télé, c'est une perte de temps, non?

3 *Que pensez-vous de cette école/ce collège?*
Etes-vous heureux/euse ici?
Si vous étiez le directeur/la directrice quels changements est-ce que vous y apporteriez?
Quelles sont les qualités d'un bon prof?
Il faut avoir des règles, non?
Vous avez des privilèges comme élève en terminale?
Les élèves de sixième sont-ils bien discipliné(e)s?

4 *Avez-vous visité la France (récemment)?*
Racontez-moi un peu votre visite
Quelles sont/étaient vos impressions des Français?
Comment avez-vous trouvé les Français?
La vie en France en quoi est-elle différente de celle en Angleterre?
La vie familiale en France est-elle différente de celle d'une famille anglaise?
Quelles différences avez-vous remarquées?
Quelles impresssions gardez-vous de l'école que vous avez visitée?
Faites quelques comparaisons avec votre école.

5 *Il y a pas mal de problèmes dans la société actuelle, à votre avis quels sont les plus préoccupants?*
Que feriez-vous si vous étiez au pouvoir/Premier ministre?
Quels remèdes y apporter?
C'est un problème insurmontable, non?
Quelles solutions apporter à long terme?

Challenging questions

You should also be prepared to be asked questions of a challenging or slightly controversial nature. The purpose of these is not to test out the content of your ideas but to see whether you can defend or support your point of view. Some of the questions above are of this kind:

C'est un problème insurmontable, non?
Il faut avoir des règles, non?

Other ways of doing this might be:

Moi, je trouve les jeunes trop/pas assez... vous ne pensez pas?
Les gens exagèrent/dramatisent ce problème, vous ne trouvez pas?
Est-ce que vous pensez sérieusement que...?
Vous avez dit que.... Vous ne pensez pas que vous exagérez un peu?
Ce n'est pas un métier pour une femme, voyons!/Peu de femmes réussissent dans ce genre de travail, vous savez

Your reaction should be to politely but firmly insist on your opinion, stating your reasons. You can say that you do not agree:

Vous avez tort
Ce n'est pas vrai
Je ne suis pas d'accord
Au contraire, c'est vous qui exagérez
Je dois insister

Or that you do not completely agree:

Je ne pense pas
Cela dépend
Cela dépend des circonstances/des cas
Jusqu'à un certain point vous avez raison
Je ne suis pas tout à fait d'accord
Je trouve difficile d'accepter cela

ENSURING SUCCESS IN THE ORAL EXAMINATION

The purpose of the oral exam is not to test your factual knowledge on a variety of topics, but to provide an opportunity for you to show how much you can say in French. The Examiner will judge your ability to communicate naturally in French. To do this he or she will take a number of factors into consideration. Grammatical accuracy is only one of these elements. More important is your ability to keep going and get him or her involved in what you are saying. So arrive with the idea that you have something interesting to communicate. Do not come with the idea that you are just going to sit there and answer questions as they come. This makes it harder work for the Examiner. A skilfully led oral exam should consist of one-third or less Examiner talking and two-thirds or more of candidate speaking.

Factors taken into consideration are the following. They are usually presented in the form of a grid with a short description that covers a range within 2–3 marks:

1 **Fulfilment of task** This applies to reporting, role-play or eliciting information tasks. It is important to do all the things included in the brief (see above). The description might range from 'Barest amount of information supplied' at the bottom of the scale, to ' most information supplied' near the top of the scale.

2 **Fluency and responsiveness** These factors describe your ability to keep going without too much help from the Examiner. Near the bottom of the scale would be something like 'Examiner can only obtain very brief replies' to 'very fluent, occasional hesitation only' near the top of the scale.

3 **Accuracy** This refers to grammatical accuracy — getting the right tenses, verb endings, agreements, genders etc.

4 **Linguistic sophistication/range** These two terms include things like range of vocabulary and structures used and the ability to switch between tenses. If you stick to simple vocabulary, the present tense and short sentences without clauses, you will score less highly. A skilful Examiner will give the candidate the chance to use more than just the present tense. The rest is up to you. If you can work in a few subjunctives it does tend to impress. So instead of:

Il faut arrêter la pollution – Il faut qu'on fasse quelque chose pour arrêter la pollution.
Ce n'est pas possible – Je ne crois pas que cela soit possible.
Je ne suis pas d'accord mais je trouve que... – Quoique je ne sois pas d'accord, je trouve que...

Here are some typical responses in an oral exam to an Examiner asking about the candidate's school:

A *Examiner* Parlez-moi un peu de cette école. Vous êtes heureuse ici?
Candidate Oui. J'aime assez bien cette école. J'y suis restée cinq ans.
Examiner Qu'est-ce que vous n'aimez pas?
Candidate Les règles, je n'aime pas les règles.
Examiner Oui, expliquez.
Candidate Les règles sont stupides. En sixième (en terminale!) les règles, c'est embêtant.
Examiner Mais quelles règles est-ce que vous n'aimez pas?
Candidate On ne peut pas sortir quand les leçons... quand il n'y a pas de leçons.

B *Examiner* Parlez-moi un peu de votre école. Vous êtes heureuse ici?
Candidate Oui, oui assez heureuse. Il y a des choses que je n'aime pas et d'autres qui sont bien.
Examiner Par exemple?
Candidate Alors en terminale, quand on est en terminale il y des règles qui sont embêtantes. On ne peut pas sortir de l'école quand on n'a pas de leçons.
Examiner Oui, c'est tout?
Candidate Ça fait cinq années que suis dans cette école. Ça fait longtemps. J'ai beaucoup d'amis ici, mais je crois que maintenant... je voudrais partir.

You will note that candidate A uses short sentences, needs prompting to carry on and expresses one thought at a time. Candidate B is ready to explain her reasons without prompting, explains both aspects of the question and uses sentences with an extra clause. Candidate A communicates adequately but what she has to say is more limited and less interesting. Candidate B is more used to thinking aloud in French than Candidate A.

5 Phonetic accuracy This refers to accuracy in pronunciation and intonation and how 'authentically' French you sound. Nearly all candidates at A-Level could improve in this aspect. It is worth remembering that the more authentic you sound, the more faults in accuracy tend to be overlooked. It is a good plan, two to three weeks before the oral exam, to enlist the help of a French assistant(e) (or native speaker) and iron out pronunciation faults. Just getting rid of one or two can make a big difference to how you sound. Common faults are: pronouncing (or not pronouncing) final consonants; not giving nasal vowels the right pronunciation; not distinguishing between adjectival endings; an English type 'r' sound; making vowels into diphthongs (e.g. *donnei* instead of *donné;* not making liaisons where a French speaker would make them); and giving an English intonation pattern (strong stress on one syllable) — French words have equal stress on all syllables with a bit more emphasis on the last one (*see* below).

3.2 PRONUNCIATION

Contents

- Intonation and stress
- Vowels
- Consonants
- Pronunciation of alphabet

Some people find it easier to acquire an authentic pronunciation than others. This is partly a question of age. The younger you are, when exposed to a second language, the more likely you are to speak it like a native speaker. As you get older, your speech organs are more likely to get set in the groove of your first language and you find it difficult to make them adapt perfectly to new sounds. Another factor is the ability to mimic. If you can imitate one or two English regional accents, you are more likely to be good at reproducing the sounds of French. Mimicry is not necessarily linked to age. Another factor is undoubtedly the amount of time you have spent listening to and speaking French.

By the time you begin your sixth-form studies, you will have had the advantage of having started to learn French at least five years previously. There will still be a number of pronunciation points that need attention. Having a good pronunciation will enhance your performance in the oral exam and it will also give you satisfaction and confidence when in France. You will benefit from working with a native speaker or teacher who can iron out some of your difficulties.

You can also do a great deal on your own by listening to French radio and to tapes as well as taking every opportunity to practise speaking. If you have access to a language laboratory, in a local university or polytechnic, working with repetition exercise tapes will help a lot. These are usually tapes of continuous French, recorded with gaps for you to repeat in. You can achieve something of the same effect by just using these with an ordinary cassette recorder; the only difference being that you will not be able to listen to your own voice. If you have the text of what is recorded, you can also try reading over the voice on the tape with the volume turned down. This gives good intonation practice.

The main pitfalls in pronunciation are caused by the differences in sounds or features in the two languages. For example, the French find it very hard to make the two sounds represented by 'th' in English simply because they do not exist at all in French. The following are some of the main areas that cause problems for English speakers.

INTONATION AND STRESS

The patterns of French and English are very different in this respect. English has strong stress which can fall on any one syllable in a word. French has equal stress for each syllable, with a slight rise or emphasis at the end of the word. For example:

English	ad–min–is–**tra**–tion	com–pos–it–ion
French	ad–mi–nis–tra–**tion**	com–po–si–**tion**

You will also notice that the syllable break is different in both languages. French tends to end with a vowel sound; English with a consonant. This has the effect of putting the vowels in a prominent place in French and giving them more importance. The even distribution of stress in French makes the overall 'tune', or pattern, of the language sound very different to that of English with its constant beat of the stressed syllable. This is one reason why French poetry has a different sound to it and why the vowels tend to carry more musical effect.

Reading over a voice on tape as suggested is good practice but also make a conscious effort to eliminate the stressed syllable of English words, particularly when they are identical or almost so with French spelling.

VOWELS

Diphthongs

A diphthong is a vowel sound made up of two vowels (e.g. English 'day' [dei] and 'now' [nau]). Eight out of the twenty English vowel sounds are diphthongs. French has sixteen vowels, none of them diphthongs. A common pronunciation fault is to give some French vowel sounds, particularly [e] and [ɛ], a double quality in words like j'**ai**, donn**é**, arriv**ait**. When you pronounce a diphthong, your tongue moves slightly in the vowel position. The trick is to first feel this happening and then to try and stop it.

When some of our politicians speak French, you will often hear quite strong diphthongization; conversely, a French person speaking English might well do the opposite and pronounce 'day' as *des* and 'lay' as *lait*.

'Tense' vowel sounds

Two things are important when making vowel sounds:

1 **tongue position** — whether the front or back is raised and how far it is up or down

2 **the shape of the lips** — whether they are rounded, narrow-rounded or stretched apart. English vowel sounds require minimum movement of the lips and tongue whilst some French vowels require quite a lot. The main ones that cause difficulty are:

- [i] in words like *lit – appétit – île de la Cité – illisible* (illegible)
Note To make this sound correctly, the lips are stretched apart and the front of the tongue is raised to nearly touch the roof of the mouth.

- [y] in words like *il a eu – j'ai pu – tu as voulu*
Note This time, the lips are narrow-rounded and protruded but the tongue is in the same position as for the previous vowel. You should hear a characteristic puff of air when this sound is made correctly. It's a bit like the action of blowing away a speck of dust!

- [y] often contrasts with the vowel [u] in a number of words. [u] is pronounced with the back of the tongue raised with lip-rounding but no protrusion. Can you hear the difference between the following:

tout – tu
roue (wheel) *– rue*
c'est vu – c'est vous
il s'est tu (he kept quiet) *– il sait* **tout**
lu – loup
une puce (flea) *– un pouce* (thumb),
au-dessous – au-dessus

147

If you are not sure, get a French speaker to say them for you, then practise yourself saying them in pairs. See if you can find other examples using the phonetic transcription in a dictionary.

Nasal vowels

There are none of these in standard English. There are four in French. A nasal vowel is pronounced by letting air flow through the nasal passage. If you want to check that you are pronouncing a nasal vowel correctly on its own, try pinching your nose. You should be able to feel a vibration through the top part of your nose. The following phrase contains the four French nasal vowels:

Un bon vin blanc

You will see that each vowel has a single 'n' following it. In a dictionary transcription, nasal vowels have a little squiggle over the top.

1. The first vowel is the least common: *br<u>un</u> – l<u>un</u>di – <u>un</u>*. It causes least difficulty.

2. The next one occurs in words like: *b<u>on</u> – <u>om</u>bre – mel<u>on</u> – v<u>ont</u> – s<u>ont</u> – d<u>ont</u>*.

3. The next in: *pl<u>ein</u> – m<u>ain</u> – mal<u>in</u> – f<u>in</u> – h<u>ein</u>*. It is represented by the letters '*-ein*', '*ain*' and '*-in*'.

4. The last occurs in: *v<u>ent</u> – ven<u>ant</u> – deux <u>ans</u> – allem<u>and</u> – cep<u>endant</u>*. It is represented by the letters '*-en*' and '*-an*'.

5. Confusion is caused sometimes by the different spellings that can represent the nasal vowels and also because of what is called 'denasalisation'. All the above vowels lose their nasal quality:

   ● when followed by another '*n*' or '*m*'

nasal	**non-nasal**
bon	*bonne*
dont	*donne*
an	*année*
mon	*monnaie*
colon (settler)	*colonne* (column)

   ● when followed immediately by a vowel

nasal	**non-nasal**
fin	*fine*
plein	*pleine*
un	*une*
brun	*brune*
pan! (bang!)	*panne*

   Try reading the words above aloud yourself. Get a French person to read them for you.

6. The nasal sounds '*-on*' and '*-en/-an*' are often contrasted. Now try saying the following aloud:

vont	*vent*
dont	*dent*
sont	*sent/sans*
violon	*violent*
tromper (deceive)	*tremper* (soak)
long	*lent*

7. Where the first syllable is '*in-*', '*im-*' and '*inn-*', '*imm-*' The rule is:
   '*in*' or '*im*' + **consonant** (except n, or m) is pronounced as nasal in **vin**
   '*inn-*' or '*imm-*' + **vowel** is pronounced non-nasally as in **colline**

ine, ime	*in, im*
innocent	*intelligent*
inégal	*intention*
inespéré	*ingénieur*

inadmissible inspirer
imminent   *impossible*
immense   *imposition*
image   *insister*
inacceptable incapable

Try reading the words above aloud. Find other examples.

Note You might also like to try the following:
A Melun (town) *il n'y pas de melons, mais il y a des moulins mêlant leur mélodie au bruit du ruisseau*

CONSONANTS

Voicing

This is the vibration you can feel when you make a continuous 'zzzz' sound and place your finger on your Adam's apple. Many consonants can either be voiced with this vibration, or unvoiced as in a continous 'ssss' sound. Voiced consonants in French tend to be more fully voiced than in English. This applies particularly to the following:

1 z (sound in) – *zéro – maison – rose – chose*

2 zh (sound in) – *j'ai – Jean – gilet – rage*

3 v (sound in) – *vous – rêve – veuve – sauver*

Try to give these sounds more vibration in order to sound more French.

4 [p] This consonant is not pronounced with a following puff of air as in English. It soun more like a 'b' sound to an English ear. The trick therefore is to think of a 'b' when pronouncing it. Try saying: *Paul part pour Paris* thinking of 'b's' instead of the 'p's'.

5 [r] The main French 'r' sound is made by raising the very back part of the tongue so that it nearly touches the uvular (the small flap hanging down at the back of the throat). This causes a vibration of air and of the uvular. Avoid the main English 'r' sound which is made by curling back the tip of the tongue towards the roof of the mouth. Try saying *rue de remarques* and *la route pour Paris* with all this in mind.

Liaison

One of the early basic pronunciation rules you probably learned was not to pronounce final consonants. But, you also found fairly soon that, in certain combinations of words, you **are** required to pronounce them. The latter cases are called **liaisons**. Leaving out liaisons, in common combinations, sounds very un-French. The simplest rules are the following:

1 Liaison occurs in **noun phrases**, between the word before the noun and the noun:
les enfants – nos étudiants – vos intentions – ses idées – trois enfants – dix ans
It often occurs between a preceding **adjective and noun**:
mes anciens amis – ces dernières années – des enfants intelligents

2 Around a verb:
nous allons – vas-y – allez-y – vous en avez – c'est un ami – c'est impossible – elle est ici

3 After adverbs and prepositions + noun, adjective etc:
très intéressant – dans un mois – chez un ami – en anglais – sous un arbre – sans intérêt

4 You can add to these some commonly used **set phrases**:
les ‿Etats ‿Unis – les ‿Champs ‿Elysées – petit ‿à petit – de plus ‿en plus – tout ‿à coup – tout ‿à fait – tout ‿à l'heure – de ‿temps en temps – mot ‿à mot – moins ‿en moins

Finally, here are some words that can cause difficulty. A rhyming word is given as a guide to pronunciation:
Adam (le premier homme) *– dent*
alcool – bol

Allemagne – campagne
allemand – banc
une aile (wing) *– elle*
ail (garlic) *– médaille*
album – homme (also like this are: *minimum, maximum, Rome* (*la ville*), *rhum* (*la boisson*))
baptême/baptiser ('*p*' not pronounced)
automne – tonne
démocratie (*cracie*)
poêle (frying pan/stove) *– voile*
un pneu (*p+n+eux*)
solennel (*-annel*)
soixante (*soissante*)
vieille (old woman) (*vi-ei-y*)
veille means the day before – the one with the two '*i*'s' in it is human!

Further reading
R Martineau and J M McGivney, (1973), *French Pronunciation* , OUP

You may be required to spell out your name or a word in French. This is a useful skill to have. This fact would be vouched for by anyone with say a name like Thoroughclough who arrives, having booked, at the reception desk of a French hotel. When asked *C'est au nom de qui?* she or he will inevitably be asked to spell out the name. *Comment ça s'écrit, madame/monsieur?* The pronunciation of the French alphabet sounds similar to the English one with a few notable pitfalls. The pronunciation is indicated below by giving a French word with the same sound or a near English equivalent.

A *as in* bas	J *as in* **gîte** *	S *as in* **ess**
B bébé	K *as in* **cas**	T *as in* **thé**
C cé	L *as in* elle	U *as in* **du***
D dé	M *as in* **Emma**	V **Vé**
E *as in* **le***	N *as in* **end**	W double vé
F eff	O *as in* **eau** (water)	X eeks
G **gé** *as in* **mangé***	P *as in* pé	Y i grec
H ach *as in* acheté	Q ku *to rhyme with* **du**	Z zed
I *as in* **six***	R **aire** *as in* **faire**	

TT *is* deux **thé**   **LL** *is* deu*x* e*ll* (deuzell)   **RR** *is* deu*x* err (deuzair) etc.
* These usually cause most difficulty

Make sure you can spell out your own name. Using a telephone directory spell out (without pronouncing) a selection of unusual names to a friend who will then do the same for you. Here is a selection of my favourite Viking names (they did exist) to test your friends with. Again you will spoil the fun if you pronounce them first:

Ragnar Hairybreeks	Bjorn Ironside	Harald Fairhair	Ketil Flatnose
Sigtrygger the Mad	Erik Bloodaxe	Harald Harefoot	Magnus Barefoot

A few French ones, but not so picturesque:

Berthe au grand pied	Pépin le bref	Louis le gros	Charles le simple
Guillaume le bâtard			

3.3 LISTENING COMPREHENSION

Understanding what someone is saying in French when you can see them is a lot easier than understanding oral a voice on tape, radio or phone. When you can't see the speaker you miss a lot of the visual clues that help you to follow what is being said.

Another factor is that when we 'listen' in English we do not have to listen to every single word. We are able to guess at or expect certain meanings because we already know something about the subject being discussed and the order in which things might occur. We may be listening just to pick out certain details and ignore anything not connected with them. If you were listening to the national weather forecast to find out if it was going to rain in your area tomorrow you would probably keep half an ear monitoring the general run of what was being said but both ears would come into operation when you heard your region of the country mentioned and you would be on the alert for words like "showers", "mainly dry", "in the morning/afternoon" etc.

Listening comprehension in French is not such a relaxed affair. Your 'half an ear monitoring' system has to be fully alert all the time in case you miss something and doubly alert for the bit of information required, since it is not always possible to tell in advance at what point this might occur. You will probably only have two or three opportunities to catch what was said. This skill needs lots of practice. Even when individual cassettes are used for the test there is a limit to how many times you can listen.

The other skill required is that of being able to take notes as you listen or during a pause. You are usually allowed to give your answers in note form. Dictionaries may or may not be permitted, depending on the Board. More about note-taking below.

The material for listening comprehension is usually taken from live, authentic sources such as radio news bulletins, advertisements, 'phone-ins', interviews and discussions. The material has always been carefully selected for level of understanding and speed and may have been edited or re-recorded. It will therefore be somewhat easier to understand than most things you may casually tune into on French radio.

THE EXAMINATION

Types of question set

These vary from Board to Board but are likely to include the following:

- Questions in English to be answered in English
- Questions in French to be answered in French
- Ticking true or false statements
- Filling in tables or grids relating to what was said
- Completing statements or filling in bits of missing text
- Summarizing in English

Some Boards make full use of the above, others use mainly questions and answers in French or English.

A few minutes are usually allowed for studying the questions before hearing the tape. There are often pauses between items and at the end of sections. You are allowed to write an answer or make notes at any time. Some Boards provide space on the answer paper for making notes.

Examination strategy

1 Make sure you know the requirements of your particular Board with respect to: the layout of the paper; where and when pauses occur; what sort of questions to expect and whether dictionaries are allowed.

2 Read through the questions beforehand and underline the key words. This will help your eye while your ear is engaged in listening. If there are any numbers involved put a big 'N' to remind you, since these always require special concentration. Look at the number of marks awarded for each item, usually given at the end of each question. This will be a good guide to how many points are likely to be required and prevent you spending too much time on questions that obviously require just a single detail. You may find it helpful to highlight, in some way, those questions that have a high mark.

3 Some questions may involve a certain amount of deduction as well as giving facts from the text. In this case, take into consideration the theme of the passage as a whole and listen carefully for the part before and after where you think the answer is contained.

④ If answers are in English, it seems logical to take notes in English. Make these as brief as possible. If you don't understand a key word or phrase, and dictionaries are allowed, jot down an approximation so that you can look it up during a pause. Answers written in French are not usually penalized for grammatical error provided that they can be understood as French.

⑤ Use the space provided for notes. If you are writing on a blank sheet, divide your page in half, (left-side for notes in pencil, right-side for answers in ink — blue or black). Make sure you cross out anything you do not want to be included as a final answer. **Don't use brackets.**

⑥ Make sure that answers you write in note form in English: make sense; are unambiguous; and show that you have fully understood. Although answers don't have to be in note form, common sense often plays a part in giving an acceptable answer. Responses like 'Open 48 hours a day' and ' Since the 40th of July' (*ULEAC A and AS-Level 1990*) could have been avoided if they had been read with a critical eye!

⑦ **Summary in English** You will probably hear the passage three times. Jot down French or English words as notes, during the first hearing, using the speaker's pauses at full stops as a guide line. Use these notes to give a framework to the summary in short phrases, leaving plenty of gaps. Use the second recording to fill in anything missing and make sure it makes sense. The third recording should be a check on the whole.

Examiners' reports, during the last two years, seem to indicate that listening skills are improving. There is a clear division between those candidates who have had sufficient practice and others who have not. Since questions in this part of the A-Level examination are closely defined, and relate directly to the spoken text, it is possible to gain full or nearly full marks. It is well worthwhile developing your skills in this area.

Finally, a comment on the listening test from ULEAC's Report on the 1990 A and AS-Level examination. Having commented on some of the problems encountered, the Report stated:

> ....candidates put on a strong performance in this test. They were clearly well-prepared and had rehearsed examination procedures so as to be able to deal calmly with the mechanics of the test: note-taking; pauses; reading the questions; and so on. There were few occasions when marks were lost because a question had been carelessly read and there was evidence of considerable presence of mind in the longer passages where, despite misunderstanding initial details, candidates were able to make sense of subsequent material and score well, rather than panicking or losing the thread.

THE CASSETTE TAPE

The tape included with this book contains listening material in two sections. Side A has material taken mainly from French radio but also includes pronunciation practice and an anecdote. Side B has material and questions from Examination Boards as they appeared in recent examination papers. In order to include the maximum amount of listening material, the recordings on the tape are not presented as exactly as they would be in an examination (i.e. with pauses and repetitions). In order to simulate as closely as possible examination practice it is recommended that you do the following:

(a) Study the questions for a few minutes before listening.

(b) Listen to the whole of one recording without stopping the tape.

(c) Stop the tape yourself in appropriate places to write your answer.

(d) Listen once more to check what you have written.

If your Board allows the use of individual cassettes you can of course listen to any part several times. Bear in mind however that you will be limited in an examination by the overall time allowance for the test.

Marks awarded for each question are given so that you can estimate the amount of material required for each answer.

You can either use the passages on this part of the tape as simulations of exam practice, or you can use them as listening practice with information to be extracted. In this case, you can listen to them as many times as you like, by stopping or replaying as required, without a time limit. A further exercise you can do is to transcribe the full text of part of any recording, stopping the tape as many times as you like. Listen again while you follow the text and try reading over the voice on the tape as suggested earlier in this book.

Side A: Practice questions

Examples of spoken French in everyday life

I   In this extract you will hear a number of news headlines. Listen to the items once through without a break and complete the following tasks as you listen:

1   Pour chaque titre écrivez le nom du pays dont il s'agit ou de la ville si cela s'est passé en France.   (10)

2   Lisez les dix phrases ci-dessous. Il y en a une pour chaque titre d'informations. Mettez-les dans le bon ordre en les numérotant 1–10.
    finale de la coupe de tennis
    continuation des grèves d'autobus
    pas d'embouteillages sur les routes
    arrestations et expulsions d'activistes
    changement de gouvernement
    un Français troisième en ski
    les soldats patrouillent dans les rues
    le mauvais temps fait des morts
    coups de fusil, deux morts
    agression et vol en pleine ville   (10)

3   Listen to the recording again and write down the French phrase that fits the English one below. There is one for each item in sequence.
    suggested to a lawyer that he forms a government
    after yesterday's riots
    the Gaza strip
    the winner of the event
    match being played at the moment
    funeral held of Lucien Toroloni
    serious damage
    well done, drivers!
    attacked in town centre
    a gang of hooligans   (10)

4   Listen to each news item again and put a tick next to those statements which are correct or a cross beside those that are incorrect.
    Lech Walesa to form new Government
    Unions claim 20 people died
    600 Palestinians expelled
    The winner was a Norwegian
    Pete Sampras will meet Michael Chang in the final
    Shoot-out was probably intended to settle old scores beween gangs
    Latest figures give 73 dead
    Motorists staggered their return home
    Claude Taittinger's name appears on bottles of his champagne
    One of the hooligans was armed with a knife   (10)

5 Listen once more to item number six.
What two events are referred to? What contrast is drawn between them.   (3)

6 Listen again to item number ten.
Explain the reason for the strike and say which bus routes are affected.   (7)

II France-Inter donne des conseils pratiques quant à la façon de soigner les animaux domestiques.

1 Répondez aux questions suivantes:

(a) En anglais
  (i) What can some dogs be like (two characteristics)?   (2)
  (ii) In which two ways are cats different from dogs?   (2)
  (iii) What do you have to teach dogs to do if you live in a town?   (1)
  (iv) What should you persuade dogs not to do when they are young?   (1)
  (v) What reason is given for doing this?   (2)
  (vi) What advice is given about barking?   (2)

(b) En français
  (i) Quels chiens sont permis dans le métro ou l'autobus?   (2)
  (ii) Comment est-ce qu'on doit surveiller son chien dans le train?   (2)
  (iii) Quelle précaution doit-on prendre avant d'amener son chien chez des amis et pourquoi?   (2)
  (iv) Qu'est-ce qu'il faut fournir à son chat avant de le laisser pour le week-end?   (3)
  (v) Si l'on est obligé de voyager avec son chat, quelles précautions doit-on prendre?   (2)

2 Comblez les blancs dans le texte ci-dessous:

Lorsque vous avez des invités, empêchez votre chat de s'installer sur leurs ———— car beaucoup de gens sont allergiques à leurs ———— ou tout simplement ne les aiment pas. Si vous avez chez vous des animaux plus ————, pensez toujours à la tranquillité de vos amis ou de vos voisins. Après tout, ce n'est pas donné à tous d'aimer les———— blanches ou les ————! Et puis, évitez d'apprendre des ———— aux oiseaux parleurs, ils les retiennent facilement et cela risquerait de vous ———— devant des invités qui n'ont pas un grand sens de l'humour.   (7)

III Vous entendrez une interview avec un ancien combattant français qui décrit sa vie dans un camp de concentration allemand pendant la deuxième guerre mondiale. Les questions couvrent trois parties de l'interview.

Section 1 Répondez en français
(i) L'âge actuel du soldat?   (1)
(ii) On l'a fait prisonnier en…?   (1)
(iii) libéré en…?   (1)
(iv) il a été capturé dans quel département?   (1)
(v) nom de la ville?   (1)
(vi) sur quelle rivière?   (1)
(vii) capturé la nuit? oui/non   (1)
(viii) par des Allemands qui parlaient français? oui/non.   (1)
(ix) l'arme utilisée dans sa capture?   (1)
(x) il était seul? oui/non   (1)
(xi) on l'a transporté directement en Allemagne? oui/non   (1)
(xii) Combien de prisonniers dans le camp de transit?   (1)
(xiii) Comment les a-t-on transportés?   (1)
(xiv) il est resté combien de temps dans son dernier camp?   (1)

Section 2 Complétez la transcription de cet extrait du texte de l'enregistrement et répondez en français aux deux questions.

A: Est-ce que cela vous a ――――― le sens de l'initiative dans le camp?

B: D'une façon générale on peut dire que le camp, on est ――――― sans rien, et par ――――― doc uns et ―――――, on était arrivé à reconstituer à l'intérieur du camp, absolument tous les ――――― dont on a besoin dans la vie sociale ―――――,

A: Vous pouvez donner un exemple?

B: Et bien il y avait un ―――――, il y avait un théâtre, il y avait ―――――, il y avait du sport, du rugby, tous les sports étaient ―――――.

A: Ahh...

B: Y compris le tennis. Il y avait ――――― des jardins potagers. (10)

(i) Qu'est-ce que les prisonniers ont même réussi à fabriquer? (1)

(ii) Nommez trois expositions montées par les prisonniers (3)

Section 3 He now goes on to describe attempts to escape before and after the initiation of a daily parade by the Germans.

Answer in English:

(i) Name three ways of escaping before the parade was initiated (3)

(ii) Give three ways the Germans used to prevent escape afterwards (3)

(iii) What method of escape was eventually devised? (1)

(iv) What help did the 'Libertas' organization provide? (2)

(v) In your opinion, why does he believe that a third world war will not happen? (2)

IV Summary in note form In the following news item you will hear about the plight of homeless families living in Paris. The item includes comment from a homeless mother and a primary-school teacher. Play the whole recording through without a break; then again, with a short pause after each piece of information required.

A First, read through the headings.
(i) Two more families are to join who? (3)
(ii) Help provided by the Emmaus organization and how life is organized. (5)
(iii) Why some families can leave from time to time. (2)

B Interview with the mother Béatrice:
(i) What further details does she add about the daily routine? (2)
(ii) What particular problems are there for Béatrice? (3)

C Interview with school teacher Jean-Paul: Tick appropriate item.
(i) 150 children are able to attend school: true/false (1)
(ii) Jean-Pierre has: (a) 35; (b) several; (c) 14 in his class (1)
(iii) Main problem with these chidren is that they are: (a) violent (b) tired. (1)
(iv) They become more alert at: (a) the end of the afternoon;
(b) the beginning of the afternoon. (1)

D Final question
How does the situation with the squatters stand as described by the news presenter at the end of the report? (3)

V 1 Vous entendrez Fabrice Lecantrac qui raconte ses impressions du Japon et des Japonais. Vous entendrez aussi une personne japonaise qui parle français.
(i) quel événement a récemment eu lieu au Japon? (1)
(ii) Fabrice, qu'est-ce qu'il vient de faire? (1)
(iii) qui a-t-il rencontré récemment? (1)
(iv) donnez deux détails sur cette personne (2)
(v) comment avait-il fait sa connaissance? (1)
(vi) donnez trois détails sur le physique de la personne (3)
(vii) pourquoi l'interviewer pense-t-elle que Fabrice a subi le charme de cette

personne? (1)
(viii) Akiko est née juste avant ou après la fin de la guerre? (1)
(ix) pourquoi Akiko n'éprouve-t-elle pas de ressentiment contre son père? (2)
(x) quel aspect est cité du caractère japonais? (1)
(xi) décrivez l'attitude des Japonais envers les Américains après la bombe atomique (2)
(xii) Quels aspects positifs et négatifs du caractère des Japonais Akiko cite-t-elle finalement? (2)

2 Listen to the next part of the interview and write down in French the phrases for which the English equivalents are given below:
(i) in effect have no memory
(ii) on the other hand
(iii) when it's over it's over
(iv) in spite of the horrors they have experienced
(v) the very next day
(vi) the guns stopped firing (6)

3 Voici une transcription de la prochaine partie de l'entrevue. Ecrivez dans les blancs les mots ou les phrases qui manquent.

Et moi ce qui m'intéresse dans ce —————, outre cette particularité biographique qui fait que cette femme est née après les bombes atomiques mais juste avant —————, alors que depuis plusieurs mois la guerre était déjà ————— en Europe, et donc elle a connu depuis lors tout ce développement du Japon, c'est le fait qu'elle ————— que, bien euh, après on est capable, on est capable d'oublier et c'est vrai que c'est à mon avis l'une des forces du Japon et des Japonais de —————, non pas en faisant table rase du passé, et disons sans s'attacher, se polariser sur des choses matérielles. On peut très bien par exemple, quand on se balade à Tokyo, voir je ne sais pas, ————— assez laid inauguré avec un écriteau 'All new'– complètement neuf – et alors ça veut dire que l'on a ————— peut-être une vieille maison en bois charmante qui était là. —————, si vous voulez on est capable de faire table rase mais en même temps on reste ————— japonais avec cette faculté de faire du neuf et d'aller de l'avant et c'est ainsi peut-être que l'on arrive à cette ironie d'histoire que ————— de la deuxième guerre mondiale, enfin l'un des vaincus, on arrive maintenant à porter ————— le trésor fédéral, le trésor fédéral américain, mais tout ça ————— et sans rancune vis-à-vis des troupes victorieuses.

(12)

VI In the following recording, you will hear part of an interview with Pierre Fabre who has just published a book on demonstrations. There are three sections. Listen to the complete text once without pausing. Listen once more with a short pause to write the answer. Listen once more to the whole of each section in order to check your work.

Section 1
(i) Describe the three different types of demonstration in France defined by Pierre Fabre and give an example of each (6)
(ii) What was the direct political effect of two particular demonstrations in France? (2)
(iii) Why were divorced fathers demonstrating? (2)
(iv) What did homosexuals hope to achieve through their demonstration? (2)

Section 2 Complétez le résumé ci-dessous de cette section en rajoutant les mots qui manquent:
A: Vous citez le cas d'un jour de mars ————— où il y a une accumulation là pendant 2 ou 3 jours assez extraordinaire.

B: Effectivement j'ai fait un reportage sur l'ensemble des manifestations qui ———— —— au ministère de la ————. On s'aperçoit que sur une période de six mois l'an dernier il y en a eu une par semaine. Alors, ces manifestations ne retiennent ... elles retiennent beaucoup moins l'attention du public... au moins des journalistes, c'est-à-dire que le public en a sans doute beaucoup moins ———— ——, à moins qu'il ne se trouve sur le passage de la manifestation ou qu'il remarque telle ou telle manifestation. Cela étant, le ministre qui est dans son ministère, il a ———— de cette manifestation. Quand les manifestations deviennent nombreuses, il y a un effet de ————, notamment d'ailleurs dans les crises, les grèves. (6)

Section 3

Répondez en français
(i) Qu'est-ce qui est dans la constitution? (2)
(ii) Cette loi date de quelle année? (1)
(iii) Quelle distinction la loi fait-elle entre le manifestant et l'organisateur de la manifestation? (2)
(iv) Dans quelles circonstances est-ce que l'autorité administrative peut interdire une manifestation? (2)
(v) Qu'est-ce qui est imprévisible dans une manifestation? (2)

Les chiffres

VII Première partie

Vous allez entendre les résultats de trois jeux de pari nationaux:
(a) **Courses de chevaux – le tiercé** Pour gagner il faut prédire les trois premiers chevaux de la course et leur arrivée dans l'ordre ou dans un ordre différent. Pour le quarté il s'agit des quatre premiers chevaux. Vingt chevaux participent à la course.
(b) **Le tapis vert** Il faut deviner quatre cartes tirées au hasard.
(c) **Le loto** Il faut prédire six chiffres tirés au hasard.

Dans chaque cas vous allez noter les chiffres des numéros sortants, le rapport pour le gagnant et la somme d'argent pariée (la mise)
(a) Le tiercé numéros gagnants: ———— rapport pour —— francs, dans l'ordre———— francs. Dans un ordre différent, ————. (6)
Le quarté: ———— rapport pour ———— francs dans l'ordre, ———— francs —— centimes, et dans un ordre différent ———— francs et —— centimes. (9)
(b) Le tapis vert: ————. (4)
(c) Le loto, premier tirage: ———— numéro complémentaire ————. (7)
Deuxième tirage: ———— numéro complémentaire ——. (7)

Deuxième partie

Pour les chiffres qui suivent vous pouvez:
(a) la première fois écrire le chiffre après l'avoir entendu
(b) et la deuxième fois prononcer le chiffre avant la voix de la bande
Il faut signaler que ce sont des chiffres qui sont souvent confondus.

6, 600, 1606, 60, 66, 676, 550, 40, 14, 1404, 91, 1981, 1.005.599

1st, 6th, 11th, 21st, in the 16th century, in the 14th century, in 2500 bc

a thousand people, a third of the population, a quarter of his time, 500 ml that makes half a litre, 2%, 5%, 3,5%, 9,3%

Pronunciation practice

VIII Intonation

Remember equal stress on each syllable, slight emphasis on last:

possibilité – administration – postérité – technologie – attention – complication

Difficult vowels
[i] Lip stretching: *appétit – au lit – il lit la liste – Italie*
[y] Narrow lip rounding with puff of air for 'u': *aperçu – voulu – perdu – vendu – il a pu*

Vowel contrasts
[u] and [y]
une roue – une rue, c'est vu – c'est vous, il sait tout – il s'est tu, au-dessous – au-dessus, il est où? – il l'a eu.

Nasals All French nasals are contained in the phrase, Un bon vin blanc
[õẽ] *lundi le vingt et un, aucun parfum, brun*
[ɔ̃] *un bon melon, ils ont, ils vont sur le pont*
[ẽ] *le vin, la main, bien, le dessein, assassin*
[ã] *le champ, un camp, deux ans, le vent*

Denasalisation
bon – bonne, fin – fine, serein – sereine, brun – brune, dont – donne, plein – pleine, colon – colonne

Nasal contrasts [ã] [ɔ̃]
le vent – ils vont, long – lent, ils sont – ça sent, violon – violent, une dent – un don (gift)

in-, inn-/im-, imm-
innocent – intelligent, inespéré – ingénieur, inacceptable – incapable, imminent – important, immense – imprimé, inimaginable – intéressant

Voicing More 'buzz' than in English
[z] *zéro, maison, rose, chose, pause*
[zh] *les jeunes gens, un agent, la rage, une cage*
[v] *un rêve, un veuf, une veuve, mauve*

Consonants [p] and [r]
[p] *Paul part pour Paris, les petits problèmes, petit à petit*
[r] *un rude hiver, rue de Rivoli, une route rurale*

Liaisons
(a) Noun phrases
   les enfants, vos intentions, trois étudiants, dix ans, les idoles
(b) Adjective + noun
   mes anciens amis, ces dernières années, de bonnes intentions
(c) Before or after verb
   nous allons, ils ont, vous en avez, allez-y, c'est un ami, c'est impossible
(d) Adverb/preposition + noun/adjective
   très heureux, dans un mois, chez une amie, sans intérêt, en anglais, trop important
(e) Set phrases
   les Etats Unis, petit à petit, de moins en moins, de plus en plus, de temps en temps, tout à fait, à tout à l'heure
(f) A few words that can cause difficulty
   l'Allemagne, allemand, une médaille, un agent, de l'argent, maximum, minimum, la démocratie, une femme, soixante, la veille (day before), *une vieille* (old woman), *de l'ail* (garlic), *une aile* (wing), *l'alcool, le baptême, l'automne, l'Europe, européen, européenne, évidemment, une grenouille, un oignon, solennel.*

IX **Histoire drôle** Ecoutez cette histoire d'abord pour la comprendre mais aussi essayez de la mémoriser pour savoir la raconter à d'autres personnes.

X Annonces publicitaires *France-Inter, octobre 1991*

Avez-vous l'oreille fine? (Have you got sharp ears?) Ecoutez attentivement les deux annonces publicitaires suivantes et pour les mots soulignés, cochez (tick) celui que vous avez entendu.

(i) A: Vie de famille

B: Vous avez un enfant de moins de <u>six/seize</u> ans et pour le faire <u>garer/garder</u> vous employez une <u>assistante/assistant</u> maternelle agréée. Nous, les allocations <u>familiales/familières</u> nous pouvons vous aider. Quelle que soit votre <u>situation/stipulation</u> familiale et le montant de vos <u>revenants/revenus</u>, nous prenons en charge les <u>qualifications/cotisations</u> sociales de l'URSAF. Alors si vous désirez en savoir plus, n'hésitez pas, <u>tapez/frappez</u> 36 15 code CAF. Vous voyez, vous faire aider à garder vos enfants, c'est aussi notre <u>rouleau/rôle</u>.

A: Allocations familiales, ça vous <u>met/fait</u> la vie plus facile.   (10)

(ii) A: Un petit <u>boulot/boule</u> par ci, une bricole par là, un mois <u>ici/aussi</u>, un mois <u>là-bas/par là</u>, et caetera, et caetera. Quand on est <u>jeune/jaune</u> et qu' on veut <u>travailler/trouver</u>, on ne veut pas traîner <u>pendant/pour</u> des années et des années. L'Exojeune c'est la <u>résolution/solution</u> pour un jeune sans <u>cotisations/qualifications</u>, d'entrer tout de suite dans la vie <u>active/fictive</u> avec un vrai salaire, un véritable emploi. Embaucher un jeune, ça n'est pas une <u>large/charge</u>.

B: Pour en savoir plus sur l'Exojeune, <u>contactez/contractez</u> votre agence locale pour l'emploi. <u>Compostez/Composez</u> le numéro vert du <u>ministère/ministre</u> du travail sur le 05 10 10 10.   (10)

Side B: Practice exam questions

Texts from Examination Boards

Note The instructions which follow are not in the exact form used on the examination papers of the various Boards. They have been adapted to suit the arrangement of material on the tape.

1 Répondez aux questions suivantes en français. Vous n'êtes pas obligé d'écrire des phrases entières, mais vous devez donner toutes les informations nécessaires. Vous avez trois minutes pour lire les questions avant d'entendre l'enregistrement.

Cet exercice consiste en trois parties: la première partie comprend deux flashs et une annonce publicitaire, la deuxième partie est un reportage et la troisième est une interview.

Première partie: *deux flashs et une annonce publicitaire. Vous écouterez chaque flash et l'annonce deux fois avec une pause. Ensuite mettez 1.30–2.0 minutes environ pour rédiger vos réponses.*

(i)   Comment cette nouvelle victime de la tempête a-t-elle trouvé la mort?   (2)
(ii)   Que faisait-il à ce moment?   (2)
(iii) Pourquoi les dernières prévisions de la météo sont-elles inquiétantes?   (1)
(iv)   Cette annonce est parue à quelle époque de l'année?   (1)
(v)   Pourquoi ce temps est-il difficile pour les parents?   (1)
(vi)   Donnez deux détails au sujet de la marchandise offerte   (2)
(vii) Comment les malfaiteurs ont-ils obtenu l'argent des automobilistes?   (3)

Deuxième partie: *un reportage sur une nouvelle entreprise appelée 'Tom et Flore'. Ecoutez une première fois et mettez quelques moments pour étudier les questions et écrire des notes. Ecoutez une deuxième fois et mettez quatre minutes pour rédiger vos réponses.*

(viii) Quel est le service spécial offert par la nouvelle entreprise "Tom et Flore"? (2)
(ix) Quand est-ce que le service est disponible? (2)
(x) Donnez trois détails de l'animation fournie par l'entreprise. (3)
(xi) Comment est-ce qu'on tâche d'avoir plus de publicité? (2)

Troisième partie: *Extrait d'une interview avec un Français qui travaille au Liban. Ecoutez une fois et mettez quelques moments pour étudier les questions et faire des notes. Ensuite écoutez une deuxième fois et mettez six minutes pour rédiger vos réponses.*

(xii) Quels sont les deux facteurs qui rendent la vie des profs insupportable? (2)
(xiii) Quelle est l'attitude des enfants vis à vis de la France? (3)
(xiv) Pourquoi est-il difficile d'étudier? (1)
(xv) Que savons-nous de la vie familiale de Houda? (4)

ULEAC

2 Listen carefully to the tape with a view to writing notes, in French, on the main points being made. Headings have been printed to help you organize your notes. You will have two minutes to study the headings before hearing the tape. Play the tape twice with an interval of one minute between the two playings. You may consult a French dictionary at any time.

Note You are not told how long to spend on finishing this question before doing the short essay [100–120 words] that follows. Total time for the paper is one hour. You should not therefore spend more than about 10–15 minutes on the listening-test questions.

Vous allez écouter la bande deux fois. Eric nous parle de sa préparation au baccalauréat. Ecoutez la bande et prenez des notes en français, sur ce qu'il dit. Vous devez mentionner:

(i) la section qu'il a choisie (1)
(ii) pourquoi il n'était pas content de ce choix (1)
(iii) pourquoi il est allé dans un lycée technique (3)
(iv) pourquoi sa section était un peu à l'écart des autres (2)
(v) l'attitude des autres élèves envers la section d'Eric (2)
(vi) ses expériences dans la classe de maths (3)
(vii) ce qu'il dit sur son professeur d'allemand (5)

SEB

3 You have two minutes to read through the questions before you listen to the tape. After the first hearing allow a pause of two minutes. Listen to the tape once more with a short pause within the text. After the second hearing you have three minutes to complete your answers. You can write at any time and use a dictionary while the tape is not playing.

The recording is an extract from a radio report on illegal and unregistered labour. Here are nine statements relating to what you are about to hear. Five of them are correct; put a tick against those five, and do not put any mark against the others. Stop the tape for thirty seconds after *non-déclarée*.

(i) Le travail clandestin diminue d'année en année.
(ii) Le travail au noir rapporte l'équivalent de ce que gagnent 30 000 entreprises de taille moyenne.
(iii) Il y aurait plus de 800 000 personnes faisant du travail de façon clandestine.
(iv) Le nombre de travailleurs au noir ne comprend ni chômeurs, ni Portugais.
(v) La grande majorité des travailleurs étrangers non déclarés sont employés dans le bâtiment, l'agriculture, le textile et la restauration des garages.
(vi) Il y a très peu de travailleurs au noir sur la Côte d'Azur.
(vii) Le Ministère du Travail a l'intention de supprimer, dans la mesure du possible, le trafic de main d'œuvre.
(viii) Le travail au noir se répand dans tous les autres pays européens.

(ix) Le renforcement des verbalisations est une des premières mesures que compte adopter le ministre. (9)

Oxford and Cambridge

4 Listen to the advertisements twice, with a short pause between them. Give yourself a minute at the end to complete and check your answers. Répondez aux questions en français.

Advertisement 1
(i) Entre quelles dates peut-on profiter de cette offre? (2)
(ii) Quel est le prix de la mini-chaîne? (1)
(iii) Notez les deux avantages de cette offre spéciale. (2)

Advertisement 2
(iv) Que pouvez-vous assurer avec l'UAP? (4 choses) (4)
(v) Nommez les deux grands projets européens dont l'UAP est l'assureur. (2)

You will now hear two news items: the first about a change in the rules of volley-ball, the second about a plane hijacking. The first requires answers in **English** the second in **French**. Listen to each one twice, with a short pause in between. Give yourself three minutes to complete and check your answers after each one.

News Item 1
(vi) Why has it been decided to change the rules of volley-ball? (2)
(vii) What is the normal procedure for scoring points? (2)
(viii) What different procedure will be applied in the fifth set? (2)
(ix) What is the highest score that can be obtained now in the fifth set? (1)

News Item 2
(x) Sur quel pays l'avion a-t-il été détourné? (1)
(xi) Sous quel prétexte a-t-il atterri? (1)
(xii) Combien de passagers se trouvaient à bord de l'avion et combien de ces passagers étaient des étrangers? (2)
(xiii) Quelle demande les pirates de l'air ont-ils faite? (2)

UCLES

5 **Item 1** In this recording you will hear a former French assistante, Nathalie, giving advice to a "would be" assistant.

(a) **Listening for gist**
Listen to the recording **once** in order to note, in English:
(i) Nathalie's overall attitude to her experience (1)
(ii) **Three** reasons for this attitude (3)

(b) **Summary**
Listen to the two sections of the recording beginning with:
(a) *Etre assistant...*
(b) *'Si je dois te parler de difficultés...*

After each section, summarize in English, the advantages and disadvantages which Nathalie mentions. Listen once more to both sections with a pause at the end to check your work.
(a) (6)
(b) (5)

(c) **Résumé en français**
Vous allez maintenant entendre Nathalie en train de parler des qualités qu'elle considère nécessaires pour être un bon assistant. Un résumé incomplet de ce qu'elle dit se trouve en- dessous. Complétez le résumé en rajoutant les mots qui conviennent.

Ecoutez une fois sans pause, la deuxième fois avec des pauses pour vous permettre d'écrire les mots qui manquent et une troisième fois pour vérifier ce que vous avez écrit.

Lisez d'abord le résumé.

Selon Nathalie, pour être un bon assistant il faut être enthousiaste, bavard, patient, curieux et un peu acteur.
Enthousiaste parce que quand on mène une classe on doit —————————
Bavard parce qu'il faut ————————————————————
Patient parce que les élèves ne font pas toujours ce qu'on voudrait —————
et on est là pour les aider et pour être patient quand —————————
Curieux du point de vue des élèves, parce qu'il faut savoir —————————
et du point de vue personnel curieux ——————————————— (16)

Item 2 In this recording you will hear Patrick Olivier being interviewed about an autobiographical book which he has just published. Read through the questions then listen to the recording straight through without a break.

(a) **Identifying information**

Listen to the tape again in three sections with a short pause after each section to write brief but informative answers in English. Play the recording straight through and allow a short pause at the end to check your work.

Section (a)
(i)   Give two ways in which the interviewer describes Patrick Olivier.   (2)
(ii) How does Olivier react to the interviewer's introduction?   (3)

Section (b)
(iii) Describe the organization which Olivier joined in 1976   (2)
(iv) Why does he now disagree with the interviewer's description of him as a mercenary?   (2)

Section (c)
(v)   What did Olivier do after Robert Mugabe's forces won the war in Zimbabwe?   (2)
(vi) What were his reasons for doing this?

(b) **Retranslation**

Listen to the last part of the interview once more in **three** short sections. After each section write down, in **French**, the phrases for which the **English** equivalents are given below. Then listen to all three sections straight through so that you can check your work.

Section (a)
(i)   I stayed an extra year.   (2)
(ii) in order to train the officers   (2)

Section (b)
(iii) The white Christian West must be defended at all costs.   (2)

Section (c)
(iv) not at all   (1)
(v)   I feel I am partly African.   (2)

NEAB

6 Candidates will be allowed a ten-minute break at the end of section two, before beginning section three.

Candidates will be allowed ten minutes to read the questions through before the tape is played and to make notes while it is being played. All questions are to be answered in English.

Section one

Listen to the conversations twice. Allow a pause of 30 seconds between the first and second time you listen. Allow five minutes after the second hearing to write your answers.

Note The French spelling of Marseilles is *Marseille.*

(a) While you are on a visit to France, you hear the following conversation between two of your French friends who have just taken the bac:
  (i) What is the girl's parents' reaction to what she has just told them? Explain this reaction. (2)
  (ii) Why does the girl say she has changed her mind about what she wants to do next year? (2)
  (iii) According to the boy, what are the disadvantages of working in a bank? (2)
  (iv) According to the girl, what are the disadvantages of a teacher's job? (2)
  (v) What arguments are used by the boy to try to persuade her to change her mind? (2)

(b) You are travelling in France in a car driven by your French friend's mother. She stops to give a lift to a young man who is hitch-hiking to his home in Marseilles. You hear the following conversation between the young man and your friend's mother:
  (i) What does the young man tell the woman about the origin of immigrants in Marseilles? (2)
  (ii) What problems does the young man say there are in Marseilles? (2)
  (iii) What does the young man say about the type of jobs done by immigrant workers in Marseilles? (4)
  (iv) How does the young man explain why many immigrants have come to Marseilles? (2)

Section two

There are **five** short news items. Listen to each one twice with a pause of approximately half a minute between the first and the second time. Then allow **one minute** after the second hearing to answer the question on that item.

Répondez en français
Flash 1 (i)   Comment Dominique Didier a-t-il trouvé sa mort? Quand est-ce qu'on a retrouvé son corps? (2)
Flash 2 (ii)   Où est-ce qu'on pourrait trouver des embouteillages ce week-end? (2)
Flash 3 (iii) Comment la vieille dame a-t-elle perdu ses bijoux? Où les a-t-on retrouvés? (2)
Flash 4   A quelle heure précisément le prisonnier s'est-t-il évadé? (2)
Flash 5   Pourquoi la circulation à Valence sera-t-elle perturbée ce week-end? (2)

Section three

Here is part of an interview with the French writer, Marcel Pagnol, first recorded some years ago and broadcast again recently on French radio as part of a programme about films which have been made recently of some of his works. Listen to the interview three times. (Allow a pause of **three minutes** between each listening. Allow a short pause of ten seconds between the second and third time you listen)
(i) Why does the interviewer find it strange that Pagnol lives in Paris? (2)
(ii) Pagnol says he is obliged to live in Paris for **three** reasons. What are these reasons? (3)
(iii) Why does he say that he divides his time between Paris and the south of France? (4)
(iv) What is the activity he takes part in while in the south of France and why is this activity particularly important there? (4)
(v) What does Pagnol say about whether Parisians are more intelligent than people from other parts of France? (4)
(vii) Pagnol gives a number of reasons why he no longer makes films. State **four** of these. (4)
(vii) What sort of films does Pagnol say he is incapable of making? (1)
(viii) What does the interviewer say about Pagnol and the 'Parisian landscape'? (1)
(ix) Why does Pagnol say he chose the hills of the *Massif des étoiles* as a location for several of his films? (4)

(x)   What does Pagnol say about the colours in the hills of the *Massif des étoiles*?

(2)

(xi)   What does he say about the rocks in the hills of the *Massif des étoiles*?   (1)

WJEC

7   You will hear two brief news items, a publicity announcement and one longer piece: an interview. Listen to each item twice. Allow yourself half a minute to study the questions before listening to each of the shorter items. Allow a forty-five second pause in between to begin your answer and just over a minute at the end to complete it. For the longer item, allow one minute to read the questions, a minute and a half in between and four minutes at the end to complete your answers. You can make notes at any time during the reading. Your answers need not be in complete sentences.

Note   Pay close attention to the number of marks given for each question as a guide to the amount of detail required.

Répondez en français

Flash 1   (i)   Qui participera au défilé de manifestation?   (2)

(ii)   Pour quelle raison est-ce qu'on manifeste?   (5)

Flash 2   (iii)   Résumez ce flash d'informations   (6)

Flash 3   (iv)   Donnez les détails de l'offre faite par Ford concernant leur voitures   (7)

Item four: interview betwen Bernard Rigoulex and Hélène Dorlach

(v)   Describe the problem outlined by Bernard Rigoulex at the beginning of the interview.   (4)

(vi)   Who is Hélène Dorlach and what action has she taken?   (5)

(vii) Bernard Rigoulex suggests that there has been a fresh outbreak of certain forms of child abuse. Which does he specify?   (4)

(viii)What is Hélène Dorlach's reaction to this suggestion?   (2)

(ix)   What measures are to be introduced?   (6)

(x)   How will the specialist teams be able to respond?   (5)

(xi)   How will the message of the publicity campaign be communicated?   (4)

AEB

FRENCH LANGUAGE

Units in this chapter

4.1 WRITING

Contents

● Letters

● Dialogue

● Narrative, imaginative and descriptive writing

● Discursive writing

Writing in French will be required for a significant part of the A-Level examination and this section usually carries between a fifth and a quarter of the total marks. For AS-Level, writing in French is required by most of the Boards (see Syllabus Analysis). For A-Level, some (or all) of the literature/topic questions may be set, and require an answer, in French. Coursework done over the two years and sent for moderation is always in French. You might also be required to write in French in response to the reading or listening test.

Almost every Board has a section of one of its papers devoted to a continuous piece of writing (of 250–300 words) called 'essay' (or 'composition') or to a report, dialogue or letter of about 200 words. It is worth remembering that in this section marks are awarded for:

● **Content** – the quality, relevance and overall structuring of the ideas

● **Range** of vocabulary, structures and idioms used

● **Accuracy** of language

The last factor is not the overriding one and often has a proportion of marks equal to each of the first two elements. It is important therefore to carefully plan the layout of your piece of writing and to be adventurous with words and expressions.

LETTERS

You will be familiar with this task from your experience at GCSE. The following points about general structure however need to be observed.

The introduction

Check to whom the letter is to be written. If it is a formal or an official letter start with the following if addressing a company:

(i)   *Mademoiselle/ Madame/ Monsieur* or *Messieurs.*

These titles are never abbreviated at the beginning of a letter.

If you know the title of the person to whom you are writing this should be given in the following form:

(ii) *Madame la Directrice*

(iii) *Monsieur le Président*

(iv) *Monsieur le Maire*

(v)   *Madame l'Attachée Culturelle*

If it is implied or stated in the instructions for the letter that you know the person quite well you may begin:

(vii) *Chère Madame* or *Cher Monsieur*

Do **not** use the form *Mon cher Monsieur* or *Ma chère Madame.*

When writing to a friend you may use *Cher* or *Chère* followed by first name or *Cher Monsieur* _____ and *Chère Madame* _____. If you want to include a whole family or group you can start *Chers amis.*

Openings

It is not possible to include here examples of all the possible beginnings for a letter since much depends on the specific instructions given. Here are some general guidelines.

Formal or official letters

The style of such letters in French often sounds a bit pompous to English speakers but this level of formality is the norm and continues to be used.

- Thanks for a letter or services already received:
  - (i)   *J'ai l'honneur d'accuser réception de votre lettre du...*
  - (ii) *J'ai l'honneur de vous remercier...*
      J'ai le plaisir de vous remercier pour...

- Asking for a service or a favour:
  - (iii) *Je vous serais très reconnaissant(e) de bien vouloir...*
  - (iv) *Je vous serais très obligé(e) de me faire savoir...*
  - (v)   *Je sollicite votre bienveillance pour me fournir des renseignements...*

- Following up:
  - (vi) *Ayant lu votre annonce parue dans le Figaro, ...*
  - (vii) *En réponse à votre annonce parue...*
  - (viii) *En réponse à votre lettre du...*
  - (ix) *Comme suite à votre demande téléphonique...*
      Faisant suite à notre conversation téléphonique...

- Opening a subject for correspondence:
  - (x)   *Je me permets de vous écrire pour/ au sujet de...*
  - (xi) *J'ai le plaisir/ l'honneur de...*

Personal letters

Distinguish between writing to a friend (or friends) of your own age and to perhaps a family you stayed with or worked for. You would probably use *'tu'* (or *'vous'* if there is more than one friend), in the first case, but *'vous'* when addressing a family. The following are some possibilities for openings:

(i)   *Je vous/ te remercie de/ pour votre/ ta lettre*
      (or if writing in more familiar style)

(ii) *Merci de ta lettre*

(iii) *Votre/ Ta lettre m'a fait grand plaisir*

(iv) *Quelques mots pour vous/ te remercier de...*
      (Or if in apology)

(v)   *Je tarde quelque peu à répondre à votre/ ta lettre*

Main part of letter

Advice on this depends very much on the brief you are given in the examination instructions and the purpose of the letter. It is important to have a **clear plan** and careful paragraphing (i.e. one idea — or subject — per paragraph). Make sure that what you write is relevant to the brief given. Do not be tempted to 'pad' your letter with, say, remarks about the weather.

The ending

Formal style

Just before signing off the following might be appropriate:

(i) *Dans l'attente d'une réponse favorable...*

(ii) *Avec mes remerciements anticipés...*

(iii) *Dans l'attente de votre réponse...*

The possibilities for the actual signing off are more formal and varied than the English 'Yours faithfully' (which normally should follow a 'Dear Sir' beginning). The following diagram gives you a basic pattern.

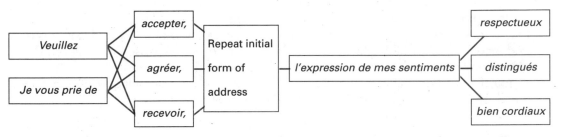

For example:

Veuillez agréer, Monsieur le Président, l'expression de mes sentiments distingués

Personal style

The following will suffice for most occasions:

(i)

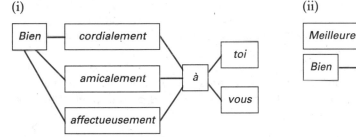

(ii)

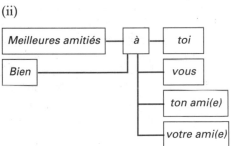

e.g. *Bien à toi, ton ami(e)*

or *Bien à vous, votre ami(e)*

Expressions such as:

(iii) *Je t'embrasse affectueusment*

(iv) *Bons baisers* (to children)

(v) *Grosses bises*

are only used between people who usually kiss each other when saying hello or goodbye.

The above framework belongs to what are known as *'les convenances épistolaires'* (the conventions of letter writing). You will find the following 'epistolary' terms useful in many cases too:

(vi) *Veuillez trouver ci-joint* – Please find enclosed

(vii) *Par retour de courrier* – By return of post

(viii) *Enveloppe timbrée à mes nom et adresse* – Stamped addressed envelope

(ix) *dès que possible* – as soon as possible

(x) *dans les delais les plus brefs* – as soon as possible

(xi) *expédier/expéditeur* – to send or post/sender

(xii) *un colis* – postal packet or parcel

(xiii) *l'emballage* – wrapping or packing

(xiv) *au déballage* – when we/I unpacked it

(xv) *Je suis au regret de vous informer que* – I regret to inform you that

(xvi) *Il faut constater que* – It must be noted that

(xvii) *Je dois vous signaler que* – I must point out to you

Note '*Signaler*' and '*constater*' are both useful words to replace '*dire*'

Illustrative questions and answers

French stimulus

The stimulus provided is usually a letter to be answered, an advertisement for a job, or an article or report in a newspaper. The letter might be formal, e.g. a job application, a letter to a newspaper or written to a friend describing something that happened to you which you have to imagine, using the material provided. Sometimes the article or report has already been part of a comprehension question.

Having a stimulus in French does have advantages. You should be able to "lift" some of the phrases used and "manipulate" some of the structures to fit into your letter. It is a good idea to mark or highlight words or phrases that you could re-use in your letter. Do not just copy out bits of the text hoping this will do the trick!

You still need of course a clear framework to your letter, a beginning, a middle and an end. Here is a typical example of this kind of letter question.

EXAMPLE 1

Pendant les vacances d'été vous avez travaillé pour une famille en France pendant quatre semaines. On avait convenu de vous verser une somme de 700 francs par semaine en récompense de certains travaux de ménage. Vous avez reçu cette somme pour les deux premières semaines mais des problèmes familiaux sont intervenus et on ne vous a pas payé pour les deux semaines suivantes. On avait promis de vous envoyer l'argent. Vous avez écrit une fois mais vous n'avez encore rien reçu. Ecrivez une lettre (150 mots) à l'agence qui vous a trouvé cet emploi pour lui expliquer la situation et lui demander quelles mesures ils vont prendre.

This kind of stimulus gives you an outline for the letter you need to write, leaving you to invent a few details. It also contains words and phrases that, with care, you could re-use. You may be asked to write on alternate lines. This is a good plan in any case since corrections are easier to insert when you are checking your answer.

Answer plan

You will need three paragraphs:

- to say who you are and why you are writing
- to explain the situation
- to make the request and sign off.

Next plan the detail. Do not be tempted to start from the beginning of the instructions. If you begin with "Pendant les vacances d' été" you will miss out the first part of your plan. When you read through the brief for the letter other French words or phrases may float into your mind, write these down before they float out again. You will have to imagine the name of the family and their "problèmes familiaux". It is a good idea to jot down French phrases for the detail of the plan. It is also helpful if you concentrate on the verbs since they are the main working part of the sentence.

A possible plan, with a few alternative words, might be the following:

Paragraph 1

trouvé/ obtenu – votre agence – quatre semaines en juillet – août – famille Legrand – Lyon

Paragraph 2
convenu de/promis de – me payer 700 francs – payé/reçu – deux semaines – problèmes familiaux
grand-mère morte/décédée – famille désolée – oublié – pas payé – on avait promis – parti vers la fin d'août – écrit une fois – pas de réponse

Paragraph 3
obligé(e)/reconnaissant(e) – m'aider – leur écrire – prendre les mesures nécessaires
If you concentrate on the verbs and the tense factor you should find that your outline reads like an abbreviated message that you can fill out.

Possible answer

The final letter, with a few comments in italics, might be as follows:

Messieurs, *(sounds business-like)*
Je vous écris *but better* Je suis obligé/je me trouve dans l'obligation de vous écrire *more forceful phrases here and official sounding* au sujet d(e) *another useful phrase, equivalent of "about", "concerning"* de l' emploi que votre agence m'a obtenu pour les vacances d'été.

J'ai travaillé au pair pour la famille Legrand à Lyon pendant quatre semaines. M. Legrand avait convenu de me verser 700 francs en échange de certains travaux de ménage. J'ai reçu cette somme pendant deux semaines mais au milieu de mon séjour, la grand-mère, qui habitait avec la famille, est morte subitement. Tout le monde était si bouleversé qu'on a oublié de me payer. Quand je suis reparti à la fin de mon séjour, ils ont promis de m'envoyer l'argent. J'ai écrit une fois mais je n'ai pas reçu de réponse.

Je vous serais très obligé(e)/reconnaissant(e) si vous pouviez prendre les mesures nécessaires pour obtenir la somme qu'ils me doivent.

Dans l'attente de votre réponse veuillez agréer, Messieurs, l'expression de mes sentiments distingués.

Note The convention for setting out this letter would be with the French address at the top **right** hand side with the name of your town and the date, but your full address on the **left** hand side as follows:

J. Lindsay	Café-Restaurant du Palais
3, Castle Street,	06000 Nice
Kilmarnock,	France
Scotland	
	Kilmarnock 16 juin 1996

Monsieur,

The convention also applies to the letter in the following example.

EXAMPLE 2

Un professeur de musique de votre lycée propose d'accompagner un groupe d'étudiants à Paris au mois d'avril. Il espère pouvoir organiser une visite à un certain musée qui l'intéresse. Il vous prie d'écrire une lettre (150 mots à peu près) au musée pour demander les détails suivants:

Heures/jours d'ouverture du musée pendant cette période
Prix d'éntrée (prix spécial pour un groupe scolaire)
Détails de ce qu'on peut y voir
Durée de la visite
Comment trouver le musée
Voici l'adresse du musée:
Musée Instrumental
14 rue Madrid
75008 Paris

WJEC

Possible answer

Towngate Comprehensive School
Newport Road
Cardiff
Wales

Musée Instrumental
14 rue Madrid
75008 Paris

Cardiff, le 8 février

Monsieur,

Je suis étudiant dans une école du pays de Galles. Mon professeur de musique a l'intention d'emmener un groupe scolaire à Paris pendant les vacances de Pâques. Pendant notre séjour, il aimerait visiter le musée instrumental. Il m'a demandé de vous écrire pour obtenir quelques renseignements afin de mettre au point les derniers détails.

Quelles sont les heures d'ouverture du musée pendant la période de Pâques et quel est le prix d'entrée? Existe-t-il un tarif réduit pour les groupes scolaires de vingt personnes?

Je vous serais très reconnaissant si vous pouviez aussi me donner des détails sur ce que nous pourrions voir dans le musée et combien de temps il faut compter pour une visite. Une dernière question: où se trouve exactement le musée à Paris? Auriez-vous un plan pour nous aider à vous trouver?

En vous remerciant à l'avance, je vous prie, d'accepter, Monsieur, l'expression de mes sentiments respectueux.

Exam practice questions

Here are more examples of examination questions requiring a letter:

1 Vous êtes un homme d'affaires et vous avez manqué un rendez-vous important à cause d'une grève. Vous écrivez une lettre à un journal national pour exprimer vos sentiments.

Oxford and Cambridge

2 Votre correspondant(e) français(e) vous a invité(e) à passer les grandes vacances chez lui (elle). Ecrivez-lui pour le (la) remercier de son invitation. Dites-lui que vous pourrez passer seulement quinze jours chez lui (elle). Expliquez pourquoi. Parlez du voyage que vous ferez pour arriver chez lui (elle). Parlez de ce que vous voudriez faire au cours de votre visite. (150 mots)

WJEC

3 Voici une petite annonce que vous avez vue dans un journal français:

Nous cherchons:

SERVEUSES/SERVEURS

pour juillet août
Ecrire ou se présenter
au

**Café – Restaurant du Palais
06000 Nice**
Clientèle internationale

Ecrivez une demande d'emploi en expliquant pourquoi vous êtes la personne qu'il leur faut et en demandant des renseignements supplémentaires. (150 mots)

WJEC

Checking your work

You will need to have a system for checking what you have written for mistakes. The following method can be applied to any piece of French you have written:

(i) **Verb**
- Does the subject (singular or plural) fit the ending? Have I spelt the ending correctly?
- Is the tense the right one? Is it an '*avoir*' or an '*être*' verb, if it's a compound tense?
- Is it an irregular verb? (e.g. the past participle may not end in *é*.)

(ii) **Nouns and adjectives**
- Check that '*s*' is there if required
- Check the gender of the noun and the adjective ending, if it needs to agree.

(iii) **Object pronouns**
- Check that they are the right ones.
- Check that they are direct or indirect as required (e.g. *le la les* or *lui leur*).
- Check that object pronouns are in their right place, before the verb if it's not in the imperative, and that they are in the right order.

DIALOGUE

You may be asked to write the dialogue for a job interview, an interview to find something out, or a conversation on a particular topic. Read the instructions carefully. You are often asked to include several points in the dialogue. Decide who will take the initiative in the dialogue and work out part of what they may ask or say first. Answers to questions will then come much more naturally. For example, in an interview for a job, the interviewer will be much more dominant at the beginning. Don't fall into the trap of starting with a list of your hobbies and interests. You don't have to tell the truth so you can invent things about yourself, provided they are relevant. The style will be conversational and should therefore follow more naturally from what you did at GCSE. Some of the dialogue will be in the present tense but the perfect and future tenses are likely to be needed. You can give the piece a brief title or make the subject clear from the opening question. Try to achieve a balance between questions and answers (i.e. not too much of one or the other). Make sure you make a neat concluding remark to an interview or a conversation.

Illustrative question and answer

1 Vous vous présentez à une entrevue pour obtenir un poste. Ecrivez le dialogue qui a lieu entre vous et le chef d'entreprise (écrivez 300 mots environ)

Possible answer

(In this case you have to invent the job!)

M. Duteuil Bonjour mademoiselle, très heureux de faire votre connaissance. Vous m'excuserez de vous avoir fait attendre. Alors, vous vous présentez comme candidate au poste de responsable d'animation dans notre village vacances.

Mlle Smith Enchantée monsieur. Oui, c'est exact, j'ai vu l'annonce dans le journal et cela m'a beaucoup intéressée.

M. D Je vois que vous parlez couramment le français. Avez-vous déjà quelque expérience de ce genre de travail?

Mlle S	Oui, le samedi je travaille dans un club de jeunes et, l'été dernier, j'ai été employée comme organisatrice dans un village vacances à Skegness en Angleterre.
M. D	Ah, bon. Vous pouvez me décrire un peu ce que vous faites au club.
Mlle S	Eh bien, en hiver je surveille les jeux et activités comme le tennis de table et le biliard et, en été, j'organise des randonnées et des manifestations sportives.
M. D	Et vous faites cela toute seule?
Mlle S	Non, non, nous sommes trois ou quatre et nous faisons cela à tour de rôle; chacun a des responsabilités particulières.
M. D	Racontez-moi ce que vous avez fait l'été dernier dans le village vacances.
Mlle S	Là-bas, il était plutôt question de surveiller des enfants et d'organiser leurs activités.
M. D	Vous n'avez aucune expérience des adultes?
Mlle S	Oui, c'est vrai. Mais, à Skegness, j'ai eu l'occasion d'observer ce qu'on faisait et le genre d'activité qui plaisait le plus.
M. D	Quel aspect du travail d'animatrice vous semble le plus difficile?
Mlle S	Pour les jeunes, il faut avoir quelques activités en réserve et il ménager quelques surprises. Le plus difficile c'est quand il pleut toute la journée!
M. D	Vous n'aurez pas ce problème chez nous! Qu'est-ce que vous avez comme diplômes?
Mlle S	J'ai mes certificats de GCSE dans huit matières et j'ai suivi des cours de secourisme. J'ai aussi l'intention de faire un stage pour animateurs qui aura bientôt lieu dans mon collège.
M. D	Et qu'est-ce que vous faites pendant vos loisirs?
Mlle S	J'aime la lecture, je fais un peu de cuisine et je joue au tennis.
M. D	Vous avez des frères ou des sœurs?
Mlle S	Oui, j'ai deux frères, plus jeunes que moi.
M. D	Vous vous en occupez beaucoup?
Mlle S	Oui, la plupart du temps, surtout depuis que mes parents sont divorcés.
M. D	Je comprends. Eh bien mademoiselle je suis très heureux d'avoir fait votre connaissance. Nous reprendrons bientôt contact avec vous.
Mlle S	Merci monsieur.

Note

(a) This example, about 350 words, is rather longer than is normally required. About 40–50 extra words are likely to be ignored as far as accuracy is concerned but will probably be taken into account for content, style and range of vocabulary. You may lose marks if you greatly exceed the stated number with some writing tasks. Check the marking scheme for your particular Board.

(b) If you are a girl, be careful of adjective and verb agreements.

(c) Miss Smith hasn't had the opportunity to ask any questions. The following might have been appropriate:

Pouvez-vous me donner des informations plus précises sur le travail?

Quelles seraient mes responsabilités?

Quelles sont les horaires de travail?

Le logement et les repas sont-ils gratuits?

J'aurais du temps libre?

Quelles activités sont disponibles pour les jeunes et pour les enfants?

Quel équipement et quel matériel sont disponibles?

Qui est-ce qui décide du programme du jour ou de la semaine?

NARRATIVE, IMAGINATIVE AND DESCRIPTIVE WRITING

Types of questions set

Here are some examples of questions that require narrative, descriptive or imaginative writing.

1 Une nuit vous êtes transporté(e) dans une autre époque. Racontez ce que vous avez vu et quels étaient vos sentiments à votre réveil.
2 Quel métier aimeriez-vous exercer quand vous aurez fini vos études et pourquoi?
3 Imaginez le texte d'une interview accordée à un présentateur de télévision par une vedette de la chanson ou de l'écran.
4 Quelle a été pour vous la journée la plus longue?
5 Composez le texte d'un dépliant publicitaire destiné à attirer l'attention des clients français sur un restaurant au Royaume-Uni. (Parlez de la situation du restaurant, de son décor, de sa cuisine, de ses spécialités, du personnel, etc)
6 Est-ce que vous croyez aux expériences surnaturelles? Décrivez ou imaginez une telle expérience.

These kinds of titles allow full range to your imagination within the bounds of the subject. You are free to enlarge on (or embellish) real experience or to invent it entirely. Keep to the format of a beginning, a middle and an end. Take care with tenses.

Question 1 for example, will require mainly past tenses with the perfect for what happened and the imperfect for describing how things were.

Question 2 contains a future perfect tense for the implied future – *quand j'aurai terminé* – when I have finished, so you will need to imitate this if you are going to write for example 'when I have left school' *quand j'aurai quitté l'école*. You are also likely to want to use the conditional – I would like to be a lawyer – *j'aimerais être avocat* (see grammar chapter pages 65–69). You could also invent some exciting career provided that you can describe its benefits and justify them.

In **Question 3** you can refer to a real personality or invented one. The interviewer is likely to use both the present and perfect/imperfect tenses – *Est-ce que vous avez parfois le trac avant d'entrer en scène? Dans votre carrière quelle réussite vous a donné le plus de satisfaction? Quels étaient vos sentiments au moment de...*

Here are some questions that might be asked in an interview with a successful pop group:

Comment avez-vous trouvé le nom de votre groupe et quelle est la signification de ce nom? Vous vous connaissez depuis longtemps? Depuis combien de temps est-ce que vous jouez ensemble? Comment avez-vous appris à jouer de vos instruments? Est-ce que vous avez pris des cours? A quel rythme est-ce que vous répétez? (how often do you rehearse?*) Vous avez un local où vous répétez?* (a place to rehearse) *Comment écrivez-vous le texte de vos chansons? Est-ce que vous vous souvenez de la date de votre premier concert? Que s'est-il passé au second concert? Quel genre de spectateurs est-ce que vous aimez le plus? Est-ce que vous êtes quelquefois découragé? Quels sont vos plans ou vos projets pour l'avenir? Est-ce que votre musique a changé au cours des années? Être célèbre, cela pose-t-il des problèmes?*

With **Question 4** it is tempting to start '*La journée la plus longue de ma vie c'était quand ....*' but this almost tells the story before you have started. Better to have a beginning like: *Une heure du matin. Rien ne bougeait dans la maison. Est-ce qu'il allait téléphoner?* – thus adding a certain amount of suspense.

Question 5 suggests details that could be included in the brochure but leaves room for further ideas. You can be really adventurous here making the setting of the restaurant really spectacular, the décor unusual, the cooking and specialities exotic, the staff speaking fluent French. The main idea of a publicity brochure is to sell the product. You could largely avoid past tenses except perhaps when saying where the chef was trained or worked before.

Question 6 requires a few opening remarks about your beliefs followed by a ghostly story or an account of a real experience. Overleaf is a possible model answer to question 6.

Illustrative question and answer

Est-ce que vous croyez aux expériences surnaturelles? Décrivez ou imaginez une telle expérience.

Si vous m'aviez demandé il y a une semaine si je croyais aux expériences surnaturelles je vous aurais répondu que non. Mais depuis samedi dernier j'ai changé d'opinion.

Samedi soir vers onze heures je suis sorti(e) comme d'habitude pour promener le chien. Il faisait très froid. La rue où j'habite est sans réverbères et normalement à cette heure il fait très noir. Mais ce soir-là il y avait un clair de lune spectaculaire. La lumière était si intense que les arbres jetaient des ombres sur la chaussée. Comme il n'y a presque pas de circulation sur cette route je laisse normalement le chien en liberté et il marche devant moi.

On avait fait quelques centaines de mètres et on était arrivés près d'une vieille maison inhabitée depuis des années. Soudain mon chien s'est arrêté tout net et a refusé de bouger. Il poussait des petits cris plaintifs et le poil de son échine était tout raide. Alors je l'ai ramassé pour poursuivre notre route parce qu'il faisait trop froid pour s'attarder. Je croyais qu'il avait peut-être vu notre voisin le renard. En le tenant dans mes bras j'ai remarqué qu'il grelottait. Nous avons continué notre chemin, lui, tenu en laisse.

Cette route est sans issue et il nous a fallu revenir sur nos pas. Je me demandais si mon chien aurait la même réaction en repassant devant la maison abandonnée. On était à 100 mètres de là quand j'ai aperçu deux formes sortir de la maison. Quelqu'un ou bien quelque chose promenait un chien! Mais le plus remarquable c'était que, malgré le clair de lune, ils ne jetaient absolument pas d'ombre. Je me suis arrêté et les deux formes ont fait halte aussi. La personne s'est retournée pour me regarder et ramassant le chien comme pour continuer son chemin, elle et l'animal sembèrent devenir plus pâles et se dissoudre dans la clarté de la lune.

Voilà pourquoi j'ai changé d'avis sur l'existence du surnaturel! (320 mots)

Note The perfect tense is used for the narrative part of the story and the imperfect for the descriptive. Also, where the sense would clearly be 'had' in English (in the opening sentence) a pluperfect is used.

Follow up task

This answer exceeds the 300 words required. What parts could you leave out or shorten without losing the sense of the story? The narrator does not describe his or her reaction to what is seen. Look up the word peur in a monolingual dictionary and find expressions to mean 'very afraid', 'terrified' and so on. Check on antonyms (opposites) for the word 'afraid'.

Exam practice questions

1 Ecrivez une lettre à un(e) ami(e) lui décrivant les sources de pollution dans votre région et les problèmes qui en résultent. *NEAB*

2 Décrivez les effets du tourisme dans votre région ou dans une région que vous connaissez. *WJEC*

3 Vous êtes témoin d'un accident. Rédigez pour la police un rapport dans lequel vous offrez une description de la scène juste avant l'accident aussi bien que les détails de l'événement et de ses conséquences. *NEAB*

Nos. 1. and 2. require mainly descriptive use of language and probably mainly the present tense. No 3. will need description but also some narration of events in the past tense.

Illustrative question and answer

Using a written stimulus

BELIER

Samedi, vous serez sans doute très énervé parce que les choses ne se passeront pas comme vous les avez programmées. Quelque chose bloquera tous vos plans: rendez-vous manqués, voyage retardé, téléphone en panne ou une lettre très urgente qui n'arrivera pas: vous allez vous fâcher contre le monde entier. Mais dès dimanche, changement radical d'atmosphère: on sera tout sourire à votre égard...

GEMEAUX

Gaieté et animation, vous ne vous ennuirez pas une seconde. Vendredi, vous serez très studieux, à la grande joie de votre professeur ou de votre patron. Et le week-end, c'est la fête! Acceptez toutes les invitations que l'on vous proposera. Un ami que vous n'avez pas revu depuis longtemps va reprendre contact avec vous. Remettez à plus tard certains travaux que vous aviez projeté de faire.

CANCER

Préoccupez-vous au plus vite des petits problèmes qui vous ennuient. Le week-end, évitez de trop sortir ou de vous coucher tard. Quelques heures supplémentaires vous feront le plus grand bien. Lundi, vous allez faire une recontre au cours d'une sortie entre amis. Ce pourrait être le meilleur moment de la semaine...

Ecrivez 200–250 mots sur **un** des sujets suivants:

1 Pour une fois, votre horoscope a dit la vérité! Bélier, Cancer ou Gémeaux – écrivez ce qui s'est passé les jours mentionnés.

ou

2 Vous lisez votre horoscope dans un magazine de la semaine passée. Comparez ce qui est en effet arrivé avec ce qu'on avait prédit.

SEB

This kind of question with a written stimulus provides a framework for your piece of writing. You just have to think up a likely chain of incidents.

Possible answer

Je viens de passer une semaine formidable. L'école a dû rester fermée du lundi au mercredi à cause d'une panne du système de chauffage. Alors mon amie et moi sommes parties* à Glasgow passer deux jours chez une de mes tantes. Là, nous avons fait les magasins de vêtements et j'ai acheté deux pantalons et plusieurs t-shirts très dans le vent. Mardi soir nous sommes allées* à un concert de rock et nous avons passé le reste de la soirée en discothèque.

Revenues* chez nous le mercredi j'étais en forme pour terminer une composition pour mon prof de français. Il a été très surpris de la recevoir vendredi matin et je crois que j'aurai une bonne note. Samedi matin j'ai joué au tennis avec Patricia. C'était l' anniversaire de mon ami Tom et il m'a invitée* le soir à sa boum. Là j'ai eu le plaisir de revoir Annick, une ancienne amie de l'école primaire. C'était vraiment chouette de bavarder avec elle. Elle a proposé de passer le dimanche ensemble et de rendre visite à d'autres amies. Je n'ai pas eu le temps dimanche de terminer tous mes devoirs mais cela n'a pas posé de problème parce que lundi et mardi c'était le demi-trimestre. (212 mots)

* C'est une jeune fille qui écrit

Try doing your own version of an enjoyable week starting with the advantage of three days off school or work.

For question 2 you can use a combination of predictions from any three horoscopes and make them come true or not as you wish. You may have to use the pluperfect tense to say what the horoscope *had* said – e.g. *On avait prédit que j'allais passer une semaine formidable.* Alternatively you could put the predictions between inverted commas – e.g. *Mon horoscope me disait "Lundi, vous allez faire une rencontre intéressante" et en effet ce jour-là j'ai revu un de mes vieux (vieilles) copains/copines.*

Writing from other stimuli – text, statistics, pictures

A few Examination Boards use a combination of text, statistical tables and pictures as a stimulus to a piece of writing in French. This kind of material gives you a theme to write about, provides some information and starts you off on a particular line or point of view. The rest is then up to you. The information is provided as a stimulus to get you going not just an outline plan with four elements so that you can write a paragraph about each one. You will need first of all to note the main ideas presented. Do this in French, note form will do.

Illustrative questions and answers

Vous allez écrire une composition **en français** de 240 à 260 mots. Vous devriez examiner les informations présentées, évaluer l'efficacité des mesures prises jusqu'ici et suggérer un plan d'action pour combattre la menace du tabac.   *AEB*

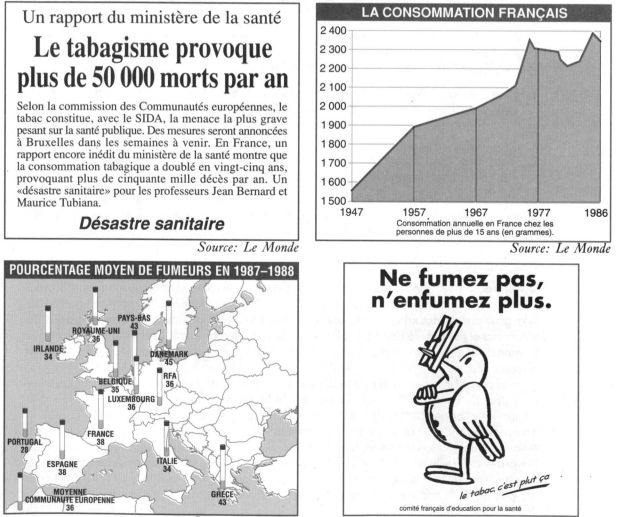

Un rapport du ministère de la santé

Le tabagisme provoque plus de 50 000 morts par an

Selon la commission des Communautés européennes, le tabac constitue, avec le SIDA, la menace la plus grave pesant sur la santé publique. Des mesures seront annoncées à Bruxelles dans les semaines à venir. En France, un rapport encore inédit du ministère de la santé montre que la consommation tabagique a doublé en vingt-cinq ans, provoquant plus de cinquante mille décès par an. Un «désastre sanitaire» pour les professeurs Jean Bernard et Maurice Tubiana.

Désastre sanitaire

Source: Le Monde

LA CONSOMMATION FRANÇAIS

Consommation annuelle en France chez les personnes de plus de 15 ans (en grammes).

Source: Le Monde

POURCENTAGE MOYEN DE FUMEURS EN 1987–1988

PAYS-BAS 43
ROYAUME-UNI 36
IRLANDE 34
DANEMARK 45
BELGIQUE 35
RFA 36
LUXEMBOURG 36
FRANCE 38
PORTUGAL 28
ESPAGNE 38
ITALIE 34
MOYENNE COMMUNAUTE EUROPENNE 36
GRÈCE 43

Source: Le Parisien

Ne fumez pas, n'enfumez plus.

le tabac, c'est plus ça

comité français d'education pour la santé

la signification des informations fournies?

– le tabagisme constitue une menace aussi grave pour la santé que le SIDA – cinquante mille décès sont provoqués chaque année par la consommation du tabac – les Français fument plus que presque tous leurs semblables européens – la consommation de tabac a doublé en 25 ans – le tabagisme peut être nuisible à la santé des non-fumeurs

efficacité des mesures?

– la consommation de tabac est en hausse perpétuelle depuis la fin de la guerre 39–45 – en revanche entre 1977 et 1982 sa consommation a légèrement baissé – il faut avouer que globalement les mesures n'ont pas été tellement efficaces – on peut influencer quand même les gens qui fument

un plan d'action

– réduire ou même proscrire la publicité pour les cigarettes à la télévision, dans la presse, et dans les rues – augmenter la taxe sur le tabac – utiliser les revenus accrus de cette mesure pour financer une campagne contre le tabagisme – souligner les dangers du tabagisme dans les écoles en commençant par le programme des écoles primaires – défendre de fumer dans tous les lieux publiques et les lieux de travail

Possible answer

En examinant de près ces informations on en tire sans difficulté la conclusion que le problème du tabagisme est aussi grave que celui du SIDA. Les 50 000 morts qui résultent du tabagisme chaque année sont non seulement tragiques pour les familles des victimes mais aussi pour l'État qui doit payer les frais de l'hospitalisation.

Ce qui est plus inquiétant c'est que la consommation de tabac chez les Français est au-dessus de la moyenne européenne. La France vient en troisième place après les Danois, les Hollandais et les Grecs. On a le droit de supposer aussi que le tabagisme surtout dans les lieux publiques peut être désagréable sinon nuisible pour la santé des gens qui ne fument pas.

Est-ce que les mesures prises jusqu'ici ont été efficaces? En examinant les chiffres on doit conclure que ce n'est pas le cas. On peut observer une légère baisse entre les années 1977 et 1982. Il est donc peut-être possible de faire quelque chose et d'alerter les gens.

Les mesures à prendre sont les suivantes: il faut réduire ou proscrire la publicité pour les cigarettes à la télévision, dans la presse et dans les rues. Il est nécessaire d' augmenter immédiatement la taxe sur le tabac. On devrait utiliser les revenus accrus pour financer une campagne de publicité contre le tabagisme. Il faut défendre aux gens de fumer dans tous les lieux publiques et dans les lieux de travail. Il est important de souligner les dangers du tabac pour la santé dans les écoles en débutant par les programmes de l'école primaire. On doit implanter chez nos compatriotes l'idée que ce n'est plus cool de fumer. (263 mots)

Note You have 2½ hours for the whole of this paper. There are 45 marks for this piece of writing. You should leave yourself at least an hour and ten minutes to complete it. Spend at least 15–20 minutes writing the notes for your answer. Put these in the right order with rings and numbers. Then write your essay. Examiners are always very impressed by well ordered answers but they tend to get frustrated by having to unravel your work for themselves.

Writing from statistics and tables

Usually requires you to write a short report rather than an essay. Your personal opinion is not normally needed unless specifically requested. You will need to be able to compare and contrast, talk about increase and decrease, most and least and so on. In the example below note the different ways of saying 'the greatest number'*

Etudiez les tableaux ci-dessous et écrivez en français un rapport (150 mots à peu près) sur le chômage de longue durée en France

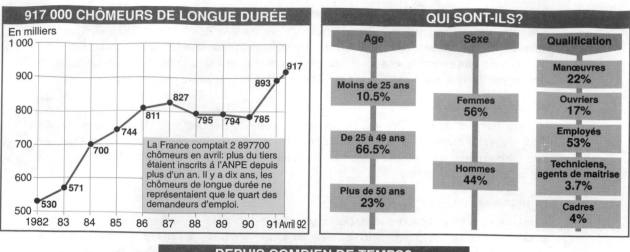

WJEC

Possible answer

LE CHÔMAGE DE LONGUE DURÉE EN FRANCE

En avril 1992 il y avait presque 3 millions de chômeurs en France. Plus d'un tiers se composait de chômeurs de longue durée, c'est-à-dire qui n'ont pas travaillé depuis plus d'un an. Le chiffre de ces chômeurs a considérablement augmenté depuis 1982, quand il y en avait 513 000, un quart seulement de ceux qui cherchaient un emploi. En 1992 leur chiffre atteint 917 000, plus d'un tiers des chômeurs inscrits à l'ANPE**.

Parmi ces gens 58,5% ne travaillent pas depuis 1 ou 2 ans, 19,8% depuis 2 ou 3 ans, et 21,7% depuis plus de 3 ans.

Qui sont ces chômeurs? La majorité* d'entre eux ont de 25 à 49 ans. 23% ont plus de 50 ans. Seulement 10,5% ont moins de 25 ans. La plupart* sont des femmes (56%). Les plus nombreux* (53%) sont les employés, et (22%) les manœuvres c'est-à-dire les travailleurs manuels. Les cadres et les agents de maîtrise ne représentent que 7,7% du total. (150 mots)

** Agence nationale pour l'emploi

DISCURSIVE WRITING

This kind of writing is usually required when you are asked to write an essay or composition which presents two sides of an argument. The ability to do this has many applications as a life-skill as well as being useful when answering questions on literary or topic-work texts. Marks are given for:

- content and organization of ideas
- quality of French in terms of structures, vocabulary and authenticity
- accuracy (spelling and grammar)

Most marks are given for (a) and (b). Therefore, it is important to have a clear plan for your essay (to make sure that the material is arranged logically) and to use vocabulary and expressions that have a genuine French ring to them rather than sounding like English translated into French and to be generally more adventurous with vocabulary and structures. You are asked to write from between 200 to 400 words, depending on the examining Board. Presenting a series of convincing 'for and against' arguments, in so few words, is more difficult than if you had more space in practice. It is important therefore to plan your essay carefully and assemble your ideas before starting to write.

Planning the structure of your essay

The simplest and most effective structure consists of:

- an introduction
- arguments for and arguments against (the main body of the essay)
- conclusion.

First plan out the 'for and against' arguments. The introduction and the conclusion will both be easier to write when you have done this. Start by writing the main idea or cause for debate (not necessarily the title) at the top of the page. Leave a gap and draw a line down the middle of the page. Label each side 'pour and contre' or 'avantages and inconvénients/désavantages'. Leave another gap for your conclusion.

Some people prefer the spider's web or bubble form of patterning for ideas. Others like to write down phrases or words that come to mind as they work through the arguments. If you choose this method leave yourself plenty of space so that you can circle phrases and link them with a pencil line. When you have finished your outline it is a good plan to number your ideas in the order you want to present them. Remember that your best ideas and strongest points are most effective when they are put last in a paragraph or list. You should therefore keep your own point of view for the second half of the essay and end with your main point. This will lead you more naturally into your conclusion.

Illustrative question and answer

La dégradation de notre planète est un processus continuel: on peut le ralentir mais on ne peut l'arrêter.

Here is a topic for debate on an environmental issue, showing how facts and ideas might be assembled.

Two columns

<u>Dégradation de la terre</u>

introduction

l'arrêter

② — Population - les gens se multiplient

③ — Industrie - pollution de l'air, de l'eau

Production de nourriture

① Instabilité de la nature
- impossible de contrôler
- tempêtes, tremblements de terre

④ — Gouvernements ne sont pas en accord

la contrôler

Contrôle de la pollution, progrès déjà faits

- Recyclage des déchets

③ — Sources d'énergie épuisables - charbon, pétrole - conserver
(- nouvelles sources)
- le nucléaire ④

① Capacité de l'homme pour la sauver

⑤ — Contrôle des naissances - action mondiale

conclusion

Spider's web or balloon-linking

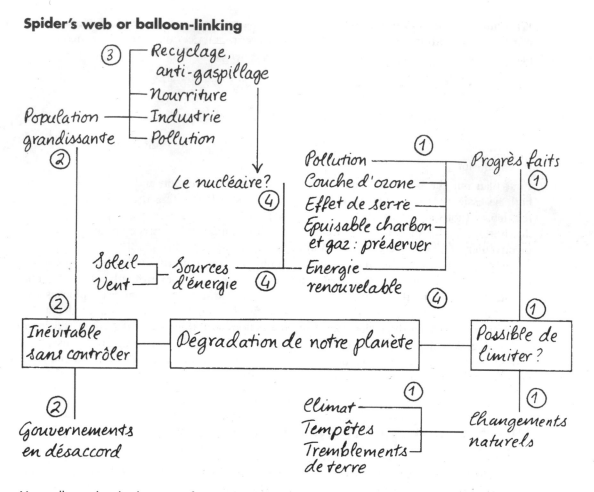

You will see that both ways of assembling ideas rely on writing down words or phrases **in French** so that you get an overview of your thinking and put some order into the ideas for and those against.

Avoid making notes in English and trying to translate them into French. This nearly always leads to anglicized French. If you have read a number of articles, and discussed the topics of essays in class, you should find that phrases stick in your mind. It helps if you make a habit of writing down useful words and phrases on various themes and if you read through these at regular intervals, including the period before the exam.

Having made your plan, and decided which side of the argument you support, you need to write an introduction. The purpose of the introduction is to present the theme which you are going to debate. It can often take the form of a restatement of the title and be expressed as a question to be answered. So taking the title of this essay you could begin:

Est-ce que nous sommes condamnés à accepter la dégradation de notre planète comme inévitable ou pouvons-nous jouer un rôle préventif en limitant autant que possible les effets de la pollution?

You could also make use of a general statement linked to the topicality of the theme:

Les médias ne cessent de nous signaler presque tous les jours de nouveaux exemples de la destruction de notre environnement

and follow this by a question:

Cette dégradation, est-elle inévitable ou pouvons-nous la limiter ou même la contrôler?

Having written the introduction, begin with the side you do not support. Present your ideas in their most effective order, keeping to one idea per paragraph. It makes a better impression if you avoid plunging in with subjective statements like: je crois; je pense; je suis convaincu; or à mon avis. Keep your personal convictions for the conclusion. You can present facts or opinions more objectively by:

(a) using an impersonal verb form
   Il est impossible d'ignorer les problèmes posés par la surpopulation

(b) using the 1st person plural of the verb
   Considérons un problème difficile à ignorer: la surpopulation

(c) using the *on* form
   On ne peut pas ignorer les problèmes posés par la surpopulation

It is better not to overwork these forms though. It is more succinct and just as impersonal to write:

Le problème de la surpopulation est préoccupant.

Having given one side of the argument you need to indicate that you are changing your viewpoint. You can do this by:

(a) the beginning sentence of a paragraph
   Ayant examiné l'impossibilité d'arrêter la dégradation de notre planète, considérons le problème sous un autre aspect/ l'antithèse.

(b) a short paragraph on its own
   Face à cette situation que faire? Accepter notre impuissance à réaliser quoi que ce soit ou adopter une attitude plus sensée en supposant que nous sommes capables au moins de minimiser la dégradation du globe.

A rhetorical question is a very useful bridging device. It is a question to which you do not give an immediate answer.

Having presented the opposing, and in your opinion, the more convincing side of the question, all you need to do is add a short paragraph in conclusion. This can:

(a) simply state your standpoint
   Quoiqu'il ne nous soit pas possible d'arrêter totalement la dégradation de notre planète, je suis persuadé que nous possédons la capacité et les moyens pour contrôler et minimiser les dangers qui menacent l'environnement

(b) point a lesson
   Un pas en arrière, deux pas en avant: cela semble résumer le progrès de notre civilisation et ce sera de la même manière qu'on arrivera à résoudre les problèmes de la dégradation de la terre

(c) express a hope
   Je préfère vivre dans la certitude que l'homme est capable de résoudre ce problème et dans l'espoir que des mesures seront prises dans un contexte mondial

Possible answers

Here are two possible responses to this theme:

1 La dégradation de notre planète est devenue un sujet de débat impossible à ignorer à notre époque. Les médias ne cessent de nous signaler de nouveaux exemples de destruction de notre environnement et de nous avertir des terribles dangers qui pèsent sur nous comme des épées de Damoclès. Faut-il accepter comme inévitable la dégradation de notre globe ou pouvons-nous jouer un rôle préventif?

L'histoire de notre planète nous fait constater que depuis sa naissance elle se trouve dans un état d'évolution perpétuelle. L'éruption des volcans, les tremblements de terre et les extrêmes climatiques nous montrent que la terre, et son atmosphère, ne restent jamais calmes. Bien avant l'arrivée de l'homme, des périodes glaciaires et des périodes de réchauffement se sont succédées à plusieurs reprises et ont apporté de profonds changements à la surface de la terre.

On ne peut pas nier le fait pourtant que c'est l'homme qui a changé et marqué le plus profondément la terre où il a fait son apparition il y a un million d'années. Notons, entre parenthèses, que la présence de l'homme est relativement récente par rapport à l'âge de la planète qui a environ cinq milliards d'années.

Depuis son arrivée il n'a cessé de se multiplier. En 1900 il y avait déjà un milliard d'êtres humains. Aujourd'hui, on en compte cinq milliards. Ce chiffre va doubler avant 2025. Pour subvenir à ses besoins, il a rasé des forêts et fait disparaître de nombreuses espèces animales et végétales: selon certains chercheurs, 75% auraient disparu. A cause des activités industrielles, il a pollué les rivières, la mer et la terre. Un bon nombre de scientifiques pensent que la dégradation de l'atmosphère a conduit le monde au bord d'une catastrophe climatique.

Le rythme de tous ces changements est d'autant plus alarmant que les gouvernements du monde ne sont pas tombés d'accord sur un plan capable de sauver notre planète.

Face à cette situation, que faire? Faut-il contempler ce scénario en spectateur impuissant ou adopter une attitude plus sensée; si l'on ne s'avère pas capable d'arrêter cette destruction il reste néanmoins la possibilité de la minimiser.

La même capacité, qui a permis à l'homme de créer et de perfectionner ses moyens de production, peut être mise en place pour résoudre les problèmes de la pollution. Des progrès dans ce domaine ont déjà porté leurs fruits.

Le recyclage des déchets s'est montré rentable et efficace; les organismes qui s'y consacrent ne manquent pas. Une attitude anti-gaspillage se manifeste dans la population mais pour tirer le maximum de résultats de tout ceci il faudrait inclure les idées anti-gaspillage plus fermement dans les programmes scolaires, surtout au niveau de l'école primaire.

Les sources d'énergie épuisables (comme le charbon, le gaz et le pétrole) doivent être contrôlées et utilisées avec prudence. En même temps, il ne fait aucun doute que les scientifiques perfectionneront les sources d'énergie non-polluantes et renouvelables en utilisant l'action du soleil, du vent ou des marées.

Dans le domaine de l'énergie nucléaire des progrès restent à faire. C'est sans doute par un hasard ironique que l'homme a d'abord fait la découverte de la fission nucléaire au lieu de trouver les secrets de la fusion. Une fois découvert, ce deuxième procédé nous fournira une énergie propre, sans les inconvénients de la radioactivité.

Le problème d'une population mondiale toujours croissante se montre très préoccupant. Des moyens existent pourtant pour limiter le nombre des naissances, que ce soit par des méthodes obligatoires ou volontaires. Mais ce sera surtout par des voies économiques que l'on trouvera une solution car les statistiques prouvent que c'est dans les pays développés que le nombre de naissances se stabilise. Donc pour établir un équilibre de la population mondiale il faudrait améliorer le niveau de vie des pays sous-développés.

Apporter tous ces remèdes s'avèrera inutile si l'homme n'accepte pas de le faire dans un contexte mondial où chaque nation assumera sa responsabilité. Bien qu'il nous semble souvent que l'humanité fasse un pas en arrière et puis deux en avant, force est de constater que finalement nous avançons. Si nous sommes encore incapables d'arrêter totalement la destruction de notre globe, la capacité et les moyens existent pour en contrôler et en minimiser les effets.

2 La dégradation de notre planète se montre le problème le plus préoccupant de notre époque. Est-ce que l'homme possède la capacité d'arrêter ce phénomène ou faut-il se contenter seulement d'en minimiser les plus mauvais effets?

La nature est instable par elle-même. Depuis sa naissance, le monde a vécu des changements fondamentaux. C'est pourtant l'arrivée de l'homme sur la terre, et son intervention, qui l'a marqué de la manière la plus profonde.

La population mondiale ne cesse de s'accroître et elle va doubler d'ici 35 ans. Par un étrange paradoxe, c'est la réussite de l'homme à se nourrir, à se protéger et à prolonger sa vie qui a amené une surpopulation impossible à contrôler.

La pollution qui résulte de presque chaque activité humaine ne cesse également d'augmenter au point que l'environnement devient inhabitable et le climat subit des changements importants. Les gouvernements ne réagissent que trop lentement devant cette situation.

Que devons-nous faire? Pratiquer la politique de l'autruche ou examiner l'horizon des possibilités.

L'intelligence humaine et la créativité peuvent être mises à contribution pour se tirer d'affaire. Non seulement faut-il économiser les sources d'énergie non-renouvelables mais aussi faudrait-il poursuivre la recherche de sources d'énergie non-polluantes.

Il est nécessaire de s'adapter à un nouveau mode de vie sur notre globe où on vivra en harmonie avec la terre. Le recyclage et l'anti-gaspillage feront partie de cette nouvelle attitude.

Des progrès dans le domaine de la prévention de la pollution ont déjà été constatés et l'on prend conscience à l'échelle mondiale de la fragilité de l'espèce humaine.

Si l'homme reste incapable d'arrêter le processus naturel de vieillissement de la terre, il possède néanmoins la capacité à contrôler et à limiter les plus mauvais effets de sa présence.

Essay phrases and vocabulary

It would be an enormous task to give a definitive list of vocabulary and phrases that could be used in any argumentative essay. The following list is based on what students have found useful in giving structure to a piece of writing. It provides only a series of signposts or markers which you will have to fill out with your own ideas and facts. You will find that these marker or structure words sometimes bring you to a halt when trying to put your ideas into order. This is because 'thinking in French' (for the purposes of writing) is often a mixture of thinking in two languages, unless you are totally immersed in them both simultaneously. So, having remembered an authentic phrase like *tous les jours la situation devient de plus en plus préoccupante*, you come to a dead stop with 'according to certain scientists' because you can't think of 'according to' (*selon certains scientifiques* or *de l'avis de certains scientifiques*) or the word for scientists does not come immediately to mind.

The following words and phrases are given with an English equivalent and sometimes given a context:

(a) Introductory paragraph
- (i) *Nous vivons dans un monde où la violence est devenue une norme* –
  We live in a world where violence has become a norm
- (ii) *Chaque année le nombre d'actes terroristes augmente* –
  Every year the number of acts of terrorism is increasing
- (iii) *Il n'est guère possible d'ouvrir le journal sans y découvrir un nouvel exemple de l'inhumanité de l'homme* – You can scarcely open a newspaper without finding a fresh example of man's inhumanity
- (iv) *La violence lors des matchs de football est désormais un problème courant* –
  Violence at football matches is a very common problem nowadays

(b) How to refer to the title as a whole if necessary
- (i) *Cette affirmation/ Cette déclaration/ Cette proposition mérite d'être examinée de plus près*
  – This statement deserves to be looked at more closely

(c) Paragraph openings
- (i) *Examinons d'abord/ en premier lieu/ l'aspect négatif de la question* –
  Let's look first of all at the negative side
- (ii) *Abordons ce problème par une étude de la situation actuelle* –
  Let's tackle this problem by looking at the present situation
- (iii) *Prenons le cas du chômage de longue durée* –
  Take the case of long–term unemployment
- (iv) *Citons l'exemple de ceux qui ont été condamnés à tort pour un crime* –
  Take the example of those wrongly accused of a crime
- (v) *On peut invoquer plusieurs raisons pour que ce problème demeure* –
  We can think of several reasons why this problem will continue

(d) Structure words within the paragraph
- (i) *Plusieurs facteurs ont contribué à la densité de la circulation en ville: **d'abord** les transports urbains ne sont pas suffisants; **ensuite** la voiture est plus confortable que l'autobus, et **enfin** le prix des carburants reste relativement modéré* – Several factors

have contributed to the density of traffic in towns: **in the first place** urban transport is not adequate; **next** cars are more comfortable than buses and **lastly** the price of fuel is relatively low

(ii) *d'une part... d'autre part...* – on the one hand... on the other hand...
D'une part nous ne comprenons pas encore tous les mécanismes de notre climat mais d'autre part certaines tendances comme les sécheresses prolongées sont bien évidentes

(iii) *cependant; pourtant; néanmoins; tout de même* – (all have the approximate meaning of) however; yet; nevertheless; all the same
bref; en un mot – in a word; in short

(iv) *Bref, quelle autre solution peut-on envisager?* –
In a word what other solution can be imagined?

(v) *quant à – en ce qui concerne ____* – as far as ____ is concerned

(vi) *dans ce domaine* – in this field, area (of thought, activity)
Je n'ose guère m' aventurer dans le domaine de la physique nucléaire –
I scarcely dare venture into the field of nuclear physics

(vii) *à cet égard* – in this respect

(viii) *par conséquent/ en conséquence* (**Not** *par conséquence*) – in consequence

(ix) *étant donné que...* – given that...

(x) *d'une façon ou d'une autre* – one way or another

(xi) *après tout* – after all

(xii) *en réalité; en effet* – in fact; in reality

(xiii) *Malgré toutes les prédictions des écologistes* – Despite all the ecologists' forecasts

(xiv) *Grâce aux actions des Amis de la Terre* – Thanks to the action of Friends of the Earth

(e) Impersonal statement introduced by 'il'

(i) *Il est évident/ possible/ probable/ certain/ clair que cette politique a échoué* –
It is possible/probable/certain/clear that this policy has failed

Note The construction here is *il est* + adjective + *que* + noun (*see also* subjunctive, page 74)

There are other examples where the construction is *il est* + adjective + *de* + infinitive:

(ii) *Il est dangereux de fermer les yeux devant cette situation*

(iii) *Il est impossible d'ignorer ces problèmes*

(iv) *Il est facile de ne rien faire*

(v) *Il est important de considérer toutes les possibilités*

Here are some other vital phrases:

(vi) *Il faut* – It is necessary

(vii) *Il nous faut* – We must

(viii) *Il faudrait* – We should

(ix) *Il nous faudrait* – We ought to

(x) *Il reste peu de temps* – There's not much time left

(xi) *Il manque des ressources* – Resources are lacking/There is a lack of....
or *Il y a un manque de ressources*

(xii) *Il s'agit/ Il est question de valeurs personnelles* – It's a question of personal values

(xiii) *Il suffit d'un sourire pour faire confiance aux gens* –
All that's needed is a smile to inspire confidence

(f) Increases/decreases

(i) *Le nombre d'accidents de la route augmente/ s'accroît* –
The number of road accidents is rising

(ii) *Le taux des naissances diminue* – The birth rate is falling/dropping

(iii) *Une augmentation des salaires* – An increase in wages

(iv) *Une baisse sur les marchés internationaux* – A fall on foreign markets

(v) *Une hausse des niveaux de la mer* – A rise in sea levels

(vi) *Le coût de la vie est en hausse* – The cost of living is up

(g) Numbers of people or things

(i) *La plupart des gens/ bien des gens* – Many people

(ii) *Beaucoup de gens ont refusé de payer leur impôt* –
Many people have refused to pay their tax

    (iii) *Certains prétendent que l'impôt est injuste, d'autres affirment le contraire* –
        Some claim the tax is unfair, others say the opposite
    (iv) *Comme nous l'avons déjà dit/signalé/fait remarquer/indiqué/affirmé/constaté/souligné*
        –
        As already stated/indicated/pointed out/shown/noted/stressed

(h) Perhaps/may be
    (i)   *Nos scientifiques ont peut-être tort*
    (ii) *Peut-être nos scientifiques ont-ils tort*
    (iii) *Peut-être qu'ils ont tort, nos scientifiques*

Inversion is needed if you begin with *peut-être*. Similarly with *sans doute*:

    (iv) *Sans doute ces opinions sont-elles mal fondées* –
        Doubtless these opinions are not well-founded

Note
    (v) *Il se peut que* – It may be that
    (vi) *Il se peut que nous ayons tous tort* – It may be that we are all wrong

(i) Times and periods
    (i)   *de nos jours/ à l'époque actuelle/ à l'époque où nous vivons* –
        at the present time, nowadays etc.
    (ii) *à l'avenir* – in the future
    (iii) *les générations futures* – future generations
    (iv) *autrefois* – formerly
    (v) *jadis* – in times past
    (vi) *du temps de mon grand-père* – in my grandfather's day
    (vii) *à l'âge de pierre* – in the stone age
    (viii)*à l'époque médiévale/victorienne* – in medieval/victorian times
    (ix) *au début de ce siècle* – at the beginning of the century
    (x) *dans les années 90* – in the nineties
    (xi) *pendant longtemps* – for a long time
    (xii) *en moins d'un siècle* – in less than a century

(j) Giving examples/quoting opinion
    (i)   *citons en exemple/à titre d'exemple* – (as titles above – **note** spelling of *exemple*)
    (ii) *prenons l'exemple de/le cas de* – let's take the example/case of
    (iii) *selon certains chercheurs* – according to some researchers
    (iv) *à en croire les experts* – if the experts are to be believed
    (v) *l'un des exemples les plus frappants* – one of the most striking examples

(k) Comparisons
    (i)   *certains disent que... d'autres prétendent que...* – some say that... others claim that...
    (ii) *Comparées à nos autoroutes, celles de France sont mieux entretenues et aménagées* –
        Compared to our motorways, the French ones are better maintained and have more
        facilities
    (iii) *faisons une comparaison entre/avec* – let's make a comparison between/with
    (iv) *si l'on compare notre époque à celle d'avant-guerre* –
        if you compare our times with those before the war
    (v) *en contraste/par rapport à la situation actuelle* – compared with the situation today
    (vi) *Le professeur français est mieux payé que son homologue britannique* –
        The French school teacher is better paid than his British counterpart

(l) Conclusions
    (i)   *tout bien considéré* – taking everything into consideration
    (ii) *en fin de compte* – when all said and done
    (iii) *il faut conclure que* – we must conclude that
    (iv) *en conclusion affirmons que* – in conclusion let us say that
    (v) *Au lieu de sombrer dans le désespoir je préfère adopter une attitude optimiste* –
        Instead of wallowing in despair I prefer to take an optimistic attitude

Further reading
R Hares and G Elliot, (1984), *Compo! French Literature Essay Writing*, Hodder & Stoughton

4.2   READING

Contents

- Reading comprehension: questions and answers in English

- Reading comprehension: questions and answers in French

- Reading comprehension: questions in French on a passage in English

Comprehension of a text is tested by a variety of different tasks: questions and answers in English, in French; translation into English; translation into French of a short piece of English based on the text; and lastly by a battery of tests that could include the following: summary in English or French; paraphrase and explanation; gap-filling; true/false statements.

QUESTIONS AND ANSWERS IN ENGLISH

One of the ways of testing understanding of a text is to ask questions about it in English. This is one of the tasks set by several Examination Boards. Questions are normally in the same sequence as the points in the text and sometimes the place in the text is indicated as is also the number of marks to be scored (by each question). The latter can be a useful guide to the relative difficulty of the question, but more importantly, a rough indication of the number of points or details that you are expected to include in your answer. Questions are usually phrased in such a way that they cannot be answered by straight translation of a piece of the text. It is of little use translating a likely bit of the text in the hope that this will somehow do. Examiners are looking for answers that show that you have understood the passage.

Very often questions will be **factual** ones requiring details to be extracted from the text. The number of facts will usually correspond with the mark allocation.

Some questions may be what are called **inference** or **interpretive** questions. This means that details will be implied rather than stated and you will have to do some deduction and use your common sense. There may also be clues in other parts of the text.

Some questions could also be **evaluative** ones. This means you are expected to be able to make your own assessment or judgement about the intentions or attitude of the author that are revealed in the way he or she has written (see *below* for examples of these).

Read quickly through the questions. They will give you some idea of what the passage is about. Then read through the passage twice. Return to the questions and read each one carefully and find the part of the text that contains the information required. Try to stand back from the text when working out your answer. Review the information given in the sentence before, as well as the one following, the place you are looking at, rather than keep on reading over the same phrase or group of words. Also, when working out your answer have a glance at the next question. You may find that you are jumping ahead with details needed for that question rather than the one you are doing. If a dictionary is allowed only use it to check the meanings of words essential to the answer or words in your answer.
"What", "how" and "why" questions usually predominate, followed in frequency by the instructions "describe", "explain" or "list". If you are not required to write in full sentences don't waste time by repeating part of the question in the answer. Marks are given for particular elements from the text required for that question. You have to show that you have understood the text and include all relevant details. Extra material is not usually penalised but you risk taxing the patience of the marker if they have to plough through a lot of words to find a relevant bit. So be brief wherever possible.

Illustrative question and answer

LA GRANDE PEUR DES TRAINS DE BANLIEUE

Toutes les statistiques de l'État ou de la SNCF n'y feront rien: on a peur aujourd'hui de prendre les trains dans la banlieue parisienne.

Que cette peur soit fondée ou non, peu importe. L'essentiel est qu'elle existe. Une partie de la population, la plus vulnérable, les femmes, les personnes âgées, sont devenues des 'exclus du train'.

Bref, la peur a envahi les trains de banlieue. C'est ce qui ressort d'une enquête effectuée auprès des usagers de la gare de Juvisy-sur-Orge, dans la banlieue parisienne. N'ont répondu que ceux qui le souhaitaient. Les réponses, dont une forte proportion émane de jeunes filles, démontrent que le sentiment d'insécurité est bien réel: un usager sur deux affirme avoir rencontré des problèmes d'insécurité. Et, même sans avoir été soi-même victime, on a peur.

La principale cause de l'insécurité c'est celle des attroupements de désœuvrés, de marginaux et de bandes à proximité des portillons de contrôle. La seconde cause qui génère ce sentiment dans les gares, c'est la fraude. «Le fait de voir régulièrement les mêmes catégories d'individus sautant par-dessus les portillons crée un sentiment de malaise. Pourquoi payer bêtement son ticket?» demande un voyageur. Et pour beaucoup la présence d'un agent SNCF, qui n'a aucune possibilité matérielle d'intervenir semble indiquer une certaine résignation officielle.

Troisième cause du sentiment d'insécurité: la malpropreté, les graffiti et les dégradations. «La sécurité, c'est aussi la propreté», assure un voyageur.

On critique aussi la déshumanisation des gares: «Le plus angoissant, c'est un train désert, dans une gare déserte. Aux heures de déjeuner, et le soir tard, il ne reste dans la gare que des bandes». Et puis, la gare franchie, il faut affronter une nouvelle épreuve, celle du train. Et là on retrouve les même critiques, le même sentiment d'isolement aux heures creuses.

Pour mettre un terme à cette panique, les voyageurs veulent la présence de policiers. «Un autre être humain est plus rassurant. Il peut intervenir immédiatement.» La peur du gendarme reste 'payante'. Aussi réclame-t-on plus d'agents de la SNCF, en uniforme: "Il faudrait que la SNCF ait des surveillants armés et accompagnés d'un ou deux bergers allemands. Tout redeviendrait calme".

UCLES

1 Répondez VRAI ou FAUX.
(a) l'insécurité dans les trains est en baisse (1)
(b) toutes les personnes sondées ont répondu (1)
(c) la moitié des usagers ont été témoins d'incidents désagréables (1)
(d) une fois dans le train, l'usager se sent plus en sécurité (1)
(e) la public voudrait que le personnel de la SNCF porte des armes (1)

2 Identifiez dans le passage un mot ou une expression correspondant à la même idée que les mots ou groupes de mots suivants:
(Exemple: faire face à…Réponse: affronter)
(a) ne changeront rien à l'affaire (1)
(b) justifiée (1)
(c) c'est la conclusion qu'on peut tirer de… (1)
(d) d'une manière stupide (1)
(e) les moments de peu d'affluence (1)

3 Answer **in English** the following questions in such a way as to show that you have understood the passage.
(a) What categories of traveller feel particularly threatened? (2)
(b) What is the principal reason for the insecurity felt by many rail travellers in the

Paris region? (2)

(c) Explain what you understand by *la fraude*, and give examples of such *fraude* and official reactions to it. (4)

(d) Describe the condition of many stations and explain how this contributes to the sense of insecurity. (3)

(e) What do passengers see as solutions to the problems described in the passage? (4)

Possible answer

1 (a) *faux* (l'insécurité est en hausse "on a peur aujourd'hui de prendre le train" cette peur "existe")*

(b) *faux* (seulement ceux qui ont voulu ont répondu "n'ont répondu que ceux qui le souhaitaient" ne...que = 'only')

(c) *vrai* ("un usager sur deux affirme avoir rencontré des problèmes d'insécurité")

(d) *faux* ("la gare franchie, il faut affronter une nouvelle épreuve, celle du train")

(e) *vrai* ("Il faudrait que la SNCF ait des surveillants armés")

* *The part in brackets is there to help you and is not required in the examination*

2 (a) "n'y feront rien" = 'will have no effect'

(b) "fondée" = 'founded, based'

(c) "c'est ce qui ressort d'une enquête" = 'this is what emerges from an enquiry'

(d) "bêtement" 'bête' = 'stupid'

(e) "aux heures creuses" = literally 'at empty times'

3 (a) This is a factual question. Two details are required: women and the elderly.

(b) Again a factual question, needing two details: large numbers of dropouts and unemployed that hang about the ticket barriers at stations.

(c) A factual and evaluative question: intentional dishonesty, deliberate breaking of the law; ticket dodgers jump over the barriers to avoid paying; railway officials, who see what is happening but cannot prevent it, create the impression of indifference to the situation.

(d) A factual and evaluative question: stations are dirty, covered in graffiti and in a poor state of repair. The poor state of repair and appearance of many stations create the impression that no one cares; this makes people feel insecure.

(e) A factual question: police presence at stations, seeing a gendarme does have an effect; more uniformed railway staff; they need to be armed and have guard dogs with them.

QUESTIONS AND ANSWERS IN FRENCH

Many Examining Boards test reading comprehension partly or wholly by asking questions about a text in French. Most of the remarks about answering questions in English also apply here. Read the passage through several times before you start writing. You will not necessarily have to understand every word fully in order to answer the questions. You will not be able to copy down a likely looking bit of the text as an answer. You may however be able to use some of the original words, provided that you make appropriate grammatical changes. Marks are usually given for conveying the details rather than for the accuracy of the French. It helps to remember this when you are trying to find your own words in French. Inference and interpretive questions might also be used, as well as evaluative ones.

An extract from the marking scheme of the Cambridge Board's Specimen Syllabus best sums up what Examiners are looking for:

"We are looking for comprehension of the text and the ability to express the content in the candidate's own words. Marks are awarded entirely for content, i.e. if the answers are clearly comprehensible and in the candidate's own French, no account is taken of linguistic error. Material may be used verbatim from from the original text as long as it is clear from the context that it is used with understanding."

Illustrative questions and answers

EXAMPLE 1

PROFESSION: CHEF DE PUBLICITÉ

Florence Ducrocq, 24 ans, travaille comme chef de publicité.
Un métier qui la passionne. Et lui donne l'envie d'aller plus loin.
Pour aborder les rivages de la publicité, Florence Ducrocq, vingt-quatre ans, s'est bien qualifiée avant d'entrer en janvier 1990 chez McCann Erickson comme chef de publicité junior.

Très vite, le métier la fascine. Elle apprécie tout particulièrement la variété des tâches qui lui sont confiées. Son rôle? Orchestrer, face au client, l'ensemble des services de l'agence afin que créatifs, média-planners et producteurs travaillent à l'unisson. En collaboration avec un chef de groupe, elle a en charge le budget Esso. "Chaque début d'année, le client fait une analyse de son marché et nous expose ses objectifs de communcation. «Chaque début d'année, Florence Ducrocq planche donc sur les dossiers marketing de la marque. "Toutes ces données bien assimilées, l'agence rédige une sorte de cahier des charges qui va fixer la cible visée par la campagne, les objectifs.»

Si le client l'accepte, s'ouvre alors le second volet du métier: le suivi de la réalisation. «Respecter les plannings, transmettre les objectifs et les contraintes de coûts de la campagne à l'équipe média. Bref, organiser et mobiliser un groupe de travail.»

Tout au long du processus, Florence Ducrocq est en relation permanente avec son client: «Mes contacts avec Esso sont presque quotidiens. Il y a toujours une opération en cours.»

Priorité au contact

Autant dire que l'aspect relationnel est essentiel, tant pour convaincre l'annonceur que pour motiver ses collaborateurs. Mais Florence Ducrocq a le goût du contact, et se sent parfaitement à l'aise dans sa fonction. «Il règne dans l'agence une ambiance conviviale, et je travaille dans un climat de confiance.» En dépit de ses horaires démentiels et de son salaire modest à l'embauche, elle est de toute évidence animée par la même passion qu'à ses débuts. Son souhait pour l'avenir: passer rapidement chef de groupe, puis évoluer jusqu'au poste de directeur de clientèle, chez McCann ou dans une autre agence. «En tout cas, c'est sûr, je resterai dans le secteur de la communication.» Quand le virus vous tient…

Questions and answers

Répondez *en français* aux questions suivantes:

1 Qu'est-ce que vous comprenez exactement par "un travail à l'unisson", et comment cette expression s'explique-t-elle ici?
You have here to understand and be able to paraphrase the phrase "un travail à l'unisson" and then find ways it is exemplified in the text.
Tout le monde travaille ensemble, c'est un travail d'équipe. Florence doit coopérer avec ses collègues et ses collègues avec elle. On travaille pour réaliser une tâche donnée. Florence doit diriger et orchestrer le travail.

2 Florence a le goût du contact avec les gens. Expliquez pourquoi cela est important dans le travail qu'elle a choisi.
Elle prend plaisir à travailler avec ses collègues et avec les clients. Elle se met en contact avec les clients pour connaître leurs besoins et établir une cible visée. Elle crée ainsi un climat de confiance mutuelle et une bonne ambiance.

3 Sans utiliser les mots du texte, expliquez ce que nous apprenons sur ses heures de travail et sur son salaire.
Ses heures de travail sont absolument folles/très longues/la plupart des gens ne seraient pas prêts à travailler tant; son salaire n'est pas très gros/elle n'est pas très bien payée.

4 Pourquoi est-elle si heureuse dans son travail?
Elle adore ce métier et le contact avec les gens. Elle aime surtout la variété des tâches. Elle est ambitieuse et voudrait progresser dans sa profession/obtenir de la promotion.

EXAMPLE 2

UN JEUNE HOMME SEUL

Il avait fait part, un soir, de sa décision à ses parents: «Je ne retournerai pas demain au lycée, je veux travailler...»

C'était au milieu de l'hiver. Il allait au lycée à bicyclette et, malgré deux paires de gants de laine, ses mains gelaient sur le guidon. Il pédalait avec une main dans la poche de son manteau; mais le froid saisissait si vite les doigts qu'avant même que la main dans la poche fût réchauffée, la main sur le guidon était déjà gelée. Au long des trois kilomètres qui séparaient sa maison du lycée, la souffrance devenait vite tellement intolérable qu'il était obligé de s'arrêter plusieurs fois, de poser son vélo contre un mur, de retirer ses gants et de réchauffer ses mains en soufflant dedans, tout en sautant sur place pour que les pieds ne gèlent pas à leur tour. Or, les ouvriers qu'il croisait et qui gagnaient leur chantier à vélo, portaient des gants de cuir. Il était visible qu'ils ne souffraient pas aux mains. Ces gants de cuir étaient en vente, mais Victoria Favart s'était refusée obstinément à donner à son fils la somme nécessaire; elle déclarait que deux paires de gants de laine suffisent assurément à protéger les doigts des plus grands froids, que le cuir relève du snobisme, que ses parents n'étaient pas des millionnaires; et qu'il devait les remercier des sacrifices qu'ils s'imposaient pour lui faire faire des études.

Eugène-Marie en était donc venu tout naturellement à envier le sort des ouvriers, qui pouvaient prendre sur leur salaire l'achat d'une paire de gants. Il était persuadé que tout ce qu'il avait appris au lycée ne comportait aucune application pratique et qu'il ne gagnerait bien sûr pas autant qu'un ouvrier.

Sa décision était donc irrévocable. Ni raisonnements, ni supplications, n'avaient pu l'amener à céder.

«Mais enfin, pourquoi ne veux-tu plus aller au lycée?» demandait son père. Il avait refusé toute explication, par honte d'avouer que c'était parce qu'il avait trop froid aux mains sur son vélo le matin. Son père s'était mis en colère. Puis il l'avait battu.

Il s'était d'abord laissé battre. Puis, soudain, il avait relevé la tête et crié: «Frappe donc, grand lâche. Quand je serai grand, je te frapperai à mon tour et bien plus fort».

NEAB

Questions and answers

1 Que pensez-vous des raisons que donne Victoria Favart dans la section "elle déclarait... relevait du snobisme" pour refuser la demande de son fils (2)
This is an evaluative question because you have to give your opinion about the mother's excuses for not buying leather gloves. It is important to make your answers clear.
C'est vrai que les gants de cuir sont plus chers, mais les autres raisons ne sont pas très convaincantes. On voit ici les préjugés de la mère.

2 Selon Victoria, son fils devrait remercier ses parents des sacrifices qu'ils ont faits. Êtes-vous d'accord avec elle? (2)

An evaluative question because you have to give a personal opinion about the mother's attitude. (2)

Vous devez être sensible aux efforts que vos parents font pour vous mais vous pouvez montrer votre gratitude de plusieurs façons.

3 Eugène-Marie refuse de donner le vrai motif de sa conduite. A votre avis, ce refus est-il raisonnable? (2)

A personal opinion is required with a reason for it.

Non, son attitude est plutôt stupide. Il devrait faire comprendre le vrai motif à son père qui va croire que c'est tout simplement parce qu'il n'aime pas l'école.

4 Si vous aviez été le père d'Eugène-Marie est-ce que vous auriez agi de la même façon? Donnez vos raisons. (2)

A personal opinion, with reasons, is required.

Non, je n'aurais pas agi comme cela. J'aurais essayé de découvrir les vraies raisons de sa conduite. Il faut être plus patient et plus, comprehensif et prendre le temps pour parler et surtout pour écouter.

5 Qu'est-ce que vous pensez du caractère d'Eugène-Marie? Justifiez votre réponse en 60 mots environ. (5)

An evaluative and interpretive question. It calls for a personal opinion based on the evidence of various parts of the text.

C'est un jeune homme, enfant unique peut-être, sans beaucoup d'expérience de la vie. Sa décision de quitter l'école est fondée sur de mauvaises raisons. Il est timide et réservé. Il a peur de ses parents. Il ne sait pas communiquer avec eux. Il est capable quand même de prendre des décisions et d'être buté. C'est sa colère refoulée qui se montre à la fin de l'extrait.

Study techniques

❶ Try every week to read part of a French magazine or newspaper. Pick out an article which interests you and make up ten questions on it. Write your answers to the questions. Then, if possible, get a friend to answer your questions. Compare your answers and help each other to produce the best possible answers.

❷ Use passages from your set texts to do the same kind of exercise. This should give you the opportunity to invent and practise 'evaluation' and 'interpretation' questions.

❸ Get from your library copies of past papers from the Board for whose exams you are preparing. Work through these. Try to find another student (or your teacher) to look at and comment on your work.

QUESTIONS IN FRENCH ON A PASSAGE IN ENGLISH

This task, used by some of the Boards, puts you in the situation of having to explain details of an article to a French person who cannot fully understand the article themselves. The task is very like the reporting one in some oral examinations except that specific questions are usually asked and these might include a résumé of part of the passage. The number of marks awarded for each answer is also given. Marks are given for: (a) content and language; or (b) accurate transmission of information, depending on the Board. The second requirement does not exclude completely considerations of language however, since you are still faced with the problem of getting the meaning across in French.

Illustrative questions and answers

EXAMPLE 1

In one of his regular letters, your French correspondent sends you this cutting from an English Sunday newspaper which he has come across in his school library.

GO FORTH AND MULTIPLY
Stubborn French ignore call to reproduce

Mother's Day in France, unlike in Britain, is a serious political occasion. On this day, in the pomp of the Elysée Palace, the Head of State receives a group of mothers who have been awarded the Médaille de la famille française. Meanwhile, across the whole country, the same ceremony takes place in hundreds of town halls. On behalf of the State, M. Mitterrand thanks the mothers for their courage, their dignity, but above all for their willingness to have a lot of children – eight or more if they are to have the Gold medal! These mothers are left in no doubt that they have guaranteed the survival of the nation.

For almost a century, France has been obsessed with raising the birth rate. Between 1946 and 1958, the French population increased by 10 million. In later life, General de Gaulle liked to claim personal responsibility for this miracle. After all it was he who had told the French, back in 1945, that 'we must have 12 million beautiful babies in the next ten years'.

But the General's speeches had much less influence than American economic aid after 1945, with the dramatic improvement in living standards that this helped bring about. As couples found they had more money to spend, they became more inclined to have children. In this, France was no different from other West European countries, but what made France unusual was its retention of repressive populationist measures from the pre-War era. A country which did not give women the vote until 1944 had no difficulty in outlawing contraceptives until 1967 and abortion until 1975. Even today, politicians periodically plead for 'le retour de la femme au foyer' – meaning 'a woman's place is in the home'.

Michel Rocard, when Prime Minister, had the courage to admit that governments can only have a marginal influence on the birth-rate, yet his government tried to stimulate the birth rate by means of extremely generous family allowances and sweeping concessions on public transport for members of large families. The ultimate purpose of such measures, however, is to halt the ageing of the French population. An element in this debate which is inevitably exploited by the National Front among others is the high birth rate of African and Arab immigrants.

Répondez en français aux questions suivantes.

1 (a) Comment voit-on que la Fête des Mères a une signification politique en France?
(4)
Parce que la Fête est marquée par des cérémonies à l'Elysée et partout en France. Le Président ou le maire remercient les mères de leur contribution à la santé et à l'économie du pays.

(b) Pourquoi le Général de Gaulle estimait-il que c'était grâce à lui que la population française avait augmenté après 1945? (4)
Parce que c'était lui qui avait encouragé les familles françaises à mettre au monde 12 million de bébés dans les dix ans après la guerre.

(c) Dans quelle mesure est-ce que l'augmentation de la population a été due à l'amélioration du niveau de vie des Français? (4)
Cette amélioration est en grande partie due à l'aide économique des Etats Unis mais il ne faut pas oublier le fait que les préservatifs et l'avortement étaient proscrits pendant cette période.

(d) Quelle avait été la politique de Michel Rocard dans ce domaine? (4)
Il avait encouragé des familles nombreuses en subventionnant pour elles le coût du transport publique pour leurs enfants et en augmentant les allocations familiales. (total 16 marks)

Note

The marking scheme for this Board in question 1 gives 2 marks for content and 2 for correctness of French. Each answer requires two statements drawn from the text and each statement is awarded 1+1 for content and language. You need to communicate the points as briefly as possible. Any French you write which is not connected with the point required will not be marked for mistakes.

2 'La politique française dans le domaine des droits de la femme a été longtemps très rétrograde... et continue de l'être.'
Relevez dans la passage quelques exemples de cette attitude et donnez vos réactions personnelles.
Ecrivez *en français* un maximum de 140 mots. (30)
UCLES

Possible answer

Je suis étonné(e) de constater que c'est seulement après 1944 que les Françaises ont eu le droit de vote. Les contraceptifs ont été proscrits jusqu'en 1967 et l'avortement jusqu'en 1975. Cela aussi est étonnant. Ces deux mesures restreignent la liberté des femmes dans un monde gouverné par les hommes. Même aujourd'hui les hommes politiques français demandent le retour de la femme au foyer. Les généreuses allocations familiales pourraient encourager les gens à procréer seulement pour obtenir l'argent de l'Etat. La fameuse médaille d'or même est décernée pour une seule activité féminine, la procréation. Douze enfants dans une seule famille c'est ridicule. Combien de gens possèdent une maison assez grande pour ce nombre d'enfants? C'est dommage que la médaille ne soit pas accordée aujourd'hui pour honorer des réussites plus valorisantes pour la femme.
135 mots (24 marks)

Note from the Board
The purpose of this exercise is to draw material from the original text, to get across the main lines of the argument in French and express personal opinions as requested. Of the 24 marks awarded, 10 are for Content, including that drawn from the original text, and 14 are for Quality of Language, divided between Accuracy and Range/Fluency.

EXAMPLE 2

BYE-BYE THE BOULANGERIE

Do you remember when *la boucherie, la boulangerie* and *l'épicerie* of your first French lessons could be found in every village in France? Not so long ago, the French countryside was full of small, family-run shops selling local products. But mass distribution has changed all that. Today, the approach to a French country town is all too often dominated by a monolithic hypermarket, with immense car park, and many of the smaller stores have closed down.

In an effort to help small businesses, the minister for business and economic development has vowed to enforce existing checks on the spread of such superstores rigorously. 'We want to keep our rural economies alive', he says.

The existing law limiting the expansion of hypermarket chains has not been effective. Big distributors dominate the market, supported by local and regional authorities keen to attract such thriving business. The number of hypermarkets has risen from 200 in 1964 to around 1,000 now. The companies involved with hypermarkets would like that number to double. The minister's announcement infuriates them. 'We denounce this return to old-style reactionary interventionism', declared the owner of the Leclerc hypermarket chain. Spokesmen for other big chains argue that jobs will be lost if their business is hurt, and that in a country where unemployment is running at more than 10% this is a key consideration. The small shopkeepers are in raptures about the government's decision. There are still millions of small shopkeepers in France, and they are overwhelmingly conservative. The decision to halt the construction of hypermarkets is above all a politically correct step. It is seen as preserving a way of life that might otherwise have disappeared and which is viewed with excessive nostalgia by young and old. The French government faces two other problems that are at least as serious as unemployment: depopulation and urban sprawl. Large areas of the French countryside are becoming deserted as their inhabitants move to larger towns which offer some limited economic opportunity. *Desertification* as the French call it, cannot be ignored, especially in a country where, experts say, at least 25% of the population is always trying to move to Paris. A French hypermarket, placed on the outskirts of a country town has what one could call the Pied Piper effect. It draws away all the economic life from the shops in the vicinity. And as the small towns around the urban centre with its hypermarket become deserted, the town boasting the hypermarket swells into an ugly urban mass. Hence the concern, voiced by the Prime Minister, to halt the desertification. 'We are not at all opposed to progress, but we would like to reconsider the system of distribution as it was conceived almost 20 years ago, to ensure that it is correctly adapted to life today.

For now, the government is supporting the traditional lifestyle, but nobody knows how long that support will last.

1 Répondez **en français** aux questions suivantes:

(a) Quelle distinction fait-on entre le petit commerce traditionnel dans une ville de province française et le commerce moderne situé en dehors de la ville?　　(4)

　　Le petit commerce est souvent dirigé par le propriétaire et sa famille et on vend des produits de la région. Le commerce moderne est très vaste, avec un grand parking et fait de la grande distribution.

(b) Quelles sont les mesures prises par le ministre, et pour quelles raisons?　　(4)

　　Il essaie d'empêcher les hypermarchés de se multiplier en imposant rigoureusement une loi déjà existante. Ces derniers font trop de concurrence. Le ministre veut porter secours aux petites entreprises et faire vivre l'économie rurale.

(c) Quelles sont les réactions des grands distributeurs face aux mesures proposées? Quelle sera la conséquence principale de ces mesures, selon eux?　　(4)

　　Ils sont furieux et considèrent ces mesures comme réactionnaires et une intervention gouvernementale qui date d'une autre époque. Ces mesures augmenteront assurément un taux de chômage déjà en hausse.

(d) Sa décision est naturellement très populaire parmi les millions de petits commerçants en France qui sont plutôt conservateurs. Le ministre rencontre beaucoup de sympathie aussi parmi les jeunes et les vieux qui ne veulent pas voir disparaître une ancienne qualité de vie.　　(4)

2 Après avoir résumé les arguments pour et les arguments contre le développement des chaînes d'hypermarchés, donnez votre avis personnel sur ce problème. Pensez-vous que cette expansion soit un signe de progrès ou, au contraire, que cette expansion détruise une qualité de vie qui existait auparavant?

Ecrivez **en français** un maximum de 140 mots　　(24)

UCLES

Possible answer

Les hypermarchés sont un grand succès et se sont répandus à travers toute la France. Ils achètent et vendent en gros, tout y est donc moins cher. Ils fournissent beaucoup d'emplois, au contraire des petits commerces.

Les petits commerces font vivre l'économie rurale et diminuent l'exode vers les grandes villes. La construction des hypermarchés entraîne une extension des agglomérations aux alentours des grandes villes et augmente la désertification de la campagne et des villages.

Je pense que les hypermarchés ont l'avantage d'être plus pratiques et moins chers. Ils représentent un certain progrès. Mais ils se trouvent souvent loin du centre ville et il faut y accéder en voiture, ce qui est difficile pour les vieux et les moins nantis. Je regretterais la disparition totale du petit commerçant obligeant et l'animation du commerce local. Il faut trouver un équilibre entre le progrès et les structures du passé.

Study skill

Make a collection of short articles in English about France. Useful sources are books on French background and the more serious newspapers. *The European* newspaper is a good source of material. Practise by reading and underlining the main points and then finding words to convey the information. It is better if you can practise brief summaries for a French person (e.g. a pen-friend).

4.3 TRANSLATION

Contents

- Translation into English
- Retranslation

TRANSLATION INTO ENGLISH

You may have to translate a whole text into English, or extracts from a text, as part of a group of language tasks. There are two aspects to this:
(a) understanding what the text means
(b) giving a version of it that sounds and reads like English.
The usual pitfalls are:

❶ Not understanding or knowing what words mean (when a dictionary is not allowed).

❷ Making a mistake with a word because it looks like another one or like an English word (e.g. *volant* – steering wheel confused with *voleur* – thief or *des milliers de personnes* – thousands (not millions) of people); or because it is a *faux ami*, exactly like an English word but with a different meaning in French (e.g. *sensible* means 'sensitive' not 'sensible' which is *sensé*).

❸ Not understanding because of grammar or syntax (e.g. *selon les informations il y aurait deux morts* – according to the news two people are supposed to have died, not 'would be dead'; *les touristes que m'envoyait le bureau* not 'the tourists that sent me the office' but 'the tourists that the office sent me' — subjects often follow the verb like this in French).

❹ Giving a word for word translation, based closely on the word order of the French. The result is something that sounds more like French than English:

A partir de ce soir, 20 heures, les usagers de la SNCF connaîtront trois jours bien difficiles – At leaving of this evening the users of the SNCF will know three days very difficult.

The latter kind of pitfall usually disappears fairly quickly with practice. You do need to read through your translation, aloud if possible and to someone else, to test whether it sounds like English. Numbers ❶ to ❸ are remedied by lots of practice and getting to know your *bons amis* and your *faux amis*.

Read through a sentence several times before attempting a translation and try to keep all the bits of meaning together in your mind before assembling them. With long sentences, it helps to read them through several times quickly in your mind, pausing at commas or semi-colons. Try to sort the sentence into natural blocks of meaning. If you get stuck on this find the main verbs and try to establish what their subjects and objects are. Remember too that there is often more than one way of translating tenses into English. The present and perfect tenses, for example, could each have three possibilities (*see* pages 49 and 52). You might find it is necessary to rearrange the order of the sentence to make it sound like good English. Another tip: English verbs, unlike French ones, are rich in their use of prepositions. Bear this in mind when reading your translation out aloud. You can often give it a more English flavour by the change or insertion of a preposition.

When you are reading through your version check that all the meaning of the original is there. Sometimes the meaning of quite small words has been confused (e.g. the definite or indefinite articles, the demonstrative adjective *ce, cette* etc. or pronouns and adjectives).

It is also worth remembering that more than one version is usually possible. The perfect translation is said not to exist although the following has been cited as near perfect:

Est-ce que la vie vaut la peine d'être vécue? Question de foi(e) –
Is life worth living? It depends on the liver

Practice questions

1 Try correcting the English of the publicity brochure below:

2 (a) Complete the same exercise as for question 1 but this time you also have the original French:

HOW TO VISIT THE EIFFEL TOWER

The most beautiful view over Paris is from the second floor. From the 1st floor, Paris seems run-over as one finds one's self at the level of the highest roofs. From the 3rd floor, everything seems too small and one cannot distinguish many of its monuments, but when the weather is clear, one has a magnificent view of the country surrounding Paris.

Forty per cent of the visitors ascend to the 3rd floor. The price of the ascent and the waits for the lifts discourage many as, in the best season, the wait to take the lift from the 2nd to the 3rd floor is often from 30 to 40 minutes.

I advise going first to the 2nd floor and making a tour of it. Then mount to the 3rd floor, tour it, and write postal cards which bear a special 'top of the Tower' stamp, and then go down to the 1st floor (you will find restaurants there suited to every pocket book).

COMMENT VISITER LA TOUR EIFFEL

La plus belle vue sur Paris est depuis la deuxième plate-forme. Au premier étage, Paris semble un peu écrasé car on se trouve au niveau des toits les plus hauts. Au troisième, tout semble trop petit, on ne distingue plus bien les monuments; en revanche, par temps clair, on a une très belle vue sur les environs de Paris.

40% des visiteurs montent au troisième étage. Le prix de la montée et l'attente aux ascenseurs en découragent beaucoup: en effet à la belle saison, l'attente au deuxième étage pour prendre l'ascenseur du troisième est souvent de 30 à 45 minutes.

Je conseille d'abord d'aller au deuxième, en faire le tour. Puis monter au troisième, bien le visiter, y écrire des cartes postales qui recevront une oblitération spéciale du sommet de la tour, puis s'arrêter au premier en redescendant et y faire un repas (restaurants à tous les prix: luxe et brasserie).

(b) How many marks out of ten would you give the original translation for:
   (i) accuracy (are any parts totally wrong?)
   (ii) style (how 'English' it sounds)

(c) Have any important bits of meaning been left out?

3 Here is part of an article singing the praises of butter:

> **QU'EST-CE QUI EST TENDRE, PUR, DOUX, FRAIS ET QUI SENT LA NOISETTE? C'EST LE BEURRE BIEN SÛR — QUI DIT MIEUX? PERSONNE CAR RIEN N'ÉGALE LE BEURRE, CE SEIGNEUR DES BONNES TABLES DONT LE NOM ÉVOCATEUR RIME AVEC SAVEUR.**

L'atout du beurre est d'être riche en vitamine A. Cette précieuse vitamine a une action polyvalente sur l'organisme. Indispensable à la croissance, elle joue un rôle fondamental dans la vision et aide l'organisme à résister contre les infections. Vitamine-beauté, elle favorise l'éclat des cheveux et la santé de la peau.

Grossir
Consommé en quantités raisonnables, sans apport d'autres corps gras, le beurre ne fait pas grossir. C'est surtout le déséquilibre alimentaire qui en est responsable, l'absorption incontrôlée de ce que l'on nomme 'les graisses cachées': charcuterie, fritures, pâtisseries, etc. consommées souvent au cours du même repas. Nous devons être vigilants afin d'utiliser les lipides dits 'visibles': corps gras d'assaisonnements (beurre)...

Quelle dose peut-on consommer?
Tout dépend de notre activité physique. Plus on est actif, plus on a besoin d'énergie: la ration quotidienne d'un athlète est estimée à 3500 kcal, dont 120g de graisses, y compris 35g de beurre environ. La suppression totale du beurre s'avère seulement nécessaire dans les cas de maladie de surcharge lipidique. Un adulte sans problème peut en consommer 30g par jour. Il s'agit évidemment de beurre cru ou fondu.

(a) Corrigez la traduction suivante de la première partie, qui a été faite par une personne sans grande connaissance de l'anglais.
   What is tender, pure, mild, fresh and smells the nuts? It is butter very sure — who says better? No person, for nothing equals butter, this lord of the table of whom the evoking name rhymes with savour.

(b) The translations of part of the second paragraph below both have their merits. Think about these and compose the definitive version:
   (i) *Consumed in reasonable quantities without being added to with other fatty substances butter does not make you fatter. It is an unbalanced diet that is mainly responsible for this: the uncontrolled consumption of what are called disguised fats: cold meats, fried foods, cakes etc. which are eaten during the course of one meal.*
   (ii) *Eaten in moderation without the addition of other fats, butter does not make you put on weight. It is especially eating in an unbalanced way that causes this: the unregulated consumption of hidden fats so called: delicatessen, fried things, pastries etc. often eaten during a single meal*

(c) 'saveur' veut dire ici *taste, flavour*. Avec l'aide d'un dictionnaire précisez la signification des mots suivants et utilisez-les dans une phrase: odeur; senteur; parfum; odorat.

(d) 'ça sent la noisette' – *it smells of hazelnuts*, so how would you express:
   It smells of onions | fish | feet | cooking | garlic

Translation into English: multiple choice option

Another way of testing translation is through a multiple choice exercise. You are given three versions of selected parts of a text. Only one of them is the appropriate one. Here is an example taken from an article entitled 'French attitudes to holidays have changed' in the Scottish Examination Board specimen questions.

Cet été, les Français ont abandonné l'étranger *pour rester dans leur pays natal.*

(a) in order to rest in their native country

(b) in order to stay in their native country

(c) in order to stay in their native countries

The correct version is of course (b). The other two contain a distractor. You might tempted to think that *rester* means 'to rest' or that *pays* is plural because of the final 's'. The better informed will know that *se reposer* means 'to rest' and that *pays* must be singular because both *leur* and *natal* are singular. Sometimes the context of the passage is needed to get the right meaning. Here are further examples from the same passage;

Sur les plages, les hors-bord et autres scooters des mers sont désormais regardés de travers par de paisibles estivants *qui aspirent au calme.* Ils sont trop bruyants, trop pollueurs pour ne pas dire dangereux. La nouvelle manie c'est de *retaper* des vieux bateaux.

(a) who long for peace and quiet

(b) who breathe in the still air

(c) who take things quietly

The correct version is (a). *Aspirer* can mean to 'breathe in' but *aspirer à* means 'to want something very much' similar to the English sense of 'aspire to something'. It cannot have the meaning in (c). Only (a) makes any real sense

(a) to retype

(b) to do up

(c) to hit again

retaper could mean any of these three things but only one of them (b) makes sense here. With this kind of task you will need to use your common sense as well as your grammatical knowledge.

Practice question

Here is some practice using a passage from Pagnol's *Château de ma mère*:

Nous déjeunâmes sur l'herbe. La conversation de Lili nous intéressa vivement, car il connaissait chaque vallon, chaque ravin, chaque sentier, chaque pierre de ces collines. De plus, il savait les heures et les mœurs du gibier: mais sur ce chapitre, il me parut un peu réticent. Il ne fit que répondre aux questions de l'oncle Jules, parfois d'une manière assez évasive et avec un petit sourire malin.

Mon père dit:

Ce qui manque le plus dans ce pays, ce sont les sources… A part le Puits du Mûrier, est-ce qu'il y en a d'autres?

– Bien sûr! dit Lili» Mais il n'ajouta rien.

«Il y a la baume de Passe-Temps, dit l'oncle. Elle est sur la carte d'état-major.

– Il y a aussi celle des Escaouprès, dit Lili. C'est là où mon père fait boire ses chèvres.

Nous déjeunâmes sur l'herbe
a) We had herbs for lunch
b) We ate some grass
c) We had a picnic

La conversation de Lili nous intéressa vivement
a) Lili's conversation was lively and interesting
b) We were very interested in what Lili had to say

c) We were interested in converting Lili

de plus
a) this was a plus
b) what is more
c) too much

mais sur ce chapitre
a) but on this subject
b) but in this chapter
c) on this chapel

Il ne fit que répondre aux questions de l'oncle Jules
a) he made no response to uncle Jules' questions
b) he tried to answer uncle Jules' questions
c) he just answered uncle Jules' questions

avec un petit sourire malin
a) with a crafty little smile
b) like a small male mouse
c) with a malicious little smile

dans ce pays
a) in this country
b) in this area
c) in this land

A part
a) next to
b) part of
c) except for

est-ce qu'il y en a d'autres?
a) there aren't any others?
b) are there any others?
c) there are the others?

Bien sûr!
a) Well surely!
b) Very surely!
c) Of course!

C'est là où mon père fait boire ses chèvres
a) that is where my father makes his goats drink
b) that is where my father takes his horses to drink
c) that is where my father takes his goats to drink

RETRANSLATION

Retranslation is a task required by a few Examining Boards as part of the written paper. It consists of a short passage of English for translation based on a text already used for other language tasks. Retranslation is a useful task because it makes you re-use words and expressions that you have met already, thus helping memorization and fluency in thinking and writing in French. Usually, about a quarter to a third of words from the French text can be re-used in the English translation. You will not however be able to just copy down chunks of the original. Tenses may have to be changed, as well as adjectives and the person of the verb. You will also have to find words from your own store to fill in the bits in between.

Before tackling the translation, read carefully through the French text again. Read the English and then the French once more, this time underlining words or expressions that seem as if they could be wholly or partly re-used. Then start the translation, paying particular attention to tenses and subjects of verbs and other words you may need.

Illustrative question and answer

LYCÉES: LES CLASSES TOUS RISQUES

La violence pure et dure est en train de gagner nos salles de classe.
Et cette fois, elle vise les profs.

Un professeur de physique, une femme, est <u>injuriée</u> par un jeune élève. Elle lui montre la porte. Il sort de sa manche un <u>tournevis</u> et <u>frappe</u>. La jeune femme s'en tire avec une lèvre éclatée et deux dents cassées. L'agresseur disparaît, la police parvient néanmoins à l'identifier: il a treize ans. Quelques jours plus tôt, les professeurs d'un collège <u>votaient de faire la grève</u> après l'impact d'un projectile venu étoiler la vitre de la salle des professeurs.

Rackets, agressions, insultes, jets de pierres: la liste de ces petits faits désormais ordinaires de la vie des écoles est longue. L'an dernier, 13,000 vols et 700 cas de racket ont été <u>recensés</u> dans les établissements français. <u>Le métier de professeur</u> est ainsi devenu un des plus exposés et un des <u>moins considérés</u>.

«Eternellement la science des maîtres passera dans le cœur des disciples, dans un grand silence attentif», proclamait l'écrivain Marcel Pagnol, au lendemain de la dernière guerre. Que s'est-il donc passé d'irréversible en un demi-siècle, derrière les murs de nos lycées et collèges?

«L'école est un lieu sur lequel les parents et les enfants comptent beaucoup comme facteur d'intégration sociale», analyse un sociologue. «A l'époque de Pagnol, l'école, obligatoire seulement dans le primaire, jouait son rôle d'intégrateur. Maintenant, les collèges et lycées surpeuplés ne parviennent plus pleinement à atteindre cet objectif dans un contexte de chômage élevé. Ceux qui n'y réussissent pas se <u>sentent exclus</u>, et <u>se retournent</u> contre ceux qu'ils estiment responsables de leur non-insertion».

<u>Tout en soulignant</u> que les <u>enfants violents</u> à l'encontre des professeurs sont ceux qui connaissent une défaillance familiale, un psychiatre fait remarquer que c'est souvent l'absence d'autorité des adultes qui précipite la violence. «Ces <u>jeunes</u> deviennent <u>agressifs</u> par besoin de punition. En l'absence de limites, ils se confortent dans des groupes dont le leader est souvent le plus malade».

On n'y voit pas le fruit du hasard. Cette violence est à la fois le fait d'enfants trop gâtés et, à l'opposé, de jeunes défavorisés des banlieues dégradées. Ces gâtés «à qui il manque quelques <u>bonnes fessées</u>» comme disaient <u>nos grands-pères</u> apprendront avec intérêt qu'un enseignant a été acquitté par la cour d'appel pour avoir <u>giflé</u> un <u>chahuteur</u>.

Translate into French
Traduisez en français le passage suivant en utilisant le texte précédent pour vous aider: Ecrivez toutes les deux lignes.

While stressing that one should punish disruptive pupils in school, a sociologist has pointed out that a good spanking will probably precipitate violence. Our grandfathers would certainly have slapped pupils if they had insulted them, but these aggressive children have turned against authority. Those who have felt themselves excluded from school life have been hitting their teachers with things such as screwdrivers. The police are recording more and more assaults and the teaching profession is therefore becoming less prestigious. From now on those teachers who hold parents responsible may decide on strike action.   (20)

NEAB

Possible answer

French version
Tout en soulignant que dans une école on devrait punir les chahuteurs, un sociologue a fait remarquer qu'une bonne fessée précipiterait probablement la violence. Nos grands-pères auraient certainement giflé les élèves si ceux-ci les avaient injuriés, mais ces enfants

agressifs se sont retournés contre l'autorité. Ceux qui se sentaient exclus de la vie de l'école ont frappé leurs professeurs avec des objets tels que des tournevis. La police a recensé de plus en plus d'agressions et pour cette raison le métier de professeur devient moins considéré. A l'avenir les professeurs qui considèrent que les parents sont responsables pourraient voter de faire la grève.

Note there are quite a few words and expressions in the original text that can be re-used. These have been highlighted.

Practice questions

The best way of practising this language task is to do lots of examples. The passages that follow have three stages of practice:
(a) phrase spotting
(b) easy retranslation
(c) more demanding retranslation

1 HOLD-UP A 14 ANS

Une adolescente de 14 ans a commis un hold-up avant-hier dans une caisse d'épargne de Hambourg, emportant un butin de 10 000DM (35 000F). La police a arrêté la jeune braqueuse peu après les faits, ainsi qu'un homme de 22 ans, qui l'attendait sur une moto, mais qui avait pris la fuite seul.

Armée d'un revolver d'alarme et coiffée d'un casque de moto, la jeune fille a fait irruption dans la caisse d'épargne et a présenté au caissier un papier sur lequel était écrit,' Ceci est un hold-up, mettez tout l'argent dans le sac et que personne ne bouge. Vite!'

En sortant de la banque, la jeune fille a été suivie par un employé qui a pu indiquer à la police une cour où elle s'était cachée.

(a) Phrase spotting Find the following words and phrases from the text:

Savings bank – arrested – nobody move – a haul – an alarm – pistol – day before yesterday – wearing a crash helmet – burst into – this is a hold-up – a piece of paper – had fled on his own – armed with – shortly after the incident – carried out a hold-up

(b) Now translate this paragraph into French:

Armed with an alarm-pistol, a young girl of 14 burst into a Hamburg savings bank yesterday and showed the cashier a piece of paper on which was written, 'This is a hold-up'. A young man was waiting for her outside on a motorbike but he made off on his own. The girl was followed by an employee when she left the bank. He was able to show the police the block of flats where she had hidden.

(c) Now translate this paragraph into French:

Two teenage girls of 14 and 15 burst into a Paris bank yesterday and got out with a haul of 100 000F. The two young gangsters had shown the cashier a card on which was written, 'This is a hold-up. Nobody move!' They were armed with alarm-pistols and were wearing crash-helmets. Outside the bank two young men were waiting for them in a car but they fled at the last moment. The police were able to arrest the girls later thanks to an employee who had followed them to a block of flats.

2 LE SIDA – FLÉAU DES ANNÉES 90

Personne n'en doute aujourd'hui: le SIDA constitue le fléau des années 90. Dans les pays en voie de développement, il frappe aveuglément, décimant hommes et femmes laissant derrière lui des cohortes d'orphelins. En Europe, aux Etats Unis, la contamination hétérosexuelle s'étend. Les femmes à leur tour paient leur tribut au virus HIV. Il y a sept ans qu'il a été découvert par une équipe de l'Institut Pasteur. Depuis sept ans, les scientifiques imaginent des parades à la maladie et à l'épidémie. Les campagnes d'information et la prévention restent indispensables. Cependant, seule la recherche apportera une arme décisive, traitement ou vaccin.

Mais chercher coûte cher. Et les scientifiques européens manquent cruellement de moyens. D'où l'idée du Pr. Luc Montagnier de faire appel à la générosité du public par le biais de la Fondation Européenne de Recherche sur le SIDA, pour donner à l'Europe des atouts supplémentaires dans cette bataille dont dépend la vie de milliers d'êtres humains.

(a) Phrase spotting

is spreading – seven years ago – indiscriminately – effective weapon – information campaign – developing countries – research on its own – on which depends the life – appeal to – killing thousands – scientists – pay their price to the virus – hordes of children – an extra advantage – was discovered – the scourge of the 90s

(b) Translate the following paragraph into French:

AIDS continues to spread in the developing countries causing the deaths of thousands of men and women and leaving great numbers of orphaned children. In Europe and the United States, AIDS is spreading amongst heterosexuals and the number of women with the HIV virus is growing. Only research can provide an effective weapon against this disease. Researchers in Europe however are desperately short of funds. The European Foundation for Research into AIDS is appealing to the generosity of the public in order to gain the upper hand in this battle for the lives of thousands.

(c) Now translate this paragraph into French:

Since the discovery of AIDS seven years ago by the Pasteur Institute the disease has continued to spread in Europe, in the United States and the developing countries. AIDS has become the scourge of our times. Contrary to the predictions of certain doctors it has also spread amongst the heterosexual population. Scientists fear an epidemic. A sad effect of the disease is to create hordes of orphan children who nobody wants to look after. Information and prevention campaigns are only partly an answer. What is needed is to discover either a treatment that is effective or a vaccine.

Illustrative question and answer

Translation into French of an unseen short passage of English

A few Examination Boards have as an option the task of translating a short passage of English into French. The passage is normally taken from a novel and either chosen for its clear English or adapted to eliminate too many bits that are difficult to translate into French. If you have a good grasp of French grammar, a wide general vocabulary and have had consistent practice in this task you could score high marks. The passage below is a good example of this kind of exercise. Try doing the translation with the help of the notes. Check your version afterwards with the sample answer.

The bus climbed[1] steadily[2] through barren[3] countryside. We could[4] see mountains coming up[5] in the South. At last we caught sight[6] of the red roofs of Burguete. We crossed[7] a bridge over a stream and the bus stopped[7]. We got out[8] and the driver handed us[9] our bags and fishing rods.

We went up[10] the street and into[10] the inn. The fat innkeeper sent a girl upstairs to[11] show us a plain[12], clean room. It was so cold that you could see your breath[13]. We washed, put on sweaters and came downstairs[14]. I went out to[11] find the woman and asked[15] her how much the room was. She looked away[16].

"Twelve pesetas."
"That's too much. We didn't pay more in a big hotel."
"We've just put in[17] a bathroom."
"Haven't you anything cheaper[18]?"
"Not in the summer. It's the big[19] season."
We were the only people[20] there. "Well, I thought[21], "it's only for a few days."
"Is wine included?"
She nodded[22].
"Well[23]," I replied, "that's all right[24]."

E Hemingway, *The Sun Also Rises*
NICCEA

1 What tense? You will need the imperfect tense for continuous action (for something that was viewed as going on) and to describe a state or something that lasted. The perfect or past historic should be used where events are completed, as steps in the action of the story. The bus 'climbing' and 'seeing' the mountains coming up are descriptive.

2 It sometimes helps to think of a synonym in English and you might find a similar word in French. Try 'bit by bit', 'progressively'.

3 Try 'arid', 'sterile', 'empty'

4 Leave out the word 'could' e.g. *Je voyais les montagnes* – I could see the mountains

5 'appearing'. The second verb in a clause is an infinitive.

6 *apercevoir*. A change of tense here, a step in the action, 'they glimpsed'. Choose either the perfect or the past historic and keep to this choice for the rest of the completed action tenses in the passage. Note that if you choose the past historic, you cannot use it in direct speech for completed action, where it is replaced by the perfect.

7 Tense?

8 to get out of a vehicle is *descendre*.

9 tendre

10 'monter' and 'entrer' 'monter' has a direct object here so it takes avoir if you are using the perfect tense.

11 where 'to' means 'in order to' translate it by *pour*

12 try 'simple'. Don't forget that most adjectives, except for a few commonly used ones, come after the noun they describe.

13 There is no really comparable expression in French. *"notre souffle se condensait"* or *"'il faisait un froid glacial dans la chambre"*

14 *'descendre'*

15 'in order to ask her' so another infinitive

16 *'détourner les yeux'*. Put it in the right tense!

17 Think of another way of saying this – 'installed'

18 eg. 'less expensive'

19 'high'

20 *personnes*

21 In reported speech (the words quoted that someone actually used) you need to invert phrases like 'she said', 'he replied' so that they become *a-t-elle dit* and *a-t-il répondu* in the perfect tense or *dit-elle* and *répondit-il* in the past historic.

22 *hocher la tête, faire oui de la tête*

23 *Eh bien*

24 'will be alright'

Possible answer

L'autobus montait progressivement dans une campagne stérile/vide/désertique. Nous voyions apparaître/se profiler les montagnes au sud. Enfin, nous avons aperçu/aperçûmes les toits rouges du village de Burguete. Nous avons traversé/traversâmes un pont sur un ruisseau et l'autobus s'est arrêté/s'arrêta. Nous en sommes descendus/en descendîmes et le conducteur nous a tendu/nous tendit nos valises et nos cannes à pêche.

Nous avons monté/montâmes la rue et sommes entrés/entrâmes dans l'auberge. La grosse aubergiste a envoyé/envoya une fille en haut/à l'étage pour nous montrer une chambre simple et propre. Il faisait si froid que notre souffle se condensait/Il faisait un froid glacial dans la chambre. Nous nous sommes lavés/lavâmes et avons mis/enfilé/mîmes/enfilâmes nos tricots/pulls et sommes descendus/descendîmes. Je suis sorti/sortis pour trouver la propriétaire et lui demander le prix de la chambre.

Elle a détourné/détourna les yeux.

"Douze pesetas."

"Ça c'est trop cher. C'est ce que nous avons payé dans un grand hôtel."

"Nous venons d'installer une salle de bains".

"N'avez-vous pas quelque chose de moins cher?"

"Pas en été, c'est la haute saison."

Nous étions les seules personnes dans l'hôtel/il n'y avait personne d'autre à l'hôtel. "Eh bien", ai-je pensé/pensai-je, "c'est seulement/ce n'est que pour quelques jours".

"Est-ce que le vin est compris?"

Elle a acquiescé/acquiesça/elle a hoché/hocha la tête.

"Eh bien", ai-je répondu/répondis-je, "ça ira ça va".

Study techniques: practising translation and retranslation

You can practise these skills by using any sort of bilingual texts; sets of instructions for the use of equipment, lists of contents of food or beauty products and labels are now often produced in more than one language. When in France you can often obtain tourist brochures in English. You might be surprised at the English in some of these, so look at them carefully! You could offer your services and do a good translation for the organization concerned. At trade fairs, brochures and publicity material are often available in several languages. When you obtain any material, like the above, read both versions and then try translating the French one into English and vice versa, glancing only occasionally at the ___. You could also use translations of your set texts for this exercise, provided the ___ not too complex or literary in style. Texts suitable for this purpose are: Pagnol's ___ aphical novels, (*La Gloire de mon père*, *Le Château de ma mère*, *Le Temps des secrets*);

Camus's *L'Etranger*; many of Prévert's poems; *Les Petits enfants du siècle* by Rochefort; and plays by Beckett or Ionesco. Other bilingual texts already mentioned are: the Press-Pocket series of English novels and the publication *La vie Outre-Manche*.

Look for suitable journalistic material. Any articles you come across in French newspapers, about aspects of life in England, can be useful because you are already familiar with the context. You could also buy English and French newspapers on the same day and compare articles on the same themes. You might sometimes find it profitable to work from French into English first.

Example: In the following extract see if you can pick out the phrases that stand for the following:

family allowances – home owners – mortgages – local authorities – council homes – above their means – social security – young unemployed – hundreds of thousands – cheap housing market – for each child – the homeless – dole mentality – evictions – repayments – interest rates – taken on – its aim was – frozen – low-income families – shrunk – according to inflation

---

TROIS MILLE SANS-ABRI — CONTRE 250 EN 1975 — DORMENT DANS LES RUES DE LONDRES ET LE PAYS COMPTERAIT NEUF MILLIONS DE PAUVRES

Les allocations familiales sont gelées depuis trois ans au même niveau et leur valeur réelle diminue donc en raison de l'inflation. Elles sont de 288F par mois par enfant.

La principale réforme de l'aide sociale a eu lieu en 1988. Elle avait pour but de concentrer les ressources sur les familles les plus démunies et les personnes âgées, tout en cherchant à éviter la création d'une 'mentalité d'assistés' chez les plus jeunes. Les allocations aux jeunes chômeurs ont ainsi été nettement réduites.

Le gouvernement s'efforce depuis onze ans de rendre les Britanniques propriétaires de leurs maisons. Des centaines de milliers de logements sociaux construits par les municipalités, surtout depuis la guerre, ont été vendus. Le parc locatif à bon marché a donc considérablement diminué.

On a assisté aussi depuis quelques mois à la multiplication des expulsions. Des familles très modestes ont contracté des prêts hypothécaires dont le remboursement se révèle au-dessus de leurs moyens: les traites varient en effet proportionnellement aux taux d'intérêt, maintenus très hauts pour combattre l'inflation.

Now translate the following:
(i)   Many low-income families have taken on mortgages that are beyond their means
(ii)   Many council homes have been sold since the war
(iii) Mortgage repayments vary according to the rate of inflation
(iv)   Family allowances are too modest for deprived families
(v)   Payments to young unemployed people have been reduced
(vi)   The interest rate has dropped
(vii) We have seen more evictions during the last few months
(viii) The government has been trying to control inflation since 1988
(ix)   The aim of many people is to own their own home
(x)   This reform was aimed at helping the homeless

Note The above passage illustrates the importance of being familiar with the context or subject matter of what you are translating. You should look through past papers from your Examining Board to see what kinds of subject matter they use. The latter may be of a documentary nature covering such things as: social and political issues; education; trade union; and environmental problems. Or they may be of a more literary nature. It is important therefore to make a habit of reading widely so that you increase your general knowledge. Pick a short article or news item, each week, about a different subject and make a list, as you read, of key words or phrases. You will sometimes find words or expressions pertaining to current matters that cannot be found easily in a dictionary!

4.4   SUMMARY AND OTHER TASKS

Contents

- Summary in English
- Summary in French of an English text
- Paraphrasing and explanation
- Gap-filling tasks: cloze tests

The skill of being able to pick out the main points of what someone has said or written and to summarise these in brief form is a very useful skill that has many practical applications in both work and study. This skill is no longer tested as a major separate task by most of the Examination Boards; instead it has been integrated into the reading and writing sections of the papers at A and AS-Level. It may also be tested in the listening part of the examination. Depending on the Board, summary in French or sometimes in English will probably feature in some part of the examination.

Whether the end result is in English or French you need to start by using your reading skills. If the text has a title or subheadings these will give you general idea of the whole subject. A quick glance at the first few lines and the last will also give you clues to what it is about and the purpose of the piece of writing. Next skim-read the passage by letting your eye run along each line without stopping at any difficult bits. You won't understand or indeed take in all the words on this occasion. If you have difficulty in skimming run your finger along a few lines below where you are reading. Now read through again, a little more slowly, marking any words or phrases that cause difficulty. Read a third time and, if dictionaries are allowed, look up anything you think is essential to the meaning. Not every word will be. Some you will be able to guess at or have a rough idea of what they mean because of the context. Leave these to last to look up and then only if they are still esssential to the summary. Next, a paragraph at a time, re-read underlining the words that contain what seems to you to be the main ideas. You may find pencil is better than a highlighter since you can rub it out if necessary.

SUMMARY IN ENGLISH

You may be required to reduce a French passage to about one-third of its original length, for example 540 words to 180. There are two main considerations here: 1) Picking out the essential information (as outlined above) and 2) writing economically in English. Both these skills are acquired through practice. Having read the text at least four times and having underlined the main points, begin writing your summary on alternate lines, paragraph by paragraph, using your underlinings as a guide but also trying to assess the whole value of each section. Do not be tempted to translate. About a third of the way through count up the words used so far to make sure you are roughly on target. If you have used too many you may have put in too much detail, so read through what is left to gauge the amount of information left to convey. Finish the summary and count up the number of words. If there are say 190 it doesn't matter too much. If you have exceeded 200 you might be at the point where you would lose marks because any ideas in the excess number of words will not be counted. You can reduce the number of words in two ways:

- Pruning the English – using one word instead of two or more, or by leaving words out, provided they don't remove important detail.

- By leaving out details that you can see are not essential to the overall meaning now that you have the whole before you.

Most texts will contain information that is either circumstantial or just an accessory to the main ideas. Sometimes lots of examples are quoted or the text simply repeats itself.

Illustrative question and answer

You work for an international company which is seeking to encourage job-sharing and part-time working. You are hoping to find evidence of the experiences of companies in France from this article in a French weekly magazine. Summarise the main points for your immediate superior.

Your summary should be in English, in continuous prose and should contain about 180 words. Indicate how many words you have used.

TRAVAIL À TEMPS PARTIEL: LA FRANCE HÉSITE

L'emploi à temps partiel. Pas d'acquéreur. Le Ministre du Travail, Martine Aubry, ressemble à un commissaire-priseur qui ne parvient pas à écouler sa marchandise aux ventes aux enchères. Elle peut bien annoncer en Conseil des ministres, le 5 août, un remboursement de 30% sur les charges sociales patronales pour toute embauche à temps partiel, mais sans succès! Les enterprises sont d'accord pour empocher le rabais, mais préviennent qu'elles ne créeront pas plus d'emplois. Le patronat compare 'temps partiel' à 'coûts supplémentaires de gestion et d'organisation'. Les petites entreprises l'envisagent uniquement comme solution d'appoint. La grande industrie le juge mal adapté au 3 × 8* et au processus de production.

Les syndicats font la moue et les salariés aussi. Il est loin le temps où l'on pouvait rêver d'horaires 'choisis' pour aménager ses loisirs. Selon une récente enquête de la Communauté Européenne, 80% des salariés (des femmes en majorité) qui exercent une activité inférieure à 32 heures par semaine en France souhaitent passer à temps plein. Seuls 12% des salariés travaillent à temps partiel, contre 25% au Royaume-Uni.

Cependant, quelques pionniers dans l'Hexagone ont fait la preuve que la flexibilité des horaires peut rimer avec la forte productivité. Chez Boiron par exemple, depuis dix ans, 20% des effectifs, y compris les cadres, travaillent moins de 39 heures par semaine. Le système obéit à deux règles: les salariés acceptent de venir à temps plein en période de forte activité et les contrats sont renégociés tous les douze mois. Le personnel (féminin à 80%) exige une organisation qui libère les mères de famille le mercredi.

La flexibilité interne peut être aussi payante pour éviter les coûts supplémentaires qui accompagnent les recrutements temporaires. Pendant longtemps, une entreprise électrométallurgique, près de Moutiers (Savoie), a eu recours à une main-d'œuvre saisonnière pour tourner à plein régime d'avril à octobre, période où les prix de l'électricité sont les plus bas. La formation de ces recrues coûtait cher et elles n'avaient pas de sécurité d'emploi. Aujourd'hui, l'entreprise retrouve chaque année les mêmes ouvriers. Ils sont moniteurs l'hiver, pisteurs ou restaurateurs dans les stations. Au printemps ils troquent leur salopette de ski contre un bleu de travail, pour être rémunérés pendant sept mois dans l'usine. Avec la garantie d'être repris l'année suivante.

Mais les essais de ce genre sont peu nombreux. Beaucoup préfèrent exercer une petite activité et puis s'inscrire au chômage. A la Compagnie industrielle des chauffe-eau, en Alsace, seuls une dizaine d'Africains se sont portés volontaires. 'Ils travaillent huit mois et retournent quatre mois au pays pour les travaux agricoles', confie Bernard Mangenot, directeur-général.

Les cadres sont, en tout cas, les derniers concernés par les expériences de temps partiel, car être cadre et se consacrer à plusieurs patrons reste, pour beaucoup, un tour de force. Néanmoins en 1985, François Boulon a quitté son patron pour devenir directeur commercial à temps partiel. Quatre petites entreprises qui n'ont pas les moyens de s'offrir un directeur à temps plein occupent chacune un quart de son emploi du temps. A 40 ans, il a maintenant derrière lui une quinzaine d'expériences commerciales et plusieurs centaines d'heures d'avion pour relier ses différents bureaux aux quatre coins de France. Cette expérience cependant reste exceptionnelle.

Le temps partiel est sans doute une superbe idée, mais qui tardera à devenir populaire.

* 3 × 8 = shiftwork

Oxford and Cambridge

Possible answers

1   The Employment Minister, Martine Aubrey, finds it difficult to persuade companies to create more part time work, even by offering them a reduction of 30% in social charges. Firms are happy to pocket the reduction but not to create more part-time jobs which entail extra running costs. Small companies regard part-time work as a secondary solution. Large firms find that it doesn't suit shift work.

Unions disapprove and despite having more leisure time many part-time employees would prefer to work full-time. Only 12% work part-time in France against 25% in the UK.

A few firms manage to combine flexible time with high production. Boiron employs 1/5 of its staff, workers and management, part-time. Two conditions apply: they agree to work full-time when production demands and women and mothers, 80% of the staff, are free on Wednesdays (a non-schoolday in France).

One electrometallurgical company in Savoie employs extra workers from April to October when electricity is cheapest. Initial training costs were high but the same workers return each year. They work in the winter sports industry for the rest of the time.

One small company employs Africans who work 8 months and return home for farming work for 4 months. Such exceptions are rare. Most prefer a small job and drawing benefit.

Part-time working at managerial level is less common and more fraught. M. Boulon however works as a manager for four small firms unable to afford one full-time. This entails air travel all over France. Part-time employment will take a long time to become popular. (260 words)

2   It is difficult to persuade companies to create more part-time work, even by offering a reduction of 30% in social charges. Firms are unhappy about extra running costs. Small companies remain sceptical. Large firms find that it doesn't suit shift work.

Unions disapprove and most workers prefer to work full-time. Only 12% work part-time in France against 25% in the UK.

A few exceptions: Boiron employs 1/5 of its staff part-time. Two conditions apply: they agree to work full-time when production demands; women and mothers, 80% of the staff, are free on Wednesdays.

One electrometallurgical company in Savoie employs extra workers from April to October when electricity is cheapest. Initial training costs were high but the same workers return each year. They work in the winter sports industry for the rest of the time.

One small company employs Africans who work 8 months and return home for farming work for 4 months. Most people though prefer a small job and drawing benefit.

M. Boulon works as a manager for four small firms unable to afford one full-time. This entails air travel all over France. Part-time employment remains unpopular. (186 words)

Note

You should read the brief for the summary carefully. In this example for instance your firm wants to know about the success or otherwise of part-time working in France. All the references to the French Minister for Employment and an auction are not needed.

The marking principles for this examination state that there are usually about 40 points contained in the passage and candidates who score 30 points get full marks. Any words in excess of 200 are not taken into account.

There are two summaries above, one which is too long and a second 'pruned' version. Read through both of them. You may consider that important details have been left out from one or the other. Opinions are likely to vary and the assessment principles for the Board take this into account.

Practising summary

Summary is not needed at GCSE Level and is therefore a new skill to be acquired for A and AS-Level. It is closely connected to reading skills (as already mentioned). You will get plenty of practice in reading literary and background texts. Make a habit, right from the start, of jotting down notes on what you are reading. Doing this regularly **in French** will help you later in answering questions in French.

You will also need more specific practice. Start by reading short extracts from French newspapers using the *'faits divers'* or *'en bref'* sections. It helps if you can imagine you are explaining the news item not to yourself but to another person, who in this case understands very little French. Aim to give as faithful an account as possible.

Example

'Le titre de 'Chanson de l'année', créé à l'initiative de la Communauté des Radios Publiques de Langues Françaises (CRPLF) qui regroupe le RSR, la RTBF, Radio Canada et France Inter, a été décerné hier à la chanson 'Hélène', interprétée par le chanteur canadien Roch Voisine. Cette chanson a été choisie par les auditeurs des quatre radios francophones, à l'issue d'un référendum au cours de l'émission spéciale programmée sur France Inter, hier, de 17 à 19 heures, en multiplex avec la Belgique, le Canada et la Suisse. L'interprète de la chanson récompensée reçoit comme chaque année, un trophée original créé par le sculpteur Christian Renonciat.

This item is about a song of the year competition that took place yesterday on four French-speaking radio channels. It was won by the Canadian singer Roch Voisine with the song 'Helène'. It was chosen by listeners during a link-up broadcast. The winner got a specially sculptured trophy. This could be condensed to:

'The radio song of the year contest was won by a Canadian singer, Roch Voisine, for the song 'Helène' chosen by listeners in four French-speaking countries during a radio–link broadcast yesterday on France-Inter.'

Deciding which bits of information to discard, and which to keep, depends partly on how short your summary needs to be and partly on how important certain details are. For example, in the above summary, the detail about the trophy has been left out.

Practice questions

1 (a) Read the following news item and select the brief English summary which seems most accurate:

DEUX ÉLÈVES JAPONAIS ENTERRÉS VIVANTS

Deux élèves japonais, âgés de treize et de quatorze ans, ont été enterrés vivants sur une plage l'automne dernier par leurs enseignants qui entendaient les punir ainsi pour avoir racketté leurs camarades. Ils ont passé plus de vingt minutes enfouis dans le sable jusqu'au menton, la tête balayée par les vagues qui venaient s'échouer sur la plage de Fukuoka, une ville située dans le sud du Japon. 'Nous pensions que nous allions mourir' a déclaré l'un d'entre eux, en précisant que lorsqu'il avait essayé de s'extirper du sable, un enseignant était arrivé aussitôt pour l'en empêcher. Sept enseignants au total auraient participé à l'incident. Le directeur de l'école les a réprimandés d'avoir agi 'de façon excessive' mais aucune sanction n'a été prise par les autorités scolaires locales.

Summaries

(i) Two Japanese schoolchildren narrowly escaped drowning after being buried alive in the sand on a beach by their teachers.

(ii) Two Japanese schoolboys were punished by being buried alive by their teachers.

> (iii) A headmaster in Japan denied a charge of excessive cruelty when seven of his teachers buried two of their pupils in the sand.
>
> (iv) Two Japanese kids were buried up to their necks in sand by their teachers to teach them a lesson.

(b) Are you satisfied completely with the summary you have chosen? If not write your own summary in not less than 25 words.

(c) The original text had a single word title. Which of the following do you think it was?

SAUVÉS ENTERRÉS PUNITION

It helps when deciding this to think of cause and effect, in other words what action preceded what action or led to another one?

2 Read the following item:

INTERDICTION D'ARROSER

Le maire informe la population que suite à l'arrêté numéro 88–002 réglementant l'utilisation de l'eau potable pendant les mois de juillet et août, il est interdit d'arroser avec l'eau potable le samedi et le dimanche de 7 à 22 heures, l'alimentation des personnes en eau potable étant prioritaire sur l'arrosage des végétaux. Il est rappelé que les contrevenants seront poursuivis conformément à la loi.

(a) which is cause and effect among the following statements?

(b) What is their most logical sequence?
Watering gardens is forbidden – You will be fined if you break the law – Providing drinking water is a priority – The Mayor has made an announcement

(c) Write a one-sentence summary of the item.

SUMMARY IN FRENCH OF AN ENGLISH TEXT

This language task is an option with one of the Examination Boards. The task is based on a practical real life skill. It puts you in the place of a bilingual person providing information for a French organisation or company from an English source which you can cope with but they cannot so easily. A similar situation is used as part of the oral test by some Boards where you have to convey information in French taken from a document in English.

Obviously you will have no difficulty in understanding the text. Read it carefully however, at least four times. The same comments about selecting the main ideas still apply. Distinguish between main or new points and just examples or minor details. Is there any repetition? Are any comparisons being made? Does cause and effect play a part?

Having marked out your text go back to the opening paragraph and its main idea. Do not be tempted to start translating. Pick a phrase, i.e. noun and adjective, subject and verb and think of the French for them. You may have already been thinking of some French words when you were underlining – these should be jotted down as you go along. Again, it helps if you can imagine that you are doing this summary for someone else. You may want to work through the whole text in phrases or you may choose to start writing the summary, a paragraph at a time, not necessarily following exactly the paragraphing of the original. Don't just translate all your underlined phrases. Try to think globally in French.

Illustrative question and answer

The following is a typical example of summary in French from an English text. The ideas have been highlighted and notes made in French:

Résumez en français (150 mots à peu près) l'article suivant.   *WJEC*

A HIGH-TECH METROPOLIS ON THE MED

The Place du Nombre d'Or in Montpellier is *far removed from those sun-baked Provençal squares*, beloved of Northern Europeans, where locals traditionally sip pastis and watch the world go by. (One thinks of the square in Arles, where Van Gogh lived – the Roman columns peek through above the modern shop fronts.)

Montpellier, in fact, for all its long history has no significant Roman connections. This has not inhibited the Catalan *architect Ricardo Bofill* from giving the town what is – Bucharest apart – the largest example of late *20th-century Classical planning* in all Europe. There are 2,300 flats, plus offices, hotels, shops, restaurants, and a building for the regional government set in a progression of squares, circuses and crescents leading down to the river Lez.

The *choice* of Bofill, more patronised in France than in his native Catalonia (where Classicism is held to have worryingly Franco-ist connotations), *was that* of the town's socialist Mayor and parliamentary deputy, M. Georges Frêche. Frêche, now in his *third term of office*, is an impressive figure, *well-connected in Brussels* and intent on *turning Montpellier* the *capital of Languedoc-Roussillon*, into a Mediterranean technopolis, the *centre* of a *new industrial region* which could become the California of Europe – and all in a city smaller than Wigan.

Thirty years ago, the place depended on tourism and the production of cheap wine. *Underpopulated* and slowly *decaying*, it must have had enormous romantic appeal. But the French are not sentimentalists. Montpellier is now developing as a centre of new industry, with *electronics* and *medical research* prominent. (Montpellier's medical school is the oldest in Europe.) The *population has more than doubled* in 30 years and is set to double again in little more than a decade. Beyond the ancient (and perfectly preserved) historic centre, new *suburbs sprawl* into the foothills of the Cevennes mountains.

Georges Frêche is determined, however, that Montpellier *shall sprawl no further* but grow in an ordered fashion. Strict planning controls which would be unthinkable in Britain are being applied and new transport links, including a metro, will be largely financed from the public purse. The Bofill scheme, christened Antigone, is just the first stage of this development programme. Bofill, it appears, hoped for further commissions, but Montpellier is now *moving away* from his bombastically baroque style and *towards* a more *pluralistic approach.*

During the 1960s the historic core was ringed with a series of *new buildings*, including the *faceless* Polygone shopping centre, which are now *widely regretted.* "In the 1960s," says Raymond DuGrand, Frêche's deputy with responsibility for planning and architecture, "there were no cultural ambitions – it was a case of development for its own sake."

Montpellier now wants to become not just large and prosperous but to develop as an *international city* with a rich and *varied cultural* life. "Only in this way can we attract people from Paris and other large cities and make them want to stay," says DuGrand.

Notes

L'architecture de Montpellier, pas typique de la Provence – style moderne classique – œuvre de l'architecte catalan Ricardo Bofill – choisi par le maire socialiste – Georges Frêche trois fois élu – contacts à Bruxelles – projets pour le futur de Monpellier – centre industriel et technologique de la région – il y a 30 ans dépendait seulement du tourisme et de la production de vin de table – sous-peuplé – aujourd'hui devient centre de recherches médicales et technologiques – population doublée – va tripler – une agglomération en expansion – maire résolu à contrôler l'urbanisme – architecture plus variée – on regrette le style des années 60 – créer une ville florissante – et riche du point de vue de la culture

Here are two versions of a summary. You will notice that the jotted notes do not all appear in the final text. The number of words used is not so crucial as in an English-from-French summary.

Possible answers

1 Montpellier ne ressemble pas aux autres villes provençales. Une grande partie est construite dans un style moderne classique, l'œuvre de l'architecte catalan, Ricardo Bofill. Celui-ci a été choisi par Georges Frêche, maire trois fois élu de Montpellier, avec beaucoup de contacts politiques à Bruxelles et ailleurs. Cet homme fort a résolu de transformer sa ville en capitale technologique de la région méditerranéenne, une nouvelle Californie. Ville autrefois sous-peuplée qui dépendait uniquement du tourisme et du vin de table, elle est aujourd'hui en train de devenir un centre de recherches électroniques et médicales (son école de médecine est la plus ancienne d'Europe). La population a doublé en 30 ans et va tripler dans les 10 ans à venir. Le maire a résolu d'améliorer les réseaux de communication, de construire un métro et aussi de contrôler plus étroitement l'urbanisme et le style de construction – on regrette maintenant le style anonyme des années 60. On vise à créer une ville non seulement grande et florissante mais également riche en culture. (171 mots)

2 L'architecture de Montpellier n'est pas typique de la Provence. Une grande partie de la ville, les nouveaux appartements, bureaux et restaurants, sont construits dans un style néo-classique moderne. C'est le maire de Montpellier, Georges Frêche, qui a choisi l'architecte de ces constructions, Ricardo Bofill. Le maire, un homme fort politique et populaire, est très ambitieux. Il est en train de transformer Montpellier en centre de recherches electroniques et médicales – son école de médecine est déjà très ancienne. En 30 ans la population a doublé et continue de croître. Les constructions de Bofill étaient seulement une étape dans le programme. On va construire un métro et améliorer les réseaux de communication. Le maire a résolu de contrôler l'urbanisme futur de la ville et le style de l'architecture. Le but est de créer non seulement une métropole technologique de pointe dans le Languedoc-Roussillon mais aussi une ville internationale riche en culture. (150 mots)

Study Techniques

1 Once a week, choose an article that interests you from a newspaper and write a summary of it in French. Check that your summary is interesting and that it contains all the important information. If possible, find a friend to read your summary to and then to tell you, in English, what he/she thinks the original was about. It would also be useful, when selecting your article, to bear in mind the interests of the person helping you. If you choose something that they know a lot about, they are bound to ask you questions or want further explanations.

2 In much writing, there are 'key sentences'. These often occur at the beginning of a paragraph. They carry the important information and the rest of the paragraph usually amplifies, re-states or gives examples. These key sentences are invaluable for the summary writer. Once a week, choose a text in English or French and underline the key sentences in it. Think what you would need to add, if anything, to make a good summary.

PARAPHRASING AND EXPLANATION

There are two main skills involved here:
(a) Reworking sentences or phrases used in a text while keeping the same meaning
(b) Explaining in your own words something already stated in a succinct or figurative way.

You may be asked, for example, to rephrase sentences 'keeping the meaning as close as possible to the original'. Sometimes a key word is provided. For example:
(a) *Le gouvernement a d'abord **minimisé** l'affaire*
    *Le gouvernement a d'abord dit que l'affaire **n'était pas très importante***
(b) *Mon grand-père me **réservait** les enveloppes que lui adressaient ses clients*
    *Mon grand-père me **mettait de côté***

There are often other ways of doing the same thing:

Le gouvernement a d'abord dit/soutenu que l'affaire n'avait pas d'importance
Le gouvernement n'a d'abord pas voulu exagérer l'importance de cette affaire

In the second example you could have written:
Mon grand-père me gardait...

You can see that words are either manipulated (e.g. with adjectives becoming nouns) or alternative words/expressions are found. Knowing the opposite of a word can be helpful; the antonym as distinct from the synonym. A monolingual French dictionary is an invaluable aid when working with paraphrase. You will discover synonyms, antonyms and paraphrases in the form of definitions of meanings. Try to build up a repertoire of words whose definitions you can give in French. Go over these each week to make sure you still know them, then learn and add ten more.

Being able to manipulate language in this way is a useful skill that has an application in many of the writing tasks you need for A-Level as well as in some of the speaking tasks which require you to do the explaining or persuading.

It is interesting to note that the word 'paraphrase' is defined in a French–French dictionary as *'explication ou commentaire diffus, verbeux, qui ne fait qu'allonger un texte sans l'enrichir'*. In other words, not to be encouraged if you want to develop a good style! *'Reformulez'*, *'transformez'* or *'trouvez un synonyme'* are closer to the English meaning. Which of the 'paraphrases' above are closer to the idea of 'reformulation'?

Being able to explain in your own words in French is like being able to think in French. It is a skill that becomes important when you try to explain to a French person some aspect of your way of life that is similar but not quite the same as theirs.

A good way into paraphrase, or explaining in French, occurs in class when words in a text you are studying are explained, in French, by the teacher rather than just translated. You can encourage this process by asking for meanings in French:
Je ne comprends pas le mot/l'expression _____
Qu'est-ce que cela veut dire?
Quelle est la signification du mot ...?

Encouraging the reverse process can also be helpful (i.e. getting you to explain simple meanings in French). Listening to someone else explaining and trying it yourself are the two processes involved. Using a monolingual dictionary is a good substitute for the first process. You will find ready-made definitions of words in rather terse and precise language. Nevertheless, by using a French–French dictionary either instead of, or in conjunction with, a bilingual one, you will greatly increase your vocabulary and ability to manipulate words.

Study skill

Work with a friend for a few minutes whenever you can. Take a short paragraph from a French newspaper and together see how many ways you can find of varying each sentence.

The following exercises are examples of other activities you and your friends can do together to help you to learn the kind of language you need for this sort of work. Using a monolingual French dictionary, you can make up many other similar puzzles for each other. You will learn equally from making up the puzzles and from doing them.

Practice questions

1   Trouvez dans les propositions ci-après une définition qui correspond à un des mots qui suivent. Attention! Il y a plus de mots que de définitions:
    épicier – supermarché – pharmacien – self-service – pharmacie – hypermarché – lycée – instituteur – mineur – collège d' enseignement secondaire – marin – instituteur – école

    (a) Grande surface qui vend des produits alimentaires en libre service
    (b) établissement scolaire pour les élèves de 15 à 18 ans
    (c) Grande surface proposant une grande variété de produits en libre service

(d) Personne qui enseigne dans une école primaire
(e) Jeune personne qui n'a pas encore atteint l'âge de 18 ans
(f) Membre du personnel d'un navire
(g) Ouvrier qui travaille dans une mine

2 Trouvez un mot anglais et un mot français qui correspondent aux définitions suivantes:
(a) Personne qui tue un être humain avec préméditation
(b) Personne qui pénètre dans une maison pour voler
(c) Pièce de métal frappée et souvent donnée en distinction honorifique
(d) Dire à quelqu'un des paroles injurieuses
(e) Répandre des matières toxiques dans la nature
(f) Opinion exprimée par chaque personne participant à une élection
(g) Esprit d'un mort qu'on suppose revenir d'un autre monde
(h) Manque presque total de produits alimentaires dans un pays
(i) Cercle imaginaire tracé autour de la terre à mi-distance des pôles
(j) Situation à laquelle on ne trouve pas d'issue

3 Expliquez en français la différence entre:
(a) Un professeur et un instituteur
(b) Un voleur et un meurtrier
(c) Un fleuve et une rivière
(e) Le football et le rugby
(f) Une église et une cathédrale
(g) Un dentiste et un médecin
(h) Un café et un restaurant
(i) Une librairie et une bibliothèque
(j) Une chemise et un chemisier
(k) La margarine et le beurre

4 Groupez chacun des mots suivants avec son opposé:
accepter – avouer – agréable – facile – privé – humide – nier – construire – parler – désagréable – se taire – refuser – détruire – difficile – trouver – libérer – public – emprisonner – augmenter – chuchoter – perdre – absence – artificiel – arriver – présence – diminuer – partir – naturel – sec – crier

5 Expliquez à une Française ou à un Français ce que veulent dire les expressions et sigles suivants:
(a) **MOT** (devant un garage)
(b) **PYO** strawberries (devant une ferme)
(c) **PLOUGHMAN'S — CHEDDAR** or **STILTON £3.50** (devant un pub)
(d) **UFO SEEN OVER SLOUGH** (dans un journal)
(e) **VAT** (sur une facture)
(f) **EARLY CLOSING WEDNESDAYS** (devant une boutique)
(g) **BEST-KEPT VILLAGE 1991** (à l'entrée d'un village)

6 Lisez le texte suivant:

DES LUMIÈRES MYSTÉRIEUSES AU-DESSUS DE LA MER

Hier soir vers 22 heures, de nombreux témoins ont observé pendant un bon quart d'heure des lumières mystérieuses qui sont apparues à la surface de la mer et se sont élevées dans l'air. Elles ont manœuvré comme pour faire plaisir aux spectateurs puis ont plané au-dessus de la plage. Parmi les témoins se trouvait René Poulain, pilote d'essai chez Aviex. Lui reste confondu. 'L'absence de tout bruit,' a-t-il déclaré à notre correspondant, 'me fait croire qu'il ne s'agit ni d'avions ni d'hélicoptères. Des ballons météorologiques ne pourraient pas faire des manœuvres aussi compliquées. Je ne trouve aucune explication à ce phénomène.' Monsieur Courtain, maire de Lacanuet, a ajouté, 'Ce n'est pas la première fois que l'on observe d'étranges lumières ou des soucoupes volantes dans cette région. Depuis des années, nous avons en moyenne un témoignage par mois en été et deux ou trois par mois en hiver. Personnellement je ne prends pas l'affaire trop au sérieux. Il doit y avoir une explication naturelle. Je ne vais pas me plaindre quand même, cela attire les touristes et notre petite ville devient célèbre.'

(a) Le sigle couramment employé pour ce genre de phénomène est OVNI. Que veut dire cette abbréviation?

(b) Trouvez dans le texte les expressions qui correspondent aux paraphrases suivantes. Elles ne sont pas dans le même ordre que dans le texte:
il reste perplexe – elles ont fait des mouvements – je n'arrive pas à expliquer – ça fait plusieurs années – il n'est pas question – ont flotté dans l'air – pour ma part – pour amuser ceux qui regardaient – c'est une attraction touristique – le silence absolu

7 Lisez le texte suivant:

LES DAMES DU CRIME

Agatha Christie aurait eu cent ans le mois prochain. La 'duchesse du crime' a fait école. Découvrez avec nous les petites nouvelles. D'autant qu'il n'y a pas meilleur cocktail que vacances, soleil et roman policier.

Agatha Christie, Phyllis Dorothy James, Mary Higgins Clark, Laurence Oriol… ces dames ont choisi de faire bouillir la marmite en mijotant de bons petits crimes que nous vous invitons à dévorer.

Drôle de genre pour une femme, pouvait-on penser dans les années vingt, lorsque Agatha Christie publia son premier roman policier *La mystérieuse affaire des styles*. Mais depuis qu'Hercule Poirot et Miss Marple, ses détectives vedettes, mènent l'enquête pas mal de romanciers ont trempé dans le crime, lui offrant une dimension toute féminine, le policier intimiste. Le crime est commis entre gens de bonne compagnie, qui se révèlent, en trois chapitres, être sans exception des modèles d'hypocrisie. L'intérêt de ce huis-clos criminel c'est que le lecteur dispose des mêmes éléments que le détective pour démasquer le coupable.

(a) Ce passage contient plusieurs phrases ou expressions au sens figuratif. Voici un commentaire numéroté présenté sous forme d'explication. Relisez le texte avec l'aide de celle-ci plutôt que d'employer un dictionnaire.

(i) *Les dames du crime* – les femmes, auteurs célèbres qui écrivent des romans policiers

(ii) *aurait eu cent ans* – c'est parce qu'elle est déjà morte

(iii) *duchesse du crime* – elle s'est fait une réputation comme femme qui écrit des romans policiers

(iv) *elle a fait école* – plusieurs romancières ont suivi son exemple avec grand succès

(v) *meilleur cocktail* – un mélange agréable de trois ingrédients: le temps libre, le soleil, et   la lecture d'un roman policier

(vi) *faire bouillir la marmite en mijotant de bons petits crimes* – dévorer.
une métaphore tirée de l'art de la cuisine: un crime qui se révèle lentement dans un récit délicieux à savourer

(vii) *Drôle de genre pour une femme* – un choix bizarre pour une femme écrivain

(viii)*détectives vedettes* – détectives renommés qui figurent comme héros dans plusieurs romans

(ix) *ont trempé dans le crime* – ont 'participé' au crime

(x) *huis clos* – monde privé et caché de la criminalité (*un tribunal à huis clos* – où le public n'est pas admis)

(b) Dans l'exercice suivant trouvez la phrase anglaise dont le sens, à votre avis, correspond le mieux au français. Il ne s'agit pas nécessairement d'une traduction fidèle. Vous pouvez adapter ou changer les traductions si bon vous semble:

(i) female crime writers – great lady crime writers – feminine writers of crime

(ii) would be a hundred – could have been a hundred – would have been a hundred

(iii) queen of crime – duchess of crime – grand old lady of crime

(iv) created a reputation – started a new trend in writing – set a precedent for other women writers

(v) (for the good reason that there is no better) mixture – combination – cocktail

(vi) slow cooking of delicious crimes – delicious aroma of slowly cooked crimes – crime that bubbles slowly and deliciously away

(vii) a funny occupation for a woman – funny kind of writing for a woman –an odd choice of subject for a woman writer

(viii) star detectives – detective heros – hero detectives

(ix) become involved in crime – got mixed up in crime – have become absorbed in crime

(x) private criminal world – hidden society of the criminal – secret world of crime

GAP-FILLING TASKS: CLOZE TESTS

These tasks are used by some Examining Boards as part of the written paper. They can take two forms:

(a) filling in gaps in a short text with no clues to the missing words

(b) filling in gaps using a list of possibilities, some of which are not appropriate
(i.e. the number of words exceeds the number of gaps)

When we read a text, or listen to speech, we do not give full attention to every word printed or spoken. Instead, we take it for granted that certain words will occur in certain places. It's a bit like listening to football results when you can predict whether the second mentioned team has won, lost or drawn from the intonation of the announcer's voice. In a printed text, several things affect our expectation of what is coming next:

(a) the general content of the passage

(b) the meaning of what has come before

(c) the sense of what follows

(d) the grammatical rules governing words and their endings.

Illustrative questions and answers

You should be able to guess many words missing from a French text. Try filling in the gaps in the following cloze tests:

EXAMPLE 1

L'AVENTURE EN AMÉRIQUE

C'est Christophe Colomb qui a (i)____ l'Amérique; depuis, beaucoup de gens y sont (ii)____ pour chercher l'aventure. Le premier homme qui a (iii)____ sur la lune (iv)____ américain. En Amérique tout est tellement plus (v)____ que chez nous! Même les champs (vi)____ immenses et pour récolter le blé il (vii)____ des douzaines de moissonneuses-batteuses*, les unes à côté des autres. Maman m'a (viii)____ des photos. C' (ix)____ impressionnant. C'est vraiment le pays de (x)____.

* de grandes machines qui coupent le blé, en détachent le grain et laissent derrière elles de grands paquets de paille.

Possible answers

(i)   *découvert* – part of a compound tense is missing, so a past participle is needed
(ii) *allés* – fits here, though partis would also: same grammatical reason
(iii) *marché* – fits the context but mis le pied would also fit: same reason
(iv) *était* – fits the sense: verb missing, a past tense required
(v)   *grand:* – adjective is missing: meaning of the following sentence gives the best clue
(vi) *sont* – verb missing, subject is plural
(vii) *faut* – 'are necessary', 'are needed' fits the sense: il doesn't refer to anything else in the sentence and so is impersonal
(viii) *montré* – fits the sense: perfect tense, so a past participle is missing
(ix) *est* – fits the sense: verb missing
(x)   *l'aventure* – though other words could also make sense: more difficult, a noun (used as an adjective with *de*)

You will see from this exercise that two things are important:

● Understanding the meaning of the words surrounding the missing ones
● Reading the grammatical clues that tell you:
     (a) What part of speech is required (verb – pronoun – adjective – noun etc.)
     (b) The tense or the part of the verb needed
     (c) What the subject is to get the agreement right

EXAMPLE 2

Essayez maintenant le même exercice avec le passage suivant en vous servant de la liste ci-dessous. Attention! il y a plus de mots qu'il ne faut. Ce sont ici les verbes qui manquent.

LES SERVICES PUBLICS

Dans chaque ville des équipes (i)____ du confort et de l'hygiène des habitants. Ils (ii)____ partie des Services publics. Tous les jours nous (iii)____ — de leur travail. Par exemple, ce matin, c'est grâce aux PTT que j' (iv)____ une carte postale de tante Marie qui (v)____ en Afrique. J' (vi)____ très content et j' (vii)____ beaucoup le facteur. Tous les jours aussi j' (viii)____ les employés de la voirie qui (ix)____ les rues et (xi)____ les poubelles. Sans eux la ville (xi)____ dégoûtante.

a reçu – s'occupe – font – bénéficient – fait – ai reçu – nettoyons – êtes – est – ai remercié – avons remercié – aperçu – nettoient – ai été – a été – serait – s'occupent – bénéficions – aperçois – vident

---

It is a good plan to cross off the words as you find a place for them. But you may find that having narrowed down the field the words left don't fit very well. This usually means that you have crossed off wrong ones earlier, so you need to go back over them.

Possible answers

This text illustrates how grammatical points are tested in this language task:
(i)   This requires a third person plural. Match the ending **and** the meaning
(ii) This is same part of the verb; *fait* won't fit;
(iii) *nous* tells you that you need a verb ending in *-ons*. Find one where the meaning fits in with the following *de* (e.g. 'benefit **from** their work')
(iv) *j'* shows a first person singular verb but which tense is suggested by *ce matin*?
(v)   *Tante Marie* is the subject, and is third person singular
(vi) This is the first person singular, what is the tense?
(vii) The sense requires a perfect tense, which first person singular verb fits the sense?
(viii) This is in the first person singular. What is the tense?
(ix) This is the third person plural. Which of the remaining verbs would fit the sense?
(x)   This is also in the third person plural. Which of the remaining verbs would fit the sense?
(xi) Which word would fit the meaning in English? 'Without them the town ____'

Note

You can see from model answer 2 that the extra words are put in for drawing a logical and usually a **grammatical** conclusion. In multiple-choice tests these are called distractors. So, don't write down the first word that catches your eye and looks as though it fits. Ask yourself the following questions:

1 Do I need a verb, noun, adjective, pronoun, preposition in this gap? If you then look at the available words, you should be able to narrow down your search.

2 If a verb, is it an infinitive? (e.g. after a preposition or the second verb in the clause).

3 If not an infinitive what is the subject of the verb? (e.g. If it's *vous* you will need a word ending in *-ez*).

4 Next check the tense. Does it fit the other tenses in the sentence and the meaning needed?

5 Is a subjunctive needed? (e.g. following another verb like *il faut que* or after a conjunction like *bien que* or *quoique*).

6 If it's a noun, check on its meaning in the sentence. If there are a few nouns to choose from, try eliminating those that don't fit the meaning.

7 If it's an adjective, check that the ending and the meaning fit.

8 Take particular care with the relative pronouns *qui*, *que*, and *qu'*. because subject and verb are frequently reversed in French. For example: *Les lettres que mon père écrivait* can also be expressed as *Les lettres qu'écrivait mon père*. So a gapped phrase like: *Le programme _____ suivaient les enfants*, with a choice of *qui* or *que* in the list, must have *que* in the gap (see also grammar section, pages 92–93).

By applying this system to the list of spare words for the gaps you can gradually eliminate the possibilities. If you tackle cloze tests systematically in this way they become like crossword puzzles!

EXAMPLE 3

For this question no words are given and only one word fits:

Sophie is discussing her winter holiday plans with her friends as she comes out of school.

D'habitude, en sortant de l'école, Sylvie passait un petit moment à bavarder avec des copines avant de _____ à la maison.

Aujourd'hui, on discutait des prochaines _____ de Noël. Brigitte et Arlette partiraient pour les sports d'hiver.

– Et toi, Sophie, tu ne vas pas _____ de ski?

– Je ne peux pas, a répondu Sophie.

– Pourquoi?

– A cause de la danse. Si je _____ cassais la jambe, toute ma carrière _____ finie.

– Alors, tu resteras à Paris pour les fêtes? a demandé Arlette.

– Non, a répondu Sophie, j'_____ au Puy, chez ma grande-mère.

Au Puy! C'est pas amusant.

– _____. C'est formidable. J'ai beaucoup d'amis là-bas.

Elle refusait de se considérer inférieure à ses copines, donc elle a ajouté:

– Mes parents passeront deux semaines à Chamonix. Ma mère skie très bien. Quand j'_____ petite, nous habitions dans les Alpes.

Personne _____ était impressioné par cette révélation. Tout à coup, Sophie a remarqué Pascal de l'autre côté de la rue. Il était, comme toujours, sans manteau et tenait un journal _____ le bras.

Toute souriante, Sophie a murmuré:

– Je vous quitte. On m'attend.

SEB

Answer plan

Vocabulary and some points of grammar are being tested in this task. Grammar points are as follows: after a preposition an infinitive is required; second verb in a clause must be an infinitive; reflexive pronouns; conditional tense; future tense; imperfect tense; negative expression requires 'ne'. The other gaps are filled by a word that makes sense. The best way of tackling it is to translate as you go through in order to find the most appropriate missing word. In nearly every case only one word will fit the sense.

Practice questions

1 (a) Essayez de combler les blancs dans le passage suivant sans l'aide d'une liste de mots.

QUE FAIRE EN CAS D'INCENDIE

- **Si vous pouvez vous enfuir**
- **Coupez le gaz**

  Dès que vous avez ____ qu'un ____ se développe dans ____ où vous ____, fermez immédiatement le ____ d'arrêt du ____ au compteur, ou ____ de la bouteille si vous n'avez pas le gaz de ville.

  En effet le ____ est certainement une des ____ principales du développement et de la propagation des incendies urbains.

- **Fermez votre porte**

  Avant de quitter votre ____, fermez-en soigneusement toute les ____ et les ____, y compris, bien sûr, la porte ____, que vous verrouillerez* avec soin pour isoler le mieux possible votre logis.

  N'____ surtout pas de ____ sur vous les ____, car les sauveteurs pourraient en avoir besoin et vous les ____.

  Enfin, il est bon de rappeler ici que vous ne ____ jamais, en aucun cas, regagner votre habitation sans la ____ expresse des ____, qui seuls peuvent apprécier le danger et les risques d'un réveil de l'incendie.

  * Means literally bolt but it is always used to mean 'lock'; mettre le verrou means specifically 'to bolt'

(b) Le passage suivant a été pris dans une autre partie de l'article d'où est tiré le texte précédant. Sans recopier le texte faites une liste des mots qui manquent. Attention! Vous ne les utiliserez pas tous.

SI VOUS NE POUVEZ VOUS ENFUIR

- **Enfermez-vous**

  (i)____ que vous avez constaté que la sortie est (ii)____ et (iii)____ vous ne pouvez fuir par (iv)____ issue, fermez votre porte et songez immédiatement à la (v)____. En effet, c'est (vi)____ et de sa résistance au feu (vii)____ dépend votre salut. Ne cherchez surtout pas à vous engager à tout prix: ce (viii)____ un véritable suicide. Agressé par les flammes, aveuglé et asphyxié par les fumées (ix)____ et les gaz chauds, (x)____ peuvent également vous brûler les poumons, vous (xi)____ en quelques instants.

  coupée – que – protéger – succomberiez – serait – aucune – qui – toxiques – que – dès – sera – de lui – sera – d'elle – succombez – coûtée – qui protège

2 Même exercice avec ce récit d'un hold-up à Bastia, en Corse:

HOLD-UP

Bastia Deux malfaiteurs, qui (i)____ de commettre un hold-up dans un hypermarché de Borgo, à une vingtaine de kilomètres au sud de Bastia, ont (ii)____ à échapper samedi aux gendarmes qui les (iii)____ en semant sur la chaussée des billets de banque qui ont (iv)_____ un important embouteillage. Vers 16 heures, deux individus armés de fusil à pompe et (v)_____ les visages étaient (vi)_____ sous des cagoules, ont (vii)_____ irruption à l'intérieur de l'hypermarché 'Corsaire' de la RN 193, et se sont fait remettre une importante somme d'argent avant de (viii)_____ la fuite sur une moto en direction du sud. Très rapidement (ix)_____ en chasse par une voiture de la gendarmerie, les malfaiteurs n'ont rien (x)_____ de mieux pour (xi)_____ de leurs poursuivants que de répandre derrière eux une pluie de billets. De nombreux (xii)_____ garaient à la hâte leurs voitures pour faire main basse sur cette manne* inespérée et pris dans un important embouteillage, les gendarmes (xiii)_____ abandonner leur poursuite.

* manne – la nourriture miraculeuse que Dieu a envoyée du ciel aux Israélites dans le désert.

provoqué – réussi – venaient – suivait – fit – réussir – dissimulés – prendre – trouvait – pris – trouvé – piétons – fallait – dissimulaient – poursuivaient – venait – fait – que – devaient – automobilistes – dont – se débarrasser – perdre

3 Faites cet exercice sans une liste de mots qui manquent:

ASSURANCES MOINS CHÈRES POUR LES FEMMES:

Elles _____ plus prudentes au volant que les hommes, et _____ moins d'accidents — les chiffres le _____. Le groupe Azur _____ donc aux conductrices de moyennes cylindrées _____ ont leur permis depuis plus de trois ans, des tarifs réduits (de 15 à 25% inférieurs aux tarifs habituels) Pour tout _____ et obtenir gratuitement un devis personnalisé, _____ 01 23 49 35.

Study techniques

1 Ask a friend or relation to choose an article at random from a French newspaper. Make two photocopies; on one copy remove every tenth word with correcting fluid. You then will have a text to work on and one to check your version. You could make it harder by having every ninth word removed! If more than every seventh word is taken out it is usually impossible – even for French people! You could also get someone to photocopy an article so that the last 2 or 3 letters on the end of each line are missing. This is not quite the same format as a cloze test but simulates what you sometimes have to do in reality.

2 Find someone to work with and make up cloze tests for each other, using newspaper and magazine articles which you think might interest each other.

3 You could also make up cloze tests with extracts from set texts. If you choose key passages, this will really help you to get to know them and you can kill two birds with one stone.

4 Word processors are very useful for producing cloze tests!

4.5 READING AND WRITING TASKS

The following exercises have been devised to practise many of the language tasks required by each Examining Board.

Exercices

1 (a) Lisez et interprétez les gros titres ci-dessous:

Le meurtrier d'un pompiste arrêté: son meilleur ami

Valise diplomatique dans le Boeing détourné sur l'Iran

Les faux policiers cambriolaient les vieilles dames

A Lyon l'ex-religieuse est accusée d'avoir détourné 900 000 francs

Réclusion à perpétuité pour l'auto-stoppeur assassin

Afflux de lettres piégées à Dublin

Deux jeunes gens tués par la drogue à Nice

Le chantage à la bombe contre 'Buckingham Palace'

Hold-up à la poste

Un incendie de trop pour le pompier pyromane

Grenades lacrymogènes au consulat italien

Assassin de sa grande-mère, on l'arrête trois jours après son crime

Métro incendié: une bouteille de gaz retrouvée sur la voie près de la porte de Vincennes

Vol de voiture à main armée

Vingt-deux tableaux dérobés dans un magasin-exposition

Sabotage sur la voie ferrée près de Montpellier

(b) Trouvez la traduction du titre ci-dessus
   (i)   Two young people die from drugs in Nice
   (ii)   Petrol pump murderer arrested: his best friend
   (iii)   Fire in the Metro: bottle of gas found on line near the Porte de Vincennes
   (iv)   Man arrested three days after murdering his grandmother
   (v)   One fire too many for the fireman arsonist
   (vi)   Former nun accused in Lyon of misappropriating 900 000F
   (vii)   Armed theft of car
   (viii) Hold-up in post office
   (ix)   Men dressed as police burgled old ladies
   (x)   Tear grenades in the Italian Consulate.
   (xi)   US diplomatic bag in Boeing hijacked over Iran
   (xii)   Hitchhiker murderer gets life
   (xiii) Spate of booby-trap letters in Dublin.
   (xiv)   Twenty-two paintings stolen from store exhibition
   (xv)   Sabotage on rail-line near Montpellier
   (xvi)   Bomb blackmail attempt on Buckingham Palace

(c) Après avoir fait ce travail, que veulent dire les mots et les phrases suivants:
   (i)   un meurtrier
   (ii)   cambrioler
   (iii)   le chantage
   (iv)   tués
   (v)   une religieuse
   (vi)   un vol
   (vii)   un incendie
   (viii) la voie ferrée
   (ix)   un piège
   (x)   un pompier
   (xi)   un pompiste
   (xii)   détourner un avion
   (xiii) détourner de l'argent
   (xiv)   réclusion à perpétuité
   (xv)   arrêté
   (xvi)   faux policiers

(d) Traduisez ces titres dans le style d'un journal anglais:
  (i) Hold-up à la poste par un pompier
  (ii) Il cambriolait son meilleur ami
  (iii) Avion détourné par une grande-mère
  (iv) Valise diplomatique volée par une religieuse
  (v) Policier tué par un pompiste
  (vi) Diplomate arrêté avec la drogue
  (vii) Grenades lacrymogènes saisies à la poste
  (viii) Vieilles dames pyromanes arrêtées avec des bouteilles de gaz devant le consulat
  (ix) Tué par une valise diplomatique tombée d'un avion
  (x) Chantage d'un pompier par une grande-mère

(e) Traduisez ces titres en français:
  (i) Killed by his best friend
  (ii) Air France plane hijacked over London
  (iii) Tear grenades seized after hold-up
  (iv) Robbery at the consulate
  (v) Life for murderer of petrol-pump attendant
  (vi) Fireman arrested with stolen paintings
  (vii) Booby-trap briefcase in post office
  (viii) Former nun blackmails diplomat
  (ix) Man posing as policeman steals diplomatic bag
  (x) Grandmothers burgle fireman's house
  (xi) Former policeman misappropriates best friend's money
  (xii) Bogus nun holds up post office
  (xiii) Murdered by ex-policeman: his best friend

(f) Try making up your own headlines, say three in English and three in French, and pass them to a partner for translating.

2 Lisez trois ou quatre fois l'article ci-dessous avant d'aborder les exercices:

Michel Leclerc l'a annoncé hier:

Une crèche bilingue, dès septembre, à Coulogne...

On en avait déjà entendu parler... Mais pas encore sur le ton péremptoire dont usa, hier Michel Leclerc, le promoteur de l'opération: une crèche bilingue sera ouverte dès le mois de septembre, à Coulogne, par l'association Eurobaby.

La nouvelle s'accompagne de plusieurs indications. En premier lieu, la crèche coulonnoise ne sera pas unique en son genre puisque Michel Leclerc annonça cinq ouvertures pour le mois de septembre, à Nice (deux), à Bordeaux, dans la réserve animalière de Thoiry et bien entendu à Coulogne.

Ces cinq crèches pourront accueillir 300 jeunes enfants au total qui pourront commencer à apprendre l'anglais, l'italien, l'espagnol et l'allemand.

Chaque crèche de 60 enfants, répartis en quatre ou cinq classes comprendra cinq moniteurs français et cinq autres ne parlant que les langues en question. Par des jeux et diverses animations, ces derniers devront amener les enfants à s'exprimer dans l'une des quatre langues 'européennes', en plus du français.

Lancée par M. Leclerc, l'association Eurobaby envisage de mettre sur pied, d'ici 1995, dans l'ensemble de la France 1000 crèches de ce type pouvant recevoir 60 000 enfants de un à six ans et employant 10 000 moniteurs dont une moitié de français et l'autre d'étrangers. Ces crèches seront gérées directement par des particuliers ou des associations avec le soutien et sous la surveillance d'Eurobaby. M. Leclerc souhaite que '30% à 50% des Français soient bilingues d'ici vingt ans' et prévoit 'd'ajouter le chinois et le russe' aux langues étrangères déjà programmées pour ces crèches. La contribution des parents, compte tenu de leurs revenus, devrait être en moyenne de 1800 francs par mois

Une des premières crèches bilingues sera donc coulonnoise ... Ou plutôt serait. Personne encore, à Coulogne ne put nous confirmer cette décision. 'Nous l'avons apprise par les médias, nous dit M. Dubut, adjoint au maire, M. Béharelle, étant en vacances actuellement. Rien n'est entériné sur le plan municipal...'

Cela dit, les Coulonnois ne semblent pas se liguer contre une telle décision... 'Nous sommes ni pour ni contre, dit encore M. Dubut. Le tout est de savoir si c'est vraiment intéressant...'

Notez Coulogne se trouve dans la banlieue de Calais

(a) Questions en anglais:
    (i) What do we know from the article about M. Leclerc?
    (ii) What does the 'Eurobaby' organization hope to achieve by the end of September?
    (iii) What are its long-term ambitions?
    (iv) How will work in the five crèches be organized?
    (v) What do M. Beharelle and M. Dubut think of the project?
    (vi) Who will be responsible for running individual crèches?

(b) Explication en français –
    (i) Expliquez en vos propres termes en français:
    une crèche – être bilingue – sur un ton péremptoire – un moniteur – la crèche coulonnoise ne sera pas unique – un adjoint au maire
    (ii) Pourquoi dans l'avant-dernier paragraphe écrit-on '...serait coulonnoise'?

(c) Questions en français:
    (i) Comment les enfants vont-ils apprendre à parler les langues en question?
    (ii) Quels détails sont donnés sur le financement du projet?
    (iii) A votre avis, est-ce que les sommes mentionnées seront suffisantes pour rémunérer le personnel.
    (iv) Que veut dire, à votre avis, le mot 'intéressant' employé au dernier paragraphe par M. Dubut?
    (v) Quelles difficultés pourriez-vous envisager pour la mise en place de ces crèches et de leur personnel?
    (vi) Un Français veut se renseigner sur les écoles maternelles en Angleterre. Quelles informations pourriez-vous lui donner?
    (vii) Mettez-vous à la place d'un parent français désirant envoyer son enfant à une de ces crèches et formulez cinq questions que vous voudriez poser à M. Leclerc.

(d) Vocabulaire –
    (i) Trouvez dans le texte l'équivalent des phrases suivantes:
    ne sera pas la seule – en somme – dont s'est servi – distribués – se faire comprendre – désire
    (ii) Faites une liste de mots dans le texte se terminant en '-tion'. Trouvez dans votre tête encore une douzaine de mots avec cette terminaison.
    (iii) Arrangez par ordre de mérite les phrases suivantes:
    Elle parle couramment le français – Elle se fait comprendre en français – Elle se débrouille en français – Elle maîtrise le français – Elle a quelques connaissances en français

3 Dans le passage suivant, une mère décrit une période difficile de la vie d'une de ses filles, Alberte. Celle-ci a commencé à voler des sommes d'argent dans la maison. Françoise, la mère, tâche d'abord de faire voir à sa fille le mal qu'elle a fait, mais sans succès. Vous allez découvrir ce qui arrive à la fin.

Alberte a traversé une période difficile. Rétive, paresseuse, elle qui ne l'a jamais été, s'est mise à dérober de petites sommes, tantôt dans mes poches, tantôt dans celles de Dolorès, puis dans le sac d'une épisodique femme de ménage. Cela finit par prendre des proportions inquiétantes: des billets de mille francs disparaissent. En même temps nous apprenons qu'elle arrive régulièrement en retard à l'école, où elle se fait conduire par des agents de police qui lui servent d'alibi et auxquels elle soutient qu'elles s'est égarée. (Elle traverse Paris en tous sens sans jamais se perdre.) Notre inquiétude grandit. Je raisonne la coupable.

'Voyons, essaie de comprendre; Christina, elle gagne cinq cents francs par heure, quand elle fait des ménages. Tu te rends compte que quand tu lui prends mille francs, tu lui voles deux heures de son travail!'

'Oui, mais tu l'a remboursée', dit-elle, butée.

'Je l'ai remboursée avec de l'argent qui représente mon travail à moi. Tu ne peux pas sortir de là.'

'Oui, mais c'est quand même plus juste...'

'Quoi?'

'Que tu me donnes ton travail à toi...'

'Que je te le donne, oui, que tu me le voles, non.'

'Est-ce que l'argent, c'est toujours du travail? Il y a des gens qui en ont et qui ne font rien.'

'Alors c'est ce qu'on appelle un capital, c'est l'argent qui travaille pour eux, quand il est placé. Mais c'est trop long à expliquer.'

'Oh! je comprends bien!' dit-elle, le visage illuminé de malice. 'C'est ces gens-là qu'il faudrait voler, hein?'

Je ne trouve pas de réponse. Inculquer à un enfant le respect du capital ne me semble pas besogne exaltante; par ailleurs, transformer ma fille en un Mandarin en jupons.... J'en suis à demander s'il faut consulter un psychologue, un psychanalyste même, quand brusquement, le remords ayant fait son œuvre (de quelle façon mystérieuse?) Alberte manifeste tout à coup, un matin, après cinq semaines de cynisme, une violente contrition, 'Je ne volerai plus, je ne volerai plus jamais!' et dépose sur mes genoux le fruit de ses rapines. Un reste de monnaie, une quantité invraisemblable de paquets de bonbons à moitié vides, biscuits et chocolats à demi rongés, un papillon artificiel en plastique, des boucles d'oreilles également en plastique, un singe mécanique qui bat du tambour, une boîte d'aquarelle, une trousse d'école en faux crocodile, et j'en passe. Que faire d'autre que de la consoler, la féliciter, prononcer un petit discours moral sur la force de la conscience (Caïn!) qui me fait rougir un peu, mais qu'Alberte approuve gravement.

Francoise Mallet-Joris *La Maison de Papier*

Quelques expressions:

rétif /rétive – une personne rétive est quelqu'un difficile à persuader ou à diriger

un mandarin en jupons – une fille ou une femme qui tient le rôle de bandit en volant l'argent des autres

(a) Questions en anglais:
  (i) Where did Alberte steal from?
  (ii) Why did she get the police to take her to school?
  (iii) Why is her mother amazed at her explanation?
  (iv) How does the mother try to convince her daughter that stealing from Christina is wrong?
  (v) What two kinds of money are referred to eventually and why is the mother lost for an answer?
  (vi) Why does Alberte suddenly change her ways?
  (vii) Judging from the things bought by Alberte with the stolen money, what age do you think Alberte is? Give your reasons.

(b) Expliquez en français Expliquez en vos propres termes en français ce que veulent dire les expressions suivantes:
  (i) une épisodique femme de ménage
  (ii) qui lui servent d'alibi
  (iii) le fruit de ses rapines
  (iv) je raisonne la coupable
  (v) inculquer à un enfant
  (vi) tu ne peux pas sortir de là

(c) Questions en français:
  (i) A votre avis, pourquoi est-ce qu' Alberte n'avait mangé que la moitié des chocolats et des biscuits qu'elle avait achetés?
  (ii) Pourquoi la mère rougit-elle un peu en parlant à sa fille après sa confession?
  (iii) Expliquez la référence à Caïn.

(d) Choisissez la traduction anglaise la plus convenable des phrases suivantes:
  (i) *Alberte a traversé une période difficile*

- It has been a difficult time for Alberte
- Alberte has traversed a difficult period
- Alberte has been through a difficult stage.

(ii) *Cela finit par prendre des proportions inquiétantes*
- It finished by taking on worrying proportions
- In the end it was getting out of hand
- Finally the thing started to get serious

(iii) *'Oh! je comprends bien!' dit-elle, le visage illuminé de malice*
- 'Oh, I understand well', she said, her face shining with malice
- 'I understand alright', she said, with a malicious look on her face
- 'I can see what you mean alright', she said her face glowing with mischief

(iv) *Alberte manifesta tout à coup, un matin après cinq semaines de cynisme, une violente contrition*
- Suddenly one morning, after five weeks of cynicism, Alberte had an attack of remorse
- Alberte suddenly one morning after five weeks of cynicism was overwhelmed by contrition
- After five weeks of cynicism, suddenly one morning Alberte was overcome by feelings of sorrow for what she had done

(v) Comment est-ce que vous traduiriez en anglais les mots et expressions suivants:

butée – l'argent... quand il est placé – sur mes genoux – un singe mécanique – que faire   d'autre que de la consoler

4 Dans le passage suivant, Françoise Mallet-Joris raconte les différentes étapes de la vie de son fils aîné, Daniel, de 5 jusqu'à 18 ans:

A cinq ans il manifesta un précoce instinct de protection en criant dans le métro, d'une voix suraiguë, 'Laissez passer ma maman.' A huit ans il 'faisait ses courses' et 'son' dîner tout seul, quand il estimait que je rentrais trop tard le soir. Il me dépassait déjà complètement. A neuf ans, nous eûmes quelques conflits. Il refusa d'aller à l'école, de se laver et de manger du poisson. Un jour je le plongeai tout habillé dans une baignoire, un autre jour Jacques le porta sur son dos à l'école: il hurla tout le long du chemin. Ces essais éducatifs n'eurent aucun succès. Du reste, il se corrigea tout seul. Nous décidâmes de ne plus intervenir.

A dix ans, au lycée, ayant reçu pour sujet de rédaction, 'Un beau souvenir', il écrivit ingénument: 'Le plus beau souvenir de ma vie, c'est le mariage de mes parents.'

A quinze ans il eut une période yé-yé. Nous collectionnâmes les 45 tours. A seize ans il manifesta un vif intérêt pour le beau sexe. De jeunes personnes dont j'ignorais toujours jusqu'au prénom s'engouffraient dans sa chambre, drapées dans d'immenses imperméables crasseux, comme des espions de la Série noire.

Il joua de la clarinette. Il but un peu.

A dix-sept ans il fut bouddhiste.

Il joua du tuba. Ses cheveux s'allongèrent.

A dix-huit ans il passa son bac. Un peu avant il avait été couvert de bijoux comme un prince hindou ou un figurant de cinéma, une bague à chaque doigt. J'attendais en silence, ébahie et intéressée, comme devant la pousse d'une plante, la mue d'une chenille.

Les bijoux disparurent. Il joua du saxophone, de la guitare. Il fit 4000 kilomètres en auto-stop, connu les tribus du désert en Mauritanie, vit un éléphant en liberté, voyagea couché à plat ventre sur un wagon, à demi asphixié par la poussière. Il constata que Dakar ressemble étonnamment à Knokke-le-Zoute (Belgique).

Il revint pratiquement sans chaussures, les siennes ayant fondu à la chaleur du désert, mais doté d'un immense prestige auprès de ses frères et sœurs. Il rasa ses cheveux et fit des sciences économiques. Voilà la saga de Daniel.

Dans tout cela, où est l'éducation? Si Daniel, qui va atteindre sa majorité cette année, est un bon fils, un beau garçon, doué d'humour et de sérieux, de fantaisie et de bon sens, y suis-je pour quelque chose? Ah! pour rien, pour rien, et pourtant pour quelque chose, une toute petite chose, la seule peut-être que je lui ai donnée, la seule, me dis-je parfois avec orgueil, qu'il était important de lui donner: la confiance.

Ce qui ne veut pas dire que tous les problèmes soient résolus. Daniel vient d'acheter un singe!

Françoise Mallet-Joris *La Maison de Papier*

Quelques explications

Jacques – c'est le mari de Françoise
la Série noire – des romans policiers dans le genre 'espionnage international'
la mue d'une chenille – une chenille c'est la larve d'un papillon
la mue – c'est le changement dans la peau de la chenille à mesure que celle-ci grandit

(a) Questions en anglais:

   (i) Why exactly was Daniel's behaviour in the underground embarrassing?

   (ii) How were Daniel's problems at the age of nine overcome?

   (iii) What decision did his parents take at that time?

   (iv) Why might the opening line of his essay have been embarrassing to his parents?

   (v) Explain what Françoise's reaction was when she wrote *j'attendais en silence, ébahie et intéressée comme devant la pousse d'une plante, la mue d'une chenille*. How apt is her use of these images?

   (vi) What countries did Daniel visit before going into higher education?

   (vii) What do you understand by the phrase *il constata que Dakar ressemble étonnamment à Knokke-le-Zoute (Belgique)*?

   (viii) What is Daniel like at twenty, according to his mother?

   (ix) What part has she played in his education?

   (x) What attitude do you think she shows in her closing remark about Daniel? Explain yourreason.

(b) Travail en anglais et en français —

   (i) Expliquez en anglais ce que vous entendez par les phrases ou les expressions suivantes:

- *un précoce instinct de protection*
- *il écrivit ingénument*
- *il eut une période yé-yé*
- *nous collectionnâmes les quarante-cinq tours.*
- *un espion*
- *atteindre sa majorité*

   (ii) Lesquelles des expressions suivantes correspondent le mieux au sens de celles d'en haut:

- *l'instinct féroce de protéger – un instinct prématuré de protection – un instinct de protection au delà de son âge*
- *il écrivit naïvement – avec toute innocence – sincèrement*
- *à un certain temps il aimait beaucoup la musique pop – chanter en s'accompagnant de la guitare – écouter la musique pop*
- *nous faisions une collection des disques à 45 tours – des disques des années 45 – des photos des châteaux de la Loire*
- *un agent provocateur – un agent secret – un agent de police*
- *avoir le droit de voter – avoir 18 ans – avoir 21 ans*

   (iii) **Traduction en anglais** Trouvez une phrase anglaise pour:
le beau sexe – un éléphant en liberté – couché à plat ventre – doué... de fantaisie et de bon sens – y suis-je pour quelque chose?

(iv) **Retranslation** Lisez le texte suivant puis relisez deux ou trois fois le passage en français. Essayez de traduire sans trop regarder le français original.

Françoise got married when she was 18. Daniel was born nine months later. Her son was a precocious child. When he was 5, he used to get his own dinner ready if he thought his mother was late in returning home. When he was 9, his parents had several battles with him. Once he refused to get washed so his mother dropped him fully clothed into the bath. On another occasion he didn't want to go to school so his father carried him there on his back. He once wrote in an essay 'The nicest thing I can remember is when my mum and dad got married'. At 16 he became very keen on girls. He went through a pop-music period. He became a buddhist and let his hair grow long. After sitting his bac exam, he hitch-hiked 4000 kilometres in Africa. When he returned home, he enjoyed great prestige with his brothers and sisters.

Today, Daniel is a handsome boy with a sense of humour but also a serious side. His mother believes they were right not to interfere too much in his life. She is proud that she has played a small but significant part in his upbringing by giving him confidence.

5 Lisez trois ou quatre fois le passage ci-dessous:

Clémentine était très adroite, mais elle trichait impudemment, et refusait d'admettre qu'elle avait perdu.

De plus, elle mentait sans cesse, pour rien, pour le plaisir.

Par exemple, venant à ma rencontre sur la pointe des pieds, elle m'annonçait à voix basse, avec des mines terrorisées, que M. le directeur était gravement malade, et que plusieurs médecins entouraient son lit. Cinq minutes plus tard, tandis que je songeais aux funérailles grandioses de ce puissant chef, M. le directeur lui-même traversait la cour, tout guilleret, et la canne à la main.

Une autre fois, un superbe tirailleur sénégalais — un sergent — était venu, disait-elle, la demander en mariage à sa mère, 'parce que dans son pays les filles se marient à douze ans'. Naturellement, sa mère avait refusé, 'parce qu'en Afrique, il fait trop chaud, et puis là-bas, ce sont les femmes qui portent les paquets'.

'D'ailleurs', ajoutait-elle, 'je suis fiancée avec un prince américain. Il gagne tellement d'argent qu'il a de grandes caisses pour le mettre. Mais ça m'est défendu de vous dire son nom'.

'Qu'est-ce que tu as? Pourquoi ris-tu?'

Mais au lieu de répondre, elle se levait d'un bond, courait prendre son balai, et elle dansait avec lui.

Un jour, dans un élan d'amitié, je lui avais dit, 'Tu aurais de beaux yeux, s'ils étaient pareils.'

Sur quoi, cette idiote avait fondu en larmes, avec des sanglots et des hoquets déchirants.

Pour la calmer, je lui expliquai que c'était un compliment, et que je trouvais avantageux d'avoir deux œils au lieu de deux yeux. Avec la rapidité d'un chat, elle me griffa la joue sous l'oreille, à quoi je répondis par une gifle absolument réussie. Elle demeura un instant comme stupéfaite, puis elle courut au platane et, le front sur son avant-bras, elle se mit à ululer si fort qu'il me parut prudent de rentrer chez moi au pas de course.

M Pagnol *Le temps des secrets*

Quelques explications
M. le directeur – est le chef d'une école primaire
un tirailleur – est un soldat de l'infanterie
guilleret – veut dire 'gai et vif'

(a) Questions en français:

   (i) Expliquez ce que vous entendez par l'expression *elle trichait impudemment*.

   (ii) Pourquoi le garçon est-ce qu'il croit au premier mensonge de Clémentine?

   (iii) A votre avis où est-ce que Clémentine a trouvé les détails au sujet de la vie des femmes en Afrique?

   (iv) Quel détail des mensonges de Clémentine trouvez-vous le plus exagéré?

   (v) Qu'est-ce que le garçon voulait dire en racontant à Clémentine qu'elle avait *deux œils au lieu de deux yeux*?

   (vi) Comment expliquez-vous la réaction de la jeune fille?

(b) **Traduction en anglais** Choisissez la version la plus convenable ou si aucune version ne vous plaît, composez en une qui convient:

   (i) *Clémentine était très adroite, mais elle trichait impudemment, et refusait toujours d'admettre qu'elle avait perdu*

- Clementine was very clever but she cheated impudently and always refused to say she had lost
- Clementine was very smart but full of impudent tricks always refusing to admit that she had lost
- Clementine was very clever but cheated shamelessly never wanting to be wrong

   (ii) *elle m'annonçait à voix basse, avec des mines terrorisées, que M. le directeur était gravement malade, et que plusieurs médecins entouraient son lit.*

- she announced in a low voice that the Headmaster was seriously ill and that his bed was surrounded by several doctors
- she told me in a whisper that the Head was gravely ill and that several doctors were standing around his bed
- she announced in a whisper that the Head was seriously ill and that several doctors were grouped around his bed

   (iii) *la demander en mariage à sa mère*

- ask her mother for her in marriage
- ask for her hand in marriage
- ask the mother if he could marry her

(c) Comblez les blancs avec un mot ou une phrase choisis dans la liste ci-dessous:

Un soir, quand elle ____ des commissions, un homme énorme, avec une barbe ____, l'avait poursuivie dans la rue. Il ____ nuit, elle ____ couru de toute ses forces. 'S'il m'avait ____, je ne sais pas ce qu'il m'____ fait'

   Paul était d'avis qu'il voulait la faire ____ dans un cirque, ou peut-être la ____ à vendre des paniers dans un pays étranger, comme Toulouse ou Avignon.

   Alors elle hôcha la tête plusieurs fois et ricana tout bas en me ____ de côté; puis elle dit, 'C'____ un enfant! Il ne ____ pas!'

aura – faisait – grande – a – dansé – rattrapé – aurait – dansant – obliger – forcer – avait – rattrapée – a fait – noire – revenait – regarder – était – comprend – est – regardant – est revenue – comprends

(d) **Retranslation:**

When I was 10 I used to play with a girl called Clementine. I remember that she was very pretty and clever but that she had the bad habit of telling lies all the time. One day, for example, she came running up to me with tears in her eyes and told me that the Headmaster was seriously ill and that the doctors said he was going to die. Imagine my surprise half an hour later when I saw the Head walking across the playground accompanied by Clementine's mother!

   One day for a joke I said to Clementine, 'You would have lovely hair if it was dark instead of blond.' She immediately burst into tears. I tried to console her by explaining that I really preferred girls with blond hair. With a speed that surprised me she turned round and scratched my face.

6 Lisez les textes suivants et répondez aux questions.

Pour ou contre?

Faut-il taxer les véhicules qui roulent au diesel?

POUR

Jean-Claude Delarue

Fondateur de SOS environnement, président de l'Association des usagers de l'administration et des services publics (Adua).
Professeur d'anglais à Paris VII, ancien membre du Conseil économique et social.

La différence de prix qui existe à la pompe entre le gazole et le super favorise l'utilisation du moteur Diesel. Aujourd'hui, en France, près de six millions de voitures particulières et plus d'un million et demi d'utilitaires roulent au gazole. Je suis pour un relèvement du prix du gazole, car ces moteurs restent plus polluants que ceux à essence. Les évolutions techniques n'évitent toujours pas au moteur Diesel les émissions de particules de carbone et d'oxyde d'azote. Or les statistiques le prouvent: quand le nombre de particules en suspension dans l'air s'accroît de manière significative, les crises d'asthme peuvent augmenter de 30%, et la mortalité pour causes respiratoire et cardio-vasculaire progresse également.

Les équipements que l'on nous présente, tels le catalyseur d'oxydation et le filtre à particules, ne doivent pas nous faire oublier la réalité quotidienne: un moteur mal réglé, même de conception moderne, dépasse les normes admises. Or, la France est le pays où il y a le plus d'écart entre la réglementation et son application. Sans nier les progrès techniques accomplis ces dix dernières années, je ne crois pas que le diesel soit une bonne solution. Pour moi, ses inconvénients sont plus nombreux que ses avantages.

En favorisant fiscalement le gazole, on a provoqué l'émergence d'un énorme parc de diesels. La France est le pays qui possède le plus au monde. Aujourd'hui, l'opinion publique s'émeut de la qualité de l'air, car les villes s'asphyxient. On s'interroge donc sur les moyens de limiter la pollution provoquée notamment par le diesel. S'attaquer à cette seule question serait une erreur: on soignerait l'effet mais pas la cause. C'est à la justification même du diesel qu'il faut s'intéresser. Economiquement, une taxe sur le diesel alimenterait les caisses de l'Etat, qui pourrait peut-être investir davantage dans l'amélioration des transports en commun. Un gazole plus cher diminuerait aussi le fret routier au profit du rail et du fleuve, plus sûrs et mieux contrôlés. Jusqu'à présent, le diesel a bénéficié de mesures économiques qui ne tiennent pas compte de l'aspect écologique et sanitaire. Il est grand temps d'inverser la tendance…

CONTRE

Jean-Yves Helmer

Directeur de la division automobile PSA – Peugeot-Citroën.
PSA est le premier constructeur mondial de moteurs Diesel. En 1994, le groupe français a produit près d'un million de véhicules Diesel.

Si le prix du gazole à la pompe rejoint celui du super, il va sans dire que les conséquences sur l'avenir du moteur Diesel seront désastreuses, avec des répercussions sur l'économie toute entière. Au nom de la pollution de l'air, on fait un faux procès au diesel, alors qu'il présente beaucoup d'avantages. Les opposants à ce moteur prétendent qu'il est très polluant. Pour ce qui concerne les émissions d'oxyde de carbone, d'oxyde d'azote et de dioxyde de soufre, un diesel est bien moins polluant à la source qu'un moteur à essence. Il a fallu que ceux-ci soient équipés de catalyseurs pour qu'ils arrivent au niveau des diesels! Et, à partir d'octobre 1996, la teneur en soufre des gazoles sera réduite, tandis que les catalyseurs d'oxydation équiperont tous les nouveaux diesels.

En fait, le diesel est incriminé du fait du rejet des résidus solides de combustion. Pourtant, en vingt ans, on a divisé par dix le niveau d'émission de particules de carbone. La conception des diesels d'aujourd'hui les rend, de fait, moins polluants qu'il y a dix ans. Ainsi, la qualité de l'air s'améliore déjà par le renouvellement naturel du parc automobile.

Mais le remède contre les particules passe aussi par une modification des gazoles. Il suffirait que les pétroliers proposent un carburant "propre" pour diminuer des deux tiers les émissions de particules de tout le parc diesel, neuf et ancien.

Par ailleurs, le diesel est un facteur d'économie d'énergie, et participe à l'augmentation de l'indépendance énergétique du pays. En effet, il consomme 25 à 30% moins qu'un moteur à essence, et le gazole est moins cher que le super. Dans quelques années, on devrait encore réaliser un gain de consommation de 10 à 15%. De plus, la durée de vie d'un diesel entretenu atteint 300 000 kilomètres.

Une éventuelle taxe fiscale sur le diesel aurait aussi des conséquences directes sur l'emploi. N'oublions pas que le moteur Diesel est une spécialité française, ce qui représente une force à l'exportation très grande.

Le diesel n'a que trente ans. En alliant les recherches des pétroliers et des constructeurs, ce sera vraiment le moteur thermique de l'avenir.

Ça m'intéresse No 175, September 1995

(a) Répondez vrai ou faux aux observations suivantes:
  (i)   Le gazole est plus cher que le super.
  (ii) Quand le nombre de particules de carbone dans l'air s'accroît les crises d'asthme diminuent.
  (iii) Le réglage des moteurs à diesel est strictement contrôlé en France.
  (iv) Un moteur Diesel est plus polluant qu'un moteur à essence avec catalyseur.
  (v)   Les voitures à diesel d'aujourd'hui sont aussi polluants que ceux d'il y a 10 ans.
  (vi) La durée de vie d'un moteur à diesel est très courte.
  (vii) Il y a plus de voitures Diesel en France qu'en Angleterre.
  (viii) Un moteur à essence consomme plus de carburant qu'un moteur Diesel.
  (ix) La quantité de soufre dans le gazole sera réduite l'année prochaine.
  (x)   On exporte de France très peu de voitures Diesel.

(b) Trouvez dans le texte l'équivalent des expressions suivantes
  (i)   une augmentation du prix
  (ii) n'empêche pas
  (iii) tout en admettant
  (iv) une manière de bien résoudre le problème
  (v)   on se demande comment on va réduire la pollution
  (vi) aborder uniquement ce problème
  (vii) a profité de
  (viii) il va de soi
  (ix) on accuse à tort
  (x)   le nombre total de voitures

(c) Complétez les phrases suivantes selon l'information du texte
  (i)   Les gens utilisent les voitures Diesel parce que...
  (ii) Malgré les évolutions techniques les moteurs Diesel...
  (iii) Les crises d'asthme deviennent plus nombreuses lorsque...
  (iv) L'effet d'accroître le prix du diesel serait de...
  (v)   Le diesel joue un rôle dans l'économie énergétique parce que...

(d) Complétez les déclarations suivantes en citant trois raisons justifiant votre opinion:
  (i)   Je n'achèterai pas de voiture Diesel parce que...
  (ii) Je n'achèterai pas de voiture à essence parce que ....

(e) En vous servant des détails donnés sur la vie et les intérêts de ces personnages expliquez en vos propres termes les raisons de leurs points de vue.

(f) Faites un résumé des arguments proposés par ces deux personnes. Ecrivez 180 mots environ.

7   ALERTE À L'OVNI SUR L'AUTOROUTE PARIS-LILLE

Le plan prévu pour la récupération d'ovni n'a été appliqué qu'une seule fois en France. C'était en 1988. et le préfet de la Somme était aux commandes
A 21 heures, le 29 septembre 1988, un automobiliste voit devant lui une boule lumineuse traverser l'autoroute Paris-Lille. Fumée, éclats de lumière..., l'objet, disparaît dans le talus. Au poste de gendarmerie de l'autoroute, le récit du témoin est pris au sérieux. Depuis plusieurs semaines une épée de Damoclès plane dans le ciel. *Cosmos 1900*, un satellite espion russe dont le radar est alimenté par un réacteur nucléaire contenant 45 kg d'uranium fortement enrichi, est en perdition. Le secrétaire d'Etat aux risques majeurs a assuré qu'une retombée radioactive était "peu probable", mais le Sepra*, chargé de suivre la trajectoire de l'engin, a mis en place, au CNES ** de Toulouse, une cellule de crise. Aussitôt prévenu, le préfet décide la fermeture du tronçon d'autoroute et l'isolement de la zone. Le Sepra, alerté par le telex de la gendarmerie, est incrédule: à l'heure indiquée, *Cosmos 1900* devrait être au-dessus de l'Océan Indien. La sécurité civile, dépêchée par le préfet de la Somme, équipe ses spécialistes de protection antiradiations. L'automobiliste est conduit à l'hôpital pour subir des examens.

La presse est tenue à l'écart

La nouvelle a filtré: TF1 diffuse un flash spécial. La presse est tenue à l'écart. Avec d'infimes précautions, compteurs Geiger à la main, les hommes de la protection civile s'approchent du fossé. Les compteurs restent muets. Dans la lumière des projecteurs, une sphère d'environ 1,50 m de diamètre, couverte d'une multitude de petits miroirs, reflète des scaphandriers aux allures d'extraterrestres. Au même moment, le musicien Jean-Michel Jarre ignore qu'il devra priver son spectacle d'une "boule de lumière". Tombée d'un camion, elle aura réussi bien d'autres effets!

* corps dont la mission première est de suivre les débris de satellite pour éviter des accidents dus à leur retombée sur terre. ** Centre National d'Etudes Spaciales

Ça m'intéresse No 175, September 1995

(a) Voici, en résumé, dix étapes principales de cet incident. Remettez-les dans le bon ordre chronologique. Il n'est pas nécessaire d'écrire les phrases: utilisez les chiffres 1 à 10.

L'automobiliste est conduit à l'hôpital
Le secrétaire d'Etat assure qu'une retombée radioactive est "peu probable"
La presse est tenue à l'écart
Les Russes lancent Cosmos 1900
Un automobiliste voit tomber une boule lumineuse
La sécurité civile est équipée de protection antiradiation
Sepra est alerté par la gendarmerie de la Somme
Les hommes de la protection civile retrouvent une sphère
Un flash à la télévision
Le préfet décide de fermer une partie de l'autoroute

(b) Répondez aux questions suivantes:
(i) Pourquoi les gendarmes prennent-ils au sérieux le récit de l'automobiliste?
(ii) Pourquoi Sepra trouve-t-il difficile de croire au télex de la gendarmerie?
(iii) Pour quelle raison est-ce que la presse est tenue à l'écart?
(iv) Pourquoi les compteurs Geiger restent-ils muets?
(v) Quelle surprise attendait Michel Jarre à Londres?

(c) Lisez les définitions de dictionnaire suivantes et trouvez dans le texte les mots qui correspondent à ces définitions:
(i) Fonctionnaire qui assume l'administration d'un département comme représentant du pouvoir central
(ii) Instrument qui mesure le niveau de radiation
(iii) Corps solidaire limité par une surface courbe dont tous les points sont à une distance égale d'un point intérieur appelé centre
(iv) L'ensemble des périodiques
(v) Information importante transmise en priorité

(d) Trouvez dans le texte une expression ou un mot qui correspond aux phrases suivantes;
on a attaché de l'importance à ce qu'il disait
n'a pas beaucoup de chances de se produire
dès qu'on l'avait informé
ne veut pas croire
qui a l'air de venir de l'espace
ne sait pas

8   **LA VALEUR DE LA FAMILLE EN FRANCE.**

Famille je vous aime! Cernés par le doute, les Français se raccrochent à la cellule de base. Et l'accomodent à leur manière.

Contestée en 1968, la famille _____ en tête des sondages. En effet, 58% des Français _____ qu'elle est la valeur la plus importante (selon un sondage _____ en janvier 1994) et réalisé pour la Croix-l'Evénement – CSA) avant l'honnêteté, la justice et l'amour.

Mais famille ne _____ plus forcément mariage. Le grand bouleversement de ces dernières années, c'est l'union libre : 1 couple sur 8 aujourd'hui, _____ 1 sur 35 en 1968. Perçue comme un mariage à l'essai, la cohabitation est en vogue chez les _____ de 25 ans. Et cette forme de vie est parfaitement _____ par la société puisque, selon l'institut de sondage SOFRES, 76% des Français _____ un couple vivant en cohabitation comme une famille. Et, _____ des contraintes institutionelles, le périmètre familal a tendance à _____ et à prendre de multiples formes, de la plus simple, monoparentale, à la plus vaste, la "tribalisation" dans laquelle grands-parents, oncles et tantes _____ à nouveau un rôle de premier plan.

Curieuse, difforme, la famille de 1995 apparaît comme un cercle à géométrie variable. On trouve des mots pour la qualifier: éclatée, recomposée, etc. Car, séparés ou divorcés, hommes et femmes tentent de refaire leur vie et de recomposer une famille avec un autre conjoint. Le ou les enfants vivent alors avec chacun de leurs deux parents et des demi-frères ou sœurs. Ils font partie de cette famille recomposée. "Plutôt que soustraction, il y a alors abondance de parents. L'enfant ne dispose plus d'un père mais de deux, un père biologique et un père social", note Martine Segalen dans *Sociologie de la famille* (éd. Armand Colin). Ballotté entre deux foyers, l'enfant souffre souvent des problèmes de références. On estime aujourd'hui à quelque 600 000 le nombre de familles recomposées en France. Et ce chiffre augmente d'autant plus que le nombre de divorces est en train d'exploser: 1 mariage sur 3 se termine aujourd'hui par un divorce, avec même une pointe à 2 sur 3 dans la région parisienne!

Ça m'intéresse Avril 1995

(a) Remplissez les blancs dans les deux premiers paragraphes du texte par l'un des mots suivants. Attention, il y a plus de mots que de blancs.

acceptée   signifie   moins   se trouve   effectué   libéré   reconnaissent   estiment   contre   affecté   après   s'étendre   jouent   se trouvent   plus   enchaîné   joue   se rétrécir

(b) Trouvez dans le texte un mot ou une expression correspondant à la même idée que les mots ou groupes de mots suivants:
   (i) une enquête destinée à déterminer l'opinion d'une population concernant un fait social.
   (ii) le cercle de la famille
   (iii) de première importance
   (iv) lieu d'habitation d'une famille
   (v) devient plus grand

(c) Answer in English the following questions in such as a way as to show that you have understood the passage.
   (i) What do you understand by *une famille recomposée*?
   (ii) Explain what is meant by the expression *l'enfant souffre de problèmes de références*?
   (iii) In your opinion why is the divorce rate higher in Paris than elsewhere in France?

CHAPTER 5

FRENCH LITERATURE

Units in this chapter

5.1 INTRODUCTION

A study of a number of books in French – novels, plays or poetry – is an option with most of the Examination Boards. Students beginning an A-Level course find this one of the most demanding tasks and a big step after the kinds of reading required for GCSE.

It is important to remember that novels and plays have a story to tell with a beginning, a middle and an end. You are presented with a series of events that unfold as you read or watch and one of the motives for reading a novel or seeing a play performed is to find out what happens next and how things turn out in the end.

For stories to work you need people – the characters, whose actions collectively or individually decide or influence what happens. To some extent they are like people you know or have met. They behave in ways that you admire or, perhaps more often, in ways you disapprove of. You may find that you have mixed feelings about many of them or that there is a certain amount of ambiguity in their behaviour. All this reflects what real life is like.

The third element to consider is that plays and novels take place against a certain background, either carefully described or vaguely referred to. The background may be a particular place with a way of life that affects to some extent the people who live there. The background could also be influenced by historical events and standards and values different at that time. War, plague or famine could also play their part. Economic conditions could also influence how people behave. Moral considerations might also have their impact on background because expectations and conventions of behaviour can change according to time and place.

Poetry is also about life. As well as being in a recognisably different form from novels and plays, poetry presents life as chunks of concentrated and intense experience. Poems are often therefore shorter than novels and plays and the language used is more concise with different shades of meaning. Some poems are nevertheless stories with characters who think and speak.

Novels, plays and poems present us with other people's experience or interpretation of life with ideas, opinions and behaviour that are partly familiar but in many ways fresh.

Reading a novel or poem, seeing a play performed becomes therefore a two-way exchange. You bring your experience into contact with that of the author. It is important to bear in mind that reading is entertainment, even if serious entertainment. It gives pleasure. Also that reading is finding out, not only what happened next or in the end but how people are, how they behave and think. With an examination in mind you also have to know your book or play quite well and be able to show that you do by writing intelligently about it.

HOW CAN I UNDERSTAND THE TEXT?

This is the difficulty experienced by all students in the transition from GCSE to A-Level and there is no short cut. You have to practise reading to get better at it. It does help though if you have an outline or an impression of the whole before you begin to read. In many ways it is easier to start with a play, if one is included in the syllabus, because of the division into acts and scenes. The list of the characters and sometimes a description of them at the beginning is also useful. The writer's stage directions can also help understanding. Some texts of plays have a synopsis of the action at the beginning.

With a novel it helps if you have some idea beforehand of the overall pattern of events in the novel. Your teacher should be able to give you this or you could look for a description or synopsis in a book of criticism. It is useful to know for example if events are linear, that is starting at one point in time and finishing at another later without interruption. Or whether the story is told as a flashback, or a series of flashbacks. It is difficult to make sense of the beginning of François Mauriac's *Thérèse Desqueyroux* unless you know that the first part of the novel is a long flashback through the events leading up to the attempted murder of Bernard.

Having got some idea of the overall pattern of the book try reading the text straight through without pausing too much over parts you don't understand or looking up too many words. With a play it is important to remember that it was written to be acted rather than read. The words have only a face value. Their interpretation is revealed by tone of voice, gesture, movement and look of the performing actors.

USING TRANSLATIONS

Most of the Examination Boards require you to write in French. Texts should be read in French. If you really do find this too difficult, you could try reading an English translation of the book first, making a chapter by chapter summary as you do so, and then read the original; as you do this, produce a summary of each chapter in French. You will find that the "value" of words in English for you is different to their value in French. You will have a large range of associations and shades of meaning that you can attach to English words but a much more restricted one, as yet, in French. If you rely too heavily on translations these values will never balance out.

Use the French text, rather than the translation, for reference, note-making and general work on the book so that you know your way around it. Write your notes and comments about the book in French; or if you do jot down things in English leave a space and look up the French later and add it. Some Boards allow you to take the text into the examination. Check the requirements of your Board.

5.2 METHODS OF STUDY

Contents
- Novels and short stories
- Drama
- Poetry

NOVELS AND SHORT STORIES

Structure

Make your own synopsis or summary of the action as you read the text a second time. You can do this according to the parts or chapters or for each story. It is also useful in some cases to give your own titles to chapters indicating roughly what they are about, or to create your own divisions in the text if none exist already. Is the story one continuous account or are there flashbacks or events subsidiary to the main action? Do the events unfold in one place or is the reader whisked from one social setting to another?

Characters

Make a list of the characters, dividing them into main, secondary and minor characters. Where large families are concerned make a family tree so that you have a visual impression of the people, their chronology and relationships. This is particularly helpful with some of Mauriac's or Zola's novels. Try to determine the function of the characters in the story. Some will be responsible for initiating and maintaining the course of events. Others may play a lesser role in influencing the action but may have a functional role in illuminating the personality or behaviour of the main characters. The guard who eventually stops the Pagnol family in *Le Château de Ma Mère* from taking their short cut along the canal is not particularly interesting as a character. He is instead a caricature of a bully and officialdom to scare the law-abiding father. He is depicted as so grotesque that we are pleased and relieved when he gets his just desserts.

It is also helpful to think of the main characters in terms of their effect upon each other by asking yourself whether they clash or complement one another. Look for any ambiguity in behaviour and also for development. Do personalities change or evolve during the period described in the book? Is change brought about by events, by others, or by the growth of a tendency within a character? Write your own brief character description of the main protagonists, illustrating your judgements with examples from the text of what people say, think or do. Take into account any details of physical appearance. Do the names of the characters have any significance?

Narration and viewpoint

Ask yourself who the narrator of the story is. It may be an anonymous person exterior to the action so that events are narrated in the third person, as in many novels by Balzac and Zola. The narration might be in the first person singular by someone directly involved in events, as for example in Mauriac's *Le Noeud de Viperes* or Camus *L'Étranger*. Another possibility is first person narration by someone close to the main characters but not of interest in themselves as in Alain Fournier's *Le Grand Meaulnes*.

Manner of narration is closely related to viewpoint in the novel. If the narrator is an outsider he or she may just describe what people say and do without giving the reader access to the thoughts of the characters. This viewpoint makes no judgements about people and is said to be more objective. If the viewpoint is from inside the story, by somone taking part in, or close to events, then their interpretation of what happens is restricted and tends to be subjective. We see everything through their eyes.

A third possibility is the viewpoint of the omniscient (all-knowing) narrator who has full knowledge of the characters, their past and present history and what goes on in their minds. Such a viewpoint is often most noticeable at the beginning of a novel. Balzac's *Le Père Goriot* and *Eugénie Grandet* are good illustrations of this technique.

Many novels and some plays have been made into films and some are available on video which is very helpful since the latter can be watched and stopped, and episodes re-run and commented on (see Appendix 2). If you do have access to a video version it can be used in several ways to improve your knowledge and understanding of a novel. You can examine and discuss how the actors or actresses interpret their roles; keep a note of any events that have been omitted and ask yourself if they should have been included. Discuss whether the film adds to the book or changes it and why. Would you have treated the book in the same way?

Setting and background

Does the background play a dominant or hardly noticeable role? Does the author sketch in just a few features to create an impression or are there long, detailed descriptions of certain places that give a sense of realism or social record? Is the setting restricted to the way of life of a certain group of people? Sometimes features of landscape are described just for their beauty. Sometimes an author might use aspects of background for symbolic purposes to mirror the state of mind or mood of the characters. The wind-bent pines and the brooding thunder storms of the Landes in Mauriac's novels or the intense heat of the Mediterranean sun in Camus *L'Étranger* spring to mind.

Meaning

You should also consider the meaning of a novel or story in terms of an author's possible motives in writing it and any message he or she may have intended. Many writers are mainly interested in illuminating a particular section of society from a critical rather than an approving point of view. If the group of people they depict is made to look ridiculous or comic then satire is being employed. Less often, a writer's motive is to celebrate or convey his delight about a period in life that has passed. Alain Fournier's *Le Grand Meaulnes* is partly about the lost experience of youth. Colette evokes the bitter-sweet emotions of awakening sexuality in *Le Blé en Herbe*. In his autobiographical trilogy Pagnol celebrates a young boy's delight and fascination as he explores the natural world of Provence. Various aspects of war are presented objectively in many of Maupassant's short stories. The author does not step into the story to tell you what he thinks. Instead he lets scenes and events unfold. We form our own impressions about the rights and wrongs.

You will be able to bring your own judgements to the novels or stories you read because you come to the text wih opinions, experiences and fantasies of your own. So, for example, as well as being delighted by Pagnol's descriptions of the Provençal countryside in *La Gloire de Mon Père* and *Le Chateau de Ma Mère* you might deplore the attitude towards shooting and trapping wild birds.

Drama

Plays can be divided broadly into two categories: plays about people and the effect they have upon one another (psychological dramas), and plays about society and its collective beliefs and the values that affect it at a particular time. Many plays reflect both these elements and the psychology of the individual comes into play with current issues of the day. Plays may be tragic and evoke emotions of anger, sympathy or sorrow. They may be comic and make us laugh at the behaviour of a particular individual or group of people. Laughter works best when other emotions are not dominant. As soon as pity, sorrow or anger creep in we tend to stop laughing. For this reason the borderline between comedy and tragedy can be a delicate one.

Make your own synopsis of the events in a play. This is often made easier by the division into scenes and tableaux. Does the action take place over a relatively short period of time or is there a time lapse at some point? Is there a single main plot or situation around which events revolve or are there subsidiary plots or intrigues enmeshed in the main one?

Characters

Divide characters into major and minor protagonists. Is the main psychological interest focussed in one or in more than one person? Do the minor characters have any depth or are they just needed at some point for the action of the play? Do characters clash or do they complement each other? Are the motives for their behaviour clear or ambiguous? Make a character sketch of the main characters finding your own words to describe features of their personality.

Action

This is the main feature of any play in terms of holding the attention of the audience. This is usually achieved by creating expectations, feelings of tension and suspense which resolve themselves in one or more climaxes or high points in the action. There might be a gradual working towards one outcome or there may be several high points or climaxes with a sense of anticlimax in between. Anticlimax might be a central feature of a play. For example in Beckett's *Waiting For Godot* expectations are created but never fulfilled.

Comedy

Comedy has its source in character and situation. Characters who make us laugh usually have one overriding obsession which creates a kind of rigidity in their personality. We laugh partly because we know how they are going to react in certain situations but also because their obsessed condition is likely to come into collision with the behaviour of more normal individuals and these clashes are funny. Comedy of situation usually has its origins in the efforts of individuals to trick, outwit or deceive each other. Laughter is caused when, for one reason or another, plans go wrong. Most comic plays exploit both character and situation. Molière's Harpagon in *L'Avare* is a good example of a man with an obsession of comic proportions but the efforts of his family and servants to outwit him also provide much of the humour. In Pagnol's *Topaze* the hero's naive dedication to the principles of "la morale", as taught to French school children, collides several times with the views and behaviour of less scrupulous people. The changed and worldy wise Topaze of Act IV is in many ways a less amusing person.

Studying seventeenth century tragedies by Corneille or Racine presents a particular challenge. You need to become familiar with some of the literary and social conventions of that period in order to fully appreciate these plays. It is important to use a critical edition of the text with a good introduction.

Meaning

Because plays are designed to make an impact within the space of one to three hours of performance their meaning or message is often closer to the surface and they are more likely to provoke an immediate reaction. The meaning or worth of a play is often on more than one level. Sartre's *Les Mains Sales* can be seen as an indictment of the Communist party's requirement of absolute adhesion to the party line even though this may be changed to suit circumstances. On a philosophical level it highlights the difficulty that the consciously willed act creates for an individual determined to justify his existence. On a human level it is concerned with the complexities of human relationships as seen in the father–son bond between Hoederer and Hugo.

Since plays are meant to be acted rather than read you can miss a good deal of their impact by just treating them as words on a page. You will find it profitable to examine selected scenes from the point of view of a stage director – you would have to decide on the positioning of the actors, their movements, gestures, eye contact, tone of voice, pauses in what they say. Some of these details may be broadly indicated in the stage directions but there will be a good deal of scope for improvisation and interpretation.

Decide first of all on the frame of mind of the characters at the beginning of the scene. Has this been influenced by events in the previous scene or is their attitude influenced by contact with each other? Decide on the positioning of the actors and how they will move at the beginning of the scene. What do they do with their hands? Who are they looking at? What facial or bodily gestures might be appropriate? Do they speak slowly or quickly? Where might there be pauses in their speech? What tone of voice would they use? Are certain words emphasised by rise and fall of intonation? Once you begin to consider some of these features you will discover that the scene can be broken down into shorter parts. Of course all this works best if the scene can then be read or acted out by a group of people. You will find that by treating parts of a play in this manner they will begin to mean much more to you and you will remember them more vividly.

Many French departments in universities put on French plays from time to time and they often choose plays used as set texts. The local branch of ALL should be able to provide details. Many plays are available on video. Failing these possibilities you could try and find other students working on the same play and organise play readings.

POETRY

Some Examination Boards offer poetry among the options for literary texts. Poems have the advantage of being shorter than plays or novels but on the other hand the language of poetry, by its nature, is more dense and the meaning therefore more difficult to penetrate.

Poetry cannot be read solely in translation because it would not have the same impact. You should always read a poem several times before looking at a translation. There are some excellent parallel texts available. Avoid those that give a translation in English verse. The attempt to make each line rhyme in English usually distorts the meaning and serves no useful purpose.

Study techniques

1 Note first of all the way a poem looks on the page. Longish looking, regular length lines that rhyme are almost bound to be 12 syllable lines called Alexandrines. Poems may be divided into stanzas ("strophes" in French) of three or four lines. They may be in pairs called couplets. A shorter line could indicate 6, 8, or 10 syllable lines. There may be a mixture of shorter and longer lines in a regular pattern. Poems made up of two, four-line stanzas followed by two of three lines are sonnets, a favourite form with many poets. Much 20th Century poetry may lack a regular pattern altogether, with lines of varied length that do not rhyme.

2 Make a note of the theme of each poem you read. This will rarely be the same as the title, if there is one. Nor will the theme be, for example, simply "love" but some aspect of this emotion or attitude towards it. If a poem is mainly descriptive it may be coloured by a certain mood or atmosphere. Group themes together so that you can see which ones occur frequently and the different ways they are treated.

3 Look at the structure of the poem. It may be presented as a scene in miniature with a stage setting, an atmosphere speaking parts and action. Many of Verlaine's and Prévert's poems follow this pattern. The poem might be narrated by an anonymous person or the voice of the poet might be strongly present.

4 Words and how they used, the imagery of a poem, is one of its most important aspects. Figures of speech are used to intensify meaning. Simile makes a direct comparison between one thing and another, and is usually signalled by the use of "comme", "pareil à" or "qui ressemble". Baudelaire turns " Ennui" into a sinister hooka-smoking person in his poem *Au Lecteur* and there are numerous examples in his poetry of the use of personnification. Figures of speech may be unusual, striking, dramatic, evocative or vivid; they may make a direct appeal to the senses of sight or touch; they may appeal chiefly to the imagination.

5 Choice of words is also an important part of imagery. What they sound like is as important as their face meaning. Look for the repetition of certain consonants (alliteration) and how harsh or soft, liquid sounds contribute to the meaning. If certain vowel sounds are repeated this is called assonance and is part of the musical effect of poetry. Apollinaire's poem *Le Pont Mirabeau* is a good example of the use of repeated vowel and consonant sounds that evoke the effect of flowing water and the passing of time.

> *Sous le pont Mirabeau coule la Seine*
> *Et nos amours*
> *Faut-il qu'il m'en souvienne*
> *La joie venait toujours après la peine*
> *Vienne la nuit sonne l'heure*
> *Les jours s'en vont je demeure*

Which vowel sounds are prominent and which consonants? What effect do they contribute to? What mood is evoked?

Rhyme is part of the overall sound attractiveness of poetry too. Try marking the ends of each line a,b,c,d, to see if there is a regular pattern. If there is, then this part of the craftsmanship of the poet and enhances the effect of the poem.

5.3 HOW TO STUDY FRENCH LITERATURE

Contents (Contenu)

- La structure
- Les personnages
- La mise en scène
- Le sens de l'œuvre

Dans la plupart des cas il faut écrire en français au sujet des livres que vous avez étudiés. Pour savoir bien aborder cette tâche, certains exercices sont nécessaires. Voici quelques conseils préliminaires:

1 Pour le premier texte choisissez un livre d'un auteur moderne plutôt dans le style de la langue parlée comme par exemple *Les Petits Enfants du Siècle* de Rochefort ou *L'Étranger* de Camus.

2 Travaillez le plus possible avec un dictionnaire monolingue.

3 Dès le début, prenez l'habitude d'écrire vos notes en français. Inutile de commencer en anglais avec l'idée de traduire cela plus tard en français.

4 Etablissez des points de repère en fonction des remarques qui suivent.

LA STRUCTURE

Si possible discutez avec votre prof pour vous renseigner en avance sur le récit et les événements – où cela se passe-t-il, à quelle époque et qui en sont les personnages principaux? Sinon trouvez dans un livre de critique un résumé du texte. Consultez, par exemple, les séries suivantes: *Profil d'une oeuvre*, Hatier; *Lire aujourd'hui*, Hachette; *Théâtre et mises en scène*, Hatier.

Vous pouvez chercher ces livres dans votre bibliothèque ou les commander par le système de Inter Library Loans. Vous pourrez aussi les trouver ou les commander à la librairie Hachette de Londres ou à la librairie de l'université la plus proche.

Au fur et à mesure que vous découvrez les textes prescrits, prenez des notes. Quand vous aurez lu tout le texte revenez en arrière et faites-vous un petit résumé des événements en soulignant les moments importants, les grands épisodes, les actions déterminantes et le dénouement final. Notez la chronologie des événements et les sauts dans le déroulement de l'action ou les retours en arrière.

LES PERSONNAGES

Faites une liste des personnages en les divisant entre personnages principaux – les héros ou les héroïnes – et ceux qui jouent un rôle secondaire. Pour chaque personne importante faites un portrait en signalant ses défauts et ses qualités. Trouvez dans le texte des exemples de son attitude, des pensées ou des jugements portés sur lui ou sur elle par d'autres personnages.

Considérez les motifs qui ont déterminé leurs actes. Ces motifs sont-ils clairs ou ambigus? Est-ce que leurs actes trouvent leur origine dans la personalité de l'individu ou sont-ils dus à l'influence d'autres personnes? Est-ce que le caractère des héros ou des héroines change ou se modifie au cours du récit? Est-ce qu'il faut tenir compte de leur âge? Essayez de vous mettre à la place de tel ou tel personnage. Est-ce que vous auriez réagi de la même façon devant un problème identique? Finalement portez vous-même un jugement sur les personnages. Les trouvez-vous sympathiques? Est-ce qu'ils sont à plaindre ou à condamner? Est-ce qu'ils méritent notre approbation ou notre réprobation. Illustrez votre opinion avec des références au texte. Quelles questions aimeriez-vous leur poser si vous aviez la possibilité de les interviewer?

LA MISE EN SCÈNE

Où a lieu le récit et à quelle époque? Dans une région de France, dans une grande ville? Dans quel milieu social est-il situé? De quelle valeur est la mise en scène, sans grande importance ou très importante? Les personnages vivent-ils en harmonie ou en désaccord avec leur environnement? Le milieu social a-t-il une influence sur leur manière de vivre? Sont-ils des privilégiés ou des défavorisés? Sont-ils relativement libres d'agir à leur guise ou se trouvent-ils en conflit avec la société? Quel rôle a joué leur naissance, leur éducation ou leur travail?

Qui raconte, qui "voit" les événements qui sont racontés? S'il s'agit d'un narrateur anonyme ou extérieur, le récit sera mené à la troisième personne. Dans d'autres cas le récit sera à la première personne et raconté par le héro ou l'héroïne comme par exemple dans *L'Etranger*, ou *Les Petits Enfants du Siècle*.

La narration est liée au point de vue de l'oeuvre. Le point de vue peut être celui d'un observateur externe qui se contente de constater les apparences sans pouvoir révéler les pensées des personnages. Il peut être interne et vu par les yeux de quelqu'un qui participe à l'action mais qui donne nécessairement une interprétation subjective. Le point de vue peut être celui d'un narrateur "omniscient" qui présente les faits sous plusieurs angles à la fois. Il lui est permis de passer sans obstacle d'une scène à une autre, de connaître le passé, le présent et le futur et de pénétrer toutes les pensées de ses personnages.

La description joue-t-elle un rôle important dans le livre? Le but de l'auteur est-il d'enchanter le lecteur par la beauté de la scène naturelle? Trouvez-vous ses descriptions poétiques? Quelle impression visuelle des paysages vous reste en mémoire après la lecture? L'auteur emploie-t-il la suggestion pour créer la mise en scène ou est-ce qu'il emploie une technique de photographie? Le résultat est-il un document de sociologie ou un film sur la nature avec flore et faune en abondance?

LE SENS DE L'ŒUVRE

Le livre présente-t-il un ou plusieurs thèmes? L'auteur délivre-t-il un message? Quelle société ou quel aspect de la société est-ce qu'il dépeint? Cherche-t-il à dénoncer, à accepter ou à approuver certaines attitudes? Est-ce qu'il cherche à en analyser les causes? Est-ce qu'il critique d'une manière directe ou est-ce qu'il présente les détails d'une manière objective? Le contexte historique est-il important pour bien comprendre le sens de l'œuvre? Le sens a-t-il une valeur aujourd'hui? Quelles sont vos réactions et vos réflexions? Sur quoi vous trouvez-vous bien informé après avoir lu le livre deux ou trois fois?

En consultant votre prof établissez une liste de sujets ou d'aspects qui pourraient donner lieu à des questions dans l'examen.

5.4 PLANNING AND WRITING ANSWERS

There are two broad approaches to literature used by the Examination Boards. With the thematic approach you study a theme and read one or more books (from a prescribed list or from free choice), that reflect this theme. The questions set are broad rather than specific and allow you plenty of scope for referring to your chosen text or texts. The other approach is to study particular books and answer more specific questions about them. In practice, both approaches lead to questions that revolve around similar aspects of the books being studied.

Typical examples of the thematic approach are the following:

- Dramatic techniques

- The portrayal of children/young people

- The portrayal of war and its effects

- The portrayal of society
- How a region is reflected in a book
- Short stories
- Characterisation and/or plot

Questions of the second kind might be as follows:

- Résumez les différences entre la plaidoirie du procureur contre Mersault et celle de l'avocat de Meursault (*L'Etranger*)
- Quelle est l'importance de la terre et du climat dans cette histoire? Est-c que Jean est conscient de leur importance? (*Jean de Florette*)
- Faites le portrait de Cécile. Quels sont ses sentiments à la fin du livre? (*Bonjour Tristesse*)

It is important to know the text and the story well, with particular emphasis on the more dramatic and important events. You need to know the characters well too and be able to say what kind of people they are and why they behave as they do. You will need to decide what the author's intentions were in writing the work. You may need to compare or contrast. You will be required to give your opinion. All opinions will be valid – provided that you back them up with reasons and clear references to the text. It is the lack of such references that examiners are always noting in their reports.

In the examination, always read all the questions through before deciding which one to do. In thematic studies not all of the questions may be appropriate to all of the books. Read the question you have chosen, carefully. It will usually ask you to do more than one thing, to explain or describe something and give your judgement.

For example: "Décrivez les personnages féminins de cette pièce (Anouilh: *La Belle Vie*). Les trouvez-vous sympathiques?" (NEAB). In this case, make sure you give space to both parts, usually in the proportion of 2 to 1. Even a question like "Quelle est votre impression des ennemis?" (UCLES: Maupassant *Boule de Suif et autres contes de la guerre*). Your answer will contain more than one part because your impression will inevitably be divided between the good and bad qualities of the German soldiers occupying France – how differences in rank affect them and how they behave collectively and individually.

With questions that ask for the candidate's personal response it is a good idea to weave into the body of the essay such phrases as "à mon avis", "je trouve que", "selon moi". Bear all these points in mind when planning and writing your answer.

Your answer should consist of:

- a brief introduction,
- discussion in paragraphs that clearly treat particular aspects, putting two points of view if required, remembering to keep the most convincing or important points until last,
- a brief conclusion. (see page 179).

If the question asks you to describe or relate and then to give your opinion, you can either work in your own ideas with the description in each paragraph, or devote a final section which is clearly devoted to giving your own viewpoint.

Marks are awarded mainly for the content of the answer. However, marks may also be awarded for the language used. The proportion can vary. Check the mark scheme for your particular Board. These two aspects go closely hand in hand. If you have had plenty of practice in discussing the texts in class, making notes on them in French and writing your own synopsis, you should be able to describe and give your own views without too much difficulty. A few incorrect genders and accents missing are not going to matter. Pay particular attention to the tenses that you use. When you are describing someone's character you will probably find yourself using the present tense. If you then refer to an incident or an event in the story, you are more likely to need a perfect or imperfect. If events before other events are mentioned you could need the pluperfect.

A comment from UCLES is instructive to both pupil and teacher:

"It was very encouraging that so many candidates could express themselves with fluency, sounding remarkably unhindered by linguistic constraints. It was also very clear that communication was least constrained where schools had provided a solid background of grammatical structures and an adequate descriptive and critical vocabulary."

A BRIEF VOCABULARY

Bonnes ou mauvaises qualités?

Lesquelles pouvez-vous attribuer aux personnages des textes que vous étudiez?

indépendant, assuré, confiant, agressif, brutal, résolu, humble, timide, modeste, souple, (*adaptable*), intelligent, habile, adroit (*clever, skilled*), maladroit (*clumsy, tactless*) incapable (*inept, useless*), rusé, malin (*cunning, crafty*), méchant (*malicious*), débrouillard (*resourceful*), sérieux (*earnest*), réfléchi (*serious, thoughtful*), limité, avoir l'esprit étroit/borné (*narrow-minded*), fantaisiste (*imaginative*), compréhensif (*understanding*), compatissant (*sympathetic*), charitable, chaleureux (*warm-hearted*), aimable, gentil, expansif (*out-going*), tendre (*loving*), innocent, naïf, impitoyable, sans pitié (*merciless*), sans scruple (*unscrupulous*), sans puder (*shameless*), sadique, cruel, joyeux, gai (*cheerful*), amusant, avoir/manquer le sens de l'humour, sombre (*gloomy*), mélancolique, triste, généreux, indulgent, avare, mesquin (*stingy*), honnête, malhonnête, menteur (*untruthful*), hypocrite (*hypocritical*), oisif, fainéant, (*idle, lazy*), travailleur (*hard-working*), énergique, passif, soumis (*submissive*), anxieux (*insecure*), insolent, rude (*harsh, severe*), grossier (*rude, coarse*), vulgaire, bien-élevé (*well-mannered*), éduqué (*well brought up*), prudent, impulsif, courageux, vaniteux (*vain*), menaçant, sinistre, optimiste, pessimiste, accepter son sort, réagir contre son sort (*accept/reject one's lot*).

Petit vocabulaire critique

les personnages (*the characters*), le caractère (*personality, character of one of the former*) e.g. il y a plusieurs personnages intéressants dans cette pièce. Ils possèdent tous un caractère très différent. Le héro, l'héroïne, jouer le rôle de... (*play the part of*) un trait de caractère (*feature of character*), contradictoire, incompatible, contraster avec, faire une comparaison avec, on peut comparer X avec Y, le conflit des opinions, être attiré, séduit par X, tomber amoureux de Y, être rejeté par Z, être abattu, démoralisé (*be downcast, dejected*) cacher ses vraies intentions, les motifs, les mobiles (*motives*)

un roman (*novel*) la pièce (*play*) un conte (*short story*), un poème, dramatique, tragique, ironique, comique

l'écrivain (*writer*) le romancier/la romancière (*novelist*), l'auteur, l'écrivain, le dramaturge (*playwright*)

dépeindre, décrire (*describe, depict*), évoquer, fait penser à, rappeler, (*evokes, makes you think of*). Le récit (*the story*) l'action se passe, les événements se déroulent en... (*action happens, events take place in*). L'intrigue devient complexe (*the action gets complicated*), le dénouement (*the outcome, conclusion*), atteindre un point culminant (*get to a climax*), un épisode qui attire notre sympathie/notre pitié, qui fait rire/pleurer, une atmosphère tendue/détendue, décontractée (*a tense/relaxed atmosphere*) l'ambiance, la couleur locale (*local colour – details that create the sense of a place or time setting*) la mise en scène (*the setting, background*), réaliste, vraisemblable (*realistic, lifelike*), invraisemblable (*unrealistic, artificial*), une scène, un épisode, un moment dramatique, des circonstances imprévues (*unexpected, unforeseen circumstances*), une tournure imprévue (*an unexpected turn of events*), un retour en arrière (*flashback*).

Illustrative question and answer

Faites le portrait de Madame Dalleray. Trouvez-vous son influence sur Phil plutôt bonne ou mauvaise?
NEAB

EXAMPLE 1

Phil rencontre Mme. Dalleray pour la première fois quand s'étant trompée de chemin elle lui demande des renseignements. Plus tard il la revoit à Ker-Anna, la maison qu'elle avait louée près de Cancale, et il lui rend plusieurs visites.

C'est une femme mûre de 30–35 ans, aux cheveux noirs et aux yeux foncés. Elle aime porter des vêtements blancs et c'est pour cela que Phil la nomme "la dame en blanc". Il faut signaler que nous observons tous les détails sur Mme. Dalleray par les yeux de Phil et donc nous n'avons que l'image que lui impose cette femme. On a l'impression d'une femme très assurée qui ne perd jamais son sang-froid. Tout ce qu'elle dit est bien pesé et même calculé. Dès la première rencontre avec Phil elle prend le dessus et il semble qu'elle joue avec lui et que ce jeu l'amuse. Se trouvant seule en vacances peut-être s'ennuie-t-elle un peu? Cette femme sensuelle aime brûler de l'encens dans la maison et se parfumer. Elle offre à Phil des boissons très fraîches et des fruit juteux. Elle est flattée par les attentions du jeune adolescent et amusée par sa maladresse. C'est elle qui prend l'initiative pourtant et joue la séductrice. Elle n'a pas d'illusions sur la profondeur des émotions de Phil. Vers la fin de son séjour pourtant, elle a l'idée d'obtenir de lui une confession de son amour, ou du moins, le faire admettre qu'il sera triste quand elle sera partie. Mais à la fin elle n'ose pas l'obliger de peur d'être blessée.

C'est par l'intermédiaire de Mme. Dalleray que Phil fait son apprentissage de l'amour sexuel et commence à découvrir la complexité du cœur féminin. <u>Je suis persuadé</u> que, sans cette expérience, Phil n'aurait pas eu le courage plus tard de prendre l'initiative avec Vinca et de lui faire l'amour. <u>Je trouve bon</u> que Phil découvre ces détails dans les bras d'une femme expérimentés. <u>A mon avis</u>, bien que Mme. Dalleray soit une séductrice, son attitude envers le garçon révèle de la tendresse et de l'estime. <u>Je trouve</u> qu'elle est pleine de tact et qu'elle prend soin de ne pas blesser le jeune garçon. <u>Il me semble</u> qu'elle joue le rôle d'une mère autant que celui d'une amante. <u>J'approuve</u> pourtant le fait que leur liaison est courte, Si Mme Dalleray était restée disponible pour le reste des vacances, <u>je ne suis pas sûr</u> ce qui aurait pu se passer entre Phil et Vinca. <u>A mon avis</u> c'est une décision volontaire de la part de Mme. Dalleray de revenir à Paris sans lui dire adieu, pour faciliter le rapport qui va développer entre ces deux jeunes personnes.

<u>Je suis convaincu</u> qu'il y a tellement du positif dans cette rencontre qu'<u>il est difficile de trouver trop de mal</u> dans l'influence que Mme. Dalleray a exercé sur ce garçon de 16 ans. Je voudrais bien savoir si au long terme cette expérience sera simplement un souvenir heureux dans sa mémoire ou s'il désirera la répéter ou la raviver.

EXAMPLE 2

Mme. Dalleray sait bien ce qu'elle fait en séduisant ce jeune garçon. <u>Je crois qu'</u>elle s'ennuie en vacances et désire s'amuser. <u>J'avoue que je trouve un peu dégoûtant</u> l'idée d'une femme mûre qui exploite ainsi un garçon de 16 ans. <u>C'est dommage</u> que ce soit là sa première expérience de l'amour. Tout est rendu trop facile pour lui. <u>Il vaudrait mieux</u> qu'il découvre les complexités d'un rapport sexuel dans les bras d'une personne qui a le même âge que lui et qui partage le point de vue et l'attitude d'un adolescent. Ce serait du moins une découverte l'une de l'autre. <u>Je crois que</u> cette première expérience pourrait bien lui donner une fausse impression et influencer plus tard ses rapports avec le beau sexe. <u>J'ai le sentiment que</u>, une fois revenu à Paris, Phil pourrait éprouver un désir très fort de revoir la femme en blanc. Ce n'est pas pour rien qu'elle lui laisse son numéro de téléphone.

Je trouve donc difficile d'approuver l'influence que Mme. Dalleray exerce sur Phil. Les impressions qu'elle laisse dans l'esprit de ce jeune homme vont revenir pour le hanter et peut-être même pour l'obséder.

A noter

1 Les phrases soulignées indiquent la manière dont on peut exprimer une opinion personnelle.
2 Vous ne serez peut-être pas d'accord avec ni l'une ni l'autre opinion exprimée à la fin de cette rédaction. Discutez ces conclusions avec votre professeur ou vos amis.
3 The Board from which this question was taken assigns marks as follows: out of a total of 50, 35 for content, 15 for language. The 35 marks are split 20:15, i.e. 20 marks for the factual response and 15 for the personal opinion.

Commentary and context questions

Commentary questions may be in English or French according to the Board. You may be asked to: "relate the passage to its context" or identify the point at which this extract occurs". This is followed by a series of tasks asking you to explain or comment on aspects of character or action revealed in the selected passage.

Situating in context means that you need to give sufficient detail for the significance of the extract to be understood. This is not an invitation to tell the whole story up to that point. You need only give enough information so that someone who knows the story can understand which part of the play the extract comes from. Quite often the reason for the state of mind of the characters at the beginnning of the passage is a good place to begin. What has made them like this? Why are they reacting in this way to what follows? With a play it is not necessary to give the number of the Act and scene from which the passage was taken. Something like:"Near the end of Act II", is quite adequate.

The other tasks usually relate only to the material in the extract itself, so make sure that what you write refers directly to this. Some Boards give the number of marks assigned to these tasks. Make sure you answer each part and be guided as to length of answer and how long you need to profitably spend on it by the number of marks indicated. You are expected to be able to explain or comment by referring to the text or show what it reveals about character or humour *but not to translate it!*

You may be be asked: "Analysez l'extrait suivant, en le situant brièvement dans son contexte". The previously stated guidelines still apply. The rest of the question will invite your comments on various aspects of the passage. You will be expected to identify the significant issues raised and show an awareness of what is happening in the text. There may be a series of questions in French that lead you into giving your reaction or expressing your thoughts about what is happening in a text. The Cambridge Examination Board's comments are helpful:

"This is not an exercise in literary criticism: Examiners should reward candidates whose answers show good understanding of how a text works and how the author has conveyed the key issues... Examiners are looking for a candidate's ability to communicate effctively and will ignore linguistic errors that do not impede communication... candidates will be required to offer intelligent comments, basing their answers on their reading rather than the literary critical approach of previous literature papers."

EXAMPLE 1

Je lui ai demandé si elle voulait venir au cinéma, le soir. Elle a encore ri et m'a dit qu'elle avait envie de voir un film avec Fernandel. Quand nous sommes rhabillés, elle a eu l'air très surpris de me voir avec une cravate noire et elle m'a demandé si j'étais en deuil. Je lui ai dit que maman était morte. Comme elle voulait savoir depuis quand, j'ai répondu: "Depuis hier." Elle a eu un petit recul, mais n'a fait aucune remarque. J'ai eu envie de lui dire que ce n'était pas de ma faute, mais je me suis arrêté parce que j'ai pensé que je l'avais déjà dit à mon patron.

L'Étranger, Albert Camus

1 Situez brièvement cet extrait dans son contexte. (2)

2 Qu'est-ce que nous apprenons de cet extrait au sujet du caractère de Meursault? (4)

3 Expliquez pourquoi cet incident joue un rôle important dans le procès de Meursault. (4)

Possible answer

1 Le lendemain de l'enterrement de sa mère Meursault va se baigner et à la piscine il rencontre une ancienne amie, Marie Cardona. Après la baignade pendant que les deux sont en train de se rhabiller Marie remarque la cravate noire de son ami.

2 On voit dans cet extrait que Meursault n'est pas préoccupé par la mort de sa mère. Il est prêt à s'amuser en se baignant, en draguant une petite amie et en l'invitant au cinéma le lendemain de l'enterrement. Est-ce l'indifférence? Il ne pense même pas à lui en parler, ce qui explique la surprise de Marie et son petit recul lorsqu'elle apprend la nouvelle que sa mère est morte le jour avant. Meursault répond "ma mère est morte" à la première question de Marie sans préciser la date. Voilà pourquoi elle doit lui demander depuis combien de temps elle est morte pensant qu'elle est décédée il y a quelque temps. Elle est tellement surprise par sa réponse qu'elle ne sait que répondre. Nous notons aussi la franchise, voire la sincérité de Meursault, qui répond directement aux questions des autres. Il est intéressant de remarquer son désir de s'excuser devant la réaction de Marie. Il ne comprend vraiment pas pourquoi elle est surprise et déconcertée. Il n'ajoute pas "ce n'était pas de ma faute'" pensant que ce n'est pas la peine de le répéter. Nous remarquons dans cet extrait le fait que Meursault ne ressemble pas à la plupart des gens, qu'il est vraiment 'un étranger'.

3 Plus tard, après le meurtre de l'arabe, Marie rend témoignage au procès de Meursault. Elle est obligée d'avouer que le lendemain de l'enterrement Meursault l'a recontrée, s'est baigné avec elle et l'a invitée au cinéma voir un film amusant. Ces détails sont cités par le procureur pour renforcer la preuve que Meursault manque de sens moral, qu'il ne possède pas les sentiments normaux d'un fils qui vient de perdre sa mère et donc qu'il est capable de tuer et coupable du meurtre de l'arabe.

EXAMPLE 2

Here is another example. The passage is from the play *Les Mains Sales* by J.P. Sartre.

Hugo   Lâchez ma main.

Hoederer   *(sans la lâcher)* Suppose que je suis devant toi, exactement comme je suis et que tu me vises…

Hugo   Lâchez-moi et travaillons.

Hoederer   Tu me regardes et au moment de tirer, voilà que tu penses: "si c'était lui qui avait raison?" Tu te rends compte?

Hugo   Je n'y penserais pas. Je ne penserais à rien d'autre qu'à tuer.

Hoederer   Tu y penserais: un intellectuel, il faut que ça pense. Avant même de presser sur la gâchette tu aurais déjà vu toutes les conséquences possibles de ton acte: tout le travail d'une vie en ruines, une politique flanquée par terre, personne pour me remplacer, le Parti condamné peut-être à ne jamais prendre le pouvoir…

Hugo   Je vous dis que je n'y penserais pas!

Hoederer   Tu ne pourrais pas t'en empêcher. Et ça vaudrait mieux parce que, tel que tu es, si tu n'y pensais pas *avant*, tu n'aurais pas trop de toute ta vie pour y penser *après*. (Un temps.) Quelle rage avez-vous tous de jouer aux tueurs? Ce sont des types sans imagination: ça leur est égal de donner la mort parce qu'ils n'ont aucune idée de ce que c'est la vie. Je préfère les gens qui ont peur de la mort des autres: c'est la preuve qu'ils savent vivre.

Hugo   Je ne suis pas fait pour vivre, je ne sais pas ce que c'est que la vie et je n'ai pas besoin de le savoir. Je suis de trop, je n'ai pas ma place et je gêne tout le monde; personne ne m'aime, personne ne me fait confiance.

Hoederer   Moi, je te fais confiance.

Hugo   Vous?

Hoederer   Bien sûr. Tu es un homme qui a de la peine à passer à l'âge d'un homme mais tu feras un homme très acceptable, si quelqu'un te facilite le passage. Si j'échappe à leurs pétards et à leurs bombes, je te garderai près de moi et je t'aiderai.

Hugo   Pourquoi me le dire? Pourquoi me le dire aujourd'hui?

Hoederer   Simplement pour te prouver qu'on ne peut pas buter un homme de sang-froid à moins d'être un spécialiste.

Hugo   Si je l'ai décidé, je dois pouvoir le faire. (*Comme à lui-même, avec une sorte de désespoir.*) Je *dois* pouvoir le faire.

Les Mains Sales, Jean Paul Sartre

1 D'après vous quelles sont les émotions de Hugo et de Hoederer au commencement de cette scène?

2 A quel moment croyez-vous que Hoederer a le sentiment d'avoir réussi à dissuader Hugo de le tuer?

3 Qu'est-ce que cette scène révèle au sujet du caractère des deux hommes?

Possible answer

1 Dès le début Hoederer est dans un état de tension. Il se doutait depuis longtemps des vraies intentions des son secrétaire Hugo, mais il vient de découvrir que celui-ci veut le tuer et qu'il est armé d'un revolver. Il croit pourtant qu'il pourra dissuader Hugo en raisonnant avec lui. Depuis le commencement de la scène Hoederer observe étroitement chaque geste de Hugo et au moment où Hugo va sortir son revolver il l'empêche de le faire.

Hugo aussi est dans un état tendu. Il trouve difficile de se donner le courage de tuer Hoederer. Il a offert de faire l'affaire pour le 'bien' du parti communiste mais aussi pour se mettre à l'épreuve et pour montrer qu'un intellectuel comme lui est capable d'agir. Mais depuis qu'il a commencé son travail de secrétaire il commence de mieux comprendre Hoederer et de respecter ses opinions politiques. Ce qu'il a résolu de faire devient de plus en plus difficile.

2 C'est peut-être au moment où Hoederer dit 'Moi, je te fais confiance' que Hugo est moralement désarmé. Hoederer comprend bien les motifs de Hugo. Il sait qu'il désire surtout être accepté et avoir quelque valeur aux yeux des autres. Il lui offre son support.

3 Nous voyons ici l'esprit tourmenté de Hugo. Il a eu le courage d'offrir de tuer pour le parti mais ses raisons sont plutôt personnelles. Il a résolu de le faire mais il ne peut pas. Il est impétueux mais il n'arrive pas à séparer l'acte de ses conséquences. Il est jeune et il a besoin d'une personne qui tient le rôle de père. Il a le sentiment d'avoir trouvé une telle personne dans Hoederer. Par respect pour Hoederer Hugo lui parle en disant vous, et ce dernier montre son affection pour Hugo en le tutoyant.

Hoederer comprend parfaitement l'esprit de Hugo et il ne le méprise pas. Il aurait pu le faire désarmer par les gardes mais il ne voulait pas l'humilier. Il parle d'un ton paternel en offrant d'aider Hugo mais on a l'impression qu'il est sincère. Tout dépend quand même du succès de ses paroles. Hoederer ne manque pas de courage, encore une raison pourquoi Hugo l'admire de plus en plus.

CHAPTER 6

COURSEWORK

Units in this chapter

6.1 *Book-based coursework*
6.2 *Subject-based coursework*

Most Examination Boards offer the option of a topic, written in French, which is set against part or all of the written literature or background papers and can count for 20% of the total marks. A topic usually consists of 2–3 extended essays of up to 2000 words in total on a theme that you have researched. The essays are spread over the two years of the A-Level course. They are usually marked by your teacher and sent to the Board for moderation. This option has the advantage of being done in your own time without the pressure of an examination. It also gives a great deal of freedom of choice. Personal research work and contact with French spoken and written sources will greatly improve your language skills. The final pieces of work are not corrected by your teacher, however, before being submitted, so they are a reflection of your own efforts. The essays are marked for content, structure, language and accuracy and are usually weighted in favour of the first two elements. You need to check the requirements of your Board.

The following extract from the Cambridge Board's Report 1990 clearly indicates the qualities that ensure high marks in this area:

> The option of Course Work was clearly popular, and, for many candidates, produced high marks. The best pieces of work were characterised by original research, a high degree of personal involvement, a very high standard of written French, and neat and thoughful presentation. It was clear that these candidates had been exposed to a wide variety of French source materials, and their learning had been strongly influenced by such exposure. Some candidates had carried out research in France, and others had carried out surveys among fellow students.

There are two broad possibilities for topic work: it may be based on a literary text or on some other subject of interest for research.

6.1 BOOK-BASED COURSEWORK

This gives you the opportunity for treating a book you have read in a less formal and more lively way than the critical literary approach. Here are some possibilities.

Book review

Imagine that you are reviewing the book for a newspaper or magazine. Describe it *briefly* under the headings of *what*, *where*, *when*, *who*. Say what you believe the author's intentions to have been in writing the book – to entertain, amuse, draw attention to some issue or problem, satirise etc. – and how successful he has been in this and why, in your opinion. What tone does the author write in – light, amused, serious, embittered? Is his or her opinion clearly evident or is it implied? Are details presented factually or are they exaggerated? Is it easy to identify with the main characters? Do you recognise them as types you have met or know of? What insight have you gained from reading the book? Would the book have a good or bad influence on readers? Say why you would urge or not recommend others to read the book.

Interview

This could be the dialogue of an interview with one of the characters for radio or television. You would have to decide what series the interview was for and who the prospective viewers might be. This will give you a purpose and an attitude to adopt for the interview. You could also think about the possible attitudes of the interviewer and interviewee. This kind of topic can go beyond what is actually stated in the text.

Diary extract

This would be from the diary of one of the characters. Decide what period is covered by the entries in the diary. Again what the character writes is based on the details of the book but you can go beyond this to explore thoughts and feelings that are otherwise only suggested or perhaps concealed.

Dramatised episode

This could be for film, television or radio. You should set yourself up as the "metteur en scène", producer and director, responsible for the details of the setting for the action and the atmosphere you wish to create. You can describe what the audience will see, what the camera shows at the beginning of the scene and subsequently. Describe where the characters are placed, how they are to move, what they are thinking and feeling, what tone of voice they use.

Report

This could be a report from a social worker, doctor, probation officer made at a given point in the book. It would try to be factual and unbiased, taking into account social conditions and environment, the influence of other people. It could outline what might happen if no action is taken and suggest what might be done.

Theme

This would deal with a theme or issue that underlies the story – social deprivation, crime, hopes and expectations of teenagers, life in an HLM, for example. You would treat the book as a source of evidence and information that helps to build up a picture. It might prove helpful to draw upon other sources such as articles or statistics to fill out your picture.

Continuation of story

This would be based on imagining what might happen to one or more of the characters later in life. You would have to decide how long after and use the book as a starting point but otherwise there is a lot of scope here for using your imagination. You could for example interview a character much later in life in the style of some TV programmes or think along the lines of a "This is your life" presenter.

Documentary

This could be for radio or television and deal with part or the whole of the book. It could be a series of episodes to illustrate a way of life, how someone got over a critical period or the attitudes of a section of the community. You could concentrate on the presenter's monologue without giving the detail of everything the viewer sees.

Speech

This could be a talk or speech given by one of the characters to a specific audience, e.g. a self-help group, a group of pupils, a speech day address, a television slot for personal opinion.

Newspaper report

You could play the part of a newspaper reporter and give an account of important events or incidents in the book as you witnesed them, for example the trial of Meursault in Camus' *L'Etranger*. How might the popular press report some of the incidents in Pagnol's *Jean de Florette* or *Manon des Sources*? Another variation on being a reporter is that of "fly on the wall" which would allow you access to any event in the books you have studied.

The above are merely suggestions and not meant to be restrictive.

6.2 SUBJECT-BASED COURSEWORK

This option offers the widest scope. You should avoid the pitfall however of the merely descriptive piece of writing that is closely based on details drawn from books. This usually leads to regurgitation of what you have read and shows little intellectual processing. Historical, geographical and biographical themes can lend themselves to this approach. The important thing to remember is to set yourself a question to be answered, something to be proved or disproved or that has two sides to it or a particular and if possible novel slant.

The following observation from the NEAB's Report on the 1993 Examination gives a helpful indication of what is required:

> High scoring candidates showed originality in their essays. This was reflected in a good choice of title, giving the candidate a novel angle on the topic. These essays were backed up by a wide variety of suitable materials which were studied and discussed in French.

A subject like "Le tunnel sous la Manche" is not so promising as "L'Eurotunnel – les dangers et les avantages" or "Le Shuttle va-t-il concurrencer la traversée maritime?" "La vie du Général de Gaulle" sounds much less adventurous than "Le Général de Gaulle – Qu'a-t-il fait pour la France?" Compare also "La révolution de '68" and "La révolution de '68 pourrrait-elle recommencer?" "Mes vacances sur la Côte d'Azur" and "Les effets du tourisme sur la Côte d'Azur". The choice of title is very important and can be responsible for sending you in the right direction from the start.

Some subjects will be interesting because they are unusual or provoke comparisons. "Le travail d'un garçon de café", "La vie d'un fermier français" or "Les rapports personnels dans une famille francophone" would have a natural interest in this way.

Research done in France in the form of opinion gathering, interviews or recordings has the advantage of being authentic both in subject and in language. Make sure that you interpret the results of any surveys you carry out and draw conclusions from them. Just quoting statistics will not earn high marks. You can of course include recorded and visual material in your study, but ensure that such material has a clear purpose and is referred to. Any research carried out in France must be carefully planned in advance. The mere fact of having been there will not ensure a high mark on its own.

You could approach project work via your own interests and by getting in touch with clubs, societies or organisations in France or making a point of contacting someone while on holiday or a visit. The internet offers the possibility of corresponding quickly with a French person.

If you are confined to seeking information without going to France, French radio and magazines and the Internet could provide project material. For example, advertising on commercial radio stations or the pictures and illustrations used to persuade purchasers in magazines. Reading a particular page or section, the *page féminine* or the *courrier du coeur* in a magazine or newspaper over a period of time and assessing the range of themes or subjects could be a fruitful area of research. *Francoscopie*, written by Gérard Mermet and published annually by Larousse, is a compilation of surveys done during the year on practically every aspect of French life. This could also be a useful starting point. It is very important to use French sources rather than English ones (see Appendix for other useful sources of information).

If you have no idea of what aspect you would like to study you could begin by looking at the main themes usually set out in Examination Board syllabuses. Here is an amalgam of some of these:

A les rapports humains

- la famille
- les jeunes et leurs problèmes
- les rapports entre enfants et parents
- la condition féminine
- le racisme

B la société

- les divisions sociales
- le chômage
- l'immigration
- la ville et la campagne
- la culture et les loisirs

C l'environnement

- les ressources naturelles
- les mesures anti-pollution
- la gestion de l'environnement
- les groupes de pression écologiste

D la vie quotidienne

- le monde du travail
- la vie politique
- la vie religieuse
- le système éducatif
- la justice et l'ordre publique
- la santé
- les médias

The above are however only broad guidelines and not meant to be exhaustive. Having chosen an area that interests you narrow down your focus onto a specific aspect. Find out what opportunities for research are available and make sure that there are enough resources for you to consult. Discuss this with your teacher or tutor. Successful studies are the ones that concentrate on a particular aspect, show personal interest and enterprise and make plenty of references to material you have consulted.

Plan and presentation

It is helpful to bear in mind the advice of a beginning, a middle and an end to the plan of your study and to pay attention to a clear introduction, paragraphing and a conclusion. Marks may not be given for presentation but how your finished study looks is an indication of how much you have been involved in it and creates a positive impression.

Pay attention to the following:

1 Attractive title page (and binder if possible).

2 Illustrations clearly labelled and positioned relevant to the text.

3 Pages numbered.

4 Footnotes or references where necesssary, at the bottom of the page or in an appendix.

5 Contents list.

6 List of sources used (avoid using English sources. This will lead to anglicised French).

Give full references – *divers* (various) will not sound very convincing, nor will "books given to me by my teacher". A full reference would be like this: *L'Express no 1563 mai 199...*, or *Francoscopie* 95, pp 267–271.

Using a word processor to write your topic essay has all the advantages of being able to manipulate text. It can also produce diagrams and tables and a legible final text. A typed essay however will not automatically earn you good marks. Unless you are quite used to typing in French you might find that all sorts of errors creep in unnoticed. There is much to recommend a neatly presented hand written version.

Note: No plagiarism! (this means copying from a source without acknowledging it). Keep quotations brief and always give their source in a footnote (as above).

APPENDICES

APPENDIX 1

The following table provides a reference to regular verbs and most irregular ones. For simplicity's sake only the present tense is given in full. The past participles are given in bold, to attract the eye. Other tenses of the verb are given in the part most frequently needed. You should be able to work out the other parts of the tense by reference to the notes on the formation of tenses given in the grammar section.

VERB TABLE

infinitive/ participles	present/		perfect/ pluperfect	imperfect/ past historic	future/ conditional	present subjunctive

REGULAR VERBS

parler	je parle	nous parlons	j'ai parlé	il parlait	il parlera	que je parle
parlant	tu parles	vous parlez	j'avais parlé	il parla	il parlerait	que vous parliez
parlé	il parle	ils parlent				
finir	je finis	nous finissons	j'ai fini	il finissait	il finira	que je finisse
finissant	tu finis	vous finissez	j'avais fini	il finit	il finirait	que vous finissiez
fini	il finit	ils finissent				
entendre	j'entends	nous entendons	j'ai entendu	il entendait	il entendra	que j'entende
entendant	tu entends	vous entendez	j'avais entendu	il entendit	il entendrait	que vous entendiez
entendu	il entend	ils entendent				

'-er' verbs with peculiarities

Verbs in '-cer'

avancer	j'avance	nous avançons	j'ai avancé	il avançait	il avancera	que j'avance
avançant	tu avances	vous avancez	j'avais avancé	il avança	il avancerait	que vous avanciez
avancé	il avance	ils avancent				

(A cedilla always comes before an '-a', '-o' or '-u' only. See also *commencer*, *menacer*, and others.)

Infinitive/ participles	present/		perfect/ pluperfect	imperfect/ past historic	future/ conditional	present subjunctive

Verbs in '-ger'

arranger	j'arrange	nous arrangeons	j'ai arrangé	il arrangeait	il arrangera	que j'arrange
arrangeant	tu arranges	vous arrangez	j'avais arrangé	il arrangea	il arrangerait	que vous arrangiez
arrangé	il arrange	ils arrangent				

('-ge' always before an '-a' or '-o'. Also *ranger* – to tidy, *venger* – to avenge, *songer* – to dream, think and others)

Verbs in '-yer'

payer	je paie	nous payons	j'ai payé	il payait	il paiera	que je paie
payant	tu paies	vous payez	j'avais payé	il paya	il paierait	que vous payiez
payé	il paie	ils paient				

('-y' changes to '-i' before a mute [unpronounced] '-e'). The forms *je paye, tu payes, je payerai* are also found. Similarly *nettoyer* – to clean, *essuyer* – to wipe, *s'ennuyer* – to be bored **but** alternative in '-y' not normal)

jeter	je jette	nous jetons	j'ai jeté	il jetait	il jettera	que je jette
jetant	tu jettes	vous jetez	j'avais jeté	il jeta	il jetterait	que vous jetiez
jeté	il jette	ils jettent				

('-tt' before mute ending. Note the future and conditional)

appeler	j'appelle	nous appelons	j'ai appelé	il appelait	il appellera	qu'il appelle
appelant	tu appelles	vous appelez	j'avais appelé	il appela	il appellerait	que vous appeliez
appelé	il appelle	ils appellent				

('-ll' before mute '-e')

Changing accents

mener	je mène	nous menons	j'ai mené	il menait	il mènera	qu'il mène
menant	tu mènes	vous menez	j'avais mené	il mena	il mènerait	que vous meniez
mené	il mène	ils mènent				

('-e' becomes '-è' before mute ending, Note the future and conditional. Also *amener* – to bring, *emmener*- to take along, *lever, geler* – to freeze, and a number of others)

espérer	j'espère	nous espérons	j'ai espéré	il espérait	il espérera	qu'il espère
espérant	tu espères	vous espérez	j'avais espéré	il espéra	il espérerait	que vous espériez
espéré	il espère	ils espèrent				

('-é' becomes '-è' before mute '-e'. Note the future and conditional. Also like this *répéter*)

MOST COMMON IRREGULAR VERBS

aller	je vais	nous allons	je suis allé	il allait	il ira	que j'aille
allant	tu vas	vous allez	j'étais allé	il alla	il irait	que vous alliez
allé	il va	ils vont				

Infinitive/ participles	present/		perfect/ pluperfect	imperfect/ past historic	future/ conditional	present subjunctive
s'asseoir s'asseyant **assis**	je m'assieds tu t'assieds il s'assied	nous nous asseyons vous vous asseyez ils s'asseyent	je me suis assis je m'étais assis	il s'asseyait il s'assit	il s'assiéra il s'assiérait	que je m'asseye que vous vous asseyiez
avoir ayant **eu**	j'ai tu as il a	nous avons vous avez ils ont	j'ai eu j'avais eu	il avait il eut	il aura il aurait	que j'aie qu'il ait que vous ayez qu'ils aient
battre battant **battu**	je bats tu bats il bat	nous battons vous battez ils battent	j'ai battu j'avais battu	il battait il battit	il battra il battrait	que je batte que vous battiez

(Also like this are: *combattre* – to combat, *abattre* – to knock down, *rabattre* – to push, force back. **Note** *bâtir* – to build is a regular '*-ir*' verb so *je bâtis, j'ai bâti* etc.)

boire buvant **bu**	je bois tu bois il boit	nous buvons vous buvez ils boivent	j'ai bu j'avais bu	il buvait il but	il boira il boirait	que je boive que vous buviez
connaître connaissant **connu**	je connais tu connais il connaît	nous connaissons vous connaissez ils connaissent	j'ai connu j'avais connu	il connaissait il connut	il connaîtra il connaîtrait	que je connaisse que vous connaissiez

(The circumflex appears only before '*-t*'. Also like this: *paraître, apparaître*)

courir courant **couru**	je cours tu cours il court	nous courons vous courez ils courent	j'ai couru j'avais couru	il courait il courut	il courra il courrait	que je coure que vous couriez
craindre craignant **craint**	je crains tu crains il craint	nous craignons vous craignez ils craignent	j'ai craint j'avais craint	il craignait il craignit	il craindra il craindrait	que je craigne que vous craigniez

(All verbs in '*-aindre* '*-eindre*, '*-oindre* follow this pattern, only the vowel '*-e*', '*-i*''or '*-a*' changes. Other verbs are: *peindre* – to paint, *éteindre* – to put out, extinguish, *restreindre* – to restrain, *contraindre* – to constrain, *joindre* – to join etc.)

croire croyant **cru**	je crois tu crois il croit	nous croyons vous croyez ils croient	j'ai cru j'avais cru	il croyait il crut	il croira il croirait	que je croie que vous croyiez
croître croissant **crû**	je croîs tu croîs il croît	nous croissons vous croissez ils croissent	j'ai crû j'avais crû	il croissait il crût	il croîtra il croîtrait	que je croisse que vous croissiez

(This verb has a circumflex over the '*-i*' whenever it might be confused with *croire*. *Croître* means 'to grow'. Other verbs like this are *accroître* – to increase, and *décroître* – to decrease. You are most likely to meet them in the third persons singular and plural, present tense.)

Infinitive/ participles	present/		perfect/ pluperfect	imperfect/ past historic	future/ conditional	present subjunctive
devoir	je dois	nous devons	j'ai dû	il devait	il devra	que je doive
devant	tu dois	vous devez	j'avais dû	il dut	il devrait	que vous deviez
dû	il doit	ils doivent				
dire	je dis	nous disons	j'ai dit	il disait	il dira	que je dise
disant	tu dis	vous dîtes	j'avais dit	il dit	il dirait	que vous disiez
dit	il dit	ils disent				

(Also like this are *interdire* – to forbid, *prédire* – to foretell, *médire* – to speak ill of, slander, *contredire* – to contradict. But the latter have *vous médisez, vous prédisez, interdisez* and *contredisez* for second person plural present tense.)

dormir	je dors	nous dormons	j'ai dormi	il dormait	il dormira	que je dorme
dormant	tu dors	vous dormez	j'avais dormi	il dormit	il dormirait	que vous dormiez
dormi	il dort	ils dorment				

(Also like this: *s'endormir* – to fall asleep.)

écrire	j'écris	nous écrivons	j'ai écrit	il écrivait	il écrira	que j'écrive
écrivant	tu écris	vous écrivez	j'avais écrit	il écrivit	il écrirait	que vous écriviez
écrit	il écrit	ils écrivent				

(Also *décrire* – to describe, *prescrire* – to prescribe, *proscrire* – to proscribe, ban, *s'inscrire* – to sign on, enroll, *circonscrire* – to circumscribe.)

envoyer	j'envoie	nous envoyons	j'ai envoyé	il envoyait	il enverra	que j'envoie
envoyant	tu envoies	vous envoyez	j'avais envoyé	il envoya	il enverrait	que vous envoyiez
envoyé	il envoie	ils envoient				

(Note the change '-*y*' to '-*i*' before mute '-*e*'.)

être	je suis	nous sommes	j'ai été	il était	il sera	que je sois
étant	tu es	vous êtes	j'avais été	il fut	il serait	qu'il soit
été	il est	ils sont				que vous soyez
						qu'ils soient
faire	je fais	nous faisons	j'ai fait	il faisait	il fera	que je fasse
faisant	tu fais	vous faites	j'avais fait	il fit	il ferait	que vous fassiez
fait	il fait	ils font				

(Also *satisfaire* – to satisfy, *contrefaire* – to counterfeit.)

falloir	il faut		il a fallu	il fallait	il faudra	qu'il faille
fallu			il avait fallu	il fallut	il faudrait	

(Only exists in the third person singular and there is no present participle. Do not confuse with *faillir* – to fail, which you will meet mainly in the perfect tense to mean – to nearly do something, e.g. *il a failli se noyer* – he nearly drowned, *j'ai failli tomber* – I almost fell.)

Infinitive/ present/ participles			perfect/ pluperfect	imperfect/ past historic	future/ conditional	present subjunctive
fuire	je fuis	nous fuyons	il a fui	il fuyait	il fuira	qu'il fuie
fuyant	tu fuis	vous fuyez	il avait fui	il fuit	il fuirait	que vous fuyiez
fui	il fuit	ils fuient				

(Also *s'enfuir* – to run away.)

lire	je lis	nous lisons	il a lu	il lisait	il lira	qu'il lise
lisant	tu lis	vous lisez	il avait lu	il lut	il lirait	que vous lisiez
lu	il lit	ils lisent				

mettre	je mets	nous mettons	il a mis	il mettait	il mettra	qu'il mette
mettant	tu mets	vous mettez	il avait mis	il mit	il mettrait	que vous mettiez
mis	il met	ils mettent				

(Also *commettre* – to commit, *compromettre* – to compromise, *permettre* – to permit, allow, *promettre* – to promise, *soumettre* – to submit.)

mourir	je meurs	nous mourons	il est mort	il mourait	il mourra	qu'il meure
mourant	tu meurs	vous mourez	il était mort	il mourut	il mourrait	que vous mouriez
mort	il meurt	ils meurent				

naître	je nais	nous naissons	il est né	il naissait	il naîtra	qu'il naisse
naissant	tu nais	vous naissez	il était né	il naquit	il naîtrait	que vous naissiez
né	il naît	ils naissent				

ouvrir	j'ouvre	nous ouvrons	il a ouvert	il ouvrait	il ouvrira	qu'il ouvre
ouvrant	tu ouvres	vous ouvrez	il avait ouvert	il ouvrit	il ouvrirait	que vous ouvriez
ouvert	il ouvre	ils ouvrent				

(Also *couvrir* – to cover, *offrir* – to offer, *souffrir* – to suffer. Unusual past participles – *couvert, offert, souffert*.)

partir	je pars	nous partons	il est parti	il partait	il partira	qu'il parte
partant	tu pars	vous partez	il était parti	il partit	il partirait	que vous partiez
parti	il part	ils partent				

(*Servir* is the same – *je sers, nous servons* etc., except that it has *avoir* in compound tenses.)

plaire	je plais	nous plaisons	il a plu	il plaisait	il plaira	qu'il plaise
plaisant	tu plais	vous plaisez	il avait plu	il plut	il plairait	que vous plaisiez
plu	il plaît	ils plaisent				

(Not easily confused in fact with the next verb. You will often hear: *Ça vous a plu?* – Did you like it?)

pleuvoir	il pleut		il a plu	il pleuvait	il pleuvra	qu'il pleuve
plu			il avait plu	il plut	il pleuvrait	

pouvoir	je peux (puis)	nous pouvons	il a pu	il pouvait	il pourra	qu'il puisse
pouvant	tu peux	vous pouvez	il avait pu	il put	il pourrait	que vous puissiez
pu	il peut	ils peuvent				

Infinitive/ participles	present/		perfect/ pluperfect	imperfect/ past historic	future/ conditional	present subjunctive
prendre	je prends	nous prenons	il a pris	il prenait	il prendra	qu'il prenne
prenant	tu prends	vous prenez	il avait pris	il prit	il prendrait	que vous preniez
pris	il prend	ils prennent				

(Also *apprendre* – learn, *comprendre* – to understand, *surprendre* – to surprise.)

produire	je produis	nous produisons	il a produit	il produisait	il produira	qu'il produise
produisant	tu produis	vous produisez	il avait produit	il produisit	il produirait	que vous produisiez
produit	il produit	ils produisent				

(Also *conduire* – to drive, *construire* – to construct, *introduire* -to introduce, *réduire* – to reduce, *séduire* – to seduce, *traduire* – to translate.)

recevoir	je reçois	nous recevons	j'ai reçu	il recevait	il recevra	qu'il reçoive
recevant	tu reçois	vous recevez	j'avais reçu	il reçut	il recevrait	que vous receviez
reçu	il reçoit	ils reçoivent				

(Also *apercevoir* – to notice, *concevoir* – to conceive.)

résoudre	je résous	nous résolvons	j'ai résolu	il résolvait	il résoudra	que je résolve
résolvant	tu résous	vous résolvez	j'avais résolu	il résolut	il résoudrait	que vous résolviez
résolu	il résout	ils résolvent				

rire	je ris	nous rions	j'ai ri	il riait	il rira	que je rie
riant	tu ris	vous riez	j'avais ri	il rit	il rirait	que vous riiez
ri	il rit	ils rient				

(Also *sourire* – to smile.)

savoir	je sais	nous savons	j'ai su	il savait	il saura	qu'il sache
savant	tu sais	vous savez	j'avais su	il sut	il saurait	que vous sachiez
su	il sait	ils savent				

sentir	je sens	nous sentons	j'ai senti	il sentait	il sentira	qu'il sente
sentant	tu sens	vous sentez	j'avais senti	il sentit	il sentirait	que vous sentiez
senti	il sent	ils sentent				

(Also *ressentir* – to feel, experience, *consentir* to consent.)

suffire	je suffis	nous suffisons	j'ai suffi	il suffisait	il suffira	qu'il suffise
suffisant	tu suffis	vous suffisez	j'avais suffi	il suffit	il suffirait	que vous suffisiez
suffi	il suffit	ils suffisent				

suivre	je suis	nous suivons	j'ai suivi	il suivait	il suivra	qu'il suive
suivant	tu suis	vous suivez	j'avais suivi	il suivit	il suivrait	que vous suiviez
suivi	il suit	ils suivent				

Infinitive/ participles	present/		perfect/ pluperfect	imperfect/ past historic	future/ conditional	present subjunctive
tenir	je tiens	nous tenons	j'ai tenu	il tenait	il tiendra	qu'il tienne
tenant	tu tiens	vous tenez	j'avais tenu	il tint	il tiendrait	que vous teniez
tenu	il tient	ils tiennent				

(Also *appartenir* – to belong, *contenir* – to contain, *maintenir* – to maintain, *soutenir* – to uphold, support, *retenir* – to retain.)

vaincre	je vaincs	nous vainquons	j'ai vaincu	il vainquait	il vaincra	qu'il vainque
vainquant	tu vaincs	vous vainquez	j'avais vaincu	il vainquit	il vaincrait	que vous vainquiez
vaincu	il vainc	ils vainquent				

(Also *convaincre* – to convince.)

valoir	je vaux	nous valons	j'ai valu	il valait	il vaudra	qu'il vaille
valant	tu vaux	vous valez	j'avais valu	il valut	il vaudrait	que vous valiez
valu	il vaut	ils valent				

venir	je viens	nous venons	je suis venu	il venait	il viendra	qu'il vienne
venant	tu viens	vous venez	j'étais venu	il vint	il viendrait	que vous veniez
venu	il vient	ils viennent				

(Also *convenir* – to agree, *prévenir* – to forewarn, *revenir* – to return, se *souvenir* – to remember.)

vivre	je vis	nous vivons	j'ai vécu	il vivait	il vivra	qu'il vive
vivant	tu vis	vous vivez	j'avais vécu	il vécut	il vivrait	que vous viviez
vécu	il vit	ils vivent				

(Also *survivre* – to survive.)

voir	je vois	nous voyons	j'ai vu	il voyait	il verra	qu'il voie
voyant	tu vois	vous voyez	j'avais vu	il vit	il verrait	que vous voyiez
vu	il voit	ils voient				

(Also *revoir*, and *prévoir* – to foresee.)

vouloir	je veux	nous voulons	j'ai voulu	il voulait	il voudra	qu'il veuille
voulant	tu veux	vous voulez	j'avais voulu	il voulut	il voudrait	que vous vouliez
voulu	il veut	ils veulent				

APPENDIX 2

USEFUL ADDRESSES AND REFERENCES

Alliance Française
Offers a wide range of courses, both intensive and
long term, in London and in France.

1 Dorset Square
London
NW1 6PU

Association for Language Learning (ALL)
The major organization for those interested in learning
and teaching languages. Language days, lectures, films
etc. Contact main office for address of your local branch.

16 Regent Place
Rugby
CV21 2PN

Association of Language Export Centres (LX)
Provides links and language services between further
and higher educational establishments and exporting
companies. Contact main office for details of local branches.

PO Box 1574
London
NW1 4NJ

Authentik Language Learning Resources Ltd
Publication of collected French news items
with audio tape. (Also German, Spanish)

27 Westland Square
Dublin 2
Ireland

BBC
The BBC publishes in the spring of each academic
year a programme of language broadcasts:
Living Languages.

BBC Education
London
W5 2PA

Also of interest: *List of residential courses*
based on BBC series and the series *Europeans*
compiled from foreign television stations.

BBC Book Enquiries
Room A3116
Woodlands
80 Wood Lane
London
W12 0TT

British Film Institute
A film and video library that has French titles

21 Stephen Street
London
W1P 1PL

British Institute in Paris
Resource packs (including cassette) for London A-Level syllabus
topics + others. Available from **London Office**

Senate House
Malet Street
London
W1E 0HU

Central Bureau (CBEVE)
A national office resonsible for providing information
and advice on all forms of educational visits and exchanges
with other countries. Many services: school and class
linking; pen-friends etc. and publications; *Working holidays*
Young Visitors' Pupil Exchange News and others.

Seymour House
Seymour Mews
London
W1H 9PE

3 Bruntsfield Crescent
Edinburgh
E10 4HD

16 Malone Road
Belfast

Centre National de Documentation Pédagogique
Textes et documents pour la classe. Project work for
French secondary pupils

31 rue de la Vanne
92120 Montrouge
France

**Centre for Information on Language
Teaching and Research (CILT)**
A national organization providing a vast amount of
information on all aspects of language learning.
Send for list of lists. Most of the latter are free.

20 Bedfordbury
London
WC2N 4LB

Commission of the European Communities
Various publications, posters and maps. Information on
education, training and youth exchanges

London Office
8 Storey's Gate
London
SW1A 3AT

Council of Europe
Many publications, reports, some available from Strasbourg
others from Sales Agents or publishers.

Publications section
F 67006
Strasbourg
France

HMSO Agency Section
51 Nine Elms Lane
London
SW8 5DR

Dial-Search
Check list and guide to radio stations in Europe.
Publication available from:

G Wilcox
9 Thurrock Close
Eastbourne
East Sussex
BN20 9NF

La Documentation Française
A government department that produces dossiers on
various aspects of French life

29-31 quai Voltaire
75340
Paris

Francoscopie — Les Français: *Qui sont-ils
où vont-ils. Gérard Mermet.* An A-Z reference to the
French and their way of life. Regularly revised.

Larousse

French Embassy Cultural Department
Bureau d'action linguistique et Service de documentation
Information on exchanges, school links, pen-friends
Information on many aspects of French society

23 Cromwell Rd
London
SW7 2EL

188 Oxford Road
Manchester
M13 9GP

BAL Ecosse
7 Bowmont Gardens
Glasgow
G12 9LR

Food and Wine from France
Main source of information and publicity on this subject.

Nuffield House
41 Piccadilly
London
WIV 9AJ

Government of Québec
Posters and information sheets.

Documentation Dept
59 Pall Mall
London
SW1Y 5JH

Institut français
A wide range of cultural activities: theatre; films;
exhibitions; lectures; secretarial courses. Membership
available. Also video and film lending service.

17 Queensberry Place
London
SW7 2DT

13 Randolph Crescent
Edinburgh
EH3 7TT

Le Journal des Journaux
*Utilisation du journal pour l'enseignement
de la langue et de la civilisation.* Publishes
an index to a selection of articles from French
press arranged under subject headings.

Département Presse
Centre international d'études pédagogiques
1 avenue Léon
Perrault
F-92311
Sèvres
France

National Council for Educational Technology
Information on task-based learning of languages with IT.

Science Park
Coventry
CV4 7EZ

Oxford University Delegacy of Local Examinations
Resource packs on a number of background
and literary themes. Information on request.

Ewert Place
Oxford
OX2 7BZ

Que sais-je? *Presse Universitaire de France.*
A French series covering a wide range of topic areas.
Distributed by:

European Schoolbooks
Ashville Trading Estate
The Runnings
Cheltenham
Gloucestershire
GL51 9PQ

Quid
A yearly analysis of events in France with statistics
and addresses of organizations. Distributor in Britain:

Grant and Cutler
55-57 Great Marlborough Street
London
W1V 2AY

Summer Academy
List of study holidays at British Universities.

Summer Academy
School of Continuing Education
The University
Canterbury
Kent
CT2 7NX

La Vie Outre-Manche
*Le magazine en français pour les lecteurs
du Royaume-Uni.* Many bilingual texts with
accompanying audio tape.

8 Skye Close
Maidstone
Kent
ME15 9SJ

World Radio and TV Handbook
Details of programmes worldwide.

Billboard, New York
Distributed by Fountain Press
Windsor

INDEX

EDUCATIONAL

A Level French Cassette

If you have purchased a copy of our Study
Guide for A Level French and would like to
buy the accompanying cassette, please
complete the order form below and return it to:

**Letts Educational
Aldine House
Aldine Place
London W12 8AW
Telephone 0181 740 2266**

Forenames (Mr/Ms) _____

Surname _____

Address _____

_____

_____

_____

Postcode _____

Please send me the following:

	ISBN	Quantity	Price (incl VAT)	Total
A Level French C90 cassette	(1-85758-815-0)	_____	£4.00	_____
Add postage – UK and ROI 75p for each cassette				_____

I enclose a cheque/postal order for £ _____
(made payable to Letts Educational)

Or charge to Access/Visa card No. ☐☐☐☐ ☐☐☐☐ ☐☐☐☐ ☐☐☐☐ ☐☐☐☐

Expiry date _____

Signature _____